APPLICATIONS SOFTWARE
PROGRAMMING WITH
FOURTH-GENERATION LANGUAGES

Other fine titles available from boyd & fraser

Introduction to Computers and Microcomputer Applications
Microcomputer Applications: Using Small Systems Software, Second Edition
Microcomputer Productivity Tools
Microcomputer Applications: A Practical Approach
Microcomputer Systems Management and Applications
Mastering Lotus 1-2-3®
Using Enable®: An Introduction to Integrated Software
PC-DOS®/MS-DOS® Simplified

Computer Information Systems

Database Systems: Management and Design
Microcomputer Database Management Using dBASE III PLUS®
Microcomputer Database Management Using R:BASE System V®
dBASE III PLUS® Programming
A Guide to SQL
Applications Software Programming with Fourth-Generation Languages
Fundamentals of Systems Analysis with Application Design
Office Automation: An Information Systems Approach
Data Communications for Business
Learning Computer Programming: Structured Logic Algorithms, and Flowcharting
COBOL: Structured Programming Techniques for Solving Problems
Comprehensive Structured COBOL
Fundamentals of Structured COBOL
Advanced Structured COBOL: Batch and Interactive
BASIC Fundamentals and Style
Structured BASIC Fundamentals and Style for the IBM® PC and Compatibles
Applesoft BASIC Fundamentals and Style
Complete BASIC for the Short Course
Structuring Programs in Microsoft BASIC

Shelly and Cashman Titles

Computer Concepts with Microcomputer Applications (Lotus 1-2-3®
  and VP-Planner Plus® versions)
Computer Concepts
Learning to Use WordPerfect®, Lotus 1-2-3®, and dBASE III PLUS®
Learning to Use WordPerfect®, VP-Planner Plus®, and dBASE III PLUS®
Learning to Use WordPerfect®
Learning to Use Lotus 1-2-3®
Learning to Use VP-Planner Plus®
Learning to Use dBASE III PLUS®
Computer Fundamentals with Application Software
Learning to Use SuperCalc®3, dBASE III®, and WordStar® 3.3: An Introduction
Learning to Use SuperCalc®3: An Introduction
Learning to Use dBASE III®: An Introduction
Learning to Use WordStar® 3.3: An Introduction
BASIC Programming for the IBM Personal Computer
Structured COBOL: Pseudocode Edition
Structured COBOL: Flowchart Edition

APPLICATIONS SOFTWARE

PROGRAMMING WITH

FOURTH-GENERATION

LANGUAGES

W. Gregory Wojtkowski
Wita Wojtkowski
both of Boise State University

boyd & fraser publishing company
Boston

Publisher: Thomas K. Walker
Editor: Marjorie Schlaikjer
Production Editor: Patricia Donegan
Director of Manufacturing: Dean Sherman
Book Design: Rebecca Evans
Cover Design: Ken Russo
Cover Photo: Clayton J. Price
Illustrations: Anne Craig

Manufactured in the United States of America

Library of Congress Cataloging-in-Publication Data

Wojtkowski, W. Gregory, 1944–
   Applications software programming with fourth-generation languages.

   Includes index.
   1. Programming languages (Electronic computers)
2. Electronic digital computers—Programming.
3. NOMAD (Computer program) I. Wojtkowski, Wita,
1944–   . II. Title.
QA76.7.W64 1989   005.13'3   88-19242
ISBN 0-87835-338-0

10 9 8 7 6 5 4 3 2 1

Figure credits from *Applications Software Programming with Fourth-Generation Languanges*

Figure 1.3 From *Managing Information as a Corporate Resource* by Paul L. Tom. Copyright ©1987 by Scott, Foresman and Company. Reprinted by permission; **Figure 1.5** Albert F. Case, *Information Systems Development: Principles of Computer-Aided Software Engineering*, ©1986, p. 12. Reprinted by permission of Prentice-Hall, Inc., Englewood Cliffs, NJ; **Figure 1.6** Albert F. Case, *Information Systems Development: Principles of Computer-Aided Software Engineering*, ©1986, p. 13. Reprinted by permission of Prentice-Hall, Inc., Englewood Cliffs, NJ; **Figure 1.9** James Martin, *Fourth-Generation Languages Volume 1: Principles*, ©1985, p. 55. Reprinted by permission of Prentice-Hall, Inc., Englewood Cliffs, NJ; **Figure 3.5** Copyright 1988 by CW Publishing Inc., Framingham, MA 01701—Reprinted from *Computerworld*; **Figure 4.24** SAS Institute Inc., *SAS/FSP® User's Guide, Version 5 Edition*. Cary, NC: SAS Institute Inc., 1985, p. 65; **Figure 4.25** SAS Institute Inc., *SAS/FSP® User's Guide, Version 5 Edition*. Cary, NC: SAS Institute Inc., 1985, pp. 314, 315; **Figure 4.26** SAS Institute Inc., *SAS/FSP® User's Guide, Version 5 Edition*. Cary, NC: SAS Institute Inc., 1985, p. 57; **Figure 4.27** SAS Institute Inc., *SAS/FSP® User's Guide, Version 5 Edition*. Cary, NC: SAS Institute Inc., 1985, p. 412; **Figure 4.28** SAS Institute Inc., *SAS/FSP® User's Guide, Version 5 Edition*. Cary, NC: SAS Institute Inc., 1985, p. 594; **Figure 4.29** SAS Institute Inc., *SAS/FSP® User's Guide, Version 5 Edition*. Cary, NC: SAS Institute Inc., 1985, p. 96; **Figure 4.30** SAS Institute Inc., *SAS/FSP® User's Guide, Version 5 Edition*. Cary, NC: SAS Institute Inc., 1985, p. 96; **Figure 4.31** SAS Institute Inc., *SAS/FSP® User's Guide, Version 5 Edition*. Cary, NC: SAS Institute Inc., 1985, p. 222; **Figure 5.1** G. B. Davis and M. H. Olson, *Management Information Systems: Conceptual Foundations, Structure, and Development*, 2nd ed., McGraw-Hill, 1985, p. 478; **Figure 5.2** Reprinted with permission of MacMillan Publishing Company from *Decision Support and Expert Systems* by Ephraim Turban. Copyright ©1987 by Macmillan Publishing Company; **Figure 5.5** Reprinted by permission of publisher from *I/S Analyzer*, United Communications Group, 4550 Montgomery Avenue, Suite 700N, Bethesda, MD 20814; **Chapter 5, Exercise 21** Reprinted by special permission from the *MIS Quarterly*, Vol. 8, No. 4, December 1984, ©1984 by the Society for Information Management and the Management Information Systems Research Center at the University of Minnesota; **Figure 6.3** Reprinted by permission of publisher from *Application Prototyping: A Project Management Perspective*, an AMA Briefing, ©1985, American Management Association, NY. All rights reserved; **Figure 7.1** Adapted from A. Milton Jenkins, "Prototyping: A Methodology for the Design and Development of Application Systems," Working Paper, School of Business, Indiana University, 1983; **Figure 8.9** Reprinted by permission of publisher from *SIM Spectrum*, Vol. 4, No. 3, ©1987 by the Society for Information Management, 111 East Wacker Drive, Suite 600, Chicago, IL 60601; **Figure 8.10** Reprinted by permission of publisher from *SIM Spectrum*, Vol. 4, No. 3, ©1987 by the Society for Information Management, 111 East Wacker Drive, Suite 600, Chicago, IL 60601.

For you, Thea and Dorothy
You are our best creative effort

Table of Contents

PART I

OVERVIEW OF FOURTH-GENERATION LANGUAGES: EVOLUTION, BASIC DEFINITIONS, AND SAMPLE SURVEYS

PART II

METHODS OF SYSTEMS DEVELOPMENT WITH 4GLS

PART III

INTRODUCTION TO A FOURTH-GENERATION LANGUAGE: NOMAD

Preface

ABOUT THIS BOOK

In today's highly competitive business environment, more and more managers are turning to fourth-generation languages (4GLs) as a means of developing computer applications. Now more than ever, students entering the work force need a clear understanding of 4GLs, coupled with a proficiency in using them effectively as business problem-solving tools. *Applications Software Programming with Fourth-Generation Languages* offers complete and comprehensive coverage of the concepts associated with these languages, in addition to providing hands-on instruction in the use of NOMAD, one of the leading 4GLs in industry today.

Applications Software Programming with Fourth-Generation Languages is ideally suited for a one-semester or one-quarter course in 4GLs. The text offers clear and concise instruction in the fundamentals of fourth-generation languages—what 4GLs are and are not, how they are used, and what factors contribute to their successful use.

The text assumes some familiarity with the Systems Development Life Cycle. Previous coursework in systems analysis and design is helpful but not necessary.

DISTINGUISHING FEATURES

Flexible Organization

This text is divided into three parts. Part I (Chapters 1-4) is an overview of basic 4GL concepts; Part II (Chapters 5-8) covers methods of systems development and prototyping. Neither of these parts is NOMAD-specific, allowing them to be used with any 4GL tool.

Part III of the text (Chapters 9-19) focuses on building a comprehensive application, the Ski Rental System, using PC NOMAD. These chapters contain enough material to constitute a separate course in and of themselves.

The text's flexible integration of theory and applications allows it to be tailored to meet the needs of any reader or 4GL course.

Project-Driven Approach

A series of ongoing projects throughout the text offers students the opportunity to build several complete computer information systems using NOMAD, one of the world's premiere 4GLs. Once proficient in NOMAD, students can easily transfer their skills to either the mainframe version of NOMAD or to any other 4GL they encounter in the business world. The project-driven approach to understanding 4GLs requires students to apply the concepts presented in the text in realistic simulated business environments, thus reinforcing these concepts.

Detailed Discussions of the Prototyping Process

The text provides thorough coverage of systems development concepts, detailed discussions of prototyping principles, and an in-depth look at managing the prototyping process.

Solid Coverage of Design Techniques

The text provides solid coverage of design techniques, with an emphasis on prototyping methodology from a management perspective. Students are also afforded an opportunity to practice these techniques themselves by generating their own applications. 4GL design techniques are compared and contrasted with those used with third-generation languages.

Examples from Popular Commercial Systems

The text introduces and illustrates the standard features and capabilities of 4GLs through examples drawn from the most popular commercial systems used in business today and surveys features common to all 4GLs.

Comprehensive Case Studies

Comprehensive case studies presented throughout the text provide students with the opportunity to relate new concepts and methods to the development of major applications.

Examines 4GLs from Historical Perspective

The text comprehensively traces the emergence of fourth-generation languages from a historical and evolutionary perspective, and shows why and how these languages have become essential tools in effectively and competitively managing business organizations today.

Free Software

Adopters of this text will receive a 7-disk implementation of PC NOMAD, the microcomputer version of NOMAD by MUST Software International. This leading fully integrated 4GL/DBMS, which has an international user base of over 100,000, offers a complete relational database management system and cooperative processing capabilities. This free educational system is limited only in file size, and otherwise offers the complete functionality of the full commercial product.

ADDITIONAL FEATURES

Exercises

Each chapter concludes with a comprehensive set of exercises. These exercises can be used for self-evaluation, student testing, or group discussion. Each serves to reinforce the concepts introduced in the chapter and to relate concepts introduced in earlier chapters.

Projects

The majority of the chapters include projects. Those following Parts I and II of the text are related to the general issues discussed in these parts of the text. Projects featured in Part III provide students with comprehensive case examples. Each chapter in Part III introduces new material and relates it to the development of the Ski Rental System Application. The end-of-chapter projects provide an opportunity for students to apply freshly introduced concepts and methods, and allow for additional practice in the use of NOMAD.

References

All chapters in Parts I and II of the text are followed by an extensive list of references and related readings. In addition, Chapter 2 includes a separate list of references related to the chapter's real-life examples of both successful and unsuccessful uses of fourth-generation languages.

Appendices

The text features six appendices, all of which the student will find most helpful. Appendices include NOMAD installation notes, notes on NOMAD's display and internal formats, NOMAD built-in functions, a glossary of NOMAD terminology, a list of acronyms used in the text, and a brief history on the origin of NOMAD.

FREE PC NOMAD SOFTWARE AND DATA DISKETTE

Adopters of this text will receive a 7-disk implementation of PC NOMAD, the microcomputer version of NOMAD by MUST Software International. This software package will also include a data diskette featuring data files for the Ski Rental System developed in the text.

All adopters who complete and return a copy of the site license agreement may duplicate the software for all students of his or her class who have purchased a new copy of the textbook.

The educational version of PC NOMAD offers a fully integrated 4GL/relational database management system. The only change in the educational version of PC

NOMAD is in file size. Otherwise, it offers the complete functionality of the full commercial product.

These ancillary materials are available from boyd & fraser publishing company, 20 Park Plaza, Suite 1405, Boston, MA 02116. You can also place your order by calling (toll-free) 1-800-225-3782.

ORGANIZATION OF THIS BOOK

The book is divided into three parts—Part I, an overview of fourth-generation languages; Part II, methods of systems development with fourth-generation languages; and Part III, an introduction to NOMAD.

Part I covers basic concepts. It provides a broad introduction to the notions that are common to all fourth-generation languages and surveys representative fourth-generation products. Case examples presented in this part provide relevant business scenarios. Students see how organizations benefit from the use of fourth-generation languages.

Part II describes concepts that are common to systems development with fourth-generation languages. Prototyping principles and issues related to the management of the prototyping process are discussed.

Part III is a tutorial treatment of the major concepts of a fourth-generation language. PC NOMAD is used as a vehicle for illustrating these concepts and for developing a complete application, the Ski Rental System. This application is developed throughout the remainder of the text and evolves and becomes more complex. The part begins with an overview of the NOMAD environment, defines the application, and describes the database definition process for it. Next, interactive and procedural data entry and file maintenance and the use of external files are covered. Detailed discussion of files manipulation is also included. Reporting is the main focus of the final section of Part III, namely standard and customized reporting. The fourth-generation nature of NOMAD is illustrated though detailed discussion of the powerful LIST command. This part concludes with an examination of integration and illustrates integration of our application.

The material can be used in sequence, but the three parts of the text are independent from one another. For example, one can use Part I (Chapters 1-4) and Part II (Chapters 5-8) and illustrate the use of a fourth-generation language product with a product other than NOMAD (adapting to what is available in a given institution). Part III can be used independently as well. One can study Chapters 9-12, consider reporting as covered in Chapters 17 and 18, return to Chapters 14, 15, and 16 to study database maintenance, data manipulation, and finish up with system integration, as discussed in Chapter 19.

Acknowledgements

It is a great pleasure to thank the many people involved, directly or indirectly, in the creation of this book. The comments and diligent work of our students were most helpful in shaping the text. Especially helpful were Marion D'Ament, Cheryl McAlister, and Brad Moor.

The book has also benefited from the comments of reviewers: Ann Burroughs, Humboldt State University; E. Reed Doke, Southwest Missouri State University; Lewis A. Myers, Texas A&M University; Jorge Moser, James Madison University; Charles Mosmann, California State University at Fullerton; Philip J. Pratt, Grand Valley State University; and Brian H. Seborg, University of Maryland, Baltimore.

We would also like to thank MUST Software International for creating an educational version of NOMAD for the PC. Special thanks go to Joan Rawlings, who helped enormously with her lucid technical reviews. We also thank Dick Rawlings and Abby Pinard for being there for us when needed. Thank you for introducing us to the NOMAD users group and for inviting us to the Fifth Annual NOMAD International Users Conference. Our conversations with NOMAD users were most valuable.

For the wonderful possibility of discussing literature, we thank our St. Ogg group, which made us realize that there are so many books but so little time. It was good to discuss Garcia Marques when having NOMAD on our minds. Our thanks go to Nancy Napier, Eve Morostica, Cheryl Larabee, Anne Carelton, Darlene Standal, and Jane DeWitte.

To our special friend, Christine Farrell, thank you for your sense of humor and for tolerating ours.

Thanks to Monty Caldwell for giving sound advice and sharing his wisdom. And we truly appreciated the hard work of Arthur Weisbach.

We both want to thank our skiing friends who missed us on the slopes. Alan and Pat Frankel and Sally and Mike Merz, thanks for waiting.

We also appreciate the work of those at boyd & fraser publishing company: Thomas Walker, Publisher, for his support, and Pat Donegan, production editor, for her fine effort in helping to bring this book to publication. Heartfelt thanks go to Margaret Hill, our copy editor, and to Michael Michaud, for bringing her to us.

Finally, special thanks go to Marjorie Schlaikjer, our editor, with whom we hope to ski someday and share the incredible beauty of Idaho.

January 1989   *Wita and Gregory Wojtkowski*
                                                                           Boise, Idaho

PART I

OVERVIEW OF

FOURTH-GENERATION

LANGUAGES: EVOLUTION,

BASIC DEFINITIONS,

AND SAMPLE SURVEYS

Part I of this book describes the concepts that are common to all fourth-generation languages (4GLs).

Chapter 1 considers the reasons for the development of the 4GLs.

Chapter 2 discusses the advent of 4GLs and the associated history of computing.

Chapter 3 describes the basic characteristics of the typical 4GL and considers ideal 4GL facilities. '

Chapter 4 surveys representative 4GLs.

The material covered in Part I is software independent. In other words, what we discuss is of general nature, and does not pertain to a specific 4GL.

CHAPTER 1

Why Fourth-Generation Languages?

More is not necessarily better, and less may sometimes be more.

Chinese proverb

1.1 INTRODUCTION

The main objective of this chapter is to help you understand the place of the fourth-generation languages in the computer information systems of contemporary business enterprises. We will consider the following specific issues:

- Why 4GLs have been developed and where they fit in the evolution of computer languages and computing
- How they relate to current system development productivity concerns
- Why 4GLs are important to you

This chapter and associated readings set the background for the remaining chapters of Part I.

1.2 BRIEF REVIEW OF PROGRAMMING LANGUAGES

This book is about fourth-generation languages (4GLs). To understand 4GLs and their use, a brief review of the levels of the programming languages would be helpful.

Languages by Level

Machine Level and Assembly Level

On this level, languages are hardware oriented. They are based on a binary code and are machine dependent; that is, programs written for one computer model usually cannot be transferred to another.

Machine languages require minimal use of hardware resources, which we will refer to as overhead. To use the language on this level requires transformations from the problem the language is to solve to an algorithm, from algorithm to machine operations, and finally from machine operations to encoding in binary. At the present time, machine language is the only language computers understand directly. Languages on all other levels must be translated one way or another into machine language. Machine languages are first-generation languages.

Assembly level languages are symbolic representations (using symbols and letters as code) of underlying machine language and thus are machine operations oriented. They require small overhead. The required transformation is from the problem to an algorithm, and then from the algorithm to a symbolic representation of machine operations. Assembly languages are second-generation languages.

Algorithm Level

On this level, languages are oriented toward procedures (algorithms) that the computer is to follow. For this reason they are called procedural languages. They require medium overhead, and are either compiled or interpreted. Examples of languages in this category are BASIC, FORTRAN, COBOL, PL/I, and APL. For these languages, the transformation is from the problem to the algorithm. One programmer instruction yields multiple machine instructions. These are third-generation languages (3GLs), often referred to as high level languages (HLLs).

Languages on this level start to be divided into general-purpose and special-purpose categories. An example of a general-purpose language is PASCAL or PL/I. A special-purpose language is, for example, Logo.

Between Algorithm and Problem Level

On this level, languages are oriented between algorithms and the problems they solve. They require high overhead, and they are compiled and/or interpreted. The high overhead is required because preparations must be made for many computing tasks, for example, opening file backup buffers, error handling procedures, automatic documentation, and automatic data integrity checks. Also, since these functions are performed automatically, whether they are needed or not, the high overhead is unavoidable.

Transformation is from the problem to the higher level algorithm. That is, a single nonprocedural statement replaces one or more sets of procedural statements. Some languages in this category may require further procedural transformations from the problem to lower level algorithms.

In essence, languages on this level provide an "already developed procedures" facility that the user can invoke interactively by issuing a single succinct command. For example, in a ski rental application, the single statement in the NOMAD language is

```
LIST BY SKI_NUM SUM(SKI_RENT_PAID) TOTAL;
```

performs several tasks such as sorting report data by ski's serial number (SKI_NUM), calculating rental fees for each pair of skis in the report data (SUM(SKI_RENT_PAID)), calculating the grand total for all fees collected (TOTAL), and finally printing a complete report that includes page numbers, column headings, and proper spacing between display columns. This single statement represents a complete procedure. Written in any 3GL, this procedure would require many lines of code.

Languages in this category are known as fourth-generation languages (4GLs), or very high level languages (VHLLs). VHLLs contain more machine instructions per programmer instruction than HLLs.

What the specific language contains depends on the user's needs. Some 4GLs can satisfy the needs of the experienced programmer; others, the needs of novice end users.

Nonprocedural 4GLs are very useful to end users and for quickly building prototypes. The fundamental concept behind a nonprocedural language is to transfer the entire issue of program flow from the user to the computer software. The need to specify low-level details such as the sequencing of computations is eliminated. Desired results, rather than actions to be taken, are specified. In essence, with a 4GL, significantly fewer programmer-written instructions are required than with, say, COBOL.

Object Level

On this level are symbolic manipulation languages. Examples are LISP and PROLOG, the languages of commercial artificial intelligence systems. In the same category are object-oriented database management system products such as GEMSTONE, which uses object metaphors for complex data structures. (For a detailed discussion, see W. B. Rauch-Hindin [20].)

LISP (List Processor) is a functional programming language. LISP programs are constructed from expressions composed of function calls, rather than statements (as in 3GLs). LISP represents objects as rules and nets as lists. These lists can be sequences of numbers, character strings, other lists, and so on. Lists can be split apart, or new lists can be made by joining old ones.

The following is an example of LISP code which defines a small database:

```
(DEFUN MAKE-DB (&OPTIONAL (SIZE 100))
    (MAKE-HUSH-TABLE :SIZE SIZE))
```

PROLOG (Programming in Logic) is a rule-based language in which a set of facts and rules can be described. These facts and rules can then be used to solve problems or answer queries. A PROLOG program is a series of statements in which logic itself is used as a programming language. The proof of the theorem using these statements serves as a way of executing them. The behavior of a program can be changed by changing one or more facts or rules. Facts are expressed as follows:

```
FEMALE (THEA)
MALE (BART)
LIKES (BART, THEA)
BOOK(FOIL FENCING, WYRICK, SAUNDERS COMPANY)
```

Rules are expressed as follows:

```
SISTER (X,Y): -FEMALE (X), PARENT (X,Z), PARENT (Y,Z)
```

The above rule states that X is the sister of Y if X is female and if the parent of X is the same as the parent of Y. Queries are expressed as:

```
? - LIKES (THEA, BART)
? - SISTER (THEA, DOROTHY)
```

The PROLOG programmer does not explicitly state the sequence in which the rules are processed. The program selects the rule it needs at each stage of the processing.

Figure 1.1 summarizes orientations, uses, and product examples for each language level.

Languages by Largest Data Structure

Another way to characterize language levels is to identify the largest data structure that is an object of the principal data handling commands of the language.

- First and second generations (machine and assembly languages)
    - Commands move, read, and write bytes, strings, numbers and symbols.
    - The largest data object is an array of numbers and symbols.
- Third generation (COBOL, for example)
    - Commands create, read and write records, arrays and files.
    - The largest data object is a record or file.
- Fourth generation (NOMAD, for example)
    - Commands create, change, sort, merge, and link database files.
    - The largest data object is a database.

Note that in 4GLs records in a database and smaller data objects are actually selected and processed as with other languages. However, this is done without the

Generation	Level	Orientation	Uses	Examples
First & Second (Pre-1950s & 1960s)	Machine Assembler (Minimal overhead)	Hardware dependent (problem→ algorithm→ machine operations→ coding)	• For frequent highly efficient use, for example, compilers	proprietary machine and assembly language
Third (1960s & 1970s)	Algorithm (Medium overhead)	Hardware independent (problem→ algorithm→ code)	• Numeric calculations • Business use • General-purpose applications • Special-purpose applications	ALGOL, FORTRAN, COBOL, BASIC, PL/I, PASCAL, MODULA-2
Fourth (1980s)	Between algorithm and problem (High overhead)	Mostly hardware independent (problem→ high level algorithm→ code)	• End-user computing • Decision support systems • Information center language • Rapid system development	NOMAD on PC EXPRESS, IFPS NOMAD IMAGINE
Fifth (1980s & 1990s)	Object (Medium overhead)	Hardware dependent (LISP machine), but mostly hardware independent (Object→ code)	• Commercial artificial intelligence systems • Expert systems • Object-oriented database management systems	LISP PROLOG GEMSTONE

Figure 1.1 Summary of the Languages Spectrum

intervention of the programmer. This specific property of the limited programmer involvement in procedural steps, that is, in transforming the problem to the higher level algorithm, characterizes 4GLs.

The largest data structure that is an object of the principal data-handling commands of a given language level is directly related to the programming process that applies. Thus the data objects of an application influence the choice of a programming language. (We will return to this subject later in discussion of the 4GL environment.)

1.3 THE SOFTWARE CRISIS

Programming languages are the primary tools for creating software. The basic challenge for business software builders in the 1990s is to build reliable software *faster*. To put this challenge in perspective, let's first look at the recent history of computing.

Some History

Computing began as a commercially viable business in about 1951. Computerization of processes such as payroll, order entry, inventory control as well as real-time control of factories, automated assembly lines, and so on are now commonplace in the enterprises throughout the world.

In the beginning, computers were thought of primarily as devices for manipulating numbers. That way of thinking about computers explains their initial use in applications that lent themselves to formula-oriented programming languages such as FORTRAN or ALGOL. In the mid-1960s, computers were much more expensive than people, and time-sharing developed as a way to distribute the expense.

Next computers were perceived as more flexible, capable of manipulating records as well as numbers. This led to record-oriented applications such as payroll management and inventory control and to the use of COBOL, PL/I, and similar programming languages. During the period of record-oriented applications, the economics of computer use resulted in the development of large centralized computer systems. Applications programming was done by centralized professional programming staffs.

By the end of 1970, many users felt, however, that it took too long to develop new applications. An application backlog of several years for both defined and explicitly expressed user's requests was not unusual. This backlog very often represented applications systems work that was important to the business operations of a given organization. The situation was made even worse by an "invisible backlog," or unexpressed users' needs. (An invisible backlog can develop for many reasons, for example, the users' inability to express a perceived information system need and management's reluctance to set priorities for applications projects.) Faced with this backlog situation, many managers of information systems were threatened with a users' revolt. Many users turned to sources outside their own information systems organizations (such as time-sharing bureaus) for help with their new applications. This sequence of events is historically considered to have given impetus to the development of fourth-generation languages.

The technological changes that came next (in the late 1970s and the 1980s) enabled many organizations to use minicomputers, microcomputers, and computer networks. This changed the economics of computing: large centralized systems are no longer perceived as efficient.

A totally new world of computing is emerging. The users of business data no longer have to rely on a centralized professional programming staff to gain access to their data. Consider that applications such as database inquiry, report generation, and spreadsheet manipulation are now regularly developed and used by the non-technical managers and professionals in many businesses.

Figure 1.2 summarizes the evolution of computer use in business.

Increasing Labor Costs

In the early days of computing, the primary concern was with hardware. Hardware development was carefully planned, but little thought was given to the software. When software was relatively simple, this approach was satisfactory.

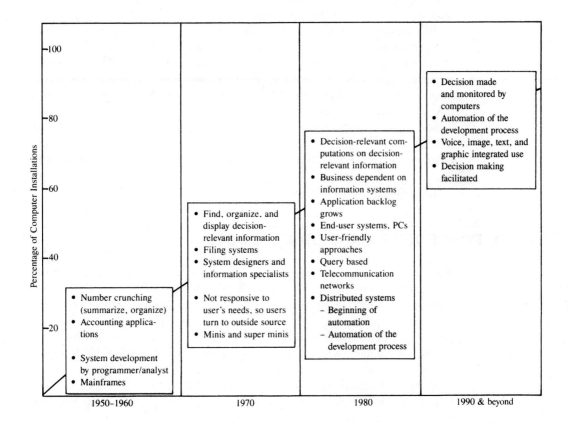

Figure 1.2   Evolution of Computer Use in Business

In the beginning, the same person routinely specified, wrote, operated, and maintained his or her programs. The very first programmers were scientists, technicians, and mathematicians who were intrigued by the idea of using computers as tools to solve some of their problems. Their software was usually one of a kind—unique to a particular problem they were solving at the time. Not until the advent of commercial second-generation computers in the early 1960s did software development start to become a distinct profession. The initial applications for these second-generation computers tended to be in areas that were already standardized as manual procedures. Procedures that were contained in written documents such as accounting ledgers and manuals that embodied custom and tradition were easily transformed into procedures that were contained in computer programs.

In the 1970s and 1980s, a steady drop in computer prices put computers in the hands of multitudes of new users. The users, in turn, needed various kinds of software. This fueled an amazing growth in the demand for software. The software that was being created was quite different from that used in earlier, straightforward business applications. Now teams of programmers were needed to tackle larger and more complex software development problems. Individual effort gave way to team effort. Coordination that once took place in the head of one person had to occur in the heads of many people. The whole process became more complicated; planning and documentation became critical. Very soon the time and cost of writing programs began to exceed the estimates. It was not unusual for the systems to cost more than twice what had been estimated and to take months (or sometimes years) longer than anyone had expected.

Making a change within a complex program turned out to be a very expensive task. To get the program to do something slightly different was so hard that it was often much easier to throw the old program out and start over. This, of course, was costly.

The software crisis had arrived!

1.4 SOFTWARE VERSUS HARDWARE COSTS

As computer technology was evolving, hardware was getting less expensive. Vacuum tubes were replaced by transistors, and then transistors were replaced by integrated circuits. Microcomputers that cost only few thousand dollars have now become more powerful than the old mainframes that cost several million dollars. As the cost of hardware was dropping dramatically, software continued to be written by humans whose wages were increasing. This trend is shown in Figure 1.3.

Software development costs have increased faster than hardware costs. Why this accelerating software cost? Because the software development, so far, has been human labor intensive.

The current relationship between labor and hardware costs makes it economical to substitute automated development (hardware) for labor. It simply makes economical sense. This relationship is shown in Figure 1.4.

Automated software development tools are just starting to be used and new ones are being developed. Engineering principles of project management and reusability of existing components are just starting to be applied to software development processes.

1.5 EVOLUTION TOWARD AUTOMATED APPLICATIONS DEVELOPMENT

By now many organizations have experienced explosive growth in the rate of proliferation of computers. With the number of computers grows the need for the software to run them.

The problem is that over the last 25 years, programming productivity increased fivefold, while the hardware price-performance ratio increased a thousand fold. In

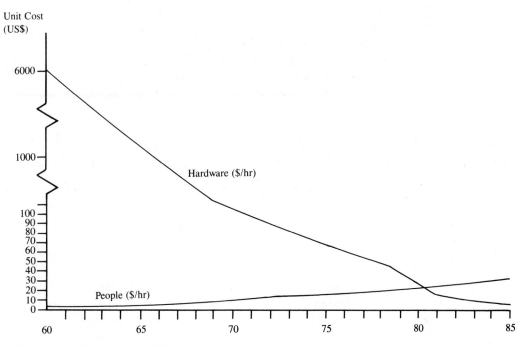

Figure 1.3   People Costs (Wages) Versus Hardware Costs

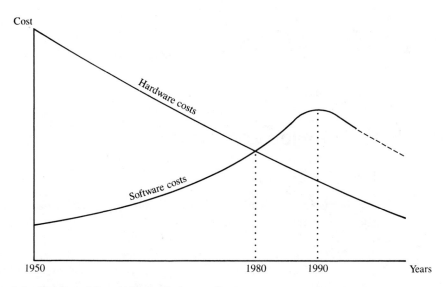

Figure 1.4   Hardware Costs Versus Software Costs

addition, the demand for software solutions to users' problems is rising faster than the supply of trained applications software programmers. What it means is that correct working systems cannot be produced at a rate equivalent to that at which new systems are needed. This situation creates a huge applications backlog.

Applications backlog exists in part because the complexity of many data processing systems has grown beyond human control. Although most standard business applications such as payroll, accounts payable, and receivables have been automated, organizational use of computers is evolving toward complex applications of both hardware and software. As the complexity of software systems grows, the need to integrate these systems to allow them to communicate with each other is also increasing.

It is more and more difficult to develop today's complex software using development tools that were designed for a simpler software world. The situation is further aggravated by maintenance problems. Many data processing departments in many businesses admit that maintenance consumes a major portion of their time. Not much time is left for programming new systems.

Since the price of hardware is declining, many new users have purchased computers. If all new computer users are to get even minimal use from their hardware, new ways of creating application software must be adopted. Just when rapidly dropping computer hardware costs seem to be opening up large markets for new applications, the continuing problems of software development are frustrating the trend. The problems with software development exist because:

■ The activity is labor intensive.

■ The tasks are getting tougher.

■ The sheer mass of data is overwhelming to old development methods.

■ There is a shortage of application programmers, and training new people is slow and expensive.

1.6 THE CONCEPT OF PRODUCTIVITY

This section is based on writings of A. F. Case from the Nastec Corporation (see [3]).

Programmer productivity is measured in terms of the functioning applications produced. This production is the end result of a lengthy process that includes analysis, design, programming, and implementation.

Improved productivity means that more functioning applications were delivered than before. This in turn is possible if one or all of the elements in the production process are performed more efficiently and in less time than previously.

Software development productivity, however, should be defined in terms of software quality, too. One measure of software quality is the absence of defects. Examples of these software defects include inaccurate calculations and unsuitable input screens. If software can be produced with the same defect rates, but faster, productivity has increased. However, poor quality software requires repairs. So, if

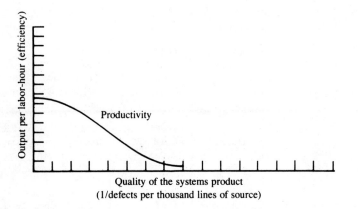

Figure 1.5   Productivity is Efficiency and Quality

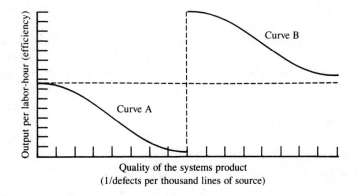

Figure 1.6   Improving Productivity by Shifting the Productivity Curve

software can be produced with lower defect rates in the same amount of time, productivity has still increased because less time needs to be spent correcting defects.

Improving productivity requires attention to both efficiency and quality. Taking actions to increase quality (spending more time on testing, for example) decreases the efficiency with which the software project is completed. Figure 1.5 presents the relationship between efficiency measured in time and quality measured in defects.

Trading off efficiency for quality keeps software developers on the same productivity curve. To move to another level of productivity requires **shift** in productivity curve. Figure 1.6 shows this shift.

If the software development process (which depends on methods, techniques, and tools) is moved from any point on curve A to any point on curve B, productivity has been improved. Discussion of this shift appears later in this chapter when we consider 4GLs and information systems.

Type	Product	Vendor
4GLs	NOMAD IDEAL ADS/ON-LINE MANTIS FOCUS	MUST, CT ADR, NY Cullinet, MA CINCOM, OH Information Builders, NY
Code Genterators	INTELLAGEN ACCOLADE PACBASE	ON-LINE SOFTWARE, NJ Computer Corporation of America, MA CGI Systems Inc., NY
Application Generators	System W EIS MODEL	COMSHARE, MI Boeing Computer Services Lloyd Bush & Associates

Figure 1.7   Examples of Programming Support Tools

To bring about the required productivity shift, new software development tools evolved. They are often grouped under the category of **automated software development tools,** which include programming support tools, design technique tools, and project management tools.

Programming support tools automate the process of writing applications software. The goals of this family of tools are to:

■ Reduce software development expense.

■ Improve programmer productivity.

■ Provide end users with development tools that will help them with their own applications needs.

Today in this category you can find:

■ Fourth-generation languages

■ Code generators

■ Application generators

Fourth-generation languages (4GLs) were developed to reduce the number of instructions a programmer must write to manipulate data. To accomplish this, 4GLs can

■ Help with application problem definition.

■ Permit definition of data in terms meaningful to the user.

■ Permit the entry, modification, and deletion of data either interactively or from existing files on traditional storage media.

■ Provide simple ways to specify the reports that are to be derived from the stored data, with flexible formats, useful summaries, and ways to make only subsets of data available to users not authorized to see all of it.

It is essential that 4GLs permit easy specification and preparation of nonstandard reports when requested. Third-generation languages (the kind of languages that are strictly procedure oriented) have great difficulty with such flexibility.

Code generators are intended to eliminate the coding step altogether.

Application generators, although still in their infancy, hold promise for going from application specification to completed application without taking any steps in between.

Figure 1.7 lists some examples of these tools and their vendors.

1.7 4GLS AND INFORMATION SYSTEMS

4GLs are effective development tools. They are now used to build information systems quickly and less expensively than in the past. They are beneficial in shifting the productivity curve because they

■ Substantially improve productivity (quality **and** efficiency).

■ Are results oriented.

■ Are easy to learn and use.

■ Are fast to program.

■ Reduce actual programming and design implementation time.

■ Allow software developers to review system models with end users to verify such items as format and functionality of system functions and input/output formats.

■ Can be used to improve old systems by adding new modules to them.

■ Can be used by end users without consulting professional programmers for such tasks as interactive ad hoc inquiry, information entry, edit, and deletion.

■ Substantially reduce the complexity of developing online and database inquiry systems making software developers more productive.

A Useful Dichotomy

A very useful dichotomy of the development of computing is proposed by James Martin in his book *Applications Development Without Programmers*. Martin has classified computing into two general categories: prespecified and user-driven. We will refer to user-driven computing as nonprespecified computing to avoid giving the impression that the second category of computing is only performed by the end users. In fact, any professional programmers develop (or help to develop) them every day.

Prespecified computing
    Formal requirement specifications are created.
    Structured development cycle is employed.
    Applications development time is many months or years.
    Initial specifications can be established with the
      help of prototypes and 4GLs.
    Programs are formally documented.
    Maintenance is formal, slow, and expensive.
Example: Airline reservations

Nonprespecified computing
    Specifications are not known in detail until initial
      version (prototype) of the system is used.
    Modifications are quick and frequent.
    Users may create their own applications or use the help
      of a professional.
    Application development time is days or at most weeks.
    Applications are created with a 4GL more quickly than
      it can be written.
    The system is self-documenting.
    Incremental changes are made constantly to the
      applications by the users or the analysts who
      assist them. Maintenance is continuous.
    A centrally administered database facility should
      be employed.
Example: Decision support

Figure 1.8   A Prespecified Versus Nonprespecified Computing

In prespecified computing, processing requirements are determined ahead of time. In nonprespecified computing, the details of what is required are not known until an approximate version (prototype) of the intended application is constructed.

In prespecified computing, applications development, if done following the traditional life-cycle development method (see Chapter 5), takes a long time— many months or even years. However, if 4GLs are used to elicit requirements specifications and to validate the design approaches (with the use of the prototyping method, which we discuss in detail in Chapters 5 through 8), the development time for prespecified computing can be drastically reduced.

In nonprespecified computing, the applications development time is usually days, or at the most weeks. With the use of 4GLs and prototyping, the system under construction is modified frequently and quickly.

Figure 1.8 presents this dichotomy.

This dichotomy makes us realize that although these two general types of computing differ, both can benefit from the use of 4GLs. 4GLs provide speed, flexibility, and ease of use. Depending on their orientation, they can be used by professional programmers as well as end users. Nonprespecified computing benefits most in applications that are subject to rapid changes or where the need for ad hoc reporting is high. Prespecified computing can use 4GLs to faster elicit system requirements.

Although 4GLs improve the productivity of applications programmers and end users, they are not applicable in every situation. To obtain the maximum benefit from 4GLs, an environment must be developed in which the 4GLs can be used appropriately. Consider the following example of such an environment.

An Example of Successful 4GL Use

Based on the case in R.H. Sprague, and B. McNurlin, *Information Systems in Practice*, Englewood Cliffs, N.J.: Prentice Hall, 1986.

Hughes Aircraft Company, with corporate headquarters in El Segundo, California, manufactures electronic products for the aerospace, military, and electronics industries. The corporate data processing and communication division, which supports end-user computing, operates in Long Beach, California.

End-user computing in this company actually started in 1973 with the formation of the business user services group. With the help of this group, users started to generate their own reports from data on corporate computers. They did it using CULPRIT, a report writer from Cullinet Software.

In 1978 a separate corporate office automation group was formed. Its main mission was to introduce word processing to the thirty-six divisions within the Hughes Aircraft organization. By 1982 this group had assumed responsibility for support of all personal computers.

In the meantime, business user services started to include statistical analysis tools, financial planning packages, project management software, and graphics software.

By 1984 the business user services and office automation groups were combined to form the corporate information center. This center now comprises three functional groups:

1. Consulting and training
2. Integration
3. Prototype systems

The consulting and training group supports mainframe end-user computing, micro end-user computing, and general word processing throughout the Hughes organization.

The integration group is responsible for mainframe-to-micro communication and for evaluating software products of interest to the Hughes organization.

The prototype system group is responsible for applications development using 4GLs and the prototyping approach.

The systems that the prototyping group develops are typically too difficult for the end users to handle, take more than two weeks to develop in 4GL, involve a large number of intended users, and perform many functions. However, the time they take and the costs they incur do not sufficiently justify developing these systems by a traditional method. All systems written by the prototyping group are turned over to the users on completion. The users must operate and maintain these systems. Many of the end users at Hughes are educated in 4GLs.

Let us examine Hughes's Offshore Supplier Tracking System as an example of how the prototyping group develops a 4GL project. The vice president of Hughes Offshore Trade requested from the corporate data processing department an information system that would track the performance of the company's offshore suppliers. He was informed that it would take three years to develop this system. No suitable packaged software could be found to meet his requirements, so the system had to be developed from scratch. The prototype system group in the corporate information center, however, could start to work on the system immediately.

A working prototype was completed in three months. Work on the complete system with all the required refinements lasted for a bit more than a year. In the end, a very sophisticated system was developed in less than half the time proposed by the data processing department. The system handles more than 150 procedures and has full online inquiry, updating, and transaction logging facilities. Moreover, it coordinates two databases. The users maintain this Offshore Supplier Tracking System and are familiar with the specific 4GL used in this system.

The prototyping group also uses 4GL tools and the prototyping methodology to perform systems maintenance. Systems maintenance in this context means rewriting existing systems in 4GL. Again, once the system is completed, the users must maintain it.

The current financial system was a good candidate for such a rewrite. It was originally developed using a database management system, but it was not enhanced over the years and it was not meeting current needs. The time and cost estimates for the proposed system overhaul were within budget of the finance group. Both the prototyping and finance groups agreed that finance people will participate in the system development and learn the specific 4GL so that they would be able to maintain the final system. A working prototype was completed in three months. The complete system took one more month to develop, at which point it was turned over to the users.

The total development cost for this system was $50,000. The finished system contained 12,000 lines of 4GL code. (In this form it is equivalent to a 60,000-line COBOL system.) So that this system could be fully maintained by the user, of the 12,000 lines of code, about 5,000 are documentation lines.

The system provides online query facilities for division executives. For group executives, it offers financial consolidation capabilities. For division personnel, it allows online updating. It has a database designed for efficiency and uses 4GL code for user maintenance.

The staff at Hughes Aircraft corporate information center realized that 4GLs are bringing to light the types of systems that users can and cannot handle by themselves. When users cannot handle the design of their systems, the prototyping group steps in. What is most important here is that if the system is written in 4GL and the users will be taking over and maintaining the finished system, the users must learn 4GL.

Disadvantages of 4GLs

Although there are many advantages to 4GLs, there are also some disadvantages. 4GLs may be a good choice for small- to medium-size end-user systems that will be subject to many changes, but they may be a poor choice for systems that must process a very large number of transactions and provide access to and maintain a very large database. Such systems need to be developed by professional programmers with professional fourth-generation tools that are not intended for the end user.

Another disadvantage is possible slow response time associated with systems that were developed with 4GLs and that service a large volume of users. (This was a serious problem with the "first generation" of 4GLs [1984]; new releases [1988] handle it much better and can be used for large volume transaction processing.)

The nature and suitability of a given 4GL product must be well understood before it is applied. Consider the following example of the misapplication of a good 4GL tool.

An Example of Inappropriate 4GL Use

Based on C. Babcock, "Big 8 Firm, Politics Tied to 4GL Snafu," *Computerworld*, Vol. 20, No. 30, 1986.

In December 1984 a test of the information system developed for the New Jersey Division of Motor Vehicles showed unacceptably slow response times. But the system was brought on line anyway. A monumental system logjam developed. It was a true disaster.

What happened is this: To speed up the development of the information system, a specific 4GL was employed without testing its suitability for the task. With the use of a 4GL, a planned 5-year project was to be completed in 2 years.

The 4GL (IDEAL) used for the development of this system proved to be entirely unsuitable. Parts of the system could have been developed in 4GL, but other parts, for which an appropriate response time was critical, should have been developed in 3GL. During the system development process, an important rule was broken: An untested 4GL was used for a project critical to the organization. As the project progressed, more limitations of the 4GL were uncovered. Vendor support of this 4GL was also inadequate.

The Division of Motor Vehicles' worst mistake was the absence of a backup plan. Despite all indications of inadequacy, the project was brought on line and it crashed. By then, the old system had been turned off.

Essentially, the mismanagement of the use of the 4GL for a critical system was at the heart of the problem. The great technical promise of the 4GL was not realized, and eventually, the transaction processing parts of the system had to be rewritten in COBOL.

1.8 WHY ARE 4GLS IMPORTANT IN YOUR CAREER?

Many organizations use 4GLs, and more plan to. The challenge is to use them effectively.

Today professional programmers use 4GLs to build complete corporate systems, or parts of these systems. An increasing number of managers, professionals, and information workers are also using 4GLs. Corporate budget planners, investment analysts, personnel managers, production schedulers, and others use these languages to become directly involved with developing applications.

Information centers and development centers grew out of the need to make data more directly accessible to users. 4GLs are ideal tools for these centers, but their advantage can only be realized if those who use them are trained in their proper use and are cognizant of possible problems.

For example, when users become directly involved in the development of applications programs many issues must be faced. One of these is: What is the impact of user-developed applications on the corporate computing facilities and staff?

Training users in 4GLs techniques, helping them develop their own applications, and making sure that they understand when the intervention of the professional system developer is needed become important.

In your professional life, you undoubtedly will be involved in helping to develop information systems and in building your own. The evolution of the use of computers in business (see Figure 1.2) would seem to support this prediction. Therefore it will serve you well to enter the job market already understanding the functions and uses of 4GLs. We hope that this book will be helpful in this endeavor.

1.9 SUMMARY

The evolution of the use of computers in business and the software crisis that developed over the years led to the development of new tools aimed at increasing the productivity of applications programmers and users. The changing relationship between programming labor cost and the cost of hardware brought about the development of 4GLs.

4GLs are well suited for the development of systems that require ad hoc reports and whose program logic, report formats, and calculations will change frequently. End users can develop systems using 4GLs as long as they are cognizant of the languages' strengths and limitations. Although 4GLs are easy to learn, understanding their place in development of information systems is important for their effective use.

EXERCISES

1. What is a programming language?
2. How can you characterize different language levels?
3. What is the largest data object manipulated by a language in each generation?

4. How would you define a procedural language?

5. Contrast a procedural language with a nonprocedural one.

6. What are nonprocedural languages suited to?

7. Is Lotus 1-2-3 a language?

8. Characterize the evolution of computer use in business organizations.

9. Why are we seeing the proliferation of programming productivity tools?

10. What is the software crisis, and how did happen?

11. Discuss programmers' work overload and its implications.

12. What is system development productivity?

13. Why are quality and efficiency important when discussing system development productivity? Be specific.

14. How can productivity be improved?

15. Is end-user productivity an important issue? Why or why not?

16. What is a 4GL?

17. Why would a 4GL make a professional programmer more productive? And an end user?

18. What impact do you suppose the use of 4GLs has on system analysis and design?

19. How would you characterize prespecified, as opposed to nonprespecified computing?

20. Consider a particular business organization with which you are familiar. If, in this organization, application systems were developed with 4GLs, do you perceive any problems?

21. When would a 4GL be an ineffective tool?

22. Can you foresee the building of "personal programs" and "little databases" by end users in organizations? Are there any problems with such systems?

23. For what types of information systems are 4GLs well suited?

PROJECTS

Contact some medium- to large-size business organizations. Interview several managers and professionals and find out the following:

■ Is end-user computing encouraged?

■ Are 4GLs available for use?

■ Who is using 4GLs and for what?

■ What training and support are available to help with the use of 4GLs?

■ What hardware, if any, is used to support end-user program development?

Prepare a brief report on your findings.

REFERENCES AND SUGGESTED READINGS

1. Bergi, W. E. "Architecture prototyping in the software engineering environment." *IBM Systems Journal*, Vol. 23, No. 1, 1984, pp. 4-18.

2. Bernstein, L., and Yuhas, C. M. "Blood from turnips?" *Datamation*, Vol. 31, No. 2, January 15, 1985, pp. 108-112.

3. Case, A. F. *Information Systems Development: Principles of Computer-Aided Software Engineering.* Englewood Cliffs, N.J.: Prentice-Hall, 1986.

4. Cobb, R. H. "In praise of 4GLs." *Datamation*, July 15, 1985.

5. Edelman, F. "Managers, computer systems and productivity." *MIS Quarterly*, Vol. 5, No. 3, September, 1981, pp. 1-19.

6. Erickson, R. W. "Tales of the DP inn." *Datamation*, Vol. 31, No. 8, April 15, 1985, pp. 168-171.

7. Ghezzi, C., and Jazayeri, M. *Programming Language Concepts.* New York, N.Y.: John Wiley and Sons, 1975.

8. Goyette, R. "Fourth generation systems soothe end user unrest." *Data Management*, Vol. 24, No. 1, January 1986, pp. 30-32.

9. Green, J. "Productivity in the fourth generation: Six case studies." *Journal of Management Information Systems*, Vol. 1, No. 3, Winter 1984-1985, pp. 49-63.

10. Gremillion, L., and Pyburn, P. "Breaking the system development bottleneck." *Harvard Business Review*, Vol. 61, No. 2, March-April 1983, pp. 130-137.

11. Jenkins, A. M. "Surveying the software generator market." *Datamation*, Vol. 31, No. 17, September 1, 1985, pp. 105-120.

12. Kohler, J. "It takes a good game plan to win savings with 4GLs." *Computerworld*, Vol. 22, No. 30, July 25, 1988.

13. Leber, J. "Application or misapplication?" *Computerworld*, Vol. 22, No. 35, August 29, 1988.

14. Lerner, N. B., Brownstein, I., and Smith, W. W. "Winds of change." *Computerworld*, Vol. 16, No. 14, March 29, 1982.

15. MacLennan, B. *Principles of Programming Languages: Design, Evaluation, and Implementation.* New York: Holt, Rinehart and Winston, 1983.

16. Martin, J. *Applications Development Without Programmers.* Englewood Cliffs, N. J.: Prentice-Hall, 1982.

17. McCracken, D. D. "Software in the 80s: Perils and promises." *Computerworld-Extra*, September 17, 1980, pp. 5-10.

18. Nolan, D. "The first two years, four months, two weeks and seven minutes of a new system's life." *Computerworld*, Vol. 20, No. 41, October 13, 1986, pp. 93-100.

19. Pratt, T. *Programming Languages: Design and Implementation.* 2nd ed., Englewood Cliffs, N.J.: Prentice-Hall, 1984.

20. Rauch-Hindin, W.B. *A Guide to Commercial Artificial Intelligence: Fundamentals and Real-World Applications.* Englewood Cliffs, N.J.: Prentice-Hall, 1988.

21. Read, N. S., and Harmon, D. "Assuring MIS success." *Datamation*, Vol. 27, No. 2, February 1981, pp. 109-120.

22. Read, N. S., and Harmon, D. S. "Language barrier to productivity." *Datamation*, Vol. 29, No. 2, February 1983, pp. 209-211.

23. Wexelblat, R. L., ed. *History of Programming Languages.* New York: Academic Press, 1981.

CHAPTER 2

The 4GL Environment

*In its simplest form, learning is the process by which inputs of
information in the past lead to images of the future in the present.*

Kenneth Boulding

2.1 INTRODUCTION

In this chapter, we present the evolution of fourth-generation languages. We
consider the evolutionary steps of any technological development and point out
that software tools evolved through similar steps to CASE (Computer Aided
Software Engineering) tools. We conclude that 4GLs were developed for data-centered information systems and that database inquiry/retrieval languages form the
foundation of 4GLs.

We classify 4GLs according to their capabilities and applications. These languages range from simple query languages that can recognize a few synonyms to
powerful integrated application generators that include tools for graphics and
financial analysis as well as statistical procedures.

We also include an extensive list of corporations that use 4GLs for their
application generation and conclude with some brief remarks on future developments in 4GLs.

2.2 THE GENESIS OF FOURTH-GENERATION LANGUAGES

Programming tools have become progressively easier to use as they evolved from
the first assemblers and compilers to today's icon-based operating systems and
window environments. The basic motivation for making the programming interface more user friendly was the need to reduce the amount of programming
required in the systems development cycle. However, the creation of applications
software that is reliable, arrives on time, and is easy to maintain is still a big
problem for many organizations.

The process of developing computer information systems involves using technology. To understand the genesis of 4GLs, it would be helpful to examine the
general pattern of technological development.

Technological development occurs in basically three stages:

1. *Tool stage,* where human intellect guides human energy; for example, a hammer.

2. *Machine stage,* where human intellect guides a non-human source of energy; for example, an automobile, a personal computer.

3. *Automated stage,* where automation, which guides itself, replaces human intellect and energy; for example, the fully automated, self-guided underground transportation system at Atlanta airport, or the (nonexistent as yet) totally automated and paperless information (office) system.

You can see the evolution of technology toward automation everywhere. Consider the proliferation of modern household appliances and, for example, the fully automated washer and dryer.

Software tools and applications development methods follow the same evolutionary path.

The notion of automating the whole system development process is now becoming a reality through computer-aided software engineering (CASE) tools. CASE tools are not yet integrated enough (see Albert F. Case reference) to completely automate the process of building computer systems. Nevertheless, they represent a profound shift in the way computer information systems are going to be developed. 4GLs are the tools of this automation.

CASE technology intends to make automating tools flexible and easy to use in order to:

■ Improve analyst and the programmer productivity (that is, both effectiveness and efficiency: doing what needs to be done and doing it right).

■ Improve software quality and reduce maintenance.

■ Increase management control over the software development process.

Thus, automated software development tools fall into the following categories:

1. Programming support tools

2. Design technique tools

3. Project management tools

Essentially 4GLs were developed as programming support tools to reduce the number of instructions required to get access to and to manipulate data. The beginnings of the 4GLs can be traced to the technological advances in access methods of the late 1950s and early 1960s, which led to the development of databases and database management systems (DBMS). Before databases and database management techniques, separate files were developed for each application. The focus was on traditional processing functions; stored data were specified and collected only after processing had been defined. The characteristics and

Computing Generator	Characteristics
First and second	Machine and assembler languages Batch systems Paper reports
Third	High-level languages: FORTRAN, COBOL Terminal access to data Disk files Centralized data processing

Figure 2.1   First Three Generations of Computing

Software	Management

• Database
• Database management system
• Data dictionary
• SQL
• 4GLs
• Distributed databases
• Cooperative processing systems
• CASE tools
• Decision support systems
• Expert systems
• Natural language
	• Information systems used
	  for strategic advantage
	• Information/development
	  centers
	• Departmental computing
	• Development by end users
	• Use of PCs
	• Proliferation of workstations

Figure 2.2   Fourth Generation of Computing

methods associated with the first three generations of computing are summarized in Figure 2.1.

Databases were developed to replace application-oriented standalone files. With a concept of a database (understood as any collection of data that is organized for access and use under user control), the emphasis shifted to the data-centered approach. This data-centered approach assumes a model that reflects the information content upon which an organization depends, that is, its business practices.

In the fourth generation of computing, data is increasingly regarded as the basic *resource* needed to operate the business. As with other resources, the management of data becomes important. The effective use of data for all the business functions in an organization (from production control to marketing) is becoming so significant that the data resource is now perceived to have strategic importance. That is why databases and their management have become one of the most important aspects of fourth-generation computing. Methods and notions associated with fourth-generation computing are listed in Figure 2.2.

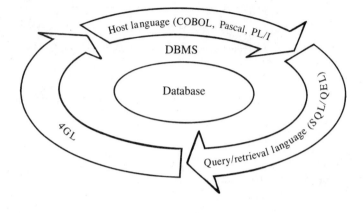

Figure 2.3 Progression to the 4GL

Databases and 4GLs

Before database systems existed, all business applications were programmed in languages such as macroassemblers, FORTRAN, or COBOL. The programmer had to decide how the programs would go about retrieving records or processing entire files. The first commercial DBMS had "hooks" to these host languages. Later developments brought about what are called query/retrieval, or database languages, examples of which are SQL and QUEL. The term query/retrieval language suggests high-level query commands in a user-friendly context. The query/retrieval language forms an additional layer of software between the DBMS and the user. Database query languages are the foundation for the development of 4GLs.

With the increasing use of query/retrieval languages, the need to devise tools for automated sequences of query language commands became apparent. This led to the creation of 4GL capabilities to support file building, file updating, and reporting that could not be executed directly under query commands. At first, 4GL software was offered as an add-on to existing DBMS packages, but it eventually evolved into 4GL packages that incorporate their own DBMS modules, including query language capabilities. Thus the next step in the evolution brought DBMS which, when combined with a fourth-generation proprietary language, permitted complete applications to be built within one programming environment. Those are called programmable database products (DBMS/4GL) or application-oriented languages.

The progression to the fourth-generation languages is shown in Figure 2.3. All the tools from host language to the 4GL on the outer shell of the data management structure in the figure allow the user to access and manipulate data. The direction of this progression is to diminish programmers' intervention in accessing data, to ultimately automate the data access and manipulation.

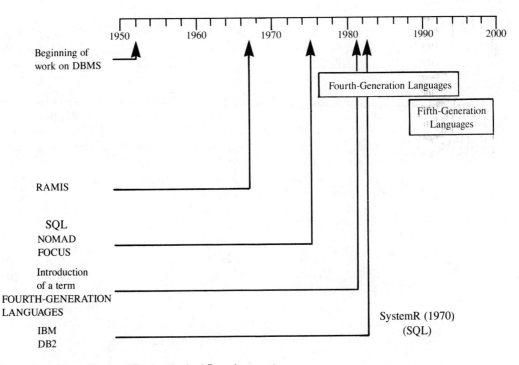

Figure 2.4   Time Scale of Technological Developments

The class of fourth-generation languages, the main topic of this book, started to appear on the market in the late 1960s.

The first commercial fourth-generation language, RAMIS (Rapid Access Management Information System), which became available in 1969, led to the development of two other fourth-generation languages: NOMAD and FOCUS. Both of these became available commercially in 1975. The term fourth-generation language (4GL) itself is attributed to Nigel Read and Douglas Harmon. It can be found in their article "Assuring MIS Success," which appeared in the February 1981 issue of *Datamation*. A time scale of the technological developments leading up to 4GLs is illustrated in Figure 2.4.

4GL Products

At first, 4GLs were available only through time-sharing. Since time-sharing users were generally unsophisticated programmers, fourth-generation language vendors had to create good user-friendly interfaces. The software vendors who developed such 4GL products fall into two categories:

1. Software vendors who developed standalone 4GLs
2. Database management system vendors who developed DBMS/4GL products

Some software vendors decided to develop products geared to a narrow class of users or problems. They covered such areas as business modeling, business graphics, statistics, and decision support systems in general. Examples of specific products in this category include IFPS, INQUIRE, and Tell-A-Graf.

Another group of vendors elected to develop products that include a broad range of integrated functions. These are primarily aimed at data processing professionals and are intended to serve as productivity tools. The basic goal was to build products that could deliver integrated complex applications. These products provide an impressive range of integrated functions, including database management systems, database query language, large-volume processing, report generation, screen generation, graphics, financial modeling, automatic documentation, application development tools, and callability to standard languages such as COBOL or PL/I. Specific products in this category include MANTIS, ADS/On-Line, NATURAL, and IDEAL (see also Chapter 4).

With only a handful of products in the beginning of this decade, the 4GL market has exploded. Currently hundreds of products are available with a constantly expanding variety of specializations.

2.3 CATEGORIES OF FOURTH-GENERATION LANGUAGES

Fourth-generation languages can be classified by:

- Language function
- Intended user
- Language characteristics

Language Function Classification

Let us consider functional classification of fourth-generation products. Limited-purpose 4GLs include:

1. **Query-and-Update Languages** allow for queries and updates of data. These vary from simple facilities that have existed since the earliest disk storage devices to complex database user languages. Examples are IBM's Query-by-Example (QBE) and SQL, and Digital's Datatrieve.

2. **Report Generators** allow data to be extracted from databases or files and then formatted into reports. Good report generators have extensive arithmetic and logic capabilities. Some are independent of databases or query facilities; others are extensions of query languages. They are generally easy to use. Examples are IBM's RPG III and ADRS, and Informatics MARK IV/ REPORTER.

3. **Graphics Languages** allow data to be graphically represented. Like report generators, some graphics languages allow extensive arithmetic and logical

operations to be performed on data. Some are designed only for graphics presentation; they create attractively laid out and labeled printouts, slides, or viewgraphs. Others are designed specifically to reveal relationships among the data they process. Since a picture can be worth a thousand words, graphics languages provide a powerful way to understand complex data. An example is the GDDM graphical data display manager from IBM.

4. **Decision-Support Products** help create systems for improving the decision-making process. They allow the user to enter formulas for calculations: to do statistical analysis, to build optimization models, and to explore what-if questions. Some of these languages incorporate a diversity of sophisticated operations research and graphics tools. An example is SAS.

5. **Application Generators** help create data processing applications. They permit data entry with data validation; file or database definition, calculations, and logic description; and output creation. An example is IBM's ADF (Application Development Facility).

6. **Application Languages** are intended for one particular application or particular application area, for example financial management, robot control, computer-aided design, and numerical control of machine tools. Examples are GPSS (used for queuing systems) and IFPS (for financial analysis).

In most applications development, limited-purpose 4GLs are used only in conjunction with other products.

General-purpose 4GLs (also referred to as full-function 4GLs) are capable of generating generalized applications. They were originally intended to substitute for COBOL as a general-purpose business-oriented computer language. The components of a general-purpose 4GLs include

1. Easy-to-use interfaces and nonprocedural facilities

2. Procedural programming facilities for complex application generation

3. A sophisticated data retrieval/management system

4. A wide range of integrated special-purpose software tools for business applications, for example:
   a. Screen design and painting facilities
   b. Report generator
   c. Graphics generator
   d. Interactive decision support tools for accounting and financial modeling and for mathematical and statistical analyses

5. Links to independent special-purpose business software tools

6. Links between micros and mainframes to facilitate distributed data processing

Examples of general-purpose 4GLs are NOMAD, FOCUS, IDEAL, and POWER-HOUSE.

User Classification

There are generally two categories within this classification:

1. Languages designed for end users
2. Languages designed for data processing professionals

Each group satisfies different management information systems needs.

End-user languages are designed to simplify data retrieval and reporting. 4GLs of this type provide an interface to users to guide them through the development of a report or screen. Because of the intended audience, these 4GLs sacrifice functionality and efficiency in favor of ease of use. They are neither effective nor appropriate for developing full-scale production applications, and they do not replace third-generation languages. (Note: these languages do not materially improve long-term professional programmer productivity—they were not created to do so.)

The other group of languages, sometimes called **development center 4GLs**, are specifically designed to simplify and accelerate the task of developing entire production systems. 4GLs of this class must perform complex screen handling and transaction processing logic, ensure data integrity, and support production-oriented file management systems—all within a multiuser mainframe environment. Development center languages are used for transaction processing systems and large databases. It is assumed that data processing professionals will be controlling the development process, and that their first priorities are power and flexibility.

Some examples for IBM 370 mainframes are: ADR/DATACOM from Applied Data Research, CA-UNIVERSE from Computer Associates, MODEL 204 from Computer Corporation of America, and IDMS/R from Cullinet Software. An example for non-IBM mainframes, specifically, the Unisys mainframes (available for the smallest to the largest mainframes), is LINC II.

There are also some independent fourth-generation products developed primarily to be used in conjunction with existing DBMS or other fourth-generation languages. Some examples of such front-end products are the QMF/QBE from IBM, which serves as an interface of DB2 (IBM database product) and the natural language-based INTELLECT, from Artificial Intelligence Corporation, which can be used with a variety of DBMS.

Language Characteristics Classification

General classification by language characteristics used to place 4GLs in the single category of nonprocedural language. But, today, 4GLs can be procedural as well as nonprocedural.

In nonprocedural languages, the user/programmer is not concerned with the low-level procedural details of **how** the system is to accomplish specific computing task. The 4GL software takes care of that. The user's concern is with the **what** of the task. However, after some real-world experience with nonprocedural lan-

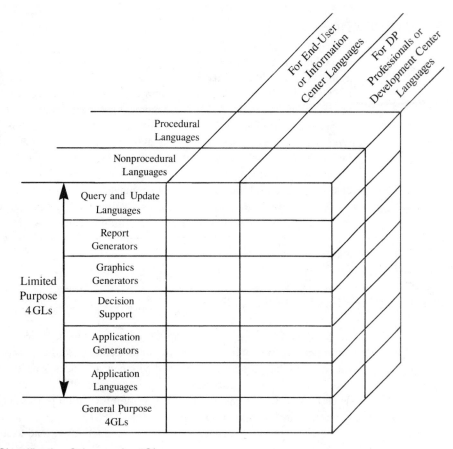

Figure 2.5   Classification Schemes for 4GLs

guages, it became clear to the users of these languages that the nonprocedural approach was imposing limitations; certain types of computing tasks could be specified only in a **how**, or procedural, code.

Procedural fourth-generation languages—seemingly a contradiction in terms—offer fourth-generation language ease of use, while also allowing users to specify detailed computational procedures, if necessary. These type of languages are now so popular that the working definition of fourth-generation languages has been changed to allow for both procedural and nonprocedural languages.

All 4GLs, whether called procedural or nonprocedural, employ very high-level instructions not present in third-generation languages. That is, programs and applications created with fourth-generation languages have fewer instructions than are needed with COBOL. Hence, 4GLs are also sometimes referred to as very high-level languages (VHLL). This is how we should generally classify 4GLs.

Figure 2.5 summarizes all the classification schemes.

2.4 STANDARDS

Procedural languages like FORTRAN, COBOL, or Pascal are subject to standards established by professional or industrial societies. For 4GLs there are no standards as yet. Each 4GL now has its own command syntax, rules, and features and many operate with their own database management software.

Standards are particularly important as aids to migration between systems. Eventually standards for 4GLs will evolve. For example the query language facilities of most 4GLs, which control the access or manipulation functions performed upon the records within a database, are now SQL based to conform to an emerging standard for database query language.

SQL is ultimately more important as a software interface than it is as a user interface. Many practitioners predict that within the next few years it will be the standard language for data access communications from one software system to another.

2.5 FUTURE DEVELOPMENTS

Since 4GL technology is still rapidly evolving, the next decade will see the introduction of many innovations and improvements. Perhaps, with the introduction of fifth-generation computers and with new advances in artificial intelligence and natural language processing, 4GLs will evolve into fifth-generation systems. Then these new systems will be not simply information processing systems, but *knowledge* information processing systems (KIPS).

New generation languages increase the productivity of end users. Since these types of workers will constitute the majority of the future work force in most developed nations, these productivity gains can have profound economic effects.

4GLs on PCs and Cooperative Processing Systems

The marriage of the PC and fourth-generation languages is now a reality. The early wave of fourth-generation languages for PCs includes PC/NOMAD, PC/FOCUS, IDEAL, CA/EXECUTIVE, and PC/POWERHOUSE.

Since data communication technology allows links from micros to minis to mainframes, cooperative processing is now possible. The concept of cooperative processing is for computers on the network to make use of each other's capabilities. Machines in the network communicate as equals. In cooperative processing, communications links are used to integrate PCs with minicomputers and mainframes so that data can be transferred (uploaded or downloaded) to where it can be processed most conveniently.

Cooperative processing is the ability to *distribute* the processing of an application across multiple CPUs. It allows you to move resource-intensive functions such as user interaction and data validation to the PC, while still maintaining the security and integrity of data in a *shared* environment, that is, the mainframe.

A typical cooperative application is one in which the user interface, action specification, and data validation take place locally on the PC. Mainframe processing then consists of transparent database access for referencing very large look-up tables, or for maintenance of data that is accessible simultaneously to multiple users.

In most applications, cooperative processing improves response time for users. One major contribution is the reduction of the information transmitted. When using a remote terminal in traditional processing, the system has to transmit both screen formats and data. Typically screen formats take many more bytes, compared to the number of bytes required for the data. Moving the resource intensive screen management function to a PC reduces the traffic over the communication link. Although the application response time is determined by the number of users, the tasks on the mainframe, and sharing the network, offloading as much of processing as possible to the PC reduces both mainframe usage and network traffic. This can contribute to a more consistent response time.

Cooperative processing is applicable to any existing or planned application. In general, to make an existing mainframe application a cooperative processing application requires moving the user interaction to the PC and adding the communications capability. Mainframe resources used by the application become reduced, and the application becomes available to a wider audience.

With the use of the 4GLs, the application building is primarily done on PCs, and database maintenance and input/output are done on bigger computers. At present the nature of the data link technology varies widely because it is new and there are no standards. However, information industry trends are such that it is quite possible that both links and PC workstations will emerge as dominant technologies by the end of this decade.

New products supporting cooperative processing are NOMAD/PC, RAMIS/PC, and IDEAL/ESCORT.

Hybrid Languages

On the horizon there is a new breed of 4GLs, hybrid languages, which combine the best of COBOL with the best of 4GLs. Although 4GL users have for some time been adding patches of COBOL to their programs wherever they wanted speed or greater sophistication, these new 4GLs will not need patching. They will simply be faster products. When those products arrive, users will have the best of both worlds for a change.

Fourth-Generation Language Cross-Compilers

Even though 4GLs reduce the time required to build new application systems, they trade development effort for computer equipment use and the ability to transport applications across different hardware architectures.

Development of a new family of cross-compilers to enable data processing professionals to translate programs written in 4GLs into standard third-generation languages or into other 4GLs automatically takes advantage of the complementary strengths of 4GLs and standard 3GLs. The first such cross-compiler is intended for translating applications written in IDEAL 4GL into ANSI Standard COBOL.

Merger of Database Machines with 4GLs

A database machine is a computer designed especially for handling large databases and for fast retrieval of data from them. Database machines can offload database management functions from a host computer to increase response time performance, but they generally are not considered user friendly. Fourth-generation languages, on the other hand, are regarded as user friendly, but they have problems dealing with large databases or with the concurrent use of data by more than one user. However, synergy is still possible between database machines and fourth-generation languages.

Database machines can offer unique advantages:

1. Multicomputer access
2. Search of very large databases
3. Good response times for large volume transaction processing

At present the only vendors of database machines are Teradata, who produces DBC/1012, and Britton Lee, who manufactures INTELLIGENT MACHINE.

Merging of database machines and fourth-generation languages is also underway. An example is an interface between NOMAD and DBC/1012.

Natural Language Processors

Natural language processing (NLP) gives users the ability to communicate with a computer in their native (natural) language. NLP offers a conversational-style interface with unrestricted syntax, as opposed to other user-friendly interfaces, such as icon-based or pointing (using touch-sensitive screen or a mouse) ones. NLP are intended mainly as an easy access (front end) to large database systems. An example of a natural language product is INTELLECT, which can interface with FOCUS and data management systems such as DB2, SQL/DS, and ADABAS. NLP typically requires a lot of main memory. We briefly review NLP and INTELLECT in Chapter 4.

Artificial Intelligence Technology

Artificial intelligence (AI) concepts will certainly work their way into fourth-generation language technology. 4GLs represent a transition into another generation of software, and by adding functionality, they should continue to evolve.

4GLs built around an active data dictionary, DBMS, and one or more development languages will also rely on expert systems that design databases, provide automatic data access methods in response to queries, and generate code from program designs. Expert systems will be embedded in DBMS, 4GLs, and full-blown applications. Natural language interfaces and speech recognition, coupled with artificial intelligence, will drastically alter end-user computing and involvement in the applications development process.

Trends for the 1990s and Beyond

Many organizations are now putting in place a new computing architecture composed of three tiers: mainframes, minis, and microcomputers. An essential aspect of this architecture is integration—the integration of mainframes, minis, and micros (functioning as workstations).

The economics of this type of integration requires that the processing load be distributed (see the discussion of cooperative processing earlier in this chapter). The cost of processing on workstations and minicomputers is much less than processing on mainframes. Applications can be built cheaper on the smaller systems. The cost of one MIPS (millions of instructions per second) processing on workstations is estimated at $4,000, whereas on a mainframe the cost of one MIPS is $16,000. This three-tiered architecture is possible because of two developments: distributed database technology and cooperative processing.

The idea behind distributed databases is to have a single logical database implemented over heterogeneous machines and different operating systems.

Distributed applications can also be built using cooperative processing systems. These systems provide 4GL applications development on workstations, coupled with an active data dictionary on a central minicomputer or mainframe. Development and execution can then be done on a distributed basis, that is, they are offloaded to smaller machines.

These two technologies—distributed databases and cooperative processing—will provide solid support for fifth-generation application development and enforce standards in local area networks (LANs), user interfaces, database access, and so on.

The one technology that essentially defines fifth-generation applications development is CASE. The ultimate goal of this technology is to attain such a level of development automation that applications can be built without programmers. The most important input to the system development will come from business analysts who understand the nature and structure of their businesses and using CASE can routinely build their applications.

The potential of CASE products comes from the data-centered approach and the concept of dictionaries/repositories. Dictionaries/repositories not only store data about data, but they also contain information about processing, screens, reports, and so on. They are active, dynamic controlling environments. They are not simply passive stores of information, but rather they are integrated with other system building tools such as query language and DBMS. By storing information in a dictionary/repository rather than in programs, reusability of information on, for example, formats of screens, reports, and so on, is possible. Such reusability brings about increased productivity.

Implementing CASE technology requires a major commitment from many organizations. It requires a shift in perceiving how to approach the development process and a commitment to and investment in training. CASE technology is revolutionary because it will allow smaller business organizations to build strategic information systems, which now cost large companies hundreds of millions of dollars.

Consider what microcomputers and minicomputers did for the processing power of small companies. The new software tools such as 4GLs will do the same in the near future for their application power. To be effective in your work, you need to know your business and to know new development tools. 4GLs are tools worth knowing.

2.6 THE USE OF 4GLS: EXAMPLES

We now present some business examples of the use of 4GLs. Our intent is to give you an idea why and where 4GLs are used. This is not a complete list of usages and languages; it is a sampling of organizations that implement a 4GL and is intended to give you a feel for the scope of the use of this tool.

Service

1. The Institute of Internal Auditors developed a software package based on 4GL to be used for audit risk analysis, planning, and management. AuditMASTERPLAN, as this package is called, is currently being used by the Marriott Corporation, a leading hotelier, to quantify possible audits, rank audits according to risk, suggest audit frequency, and to do long-range planning by audit year. Use of this package has contributed to the success of Marriott in long-term planning and budgeting.

2. Chedoke-McMaster Hospitals in Ontario, Canada, are using a 4GL to reduce applications backlog. They were faced with demands beyond the capacity of their limited resources of the Laboratory Computer Services (LCS), which provides computer services to the hospitals. In 1981 they made a strategic decision to replace FORTRAN and COBOL with a 4GL. They decided to use POWERHOUSE from Cognos. About 20 systems were built with this tool. The largest and most complex system is the microbiology information system, which uses 70 screens and generates 50 different reports. When the hospitals converted to Digital Equipment Corporation (DEC) VAX 11/750 computers in 1985, the conversion was not difficult because POWERHOUSE is supported on the DEC hardware.

Government

1. The data processing department for the City of Buffalo, New York, serves all the city's municipal departments. When the department was computerized 10

years ago, it was adequately served by 3GLs. However, the quantity and diversity of data files that the department has to access have grown beyond all expectations. It receives more than 20 requests a day from different city departments to extract data and issue reports.

In 1986, the City of Buffalo contracted to test a 4GL that would allow the data processing department to access multiple files across previously incompatible databases. The product they tested and eventually purchased (because it worked well, was easy to learn, and was cost effective) was MAGNA 8 4GL from Magna Software Corporation. The department now delivers reports in 24 hours, rather than 10 days.

2. The Department of Central Management Services (CMS) for the State of Illinois has an annual budget of $650 million, employs 13,000, and administers a wide variety of support functions. Some of the support functions are: personnel recruitment, jobs classification, labor relations, employee benefit programs, central purchasing, operations, and maintenance of state buildings and vehicles. CMS manages the state's computer and telecommunications operations as well, including the procurement of all computer hardware and software.

CMS became concerned about the problem of supporting end-user computing with too many computing tools, especially the issue of training and support when many different tools are used. Management decided to look into a 4GL that could be used as the application development tool for all the agencies, so a 4GL search committee made up of interested agencies and CMS staff was formed. The selected product was to increase the productivity of the applications development staff, and to give end users an interactive, easy-to-use tool to access and manipulate data. NOMAD from Must Software International was chosen for its flexibility and was installed for a 60-day trial period. The development of six applications of varying degrees of complexity began. Although many of CMS' NOMAD users are small agencies with user-developed desk-top applications, one agency (Illinois Department of Public Health) has a NOMAD database containing 13 million records. CMS now runs one of the country's most sophisticated and ambitious end-user computing programs whose primary tool is a 4GL.

Manufacturing

1. Kawasaki Motors Corporation USA needed to solve their application backlog problems with a 4GL. A decision was made to use PROIV from PRO Computer Sciences Inc. Initial use of this 4GL was limited. The use of the PROIV increased rapidly (after a rather slow start) when the management realized that the introduction of a 4GL required investment in staff training. Conservative estimates indicate that productivity increased by a factor of 5. Application backlog was reduced substantially.

2. A customized software program has improved communications, productivity, accuracy, and efficiency at the Fairchild Control Systems' Manhattan Beach,

California, manufacturing facility. A customized inventory control system was built using a 4GL from Mitrol Inc. Fairchild's business base consists mainly of high-technology, low-quantity production items. The first step in implementation of this software system was to form a team of production control, material control, purchasing, receiving, accounting, and data processing personnel. They worked together to establish four functional areas of the inventory control system: data entry, query, data verification, and report generation. One important feature of the system is that anyone with the proper access rights can use real-time data. Use of the 4GL enables users to develop new reporting formats easily.

3. Timex Corporation, one of the world's leading producers of time pieces, headquartered in Middlebury, Connecticut, has manufacturing facilities around the world. Most of these plants have their own computer facilities and are linked to Middlebury via the Timex Communications Network.

In the middle of 1984, Timex realized that it had a problem with its distribution system. The sales department wanted a more accurate and flexible way of releasing orders to customers on a more timely and direct basis. The development of this new system had a tight deadline; it had to be operational by January 1985.

Writing a system in a 3GL would have taken too long and would have been too costly to maintain in the face of constantly changing conditions that affect the release of orders. In addition, lots of reporting was required, much of it ad hoc. The only way that the system could be up and running quickly was to use a 4GL. The 4GL required was one that had good procedural language capabilities, and did not need to branch to PL/I or COBOL routines. The MIS professionals decided to use NOMAD from Must Software International.

Two of Timex's most experienced users were assigned to the development of the new order release database and reporting system. After some initial training, they developed the schema, screens, and report generators in three months. Next the MIS staff built the necessary interfaces to the existing system. The completed system was delivered two months before the deadline.

Natural Resources

1. Chevron currently maintains an internal time-sharing system that services more than 12,000 end users throughout North America. The company's information center, consisting of two data centers, handles the diverse and often sophisticated needs of its end users quickly and efficiently. Staffed by 1200 data processing and support personnel, the centers handle a variety of computer needs. Six large mainframes are dedicated to the company's internal time-sharing services. Another six are used for large online systems and batch processing jobs such as payroll. The time-sharing network offers a selection of languages, but the greatest share of the work goes to a 4GL, NOMAD. NOMAD applications, for example, monitor worldwide oil flow and information on company patents and machinery.

2. Oil Sands Group of Suncor Inc., one of Canada's largest integrated oil and gas companies, switched from traditional software to a 4GL using prototyping. The software they use is POWERHOUSE. Suncor used prototyping as a selling tool to get new projects off the ground and to build functional models of its new maintenance and materials management systems. Although the users did not have a lot of experience with computer systems, they had the opportunity to review the progress of the system development and to make changes along the way through weekly meetings with system analysts.

Insurance

1. Crawford & Co., headquartered in Atlanta, Georgia, provides risk management services to both corporate and insurance markets through over 700 branch locations in the United States, Canada, and Puerto Rico. One of its services is rehabilitation, which includes rehabilitation counseling.

   Crawford & Co. is now better able to find suitable work for recently rehabilitated workers because of 4GLs. Crawford has about 250 rehabilitation counselors offering services required under the Workers' Compensation Act. Before the computerization, the counselors gathered and analyzed data manually and compiled a list of occupations that the rehabilitated claimant could perform. A request to the information resources division resulted in the decision to use 4GL to develop a computerized system from scratch.

   The decision was made to use NOMAD, a 4GL/DBMS from Must Software International. Using NOMAD, one senior system analyst working with the rehabilitation specialist was able to complete the prototype of the occupational system in 4 months. (The analysis and design group has estimated that to do the same work with a 3GL such as COBOL would take at least 2 person-years.) The new computerized occupational system, built entirely using NOMAD has resulted in a dramatic increase in job placements.

2. The Travelers Corporation's MIS department no longer generates ad hoc reports, but rather teaches 4GL to end users so that they can create their own reports. The needs of different users are studied and the customized training program teaches them only the necessary skills. The use of 4GLs allows the users to be programmers in a limited way, which decentralizes database access and frees up the MIS staff.

3. The Equitable Life Leasing Corporation uses structured programming techniques with 4GL to develop complex applications. Projects are first broken down into small processing modules with an automated design tool (Life Cycle Manager from Spectrum International), and programming is done with IDEAL from ADR.

4. At American Family Mutual Insurance, 4GLs help provide faster policy writing, more active participation in data calculation and verification, and improved data management and processing. Products used are the DBMS/4GL, ADABAS, and the 4GL, NATURAL. These products offer flexibility in designing systems and help reduce maintenance of new systems.

Transportation

The rapid transit system of Ontario, Canada, depends on Ottawa-Carleton Regional Transit Commission computers and the software that drives them. The transit system carries 90 million passengers every year. It has an online, real-time radio communications system, which integrates voice communication with bus tracking and scheduling. Customers can determine bus arrival times at their stops over the telephone. When the Regional Transit Commission decided to change from IBM to VAX hardware, they also decided to rewrite existing interactive programs in a 4GL inhouse. The tool they chose for this transition was Cognos' POWERHOUSE. This software is said to meet at present 80 percent of their needs.

Banking

1. Commodore Saving Association uses ADABAS DBMS/4GL from Software AG to reduce its applications bottleneck. Use of the DBMS brings all the important information into an integrated repository where it can be managed and where access by all end users can be controlled. The ease of writing applications is achieved with the 4GL.

2. Citicorp Investments Bank's group human resource office in New York has succeeded in decentralizing its operations and giving reporting capabilities to its individual businesses. In the past, personnel data for all the businesses were centralized at the group level. As business expanded and became more decentralized, reporting needs began to exceed the capacity of the system.

   To allow for decentralization, the human resource information system is running a 4GL (FOCUS) on networked PCs and an IBM 4341 mainframe. The data in this system fall into four categories: corporate data, local data, compensation data, and salary history. Assuring the security and confidentiality of information is accomplished by encrypting all masters and using security features built into the FOCUS files. Responsibility for downloading data and reporting data into the mainframe rests with the individual businesses.

3. The Meridian Bank Corporation always performs a cost justification step before selecting a system. Cost justification requires very different procedures and a different perspective than the system selection process. The cost justification for the use of DBMS/4GL tool allowed Meridian to identify the cost savings associated with shorter coding time, reduced applications backlog, and lower applications development costs. Meridian decided to use NOMAD (from Must Software International) for all their new applications.

Academia

1. The University of Texas at Austin shifted its administrative data processing from a traditional, centralized COBOL shop to a distributed resource operation by using 4GLs and fourth-generation development tools. Problems with

applications backlogs led the university to decide to distribute a large part of the work to end users through the use of a DBMS/4GL, ADABAS, and the 4GL, NATURAL, from Software AG. The synergy of cooperation and communication between end users and the data processing department was achieved using these tools. In addition, the data processing department now spends only about 35 percent of its time on maintenance.

2. The State University of New York (SUNY) tested its DBMS and 4GL on the task of keeping track of crimes on its 29 campuses located throughout New York. SUNY security staff members report crime data to the state computer center in Albany. To satisfy crime statistics requirements, the computer center processes the information and sends it to the state's criminal justice department once a month. When the university acquired Datacom's DBMS and the 4GL IDEAL, SUNY'S security officers requested a new crime reporting system that not only could handle the statistics for the criminal justice department, but also would allow the officers to enter data interactively and to generate ad hoc reports for their own use.

Electronics Industry

1. Apple Computer is a decentralized organization functioning in a rapidly changing and highly competitive marketplace. To support its flexible organization, Apple employs a number of different computer information systems, including a general ledger system at 35 sites, forecasting models for 15 divisions, and three distribution vendors with their own computer system feeding into a central sales and marketing system. The data from all these diverse systems had to be made available to top financial management for the development of consolidated financial and forecasting reports.

   The proposed system solution, a Consolidated Reporting and Evaluation System (CORE), had these objectives:

   ■ Consolidate data from the general ledgers, the forecast subsystem, and the sales and marketing reporting systems

   ■ Allow for different business "views" of data

   ■ Generate flexible reports

   A team made up of finance department and MIS staff, along with consultants from Arthur D. Little, interviewed division managers, established systems requirements, and put together a functional design of a proposed system. They identified a 4GL as the primary tool for the delivery of the consolidated data.

   The main reason that a 4GL was identified as the best solution was the need for short development time. Apple needed a tool that would allow them to change systems easily and rapidly. The 4GL they chose was NOMAD because it represented the best fit of the functions it represented with the needs of the system to be developed. Apple needed a professional programmer productivity tool that was also easy for the user to use.

During the first year and a half that the system was in place, the internal processing was rewritten 100 percent. These changes were transparent to the user. This degree of needed change is typical of management reporting systems.

2. The LSI Logic Corporation is a highly specialized supplier to the Computer Aided Design (CAD) and Application Specific Integrated Circuit (ASIC) markets. Headquartered in Malpitas, California, LSI Logic sells both custom and semicustom software and design services. The company operates in Europe, Canada, Japan, and the United States. A strategy developed by this company is to distribute its design capabilities such that a design begun in one location can be completed in another, if necessary. Under those circumstances, communication between the operating companies is critical. LSI Logic's operations require many analytical reports and ad hoc requests for data and reports.

The company wants to keep its MIS staff small and yet capable of responding to end users' requests quickly. In its search for appropriate computing tools, LSI Logic looked at 4GLs. It chose NOMAD from Must Software International because of its broad capabilities, ease of use, and support on both corporate and local levels.

First they have expanded and made more flexible an old version of the order entry application using NOMAD. The new version of the system was developed by two people working for two weeks. Since then, NOMAD has been used to develop several systems for manufacturing and business data processing. The developed Computer Aided Manufacturing System runs on Digital's VAX systems, whereas business applications run on an Amdahl mainframe. NOMAD allows them to communicate with each other and the 4GL provided the basis for computer-integrated management.

2.7 SUMMARY

4GLs were developed for data-centered information systems. Databases and database management systems (DBMSs) form the basis of data-centered systems.

DBMSs allow access to a database through the development of application programs written in traditional file processing languages such as COBOL, through the use of a high-level query language, or with 4GLs.

A query language is a set of individual commands entered and executed individually by the user. By contrast, a 4GL represents higher level programming capabilities. In a 4GL, mechanisms are provided for specifying processing sequences; these sequences control processing of complete applications.

4GL capability adds to the automation tools available to the user of the data-centered information system.

Present-day 4GLs are varied. They can be classified by language function, by intended user of the language, and by general language characteristics.

The future of 4GLs is related to developments in new technologies. CASE technology, as well as developments in DBMSs (such as database machines, cooperative processing systems, and distributed databases) already have had an impact. Perhaps in the future, expert systems and AI technology will be embedded in a new generation of 4GLs.

EXERCISES

1. What is the genesis of 4GLs?

2. How would you define a computer language? Give as general definition as you can. For example, first explain what makes a computer language a language. Then tell whether the word "language" is really appropriate. (Consider what it means in English.)

3. What is an application package (for example, Lotus 1-2-3, dBASE III PLUS, or ENABLE)? Is an application package also a language? If so, why? If not, why not?

4. How do 4GLs relate to the development of databases?

5. What were 4GLs developed for?

6. List classification schemes for 4GLs and briefly describe each group.

7. Why do end-users find fourth-generation languages easy to use even if a specific product contains very complex facilities?

8. What is a development center 4GL? Give examples.

9. What are CASE tools?

10. Why were CASE tools developed and how does their development relate to the evolution of any technology?

11. List categories of automated software development tools.

12. Do 4GLs represent CASE tools? Elaborate.

13. In a computer publication such as *Computerworld,* identify a 4GL used on:
    a. A mainframe
    b. A mini
    c. A micro
    Compare and contrast each product addressing such issues as hardware requirements, what operating environment each product is portable to, who is anticipated to be a typical user, with what DBMS is it integrated if at all, if it uses menus and prompts, if it uses windowing for development, and if it supports SQL. And, finally, compare price.

14. In the most current issue of the *Computerworld,* find 4GL products that support cooperative processing. What is cooperative processing?

15. Refer to one of the many books on databases (C. J. Date's book, for example) and list the attributes of distributed database processing. Contrast distributed database processing with cooperative processing.

16. How would you characterize the building and execution of applications over distributed heterogeneous computers?

17. Can the database access tool that allows the PC user easy access to corporate data stored on distributed databases be called a cooperative processing tool?

18. Can you foresee any problems with the use of such a tool?

19. What is a database machine?

20. Comment on why the database machine/4GL interface can be useful for large scale database applications.

21. Can expert systems and 4GLs work together?

22. Do you think that 4GLs can be embedded in CASE tools needed for systems planning? If so, what function do you foresee for them? If not, why not?

23. Comment on the future of 4GLs.

REFERENCES AND SUGGESTED READINGS

1. Abbey, S. G. "COBOL dumped." *Datamation*, January 1984, pp. 108-114.

2. Bernknoph, J. "A 4GL by another name would not be COBOL." *Information Center*, October 1985, pp. 21-28.

3. Boulding, K., *The Image: Knowledge in Life and Society*. Ann Arbor, Mich.: Ann Arbor Paperbacks, 1961.

4. Case, A. F. *Information Systems Development: Principles of Computer-aided Software Engineering*. Englewood Cliffs, N.J.: Prentice-Hall, 1986.

5. Date, C. J. *An Introduction to Database Systems*. Vol. 1, Fourth edition, Reading, Mass.: Addison-Wesley, 1986.

6. Cobb, R. H. "In praise of 4GLs." *Datamation*, July 1985, pp. 90-96.

7. Grant, F. J. "The downside of 4GLs." *Datamation*, July 1985, pp. 99-104.

8. Gremillion, L. L., and Pyburn, P. "Breaking the systems development bottleneck." *Harvard Business Review*, March-April 1983, pp. 130-137.

9. Horowitz, E., Kemper, A., and Narasimhan, B. "A survey of application generators." *IEEE Software*, January 1985, pp. 40-53.

10. Inmon, W. H. "Fourth generation technology—A management assessment." *Auerbach*, January 1986.

11. Kolodziej, S. "The fate of 4GLs: Hard to define, They fight for credibility." *Computerworld*, Vol. 22, Feb. 3, 1988, pp. 25-28.

12. Martin, J. *Application Development Without Programers*. Englewood Cliffs, N. J.: Prentice-Hall, 1982.

13. Martin, J. *Fourth Generation Languages: Volume 1*. Englewood Cliffs, N. J.: Prentice-Hall, 1985.

14. Martin, J., and Leben, J. *Fourth Generation Languages: Volume 2*. Englewood Cliffs, N. J.: Prentice-Hall, 1986.

15. Parmesano, P. M. "Tools for the big application." *Business Software Review*, Vol. 6, No. 11, Nov. 1987, pp. 43-50.

16. Read, N. S., and Harmon, D. L. "Assuring MIS success." *Datamation*, February 1981, pp. 109-120.

17. Sippl, R. "Tools of the Trade." *UNIX Review*, Vol. 5, No. 11, Nov. 1987, pp. 61-67.

18. Spotlight (Anonymous), "Programmer productivity tools: Fourth generation languages." *Computerworld*, July 25, 1988, pp. 60-62.

19. Necco, C. R., and Tsai, W. N. "Use of fourth generation languages: Application development and documentation problem." *Journal of System Management*, August 1988, pp. 26-33.

REFERENCES FOR CASES OF 4GL USE

1. Anonymous. "Fourth Generation DBMS Delivers Speed, Efficiency to Large Info. Center." *Data Management*, Vol. 22, No. 11, November 1984, pp. 34-35.

2. Anonymous. "Citicorp focuses on personnel." *ICP Banking Software*, Vol. 11, No. 2, Summer 1986, pp. 16.

3. Baily, J. "4GL slashes backlog. "*ComputerData (Canada)*, Vol. 12, No. 10, October 1987, p. 17.

4. Caradonna, L., and Hyman, J. P. "How useful is your DBMS? It depends on the proper tools/MIS dept. eases programming, marketing burdens with DBMS." *Bank Systems and Equipment*, Vol. 23, No. 11, November 1986, pp. 72-76.

5. Dunmore, D. B. "Using AuditMASTERPLAN." *Journal of Accounting and EDP*, Vol. 3, No. 4, Winter 1988, pp. 30-34.

6. Harm, L. W. "Innovating at the Equitable." *ICP Insurance Software*, Vol. 9, No. 4, Winter 1984, p. 9.

7. Hurst, R. "Users debate 4GL virtues." *Computerworld*, Vol. 21, No. 27A, July 8, 1987, pp. 49-50.

8. Kolodziej, S. "Users shine at lone star campus." *Computerworld*, Vol. 20, No. 27A, July 9, 1986, pp. 43-44.

9. Kolodziej, S. "The fate of 4GLs: They fight for credibility." *Computerworld*, Vol. 22, No. 5A, February 3, 1988, pp. 25-28.

10. Krepchin, I. P. "Custom software ups accuracy, efficiency." *Modern Materials Handling*, Vol. 41, No. 12, October 1986, pp. 95-98.

11. Lawson, K. "4GL paves the way for city's advanced data integration." *Data Management*, Vol. 25, No. 8, August 1987, pp. 15-16.

12. Lynch, B. "Job matching by computer." *Best's Review (Prop/Casualty)*, Vol. 87, No. 12, April 1987, pp. 84, 86.

13. Raimondi, D. "Computer collects campus crime statistics." *Computerworld*, Vol. 18, No. 48, November 26, 1984, pp. 34-35.

14. Rajala, W. "Suncor fixes problems by prototyping." *Computing Canada*, Vol. 11, No. 19, September 19, 1985, pp. 14-15.

15. Robinson, A. "Keeping transit rapid: PowerHouse is a Powerhouse in Ottawa." *Computing Canada*, Vol. 13, No. 4, February 19, 1987, pp. 26-27.

16. Roman, D. "A marriage of convenience." *Computer Decisions*, Vol. 18, No. 8, April 8, 1986, pp. 40-44.

17. Rossell, G. G. "So you've chosen your 4GL—now can you cost justify it?" *Computerworld*, Vol. 19, No. 37A, September 18, 1985, pp. 35-36.

18. Stevens, L. "Every user a programmer." *Computer Decisions*, Vol. 18, No. 18, August 26, 1986, pp. 56-61.

CHAPTER 3

Principles of 4GLs

*The level of change involved is so fundamental yet so subtle that
we tend not to see it, or if we see it, we dismiss it as overly
simplistic, and then we ignore it.*

John Naisbitt

3.1 INTRODUCTION

In this chapter, instead of giving a precise definition of 4GLs, we briefly review
their essential characteristics. We concentrate especially on the 4GL facilities that
are useful in transaction processing systems, and on the 4GLs that are useful as
tools for constructing decision support systems.

We also look at ideal 4GL facilities and required infrastructure support
facilities. Finally, we offer guidelines to help you select a 4GL for a specific
application.

3.2 GENERAL REMARKS

As we have seen, commercial 4GLs represent still-evolving software technology.
Any rapidly evolving technology is difficult to define precisely. There are as yet
no industry-wide standards.

Generally defined, a 4GL is the user interface to an application generator. The
nature of the interface depends on the user for whom it is intended. 4GLs employ
what is called a graded-skill user interface, which provides a different access mode
to different levels of users.

One of these interfaces is a proprietary programming language (procedural
language) that is specific to the particular 4GL and whose operations include the
usual arithmetic and control facilities of conventional languages (such as COBOL
or PL/I) as well as facilities for database definition and access, screen data
manipulation, screen input/output, and so on.

In other (nonprocedural) interfaces, the user does not need to write code in any
conventional manner at all, but rather can merely conduct some form of interactive
dialogue with the system.

We illustrate these interfaces in Chapter 4, when we review some of the 4GLs products. We show how to use these interfaces in the last part of the book, when we show concrete examples of the use of a specific 4GL, that is, NOMAD on PC.

Since database processing (with appropriate control and manipulation of data) plays a central role in contemporary business systems, the intent of the majority of 4GLs is to facilitate this type of processing with all graded-skill user interfaces available in a given 4GL.

3.3 BASIC CHARACTERISTICS OF 4GLs

For the language to belong to the fourth generation, it should have the following four characteristics:

1. User friendliness
2. Data accessibility
3. Flexibility of processing
4. Development and programming productivity improvement

User Friendliness

Each 4GL is designed for a particular type (or types) of users. These different types could be end users with minimal computer experience, end users with substantial experience, analysts, low-level programmers, applications programmers, or system programmers. As we have already seen, some 4GLs have a nonprocedural part intended for the inexperienced user (this may include a special purpose language, perhaps forms- or menu-based) and a procedural part (a proprietary programming language) useful to the very experienced users and programmers. The degree and the type of user friendliness a given 4GL exhibits depends on the intended or "target" users.

Data Accessibility and Flexibility of Processing

4GLs should facilitate access to data. The object is to minimize the number of programming obstacles between the user of the data and the desired results.

The majority of commercial 4GLs are built to facilitate access to data in a database because database processing (especially a relational model) plays a central role in current computerized business applications.

We now briefly review basic database concepts, concentrating on the relational model. This discussion is intended only to help anchor our discussion of 4GLs. There are many database textbooks you can consult for a in depth treatment of the subject.

On Databases

The database is the foundation upon which the majority of the computer applications in many business organizations are now developed. The database can be considered a repository of information about an organization. In our opinion, the best definition of the database is offered by James Martin in his *End Users Guide to the Database* (Prentice-Hall, 1981):

> A database is a shared collection of interrelated data designed to meet the needs of multiple types of end users.

This shared collection of interrelated data needs to be first constructed and then appropriately managed. This is accomplished by a software system that integrates the organization's data, provides different views of these data to its different users, and manages their access and use. This software system is called a Data Base Management System (DBMS).

A DBMS is an outer "shell" to the database, serving as an interface between the database and its users. It offers a mechanism through which users access and manipulate data. Data stored in a database are protected through data management functions such as backup, recovery, integrity checks, security, and so on. It has facilities for allocating disk storage space for new files; for entering data into those files; for changing, deleting and inserting records; and so on.

The database itself can be structured on one of three data models: hierarchical, network, and relational. Some 4GLs include a DBMS; some do not. Those that do can support up to all three data models. How many and which ones depends on the particular 4GL product. Since most recent products support the relational data model, we briefly consider it now.

A relation constitutes the fundamental organizational structure for data in the relational model. A relation is a two-dimensional table (rows and columns). In a relational context, the words **relation** and **table** are often interchanged. Each table stores data concerning **entities**. Entities can be products, bank account numbers, manufacturers of equipment, customers, addresses, and so on. Thus, entities constitute organizational data.

The columns in a table represent the characteristics of an entity. These characteristics are referred to as fields, or data items, or attributes. The rows in a table represent records, which are referred to as specific occurrences of an entity. A specific row in a table is identified by a primary key, that is, the attribute (or attributes) whose value uniquely identifies a specific row in a table. For example, a social security number is normally used as a primary key (a unique attribute) for personnel records. Each row in a table must be unique.

Each table represents data as a two-dimensional table, and each table provides a structure for storing data concerning some entity within an organization.

A database in a relational model consists of many tables, each table representing a different entity. For example, since entities are data that a given enterprise

SKI INVENTORY RELATION

Inventory Number	Ski Type	Ski Size	Price	Quantity
00237800	DYSL	195	420.50	15
00245560	DYSL	205	455.00	25
01111145	DMSL	200	425.00	38
02238900	DMDH	215	525.00	5
13333899	RSSL	200	460.00	45

SKI BRAND NAME AND MANUFACTURER RELATION

Ski Type	Type Name	Manufacturer Name
DYSL	Dynastar Slalom	Dynastar Ski Co.
DMSL	Dynamics Slalom	Dynamics Inc.
DMDH	Dynamics Down Hill	Dynamics Inc.
RSSL	Rossignol Slalom	Rossignol Inc.

Figure 3.1   An Example of Relations from the Ski Inventory Database

chooses to collect, let us consider the data needed in the simple ski inventory system. Figure 3.1 illustrates two relations. The first one contains the data on the ski inventory; the second contains the brand name and manufacturer of the skis.

An important characteristic of the relational model is that records stored in one table can be related to records stored in other tables. Data in different tables can be integrated by matching common data values from the different tables. For example, in the tables of Figure 3.1 we can combine information from both relations with the Ski Type Code.

The various tables that store information related to the database (the tables' names, definitions, contents, structure, and so on) form what is called a data dictionary. Essentially the data dictionary is a database about the database. Software used to maintain the data dictionary is called the data dictionary control program, which may be embedded within a database. Data dictionaries can be passive or active.

A passive data dictionary maintains (catalogs and standardizes) data definitions but has no control over database system access. That is, a passive dictionary is independent of the database system (decoupled from it). The advantage of a passive dictionary is that it does not need to be reconstructed if the database system is changed. Its disadvantage is that the data standards included in the data dictionary are not imposed on the database system.

An active data dictionary maintains data definitions and controls access to the database system. That is, an active dictionary is an integral part of the database system (coupled to it). All processes that access the database must interact with the active data dictionary. The active data dictionary provides a data reference system that controls access to the database and reinforces data standards throughout.

A good data dictionary should:

- Maintain and provide (to application programs that use it) standard definitions of data, including data formats and data types.
- Maintain a cross-reference list of data used by applications programs and programs using given data.
- Maintain data on system-related items, including number of users, number and size of buffers, which terminals are connected to the system, which programs and users are affected by proposed changes to the system, and so on.

The content of a data dictionary can be regarded as comprehensive data about the data and system, which also includes cross-reference information on which programs use which fragments of the database. A data dictionary of this type is sometimes referred to as a common data dictionary (CDD).

Data dictionaries have evolved to a point where they can be used in many stages of the system development life cycle, supporting applications development and maintenance. When 4GLs are used, the process of applications development is substantially accelerated. With a 4GL, data characteristics such as content, form, and order of presentation can be changed quickly and easily. For example, to change any characteristic of data in NOMAD on a PC the only thing required is to change its definition (in the data dictionary) with the source code editor. Once this is done, a single restructuring command not only changes file structures, but puts all the existing physical data in a new format. The CDD ensures that specified data types match. The user, for example, can select fields that should be updated. The facility then requests the details of integrity checks: range and data types checks, checks for permissible values, and checks involving cross-references to other data.

Chapter 9 gives an example of a CDD for a specific 4GL, that is, NOMAD on a PC.

On Database Systems and their Relation to Organizational Information Systems

Databases and DBMSs provide an infrastructure on which many information systems in organizations are built.

Production data in many business enterprises are processed by a transaction processing systems (TPS), for example, inventory maintenance, accounting functions of different types, and so on. A TPS is often called a production system.

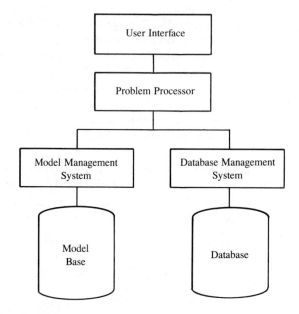

Figure 3.2 Essential Components of a DSS

These types of transactions, in turn, provide most of the internal organizational data used as a basis for generating information for well-structured managerial decision making. These are mostly report-oriented management information systems (MIS), for example, standard reports to be produced periodically to support such tasks as budget or personnel decisions.

When decision making does not call for clear-cut anticipation of information needs, flexible and adaptable systems, referred to as decision support systems (DSS), are needed. These systems often use mathematical and statistical modeling techniques to manipulate data. Most of the current DSSs rely on data extracted from database systems, especially those using a relational data model. (For more details on DSS, see [17].) With the use of a 4GL, the user of a DSS can quickly analyze data from different perspectives, sort on different criteria, and so on.

The essential components of the DSS are the DBMS, a model management system, a user interface, and the problem processor, which links all the other components. This is shown in Figure 3.2.

Database, DBMS, and 4GLs

The route to the 4GL environment is provided by tools built around a database and a DBMS. This route has four stages.

The first stage allows the application developer to produce applications by having "hooks" to the DBMS via a 3GL. The 3GL function calls into the DBMS would allow, for example, the creation, insertion, modification, and deletion of data in the applications database.

The second stage involves report and forms generation. The developer can interactively "paint" customized or default screens and reports. Screens are to be used, for example, for data insertion, deletion, modification, and so on. Reports can be generated by the use of the report writer definition language (such as RPG) or a forms-based procedure. Forms processing and reports are, however, integrated by using a 3GL.

The third stage provides a nonprocedural query language with which the database can be manipulated without recourse to the programming language. The query language enables the user to obtain standard and ad hoc queries on the database as and when needed. Initially each DBMS vendor provided a proprietary query language, but these have been superseded by an industry standard query language (SQL).

The fourth stage involves a general procedural language that links the forms generator, report generator, and all the other tools in order to tie the application together. These procedural languages are usually proprietary to the vendor of a given 4GL, but there is a tendency among the vendors to base them on SQL.

As a matter of fact, most of the 4GLs currently on the market evolved from database languages and database systems, and they represent extensions of the database technology.

In reality, 4GLs represent a whole spectrum of products. On one end of this spectrum are 4GLs, which comprise only programming languages. On the other end are very complex products including automated application development tools, programming languages, a sophisticated proprietary DBMS, direct links to other, external DBMS and communications network management software.

Development and Programming Productivity Improvements

No matter what the complexity of a 4GL product, its main objective is to help accelerate the development of computer application systems by speeding up and simplifying the programming process. In addition, it is hoped that the maintenance of programs is made easier by the more standardized code design and the clarified functions of the program fragments.

As an example, assume that you have to write a commonly used subroutine to open a database. In a typical 3GL this routine might take several pages of low-level code to ensure that all errors are checked and that error conditions are handled. In a 4GL this entire procedure might be collapsed into a single statement. Since the same single statement can be used in all other applications it will be easy to understand and maintain another person's code.

4GLs are intended to improve system development productivity for applications programmers as well as for end users. Most applications should be developed with a 4GL in at least one order of magnitude less time than with, for example, COBOL, and have one order of magnitude fewer instructions than in COBOL. To illustrate this point, consider the following simple problem (adapted from *Structured COBOL* by C. R. Litecky and G. B. Davis, McGraw-Hill, 1987).

An organization has just taken a physical inventory, and for every item in inventory, a record containing bin number (a field 3 characters long), part number (a field 5 characters long), and actual quantity on hand (a 5-digit integer) has been prepared. The bin number is used for locating the item in inventory. The transactions are in random order. The inventory manager needs a simple list of these transactions by part-number order.

Figure 3.3 shows a listing of the COBOL program that accomplishes this task. The program reads inventory transactions, lists them, sorts them by part number, and prints them.

Now, let us do the same task in NOMAD. First assume that the inventory transactions are stored in the NOMAD master containing fields with the following names:

- `PART_NUMBER`
- `BIN_NUMBER`
- `QUANTITY`

To create the list of inventory records that our manager requires, we only need one NOMAD statement:

```
LIST BY PART_NUMBER BIN_NUMBER QUANTITY ON PRT;
```

In this statement BY `PART_NUMBER` sorts transactions. `PART_NUMBER`, `BIN_NUMBER`, and `QUANTITY` are the report columns. `ON PRT` sends the report to the printer. (If `ON PRT` is omitted, the report is displayed on the CRT screen.)

This one statement takes place of COBOL's 131 lines of coding. But you say that to do what the COBOL program does, you have to have the inventory transactions in a NOMAD database and perhaps this may be a complicated process.

So let us start from the beginning. Assume, as the COBOL program does, that the inventory records are stored in the external file (with three fields). We need NOMAD statements to perform the following tasks:

1. Define the NOMAD database containing our data.
2. Initialize the NOMAD database.
3. Load the data from the external transaction file into the NOMAD database.
4. Create the required listing of inventory transactions.

Figure 3.4 presents a listing of all the NOMAD statements required to perform these tasks. As you can see, even in this case we needed only 11 NOMAD statements in contrast to 131 COBOL lines.

Even though 4GLs allow fast creation of programs with fewer lines of code, it is still necessary to assure that the programs are sound and that they accurately process the data. Remember that powerful 4GLs not only can make big mistakes, but can make them faster, too. Users of 4GL, no matter what their level of sophistication, must take this into consideration. For example, in Chapter 1 we discussed the inappropriate use of a 4GL for an information system (the New

```
00001          IDENTIFICATION DIVISION.
00002          PROGRAM-ID. DL06BC.
00003          AUTHOR. NANCY KELLY BOSTROM.
00004          REMARK. PROGRAM TO SORT INVENTORY FILE.
00005                  UPDATED BY CHUCK LITECKY.
00006          *
00007          ENVIRONMENT DIVISION.
00008          *
00009          CONFIGURATION SECTION.
00010          SOURCE-COMPUTER. IBM-370.
00011          OBJECT-COMPUTER. IBM-370.
00012          SPECIAL-NAMES.
00013              C01 IS TOP-OF-PAGE.
00014          INPUT-OUTPUT SECTION.
00015          FILE-CONTROL.
00016              SELECT   INVENTORY-FILE-IN        ASSIGN TO UR-S-SYSIN.
00017              SELECT   INVENTORY-FILE-SORTED    ASSIGN TO UR-DA-S-UMCSC2.
00018              SELECT   INVENTORY-FILE-SORT      ASSIGN TO UR-DA-S-UMCSC3.
00019              SELECT   PRINT-FILE               ASSIGN TO UR-S-SYSPRINT.
00020          *
00021          DATA DIVISION.
00022          *
00023          FILE SECTION.
00024          FD  INVENTORY-FILE-IN
00025              LABEL RECORDS ARE OMITTED
00026              DATA RECORD IS INVENTORY-FILE-IN-REC.
00027          01  INVENTORY-FILE-IN-REC       PIC X(80).
00028          *
00029          FD  INVENTORY-FILE-SORTED
00030              LABEL RECORDS ARE OMITTED
00031              DATA RECORD IS INVENTORY-FILE-SORTED-REC.
00032          01  INVENTORY-FILE-SORTED-REC   PIC X(13).
00033          SD  INVENTORY-FILE-SORT
00034              DATA RECORD IS INVENTORY-FILE-SORT-REC.
00035          01  INVENTORY-FILE-SORT-REC.
00036              05  S-PART-NUMBER           PIC X(05).
00037              05  FILLER                  PIC X(08).
00038          FD  PRINT-FILE
00039              LABEL RECORDS OMITTED
00040              DATE RECORD IS PRINT-LINE.
00041          01  PRINT-LINE                  PIC X(132).
00042          *
00043          WORKING-STORAGE SECTION.
00044          *
00045          01  LINE-COUNT                  PIC 99.
00046          01  MORE-DATA                   PIC X(101)    VALUE 'Y'.
00047              88  THREE-MORE-DATA                       VALUE 'Y'.
00048              88  NO-MORE-DATA                          VALUE 'N'.
00049          01  WS-INVENTORY-RECORD.
00050              05  PART-NUMBER             PIC X(05).
00051              05  BIN-NUMBER              PIC X(03).
00052              05  QUANTITY-ON-HAND        PIC 9(05).
00053              05  FILLER                  PIC X(67).
00054
00055          01  COLUMN-HEADING.
00056              05  FILLER                  PIC X(36)     VALUE SPACES.
00057              05  FILLER                  PIC X(21)     VALUE
00058                              'PART NUMBER              '.
00059              05  FILLER                  PIC X(20)     VALUE
00060                              'BIN NUMBER           '.
00061              05  FILLER                  PIC X(16)     VALUE
00062                              'QUANTITY ON HAND'.
00063              05  FILLER                  PIC X(39)     VALUE SPACES.
00064          01  AFTER-SORT-HEADING-1.
00065              05  FILLER                  PIC X(50)     VALUE SPACES.
```

Figure 3.3 Listing of Program in COBOL to Sort and Print Inventory Records

```
00066              05  FILLER                    PIC X(28)     VALUE
00067                            'INVENTORY LISTING AFTER SORT'.
00068              05  FILLER                    PIC X(54)     VALUE SPACES.
00069      01  AFTER-SORT-HEADING-2.
00070              05  FILLER                    PIC X(54)     VALUE SPACES.
00071              05  FILLER                    PIC X(21)     VALUE
00072                            'SORT BY PART NUMBER'.
00073              05  FILLER                    PIC X(57)     VALUE SPACES.
00074      01  INVENTORY-DETAIL-LINE.
00075              05  FILLER                    PIC X(39)     VALUE SPACES.
00076              05  D-PART-NUMBER             PIC X(05)
00077              05  FILLER                    PIC X(16)     VALUE SPACES.
00078              05  D-BIN-NUMBER              PIC X(03)
00079              05  FILLER                    PIC X(19)     VALUE SPACES.
00080              05  D-QUANTITY-ON-HAND        PIC ZZ,ZZ9.
00081              05  FILLER                    PIC X(44)     VALUE SPACES.
00082      *
00083      PROCEDURE DIVISION.
00084      *
00085      MAIN-CONTROL-ROUTINE.
00086          PERFORM SORT-ROUTINE.
00087          PERFORM SORTED-INITIALIZATION.
00088          PERFORM SORTED-PROCESS UNTIL NO-MORE-DATA.
00089          PERFORM SORTED-CLOSING.
00090          STOP RUN.
00091
00092      *
00093      SORT-ROUTINE.
00094          SORT  INVENTORY-FILE-SORT
00095                ASCENDING KEY S-PART-NUMBER
00096                UNSING  INVENTORY-FILE-IN
00097                GIVING  INVENTORY-FILE-SORTED.
00098      *
00099      SORTED-INITIALIZATION.
00100          OPEN INPUT INVENTORY-FILE-SORTED, OUTPUT PRINT-FILE.
00101          MOVE 'Y' TO MORE-DATA.
00102          PERFORM SORTED-NEW-PAGE-ROUTINE.
00103          READ INVENTORY-FILE-SORTED INTO WS-INVENTORY-RECORD
00104              AT END MOVE 'N' TO MORE-DATA.
00105      *
00106      SORTED-PROCESS.
00107          IF LINE-COUNT GREATER THAN 55
00108              PERFORM SORTED-NEW-PAGE-ROUTINE.
00109          MOVE PART-NUMBER TO D-PART-NUMBER.
00110          MOVE BIN-NUMBER TO D-BIN-NUMBER.
00111          MOVE QUANTITY-ON-HAND TO D-QUANTITY-ON-HAND.
00112          WRITE PRINT-LINE FORM INVENTORY-DETAIL-LINE
00113              AFTER ADVANCING 2 LINES.
00114          ADD 2 TO LINE-COUNT.
00115          READ INVENTORY-FILE-SORTED INTO WS-INVENTORY-RECORD
00116              AT END
00117                  MOVE 'N' TO MORE-DATA.
00118      *
00119      SORTED-NEW-PAGE-ROUTINE.
00120          MOVE SPACES TO PRINT-LINE.
00121          WRITE PRINT-LINE AFTER ADVANCING TOP-OF-PAGE.
00122          WRITE PRINT-LINE FROM AFTER-SORT-HEADING-1 AFTER
00123              ADVANCING 2 LINES.
00124          WRITE PRINT-LINE FROM AFTER-SORT-HEADING-2 AFTER
00125              ADVANCING 1 LINES.
00126          WRITE PRINT-LINE FROM COLUMN-HEADING AFTER
00127              ADVANCING 2 LINES.
00128          MOVE 7 TO LINE-COUNT.
00129      *
00130      SORTED-CLOSING.
00131          CLOSE PRINT-FILE, INVENTORY-FILE-SORTED.
```

Figure 3.3 *continued*

```
master INVENTORY      keyed(PART_NUMBER);
      item PART_NUMBER   as A5 heading "PART NUMBER";
      item BIN_NUMBER    as A3 heading "BIN NUMBER";
      item QUANTITY      as 99,999 heading "QUANTITY ON HAND";
end;



      !These statements define NOMAD database structure.!
      !This structure will be stored in the file CASE1.SCH.!




schema CASE1;

      !This command creates the NOMAD database!
      !of our example.!


database CASE1;


      !This statement initializes our database.!


File define INVENTORY_TRANSACTIONS = C: TRANSAC.DAT;
Load INVENTORY
      Read INVENTORY_TRANSACTIONS
      Set &PART_NUMBER form A5
          &BIN_NUMBER form A3
          &QUANTITY    form N5
Print "RECORDS READ: " (&READS)
      Fold "RECORDS INSERTED: " (&INSERTS);


      !These statements load inventory information!
      !from the external transaction file into NOMAD!
      !database. The number of records read and the number!
      !of records inserted into database is printed.!


List by PART_NUMBER BIN_NUMBER QUANTITY on prt;


      !This statement creates the required inventory report.!
```

Figure 3.4   Listing of NOMAD Statements to Accomplish the Same Task as Program in Figure 3.3

Jersey Motor Vehicles Department case). The disastrous logjam happened because the whole application was written in 4GL, which used machine resources inefficiently and exhibited degrading response time when the volume of processed data increased significantly. Perhaps certain parts of the system could have been written in 4GL (definitely, the initial prototype of the system). Other parts of the system required a 3GL or even a 2GL to ensure proper response times and, as required in the application, very efficient heavy-volume data processing.

One of the most attractive characteristics of any 4GL is that changing an application is generally easy. Anyone who has spent months developing a software system only to discover that it fails to meet the user's needs or to learn that the user has changed the design requirements after having seen the original specification in action will appreciate the value of this characteristic. It is, for example, a particular advantage in building prototypes with 4GLs. (We discuss the prototyping process in Chapters 5 through 8.)

3.4 4GL FACILITIES

As noted before, 4GL technology is rapidly evolving. Fourth-generation products are known by various names: development workbenches, fourth-generation languages, program generators, and programmer's productivity tools. At present, some 300 vendors offer such tools for mainframes and minis; another 150 produce them for micro-based systems. A partial list of 4GL products including such characterizations as to what environment the product is directly portable; who its typical users are; whether or not it is integrated with a data dictionary, with a DBMS, or with an application generator; or whether or not it supports cooperative processing, is presented in Figure 3.5. As if the sheer number of available products were not enough, these tools also employ different approaches (see Chapter 4) to the tasks of application's development.

Seeing this maze of products, one might very naturally wonder what features the 4GL should provide. Since the answer depends on the specific application, we concentrate on two types of the most common types of computerized business applications: medium-sized transaction processing systems and decision support systems. We first discuss what functions a 4GL that is useful for these two types of applications should have, and next, we combine these functional features into an integrated fourth-generation facility.

4GL Facilities For Transaction Processing Systems

The central facility of the 4GL for medium-sized transaction processing systems is a sophisticated DBMS to which are added database creation tools, data input tools, application generator tools, and decision support tools.

Database Creation Tools

To make a database management system easy to use, it must include certain tools:

- An *online data dictionary/directory* to support data element/field description, record and file/database definitions, and maintenance capabilities.
- *Data analysis tools* to monitor performance and to enhance and analyze user views of data.
- *Data modeling and database design tools* to help speed up the system building.

Company	Product	Hardware Platform	Direct Portability to What Operating Environments	Supports Cooperative Processing	Typical User	Integrated with DBMS	Integrated with Data Dictionary	Integrated with Application Generator	Compiled/ Interpretive/ Compiled Language	Automatic Syntax Checking	Uses Menus/ Prompts	Uses Windowing for Development	Incorporates Windows in Created Applications	Supports SQL
Adrem, Inc.	Goesi-IDT	IBM mainframes	MVS, VSE, VM/CMS	No	Programmer	No	No	No		Yes	Menus	No	No	ANSI standard (late this year)
Applied Data Research, Inc.	Ideal	IBM 370 architecture, PCMs¹	Between all operating environments supported	Yes	Programmer	Datacom/DB, DB2	Yes	NA	Compiled	Yes	Both	Yes	No	DB2
Apacore International, Inc.	Cue-Bic	Independent	Unix, VM, MVS, Dos, VMS via Pick	Yes	Programmer	Pick	Yes	Yes	Both	Yes	Both	Yes	Yes	No
Business Computer Solutions, Inc.	Ziour	Any running Unix, Xenix, DOS, VMS	Between all operating environments supported	Yes	Programmer	Ziour	Yes	Yes	Compiled	Yes	None	Yes	Yes	ANSI
Carleton Corp.	CQS-INFOTEC	IBM 9370: 4300 series: 3000; 370; IBM PCs	Honeywell	Yes	Both	IMS/DL1, IDMS/R, Datacom/DB, Adabas, Total/ Supra, DB2	Yes	Yes	Compiled	Yes	Both	No	No	ANSI
Certified Software Specialists	ACT/1	IBM mainframe	MVS/XA, ESA, MVS/SP, OS/VS1, VM/SP, VM/XA, VSE/SP, DOS/VSE, SSX/VSE	No	End user	No	No	Yes	Table driven	Yes	Both	No	Yes	NA
Cincom Systems, Inc.	Mantix	IBM MVS, DOS/VSE, VM/CMS, VSE, PC-DOS, OS/2, DEC VMS, Wang VS; NCR VRX/MCS; VRX/Tranpro III; Siemen's POS 2000; ICL TPMS, TPS	Between all operating environments supported	Yes	Programmer	Totsl, Supra, DB2, IMS, D4, IDMS, IDMS/R, Adabas	Yes	Yes	Interpretive	Yes	Both	Yes	Yes	ANSI
Cognos Corp.	Powerhouse	VAX; DG Eclipse/MV; HP 3000: IBM PC-AT or compatibles	Between all operating environments supported	Yes	Programmer	RDB/VMS, RMS, Infos, DG/SQL, Turboimage, KSAM	Yes	Yes	Compiled	Yes	Both	No	Yes	NA
Compuserve Data Technologies	System 1032 4GL/DBMS	VAX	None	No	Programmer	System 1032	Yes	Yes	Compiled	Yes	Both	No	Yes	No
Computer Corporation of America	User Language	IBM 370 architecture, PCMs	MVS, MVS/XA, VM/CMS, DOS/ VSE	Yes	Programmer, end user	Model 204	Yes	Yes	Interpretive	Yes	Both	No	No	No
Computer Techniques, Inc.	QUEO-V	IBM-PCs or compatibles; Prime; DG	Between all operating environments supported	Yes	Programmer, end user	QUEO-V	Yes	Yes	Compiled	Yes	Both	No	Yes	No
Concept Omega Corp./ Thoroughbred division	Thoroughbred IDOL-IV	AT&T 3B series; 80386 super-micros; HP 9000 series; IBM PS/2 Models 50, 60, 80; 68020-based minis	Unix, Xenix, DOS, Thoroughbred/OS	Yes	Programmer	Thoroughbred IDOL-IV DBMS¹	Yes	Yes	Compiled	Yes	Both	Yes	Yes	No
CRI, Inc.	Graf	HP 3000	None	No	End user, programmer	Relate	Yes	Yes	Interpretive	Yes	Both	No	No	No
Cullinet Software, Inc.	ADS/Online	IBM 370, 3080s, 3090s, 4300, 9370 series or compatibles; Siemens 7500, 7700 series	Between all operating environments supported	Yes	Programmer	IDMS/R	Yes	Yes	Compiled	Yes	Both	No	No	No

Figure 3.5 Partial List of 4GL Products

Company	Product	Hardware Platform	Direct Portability to What Operating Environments	Supports Cooperative Processing	Typical User	Integrated with DBMS	Integrated with Data Dictionary	Integrated with Application Generator	Interpretive/ Compiled Language	Automatic Syntax Checking	Uses Menus/ Prompts	Uses Windowing for Development	Incorporates Windows in Created Applications	Supports SQL
Datatron, Inc.	Datatron	IBM-PC, XT, AT or compatibles, IBM mainframe. Honeywell mainframes	OS/DOS, CICS	Yes	End user, programmer	No	Yes	Yes	Interpretive	Yes	Menus	Yes	No	No
Digital Equipment Corp.	VAX Rally	VAX/VMS	None	No	Programmer	RDB/VMS	Yes	Yes	Table driven	No	Both	No	Yes	No
ESI	Group Four Application Generation System	Unisys A/V series, B1000, IBM-PC or compatibles	Unisys MCP, MS-DOS	Yes	End user, programmer	Unisys DMS II	Yes	NA	Compiled	Yes	Both	No	No	No
Execucom Systems, Inc.	IFPS/Plus	IBM-PCs or compatibles; Prime; DEC; Honeywell Bull; HP 3000; Sun Unix Model 3, 3861; Apollo Domain 3000, 4000	NP	Yes	End user	NP	Yes	Yes	Interpretive	NP	Menus	No	No	IFPS modeling
Flexware	Flexware Development System	Mac Plus, SE, II	MS-DOS, VAX/VMS	No	Programmer	Flexware	Yes	Yes	Compiled	Yes	Both	Yes	Yes	No
Help/38 Systems, Inc.	Open	IBM System/38, AS/400	CPF, AS/400	Yes	End user	CPF, AS/400	Yes	No	Compiled	Yes	Both	Yes	No	No
Henco Software Inc.	Info	Prime running Primos; Harris running VOS, Honeywell Bull running CGOS6, HV56; DG running AOS/VS; IBM running MS-DOS	Between all operating environments supported	Yes	Programmer, end user	No	No	No	Compiled	Yes	Both	No	Yes	No
Hewlett-Packard Co. Contact local dealer	Allbase/4GL	HP 3000 series 900, HP 9000 series 300, 800	MPE XL, HP-UX	No	Programmer	Allbase	Yes	No	Interpretive	Yes	Menus	No	No	ANSI
Honeywell Bull, Inc.	IQS	DPS7, DPS7000	NP	Yes	End user	IDS II	Yes	No	Compiled	No	Both	No	Yes	No
	System 80	DPS6, 6 Plus, 8, 80, 8000, 90	NP	No	Programmer	IDS II	Yes	No	Compiled	Yes	Both	No	No	Yes
IBM Contact local sales office	Cross System Product	IBM/370; 3000 series, 9370; 4300; 8100; IBM-PC	IBM only	No	Programmer	DB2, SQL/DS	No	Yes	Interpretive	Yes	Menus	No	No	Yes
Information Builders, Inc.	Focus	IBM running MVS, VM/MSE; DEC running VMS/Decnet; Wang VS; PCs running MS-DOS, PC-DOS, OS/2; Apollo running Unix; AT&T 3B; IBM RT; Motorola series 8000; NCR Tower; Phillips 9070	Between all operating environments supported	Yes	Programmer, end user	Focus, DB2, IMS, VSAM, IDMS/R, Adabas, Dbase, Ingres	Yes	No	Interpretive	Yes	Both	Yes	Yes	ANSI
Information Resources, Inc.	Express	IBM running MVS, VM; VAX/VMS	None	Yes	End user	Express	Yes	No	Both	Yes	Prompts	No	Yes	No
	PC/Express	IBM-PC, PC-XT, AT, PS/2 or compatibles	None	Yes	End user	Proprietary	Yes	Yes	Both	Yes	Both	No	Yes	No

Figure 3.5 continued

62

Company	Product	Hardware Platform	Direct Portability to What Operating Environments	Supports Cooperative Processing	Typical User	Integrated with DBMS	Integrated with Data Dictionary	Integrated with Application Generator	Interpretive/Compiled Language	Automatic Syntax Checking	Uses Menus/Prompts	Uses Windowing for Development	Incorporates Windows in Created Applications	Supports SQL
Informix Software. Inc.	Informix-4GL	IBM-PC, XT or compatibles. Altos 3068. VAX. Cray-2	DOS, OS/2, Unix. VMS	No	Programmer	Proprietary	Yes	No	Compiled	Yes	Both	No	Yes	ANSI
	Informix-4GL Rapid Development System	AT&T 3B2, 3B20, 3B4000 series. Altos 3068. Amdahl 580. Microvax. Intel 386/320. HP Series 9000. Sequent Symmetry. Sun 3 Series. Unisys 6000/50	DOS, Unix	No	Programmer	Proprietary	Yes	No	Interpretive	Yes	Both	No	Yes	ANSI
Intelligent Information Systems, Inc.	IIS/Destiny	VAX/VMS	None	No	Programmer, end user	Proprietary	Yes	Yes	Compiled	Yes	Both	Yes	Yes	No
Intersystems Corp.	M/SQL	VAX, PDP-11; DG Eclipse MV; IBM-PC, mainframes; Altos 386 series 1000, 2000	VMS, AOS/VS, PC-DOS, MS-DOS, VM, Unix	Yes	Programmer	M/SQL	Yes	Yes	Compiled	Yes	Both	Yes	Yes	ANSI
I. P. Sharp Associates, a Reuter Co.	Viewpoint	IBM 370, P9070	None	Yes	End user	Proprietary, DB2, Adabas	No	Yes	Interpretive	Yes	Both	No	No	No
Koala Development Corp.	Add system	IBM System/34, 36, PC, AS/400	PC, System/34, MS-DOS, AS/400	No	Programmer, end user	No	Yes	Yes	Compiled	Yes	Both	No	No	No
Magna Software Corp.	MAGNA	CDC Cyber series	NOS, NOS/VE, NOS/BE	Yes	End user, programmer	No	Yes	Yes	Compiled	Yes	Prompts	No	No	No
McCormack & Dodge Corp.	Millennium; Systems Development Tool	IBM, Fujitsu, ICL.	MVS, OS, DOS, VSE, ALM, VME	No	Programmer	IBM, DB2	Yes	Yes	Interpretive	Yes	Both	Yes	Yes	ANSI
McDonnell Douglas Information Systems Group	Pro-IV	AT&T 3B1, 3B2, Microvax; Honeywell Bull DPS 6 series; IBM-PC-XT, AT, PS/2, 3030, 3080, 3090, 4300 series, 9370; NCR Tower 32, Mini XP; Plexus P15-75	All attached environments	NP	Programmer	No	Yes	No	NA	No	Both	No	No	ANSI
MDBS, Inc.	Knowledgeman/2	IBM-PCs or compatibles; VAX	VNS	No	Programmer	Knowledgeman/MDBS III	Yes	No	Interpretive	No	Both	No	No	IBM
Multisoft, Inc.	Infront	IBM-PC, PC-XT, AT, PS/2 or compatibles	None	Yes	Programmer	Infront B-tree database	No	Yes	Compiled	Yes	Both	Yes	Yes	No
MUST Software International	Nomad	IBM 370, PC-AT, PS/2 or compatibles; VAX	VM/CMS, MVS/TSO, MVS/XA, PC-DOS VMS	Yes	Programmer, end user	Nomad	Yes	Yes	Compiled	Yes	Both	Yes	Yes	Extended ANSI
National Information Systems, Inc.	Accent R	VAX	RMS, A/UX	No	Programmer	Accent R's DBMS, Britton Lee shared database	Yes	Yes	Compiled	Yes	Both	Yes	Yes	No
Netron, Inc.	Netron/Cap Development Center	IBM mainframes. PCs; VAX; Wang VS	MVS/TSO, VM/CMS, VAX/VMS, Wang VS	Yes	Programmer	No	No	Yes	Compiled (COBOL)	Yes	Both	No	Yes	ANSI

1 American National Standard Institute   2 Plug-compatible mainframes   3 Database management systems

The companies included in this chart responded to a telephone survey conducted by *Computerworld*. When a vendor is unable to provide specific information about its product, this is designated NP (not provided). When a question does not apply to a vendor's product, this is designated NA (not applicable). Further product information is available from the vendors.

Figure 3.5 *continued*

63

Data Input Tools

The data input tools include:

■ *Screen design and painting facilities*, which are the most important data input tools. The screen painter tools should be able to create, for example, highlighting, color blocks, reverse video, fields for user data entry, and fields to display variables.

■ *Data security and integrity controls*, which should be automatically invoked. Necessary information for the checks should be received from the system's dictionary or be requested from the user. These should include security details such as, for example, checks on whether the specific user has rights to input or update given fields, records, files, or databases; range and data-type checks; checks for permissible values; and checks involving cross-references to other data.

■ *Audit controls*, which should be easy to use or automatic. Audit controls will allow one to store information on who read, created, updated, or deleted data items.

■ *An online HELP facility*, which the user should be able to invoke.

All these data input tools allow a user to automatically generate good human engineered screen layouts and interactions. The ultimate benefits are much better designed systems and a much lower rate of error in data-entry and data-update dialogues.

In addition to the normal online data entry, the capability for accessing data from databases and files created by 3GLs or by the batch data entry should also be available.

Application Generator Tools

The application generators tools include:

■ *A query language,* which is required either for simple queries that display a single record or for complex queries that display the data that were projected, joined, or searched, with various conditions applying. A user should be able to store queries for future use and edit them as needed.

■ *A report generator facility*, which provides the user with simplified means of generating and formatting reports. The default values provided allow standard reports to be produced with a minimum of specifications. If nonstandard reports are required, custom formats can be designed with the use of procedures. Any user should then be able to build complex reports very quickly and store their format code for any future use. Often the report generator can perform simple arithmetic functions such as averaging, calculating percentages, and finding maxima and minima.

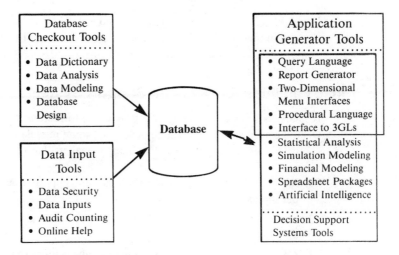

Figure 3.6   4GL Facilities for Production Systems

■ *A graphics generator*, which can adjust the formats, color, shading, scale, and labeling of the graphs and help create well-designed graphical outputs. Graphical presentation routines can be supplemented by graphic editors and languages to facilitate the creation and manipulation of custom graphics.

■ *A two-dimensional menu interface facility*, which should help generate menu dialogues, command-and-response dialogues, and any other types of user-machine dialogue. It may be an extension of the screen painter.

All the facilities just described should be nonprocedural and therefore easy to use. Remember, though, that not all data processing applications can be built with nonprocedural facilities. For example, parts of some applications may require structures with complex control commands, loops, and nested routines, and that can be done only with a procedural language. Ideally this procedural part of a 4GL should be compatible in syntax with its nonprocedural part.

Interface to high-level procedural languages, such as COBOL, PL/I, FORTRAN, C, and APL, and *interface to low-level procedural languages* such as ASSEMBLER are very useful. For example, it should allow a user to write third-generation routines for heavy computational work and optimize the use of computer resources. Figure 3.6 illustrates ideal 4GL facilities for production systems.

Some evolving issues that are relevant to 4GLs:

■ *Portability* is an important consideration for a 4GL, especially in distributed environments where it is important that the product can be used on hardware from different vendors.

■ *Reusable code* usage is encouraged by the functionality of 4GLs. This is an evolving programming practice in which modules of created code can be quickly retrieved from storage, changed if needed, and used in a new program or programs. An online *software development library* of such modules and other 4GL tools allows rapid creation of systems.

4GL Facilities for Decision Support Systems

A decision support system (DSS) provides information to help make decisions when the need arises. We will consider the Simon model of decision making (see [18]). This model, which is used by many managers, has three stages:

1. *Intelligence stage*—identifies problems and opportunities associated with the decision situation.
2. *Design stage*—identifies alternative courses of action and evaluates each alternative.
3. *Choice stage*—selects the best decision alternative.

Since a DSS should support the way decisions are made, we will use the Simon model to categorize ideal 4GL tools useful for building decision support systems. 4GLs can be though of as DSS tools.

Intelligence Support Tools

All application generator tools such as *query languages*, *report generators*, *graphics generators*, are needed in the intelligence stage. These tools allow the decision maker to search the files and databases for potential problems and decision opportunities.

For example, query languages allow the decision maker to make the request: LIST ALL PARTS FOR PONTIAC FIERO THAT HAVE QUALITY CONTROL REJECT RATE GREATER THAN TEN PERCENT. Obviously, the response identifies a decision opportunity.

Report generators allow the decision maker to quickly create new reports using old data. Such reports can confirm or deny a suspected problem or identify a new problem.

Graphics generators can summarize data into graphs and charts that may trigger decisions.

Finally, *statistical analysis packages* help to analyze data in order to isolate or confirm problems.

Design Stage Support Tools

In this decision stage, *simulation* and *modeling tools* as well as the tools just discussed are needed.

Query languages and *report generators* can generate alternative decision choices and pertinent data required for those choices. *Statistical* and *graphics tools* may help analyze decision alternatives.

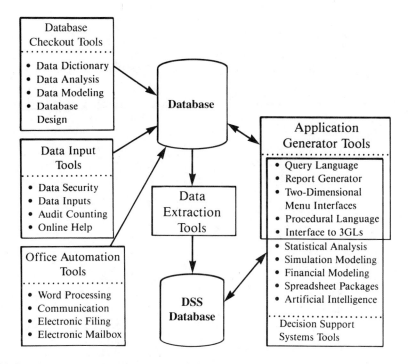

Figure 3.7 4GL Facilities for Decision Support Systems

Simulators and *modeling tools* allow answers to what-if questions. Simulations allow the decision maker to predict the outcome of some major decisions with respect to productivity, cost, and profits, for example, without actually implementing these decisions—just *simulating* their implementation. They are most useful in forecasting, optimization, and so on. The most popular modeling tools at present are *financial modeling* and *spreadsheet packages*.

Choice Stage Tools

This decision stage is only beginning to be supported by computerized tools. These are artificial intelligence technology tools. Artificial intelligence is the ability of a computer to perform certain human functions such as reasoning, learning, and decision making. Artificial intelligence tools employed at this stage could guide users through complex decision-making processes.

The data needed for the decision-making process are usually captured by production systems. (Production systems are computer applications that involve processing of organizational "production" data.) Tools that can transfer data from a production database into a decision support system database are *data-extraction aids*. These special tools are required because efficient *decision support database* structures are usually separate from production database structures. Figure 3.7 shows 4GL features needed for decision support systems.

3.5 INTEGRATION

The general-purpose 4GL facilities described in Chapter 2 (in the section on language function specification) should have a common syntax and style of operation. They should be integrated in one package so that the user will be able to learn the complete package step by step, in a graded-skill fashion. Beginning users, for example, can be exposed initially to only a database query language and report generator. When they are completely familiar with this level, they can master the next level, and so on. You can imagine that this "subsetting," often called "graded-skill user interface," can be very important. It can help a given 4GL gain wide acceptance, because novice users tend to reject any 4GL that appears to be too complex right from the start.

To make integrated systems really user friendly an ideal 4GL facility should include such aids as online documentation creation tools, HELP files, human language interpreters, and computer-based teaching. To help in the design of computer systems, the integrated package should have *graphics design aids*, tools such as computer-aided design, a data model editor, and decision tree tools. *Office automation tools* should also be integrated into 4GL features to provide word processing for creating specifications and documentation. Additional features such as electronic filing, communications, and mailbox facilities help improve information dissemination among application users in a given business.

Figure 3.8 shows an ideal fully integrated fourth-generation facility.

3.6 INFRASTRUCTURE SUPPORT FOR 4GLS

To function properly in the data processing department of any organization, a fully integrated fourth-generation language requires some additional organizational infrastructure, including:

- Multisystem infrastructure
- Personal computer infrastructure
- System controls infrastructure
- Code generation and checking infrastructure

The proliferation of computers in many organizations has led to a need to access multiple data sources located on different computers. Users found that they needed to be able to extract information using data extractors; send information via local area networks (LANs) or data transmission networks; and control data flow on multiple computers with distributed system architecture and distributed databases. All these facilities represent the *multisystem infrastructure*.

The introduction of large numbers of personal computers into the corporate world changed their function in many organizations. Personal computers are becoming workstations supported by a large numbers of diverse software products. Furthermore, beyond the common PC spreadsheet and database software, 4GLs are

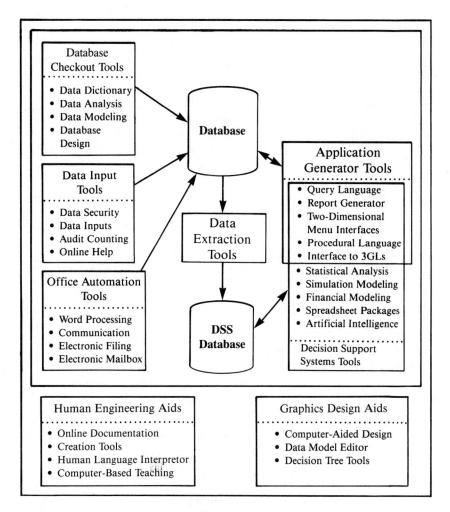

Figure 3.8   Fully Integrated Ideal Fourth-Generation Facilities

now also available on PCs. Many of these PC 4GLs have the same command structure as their mainframe counterparts. The decision support tools are also available in their PC versions. Workstations are integrated with the computer networks of many organizations. Micro-mainframe interaction and data extractions to PCs are common occurrences in many organizations. Facilities of this type represent the *personal computer link infrastructure.*

Certain facilities can permit several users to access a given system at the same time:

■ Concurrence controls to prevent invalid updating of the data

■ Checkpoint/recovery controls to permit system recovery from system failures

■ Security and auditing tools to control working systems

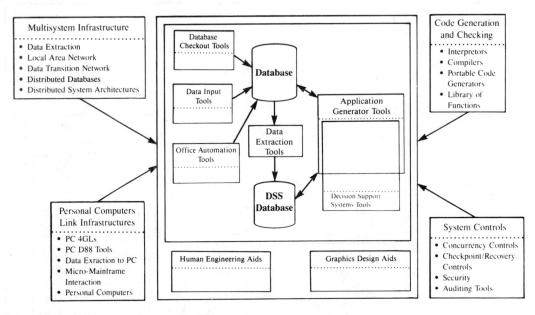

Figure 3.9   Infrastructure Support for 4GLs

All these facilities represent *system controls infrastructure.*

Interpreters and compilers are needed to convert 4GL code into executable code, and in the case of large production systems, to compile them to improve processing efficiency. To be able to transport code to different manufacturers' computers, portable code generators are helpful. Libraries of functions, routines, and data types are useful in any organization because they can substantially speed up the process of application generation. Facilities of this type represent the *code generation and checking infrastructure.*

Figure 3.9 illustrates infrastructures useful in the data processing departments of many organizations.

3.7 SELECTION CRITERIA FOR 4GLs

There are many 4GL products on the market. There are products suited for inexperienced end users (nonprogrammer) as well as products specifically developed for data processing professionals.

4GLs vary in options, efficiency, reliability, and cost. If you need to evaluate a specific 4GL, you must focus on the facilities you and your organization need rather than on attractive functions the 4GL may offer but you might use infrequently. For example, an organization doesn't need a fourth-generation language that handles transaction processing if it's going to use this 4GL only for information retrieval.

A well-planned, carefully executed selection improves the chance of finding the right language. The selection process includes four phases:

- Objectives definition
- Evaluation planning
- Evaluation
- Decision

In the following descriptions of these four phases, we will assume that you are working for an organization that wants to acquire a 4GL, and you are responsible for an evaluation. In other words, you are a designated evaluator.

Objectives Definition Phase

In defining selection objectives, the evaluator should consider all the current data processing needs of the organization. He or she should also keep sight of possible future data processing considerations and must fit them with the organization's other systems plans, for example, a scheduled change in operating, a plan to acquire a new computer (perhaps from a different vendor), or a change of database management system.

There are many factors to consider. Objectives should be defined with users, applications, efficiency, need for integration with other software, any hardware and reliability requirements as well as costs in mind.

Evaluation Planning Phase

The primary objective of the evaluation planning phase is to identify the small number of *critical factors* that differentiate an appropriate from an inappropriate language for specific computing requirements arrived at in the objectives definition stage. (Those factors are presented in the following sections.)

The selection process should have some time limit imposed on it. An evaluator should avoid "analysis paralysis". If the selection process drags on, new selection objectives and new 4GL products may arrive. Waiting for and reacting to new developments can stall the selection process indefinitely. An evaluator can avoid that trap by setting a time schedule and sticking to it. The critical factors may be selected from the set described in the following sections. This set can be classified into the following groups:

- User needs
- Application needs
- Efficiency

■ Hardware requirements

■ Reliability requirements

■ Cost consideration

User Needs

User needs should be met whether the users are novices, data processing professionals, or a combination of both.

If a novice is the primary 4GL user, ease of use is most critical. Ease of use will be ensured by the nonprocedural form of the language and, if available, a natural language interface. Built-in HELP and tutorial functions will help novices do their own computing. In addition, a highly integrated 4GL set of tools is a better choice for the novice than multiple specialized tools. With an integrated set of tools, the user learns only one command language. The movement of data within an integrated tool is much easier than the transfer of data between multiple tools that were not designed to operate within a single integrated environment.

On the other hand, in order to meet the needs of the very experienced user, the 4GL must offer advanced tools and have the power of the procedural language.

HELP facilities such as detailed error messages or layers of menus that cannot be avoided by shortcuts are an enormous hindrance for an experienced data processing professional. They become a hindrance for the novice user as well when this user becomes more experienced.

If both novices and data processing professionals plan to use the same 4GL tools, both procedural and nonprocedural facilities should be part of a language. Moreover, the language might include HELP and tutorial facilities that could be switched on and off.

A 4GL should support prototyping. This will enable an experienced data processing professional to interact closely with users during the design and testing stages of an application development cycle. A 4GL should produce documentation for the application, including specifications, documenting history of changes, and different versions of the application reports.

Application Needs

Just as the language should be appropriate for the type of user for whom it is intended, it should also satisfy application objectives:

1. Whether the language should employ compilable code, which is more resource efficient, or interpretive code, which is usually easier to use. Choosing the wrong language type can have disastrous consequences. A production program that calculates payroll, for example, will overwhelm processing resources if it is developed with an interpretive language.

2. Which processing facilities the language should include. Obviously, this will depend on the nature of the intended application. The processing facilities of most common concern are programming loops, array processing, computational functions, type of databases and files, and volume of data processing.

Very experienced programmers might be able to work around a 4GL's lack of a specific processing function. However, the coding produced would be so convoluted that the primary benefit of the 4GL's code simplicity would be lost. That would make program maintenance much more difficult. Under those circumstances, for example, a plan to replace a third-generation application with fourth-generation programming expressly to reduce maintenance costs would be a big disappointment.

3. What type of processing the 4GL supports. This concerns the nature of intended applications, that is, whether processing is going to be batch, online, or exploratory (for example, decision support systems).

Efficiency

A 4GL should provide the execution performance that was established in the objectives definition phase.

The vendor of the given 4GL should be able to specify the amount of memory, the number of disk drives, and the communications facilities an organization will need when it implements the particular 4GL. The language's efficiency, the number of users, the size and nature of applications, and desired response time determine the need for resources.

Although a specific 4GL may work under several operating systems, its efficiency will vary from one system to another. For that reason, the language's efficiency characteristics must apply to the appropriate operating system.

Hardware Requirements

The 4GL should be flexible enough to work in various hardware or software environments of the organization for which that specific 4GL is evaluated. The selected language should meet the needs of the environment, rather than forcing the environment to adjust to suit the language.

Since many PCs are used in today's organizations, an evaluator should look at 4GL distributed processing capabilities. Selection factors for these capabilities include:

1. The language should allow the PC user to query and extract mainframe data, download the data to the PC, and manipulate the data locally with standard PC tools or with a PC version of the mainframe language.

2. The application developer should be able to develop and test an application on a PC and later upload to the mainframe for the production runs.

Reliability Requirements

All complex software harbors errors that can cause crashes ranging from annoying to devastating. To reduce the possibility of a major crash, an organization can set reliability objectives. It can require, for example, that the language exhibit a certain mean time for failure, or it can specify an acceptable failure rate for crucial commands or applications.

An organization can determine failure rates by testing the language or by talking with other organizations that use this particular language. If tests uncover a high failure rate, the fault may lie with the product or with the way it is being used. In the latter case, problems should fade as users become more proficient in the use of the language. On the other hand, improper use of the language may reflect poor documentation or design.

The evaluator also should check the reliability of the 4GL vendor to ensure that the language will receive adequate support. An evaluator may require that the vendor have been in business for a specified period, have a good track record for meeting production-release dates, and supply the names of organizations where it has installations. An evaluator may also establish criteria for good documentation.

Finally, the evaluator should look at how the vendor improves the product when new technologies are introduced. That may mean selecting a vendor that allocates perhaps a minimum of 10 percent of its revenue to enhance its products. The vendor should be known for maintaining compatibility between product releases. The number of releases alone does not necessarily indicate a vendor's ability to keep up with developments—new release can represent an enhancement or an effort to patch up problems in an earlier version. It can also be a poorly tested, rushed response to competition.

Cost Consideration

Of course, the bottomline for any purchasing decision is cost. The final cost of the 4GL may be significantly higher than the product's price because of the additional hardware, system software, and skilled personnel needed to implement the language.

Determining the final cost of a language is further complicated by vendors' pricing structures. Many vendors split costs among components and charge extra for options.

A summary of the selection criteria is shown in Figure 3.10.

Evaluation Phase

Once an organization decides what type of 4GL it needs, evaluation can begin. There are two evaluation types: static and dynamic.

Static Evaluation

A static evaluation involves accumulating as much information as possible about a product short of running it. Static evaluation is a relatively inexpensive way to narrow the field of proper 4GLs. It involves collecting literature from vendors, compiling information from publications and directories, and talking to user organizations that have similar systems. (4GL vendors should be able to provide comprehensive customer lists so that an evaluator can randomly select organizations to interview.)

Finally, demonstrations, however time consuming and slanted away from the language's shortcomings, provide a reasonable view of the way a product works.

USER NEEDS	APPLICATION NEEDS
User friendliness	
Menus and prompts	**Hardware & Operating Systems**
Integration across modules	
Default report formats	Mainframe, mini, macro
Help facility	compatibility
Clear error messages	Operating system compatibility
Full screen data entry and	Resource use: CPU, Memory,
editing	storage
Novice and expert mode	
(procedural and non-	**Communication Linkage**
procedural mode)	
Supports prototyping	Other databases
Clear and helpful	Other computer languages
Documentation	Special-purpose software
Initial license, installation	Other computers
and annual costs	Costs and resource usage
Vendor Support	**Language**
	Procedural/nonprocedural
User training	Compiled/interpreted
Applications consulting	Customized menus, prompts,
Hotline and technical support	forms, warnings, errors
Product updates	messages, and reports
User groups	Standard symbols and conventions
Number of installations	Common and user defined
Time-sharing access	functions
Efficiency and reliability	
Data	**Data Management**
Support Cost	
Pricing Structure	Data dictionary
	Common DBMS
	Other DBMS
	Data types
	Simultaneous access
	Data security

Figure 3.10   Selection Criteria for 4GLs

Vendors of 4GLs usually offer demonstrations at a customer's site, at trade shows, and at seminars. Often the vendor's technical staff is on hand to provide information not included in the product literature and to answer questions the potential users may have. However, static evaluation is not a substitute for a dynamic evaluation.

Dynamic Evaluation

A dynamic evaluation involves actually testing the language by running it. It can take the form of a benchmark test, a pilot project, or trial runs. These procedures differ in length and scope.

A *benchmark test* entails comparing how well languages perform on limited applications designed to measure their key characteristics. It is the shortest procedure for evaluation.

For the benchmark to be valid and reliable, each language must be applied to the same set of problems. Vendors may act as advisors in designing the benchmark

Static Evaluation	Dynamic Evaluation
Survey of vendor literature	Benchmark test by prospective users
User groups survey	No vendor involvement
Size of installed customer base	
Local branch office support	
Product demonstration by vendor	Leads to 1–2 choices
Assessment of vendor support in:	
User training	Pilot project on leased software
Hotline and technical support	
Applications consulting	
Product improvements	Trial run on variety of applications
Leads to 6–12 choices	

Figure 3.11   Static Evaluation Versus Dynamic Evaluation

and should set up the test. Otherwise, it would be too time consuming for an evaluator to learn to use the language before testing. Prospective users should maintain control over the test to ensure that it is not biased in favor of the language's strengths.

Pilot projects use broader applications than benchmarks to test languages. As a result, they take longer to complete, usually about three months. In a pilot project, software is leased or rented. An investment in a pilot test is worthwhile, especially if a language proves to be inappropriate for the planned application or simply disappointing. It's better to discover this after spending modest amount on a lease or rental than after paying a lot to purchase the language.

A *trial run* allows an organization to evaluate a product's performance on a variety of applications. The obvious advantage this method offers over a pilot test is that it yields more information from more users. It can sometimes complicate a decision process, however, when there is a difference of opinion. Whatever language an organization selects, it is possible that some users will be pleased, and others disappointed.

Figure 3.11 gives a comparison of the static and the dynamic evaluation processes.

Decision Phase

After this thorough evaluation of 4GLs, an evaluator should be able to select a language confidently. Figure 3.12 summarizes steps needed in the 4GL selection process.

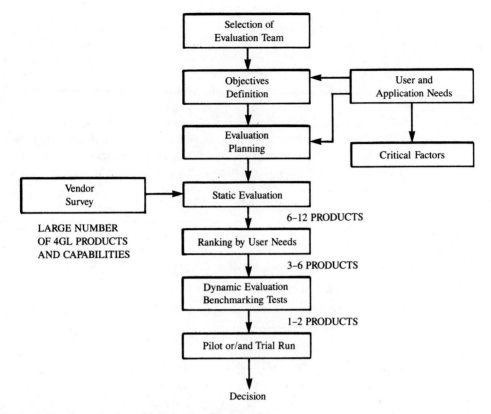

Figure 3.12   Steps in the 4GL Selection Process

3.8 SUMMARY

4GLs represent an evolutionary step in the development of computer languages, in that they are anchored in the database processing environment.

The basic objectives of the constructs they offer are: data accessibility, productivity improvements in programming as well as in the design of systems, flexibility of processing, and user friendliness.

4GLs are still evolving. The products that are available on the market cover the spectrum from the standalone programming language using 4GL constructs to a very complex DBMS combined with a network management system.

Different types of 4GLs can be used for different types of information systems. We discussed the tools needed for transaction processing and decision support system. An ideal 4GL facility integrates all the tools.

When evaluating a 4GL, one should establish selection criteria and consider a specific selection process in order to make an informed choice of a fourth-generation product. The selection process should include: identifying the application objectives, planning the evaluation process, actually evaluating and finally, deciding. Before a final decision is made, the evaluation of a 4GL product should be performed in a dynamic as well as in a static manner.

There is no 4GL product on the market as yet that can be used for all types of applications. Nonetheless, existing commercial 4GLs are capable of supporting a substantial portion of the applications development in many organizations. In Chapter 4 we look at the 4GL environment, using some of the currently available 4GLs as examples.

EXERCISES

1. What is a fourth-generation language? Is it easy to define?

2. Give some names that have been used to refer to 4GLs.

3. What properties are of importance for a 4GL?

4. How would you characterize the difference between an application generator and a program generator?

5. Why do you suppose a DBMS is at the heart of a fully integrated 4GL?

6. Assume that a manager at your company knows that you are a computer whiz. Since she is impatient and very busy, she always demands clear, concise answers. She asks you: "What is it with these new 4GLs on PC? Are they good for us? Could you tell me why?" What would you say? Do you have any questions for your manager?

7. Can a 4GL be classified as a user's interface to an applications generator? Why or why not?

8. How would you explain the advantages of using 4GLs to a company's board of directors? (Assume that these people know very little about computer languages and do not want to be bothered with the technicalities of data processing.)

9. What factors do you need to consider in choosing a 4GL?

10. Summarize the advantages of using 4GLs.

11. Summarize the disadvantages of using 4GLs.

12. For whom are 4GLs intended?

13. Assume you are the manager of a programming group that is charged with the design of a decision support system that is going to be used daily. The functioning of this system depends on complex mathematical procedures being performed repeatedly. The system must provide outputs for each solution in no more than few minutes. Which programming language would you recommend?

14. A crisis situation developed in your organization. A system that is going to be used three times a year and requires a large amount of data (computation time is not critical and is not an issue for this system) must be developed now, within few days. What do you recommend?

15. Are there industry standards for a 4GL?

16. How would you choose a 4GL? What would you need to consider?

17. What are the phases for selecting a fourth-generation language for a specific application? Give a short definition of each phase. Consider any possible problems.

18. When would static evaluation be adequate?

19. Why and when would you consider dynamic evaluation?

20. In your organization you are responsible for the evaluation and recommendation of the new application generation tools. In the past, with some of the marketed systems evaluated already by the broad base of users, you were able to get some recommendations from your counterparts in other companies. But what do you do about the newest releases and the newest tools? Comment.

21. In publications such as *Computerworld* or *Datamation* find and analyze an advertisement for a 4GL. What 4GL features are emphasized? What type of a 4GL is it? How do these features compare with those needed for a production or a decision support system? How would you go about evaluating this product? What will it depend on?

REFERENCES AND SUGGESTED READINGS

1. Alloway, R. M., and Quillard, J. A. "User managers' systems needs." *MIS Quarterly*, Vol. 7, No. 2, June 1983, pp. 27-41.

2. Babb, D. "Increasing productivity with the application generation interface." *Journal of Information Management*, Spring 1985.

3. Babcock, C. "Big 8 firm politics tied to 4GL snafu." *Computerworld*, Vol. 20, No. 30, July 28 1986, pp. 1-4.

4. Cobb, R. "In praise of 4GLs." *Datamation*, July 1985.

5. Connor, A. J., and Case, A. F. "Making a case for CASE." *Computerworld-FOCUS*, July 9, 1986, pp. 45-46.

6. Davis, M. *Applied Decision Support*. Englewood Cliffs, N.J.: Prentice-Hall, 1988.

7. Grant, F. "The downside of 4GLs." *Datamation*, July 1985.

8. Jenkins, M. "Surveying the software generator market." *Datamation*, September 1985.

9. Kull, D. "Anatomy of a 4GL disaster." *Computer Decisions*, January 11, 1986, pp. 58-65.

10. Martin, J. *Fourth-Generation Languages, Volume I: Principles*. Englewood Cliffs, N. J.: Prentice-Hall, 1985.

11. Meador C., and Mezger R. A. "Selecting an end user programming language for DSS development." *MIS Quarterly*, Vol. 8, No. 4, December 1984.

12. Parmesano, P. M. "Turning PCs into programming powerstations." *Business Software Review*. Vol. 7, No. 1, 1988, pp. 22-30.

13. Sprague, R., and Carlson, E. *Building Effective Decision Support Systems*. Englewood Cliffs, N.J.: Prentice-Hall, 1982.

14. Stott, J. "Planning and designing of an enterprise software development library." University of Hawaii Working Paper No. 85-1, 1985.

15. Snyders, J. "In Search of a 4th generation language." *Infosystems*, October 1984, pp. 28-32.

16. Tinnirello, P. "Making a sensible 4GL selection." *Computer Decisions*, July 30, 1985.

17. Turban, E. *Decision Support and Expert Systems: Managerial Perspective*. New York: Macmillan Publishing, 1988.

18. Whitten, J. L., Bentley, L. D., and Ho, T. I. M. *System Analysis and Design Methods*. St. Louis: Times Mirror/Mosby, 1986.

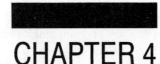

CHAPTER 4

Some Fourth-Generation Languages

The trick to problem solving is not just "know how," but "know when"—which lets you adapt the solution method to the problem and not vice versa.

Gerald M. Weinberg

4.1 INTRODUCTION

This chapter briefly describes the functional characteristics of selected fourth-generation products. The main objective is to give you a general feel for what these fourth-generation products have to offer. It is not our intention to evaluate the products.

The 4GL products described here were chosen because their development continues to anticipate business user's and professional programmer's future needs, especially networking, cooperative processing, and distributed databases. (A good source of information on current developments in 4GLs is the National Database and 4th/5th Generation Symposium held twice a year, see reference [5].)

The chapter begins by describing the advantages of 4GLs and proposing a general way to categorize the many 4GLs on the market. It continues with the specific 4GL products, defining the mode of use for each product and presenting coding examples for some. This chapter should help you better understand what 4GLs are and make you aware that for the many 4GL products there are at present no standards.

4.2 APPROPRIATE TOOL SET

The benefits of using a 4GL over a 3GL can be summarized as follows. With 4GLs:

1. Application systems can be build quicker.
2. Application systems can be fine tuned more easily.

3. Maintenance of application systems becomes easier.

4. End users can do some programming and develop their own systems.

Further goals of 4GLs (see reference [14]) are:

1. *Maximum results.* To be able to develop applications that are as powerful and as useful to future users as possible.

2. *Minimum time.* To be able to develop applications quickly.

3. *Minimum work.* To be able to accomplish work with the minimum effort; to reduce long and complex training required in mastering programming and development tools.

4. *Minimum error.* To use techniques that reduce the probability of human error; to catch those errors that occur automatically.

5. *Minimum maintenance.* To be able to accommodate the changing needs of an application by allowing for easy modifications.

These advantages are also advantages of the CASE tools, of which 4GLs are part. Most product groups marketed as 4GLs fall into one of two general categories:

1. End-user/decision support productivity tools, which concentrate on visual and simple command-driven interfaces.

2. Professional programmer tools, which offer powerful applications development tools.

The distinction between the two categories, however, can become hazy when one looks closer at any 4GL product because vendors of both product groups are attempting to give them universal appeal. This universal appeal is offered through the graded-skill user interface.

Graded-skill user interface of a 4GL product is intended to offer different access modes in one system. It attempts to address different levels of programming skills and different applications needs of the product users. On the lowest level, it may provide the capability to instruct the system by visual means (for example, screen painters) and by natural language interface (for example, English-like requests to the database). On the next level, it can include a dialogue-based program generator (for example, prompting forms). An interactive command language for the advanced user can be on the next level (for example, the interactive access to the system development tools). Finally, the highest level can include standard procedural language features intended for the experienced programmer (for example, control statements, conditional statements, and assignment statements).

There is no single 4GL product, as yet, that is powerful enough to be used in building a complex application and yet simple enough to allow an unsophisticated business user to feel comfortable working with it.

Thus, there are different types of 4GLs. The variety and diversity of 4GL products present in the marketplace is quite confusing. Individual 4GLs differ

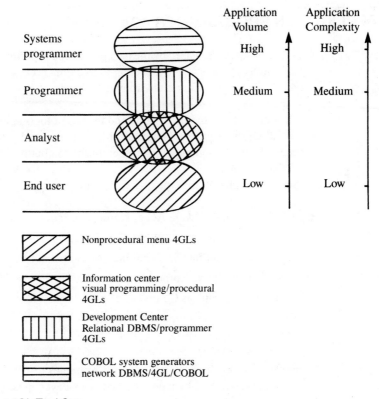

Figure 4.1   Different 4GL Tool Sets

greatly in their capabilities. In addition, 4GLs are changing and improving quickly, and what was appropriate last year may well have been superseded this year.

As discussed in previous chapters, the orientation of a product marketed as a 4GL depends on:

■ For whom it is intended, that is, its ultimate user (end user, analyst, programmer, or system programmer).

■ The nature and complexity of an application for which the 4GL can be effectively used. That is, is it intended for the development of a transaction processing system with multiple concurrent users, on one end of the spectrum, or for simple reports from a personal database, on the other end of the spectrum.

■ Application volume (low, medium, or high) for which it is appropriate.

In reality, even with a graded-skill user interface, a 4GL cannot be all things to all users, for all types of applications. Many products, of course, overlap certain domains. This situation is represented in Figure 4.1.

4.3 APPLICATION PROGRAMMER 4GL

This type of software is used by the data processing departments of many business organizations. It is used to develop transaction processing systems or large databases in the mainframe environment, that is, it is used for company-wide systems.

Most of the time, the installation and the use of tools associated with products in this category require a highly technical staff. Usually this software is very procedural and too complex for most end-user computing. Its use calls for rather extensive training.

Some examples of this type of software are:

- ADABAS from Software AG of North America
- ADR/DATACOM from Applied Data Research
- IDMS/R from Cullinet Software Inc.
- LINC II from Unisys Corporation
- MAPPER from Unisys Corporation
- MODEL 204 from Computer Corporation of America
- ORACLE from Oracle Corporation

Some of these products (ORACLE, for example), can be used by application programmers as well as by highly trained users-developers.

4.4 ORACLE

ORACLE was originally developed in 1979 as a relational database management system for the IBM mainframes environment. It uses SQL for all data usage operations: data definition, data control, data query, data manipulation, and so on. (A brief comment on SQL is given when we show examples of the ORACLE code.)

ORACLE evolved into a 4GL product that can run on a variety of mainframes, minis, and personal computers. It supports a large number of operating systems such as MS-DOS, UNIX, VM/SP, MVS/SP, MVX/XA, and VMS. In mainframe environments it is able to manage large databases with multiple concurrent users. The distributed version of ORACLE allows transparent access to ORACLE applications on a network. The microcomputer version of ORACLE has all the functions of the mainframe version. The ORACLE system structure is shown in Figure 4.2.

The center of ORACLE is a relational database management system (RDBMS). It includes a multiuser support facility, data dictionary, and security and auditing facilities.

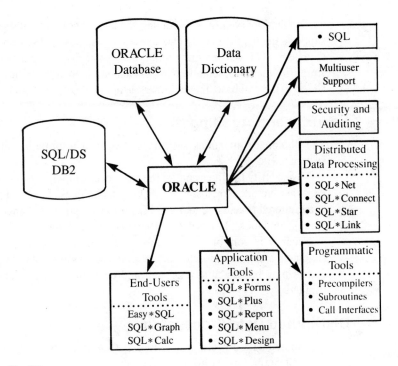

Figure 4.2 Oracle Facilities

Data Structure and Capabilities

ORACLE database structure is uncomplicated. The physical file unit, a relation, is a simple two-dimensional table. Logical files are of two types:

1. Store tables, which contain data, indexes, and a data dictionary.
2. User views, which are virtual tables that behave as store tables but do not exist in the storage space.

Multiuser Support

ORACLE has a multiuser support facility. The same application can be run by many users at once.

Data Dictionary

ORACLE has an integrated (with the rest of the system) data dictionary that provides basic interface between the SQL and the database.

The dictionary defines the tables, the table's columns, and user's views. It also supports the detailed comments about any database entity down to the individual data items. This documenting function helps keep track of data information, which simplifies the documentation process and maintenance. As new tables or users are added to the database, the dictionary is updated automatically.

Security and Auditing

The dictionary maintains security and control information on the data and the system users.

The security facilities control the data access, manipulation, and creation. These facilities include, for example, locking techniques that bar users from the data being altered (exclusive lock) and features that prevent changes to the data being read (shared lock). Locks can be applied to the tables and to the rows within tables.

Security is controlled by each data owner (table creator). Through an audit statement a user can monitor all attempted access and data usage. All types of file access may be selectively defined and controlled. These functions can be distributed.

Distributed Data Processing

Distributed data processing facilities are supported by SQL*Net, SQL*Connect, SQL*Star, and Easy*Link.

SQL*Net

SQL*Net is an interactive facility that handles all communications between ORACLE processes on various computers. It permits connections within a specific computer network or among a series of networks. It is designed to support major communication protocols and a network of similar and dissimilar computers, for example, PC to VM/CMS or PC to Digital Equipment VAX/VMS.

SQL*Connect

SQL*Connect allows users to access IBM mainframe databases from ORACLE applications. This access is to DB2 and SQL/DS databases, which are based on the relational model. Both products are similar but work on different IBM operating systems. With this facility, users do not need to convert DB2 or SQL/DS data into ORACLE tables. For example, users can call DB2 tables, and SQL*Connect retrieves these data automatically.

SQL*Star

SQL*Star is built on top of SQL*Net and SQL*Connect. With SQL*Net, users can access ORACLE databases housed on computers of various types (not only IBM). With SQL*Connect, non-ORACLE DBMSs are accessible. Thus SQL*Star allows physically distributed databases to appear as one logical database. This is represented in Figure 4.3.

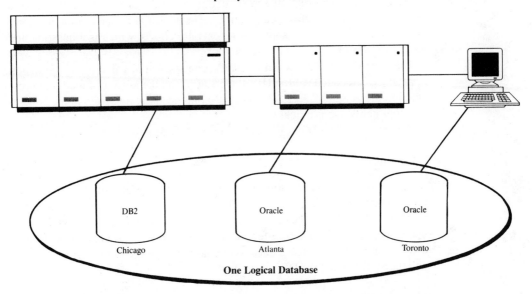

Figure 4.3 SQL*STAR Provides the Capability to Make Physically Distributed Databases Appear as One Logical Database

Easy*Link

Easy*Link provides the mainframe-to-microcomputer link. It allows the micro-computer user to transmit extraction statements to mainframe databases for down-loading of information. It also supports uploading operations.

Programming Tools

The programming interface allows application programmers to access ORACLE data from within third-generation languages. This interface supports languages such as COBOL, C, BASIC, FORTRAN, Ada, PL/I, and Pascal.

Application Tools

This set of tools is designed to substantially speed up the process of building computer applications. These facilities are: SQL*Forms, SQL*Plus, SQL*Report, SQL*Menu, and SQL*Design Dictionary.

SQL*Forms

SQL*Forms allows the quick development of forms-based applications. A user develops applications by making menu choices and using a screen painter. The SQL*Forms facility combines a user's instructions with the information from the ORACLE data dictionary to generate applications.

SQL*Forms supports full-screen definition and development. It supports records insertions, updates, and deletions. The screen is defined through a form entered into an interactive application generator (IAG), which is a question and answer session.

The form defines screen fields, fields prompts, initial values, data validation parameters, calculated values, HELP messages, and the range of functions accessible to the operator. Thus, SQL*Forms' nonprocedural approach allows one to prototype applications quickly.

(Later in this chapter we give an example of the SQL*Forms application.)

SQL*Plus

SQL*Plus is a fourth-generation language (essentially SQL with additional features) designed to manage all interactions within ORACLE. It allows the user to create, modify, and join the database tables; control database access; create ad hoc reports and enquiries; and transfer data among the ORACLE systems distributed on different computers. It includes a command-oriented report writer compatible with the SQL/DS and the DB2 as well.

SQL*Report

SQL*Report formats outputs of database queries into fully formatted reports.

The user has complete control over the format of the report. A text preparation extension allows the user to combine both text and the result of multiple SQL queries into a single report. For example, the user can merge a form letter with selected names from the ORACLE database tables or write textual reports that pull required numbers from the ORACLE database.

SQL*Menu

SQL*Menu allows the creation of customized menu systems. It provides uniform access to all parts of ORACLE, including forms, reports, and commands. It is a menu environment that controls and provides security for the way in which the tasks are carried out.

SQL*Design Dictionary

The SQL*Design Dictionary is a design, development, and documentation tool that helps manage ORACLE applications from the initial analysis to running and maintenance. It is a CASE tool.

The SQL*Design Dictionary automatically produces technical documentation for applications by examining the ORACLE database. It has the capability to generate relational DBMS table definitions when a new application is started by the user.

Automatic documentation and execution tracing provide the user with the information needed to maintain systems easily.

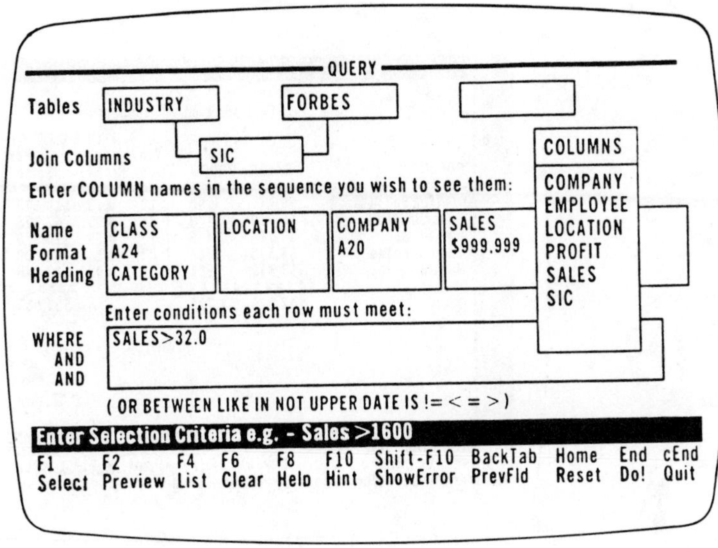

Figure 4.4   An Example of EASY*SQL Menus Screen

End-User Tools

This class of tools provides straightforward interface to ORACLE's databases. These tools are designed for casual users and for those who are just starting to use ORACLE. There are three tools in this class: Easy*SQL, SQL*Graph, and SQL*Calc.

Easy*SQL

The Easy*SQL is designed to assist nonprogrammers in developing SQL statements through full-screen interactive forms, pop-up selection menus, and windows. It allows the user to:

- Enter the data simply by filling in the blanks.
- Formulate queries.
- Create, modify, and join tables and user views.
- Produce and modify database reports and graphs.
- Manage the databases and pass the data to other software applications and computers.

Online HELP facilities as well as menus for access to other ORACLE utilities are part of this tool. In addition to supporting standard keyboard entry, Easy*SQL supports mouse input. An example of the EASY*SQL screen is shown in Figure 4.4.

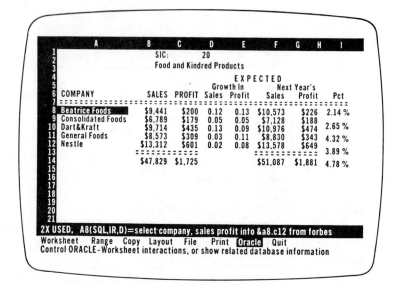

Figure 4.5 An Example of the SQL*CALC Worksheet Screen

SQL*Graph

SQL*Graph is an interactive graphics facility that creates pie, bar, and line charts from the data that the user extracts from the ORACLE database. For a customized graph it has commands to change the color, pattern, size, and orientation of any graph element. Finished graphs can be saved, edited, and reused. The user can query, update, modify, and perform mathematical operations on information stored anywhere in the graphics database.

SQL*Calc

SQL*Calc is a spreadsheet. It is possible to access any ORACLE database directly from the SQL*Calc spreadsheet by entering an SQL statement into a spreadsheet cell. Commands are entered in the same manner as the formulas in a conventional spreadsheet. They can be copied, moved, saved, and edited. Users can manage hundreds of thousands of rows of data, or combine information from several databases onto one spreadsheet. The ORACLE worksheet interaction control screen is shown in Figure 4.5.

Examples of ORACLE Code

We now give elementary examples of the ORACLE code. We consider two facilities: SQL and SQL*Forms. We chose to show an example of the use of SQL because it continues to gain acceptance as the database language of many 4GLs. In 1986 the American National Standards Institute (ANSI) approved SQL as the

SKI INVENTORY FILE STRUCTURE

Inventory Number	Ski Type	Ski Size	Price	Quantity

SKI BRAND NAME AND MANUFACTURER FILE STRUCTURE

Ski Type	Type Name	Manufacturer Name

Figure 4.6   The Structure of Files from the Ski Inventory System

standard relational database language. We briefly demonstrate the SQL*Forms facility to illustrate the use of a visual programming tool suitable for end users.

Before we begin the two examples, we should define our application as we will use it throughout this chapter. The business problem is a SKI INVENTORY control system for a large sporting goods retailer.

For now we will only define the structure of the database for the SKI INVENTORY system. Other requirements will be stated as they are needed. The SKI INVENTORY system database contains two main tables (files):

1. Ski Inventory

2. Ski Brand Name and Manufacturer

The structure of these files is given in Figure 4.6.

SQL

The SQL database language permits users to define, access, and manipulate data stored in the database. We show how to use SQL to:

■ CREATE a table (file).

■ INSERT rows (records) into a table.

■ SELECT rows from a table.

Table Creation

First, we need to name our tables. Let the table for the Ski Inventory be called INV1 and the table for the Ski Brand Names and Manufacturer be called NAM1.

To create a table in SQL, we use the following CREATE TABLE command.

```
user:      CREATE TABLE INV1 (INVNO NUMBER(5),
                  SKITP CHAR(4),
                  SKISZ NUMBER(3),
                  PRICE NUMBER(6,2),
                  QUANT NUMBER(5));
system:    Table created.
```

Even if you had never used SQL before, you could, by analyzing the structure of this command, decipher what it is to accomplish.

First, you indicate what you want to name your table. In our case, it is INV1. Next (this is a part of your create command) you specify the columns (fields) of your table. This specification contains column name, the type of data it will contain, and the field length.

In this example, the column names are: INVNO, SKITP, SKISZ, PRICE, and QUANT. The command syntax requires that you start with the open parenthesis "(". Note also the closing parenthesis ")" at the end of the command.

After naming the column, we need to specify the type of data that each column is to contain. For example, we used CHAR to specify that the SKITP column can contain any character data, that is, we allow letters, numbers, or punctuation marks in this field. We used NUMBER to specify that the INVNO, SKISZ, PRICE, and QUANT columns are to contain just numeric data.

Next we specified field length, that is, the maximum length of any value that can be stored in this column. For example, we used NUMBER(6,2) to specify that the PRICE column is to be numeric with a maximum length of 6 digits, 2 of which are to the right of the decimal point. For the SKITP column, we used SKITP CHAR(4) to require that it be a character field no longer than 4 characters.

Note: Pay attention to the punctuation marks: there is a comma after each column specification and a semicolon at the end of the command. Also note the placement of brackets.

After the CREATE TABLE command is successfully executed, the "Table created" message appears. Tables created with the CREATE TABLE command are referred to as base tables. The table definition is automatically stored in a data dictionary referred to as the system catalog. This catalog is made up of various tables that store descriptive and statistical information related to the database.

To create the NAM1 table, use the CREATE command as follows:

```
CREATE TABLE NAM1 (SKITP CHAR(4) UNIQUE,
                   TPNAM CHAR(15),
                   MFNAM CHAR(35));
```

For the SKITP column of the NAM1 table, you include the UNIQUE specification to prevent a possible double record entry for the same ski type.

In general, the UNIQUE specification automatically prevents two rows of the table from having the same value in the same column. (Note that no data is stored in the table at the time it is created.)

Inserting Rows (Records) Into a Table

As soon as you have created a table, you may begin entering rows of data by issuing the INSERT INTO command.

To enter the first row of data into the INV1 table, we issue:

TPNAM	SKISZ	PRICE	QUANT
Dynastar SL	185	324.50	121
Dynastar GS	205	420.00	10
Dynamics D	225	385.20	5

Figure 4.7 The Output from the SELECT Query

user: INSERT INTO INV1
         VALUES (12500,'DSGS',185,325.50,34);
system: 1 record created.

Consider the structure of the INSERT INTO command.

First, identify the table name into which your row of data is to be inserted. Next, list the data values that are to go into each column, by specifying the VALUES parameter. In our example, those are: (12500,'DSGS',185,325.50,34). Note that the character data item is enclosed in single quotes. After the successful execution of the INSERT INTO command the "1 record created" message appears on the screen.

To add a second row into the table, enter the INSERT command again, specifying data values to be inserted, and so on.

Selecting Data From a Table

After the tables have been created and populated with appropriate data values, you can issue requests for information from a database. Retrieving data from the database is the most common SQL request operation. A database retrieval is called a **query**.

To issue a query, use the SELECT command. The basic SELECT command has two parts, called clauses:

1. SELECT, which contains some data (column name(s))
2. FROM, which contains a table or some tables (table name(s))

The order in which the column names appear after the SELECT clause is the order in which the columns will be displayed.

Let us say that you want to retrieve and list data contained in columns TPNAM, SKSZ, PRICE, and QUANT from both the INV1 and NAM1 tables. The SQL command that will give you this listing is:

    SELECT TPNAM,SKISZ,PRICE,QUANT
    FROM   NAM1,INV1;

We obviously assume here that both tables are already populated with appropriate data. Displayed on the screen, the output from SELECT query looks like table in Figure 4.7.

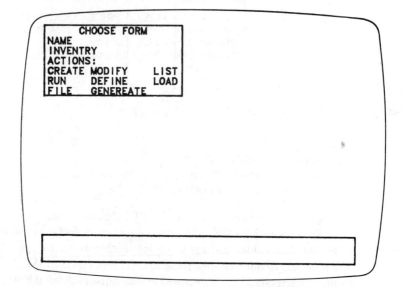

Figure 4.8   First Menu in the SQL*FORMS

Note that the column name is automatically used as the column heading. In this example, the TPNAM column comes from the NAM1 table, and the SKISZ, PRICE, and QUANT columns are from the INV1 table.

SQL*Forms

Recall that this end-user tool helps to develop *forms-based* applications. It is an example of a visual programming tool. It is especially useful for entering, querying, updating, and deleting data. With SQL*Forms we show (see the next section) how to quickly construct the Data Entry form for the Ski Inventory table.

Default Form Creation

When we created the INV1 and NAM1 tables, their definitions were automatically entered into the data dictionary. SQL*Forms uses this information.

Your work is done through the menu dialogue. You start by defining the menu (First menu). (Figure 4.8 illustrates the format of the First menu.) This First menu requires you to name the form with which you want to work. Only 8 characters are allowed in this name. In the example in Figure 4.8, we named the data entry form for the Ski Inventory System INVENTRY (remember to use only 8 characters).

After this is done, you are requested to take an action pertaining to the entry form just named. You can CREATE, MODIFY, LIST, RUN, DEFINE, LOAD, FILE, or GENERATE the form.

Since the INVENTRY form does not exist yet, you select the CREATE action. This brings you to the Second menu, illustrated in Figure 4.9. On this menu the

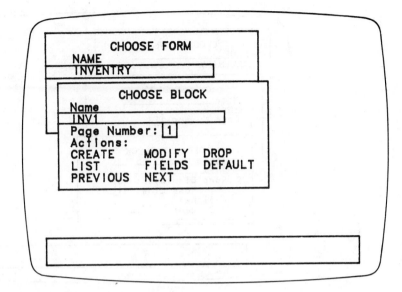

Figure 4.9   Second Menu in SQL*FORMS

name of our INVENTRY form appears automatically in its CHOOSE FORM pop-up window. The action required is to choose a block.

A block is an extension of the idea of the table. A block may contain calculated (derived) fields. In a given form, you can use as many tables (or blocks) as you need.

In our example you only need to name one table, the INV1 table. Next, you are prompted to select an action. If you select DEFAULT, SQL*Forms defines the format of INVENTRY automatically. The next menu (the Third menu) then appears. (Figure 4.10 illustrates this menu.) The last step in creating this form is to specify how many rows of INV1 table data you want to have on the screen at the same time. For example, if 5 rows are required, type 5 when you are prompted for the number of rows to be displayed.

The data entry form is now ready. Note what we have accomplished. We have created a fully functional application form INVENTRY to be used for the entry of data into INV1 table. We have done it by:

1. Typing in the form name.
2. Typing in the table name.
3. Choosing the number of rows of data to be displayed at once.

We did not have to identify each column in the INV1 table. SQL*Forms took all the required information from the data dictionary and created the form. It automatically generated the INVENTRY form with the proper headings and column sizes. The

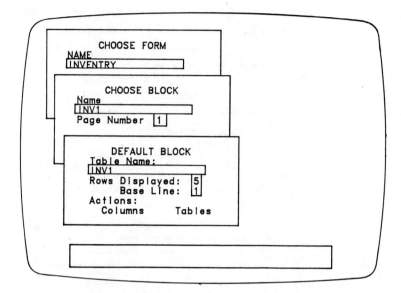

Figure 4.10 Third Menu in SQL*FORMS

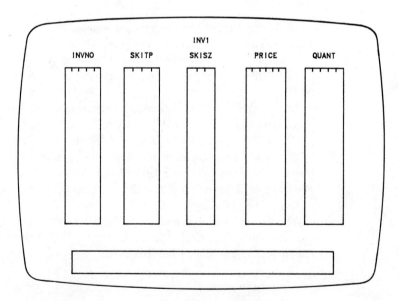

Figure 4.11 Fully Functional Data Entry Form for the Ski Inventory System

number of rows displayed on the screen at once will correspond to the number specified in step 3. Figure 4.11 illustrates the INVENTRY form to be used for the data entry into the INV1 table.

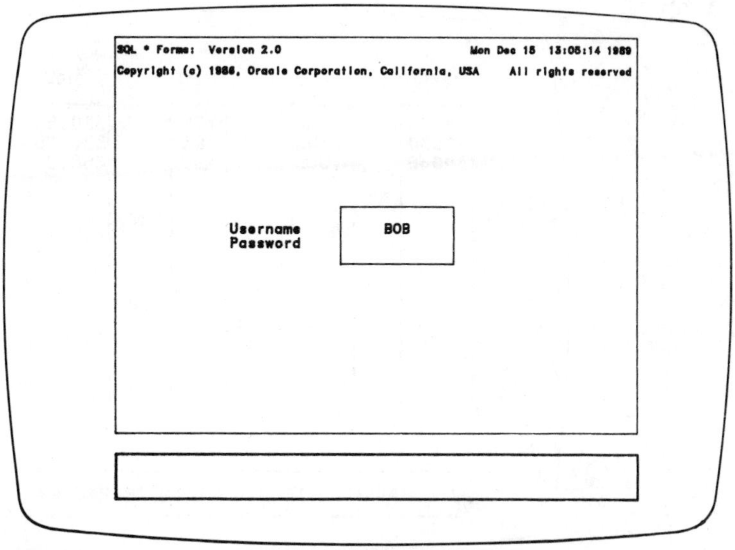

```
SQL * Forms:  Version 2.0                          Mon Dec 18  13:08:14 1989
Copyright (c) 1988, Oracle Corporation, California, USA    All rights reserved




                          Username        BOB
                          Password
```

Figure 4.12 The Password Screen

Running a Form

The INVENTRY form just created gives you complete data entry, query, update, and delete facilities, not only for one user, but for multiple, concurrent users as well. The next example demonstrates the use of this form for data entry and query.

When you start to run your form, the first screen you encounter is the Password screen. This screen represents the security control. Form users can be authorized to perform all functions on specified data, or they can be allowed to perform only selected entry, query, update, or delete functions. The nature of this authorization is defined in the data dictionary, together with the assigned password. Figure 4.12 illustrates this Password screen.

Data Entry

To enter the data, type into the fields on the form. The validation restrictions on all data inputs are automatically enforced. For example, the data dictionary is consulted to establish which data type (alphanumeric, numeric, or date) the fields must be. Figure 4.13 illustrates an example of the Input screen with an entry error in the third record and a statement describing the error.

Data Query

A query-by-example approach allows novice and casual users to retrieve specified data without having to learn a formal query language. To use this approach, execute the QUERY function and type your selection criteria into the appropriate columns of the form.

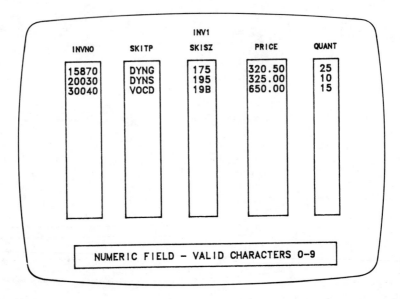

Figure 4.13 The Input Screen

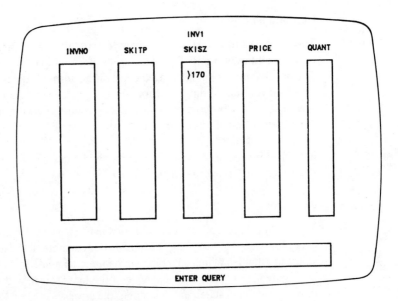

Figure 4.14 Sample Query-by-Example Screen

For example, say that you want to retrieve the list of skis that are longer than 170 cm. Simply invoke the QUERY function and type 170 into the SKISZ (ski size)

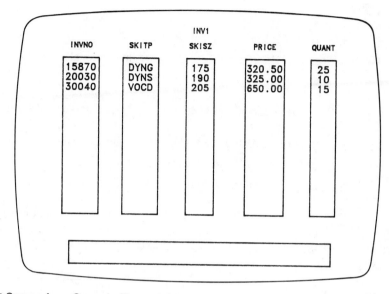

Figure 4.15   Output Screen from Query in Figure 4.14

column. (Figure 4.14 shows the screen.) After this query is executed, the list of all skis that meet the query specification is displayed on the screen (see Figure 4.15).

This ends our examples of ORACLE code. These simple examples are intended to give you a feel of how this software works. In reality, to do what we have described so far will only take a minute or two—much less time than it takes to describe how to do it.

4.5 GENERAL-PURPOSE 4GLS

There are two categories of products in this group: those that comprise both DBMS and a 4GL and those that do not have a proprietary DBMS.

DBMS/4GLs are often called the development/information center 4GLs. Some are used by professional programmers only; others can be used for departmental computing by the end users as well. Products in this category include:

- EMPRESS from Empress Software
- FOCUS from Information Builders
- IDMS/SQL from Cullinet Software
- INFOCEN from 3CI
- INGRESS from Relational Technology
- NOMAD from MUST Software International

- PROGRESS from Progress Software Corp.
- PACE from Wang Laboratories
- RAMIS from On-Line Software International
- ZIM from Zanthe Information Inc.

In the category of 4GLs without a proprietary DBMS are:

- APPLICATION FACTORY from Cortex Corporation
- INTELLISYS from Genex Technology Group
- POWERHOUSE from Cognos Corporation

To give you a feel for what these products offer we briefly review two examples of the DBMS/4GL and a 4GL useful to both application programmers and end users. These products are NOMAD and POWERHOUSE.

4.6 NOMAD

The DBMS/4GL product called NOMAD is especially useful for developing departmental information systems. It is query and reporting oriented.

NOMAD has been used since 1975. It was the first relational DBMS and 4GL with wide availability. With enhancements brought out during 1988 this product is a general-purpose 4GL.

NOMAD is useful for processing business data, especially in combination with DBMS such as SQL/DS and DB2. It has facilities that can serve the end users as well as application programmers. Its language has both procedural and non-procedural components. NOMAD is emerging as a technology leader in:

- More functional DB2/SQL/DS interfacing
- Communication capabilities for developing cooperative processing applications among mainframe, mini, and micro
- Degree of integration throughout the package
- Consistent syntax in both mainframe and PC versions

NOMAD is designed to run on IBM or IBM-compatible mainframe computers under the VM/CMS and MVS/TSO operating systems. This software can be also ported to Digital Equipment's VAX.

Its microcomputer version has windowing capabilities and is highly compatible with its mainframe version. In fact, the NOMAD windows interface is the standard for all NOMAD user interfaces.

Figure 4.16 illustrates the integrated components of NOMAD.

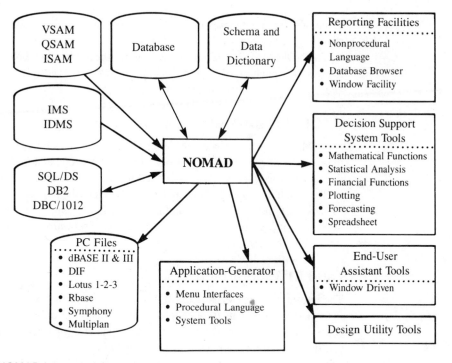

Figure 4.16 NOMAD Integrated Components

NOMAD Data Handling Facilities

At the center of NOMAD is a database management system. It supports both hierarchical and relational access to data. According to 4GL evaluators (see reference 16), although NOMAD can be used for other data models, its support for a true relational model is significantly greater than its competitors FOCUS and RAMIS. NOMAD on a PC supports the relational model only.

NOMAD DBMS Facilities for the Data Processing Professional

NOMAD has read/write interfaces with the DB2 and SQL/DS database management systems. It also can interface with Teradata's DBC/1012 database machine. Read-only interfaces exist for the IDMS and IMS database management systems.

NOMAD DB2 and SQL/DS Interface

The NOMAD DB2 interface couples a fourth-generation language of NOMAD with IBM's DB2 relational database management system. DB2 provides the power to support large databases (up to 64 billion bytes), while NOMAD provides the tools to generate the user's applications.

The NOMAD SQL/DS interface provides the application developer with a tool to create a sophisticated system. Concurrent access by multiple users, data sharing and sorting, and global changes and deletes are handled by the SQL/DS.

DBC/1012 NOMAD Interface

A NOMAD interface to a database machine (Teradata's DBC/1012) allows users to solve their problem of managing very large, shared databases while providing the easy-to-use features of the NOMAD fourth-generation language.

The parallel structure of the DBC/1012 provides the power to manage terabytes (that is, trillion bytes) of information and supports concurrent users with a very high level of performance, important for the general-purpose transaction processing system builder.

IMS and IDMS Interface

The interface to the IMS and the IDMS allows users to access data that are stored in these databases. The users then have the ability to describe the database, control access, and run an application in more than one environment. For example, users can run batch report applications while updating and set limits on the number of accesses.

Data Dictionary

The mainframe version of NOMAD has a partially active, partially passive dictionary. The microcomputer version has a fully active data dictionary. The data dictionary provides:

1. One command to load the database or procedure
2. The ability to create schemas for use outside the data dictionary
3. The facility to report information stored in the data dictionary
4. The ability to create a cross-reference file during program execution
5. Ad hoc analysis of the data dictionary and cross-reference file
6. Automatic documentation of the databases and procedures

The data dictionary facility substantially simplifies data administration as well as the development of applications. (See Figure 4.17.)

Decision Support System Tools

NOMAD has over 140 mathematical and financial functions such as depreciation calculations, time-value of money analysis, time-series analysis, and statistical analysis for forecasting and data analysis.

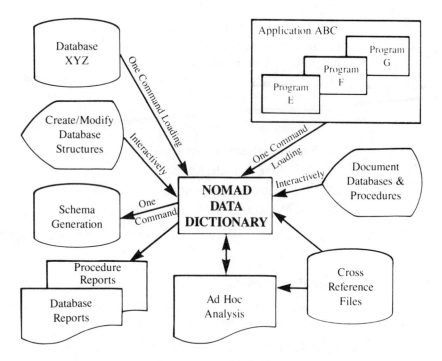

Figure 4.17   NOMAD Data Dictionary

The GOAL SEEK command can help users plan financial strategies. It determines how much a variable must change to reach a specified goal. If the stated GOAL is to increase net income, for example, by 10 percent, SEEK will show the necessary increases in sales.

The WHAT IF command allows users to manipulate their data to see how a change in one or more variables will affect other variables. It is very useful for forecasting; for example, WHAT IF investment increases by 5 percent? How does that affect the rate of return?

When these decision support capabilities are combined with the reporting facilities briefly described in the next section, users can format special financial reports; for example, variance reports, exception reports, or comparative financial statements.

End-User Assistant Tools

Reporting Facilities

The database browser allows totally nonprocedural access to the data. This is accomplished through a function-key-driven system. NOMAD's nonprocedural language enables end users to create custom reports.

For the casual NOMAD user there is an easy-to-learn, window-driven user interface. This interface uses the point-and-pick approach. That is, it can guide the user through a series of screens to create reports from existing databases. This facility can serve as a learning tool for the new language user. The commands generated by the point-and-pick method are saved and displayed in a special command window.

An automatic catalog maintained for each user tracks:

1. Source databases the user frequently accesses.

2. Reports the user selects to keep.

3. Files created during reporting which the user chooses to keep.

4. Other NOMAD procedure files required by the user.

The user can at any time recall, revise, or run any cataloged report from menus and windows.

Other Facilities

There are also some other facilities and productivity tools that help in the design of user applications. Some are actual **commands**:

- *DIAGRAM command*, which produces a pictorial representation of the database, including the names of all the items.
- *SPROMPT command*, which provides screen-based prompting for the interactive database maintenance, for quick application prototyping or for building dialogues in the applications.

Others are **tools**:

- *MAKEM tool*, to build procedures for updating a database.
- *MAKEFORM tool*, to build and update forms descriptions.
- *CHOICE* and *EZHELP tools*, to give application developers ready functions for menu processing and online application HELP facilities.
- *BEAMIT tool*, to allow PC users to select and extract the data from the mainframe databases. The extracted data is automatically formatted for the user with such microcomputer software as dBASE II and III, Chart-Master, Lotus 1-2-3, R:BASE 4000 and 5000, Symphony, and Multiplan.

In the last part of this book we show several examples of how this powerful collection of tools is used on a PC, so we will omit any examples of NOMAD coding here.

4.7 POWERHOUSE

POWERHOUSE is an advanced development language for creating business applications on minicomputers. It was released in 1982 and is running on Hewlett-

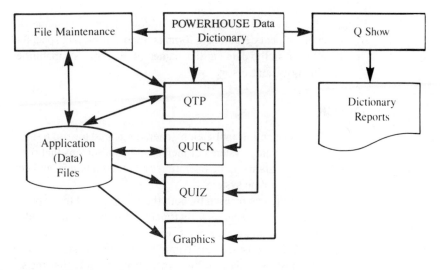

Figure 4.18   Powerhouse Components

Packard HP-3000s, Digital Equipment Corporation (DEC) VAX machines, and Data General machines.

POWERHOUSE does not have its own database management system. However, it supports, for example, HP IMAGE and other file structures offered by Hewlett-Packard as well as FMS, TDMS, and RMS files on the DEC's VAX machines.

POWERHOUSE is the most widely installed 4GL on Hewlett-Packard minicomputers, and is becoming very successful on Digital and Data General minicomputers. Its high-level, nonprocedural statements are designed for the data processing professionals, but they can also be used by individuals of all levels of experience (particularly in the area of report writing, as shown in the examples that follow).

POWERHOUSE consists of several integrated processing components that match the structure of commercial applications: online transaction processing, adhoc and production reporting, and graphics. Figure 4.18 illustrates the POWERHOUSE components.

Data Dictionary

The POWERHOUSE data dictionary is a central depository for definitions of the basic elements needed to define the data for an application system or systems. The data dictionary schema can be written using nonprocedural statements. (When we consider the nature of the POWERHOUSE code later in this chapter, we show how to create the data dictionary schema for our Ski Inventory System application.) The data dictionary can also be created and maintained through an elaborate system of screens.

The dictionary allows the definition of many system-wide parameters, for example, global default date formats, report titles, and special characters that will be allowed in the data entities names. It also offers capabilities for data security and integrity controls.

QUICK

QUICK is an online application generator geared toward transaction processing. It is used to develop systems of menus and data screens that read from and write to files, run programs, issue operating system commands, and control the operation of the entire online system.

This utility can be used by both the end user and the experienced programmer. The end user can generate fully functional screens that can add new records to the file or retrieve and update/delete existing ones. The experienced programmer can use QUICK to construct very complicated screens that perform extensive edits and calculations and update multiple records in multiple files the same time.

QUICK has three levels of programmer support:

1. *Design Statements Level*—where nonprocedural specifications define the format and functions of the application screens. One-word design commands used on this level are equivalent to many lines of procedural code. Design statements allow users to specify, for example, default values, required fields, table lookups, screen linkages, and operating system commands.

2. *Procedural Section Level*—where simple syntax and English-like words perform logical high-level functions. For example, one verb, PUT, can control locking and updating of all supported files on a specific computer. This level supports IF-THEN-ELSE logic and repeating FOR construct.

3. *External Programs Section Level*—where external programs can be viewed as subroutines in that the data can be passed to and received from them. This capability allows access to the applications library as well as to third-generation languages. For example, the ability to call external programs allows a specific application to perform calculations too difficult or perhaps not even possible in POWERHOUSE.

QUIZ

QUIZ is the POWERHOUSE report writer and query processor. The basic use of QUIZ is simple. For example, to create a fully formatted report requires only three statements:

1. ACCESS—a file where the data needed for the report resides.
2. REPORT—a list of items to be extracted from the ACCESS file and put on a report.
3. GO—to execute the request.

QUIZ automatically extracts all the necessary dictionary information such as the report title, headings, and so on. It formats the report, including a page title, column headings, page breaks, and page numbers.

Experienced programmers can produce complicated reports using this facility. Multiple files can be accessed simultaneously, records can be sorted, and control-break headings and footings (with summary operations) can be generated.

QTP

QTP is the POWERHOUSE volume transaction processor intended for data processing professionals. This facility can access many files, apply selection criteria to the records it reads, sort them, establish control breaks, and update files. It automatically generates a default locking strategy. It has special logic that guards against potential problems in multiple file updates.

With QTP the application designer has control over the locking strategy. For example, all files in a run can be locked for the duration of the entire run, or locking can be implemented around each record as it is updated. Locking can also be turned off entirely.

The QTP code can be run uncompiled or compiled. Both the source and the compiled modules can be saved for later reuse. This way QTP becomes an applications development productivity tool in that its use avoids reinventing modules of code.

Graphics

POWERHOUSE graphics can produce fifteen different types of graphs or graph combinations. At its most advanced level, it can be used interactively by professional programmers and experienced users to produce complex graphs and reports. At its simplest level it is a fast, online graphing system.

For example, to create a simple bar graph requires only three statements:

1. ACCESS FIL1, where FIL1 is the name of the file where your data is stored.
2. GRAPH NAM1 VS NAM2, where NAM1 and NAM2 are the names of the variables you want to graph. NAM1 is the variable on the x-axis; NAM2 is the variable on the y-axis.
3. GO (to execute the request)

Sample POWERHOUSE Code

We refer to our Ski Inventory application and through it show examples of POWERHOUSE code. Our intent is to show you its flavor.

We first create the data dictionary, the physical files, and the data entry screen. Then we show how to enter the data. Finally, with the use of the POWERHOUSE code, we show how to create simple reports.

```
TITLE "BOB'S SKI SHOP INVENTORY SYSTEM"
        FILE SKI ORGANIZATION INDEXED
        FILE BRAND ORGANIZATION INDEXED
        ELEMENT SKI-TYPE X(4)
        ELEMENT TYPE-NAME X(15)
        ELEMENT MANUFACTURER X(35)
        ELEMENT INVENTORY-CODE 9(5)
        ELEMENT SKI-SIZE 9(3)
        ELEMENT SKI-PRICE 9(4)V9(2) PICTURE "^,^^^.^^"
        ELEMENT SKI-QUANTITY 9(5) PICTURE "^^,^^^"
        RECORD SKI
          ITEM INVENTORY-CODE   UNIQUE KEY
          ITEM SKI-TYPE
          ITEM SKI-SIZE
          ITEM SKI-PRICE
          ITEM SKI-QUANTITY
        RECORD BRAND
          ITEM SKI-TYPE UNIQUE KEY
          ITEM TYPE-NAME
          ITEM MANUFACTURER
```

Figure 4.19 Powerhouse Data Dictionary for Our Application

Creating the Data Dictionary

We create the data dictionary by using nonprocedural statements. The set of statements needed to create the dictionary for our application is shown in Figure 4.19. If you analyze this set of statements, you can see that first we specified the title. Thus, the title "BOB'S SKI SHOP INVENTORY SYSTEM" will automatically appear as the heading on all reports requested from this database.

Next, the files are described with the FILE statement. Each file is given a name. (The file names for our application are SKI and BRAND.) The file organization also is specified (the organization for both files in our application is indexed).

Next, each field in these files is described using the ELEMENT statement. Each statement contains the ELEMENT's name and its attribute. For example, an attribute expressed as 9(4)V9(2) means that this element is numeric with 4 places to the left of the decimal point and 2 places after the decimal point. (In some element statements we used PICTURE to define the image of the element for display in reports and screens, with the appropriate commas and decimal points shown for numeric displays.)

Because the ELEMENTs are independent of any particular file, the order in which they are listed is not important. Moreover, in the data dictionary, the ELEMENT needs to be listed only once, even if it is a member of multiple files.

Next, we define the record structure. We begin each record structure definition with a RECORD statement in which we name the file to which the particular record belongs.

The particular record structure is defined by the sequence of the ITEMs in the data dictionary. Only the ELEMENT's name needs to be used in the ITEM statement. (All the other data attributes have been defined already.) We can add attributes to the ITEMs to fit the needs of a particular record structure. For example, we defined the item INVENTORY-CODE as a unique key. This means that the value for this ITEM can appear only once in the SKI file. To keep our example simple, we specify a minimum number of parameters. We omit, for example, security controls, headers, validation checks, and HELP information, all of which can also be defined in the dictionary.

Now we compile the code we have created using the data dictionary maintenance program called QDD. The steps involved are as follows:

1. Initiate QDD.
2. Bring the copy of the dictionary code into working storage by executing the USE statement and specifying the name of the physical file where the code is stored. When the code is read into working storage, it is checked for errors.
3. If no errors exist, the dictionary is compiled by executing the BUILD statement.

For our example, assume that F1 is the name of a physical file where the copy of the data dictionary source code is stored. To compile our code, we follow the three steps:

```
: QDD
> USE F1
> BUILD
```

Creating Physical Files

To create physical files for your application, you need the utility program called QUTIL. After this program is initialized, you need to execute only one command: CREATE ALL. This corresponds to:

```
: QUTIL
> CREATE ALL
```

The CREATE ALL command uses information from the compiled data dictionary and creates all the necessary files—in our case the two files SKI and BRAND.

Creating the Data Entry Screen

To construct the data entry screens, program called QDESIGN is used. Our example requires only four statements:

1. SCREEN (to name our screen)
2. FILE (to indicate which file we want)
3. GENERATE (to generate the fields our screen will include)
4. BUILD (to build our screen)

```
: QDESIGN
     > SCREEN SKIUPDAT
     > FILE SKI
     > FILE BRAND REFERENCE
     > GENERATE
  FIELD INVENTORY-CODE OF SKI REQUIRED NOCHANGE LOOKUP NOTON SKI
  FIELD SKI-TYPE OF SKI LOOKUP ON BRAND
  FIELD SKI-SIZE OF SKI
  FIELD SKI-PRICE OF SKI
  FIELD SKI-QUANTITY OF SKI
     > BUILD
```

Figure 4.20   Powerhouse Commands Generating the Data Input Screen

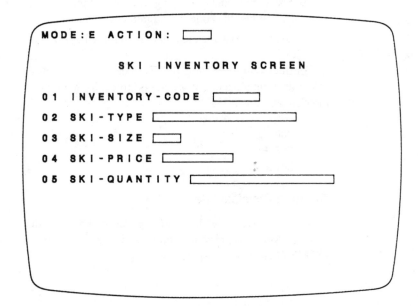

Figure 4.21   Data Entry/Edit Screen Created for Our Application

The information that the GENERATE statement needs is obtained from the data dictionary. The GENERATE statement generates the required FIELD statements.

Let the name of our input screen be SKIUPDAT (for the update of the SKI file). A screen generating session is shown in Figure 4.20. All of the FIELD statements (after the GENERATE command) are automatically generated from the definitions in the data dictionary. The created data entry screen is shown in Figure 4.21.

Entering the Data

With the data input screen created, you can quickly enter the application's data. To enter the data, the QUICK program is invoked and the input screen is identified by name. Our input screen is SKIUPDAT (see Figure 4.20).

```
PAGE  1    BOB'S  SKI  SHOP  INVENTORY  SYSTEM      DATE  09/12/89


   SKI-TYPE              SKI-SIZE     SKI-QUANTITY        SKI-PRICE
- - - - - - - - - - -    - - - - - - - -   - - - - - - - - - - - -    - - - - - - - - - - -
DYNASTAR  SL               175              53             258.70
DYNAMICS  GS               190             123             310.00
DYNASTAR  DH               205              15             415.50
```

Figure 4.22   Simple Report Generated by Powerhouse

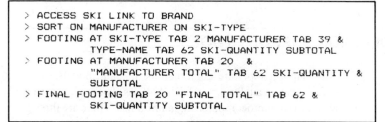

```
>  ACCESS SKI LINK TO BRAND
>  SORT ON MANUFACTURER ON SKI-TYPE
>  FOOTING AT SKI-TYPE TAB 2 MANUFACTURER TAB 39 &
            TYPE-NAME TAB 62 SKI-QUANTITY SUBTOTAL
>  FOOTING AT MANUFACTURER TAB 20  &
            "MANUFACTURER TOTAL" TAB 62 SKI-QUANTITY &
            SUBTOTAL
>  FINAL FOOTING TAB 20 "FINAL TOTAL" TAB 62 &
            SKI-QUANTITY SUBTOTAL
```

Figure 4.23   Powerhouse Code that will Generate a Report with Subtotals and Totals

First you enter E (for the Entry mode) alongside the word ACTION at the top of the screen. Then you enter your data. All the information entered goes first into the update buffer. When you have finished entering records, type // to get back to the Action field.

To store all records permanently and finish the entry session, type UR (for the Update and Return) in the Action field. This ends the data entry session. The records will now be stored in the appropriate physical file.

Creating Simple Reports

The QUIZ program requires only three commands to create simple reports. The code that will generate the report is as follows:

```
> ACCESS SKI
> REPORT SKI-TYPE SKI-SIZE SKI-QUANTITY SKI-PRICE
> GO
```

The created report is in Figure 4.22.

Let us say that we want our report to be a bit more complicated. We want to report the total number of skis by manufacturer and by ski type. The code that will create this report is shown in Figure 4.23 and resulting report in Figure 4.24. The FOOTING statements report subtotal quantities each time the ski type or the manufacturer change. The FINAL FOOTING reports the grand totals.

```
PAGE  1   BOB'S  SKI  SHOP  INVENTORY  SYSTEM      DATE  09/12/89

DYNAMICS             DYNAMICS  SL              15
                     DYNAMICS  GS              25
                     DYNAMICS  DM              16
                     MANUFACTURER  TOTAL       51
DYNASTAR             DYNASTAR  SL              28
                     DYNASTAR  GS              32
                     MANUFACTURER  TOTAL       60

                     FINAL  TOTAL             111
```

Figure 4.24   Quiz Report with Subtotals and Total

4.8 4GL DECISION SUPPORT TOOLS

Decision support tools are combinations of data models, simulation languages suited for decision analysis, and DBMS/4GLs. These tools run on a broad range of hardware, from microcomputers to mainframes. There are three general categories of decision support tools:

1. *Modeling Languages*—nonprocedural languages for modeling and decision support system generation. Examples of these tools are:

■ SYSTEM W from Comshare

■ IFPS from Execucom Systems Corporation

2. *DBMS/4GL with Operations Research Tools*—DBMS/4GLS with embedded operations research tools and decision support system generators. Examples of these are:

■ EXPRESS from Information Resources

■ SAS from SAS Institute

3. *Executive Information Systems (EIS)*—essentially packaged decision support applications that can be used directly by management executives. Those are designed as true end-users tools with menu and graphical interfaces. Examples of this type of tools are:

■ COMMANDER EIS from Comshare

■ OPN from Lincoln National Information Services

■ DirectLine from MUST Software International

4.9 SAS

This product started out as a straightforward statistical and mathematical analysis tool. It works with many different arrangements of hardware and operating system

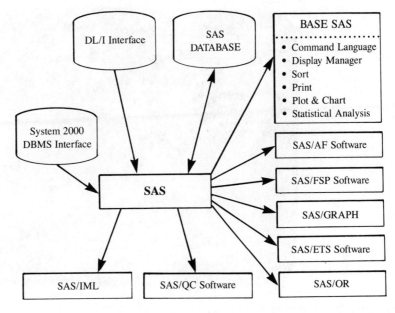

Figure 4.25   SAS Components

software. Essentially it is a software system for data analysis. It is a very sophisticated set of tools used in research, manufacturing, medicine, and business.

We do not give examples of code for this product. This brief description of SAS is included here to give you a feel for the variety of available approaches.

The capabilities of the SAS system's database management, query, report writer, graphics support, financial planning, statistical analysis, operation research, and screen display/editing are molded together to support almost any type of the data management operation: from simple business calculations to sophisticated scientific data analysis. In general, the SAS system comprises:

■ Applications development tools

■ Data entry, retrieval, and management

■ Report writing and graphics

■ Statistical and mathematical analysis

■ Business planning, forecasting, and decision support

■ Operations research and project management

Components of the modular SAS system are illustrated in Figure 4.25.

Base SAS Software

The foundation of the SAS system is the Base SAS Software used for general data management analysis and reporting. There are two basic groups in the Base:

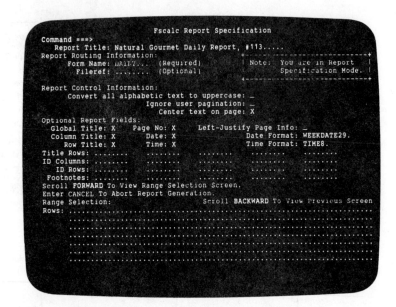

Figure 4.26   An Example of the Report Specification Screen

1. Database creation tools
2. Procedures that process the data

The following sections describe briefly other SAS system software.

SAS/AF Software

The SAS/AF system is an online facility. It is used in applications development for menu and screen building. This facility allows novice users to access the power of SAS without the need to learn its syntax. Predefined procedures are used to construct screens, control the user's path through an application, and transport screens between operating environments. Online HELP and query are available at any point in the operation. An example of the Report specification screen is shown in Figure 4.26.

SAS/FSP Software

This facility is useful for handling large amounts of business information efficiently. It has full-screen, interactive data entry, editing, and querying capabilities. A letter composition and storage facility allows the user to produce personalized letters without the need for repetitive typing and error checking (see Figure 4.27).

A procedure for creating electronic spreadsheets allows the user to design, build, consolidate, and save spreadsheets. The user can perform "what if" analyses,

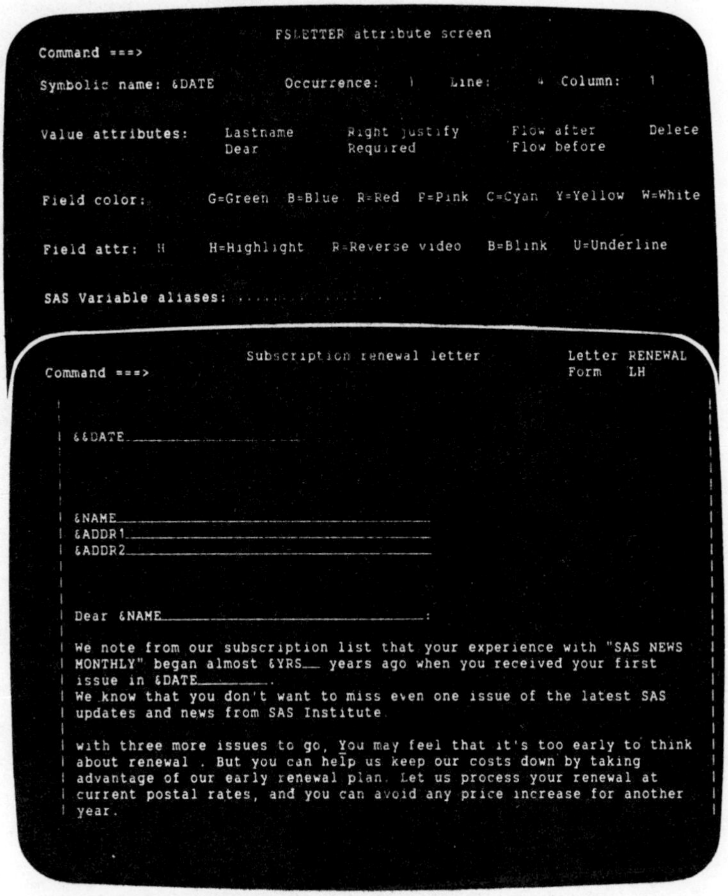

Figure 4.27 Examples of Letter Composition Screens in SAS/FSP

read in collected data, and display multiple spreadsheets simultaneously (see Figure 2.28).

SAS/GRAPH

This facility provides color graphics on a variety of terminals, pen plotters, laser printers, and cameras. Integration of GRAPH with data handling capabilities allows users to access any amount of data, from any file, summarize data in any form, and then present the data in any type of graph. Color output is limited only by the hardware itself. The user can superimpose two or more plots and display charts horizontally or vertically. An example of the SAS graph display is shown in Figure 4.29.

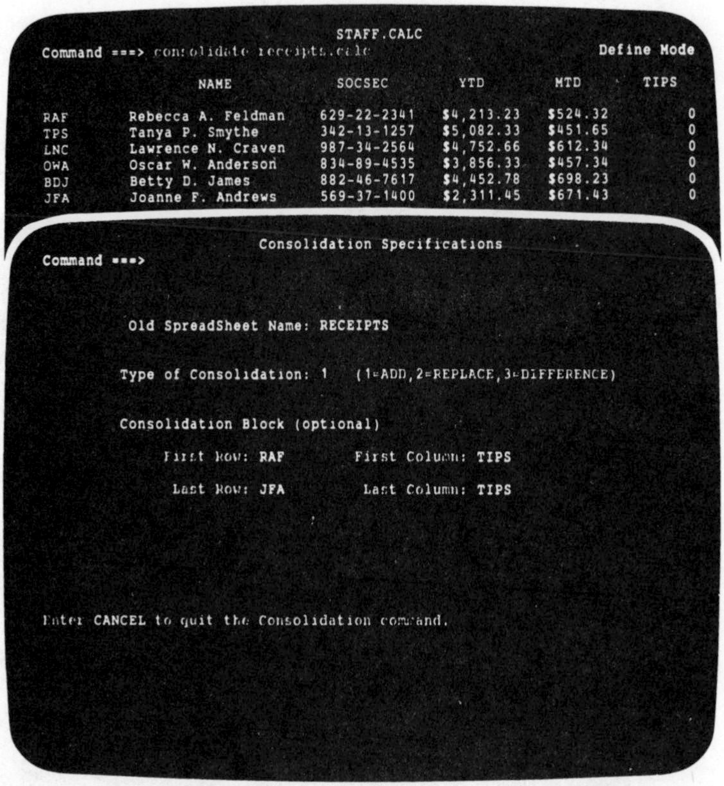

STAFF.CALC
Command ===> consolidate receipts.calc
Define Mode
NAME
SOCSEC
YTD
MTD
TIPS
RAF Rebecca A. Feldman 629-22-2341 $4,213.23 $524.32 0
TPS Tanya P. Smythe 342-13-1257 $5,082.33 $451.65 0
LNC Lawrence N. Craven 987-34-2564 $4,752.66 $612.34 0
OWA Oscar W. Anderson 834-89-4535 $3,856.33 $457.34 0
BDJ Betty D. James 882-46-7617 $4,452.78 $698.23 0
JFA Joanne F. Andrews 569-37-1400 $2,311.45 $671.43 0
Consolidation Specifications
Command ===>
Old SpreadSheet Name: RECEIPTS
Type of Consolidation: 1 (1=ADD,2=REPLACE,3=DIFFERENCE)
Consolidation Block (optional)
First Row: RAF
First Column: TIPS
Last Row: JFA
Last Column: TIPS
Enter CANCEL to quit the Consolidation command.

Figure 4.28 An Example of Spreadsheet Consolidation Command Screens in SAS/FSP

Iris Species Classification
by Physical Measurement
Source: Fisher (1936) Iris Data
SPECIES: VIRGINICA
VERSICOLOR
SETOSA
SEPALLEN
80
60
40
20
0
70
50
30
10
PETALLEN
25
17
PETALWID
9
1
PETALLEN: Petal length in MM.
SEPALLEN: Sepal length in MM.
PETALWID: Petal width in MM.
Sepal width is not shown

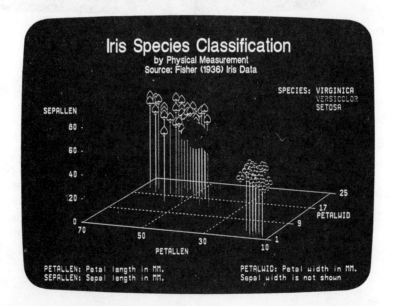

Figure 4.29 An Example of SAS/GRAPH Display

```
                            CITIBASE/CITIBANK ECONOMIC DATABASE
                            QUARTERLY EXAMPLE SHOWING STANDARD TABLES

F 2 SUMMARY MEASURES
AVG. ABSOLUTE PER CENT CHANGE OVER INDICATED SPAN
SPAN
  IN      B1       D11      D13      D12      D10      F1       E1       E2       E3
QUARTERS   O       CI        I        C        S      MCD      MOD.O   MOD.CI   MOD.I
    1   317.720  222.064  228.317   40.510   53.407   27.792   97.536   58.141   19.157
    2   210.803  246.695  154.497   85.739   15.725   56.148  139.883  118.802   19.254
    3   481.843  345.756  140.745  130.265   54.646   83.460  246.476  172.471   17.750
    4   502.426  504.754  168.070  155.909    2.860  101.538  223.133  217.806   20.229

REL. CONTRIBUTIONS OF COMPONENTS TO VARIANCE IN ORIG. SERIES
SPAN IN     D13      D11      D10                RATIO
QUARTERS     I        C        S      TOTAL      (X100)
    1      92.064    2.898    5.037  100.000     56.091
    2      75.853   23.361    0.786  100.000     70.813
    3      49.816   42.674    7.510  100.000     17.127
    4      53.740   46.244    0.016  100.000     20.823




AVERAGE DURATION OF RUN
      CI       I        C      MCD
    2.556    1.533    3.286    2.857
I/C RATIO FOR QUARTERLY SPAN
     1       2        3        4
   5.636   1.802    1.080    1.078
QUARTERS FOR CYCLICAL DOMINANCE       4

AVG % CHANGE WITH REGARD TO SIGN AND STD. OVER SPAN
 SPAN     A1                  D13                  D12                  D10                  D11                  F1
  IN      O                    I                    C                    S                    CI                  MCD
 QRTS   AVGE     S.D.      AVGE      S.D.      AVGE     S.D.      AVGE     S.D.      AVGE      S.D.      AVGE     S.D.
    1  265.950 1033.314   201.118  958.914   12.889   54.277   12.440   57.704   183.113  766.272    8.197   34.103
    2  166.190  441.988   136.099  607.226   45.564  121.735    1.634   23.177   203.203  633.047   25.452   69.809
    3  424.358 1216.698   122.399  545.565   84.233  196.142   12.260   60.006   295.042  845.155   43.111  111.021
    4  451.929 1310.987   147.794  638.233  108.585  239.735    0.470    3.636   453.915 1336.571   55.301  145.876
```

Figure 4.30 An Example of Output from SAS/ETS

SAS/ETS Software

This is a tool for forecasting and econometric analysis. Forecasters and planners can use this software to handle routine projections as well as sophisticated econometric models. ETS contains a library of procedures designed for use by a statistician or mathematician involved in business analysis, planning, and modeling. An example of output from ETS is shown in Figure 4.30.

SAS/OR

SAS/OR is a decision support and data analysis tool that can help managers to plan and schedule complex projects, solve assignment problems, and determine cost effective distribution and transportation strategies. For example, a high-resolution

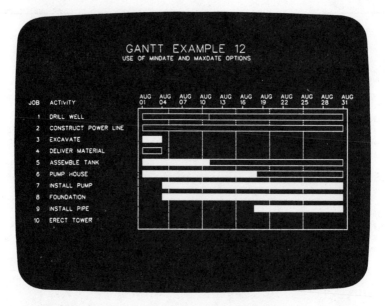

Figure 4.31 An Example of GANTT Chart Produced with SAS/OR

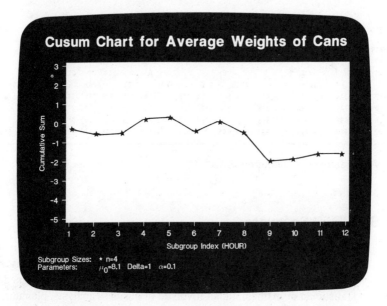

Figure 4.32 Quality Control Data Obtained from SAS/QC

```
SAS (invoke the SAS System)
SAS messages
*ENTER DATA?
DATA MAP.WEATHER;
*ENTER DATA?
INFILE DAILY RECFM=recfm BLKSIZE=blksize LRECL=lrecl;
*ENTER DATA?
INPUT TEMP PRECIP SUNHRS;
more SAS statements and messages
*ENTER DATA?
ENDSAS;
```

Figure 4.33 An Example of a Fragment of a Session with SAS/IML

plotting procedure can help to plot project schedules in the form of a Gantt chart. An example of such output is shown in Figure 4.31.

SAS/QC

SAS/QC is designed for the statistical quality control problems. It is used to organize and analyze manufacturing data. The software includes procedures and graphic tools for determining how well manufactured output meets quality control specifications. An example of SAS/QC output is shown in Figure 4.32.

SAS/IML

SAS/IML is an interactive programming language whose data elements are matrices. It has the most commonly used mathematical and matrix operations built directly into its software. The user never has to declare or allocate storage for any data item. Since the variables refer to the entire matrices of values, a single statement can operate on one or thousands of values. An example of an SAS/IML session is shown in Figure 4.33.

4.10 4GL WITH ARTIFICIAL INTELLIGENCE TECHNOLOGY

Artificial intelligence technology is now being used to enhance existing 4GLs to make them friendlier and perhaps smarter. Examples of such products are:

- ENGLISH from Mathematica
- INTELLECT from Artificial Intelligence
- THEMIS from Frey Associates

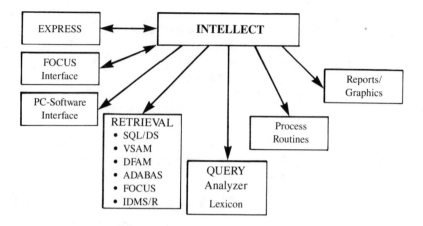

Figure 4.34 Intellect Components

4.11 INTELLECT

INTELLECT was released for commercial use in 1981. It enables business users to access and analyze information contained in a corporate database using conversational English requests.

It is a system that embodies both the knowledge and abilities of a skilled computer programmer and a knowledge of the English language.

It does its work by using artificial intelligence techniques to translate English-language questions into coded instructions that the computer understands, a process that previously required the services of a trained data processing professional.

INTELLECT runs on IBMs and compatible computers under the MVS/TSO, MVS/CICS, and VM/CMS operating systems. It also runs on DEC's VAX systems under VMS operating system. Components of INTELLECT are illustrated in Figure 4.34.

INTELLECT's Natural Language

Being able to "talk" to computers in normal English represents a dramatic breakthrough in user-machine communication. INTELLECT recognizes many different ways of expressing the same thought. You do not have to remember any key words. For example, an user can ask for the same information in any of the following ways:

```
What were the total sales of salesman in district ten for
last year?
```

or

```
In district ten, last year's total sales for salesman.
```

or

```
District ten salesman total sales last year.
```

No matter how the user phrases it, INTELLECT will interpret this query and deliver the required information.

INTELLECT understands a large vocabulary consisting of:

1. Its own built-in dictionary of basic English words and a complete set of grammatical rules.
2. The names of user data fields, alternative names, and other information automatically extracted from the user's DBMS schema.
3. Actual data values in the user's database.

These vocabulary elements form the application's lexicon. Users can then augment this lexicon with synonyms, calculations, and other concepts.

INTELLECT learns from those who use it. By referring to the word that it does not recognize, it will ask a user either to correct its spelling or define the new word in terms it already knows. It allows the user to store this new definition in either the application's base lexicon or in the user's private lexicon.

This software can recognize ambiguous or unclear queries by considering available data, information on a particular application, and the context of the query. For example, if the user asks "List electronic companies in Idaho and Washington," INTELLECT determines that the user is referring most likely to Washington State, not the city, because it understands the context of the user's question. If INTELLECT has many possible interpretations for the query, it searches its database in an attempt to discover the user's intended meaning. In case the available information is insufficient, it consults the user.

INTELLECT is capable of accepting ungrammatical or partial sentences. (A simple illustration of INTELLECT in action will be shown later in this discussion.)

PGF Graphics

This is an interface to the Presentation Graphics of IBM's Graphical Data Display Manager (GDDM). It allows users to create presentation-quality graphs by asking for them in English. For example, in the case of our SKI INVENTORY application, you could simply ask:

```
SHOW ME A PIE CHART OF SKI QUANTITY BY SKI MANUFACTURER.
```

The pie chart will be created without any additional commands.

PC Link

This facility is a mainframe-to-microcomputer link. INTELLECT downloads output to a PC via simple English requests. For example, if you had the data on our

SKI INVENTORY application on a mainframe computer and you wanted to download a report to the PC connected to this mainframe, you could issue the following request:

```
REPORT OF SKI INVENTORY BY SKI INVENTORY NUMBER TO PC.
```

PC Link can also be used for such tasks as loading the data from the mainframe into a PC spreadsheet, word processor, or database management system.

Database Interfaces

INTELLECT has interfaces to several mainframe database management systems. Some examples are as follows:

- *DB2 Database Interface*—converts English user requests into the SQL queries to be applied against the user's DB2 databases.
- *SQL/DS Database Interface*—allows the user to interface SQL/DS directly. (This is similar to the DB2 interface.)
- *DBC/1012 INTELLECT Interface*—supports the parallel processing architecture of the DBC/1012, the database machine.

Personal Vocabulary

The Personal Vocabulary facility helps users personalize their applications. It enables users to maintain a common base lexicon for an application. At the same time it allows individuals to establish personal extensions to the base lexicon to reflect their own usage and concepts.

Examples of the INTELLECT Code

To give you a feel for how the INTELLECT works, we start with a simple query. We illustrate how INTELLECT resolves the built-in ambiguities of the English language. We close with an example of mathematical processing.

Query

For our ski inventory application we want to know how many skis in our inventory were produced by the DYNASTAR Company. Assume that to obtain this information you typed in the following query:

```
WHAT IS THE QUANTITY OF SKIS FROM DYNASTAR?
```

```
user:       WHAT IS THE QUANTITY OF SKIS FROM DYNASTAR?

system:     I'M NOT FAMILIAR WITH THE WORD "DYNASTAR".
            IF IT'S A WORD YOU EXPECT TO FIND IN THE FILE
            HIT THE RETURN KEY.
            OTHERWISE EITHER FIX ITS SPELLING OR ENTER A
            SYNONYM FOR IT.
```

Figure 4.35 An Example of a Query and Response During the Intellect Session

The INTELLECT software verifies that you have access to the SKI INVEN-TORY file and it echoes the request and gives the following answer:

```
TOTAL SKI QUANTITY WITH MANUFACTURER = DYNASTAR
ANSWER:  124
```

In this example we assumed that INTELLECT's database included the word "DYNASTAR" as the name of the manufacturer. If this is not so, the INTELLECT response will be as described in the next section.

Handling Unfamiliar Words

Assume that you did not define the word "DYNASTAR" to INTELLECT and you are seeking the same information. In this case, the query and the response will look as in Figure 4.35.

If you press the RETURN key, INTELLECT responds with the following request:

```
WHAT FIELD SHOULD IT APPEAR IN?
```

You type the response, and INTELLECT responds with:

```
MANUFACTURER
TOTAL SKI QUANTITY WITH MANUFACTURER = DYNASTAR
ANSWER: 124
```

You can avoid extra work by wording your queries in such a way that INTEL-LECT has enough information to interpret them properly. For example, you could have worded last query as follows:

```
WHAT IS SKI QUANTITY MANUFACTURED BY DYNASTAR?
```

With such a query, INTELLECT would know that DYNASTAR is the data value associated with data item MANUFACTURER and it would not need additional information.

```
user:      HOW MANY DIFFERENT MANUFACTURERS ARE THERE?

system:    COUNT UNIQUE MANUFACTURER SORTED BY MANUFACTURER
           OF ALL SKIS IN THE INVENTORY.
           THE NUMBER OF RECORDS TO RETRIEVE IS 953
           ANSWER: 8
           NEXT REQUEST.
```

Figure 4.36   An Example of an Intellect Process Query and Response

INTELLECT Processes

INTELLECT has several routines called *processes* to handle queries. These processes can be divided into two classes:

1. Arithmetic and logical

2. Output definition

INTELLECT selects the specific process by using root words of each query. For example, "how many" is interpreted as a COUNT process.

For our next example we select the counting of unique records in the file. When INTELLECT sees the root words "how many different" in a query, it interprets them as a request to count only the unique occurrences of records and ignore duplicates. When INTELLECT uses the unique count process, the query and response can look like that in Figure 4.36.

4.12 SUMMARY

Because of the competitive and dynamic nature of the software industry, the specific features and hardware environment for which a given 4GL product is intended, changes rapidly. It is rather difficult to review all products available on the market. New products appear monthly, and some of the older ones are incorporated into new integrated and complex development systems.

In this chapter we have attempted to give you a feel for a variety of the 4GL products. The products discussed have been in service for several years across a broad user base and have established customer support facilities.

We summarize and conclude this chapter with a list of sample products mentioned in this chapter. (See Figure 4.37.)

3GL languages such as COBOL or Pascal or PL/I are subject to standards established by industrial and professional societies. 4GLs lack such standards. As a result, as you saw in the brief examples of this chapter, each 4GL has its own command syntax, rules, and features. Some of the 4GL products attempt to overcome this problem by providing optional approaches to the user interface.

	SYSTEM	VENDOR
Application Programmer 4GL	ADABAS ADR/DATACOM IDMS/R LINC II MAPPER MODEL 204 Oracle	Software AG Applied Data Research Cullinet Software Inc. Unisys Corporation Unisys Corporation Computer Corporation Oracle Corporation
DBMS/4GL	EMPRESS FOCUS IDMS/SQL INFOCEN INGRESS NOMAD PROGRESS PACE RAMIS ZIM	EMPRESS Information Builders Cullinet 3CI Relational Technology MUST International Software Progress Wang On-Line International Zanthe Information
General-Purpose 4GL	APPLICATION FACTORY INTELLISYS POWERHOUSE	Cortex Genex Technology Cognos
Decision Support 4GL	EXPRESS IFPS SAS SYSTEM W	Information Resources Execucom SAS Institute Comshare
4GL with AI	ENGLISH INTELLECT THEMIS	Mathematica Artificial Intelligence Frey Associates
Executive Information Systems (EIS)	COMMANDER OPN RAPID IPS	Comshare Lincoln MUST International Software

Figure 4.37 Summary of the Sample 4GL Products

Especially the potential behind natural language processing and graphical-icon-based inputs is being recognized. Although these types of applications are still in their infancy, advancements over the next few years are very likely to benefit the 4GL market as well as the development of new support tools such as EIS.

We conclude this sampling of 4GLs with a few miscellaneous observations:

1. 4GLs attempt to provide a graded-skill interface and visual programming aids of varying complexities.

2. 4GLs support different database structures: some come with their own database management system; others use external ones.

3. There is no standard 4GL approach.

4. 4GLs are still evolving.

5. In one way or another, 4GLs are built to facilitate the manipulation of data in databases.

EXERCISES

1. Comment on the need for the variety of 4GL products. Can there be a standard for a 4GL?

2. What types of applications may not be suitable for coding in a 4GL as opposed to, for example, COBOL?

3. Why do you suppose end users could find 4GLs easy to use even if they contain very complex facilities? What would they use a 4GL for?

4. Assume you are programming in a 4GL and have come to a part of the problem that you know this 4GL will handle inefficiently. Comment on the following alternatives:
   a. Use the 4GL and take the inefficiency.
   b. Use the available facilities of the 4GL and incorporate the COBOL routine into the system written in 4GL to do the processing in question.
   c. Do the entire application in COBOL.

5. When are form-based systems appropriate?

6. In your opinion, what are the best features of ORACLE?

7. Briefly describe the main features of NOMAD.

8. For what type of applications would you use NOMAD?

9. What type of 4GL is POWERHOUSE? How would you characterize it? In what environment and for what applications, in your opinion, should this 4GL be used?

10. Why is SAS useful as a decision support tool?

11. In your opinion, what is the strength of INTELLECT?

12. In what environment would INTELLECT be the best application tool?

13. You are the MIS director in a medium-sized firm. Several end-user departments have asked you to help them locate and evaluate various end-user computing tools. What criteria would you use?

14. What is a command-driven interface?

15. Give an example of the menu- and forms-driven interface. When would it would be useful? Comment on any possible disadvantages.

16. How is the menu- and form-driven interface different from the command-driven interface?

17. Give an example of a 4GL product that has both command driven and form- and menu-driven interfaces.

18. What is a natural language interface? Can it allow the user to apply automation directly into the decision process? For what type of DSS would you use it? For whom in your organization?

19. Comment on any possible disadvantages of the natural language interface.

20. All the hardware in your organization is from the same vendor and uses the same operating system. You are asked for an opinion about the programming language and development tools required for an information system that is to support a large-scale distribution process important for your organization. This system is expected to require a significant amount of the text manipulation and many analytical procedures. This system is projected to respond to the needs of the changing business of your enterprise and thus will require frequent upgrades and revisions. What type of product would you recommend? Defend your recommendation.

PROJECTS

1. Review the most current issues of the *Computerworld* and *MIS Week* to find articles on the use and the new releases of 4GL products. Write a brief on trends you detect. Analyze the trend's significance to the development of information systems.

REFERENCES AND SUGGESTED READINGS

1. Codd, E. F. "Relational database: A practical foundation for productivity." *Communications of the ACM*, Vol. 25, No. 2, February 1982, pp. 109-117.

2. Date, C. J. *A Guide to DB2*. Reading, Mass.: Addison-Wesley, 1984.

3. Date, C. J. *A Guide to INGRES*. Reading, Mass.: Addison-Wesley, 1987.

4. Date C. J. *An Introduction to the Database Systems*, Vol. 1, Fourth Edition. Reading, Mass.: Addison-Wesley, 1986.

5. Digital Consulting Associates, Inc. "The 1989 National database and 4th/5th generation language symposium: Proceedings." Published Semiannually.

6. Hardele, D. J., and Jackson, R. D. "IBM Database 2 Overview." *IBM Systems Journal*, Vol. 23, No. 2, 1984, pp. 112-125.

7. Jenkins, A. M., and Bordoloi, B. "The evolution and status of fourth generation languages: A tutorial." IRMIS Working paper #W611, Indiana University, 1986.

8. Lukac, E. "The impact of 4GL on hardware resources." *Datamation*, October 1, 1984.

9. Manuals on INTELLECT from Artificial Intelligence Corporation, 100 Fifth Avenue, Waltham, Mass.

10. Manuals on NOMAD from MUST Software International, 187 Danbury Road, Wilton, Conn.

11. Manuals on Oracle from Oracle Corporation, 20 Davis Drive, Belmont, Calif.

12. Manuals on POWERHOUSE from Cognos Corporation, 2 Corporate Place, I-95, Peabody, Mass.

13. Manuals on SAS from SAS Institute Inc., Box 8000, SAS Circle, Cary, N. C.

14. Martin J., and Leben J. *Fourth-Generation Languages Volume II. Representative 4GLS*. Englewood Cliffs, N. J.: Prentice-Hall, 1986.

15. Sandberg, G. "A primer on relational data base concepts." *IBM System Journal*, Vol. 20, No. 1, 1981, pp. 23-40.

16. Schussel, G. "Shopping for a fourth generation language." *Datamation*, November 1, 1986.

17. Stonebraker, M. R. *The INGRES Papers: Anatomy of a Relational Database System*. Reading, Mass.: Addison-Wesley, 1986.

PART II

METHODS OF

SYSTEMS DEVELOPMENT

WITH 4GLS

Part II of this book describes the concepts that are common to systems development with 4GLs.

Chapter 5 considers the system development process, prototyping, and 4GLs.

Chapter 6 discusses principles of prototyping.

Chapter 7 presents a general description of the prototyping cycle.

Chapter 8 analyzes successful prototyping processes.

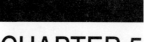

CHAPTER 5

Systems Development and Fourth-Generation Languages

Beauty requires both sun and rain—and is more rooted in a familiar surroundings than we'd like to think.

G. M. Weinberg

5.1 INTRODUCTION

The development of information systems is a complex undertaking. The classical system development life cycle represents a disciplined approach to mastering this complexity. Structured development methods are enhancements of this disciplined approach.

The increase in systems development productivity represents a critical issue for many organizations. In this chapter we consider 4GLs and prototyping both of which contribute to the improvement of productivity in the systems development process.

5.2 THE DEVELOPMENT PROCESS

The System Development Life Cycle (SDLC)

The development of computer information systems is a complicated process. It involves issues ranging from the technical, such as database structure, to the behavioral, such as the nature of the user interface. The combination of application characteristics, human characteristics, and information determination strategies is represented in Figure 5.1.

Although the many types of computer information systems (discussed in Chapter 1) are interrelated, they can be viewed as unique classes of information technology. The development of many Transactions Processing Systems (TPS),

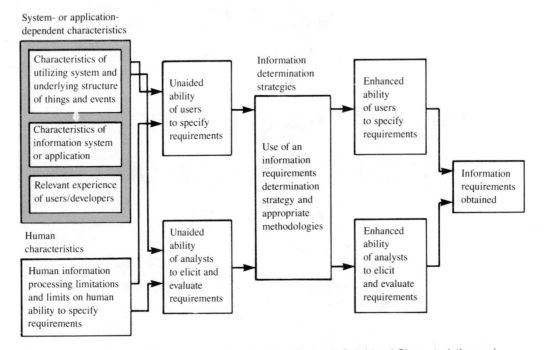

Figure 5.1 Applications Requirements are Obtained Through Combined Characteristics and Strategies

Management Information Systems (MIS), and some of the Decision Support Systems (DSS) follows a lengthy and linear process termed the system development life cycle (SDLC). (For details, see references [9] and [11]). The life cycle process is summarized in Figure 5.2.

The class of applications that are large in scope and highly structured requires this linear development strategy. Applications of this type correspond to categories of *prespecified computing*. For such applications, the processing requirements are determined well ahead of time.

For prespecified computing:

1. Application systems are large and highly structured.

2. The application development time is many months or years.

3. Formal requirements specifications are created.

4. The classical system development life cycle is employed.

5. Programs are formally documented.

6. Maintenance is very formal, slow, and expensive.

The classical development life cycle offers an assurance strategy. Each stage of the development is well defined and has clear and straightforward expectations.

Phase	
1. System analysis and planning	Documenting and analyzing existing systems, needs analysis defining performance requirements, feasibility analysis (technological, economical, behavioral). Develop a conceptual design of a system. Development of a master plan (objectives, structure, resources, control). Analyze problems and opportunities, (e.g., using "Critical Success Factors").
2. Design	Identify information requirements logical system design, input, process, and output design. Identify the components of the system. Design physical system (hardware, and software). Determine how the components will work together.
3. Construction and testing	Write software, test software and hardware, debug, improve system.
4. Implementation	Site preparation, installation, testing and debugging, training, conversion (e.g., in parallel systems), phase in new system, documentation, and overcome resistance to change.
5. Operation and maintenance	Maintenance security, backup, error detection.
6. Evaluation and control	Progress review, acceptance test, post-installation review, cost-benefit analysis, audits, performance monitoring.

Figure 5.2   Computer Information Systems Development Life Cycle

Prespecification of the requirements is assumed, and the basic expectation is to do things right the first time.

Shortcomings of the Life Cycle Approach

The major drawback of the life cycle approach is in the development time involved and amount of documentation produced when this methodology is used. Since correct prespecification of requirements is assumed, any mistakes are costly and difficult to correct, especially when they occur late in the process.

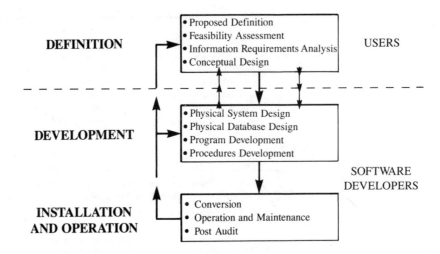

Figure 5.3 Communication Barrier Between Users and Software Developers

System development is supposed to begin when users deliver (presumably) correct and complete definitions of the users' requirements to the developers of the system. However, instead of initiating the development of the system, this requirement's documentation often triggers many rounds of revisions.

Typically, the documents describing the intended system are passed back and forth (to be revised) between users and designers of the intended system. On the one hand, the users often find it hard to state their information needs precisely; on the other, the developers often use technical jargon to communicate information to the users. Thus, an invisible, but real, communication barrier develops between users and developers because of the frustrating lack of clear communication and understanding of each others "business." This situation is represented in Figure 5.3.

Users often have difficulty with abstract descriptions of the proposed system. They cannot clearly assess whether or not the proposed design meets their needs. In addition, the degree of user involvement in the design of the system can diminish dramatically when users are faced with the analysis of many documents (and those are not clearly understood). Communication problems like these often lead to incomplete system specifications.

Problems surface later in the life cycle, often in the programming phase. Specifications changed or modified at this phase lead to extensive reprogramming efforts and increased costs, and bring about serious delays.

Some of the possible reasons for design errors are:

1. Users may be unable to express information needs adequately.

2. Analysts may misinterpret user needs.

3. Analysts may fail to uncover all of the users' problems.

4. Analysts may misinterpret the actual, specified requirements.

5. Analysts may fail to identify trade-offs that must be considered.

6. Analysts and users may choose the wrong trade-off.

7. Details of the system functioning are wrong due to inaccurate translation of system objectives into precise *descriptions* of system behavior, from the user's point of view.

As a defense tactic, users may provide much broader specifications than those required in the basic application. For example, when users are not certain of all the functionality needed from the system they require, they include all they can possibly foresee, even if they do not need it at the present time. This posture is simply: "I do not need it now, but perhaps I will need it in the future; please build it into the stem now so I do not have to ask you for it later."

Adapting this posture, users protect themselves from future conflict with the designers of the application, who may have difficulty implementing changes later in the development process. Designers, on the other hand, may accept this tactic to guard against changes in specifications later in the development process.

Summary of the Life Cycle Approach

To summarize, the life cycle development of computer information systems is based on the implicit assumption that an effective system can be constructed from predefined users' specifications. However, serious problems can surface *later* in the development process when the differences between what the users expected and what the system delivers become apparent. Any corrections that late in the process are very expensive.

The process described in Figure 5.2 is appropriate in situations when application needs as well as user needs are well understood or the systems to be designed are very complex. The key to success in this sequential iteration of the design life cycle is to do it right the first time. There is little latitude for mistakes and thus hardly any opportunity to learn from them. Learning is not explicitly integrated into the traditional life cycle design approach.

Structured Approach

The structured approach to building computer information systems (originated by Yourdon [32], Warnier [28], Orr [26], Gane and Sarson [15], and DeMarco[10]) can be considered a supplement to the life cycle development approach (for system analysis and design phases) of large and complex systems.

The structured approach can be described in terms of concepts and tools. The main idea in the structured approach is to decompose system complexity. Systems are analyzed and designed from the global, abstract level to the detailed level. The description is in terms of data flow diagrams, structure charts, data dictionaries, and process descriptions.

Data flow diagrams and structure charts are developed for each level into which the system is partitioned. These diagrams are supported by a data dictionary that describes data stores, data flows, and data elements and by process descriptions written primarily in structured English or pseudocode.

Many organizations are developing computer-based information systems using structured methods of analysis and design. However, these methods also suffer from problems similar to those encountered with classical life cycle (Figure 5.3). The specific problems are:

- The users' involvement being hindered by the technicality of approaches.
- The system development exceeding the estimated time schedule.
- Late and expensive changes and modifications being requested.
- The systems developed not meeting users' specifications.

5.3 PROTOTYPING

The development strategy which explicitly integrates learning into the design process is called *prototyping*. (Names such adaptive design, incremental design, iterative design, and so on also are used to describe this development process.)

What distinguishes this strategy from the traditional one is the explicit inclusion of learning in the design process. In addition there is no built-in expectation of doing things right the first time. During the prototyping process of system development, designers as well as users of the system expect to make mistakes. They attempt, however, to learn as much as possible from such mistakes, because the underlying assumption is that the initial analysis of the system is always incomplete and needs to be revised.

A prototyped system is built and evaluated. The necessary corrections and enhancements are determined, then the prototype is evaluated again. There is recycling and looping to earlier stages of the system development until the users and builders of the system agree that the requirements are specified. Prototyping essentially bypasses the life cycle stage of the information requirements definition. Users' needs are clarified by actively involving them in a fast (with feedback) development process.

A key aspect of prototyping is the short interval between iterations. For the prototyping to work, the feedback from the system evaluators must be given relatively quickly. The system evaluators are its intended users. (The users are people outside the formal data processing or information systems areas of an organization who use computers to solve problems or enhance productivity.) Besides the short intervals between iterations, an advantage of prototyping is the low cost of the initial prototype. Thus the process of prototyping becomes "a quick and inexpensive process to develop and test a trial balloon" (see Edelman [13]), which later can be extended and enhanced (see Jenkins [20]).

Another important aspect of prototyping is the users' active participation in the prototyping process. Prototyping assumes that users must actively participate and

Prototype use	Where used in life cycle
Demonstrate to management	Planning (start)
Requirements specification	System analysis and planning (at end) and design (at start)
Design selection	Design
Test system components	Construction and testing
Test completed system	Design (at end) implementation (at start)
Train users	Implementation (at end) Operation (at start)

Figure 5.4   Prototype and the Life Cycle

direct the system design. It is explicitly assumed that a successful implementation is achieved with the active involvement of users in evaluating iterations of prototypes.

Prototyping is useful within the traditional life cycle as a method for:

1. Verifying that the needs of the user(s) are met.
2. Verifying that the intended design meets the specifications.
3. Selecting from among a number of alternative design solutions.
4. Testing a design under varying environmental conditions.
5. Testing novel design solutions.
6. Training users in the use of the system.
7. Demonstrating a prototype of the system to upper management to gain approval for a full-scale development effort.

In addition, an information system prototype can be used when:

1. The information requirements needs of the application are unclear.
2. The use of the application can be highly variable and uncertain.
3. The traditional life cycle approach will take too long.
4. The users cannot communicate their needs clearly, or they do not know what they need.

In summary, the prototype is used to clarify user requirements, to verify feasibility of the design, to train users, and to create the final system. Figure 5.4 shows what a prototype is used for and where it fits in the system development life cycle.

The application development cycle using prototyping differs from the conventional process in three ways: in the procedures followed, in the skills needed, and in the tools used.

In the conventional life cycle, user requirements are defined in a specification document. This document must be signed and approved by all involved. Only after that phase is completed does the design of the system begin.

In prototyping, the requirements definition and design evolve at the same time since the development of the prototype deals jointly with requirements from the users' view and the design from the designers' view.

All the requirements do not have to be specified at the beginning of the process. As a matter of fact, prototyping assumes that requirements can be known only partially at the beginning of the system development. Each version of the prototype clarifies the users' requirements.

From developers prototyping requires far less coding (when fourth-generation tools are used). Since users are actively involved in the design process, developers need more "people" skills than in a traditional development.

From users, prototyping requires knowledge of the functional business area for which the system is to be developed. Their participation in the prototyping process is active and requires from them the commitment of time and effort in evaluating an evolving prototype. The risk of developing systems using the prototyping approach is reduced. If the system appears to be, for example, too costly for the possible benefits to be received, it can be discarded in the prototyping stage.

Prototyping is characterized by:

1. Rapid development
2. High user involvement
3. Decreased system development time and cost
4. Reduced risk
5. Clearer definition of project boundaries and scope
6. High management visibility and smoother implementation of production systems

Prototyping differs from life cycle methods in that it focuses on the process and the production of a product, rather than on the sequencing of work leading to the ultimate system. However, prototyping and life cycle methods are complementary rather than alternative approaches to development of information systems. They can be used separately or in tandem in a variety of different combinations. The summary of information systems prototyping is presented in Figure 5.5.

The main issues surrounding the prototyping approach are how to tell the system for which the approach is most applicable, the types of results to expect from prototyping, and potential problems when this approach is used. We address these issues in the next three chapters.

Advantages of Prototyping

Prototyping Decreases Communication Problems

Prototyping improves communication not only between the user and the designer, but also among the technical people involved in designing the system. The prototype itself is the main medium of communication of system functions. It can be used to improve the external design of the system, that is, what the end user sees,

- The software prototype is *a live, working system*; it is not just an idea on paper. Therefore it can be evaluated by the designer and the end users through its use in an operational mode. It performs actual work; it does not just simulate that work.

- The prototype *may become the actual production system*, or it may be replaced by a conventionally coded production system. Thus, the prototype may or may not be discarded.

- The purpose of a prototype is *to test out assumptions,* about users' requirements, and a system design architecture, and perhaps even the logic of a program.

- A prototype is a software system that *is created quickly*—often within hours, days or weeks—rather than months or years. With only conventional programming methods available, it was much too expensive to create both a prototype and a production version. So only production systems were developed, and they had to be done right the first time around. Now more and more users are making innovative use of software tools, such as 4GLs and application generators to get prototypes up and running quickly.

- The prototype *is relatively inexpensive to build,* meaning less expensive than coding in a conventional high-level language. The reason the software tools make prototyping less expensive is that they create most, if not all, of the code necessary from source specification statements.

- Prototyping *is an iterative process*. It begins with a simple prototype that performs only a few of the basic functions in question. Through the use of the prototype, system designers or end users will discover new requirements and refinements that will then be incorporated into each succeeding version. Each version performs more of the desired functions and in an increasingly efficient manner.

Figure 5.5   Summary of Information Systems Prototyping

because the user can easily tell the designer what he likes and dislikes about an existing dynamic model of the system (see Jenkins [20]).

The prototype can help to verify and improve the internal design of the system as well. Good new ideas come much faster when builders can experience the working dynamic model of the system.

The prototyping approach can be used in other circumstances. For example, if a company wanted to integrate several off-the-shelf application packages into one system, they could use the prototyping approach to experiment with different ways of linking the packages.

Prototyping Reduces Design Errors

Prototyping reduces the possibility of design errors and allows changes to the system to occur in the development cycle. Most of the time, the design errors are the result of an incomplete or inaccurate translation of the users' requirements. Inaccurate translation of the user's requirements is a communication problem. This problem is substantially reduced when prototyping approach is used.

Prototyping Increases User Satisfaction

When the user is not sure of the initial systems requirements, experimentation with the "life" model of the system is more fruitful than attending system requirements meetings and reviewing static screen and report layouts and signing off various documents, many of which the user may not fully understand. Active user involvement and fast builder's response to user's criticism create a productive environment.

Prototyping Produces the Right System

With prototyping, the requirements of the final system are not merely theoretical. They are developed from actual experiences with the prototype; they correctly model information needs of the users. With improved communication between system designers and system programmers, the right technical solutions can be created for difficult parts of the final system.

Prototyping Reduces Calendar Time

With prototyping, less time is required to complete and implement the final system. Much less rework of the system is necessary since the designers and the users communicate about their needs and problems better than when static techniques of systems design are used. In addition:

1. Excessive documentation is not needed. Although documentation is a part of the prototyping technique, the work required to produce documentation for the protection of users and designers does not need to be done.
2. No last-minute surprises requiring major modifications turn up. Constant incremental development and testing, which are very important aspects of prototyping, keep the likelihood of finding major system flaws very low.
3. Much of the users' training is a by-product of system development, not a separate implementation phase. Users are trained continually; they evaluate prototypes for their appropriateness and completeness.

Prototyping Reduces Development Risk

Medium to large systems development is a high-risk undertaking. To minimize such a risk, prototypes can be used to test ideas and solutions. Only when the risk level has been diminished by arriving at the consensus of the developers and users evaluating the prototype, can major resources be committed to the building of the full and final system.

Prototyping Reduces Users' Training Time

Reduced training time naturally follows when the users are extensively involved in the development of the information systems, as is the case with the prototyping technique. In addition, once a definitive working prototype is developed, it can also be used to train other users.

Prototyping Simplifies Management

Prototyping can simplify the management of building information systems. A status report can be an actual demonstration of the revised working prototype.

Prototyping Lowers System Cost

First, prototyping reduces the number of reports and screens needed in the final system. When the life cycle technique of system development is employed, users often request reports or screens they know they may never use after the finished system is installed. When the life cycle technique is used, both the users and the designers know that if hypothetically useful reports or screens are not requested during the system design stage, adding or changing them will be very costly once the system is implemented. Moreover, the cost of repairing the omissions and implementing the changes will be blamed on the users, not on the designers. On the other hand, systems developed through prototyping usually do not produce unnecessary reports or screens. The system requirements are produced incrementally using dynamic prototypes, and any required changes can be implemented without exorbitant costs. There is no pressure to design for all possibilities.

Second, systems designed using prototyping contain fewer validation steps and unnecessary controls. The users have a better understanding of what it will cost and the time it will take to add validations that are nice to have but not absolutely necessary. The designers do not add controls that they might have added otherwise because they did not know how users would operate the final system. With prototyping, users know how the system operates, with all controls and validations they truly require.

Third, the use of a 4GL is not a mandatory part of the final system. If operational efficiency is a required criterion for a system, and if the use of a specific 4GL will prevent optimal efficiency, then the system should not contain programs written in this language.

Prototyping Serves as a Learning Vehicle for All Involved in the Process

No matter how experienced and skilled the designers are, they inevitably learn during the system development. Specifically, they learn about the dynamics and the social context of the specific application environment.

The users involved in system design very often gain new insights into their own work and perhaps even learn of other ways of doing things. They also learn about data processing, both specifically, in formalizing their own tasks, and generally, by taking an active role in the system development effort.

A summary of the benefits of prototyping is presented in Figure 5.6.

Shortcomings of Prototyping

Some problems are associated with prototyping. Prototyping may encourage inadequate problem analysis. As is often pointed out by data processing practitioners, prototyping still requires a disciplined analysis of the problem. Prototyping is not a substitute for analysis, it supports it. Since building a model of a system quickly with the help of a 4GL does not guarantee that the model is adequate, the time required to finally fix the problem can exceed the time required to perform a detailed analysis.

> Decreases communication problems
> Reduces design errors
> Increases user satisfaction
> Produces the right system
> Reduces calendar time
> Reduces users' training time
> Can simplify the management of building of information systems
> Lowers system cost
> Serves as a learning vehicle for all involved in the process

Figure 5.6   Benefits of Prototyping

Users may not adequately understand the prototyping process and may be unwilling to give up the prototype. For example, when users see the prototype running, they may assume that it is ready to be used in a production mode. They may not realize that edit and validation routines have not been included, backup and recovery procedures have not been added, and so on. Users may become impatient waiting for a final version of the system, because the prototype took a short time to construct. Thus they may resist having anyone work on the production version of the system, erroneously assuming that the prototype is adequate.

Prototyping and 4GLs

Prototyping requires software tools that allow builders to create model systems in a very short time and to revise them easily. Prototyping works well in an environment with changing requirements. It is also useful in what is called an information center approach to the development of information systems. In the information center approach, a staff of data processing specialists assists users with their own applications development. The main technologies supporting this concept are 4GLs and prototyping.

Prototyping is useful in organizations in which databases and DBMS are well established because it is then possible to build upon existing data resources. If an appropriate database is in place and steps are taken to ensure that this database's integrity will not be compromised by the users' intended application, user-developed systems can be constructed with database tools such as 4GLs. The data processing professional then becomes a consultant who assists users in developing their own systems. Development time is reduced greatly, and users are involved from start to finish. With 4GLs, designs for new applications can be implemented by executing commands directly upon a database that is already designed, implemented, and in place.

The advantages of tools such as 4GLs lie in the ability of users and data processing professionals to work, so to speak, closer to the application. Their attention is focused on what happens rather than on how to get a computer to make it happen.

4GLs are prototyping tools because:

■ They make it easier to create and manipulate data.
■ The code they create is essentially self-documenting.
■ They reduce programming time for end users as well as for programmers.

4GLs, however, are not substitutes for good program design; they are tools to support it.

5.4 SUMMARY

The life cycle system development approach is useful for prespecified computing, which is appropriate for highly structured, large, and complex applications. The life cycle consists of three major stages: definition, development, and installation/ operation. Each stage is composed of specific phases that provide a basis for the management and control of development by breaking the process down into well-defined segments. An implicit assumption for this approach is that developers can produce an effective system from predefined user specifications. Problems with this approach are long development times and difficulties with users' involvement in the process.

To deal with problems of this sort, the prototyping development approach can be used when prespecified computing does not apply. 4GLs are tools of the prototyping approach. Prototyping aims to:

■ Shorten development time.
■ Improve users' understanding of systems requirements needs and capabilities by presenting them with a model of the system.

Prototyping is used to:

■ Clarify user requirements.
■ Verify feasibility of the design.
■ Create the final system.

A distinctive feature of prototyping is the explicit integration of learning (for users as well as builders) into the system development process. Moreover, the user must actively participate and direct the design of the system.

There are also disadvantages to the prototyping process. When such an approach is used, the gains obtained from the discipline of the life cycle approach may be lost. Prototyping may encourage inadequate problem analysis. In addition, users may not fully understand the nature of the prototyping process and be unwilling to give up the prototype before development is completed.

Prototyping and 4GLs are tools that support analysis, design, and programming. Prototyping can improve analysis and design. 4GLs speed up programming. They are complements to the life cycle process and serve also as aids in the final system implementation.

EXERCISES

1. Describe outputs from the main stages of the system development life cycle.

2. Consider some reasons why planning is essential to the successful development of information systems.

3. In your opinion, how important is planning for prototyping and during the prototyping process?

4. You are a member of the MIS steering committee in your organization. Lately the meetings have deteriorated into gripe sessions. Some managers of functional units in your organization are complaining loudly about their pet information system projects that are behind schedule in development. Others complain bitterly about systems failures. It is becoming obvious to you that the steering committee is not functioning effectively. What suggestions do you have for this group?

5. Why is active user participation in system development often difficult?

6. You are a member of a panel discussing prototyping as the key to the success of the development of computer application systems. One of the panelists made the following statement: "Unfortunately, when a software developer uses modern techniques, success is only likely when the application is both well understood and supported by previous experience. The current rate of growth in hardware acquisition means large numbers of end users are demanding more new applications each year. In order to develop these systems, the old knowledge is inadequate. Prototyping can tackle some of these problems." Discuss how prototyping can do that. Be as specific as you can.

7. Elaborate as fully as you can on this question: Should managers be involved in the design and implementation of systems in their area of responsibility?

8. How does prototyping differ from the classical and structured approach?

9. How are the traditional life cycle methods and prototyping complementary and how are they not? Comment on this as fully as you can.

10. What would you consider a prototyping environment?

11. What is prototyping characterized by?

12. Why is inclusion of learning in the system development process of importance? Under what circumstances is it critical?

13. What is the fundamental problem between system users and systems developers that frequently leads to misunderstanding and unrealistic expectations? What are some of the causes for this basic problem?

14. What is it about the process of prototyping that allows developers to clarify the user's information system needs?

15. Do you think that the library of prototypes could be useful to the data processing departments of business organizations? Why or why not?

16. Can a prototype be used for future enhancements of a system under construction?

17. How can prototyping shorten the development cycle?

18. How can prototyping be used to improve communications between designers of the system?

19. If the system is expected to change very much in the future, should its development use the prototyping approach? Specify your position in detail.

20. If the system is expected to change very much in the future, should most of it be written in 4GL? Why or why not?

21. In the book *Decision Support Systems: Putting Theory Into Practice* by R. H. Sprague and H. Watson, published by Prentice-Hall in 1986, on page 189, you can find a table listing sample criteria for evaluating DSS tools. Here is the table:

A. FUNCTIONS AND FEATURES
  1. Modeling-able to calculate with the information in the system, do optimization, "what-if" analysis.
  2. Procedurability-ability to solve equations independent of their ordering symbolic reference of data.
  3. Data management-number of dimensions, handling of sparse data, ad hoc inquiry.
  4. Report generator-ability to produce high quality formal reports quickly and easily.
  5. Graphics-line, pie, bar, quality of output
  6. Statistics & analysis-descriptive statistics, regression, significance tests
  7. Project management-PERT/CPM, multi-level work breakdown structure
  8. Operations research-linear, integer, dynamic programming
  9. Forecasting & Econometrics-time series analysis, seasonalization, smoothing
  10. External database & interfaces
  11. Security-database, file, model, class of user

B. EASE OF USE
  1. End user-analysis performed directly by person who needs the information
  2. Programmer/analyst-interested in the quality of the editor, data management, report writer, etc.
  3. Ad Hoc inquiry-end user answering questions for which no standard report is available

C. FACILITIES
  1. Documentation-for user, programmer, operations
  2. Training-novice/advanced, system/user
  3. Support-consultant, hot line
  4. Host hardware-computers supported
  5. Operation Environment-operating systems, disk requirements, etc.
  6. Available-in-house & on timeshare

D. MARKET POSTURE
  1. Pricing-lease, rent, purchase
  2. Installations-numbers of users, length of use
  3. Target Market-type of business actively pursued the the vendor
  4. Plans-commitment to DSS as a business area, amount of R&D
  5. User Perceptions-degree of use and support, functions used
  6. Vendor viability-size of company, revenues, etc.

Could the prototyping approach be used in building DSS with such tools. Why or why not?

22. Briefly describe the benefits of prototyping.

23. Briefly describe the problems associated with prototyping.

24. Can prototyping be a substitute for system design and requirements definition?

25. Comment on the impact of prototyping on the skills and attitudes of users and professional programmers.

26. Assume that in an organization there exist a portfolio of design and code modules, but the prototypers are not aware of this. Comment on the consequences of this lack of knowledge on the prototyping process.

27. Why are 4GLs tools of prototyping?

28. Can poorly designed programs benefit from the use of 4GLs?

29. Comment on the following statement: The systems requirements definition technique used (for the development of new applications) depends on the ability of the system development participants to specify requirements.

30. Is it possible that successful prototyping depends not so much on the selection of prototyping tools but on corporate culture? Discuss.

PROJECTS

1. Locate the article:
   Cervthe, R. P. et al. "Why software prototyping works." *Datamation*, Vol. 33, No. 16, August 1987, pp. 97-99.
   a. What questions do the authors explore concerning prototyping?
   b. In the opinion of the authors:
   ■ How does prototyping fit into the traditional lifecycle development methodology?
   ■ How should prototyping be used?
   ■ What are the benefits of prototyping?

   Prepare a brief answering these questions and evaluate opinions expressed in this article.

2. Consider a basic business application with which you are familiar. Use this application to describe how system development would proceed under the prototyping approach. Explain the advantages (if any) of using the prototyping approach.

REFERENCES AND SUGGESTED READINGS

1. Adamski, L. "The prototyping process," *Systems International*, Vol. 13, No. 6, 1985, pp. 91-92.

2. Barnes, J. "Giving prototyping free rein and just due." *Computerworld*, Vol. 21, No. 36, September 7, 1987, pp. 21-22.

3. Boggs, R. A. "Microcomputers, prototyping, and the life Cycle." *The Journal of the Computer Information Systems*, Vol. 27, No. 3, Spring 1987, pp. 8-11.

4. Bruch, J. G., and Grudnitski, G. *Information Systems: Theory and Practice*. New York: John Wiley and Sons, 1986.

5. Cerveny, R. P., Garity, E. J., and Sanders, G. L. "The application of prototyping to system development: A rationale and model. *Journal of Management Information Systems*, Vol. 3, No. 2, 1986, pp. 52-62.

6. Cervthe, R. P. et al. "Why software prototyping works." *Datamation*, Vol. 33, No. 16, August 1987, pp. 97-99.

7. Colter, M. A. "A comparative examination of system analysis techniques. *MIS Quarterly*, Vol. 8, No. 1, March 1984, pp. 134-147.

8. Couger, R. W., Colter, M. A., and Knapp, R. W. *Advanced System Development/Feasibility Techniques*. New York: John Wiley and Sons, 1982.

9. Davis, G. B., and Olson, M. H. *Management Information Systems: Conceptual Foundations, Structure, and Development*. New York: McGraw-Hill, 1985.

10. DeMarco, T. *Structured Analysis and System Specification*, Englewood Cliffs, N.J.: Prentice-Hall, 1979.

11. Dickson G. W., and Wetherbe, J. C. *The Management of Information Systems*. New York: McGraw-Hill, 1985.

12. Doke, E. R., and Myers, L. A. "The 4GL: On its way to becoming an industry standard?" *Data Management*, Vol. 25, No. 5, 1987.

13. Edelman, F. "Managers, computer systems, and productivity." *MIS Quarterly*, Vol. 5, No. 3, 1981, pp. 1-19.

14. Edwards, P. *System Analysis Design And Development with Structured Concepts*. New York: Holt, Rinehart and Winston, 1985.

15. Gane, C., and Sarson, T. "Structured methodologies: What have we learned." *Computerworld/Extra*, Vol. 14, No. 38, September 1981, pp. 52-57.

16. Ginzberg, M. J. "Key recurrent issues in MIS implementation process." *MIS Quarterly*, Vol. 5, No. 2, June 1981, pp. 47-60.

17. Harrison, R. "Prototyping and the system development life cycle." *Journal of System Management*, Vol. 36., No. 8, 1985, pp. 22-25.

18. Henderson, J. C., and Ingraham, R. S. "Prototyping for DSS: A critical appraisal." In *Decision Support Systems*, Ginzberg, M. J. et al. (eds.), New York: North-Holland, 1982.

19. Janson, M. A., and Smith, L. D. "Prototyping for system development: A critical appraisal." *MIS Quarterly*, December 1985, pp. 305-316.

20. Jenkins, A. M. "Prototyping: A methodology for the design and development of application systems." *Spectrum*, Vol. 2, No. 2, 1985.

21. King, D. *Current Practices in Software Development*. New York: Yourdon Press, 1984.

22. Klinger, D. E. "Rapid prototyping revisited." *Datamation*, Vol. 32, No. 20, 1986, pp. 131-132.

23. Lantz, K. E. *The Prototyping Methodology*. Englewood Cliffs, N.J.: Prentice-Hall, 1986.

24. McKeen, J. D. "Successful Development Strategies for Business Application Systems." *MIS Quarterly*, Vol. 7, No. 3, September 1983, pp. 47-65.

25. Powers, M. J., Adams, D. R., and Mills, H. D. *Computer Information System Development: Analysis and Design*. Cincinnati: South-Western Publishing Co., 1980.

26. Orr, K. T. *Structured System Development*. New York: Yourdon Press, 1977.

27. Schultz, H., and Eierman M. "Information centers, prototyping, and fourth generation languages." *Data Management*, Vol. 25, No. 4, April 1987, pp. 26-31.

28. Warnier, J. *Logical Construction of Systems*. New York: Van Norstrand Reinhold, 1981.

29. Weatherbe, J. C. *System Analysis and Design: Traditional, Structured, and Advanced Concepts and Techniques*. St. Paul, Minn.: West Publishing Company, 1984.

30. Weatherbe, J. C. "Advanced system development techniques avoid 'analysis paralysis'." *Data Management*, Vol. 22, No. 2, February 1984, pp. 49-52.

31. Zmud, R. D., and Cox, J. F. "The implementation process: A change approach." *MIS Quarterly*, Vol. 3, No. 2, June 1979, pp. 35-43.

32. Yourdon, E., and Constantine, L. *Structured Design: Fundamentals of a Discipline of Computer Program and System Design*. Englewood Cliffs, N.J.: Prentice-Hall, 1979.

CHAPTER 6

PRINCIPLES OF PROTOTYPING

Think of things in themselves.

Virginia Woolf

6.1 INTRODUCTION

This chapter is based in large part on work of R. Budde et al.

We start with an actual business case in which prototyping was used, almost by accident, as a necessary response to a crisis that developed. It will give you an idea how and why the prototyping process works.

Prototyping is widely applied in many organizations for several reasons, including the availability of 4GLs, the trend toward increased user involvement in system development, and the benefits demonstrated by many prototyping efforts.

The information system prototype may or may not be implemented, depending on its intended use, completeness, and operational efficiency. At one extreme of prototype types is the construction of mock-up screens and reports; at the other is the building of successive versions of the functional final system.

Instead of a single prototyping methodology, there are several, each with its unique characteristics and objectives. This chapter focuses on methodology, and in Chapters 7 and 8 we address technique and tools.

6.2 BUSINESS CASE

In one of the divisions of the largest ski manufacturer in the United States, a data processing crisis erupted. Although it was not the first crisis, nor the last, nor even the largest ever to occur, this case is very interesting because of the way in which it was eventually resolved.

For some time, the manufacturer's traffic department had requested that the data processing department develop an in-house, online traffic management system to manage millions of dollars in fright charges. The system in use was an inadequate and outdated batch system run by a service bureau. Meanwhile, relations with the service bureau had been deteriorating for the last two years. However, due to the project's backlog in the company's data processing department, the in-house system was not scheduled to be developed until the next budget year.

Then the crisis hit. Without warning, the service bureau announced that it would no longer run the company's traffic system, because the bureau was switching to a new computer system. Knowing that the ski manufacturing company was planning to terminate their contract eventually, management of the service bureau decided that rewriting the traffic system would be unprofitable for them.

The ski manufacturer, with hundreds of shipments being consigned weekly, could not afford the immediate loss of even an inadequate computer system. Such a situation would result in complete chaos. The estimated time to develop a new system with the team of three programmers was seven months. The manufacturer's traffic department could function without the system for approximately two weeks. Panic was setting in.

As is often the case, emergency situations provide the opportunity to use radically different approaches to the problem at hand—approaches that might never have been tried otherwise. Dire circumstances can provide a catalyst for the most enlightening discoveries. And so it was that time.

It so happened that a certain information systems consultant, who had long experience in applications development and who understood the relation between an effective system development process and good communication between systems users and data processing departments, was involved in several other development projects for the company. Therefore, in the crisis that developed, the vice president of the company naturally instructed the consultant to cease all other activity and try to find a solution as quickly as possible.

It was obvious to the consultant that the only hope of shortening the development cycle and improving the quality and acceptance of the end product was to communicate the application specifications faster and better. To communicate these specifications, he selected the technique of modeling the application as opposed to using tediously written, and often misunderstood, functional specifications as they are used in SDLC. The term "prototyping" (building models) was hardly a household word then among data processing professionals. The general principles of the process were all sound, however, and some successes in building information systems had already been recorded.

The summary of the situation is presented in Figure 6.1.

The consultant began by interviewing the manager and several key personnel from the manufacturer's traffic department. The consultant wanted to establish what an online traffic management system should essentially do. However, there was much disagreement on how it should be done.

To bring about a more productive atmosphere, the consultant decided to explain the prototyping philosophy to the users. He emphasized that detailed specifications were now unnecessary; they would be using a working model of the new system to help them formulate suggestions from the users. If this approach did not work, the consultant assured his clients that he would restart the project using more conventional means. He took the blame for any possible failure since the new

Industry	Ski Manufacturer
Problem	Information system for the traffic department.
Genesis of the problem	Old batch traffic system, managing millions of dollars run by the service bureau (SB), preceived as inadequate. Relations with SB poor. Management of the enterprise is contemplating possible phasing out of the SB services. SB aware of the pending decision.
DP department	Serious backlog of work. Outside consultant advising on information processing needs for the enterprise. Traffic department requests from the DP an on line traffic management system to be built in house.
Crisis	SB abruptly terminates services. Development of the new system estimated to take 3 programmers 7 months. Traffic department can function without information system for 2 weeks.
Management solution	Request to the outside consultant to drop all other commitments to the enterprise and to concentrate on the problem with the traffic department.
Consultant's approach	This crisis requires special tactics because of the need for the shortest possible development time. Specifications for the new system to be communicated well and fast.
Tactics	Use a model of the application, utilize prototyping methodology.

Figure 6.1 Problems with the Information System for the Traffic Department of the Ski Manufacturing Organization

approach had been his idea. This relieved much of the tension and went a long way toward establishing open relationships that are necessary for prototyping to work.

After about two days, the first prototype screens and processes were programmed and running. The consultant revised and improved upon them according to hands-on demonstration sessions for users that were conducted daily at first, and then several times each day. If a mistake was found, he corrected it immediately.

The system was operational and in a production mode by the end of the two-week period, and it was heartily accepted by the users. The consultant, with the help of the users, produced a superior traffic management system in a fraction of the estimated development time.

The steps taken by the consultant to implement prototyping are summarized in Figure 6.2.

To understand why the system development process employed in this case was successful, we turn now to the study of the prototyping method: its objectives, techniques, and necessary tools. In the next several chapters we consider why prototyping works as well as it does and when it should be used. We look at possible pitfalls of prototyping and consider some management issues.

Tactic	Interview key decision maker and key personnel.
Objective	To elicit perceptions and ideas of what the system should do.
Tactic	Explan the prototyping process to the key users. Assurance given that the new process will be assessed and if perceived as failing, old methods will be implemented. Striving for the attitude of an openess and trust from all involved. Initial responsibility shifted to the consultant.
Objective	To prepare for the use of the working model of the new system and the elimination of the detailed written specification process.
Tactic	Deliver prototype basic functions and screens fast (two days) and demonstrate to the key users. Use hands-on approach.
Objective	To build up trust in the process and to start to elicit detailed specifications.
Tactic	Correct any problems immediately and speed up the prototyping. Initially meet the users every day, eventually when the process is on the way, consult them several times a day.
Objective	To demonstrate efficacy of the process and appropriateness of the tools used.
Tactic	Make the system operational in a two week period. Involve users extensively throughout the process.
Objective	To assure that users contribute constructively to the process and "own" arrived at solution (since they understand the information system problem well). Assure that users accept the new system heartily. By speedy development process give credence to the prototyping methodology.
Outcome	Superior on-line traffic system produced in record time.

Figure 6.2 Consultants Steps to Implement Prototyping

6.3 APPROACH

We first need to define the terms methodology, technique, and tools, as they pertain to information systems prototyping.

Prototyping methodology represents the analysis of concepts and principles associated with prototyping. It is concerned with major issues of prototyping, relationships between them, and the expected outcomes. When methodology is discussed, questions like the following are asked:

■ What factors are important?

■ What are the relationships among these factors?

■ What are the desirable outcomes?

Prototyping technique concerns itself with the procedures needed to accomplish the desired outcomes. Technique deals with *how* to perform a prototyping activity.

In particular, it specifies the steps needed as well as the necessary inputs and results from each step. Questions like the following are asked:

- What sequence of steps is needed for a given activity?
- What are the required inputs to a specific step?
- How are the desired results obtained?

Prototyping tools are aids (in a form of, for example, software tools such as 4GLs) needed in creating prototypes of the computer information systems. The objective of using a specific tool is to help to produce a prototype.

6.4 PROTOTYPE AND PROTOTYPING

The word "prototype" literally means "first of the type." A prototype can reflect any of the following concepts:

- A model on which something is patterned (for example, a wooden prototype of a car).
- The first, full-scale, and (possibly) functional form of an object (for example, a prototype of an airplane).
- A new design or a construction of an object (for example, the space shuttle).

The terms "prototype" and "prototyping" are not context free. The meaning of the term depends on where and to what it is applied.

In engineering, prototyping refers to a well-defined phase in the production process. The engineering manufacturer's aim is to mass produce goods of the same type. The original *model* of a product is constructed, with all the essential features of the final product, in advance of mass production. Most often, the prototype is intended for use as a test specimen, to improve and guide future production. This type of prototype development occurs over a long period of time and costs more than the final production version of a product; for example, a prototype of a new airplane.

The manufacture (development) of computer information systems (for example, the development of computerized production planning system) differs from the manufacture of engineering products (for example, the manufacture of cars) in important ways. The development process of computer information systems leads to one product. Here prototyping, in general, refers to a process of building a "quick and dirty" version of information system. Moreover, with the information system prototype, it is not always clear how the prototype will relate to the final product.

When prototyping, the information system developer focuses on the prototyping *process* itself essentially because the prototyping process helps the system builder elicit the design requirements from the intended users of the system. The underlying assumption is that users know better than system builders what the

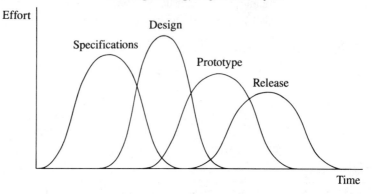

The Engineering Project Life Cycle

Figure 6.3 Prototyping as the Central Step in any Engineering Discipline

target information system should do. They know better because they are specialists in the functional business area for which a given information system is intended (for example, production planning).

Information systems prototyping enables the system builder to present a prototype of an application (albeit often very incomplete) to the user. The prototype is demonstrated on the computer.

A successful use of software prototypes exploits the following: Users of the application software can point to features they don't like about an *existing* system or indicate when a feature is missing more easily than they can describe what they think they would like in an *imaginary* model. The computer system prototype serves as an existing, dynamic model.

Consider the analogous dichotomy of trying to understand football by going to the game versus by looking at a series of still pictures of the game. One method represents the dynamic model; the other, a static one.

Prototyping in Traditional Engineering and Software Engineering Disciplines

Prototyping is central to the engineering life cycle. (This is represented in Figure 6.3.) Since computer information systems development is evolving into the software engineering discipline (consider the CASE methods mentioned previously), building a prototype before proceeding with the final product is becoming a pivotal step in the development of many information systems, especially for interactive computer information systems intended for human work. Systems of this type are characterized by an interactive user interface that cannot be easily considered in the static manner.

The Software Engineering Life Cycle

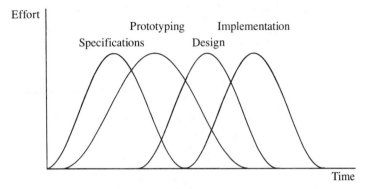

Effort

Specifications   Prototyping   Design   Implementation

Time

Figure 6.4 Prototyping as Part of Each Step of the Project

Moreover, many highly structured and complex systems such as nuclear power stations monitoring systems or air traffic control systems contain a large component of interactive user interface. The interface can be prototyped during specification and during the design stage.

Prototyping for interactive information systems serves to enhance communication between system builders and users. Software engineering uses prototypes before or during the design stage and after or during the specifications stage. The part that prototyping plays in the software engineering life cycle is presented graphically in Figure 6.4.

Types of Prototypes

Essentially two kinds of prototyping are recognized: the throwaway and the evolutionary. Both approaches use modern software tools such as 4GLs to create prototype systems quickly.

The *throwaway* concept is based on an initial test idea of engineering. Once the test is done, the prototype is discarded and a preliminary design takes place. The test's goal is to achieve a better understanding of the users' requirements and of system performance because initially the users may not be able to clearly define their requirements.

The *evolutionary* approach refines the system iteratively, over repeated trial periods. It is based on the iterative product development idea of engineering. The system is constructed rapidly, and then it is enhanced and changed as it is used. The goal is to deliver a working model of the system to try to react to it iteratively. This iteration is planned, an thus as subsequent versions of a working system evolve, they come closer to what user really wants.

When is discarding a prototype appropriate? When is evolutionary approach better? Which prototypes can become final production systems? We consider these questions later in this chapter.

Methodology of Information System Prototyping

Prototyping comprises methodologies that involve an early practical demonstration of relevant parts of the information system on the computer, to be combined with other processes in the system development. There is little agreement at present regarding the taxonomy of prototyping. Several methodologies, however, are recognized. There are four general phases to prototyping:

1. Functional selection
2. Construction
3. Evaluation
4. Further use

Functional Selection

The range of functions present in the prototype of the system is not the same as that in the final system. Two approaches are usually considered:

1. Functions are implemented in the prototype in an incomplete form; part of their effect is simulated because they are used for demonstration purposes only.
2. Only selected system functions are implemented in the prototype in their final intended form.

These two approaches can be combined in different parts of one system prototype.

Construction

This refers to the effort and time required to build a prototype. Construction of the prototype takes much less time and requires much less effort than the construction of the final system. Appropriate functional selection and exploitation of specific prototyping techniques and tools assures this. The emphasis in construction is on the users' evaluation of the prototype.

The prototype is constructed in such a way that certain quality requirements such as data security and efficiency needed in final product are not included. These requirements can be disregarded unless they are a part of what the prototype is supposed to demonstrate. For example, if the prototype is to be used for finding out whether the response time of the system is suitable for desired work load, then efficiency is an essential aspect of the prototype and cannot be neglected. However, if the response time of the system is not as important, prototype efficiency can be ignored.

Evaluation

This is a very important aspect of prototyping because it involves all the participants of the prototyping process and provides feedback to the system development as a whole. It allows systems to be designed iteratively. The user evaluates the prototype, determines necessary enhancements, and returns it to the builder. The builder updates the prototype and returns it to the user for more evaluation.

Phase	Description
Functional selection	Only selected functions of the system or incomplete, simulated functions are included.
Construction	Quality requirements such as efficiency and security are included only if the prototype is to demonstrate these requirements; otherwise they are not included.
Evaluation	Central to the process. Serves as a learning vehicle about system requirements for both builders and users.
Further use	Prototype throw away or evolve to final system.

Figure 6.5   Summary of Phases of Prototyping

The iterative evaluation aspect of the prototype serves as a learning vehicle for both the builders of the system as well as its users, providing precise ideas about what the intended system should be like. The prototyping process is basically a learning process and is often designed as such. The essential aspects of this process are:

- Early availability of the prototype and short intervals between iterations
- The demonstration of the prototype to the users
- Users' commitment to the prototyping process
- The use of the successful prototype as a teaching tool

The prototype should be available very early in the development process for users to evaluate. The assumption here is that, when system development begins, the requirements are only partially known. Iteration implies that system requirements evolve as experience is gained, and looping back to initial stages relates to the ongoing learning process. Timely feedback is essential to effective learning.

The demonstration of the prototype for users involves the demonstration of nontrivial problems, which makes evaluation relevant. Revising and adding new features to the prototype is facilitated by exploiting existing technology. This relates directly to the need for short intervals between evaluations.

Commitment by the users to the prototyping process is essential. Users must actively participate in the prototyping process and direct the design of the system since successful implementation of the final system depends on their active involvement. Explicit consent of the users is required for each essential modification of the prototype.

After evaluation and modification, a successful prototype can serve as a teaching tool. It can prepare prospective users for their work with the final, completed system.

Further Use

Further use of the prototype depends on the experience gained with the prototype and the type of prototyping used (see the discussion of types of prototypes in the next section).

The arrived at prototype may be thrown away, serving only as a learning vehicle to be discarded after the prototyping process is finished, or it may be used fully or partially as a component of the final implemented system.

A summary of the general phases of prototyping is presented in Figure 6.5.

6.5 APPROACHES TO PROTOTYPING

We consider three broad approaches to prototyping.

1. *Prototyping for Exploration*—emphasis is on clarifying requirements and desirable features of the final system and on exploring possible alternative system solutions.

2. *Prototyping for Experimentation*—emphasis is on determining the adequacy of a proposed solution before investing in a large final system (as in a pilot project for engineered goods).

3. *Prototyping for Evolution*—emphasis is on gradually adapting the system to changing requirements, which cannot reliably be determined in the early phases of system development.

Although the distinction between exploration and experimentation can sometimes be fuzzy, it is useful for clarifying the relation between prototyping and the system development process as a whole.

For each prototyping type, we discuss the relation between the prototype of the system and the final system.

Exploratory Prototyping

The focus is on the problems of communication between developers and users of the prototype.

When the process of system development is originated, quite often the developers have little knowledge of the application field and the users have no clear idea of what the computer can do for them. A practical demonstration of possible system functions promotes understanding and creativity and keeps good ideas flowing. The designers do not focus on one particular solution, but discuss the merits of different alternatives with the users.

The exploratory prototyping approach is generally very informal; there are no strict rules on how to proceed. Essentially, both parties are free of any regimented methods, and this freedom allows them all to be very creative. Although exploratory prototyping is informal, the developers should be aware that users' expectations concerning the system under development will be influenced by their exposure to the prototype.

For example, designers can start with all the functions for a specific work task the user requires. With the help of this initial prototype, the user can assess the suitability of the proposed partial solution and also generalize to broader solutions by looking at analogies and dissimilarities to other work tasks.

For this exploration to succeed, the user must understand that there is no commitment to reproducing the prototype in the final system. The commitment is to incorporating any good ideas from the prototyping model into the final system. That is why it is important for the designer to be sure of what the user likes or dislikes about the prototyped system feature.

Exploratory prototyping is compatible with the classical life cycle technique of developing computer information systems and serves to enhance its two early phases: requirements definition and functional analysis.

This approach can be helpful during rapidly changing market or business conditions or during the establishment of a new business function or department. A prototype of this type can be used to approximate an initial solution to the information system problem quickly, say, in one to three months.

The user operates the prototype for a period of time, analyzes feedback, makes refinements, and the process continues until a stable set of business requirements can be established. Then the prototype is discarded, and a more conventional development process is initiated using the results of the requirements prototyping process as the actual specification. In this case, prototyping is a tool that is used for requirements analysis, leaving the remainder of the application development process intact.

The exploratory prototyping approach is illustrated in the following example.

Example: **An Expert System for Agricultural Management** This example is based on R.G. Hopmans [9]. Brant Computer Services Ltd. was commissioned by Professional Agricultural Management Inc. to build an expert system that could demonstrate the applicability of the artificial intelligence (AI) techniques to its business applications. The user as well as the developer were new to applying AI technology to the management of the agricultural business. Although it is a monumental task to build a complete expert system, it was possible to build a quick working model using the prototyping approach. The developer and the user chose to develop an Irrigation Event Scheduler. The problem of what to include in the knowledge base was solved by using exploratory prototyping.

The prototype was used explicitly to establish a usable framework to represent required knowledge appropriately. The first step was transferring human problem-solving expertise to the computer and to experiment with what part of human knowledge was to be transferred. An exploratory prototype of the complete system was developed in three weeks. Essentially, the knowledge base was gradually established and, through refinements, the expert system become usable within less than a year.

Experimental Prototyping

Experimental prototype is the closest to the meaning of the word "prototype": The evaluation of computer solutions to the user's problems is done by experimentation.

This approach is essential in some areas of the system development process. For example, only through experimenting can the issues of transparency and ease of use of the man-machine interface be resolved. Other instances of the use of experimental prototyping are the cases of determining the acceptability of a proposed system performance or feasibility of a given solution when resources are limited.

Experimental prototyping is appropriate in any development phase after the initial specifications have been established. This type of prototyping should always be regarded as an enhancement of the final system's specification. Depending on the phase in the development process in which this mode of prototyping takes place, the prototype could serve as a complementary form of specification, a form of refinement of the specification, or an intermediate step between specification and implementation. The developed prototype is discarded.

The details of the experimental prototyping process vary depending on the nature of the experiment and the strategy selected to carry it out. There are several different types of experimental prototyping (simulations):

- Human interface (front end) simulation
- Skeleton simulation
- Base machine construction
- Partial functional simulation
- Full functional simulation

Human Interface (Front End) Simulation

This simulation gives the users the intended feel for the proposed man-machine interface. This can be in the form of dialogues, screens, and menus to be used in the final system. A mock-up is used for all other parts of the system. In this type of simulation, users see what looks like a real system, but there may be no real data behind the prototype and there is minimal validation of the input.

Skeleton Simulation

This simulation is intended to establish the overall structure of the final system. It is to be based on a few essential system functions. The object is to design the whole system, but to implement only a reduced functional scope. In this type of prototype, the included functions allow users to perform some of their work tasks completely and to draw analogies to other work steps not yet supported by the skeleton prototype.

For example, consider a system developer who is responsible for building an online school supplies inventory system for a large school district. The important design criterion is to build an easy-to-use system because its intended users are inexperienced in the use of computers.

The most sensitive operation of this inventory system is the processing of the orders placed by the individual schools. The designer decides to build a skeletal prototype that includes only one function: the processing of orders for school supplies. Using a skeletal prototype, the designer is able to properly estimate the satisfactory response time for all the users in the school district.

Starting with this information, the design of all the other parts of the system (which will satisfy the minimum system efficiency acceptable to all the users) can commence.

Base Machine Construction

This form of prototyping implements the basic functions of the final system and combines them into higher level functions (a driver). The base machine construction approach is extremely useful in establishing system requirements when the final application system is to be used by diverse users whose needs do not exactly coincide.

For example, consider the budgeting system to be designed and implemented for the legislature of a western state. This system is to be used by legislators who have varied information needs. The same system is to serve the governor's budget office and all of the state agencies as well. The problem for the designer is to come up with system specifications for this diversified group of users, and to do it in a timely manner.

The designer decides that the easiest way to proceed is to develop several modules comprising basic budgeting functions: a reports module that summarizes budget data related to different legislative rules, a graphic module that graphically presents the same data as that contained in the reports module, a module of retrieval routines that select different sets of budget data, and so on.

The designer also constructs the system driver. The driver simply combines all the primitive system functions (data selection, reporting, and graphics) with all the high-level functions (specific requests for information by legislators, administrators, and the governor).

By prototyping the various combinations of primitive functions and the system driver, the designer finally selects the one combination of modules that fulfills the statewide budgeting system requirements that in turn satisfy the needs of the diversified group of users. The selection of a specific combination (a base machine construction) is accomplished through the users' evaluation of the prototypes.

Partial Functional Simulation

This simulation is used to test for specifics about the final system. For example, this type of prototyping can be used to test if specified algorithms employed in the system give satisfactory results and use the expected amounts of resources.

Full Functional Simulation

This simulation is based on a prototype having all the functions of the final system. 4GL is often used to arrive at a needed code faster than would be possible with a traditional language. The requirements are translated into an operational system that *simulates* the production environment. The prototype is functional.

In constructing such a prototype, the ease of implementation and modification, rather than the efficiency required of the final system, is sought. Such a prototype may not be used as a production system because it lacks efficiency or does not include functions necessary for handling errors, security, or special cases.

Selection of a particular prototyping method depends on the communication needs of a given development case as well as on the availability of resources and tools. There is no clear agreement between practitioners on which is best.

The experimental prototyping approach is illustrated in the following example.

Example: **Marketing Research and Corporate Planning** This example is adopted from M.A. Janson [10]. A large mid-western insurance firm approached several university faculty members about a joint effort to develop a decision support system for marketing research and corporate planning. The primary goal was to produce reports and geographic maps that summarized the company's past performance statistics. The idea was to enable the management of the insurance firm to compare the company's performance relative to its competitors.

The fourth-generation tool SAS was thought to be particularly applicable in light of the stated systems requirements. (Recall from Chapter 4 that SAS has excellent mapping and report generating capabilities, a wide range of modeling capabilities, a file management system, and so on.)

This project required the construction of several independent prototypes. Each prototype was different in nature because it performed a different set of functions. For example, the development of predictive models was supported by a partial functional simulation. This facilitated testing of possible modeling technique. Prototypes operated on a small subset of the corporate data with a file structure that differed from that of the corporate database. In this way modeling technique selection was insulated from modifications of and additions to the corporate database. Prototype testing and evaluation was simplified.

Once a modeling technique had been chosen, a second prototype was built to aid variable selection and parameter estimation of the predictive model. In addition, this prototype was used to demonstrate the input, output, and operating features of this part of the system. Partial functional simulation was used.

A full functional simulation prototype was done next. This prototype (of the decision support system) operated under conditions similar to those of the corporate computing environment. The main function of this prototype was to demonstrate the system to the user. The main objectives were to use it as a learning vehicle and to eventually achieve successful systems implementation at the corporate facilities.

Using the prototyping approach, the design and construction of this information system was accomplished within three weeks.

Essentially, an experimental prototype should be an enhancement tool for the final system's specification. It can serve as:

1. A complementary form of a specification.
2. A form of refinement of specification or parts of specification.
3. An intermediate stage between specification and implementation.

Evolutionary Prototyping

This approach to prototyping is the most powerful, but at the same time it is the furthest away from the original definition of the term "prototype."

Evolutionary prototyping is a *dynamic* strategy that views the final system itself as a sequence of contiguous versions of the system. Each version is evaluated when completed, and it serves as a prototype for its successor. This strategy is especially useful when applied to the development of interactive application systems.

Evolutionary prototyping recognizes that:

1. The environment surrounding the interactive application system continuously evolves and new requirements emerge.
2. The interactive application system transforms the surrounding environment and causes the emergence of new requirements.

Evolutionary prototyping is characterized by an evolving approximation of the solution to the problem, where the initial prototype becomes the nucleus of the evolving system. Each evolutionary prototyping cycle adds more system features. Thus this type of prototyping becomes a replacement for the entire development process, and the model eventually becomes an operational system.

The evolutionary prototyping approach is illustrated in the following example.

> *Example:* **Job Hunting Information System** This example is adopted from B. Lynch [13]. Crawford & Co. is now able to do a better job of finding suitable work for recently rehabilitated workers thanks to the information system they developed using evolutionary prototyping.
>
> Crawford has about 250 rehabilitation counselors offering services required under the Workmen's Compensation Act. Before the computerization, the counselors used a manual system for data gathering and analysis that resulted in a list of occupations that the rehabilitated claimant could perform. The project to computerize the system began when one senior system analyst, working with rehabilitation specialists, developed an initial prototype (using a 4GL NOMAD). In the next three iterations, he added more features to this nucleus of the system. The final functional system was completed in four months.
>
> The new system has resulted in a dramatic increase in job placements, and there are even plans to extend this system to allow for national job searches.

Evolutionary prototyping can be classified into the two following forms of system development:

1. Incremental system development
2. Evolutionary system development

Incremental system development, also called "slowly growing systems," is used in solving complex system design problems that require integration. The underlying idea is that complex problems are dealt with by extending (in a stepwise fashion) the first approximation to the solution.

For example, the strategies of the existing interactive information system can be taken as a base solution for the evolving system. Then, only limited numbers of existing elements are exchanged with new ones. The focus is on the long-range development strategy and final design. The design of the new system is accomplished gradually through the process of learning.

In the successful incremental system development process, each stepwise extension of the solution is carefully geared to the work tasks to be supported by the future system. This approach allows users to become involved in the system development process gradually, with the obvious benefits of improving communication among the system developers as well as the users.

The evolutionary system development process views system development as a sequence of cycles: design, implementation, and evaluation. (As a matter of fact, any prototyping development, by permitting revision of requirements, contributes to the evolution of the prototyped system.) The final product here is viewed as a sequence of versions. Exploratory and experimental prototyping modes can be incorporated into this process in its early cycles.

From both the developers of systems and the users it requires a willingness to change the way information systems are built. Developers must accept the necessity of revising their own programs repeatedly; this calls for a very high work discipline. Users, on the other hand, must be willing to accept repeated system changes, which calls for frequent new learning and invariably affects the users' work.

When evolutionary prototyping is used essentially there is no maintenance stage. System maintenance is replaced by a consecutive development cycle, based on the existing version of the system and on evolving new requirements.

Final Thoughts on Prototyping Approaches

Figure 6.6 summarizes our discussion of prototyping approaches.

The number of prototyping approaches and iterations involved in the creation of a final system can be tailored to the needs of the situation at hand. The prototyping process, no matter what approach, is basically and naturally evolutionary. This evolutionary nature permeates the process whenever prototyping occurs.

For example, there can be one or two cycles of exploratory prototyping to facilitate better communication during requirements analysis, one or more experimental prototypes to check the validity and correctness of solutions to difficult technical problems encountered during the design stage, and incremental system development employed during the implementation stage to better handle the dynamic and changing work environment.

Prototyping	Enhances	Type
For exploration	Requirements definition Functional analysis	User-view
For experimentation: • Front-end simulation	mock-up of the human-machine interface, reports, etc. Requirements definition Functional specifications	User-view
• Structure simulation	Essential system functions (structure) implemented	User-view and functional
Base machine construction	Basic functions of the final system together with a facility integrating them into higher functions (for multiple users). Refinement of specifications & functional	User-view and functional
Partial Functional simulation	Test for specifics of final system performance Functional analysis	Functional
Full functional simulation	All functions of final system without efficiency required of production system Functional analysis Intermediate step to implementation of the final system	Functional
For evolution: • Incremental	Fully functional, replacing part of the existing system implementation	Functional
• Evolutionary	Exploratory and experimental modes incorporated into development process in early cycles Evolving requirements	User-view and functional

Figure 6.6   Summary of the Prototyping Approaches

A warning is in order here. Prototyping should not compensate for a lack of analysis and design in system development. Such misapplication of prototyping methodology will turn computer information system development into a mismanaged and aimless trial-and-error process. This can be an invitation to disaster.

6.6 SUMMARY

Prototyping is a process of building functional and semifunctional models of application systems during the development process. Prototyping is a language independent process and can be accomplished with 2GLs, 3GLs, or 4GLs. With the use of 4GLs in the prototyping process, the programming and design implementation time is reduced. Simulated systems can be developed very quickly.

The basic premise of the prototyping methodology is that building the system from the visible model is easier than building one from paper specifications.

Information systems prototyping is a method used to determine system requirements and in which the user needs are extracted, presented, and developed by building a dynamic working model of the target system. The working model is used to enhance communication between the developers of the system and its future users. The model is gradually expanded and refined as project participants (developers and users) increase their comprehension of the information system under construction.

In general, prototypes can be classified as requirements (user views) prototypes that do not function as an application and functional prototypes that simulate production systems. Specifically, prototyping is done for:

- **Exploration**—clarifying the nature of requirements and desirable features of the final system.
- **Experimentation**—determining the adequacy of a proposed solution before investing in a large final system.
- **Evolution**—adapting the system gradually to changing requirements that cannot be reliably determined in the early phases of the system development.

Prototyping in any form is a vehicle for the learning process that occurs during system development.

Prototyping helps establish what needs to be built. Together with 4GLs, prototyping supports accelerated analysis, design, and programming, but it does not replace disciplined analysis process. Essentially, prototypes serve to aid in the final implementation of the information systems.

EXERCISES

1. Describe the nature of the difficulties with information systems in the traffic department of the ski manufacturer. Was the service bureau responsible? Ultimately, who is responsible for the crisis that developed?

2. Summarize the steps taken by the consultant to implement the prototyping method. Can you identify critical factors, if any, that are responsible for his success?

3. What is a methodology? Give some examples of methodologies with which you are familiar from your studies of other academic subjects.

4. Contrast the notion of a methodology with that of a technique. Give an example of each.

5. For an engineered product, what is its prototype?

6. A prototype is a physical model. Do you agree with this statement? Why or why not?

7. In your opinion, how does the manufacture of information systems differ from the manufacture of engineered products?

8. How does the prototype of an information system relate to a final product? What does it depend on?

9. Discuss this statement: "Prototyping is a basis-for-action technique that trades a conjecture of prespecification for hands-on experimentation."

10. What underlying assumptions are present in the application of the prototyping methodology to the information systems? Is it a strategy? If so, why would you consider it a strategy? If not, why not?

11. Contrast a static model of the system with a dynamic one. What tradeoffs can you foresee for each? Discuss.

12. When would a static model be of use? When would it be absolutely necessary?

13. What types of systems would be good for prototyping? Why?

14. What is throwaway prototyping? Why would you use it?

15. How would you characterize evolutionary prototyping?

16. Comment on this statement: "Prototyping has always been desirable, but it has only recently become possible." Is this statement correct? Defend your position.

17. Why is an evaluation such an important aspect of the prototyping process? What is being evaluated?

18. Are prototypes always used? What does it depend on?

19. This statement about the prototyping is often made: The entire assumption about the prototyping process is that misunderstandings will occur. Elaborate on what possibly is meant here by misunderstanding—between whom? Give examples.

20. Success rests on a series of step-by-step formulas. Does this apply to prototyping? If so, where? If not, why and where not?

21. Characterize basic differences between prototyping for exploration and prototyping for experimentation.

22. Do you suppose that the terms "exploration" and "experimentation," when describing prototyping, are used in a strict technical sense? Especially, are "experiments" based on any rigorous theory? Discuss.

23. Can evolutionary prototyping contain both exploratory and experimental prototyping as part of an overall system development strategy? Elaborate.

24. Consider this statement: "The borderline between exploration and experimentation is fuzzy." Explain what it means in the context of prototyping.

25. What is incremental system development and why can it be characterized as a "slowly growing" method? Give examples.

26. What are versions of the system? Why would you need them?

27. Comment on this statement: "There can be one or two cycles of exploratory prototyping during requirements analysis, one or more experimental prototypes during design, and incremental system development during implementation." Where is there a transition between a prototype and the final production product? Is a standard life cycle used here?

28. Discuss under what conditions people tend to select: exploratory prototyping, experimental prototyping, and prototyping for evolution.

PROJECTS

1. In your library locate these two articles:

   ■ From *MIS Quarterly,* June 1985, the article by M. E. Shank and others, titled "Critical Success Factor Analysis as a Methodology for MIS Planning."

   ■ From *Infosystems,* July 1985, the article by A. D. Crescenzi and R. H. Reck, titled "Critical Success Factors Helping as Managers Pinpoint Information Needs."

   On the basis of these two articles prepare a brief on how critical success factors and prototyping can be combined. Focus especially on where prototyping of this type fits in the life cycle development process.

2. For an organization with which you are familiar discuss a recent system design and implementation project with:

   ■ One of the key users of the system

   ■ One of the MIS department members of the team

   Prepare a brief on the following:
   a. Ask them to describe the process that was followed.
   b. Was a prototyping method used? If not, why not?
   c. What would they have done differently, knowing what they know now?
   d. Do they have a different opinion of what went well and what did not? If yes, briefly state your perception concerning the source for these differences.

REFERENCES AND SUGGESTED READINGS

1. Andrews, W. C. "Prototyping information systems." *Journal of Systems Management*, Vol. 34, No. 9, 1983, pp. 16-18.

2. Alani, M. "An assessment of the prototyping approach to information systems." *Communications of the ACM*, Vol. 27, No. 6, June 1984, pp. 556-563.

3. Boar, B. H. "Application prototyping: A life cycle perspective." *Journal of System Management*, Vol. 37, No. 2, 1986, pp. 25-31.

4. Budde, R., Kuhlenkamp, K., Mathiassen, L., and Zullighoven, H. *Approaches to Prototyping*. Berlin: Springer-Verlag, 1984.

5. Canning, R. G. "Developing systems by prototyping." *EDP Analyzer*, Vol. 19, No. 9, September 1981, pp. 1-14.

6. Cerveny, R. P., Garity, E. J., and Sanders, G. L. "The application of prototyping to system development: A rationale and model." *Journal of Management Information Systems*, Vol. 3, No. 2, 1986, pp. 52-62.

7. Edelman, F. "Managers, computer systems, and productivity." *MIS Quarterly*, Vol. 6, No. 3, September 1981, pp. 1-19.

8. Gremillion, L., and Pyburn, P. "Breaking the systems development bottleneck." *Harvard Business Review*, Vol. 61, No. 2, March 1983, pp. 130-137.

9. Hopmans R. G. "Prototyping an expert system." *Computing Canada*, Vol. 13, No. 17, August 1987, pp. 20-21.

10. Janson, M. A. "Applying a pilot system and prototyping approach to system development and implementation." *Information and Management*, Vol. 10, No. 4, 1986, pp. 209-216.

11. Jenkins, A. M. "Prototyping: A methodology for the design and development of application systems." *Working Paper*, School of Business, Indiana University, April 1983.

12. Kraushaar, J., and Shirland, L. "A prototyping method for application development by end users and information systems specialists." *MIS Quarterly*, Vol. 9, No. 3, 1985, pp. 189-197.

13. Lynch, B. "Job matching by computer." *Best's Review*, Vol. 87, No. 12, April 1987, pp. 84-86.

14. Mahhmood, M. A. "System development methods—A comparative investigation." *MIS Quarterly*, Vol. 11, No. 3, 1987, pp. 293-311.

15. Nauman, J. D., and Jenkins, A. M. "Prototyping: The new paradigm for system development." *MIS Quarterly*, Vol. 6, No. 3, September 1982, pp. 29-44.

CHAPTER 7

The Prototyping Cycle

Little islands out at sea, on the horizon
keep suddenly showing a whiteness, a flash and a furl, a hail
of something coming, ships a sail from over the rim of the sea.

D. H. Lawrence

7.1 INTRODUCTION

This chapter is based on the work of Jenkins [7]. This chapter presents a general description of the prototyping cycle, without identifying a prototyping method. Identified participants, their tasks and responsibilities can be generalized to any prototyping approach.

7.2 THE PROTOTYPING CYCLE

We now describe a generalized prototyping approach, identifying the specific steps of this process and examining the tasks needed in each phase. The prototyping environment should have these components:

- Well-managed data resources for easy access to organizational data.
- A 4GL or other development tools for quick creation of the prototypes.
- Users knowledgeable in their business area, informed about the prototyping process, and willing to use new tools to solve their information system problems.
- A prototype builder—a data processing professional knowledgeable about organizational data resources, prototyping approaches, and tools.

The prototype is developed with the help of the intended user of the system, who also functions as the *designer* of the application (user/designer), working side-by-side with the systems professional, who functions as the system *builder* (analyst/builder). From the practitioner's point of view, the most productive prototyping arrangement is one in which there is a separate person for each role, that is, the prototype is developed by one builder and one designer.

The prototyping cycle consists of four steps that essentially focus on the construction of the working prototype of the required computer information system as quickly as possible. The four steps of the prototyping cycle are illustrated in Figure 7.1 on page 177. For each step of the prototyping cycle the following sections state the objectives, basic prototyping activities and principles, and responsibilities required of the user/designer and of the analyst/builder.

Step 1: Identify Basic Information Requirements of the User/Designer

The purpose of Step 1 is to develop sufficient knowledge of the user/designer information system needs so that the initial prototype can be built.

Objectives

The objectives of Step 1 are as follows:

1. To discuss the prototyping process with the user/designer. A good understanding of the prototyping process on the part of the user/designer speeds up the prototype construction process and improves communication between the user/designer and the analyst/builder.
2. To discuss the possible use of the prototype. This includes explaining to the user/designer that the prototype may not be reproduced in the final system. The essential goal is to incorporate good ideas generated by the prototyping process into the functional specifications of the final system.
3. To write a brief description of the essential user/designer requirements for the intended information system.
4. To establish a set of required data elements and their logical relationships.
5. To determine the availability of this data.
6. To define the tasks and estimate the cost of an operational prototype.

Basic Prototyping Activities and Principles

After establishing the ground rules for the prototyping process, the builder and the designer define the basic requirements of the user's information system. Specifically how this is done depends on the nature of the user's application and on the development tools available to the builder. The analysis in Step 1 must include the identification of logical relationships and sources of the critical data elements. The multiple information requirements, if they exist, must be ranked.

To prevent problems with future implementations of the prototype, the scope of the system and the desired functionality must be clearly defined and mutually understood by the user/designer and the builder. To this end, the builder needs to carefully consider the scope of the system, including its intended use. These factors are most important in estimating the prototype's costs and the delivery time.

The following prototyping principles are applied in Step 1:

1. The use of computer and data processing jargon is avoided.
2. The process is completed in one meeting, two at most.
3. All models used in the initial prototype are simple or are simple adaptations of the existing models.
4. The necessary data elements are limited and the data structures are kept simple.

Responsibilities of the Prototyping Participants

The principal responsibilities in Step 1 are as follows:

- *User/designer*—To articulate the nature of the the desired system.
- *Builder*—To establish realistic user/designer expectations and to estimate the cost of developing an operational prototype.
- *Joint*—To consider the scope of the system, including its intended use and determination of data availability.

Step 2: Develop the Initial Prototype

The objective of Step 2 is to build a working interactive prototype of the application system that meets the basic information requirements established by the user/designer and the builder in Step 1.

Basic Prototyping Activities and Principles

Although the specific activities vary depending on the fourth-generation tools in use, the following general activities usually occur:

1. Preliminary logical design of the required database.
2. Construction of the data transfer or data generation modules.
3. Physical development and loading of the prototype database.
4. Building of appropriate menus or command language dialogues to make the prototype's input/output user friendly.
5. Development of the required application program modules.
6. Delivery of the initial prototype to the user/designer and the demonstration of how it works. Here, the builder makes sure that the user/designer's basic information needs are met, that the prototype's interface and features are fully explained and understood, and that the user/designer is comfortable using the prototype.

The prototyping principles applicable to Step 2 are as follows:

1. Speed of building, not efficiency of operation, is the critical factor. The quicker the initial prototype is delivered, the better.
2. The user/designer's basic requirements must be met by the initial prototype.
3. The initial prototype is incomplete by design; it responds only to the user/designer's basic known requirements.
4. The user/designer must be comfortable in using the initial prototype.
5. The code is functionally decomposed to modules of one page or less.
6. The builder avoids writing traditional programs and, instead, assembles and modifies existing modules.
7. The builder exploits available fourth-generation technology.
8. The user-system interface is simple enough so as not to inhibit the user/designer in working with the initial prototype.

Responsibilities of the Prototyping Participants

The principal responsibilities in Step 2 are as follows:

- *User/designer*—No clear-cut responsibilities.
- *Builder*—To construct the initial working prototype (including interactive dialogues and menus that fit the user/designer's needs and abilities) and to capture the user/designer's reactions to the initial prototype.

Step 3: Use the Prototype To Refine the User/Designer's Requirements

The purpose of Step 3 is to refine the user/designer's requirements by using the working prototype of the system.

Objectives

The objectives in Step 3 are as follows:

1. To allow the user/designer to gain experience with the prototype of the system in order to specify more complete information needs along with the system features that best meet these needs.
2. To capture what the user/designer does and, more importantly, does not like about the current prototype system.
3. To determine if the user/designer is satisfied with the existing prototype.

The builder does not proceed further until the user/designer documents the inadequacies, undesirable features, and information shortcomings detected while using the current prototype of the system.

Basic Prototyping Activities and Principles

The basic activity in Step 3 is the capture of the user/designer's reactions to the current prototype of the system. Several techniques may be used for this purpose:

1. Use of the log book to capture comments.
2. Capture of the user/designer's reactions using the prototype itself by having the user/designer key in the messages.

The principles applied in Step 3 are as follows:

1. Hands-on experience with a real system leads to a real understanding of the system.
2. The user/designer always finds problems with the first version of the system—prototyping exploits rather than is inconvenienced by this behavior.
3. The user/designer determines when changes are necessary and thus controls the overall development time.
4. If the user/designer does not contact the builder within a reasonable time, the builder should contact the user/designer.

Responsibilities of the Prototyping Participants

The principal responsibilities in Step 3 are as follows:

■ *User/designer*—To use the prototype and to react to its features. This includes documenting perceived inadequacies and undesirable features.

■ *Builder*—To wait for and analyze the user/designer reactions to the prototype, and then discuss any desired changes with the user/designer in an effort to identify all requests clearly.

Step 4: Revise and Enhance the Prototype System

The sole purpose of Step 4 is to modify the prototype in such a way as to correct undesirable or missing features identified by the user/designer in Step 3.

Basic Prototyping Activities and Principles

The specific activities in Step 4 will vary depending on the nature of the changes requested by the user/designer. They may, for example, involve modification of the database, changes to the existing programs, and the development of additional program modules. Regardless of the nature of the requested changes, the prototyping activities are identical to those identified for Step 2.

The following principles are applicable in Step 4:

1. Existing program modules are assembled and modified; writing of new programs is avoided.
2. If the module is too difficult to change, it is rewritten.
3. If the user/designer does not want it fixed, it is not fixed.
4. The scope of the system is not changed without an appropriate modification of the estimated cost of the operational prototype.
5. Speed in modifying and returning the prototype system to the user/designer is critical; the sooner, the better.
6. If any requested changes cannot be made, the builder contacts the user/designer immediately.
7. The user/designer must be comfortable in using the enhanced prototype.
8. Available fourth-generation technology is exploited.

Responsibilities of the Prototyping Participants

The responsibilities in Step 4 are similar to those in Step 2:

- *User/designer*—No responsibilities.
- *Builder*—To construct a modified working prototype of the system and re-examine the methods used for capturing the user's/designer reactions.

General Comments on Steps 3 and 4

Steps 3 and 4 are iterative as can be seen in Figure 7.1. The number of iterations will vary and will depend on the specific application. Most applications average five iterations (see Stroka and Rather [12]).

There are two instances when the iterations stop:

1. When, based on what has been learned during the prototyping process, the user/designer determines that the application system under development will not be of value after all. In this case, the enhanced working prototype is simply discarded and the whole process is finished.
2. When the application's user/designer is satisfied with the operation of the initial prototype, and this initial prototype becomes an operational one.

When the builder determines, during the prototyping process, that the prototype should be modified to enhance efficiency or to facilitate future modifications, such changes should be transparent to the user/builder but not of concern. They are the responsibility of the prototype builder.

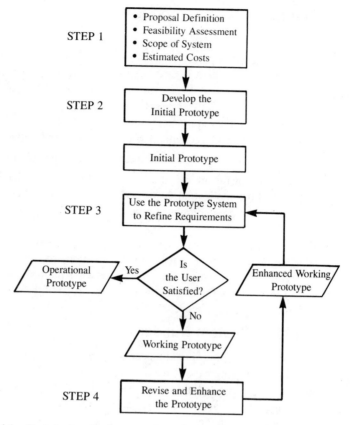

Figure 7.1   The Model of the Prototyping Cycle

7.3 VARIATIONS IN THE GENERAL PROTOTYPING PROCESS

There are several variants of the prototyping process, the most common of which are the direct result of the differences in the number of people involved. They are:

1. Prototyping with multiple users/designers.
2. Prototyping with multiple system builders.
3. Prototyping when a system builder is functioning as both the builder and the designer.
4. Prototyping when a user/designer is functioning as both the builder and the designer.

Although each of these variants diminishes the basic effectiveness of the prototyping process, there are situations for which each of them is quite appropriate.

Multiple Users/Designers

The need for this prototyping situation occurs when the application system under construction is perceived as being potentially useful to many diverse users or the application system is so complex that it requires specialists from multiple user communities. In this case, the prototyping process is affected as follows:

1. The initial requirements will take longer to define (Step 1). Multiple meetings will be required with or without the system builder.
2. The time required to define desired changes will be longer (Step 3).
3. During the prototyping iterations, there will be a tendency to expand the scope of the application. More time will be required between iterations, and generally more iterations will be required.

The additional development cost for this prototyping variant is in the extra time required. The time is used for the additional communications, negotiations, and compromises that are always required when multiple users/designers are involved. This cost is borne largely by the users' group of the organization.

Multiple System Builders

This prototyping situation occurs when the required technical and analytical skills or prototyping experience are not available in a single builder. As with multiple users/designers, multiple builders affect the prototyping process by requiring more time. Which activities will require additional time depends on how the system builders work together.

For example, if the system builders function as specialists in separate areas, one handling the user/designer contacts and one handling the technical system development, the development time will generally increase for Steps 2 and 4 of the prototyping process. On the other hand, if they function as a team, the increases in development time will be spread more evenly over all the prototyping steps and the development time for Steps 2 and 4 might even decrease.

The procedure recommended most often is to function as a team because this approach can bring about the following advantages:

1. Quicker turnaround to the user/designer by reducing the time required for Steps 2 and 4, hence greater user/designer satisfaction.
2. Improved skill levels for both prototyping participants.

System Builder as Both Builder and User/Designer

This prototyping situation occurs when the builder perceives that he understands the user/designer's needs well enough to exploit the opportunity in the user/designer's environment without consulting the user/designer or when very unclear or unnecessarily complicated information requirements specifications have been generated during the definition phase of the life cycle development methodology.

Both of these situations obviously result in a compression of the prototyping process. This compression can occur at two levels:

1. When the system builder generates only an initial prototype. Here, the system builder develops the initial prototype without the benefit of a statement of need from the user/designer. The designer gets involved in the prototyping process only from Step 3 and remains involved as the operational prototype is developed. The advantage of this approach is in the speed with which the initial prototype is delivered. However, the builder risks not really understanding the user/designer's basic information needs or the desired scope of the application.

2. When the system builder continues the prototyping process in isolation from the user/designer, by completing several iterations for Steps 3 and 4. Here, the development process is totally compressed. The system builder presumably has developed an operational prototype without the benefit of a statement of need from the user/designer. The advantage of this approach is the speed with which the operational prototype is generated.

However, when the system builder assumes the role of the user/designer, the continual and very real risk exists that the system builder will not really understand the users' information needs and will deliver system that is essentially unusable to the intended user.

User/Designer as Both Builder and Designer

This prototyping situation may occur under several circumstances:

1. When the user/designer perceives an opportunity in his or her own environment and is unable to obtain timely assistance from the MIS organization.

2. When the user/designer has been involved in a project team activity under the life cycle development methodology and perceives that the time required until the system is complete is unacceptable given his or her current information needs.

3. When the user/designer is experienced with the fourth-generation language available in his or her organization and has access to the necessary data.

Under all these circumstances, the user/designer must have some minimal level of computer/system skills and have access to computing and information/data resources.

This set of circumstances also leads to the compression of the prototyping process. As was the case with the prototyping variant in which the system builder functions in both roles, that of the builder and the user/designer, the development risks become greater as the compression increases. The nature of the risks is, however, quite different. The risks associated with the user/designer developing a prototype alone are:

1. Unnecessarily high operating costs.
2. Lack of data integrity, including accuracy, currency, and consistency.
3. Lack of program integrity, neglect of program testing, and possible logic and coding errors.
4. Lack of proper system documentation.

All these risks are usually associated with the lack of professional system skills. Just as the system's builder may underestimate the importance of the users' perspective in defining the information needs, the user/designer may underestimate the importance of MIS controls and procedures.

7.4 SUMMARY

There are four basics steps in the prototyping process.

1. Identify user requirements.
2. Develop a working prototype.
3. Evaluate and use the prototype.
4. Refine the prototype.

Steps 3 and 4 are repeated until the system requirements are met.

Each step of the prototyping process has its objectives and principles. For the process to be a success, its participants must adhere to their responsibilities.

EXERCISES

1. Why is project management important for prototyping?
2. Who should establish project plans and why?
3. Why are project plans important?
4. Do you think that project plans should be revised? Explain your answer.
5. Do project plans depend on the development approach taken?
6. Why should prototyping process participants estimate the cost of an initial prototype?
7. Why should the builder of the prototype be concerned with the scope of the system under development?
8. What factors should be considered when making cost estimates?

9. Why do you suppose the most efficient way to build prototypes is to involve only one user/designer and one analyst/builder?

10. Why is a user considered a designer when he or she is engaged in the prototyping process?

11. Summarize the steps of the prototyping process.

12. Define objectives for each step of the prototyping process.

13. Specify the responsibilities of the participants for each step of the prototyping process.

14. For large systems, would you recommend a one analyst/builder, one user/designer arrangement? Explain your answer.

15. What are the most important responsibilities of the participants in the prototyping process during the step of developing a working prototype?

16. Why should the builder not proceed with the prototyping process until the user/designer has documented the inadequacies, undesirable features, and information shortcomings detected while using the current prototype of the system?

17. Comment on the following statement: "The user/designer determines when changes are necessary and thus controls the overall development time."

18. What would happen to the prototyping process if the control of the development time were the sole responsibility of the analyst/builder?

19. List the circumstances in which the prototyping process stops.

20. List the possible variants of the prototyping process, and briefly describe the circumstances under which these variants apply.

21. When the prototyping process involves multiple users/designers, why is the development time usually expanded?

22. When the prototyping process involves multiple analysts/builders, why is functioning as a team the procedure most often recommended?

23. What are the risks of developing a prototype by a user who is functioning also as a builder?

24. Comment on the risk of building a prototype without user involvement.

PROJECTS

Consider a particular business with which you have an ongoing contact or for which you have worked in the past. Briefly describe the management problems (if any) you perceive with applying a prototyping approach to the development of new applications in this organization. Would it be easy to monitor the prototyping development process? What variant of the prototype building approach is most appropriate there? Why? Would it depend on the nature of the application? Prepare a brief on the management issues of the prototyping process in this organization.

REFERENCES AND SUGGESTED READINGS

1. Alavi, M. "An assessment of the prototyping approach to information system development." *Communications of the ACM*, Vol. 27, No. 6, 1984, pp. 556-563.

2. Aptman, L. H. "Project management: Process to manage change." *Management Solutions*, Vol. 31, No. 8, 1986, pp. 30-34.

3. Boer, B. H. *Application Prototyping*. New York: AMA Management Briefing, 1985.

4. Boehm, B. W. *Software Engineering Economics*. Englewood Cliffs, N.J.: Prentice-Hall, 1981.

5. Cleland, D. I, and King, W. R. *System Analysis and Project Management*. 3d ed., New York: McGraw-Hill, 1983.

6. Hannan, J., ed. *A Practical Guide to System Development*. New York: Auerbach, 1982.

7. Jenkins A. M. "Prototyping: A methodology for the design and development of application systems." *SIM Spectrum*, Vol. 2, No. 2, 1985, pp. 1-8.

8. Kean, J. F., Kean, M., and Teagan, M. *Productivity Management in the Development of the Computer Applications*. Englewood Cliffs, N.J.: Prentice-Hall, 1984.

9. King, D. *Current Practices in Software Development*. New York: Yourdon Press, 1984.

10. Lackman, M. "Controlling the project development cycle: Part 3—Tools for successful project management." *Journal of Systems Management*, Vol. 38, No. 2, 1987, pp. 16-27.

11. Staw, B. M., and Ross, J. "Knowing when to pull the plug." *Harvard Business Review*, Vol. 65, No. 2, 1987, pp. 68-74.

12. Stroka, J. M., and Rader, M. H. "Prototyping increases chance of system acceptance." *Data Management*, Vol. 24, No. 3, 1986, pp. 12-19.

13. Wolff, M. F. "Rules of thumb for project management." *Research Management*, Vol. 27, No. 4, 1984, pp. 11-13.

CHAPTER 8

How to Prototype

*Let me think, I said to myself. I am bouncing round a bit, but there
is nothing abnormal about that.*

Antoine De Saint-Exupery

8.1 INTRODUCTION

The main objective of this chapter is to analyze successful prototyping. Successful
prototyping starts with clarifying objectives and planning the process.

Essentially, the management of prototyping is based on the fundamental
management principles used in developing computer application systems.
Management issues unique to prototyping are:

- Specifications management
- Change management
- Staffing of the prototyping projects
- Delivery intervals

An important underlying concept is that the management of prototyping is a
management of fast-paced change.

8.2 PROTOTYPING OBJECTIVES AND PLANNING

Chapters 6 and 7 considered the prototyping concepts and procedures that make
this approach effective. Practitioners of this approach maintain that it is the best
answer to the existing development backlogs. Others claim that it is an essential
tool needed for extraction of the systems requirements definition. Still others
advocate it as a panacea for the problem of adequate users' involvement. As we
discussed in previous chapters, prototyping does have its problems. In addition,
there is no such thing as a single application prototyping approach or methodology;
numerous versions and strategies abound.

Do all these possibilities and strategies mean that application prototyping is too
confusing for us to make the proper choices? (For example, whether or not to use

prototyping, what approach to take.) Not necessarily. It just means that if we are considering application prototyping, we should look before we leap.

Application prototyping should especially be used when new ideas have to be tried out, when new technologies are brought into use, or when new organizational environments are created. Consider the following case studies:

Case 1: **Marketing Administration System for NCR International** This case is based on a paper by B. Livesey [4]. The Information Systems and Services Group of NCR Ltd. is responsible for providing internal management services to the British division of NCR Corporation. It also has a responsibility for developing systems to be implemented within world-wide divisions of the NCR Corporation. Their assignment was to develop a marketing administration system (namely, order processing, billing, and inventory management) to be introduced in multinational divisions.

Previous systems development work took more than two years (from the time the need for an operational system was identified until the system was implemented) on one site. Up to four years could pass until the divisions in all countries within the NCR Corporation had implemented the final system. The implication here is that the business needs were to remain static for the duration of these four years. In the computer industry in which NCR operates, this clearly is not the case. NCR technology products have a short life cycle. It seemed ironic and unacceptable for the computer systems development cycle to take longer than the products cycle.

To adapt to the fast-changing business environment in which NCR operates, the information systems development team decided to use the prototyping approach in hopes of substantially reducing development time. The final system was implemented after four prototypes were created and tested over a period of one year. This substantial reduction in development time led NCR Corporation to rethink their strategy for developing computer systems.

Prototyping, when used well, can lead to a better understanding of the actual application area, especially when it is a complex one. Prototyping can help system designers arrive at the correct initial versions of the system, before the commitment to the final construction of a complicated system is made. This is achieved by experimenting with a proposed design, as shown in the following case.

Case 2: **An Interactive Decision Support System for the Energy Policy Analysis (EPLAN)** This case is based on an article by L. R. Medsker [14]. The National Audubon Society is involved in an ongoing project to develop an interactive computer system that models the impact of various public policies on U.S. energy demand. The system (EPLAN, or Energy Policy Analysis Plan) uses a decision support system that assists the user by managing a large amount of engineering, and economic data, performing calculations, permitting the evaluation of different energy use scenarios, and keeping track of various constraints. Such diversified functions made available to the user make this system very complex. The system implementation team used the prototyping approach to handle this complexity..

As a first step, the skeletal prototype of the whole system was built. After testing, to verify structural accuracy, parts were added to represent, for example, calculations of energy consumption for each of the fuel types.

The rest of the project involved adding detailed calculations, providing constraints and dependencies among competing fuel uses, and creating needed displays. Systematic testing ensured that each implemented prototype was error free before the next layer of complexity was added.

With this evolutionary prototyping, the development team was able to manage growth in system complexity without introducing untraceable bugs.

The process of attaching more and more functionality to a kernel of the system is not unique to prototyping. This process has been used for years in software design with other methodologies. Prototyping exploits this approach.

The most important feature of all the prototyping approaches (exploratory, experimental, and evolutionary; see Chapter 6) is that a tangible model (prototype) is used as a feedback mechanism to help define the final system solution. The questions then arise: Can prototyping, an apparently productive tool, lead to failure? To the wrong system? To a system that falls short of user expectations? To cost overruns and schedule delays? Prototyping failures are usually caused by one or more of the following problems:

- Selecting an inappropriate business problem for prototyping.
- Not having the proper technical environment to support the prototyping process.
- Not having effective management methods and controls for prototyping.
- Dealing with users who are uninformed about the prototyping process.

To avoid problems with the prototyping approach, prototyping should be planned. This planning process has five essential steps.

1. Assess the nature of the application to see if gains will be made from the prototyping.
2. Develop and document a prototype life cycle model that makes sense for a particular environment.
3. Acquire the appropriate software tools and train the technical staff in their use.
4. Establish management and control procedures for the system development process.
5. Train both users and technical staff in the application prototype development procedures chosen.

8.3 SELECTING A PROJECT FOR PROTOTYPING

It is important to remember that the traditional or the structured approaches to systems development are very acceptable in some cases. In fact, under certain circumstances, they may even be superior to prototyping, because as with everything else, there are good prototyping applications and there are bad ones. Essentially, the success of prototyping very much depends on the application.

Factors Favoring Traditional Systems Development (SDLC)	Factors Favoring Prototyping
Data needs are clearly defined.	Users requirements are uncertain.
System has long life expectancy.	Procedure changes are extensive.
Tight controls are required.	User environment is volatile.
Development risks are clearly defined.	System has relatively short life expectancy.
Essential system features are known in advance.	System needs to be operational in short period of time.
Operational characteristics are well understood.	Changes in specifications are anticipated.

Figure 8.1   Project Characteristics Favoring SDLC Approach Versus Prototyping

Where should prototyping be used and on what type of projects? Some computer information specialists would limit the use of prototyping to the development of systems that are poorly defined. Others would limit it to systems that are relatively small. In fact, some claim that the use of prototyping tends to keep projects smaller and thus more manageable.

Good applications for prototyping are those that tend to be dynamic and those that require extensive use of user dialogues.

Poor applications are those that tend to be batch oriented, extremely large, and involving little or no user interface. Applications that require real-time capabilities or focus heavily on number crunching such as numerical analysis or statistical algorithms also are not prime candidates for prototyping.

In Figure 8.1 we list the project characteristics that make a project suitable for traditional system development methodology (SDLC) and those that make the project suitable for the prototyping approach.

Being a poor candidate for prototyping does not automatically mean that the prototyping approach should not be attempted. On the contrary, prototyping, if properly managed, can be very beneficial, improving the productivity of those who are developing the system.

Specifically, prototyping can be useful in the following application areas:

- Development of
    - Online systems
    - Certain batch systems
    - Certain real-time systems

- ■ Systems based on software packages
- ■ Decision support systems
- ■ Enhancement and modifications of existing systems
- ■ Selection of packages

Prototyping is especially useful in developing *online systems*. These types of systems are difficult even for system designers to visualize if they are working only on paper. Using some kind of prototyping (for example, exploratory or experimental prototyping), at least for the flow of information to and from screens, helps in visualization. Many system designers started prototyping when they realized that the screen design facility, part of the fourth-generation language they had acquired, significantly helped them design and implement systems.

Prototyping's usefulness in the development of *batch systems* is a more complex issue. Nevertheless, the same problems arise in the development of batch systems as in that of online systems. Quite often users have difficulty visualizing what they want a system to do, and they especially have problems evaluating requirements documentation. Exploratory prototyping, which focuses on the basic problems of communication between system developers and prospective users, particularly in the early stages of the software development process, can help with these difficulties.

Prototyping can also enhance the development of *real-time systems*. Experimental prototyping can be used to simulate the operation of the final system to specifically check for appropriateness or efficiency of proposed solutions.

Prototyping is useful for developing *systems based on software packages*, especially when users integrate the package into other applications and modify the package. Building a prototype that consists of the package with its modifications, including options, exits, preprocessors, and postprocessors, provides all the advantages of prototyping. Installing it first as a prototype with test data enables system designers to test it to ensure that it meets user's needs, to train key users, and to determine whether it interrelates well with interfacing systems.

All the prototyping approaches discussed in Chapter 6 are very useful for the creation of *Decision Support Systems*. For example, exploratory prototyping can be used to test and evaluate different user interfaces into the system; experimental prototyping can be used to establish which analysis technique is correct; and evolutionary prototyping can be used to gradually introduce options when dealing with a complex decision system.

Prototyping is very useful in situations requiring *enhancements and modifications of existing systems*. Information systems developers need only prototype that part of the system that needs changes. If an enhancement or modification is to be relatively minor, bringing up a prototype of it is a minor task. If the proposed change is large, the benefits of prototyping can be very substantial.

The *package selection* process is also enhanced by using prototyping. Most vendors allow a trial use before purchase or at least before the purchase is final. Use in the prototype version can help evaluate the package's strengths and weaknesses and helps users make a good, informed choice.

System Type	Protyping Purpose	Prototyping Methodology	Where Used in Life Cycle
Development of online systems	• Establish user needs • Design screens and data flow	Exploratory Experimental	Requirements Specification Design stage
Development of certain batch systems	• Establish user needs • Improve communication between developer and user	Exploratory	Requirements Specification
Development of certain real-time systems	• Simulate operation of a system • Check correctness of proposed solutions • Check efficiency of proposed solutions	Experimental	Design stage Programming
Development of systems based on software packages	• Test if it meets user needs • Train key users • Check whether it interrelates well with other systems	Experimental	Testing Implementation stage
Development of decision support systems	• Specify user need • Specify design • Select modeling technique • Gradually introducer of complex system	Experimental Evolutionary	Intelligence stage Design stage Implementation stage
Enhancement and modification of existing systems	• Check correctness of proposed changes	Experimental	Maintenance
Selection of packages	• Evaluate package	Experimental	

Figure 8.2   Summary of Prototyping Approaches and Their Applicability to the Development of Different Classes of Systems

A summary of prototyping approaches and their applicability to the development of different classes of computer information systems is shown in Figure 8.2.

8.4 LIFE CYCLE MODELS FOR PROTOTYPING

Once it is clear that prototyping might apply, the second step in prototyping planning is to identify a life cycle model for the specific development case. Without a development model, prototyping is just uncontrolled development that often leads to failure. The model, which helps to define how software development will be managed later on, also allows the users and the data processing specialists to establish their roles and responsibilities.

There are three major types of life cycle models of prototyping: exploratory, experimental, and evolutionary. In the first two life cycle models, the prototypes are regarded as throwaways (also called disposable models), to be discarded when the real production system is implemented. In the third model, prototypes wind up as the end product: prototypes that actually become the final production system (called nondisposable or operational models).

Recall again that the discarded prototype models facilitate the development of a clear, concise definition of requirements. The throwaway models provide the users with valuable hands-on experience that increases the chances that the resulting requirements will be more accurate and complete.

Prototypes are also used as a communication vehicle between system developers to help them better understand proposed technical solutions.

Exploratory Prototyping Models

The exploratory prototyping (also called requirements prototyping) approach is used when no conventional requirements analysis can satisfactorily identify and validate the true business requirements. We identify two possible variants of life cycle models.

The first variant is defined as including:

■ Preliminary analysis

■ Requirements definition

■ Design prototype

■ Code prototype

■ Use prototype

■ Iteratively refine prototype

■ Code production system

■ Production

■ Maintenance

This variant of the life cycle model is illustrated in Figure 8.3.

The second, slightly more complex model of the requirements prototyping includes:

■ Preliminary analysis

■ Requirements definition

■ Design prototype

■ Code prototype

■ Use prototype

■ Iteratively refine prototype

■ Refine system requirements

■ Design production system

■ Implementation

■ Maintenance

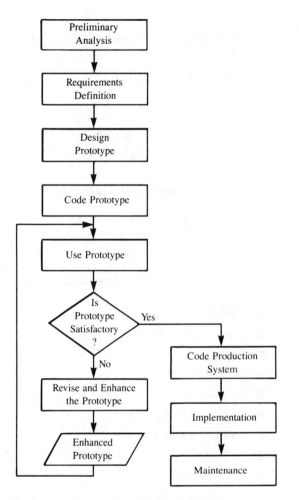

Figure 8.3   First Variant of the Exploratory Prototyping Life Cycle Model

This life cycle model is illustrated in Figure 8.4.

The phases outlined for these two life cycle models are quite similar. One subtle difference, however, appears at the production system design phase. The first model proceeds to the production system implementation phase immediately after the user's acceptance of the prototype, whereas the second makes a distinction between the design of the prototype and the design of the production system.

Depending on how closely available prototyping software tools match available production system software tools, either model may be appropriate. For instance, if the prototype is built using a fourth-generation language with limited functionality and efficiency and the prototype is not an operationally efficient system, chances are that prior to implementation some redesign work in a third-generation language will be needed. In this case, we should deal with the second model we have described.

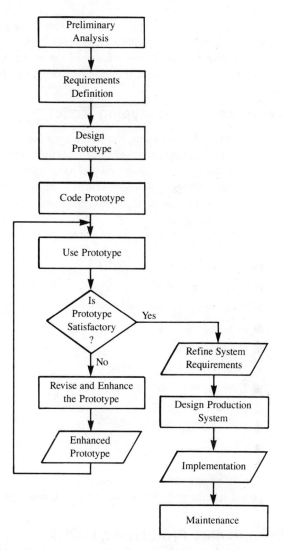

Figure 8.4   Second Variant of the Exploratory Prototyping Life Cycle Model

On the other hand, if the prototype system is coded using a fourth-generation language and functionality and performance are sufficient for the given application, extensive redesign may be unnecessary. Here, the first life cycle model is applicable.

The use of throwaway prototypes almost always involves an iterative process of analyzing, designing, coding, testing, and modifying the prototype. The details of this process were described in Chapter 7.

The iterations are stopped when all the user's requirements are identified and met. In essence, requirements prototyping is the system analysis technique that involves an elaborate simulation of system features and intense user involvement. Once the prototyping phase is complete, system designers concentrate on the production system. The reminder of the production software development life cycle usually follows the traditional or structured approach.

Experimental Prototyping Model

Experimental prototyping should be used especially when there is a need to test acceptability of the proposed system performance or to aid communication within the developers' team. Experimental prototyping also helps to structure the implementation of large systems. In addition, this mode of prototyping is also applicable when there is a need to assess the feasibility of a proposed solution against available resources.

The experimental prototyping life cycle model is defined as follows:

- System analysis
- Requirements definition
- Design production system
- Design prototype
- Code prototype
- Experiment with prototype
- Evaluate outcomes of experiment
- Improve design of production system
- Implementation
- Maintenance

This life cycle model is illustrated in Figure 8.5. It should always be regarded as an enhancement of the production's system design.

Evolutionary Prototyping Model

The evolutionary prototyping approach recognizes the inherent failure of many approaches to manage change. The life cycle model for this case includes the following phases:

- System analysis
- Requirements definition
- Develop initial prototype
- Use prototype to refine requirements
- Iteratively refine prototype
- Modeling and benchmarking

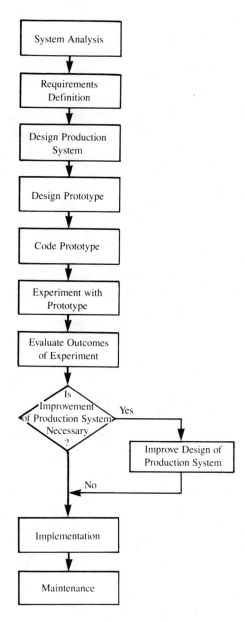

Figure 8.5   Experimental Prototyping Life Cycle Model

■ Implementation

■ Maintenance

Figure 8.6 illustrates this model.

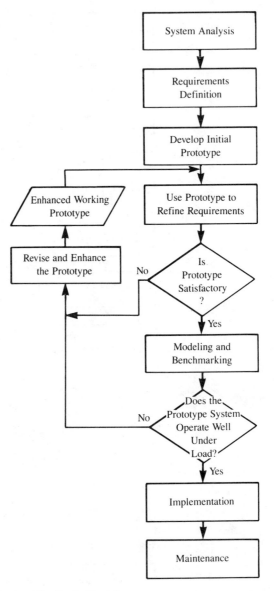

Figure 8.6   Evolutionary Prototyping Life Cycle Model

8.5 SOME THOUGHTS ON MODELING PHASE

The modeling phase is probably the most important for the prototype-as-end-product life cycle model. Quite often, initial prototypes may be very slow, and they can consume inordinate amounts of system resources. If the prototype (even a modified one) is to run as a production system, it must perform acceptably. Modeling or benchmarking is critical here. The prototype system must be tested to see if it can handle the expected maximum data load. If it performs well under that load, it can be considered for use as the production system. Other tasks such as maintenance documentation, user documentation, and site testing must also be done before the system is suitable for production use.

If portions of the prototype do not hold up under stress testing, these subsystems, programs, or modules may need to be redesigned and replaced with third-generation language counterparts. As in the prototyping phases, the modeling and implementation phases also can be iterative.

Regardless of the prototyping approach, once the model passes through all the required phases, can it really work? Do such systems exist in production? The last section of this chapter shows examples of successful prototyping. We contend that it is possible to develop a major system that consists of a hybrid of fourth-generation language, third-generation language, and even second-generation language software.

8.6 PROTOTYPING TOOLS

The third step in prototyping planning involves the selection of the technical environment in which the prototyping process is to be carried out. This includes acquiring the proper software tools and training the staff in their use.

Managers of the system development process should be prepared to evaluate, select, and purchase some software development tools that could be quite expensive. They have to be aware that no matter which prototyping life cycle model they will use, no single fourth-generation tool on the market can be all things to all developers for all applications. Nevertheless, there are key features to look for:

1. *Online interactive system.* In prototyping, the builder and the prototype itself must respond rapidly to change.

2. *Sophisticated database management systems.* Preferably these should be of the relational type, with a natural-language-based retrieval process. Such database management systems provide most of the functions of managing the data, in contrast to a traditional system design, where a substantial amount of time and effort is expended to define access methods, physical storage structures, back-up, integrity, and security.

3. *Integrated data dictionary or directory.* It should be actively coupled to the database management system to control data integrity.

4. *Ad hoc query language.* If possible, this should have English-like syntax.

5. *Fourth-generation nonprocedural language.*

6. *Screen generation and management facility.*

7. *Batch report generator.*

8. *Support.* This is needed for various procedural and nonprocedural language interfaces.

9. *Text editing and word processing.*

Other desirable features include supplemental security, cataloged command procedures, statistical packages, back-up/recovery, documentation report/generator, online HELP, business graphics, spreadsheet analysis, access to other database management systems or files, and micro to mainframe connection. [The majority (but not all) of these features can be found in the fourth-generation languages described in the first four chapters of this book.]

8.7 MANAGEMENT ISSUES IN PROTOTYPING

The fourth step in prototyping planning is to establish the management and control procedures for the system development process.

Management and Controls of Prototyping Process

Prototyping-oriented project management is easier than that of a conventional software development process because a prototype demonstrates meaningful performance at each stage of the project. It may perform poorly, but it does perform.

There is a conventional perception that a prototyping project is essentially uncontrollable. In fact, large-scale prototyping requires the use of proper project management techniques to increase the likelihood of success. Most of these techniques derive from common sense; they are normal practice among experienced project managers.

It is essential that the prototyping project manager identify key users and decision makers. These people will ultimately be the ones who decide whether the application truly meets their requirements and whether additional expenditures are justifiable.

The users must take an active role in the prototyping process. Without interested and active users, the demonstration and use phases can become ineffective. Fortunately, the process of interacting with the prototype early in the application development life cycle usually serves to stimulate interest among users.

Another critical aspect of successful prototyping management is the isolation of the prototyping team during the construction and revision (but not the demonstration and review) cycles of the prototyping project. Usually the team is expected to develop a model of a significant application very quickly. It can function best in an environment that enhances efficiency.

Isolation from distractions by the users' community and by other activities going on within the data processing organization (such as maintenance of existing applications) is essential to the rapid building of large application prototypes. Demonstration and review sessions with the users need to be structured. This structuring requires that the users operate the model rather than simply observe it.

Good project management sets up demonstrations and review sessions in such a way that they conclude with a consensus meeting in which the revisions to the model are reviewed with all the users to ensure concurrence and understanding.

Special care has to be taken to prevent so-called paralysis within the prototyping effort. This problem arises most commonly when the users refuse to reach a decision as to whether one technique or another is more appropriate. As a consequence, the prototypers are asked to implement solution A, followed by solution B, followed by solution A, and so on. This is one of the circumstances where, if the users themselves will not resolve the indecision, the users' management needs to be encouraged to do it for them.

Prototyping project managers must also guard against continuously expanding the application's scope during the design effort. The prototyping team, in its effort to satisfy user requirements, could presumably include diverse functionality requirements within the prototyping model of the application. Although there is nothing inherently bad with providing all the functionality anyone ever dreamed of in an application, including all related and subordinate functions in a prototype defeats the purpose of its use. In addition, the cost associated with this expanded system will exceed initial estimates. This situation can make the users' management very unhappy, and the resulting disillusionment by the user's management can often defeat the acceptance of prototyping as an effective tool within the organization.

One technique for dealing with this phenomenon is for the project manager to recognize and report changes in the scope of the application back to the users' management. The users' management can always be given the option of reconsidering final system costs including such expanded scope.

A summary of general prototyping project manager responsibilities is given in Figure 8.7.

Managing Prototyping

Like all innovations that promise big payoffs, the development of systems using prototyping is a risky business. Assume that you must convince your management that prototyping will be the answer to managing the development of information systems to solve problems they currently have. You must be in a position to spell out how you intend to control and minimize possible risks if you want to implement the prototyping methodology. Strong project management practices and tools are essential here.

It is important not to overcommit prototyping. To start with, you may want to try to get management approval of the initial prototyping work to be done on small, less visible applications (not to oversell prototyping, and to start with projects that are not critical to management as yet). Small projects will help ensure that the adopted prototyping approach can be controlled. Also, this should give all concerned enough time to get used to the prototyping process.

Next, the biggest thing to watch out for is the natural tendency to continually expand the original system prototype. It is easy to change the prototype or to add fancy functions, but it is also easy to get carried away with such indiscriminate changes. It is even quite possible to continually add new functions to the system, without making any real improvements. In such cases, the prototyping participants are playing with technology rather than applying it. If this is allowed, the project cannot maintain its objectives, establish clear milestones, or demonstrate that it is being managed effectively.

Standard project manager responsibilities
....

- Setting Objectives
- Developing plans
- Establishing schedules
- Setting controls
- Performing operations
- Gathering information
- Preparing reports

Project manager responsibilities to prototyping
....

- Identify key users and decision makers
- Serve as coordinator, arbitrator, counselor and diplomat to the larger degree than for standard projects
- Resolve disagreements as quickly as possible to prevent an antagonistic atmosphere from developing
- Isolate the prototyping team from distractions
- Set up demonstrations and review sessions
- Guard against continuously expanding application's scope and endless iterations
- Guard against stifling the creative efforts of users in an attempt to meet project deadlines
- Be aware of the relationships between the user groups and the prototypers
- Determine the format and extent of the documentation
- If necessary, make a decision to abandon the project

Figure 8.7 Responsibilities of Prototyping Project Manager

Managing a prototyping project, in general, includes three major concerns: general project management, specifications management, and change management.

Project Management

While the prototyping method itself does not guarantee a project's ultimate success, proper project management is a necessary ingredient for successful project implementation.

Project management starts during the feasibility study phase of the process. The following management tasks are initiated:

1. Selection of the personnel for the application development team.

2. Definition of the set of appropriate benchmarks, tests, and performance evaluation procedures.

3. Identification of the intermediate milestones for the proposed application.

Managing prototyping projects is, to some degree, easier than managing systems developed by conventional methods such as SDLC. Even an initial prototype gives the user a meaningful working model of the project rather than a dry, dull report of, say, specifications, and that certainly makes everyone more interested and engaged. The prototype may perform poorly in terms of the final system scope or required running time, but it does perform. With a good development team and initial specifications in place, it is possible to produce a prototype that demonstrates the feasibility of the entire project.

Specifications Management

Recall that the prototyping methodology does not rely on complete, precise system specifications. This is in contrast to the SDLC development method where such specifications are created prior to system's design work.

However, this does not mean that prototyping does not require specifications. On the contrary, clear initial specifications are essential to successful system development using the prototyping methodology. Remember, though, that these specifications remain incomplete and imprecise through the stages of the system development process. They are refined and elaborated on simultaneously with the prototype development as the project proceeds.

In terms of specifications management, prototyping specifications are created to be changed and updated, but they must be constantly maintained. They must be documented and then approved by all participants: funding management, prospective users, system project management, and system designers.

Change Management

In the prototyping environment, change is not incidental—it is essential. It must be planned for and built into all strategies and schedules. In other words, change must be managed.

The elaborate project management control present in SDLC is not appropriate for the prototyping methodology. Each prototyping cycle is relatively quick. In a very short time, it becomes quite obvious if those who are charged with constructing the prototype do not deliver an acceptable model. It becomes apparent very quickly if users do not adequately contribute to the prototype review sessions. A prototype demonstration of what is currently working can easily serve as a status report (an element of the project management control).

When the decisions concerning a proposed application system have to be made by many people, change control procedures become a problem, however. For example, change control procedures must include such questions as: Who decides what changes should be made to the prototype? Do all users have equal authority to request changes?

The most practical solutions for change management problems are to function with only a small group of users who will have sole authority to approve or disapprove changes and to insist that decisions be made quickly in order to maintain the momentum of the prototyping process.

Staffing Prototyping Projects

Building computer systems is a complex task. Establishing systems requirements is difficult, and doing it fast is quite demanding. Prototyping puts special demands on the prototyping staff. It requires fast adaptation to change.

Members of the prototyping team must be able to accomplish the entire development process in a short period of time. All the necessary tasks such as analysis, design, programming, generation of screens and reports as well as the inclusion of user interfaces must be done while maintaining the prototype's conceptual unity.

The prototyping team should be few in numbers, generally not more than two or three. The small size team forms an efficient group with a focused set of objectives.

During most of the prototyping effort, the design team has to concentrate on the delivery of the functional application with little regard for performance of the prototyping model. Performance considerations are best addressed after the requirements are well understood.

The prototyping design group cannot be a committee. "Fast" and "committee" are two essentially contradictory terms. Who should be a member of this team? A design generalist, that is, a person with the following characteristics:

1. Experienced in the development and design of computer applications.
2. Competent (but not necessarily an expert) in many areas, such as communication, numerical methods, database design, and user-machine interface.

Specific areas of competence depend on the application.

Delivery Intervals

The prototyping life cycle involves relatively short delivery cycles (intervals), which are cycles of interactions with the users. In each cycle a tangible system model is delivered. The essential objective here is to build and maintain a high level of interest on the users' part for the application under construction. For the typical prototyping process, the delivery intervals are measured in days; for very complex prototyping projects, in no more than a few weeks.

The pace at which the prototype is being built frequently precludes precise completion of the major security features within it. Elaborate algorithms whose functionality is not absolutely essential are also not included. This is only possible within the prototyping context since the basic goal is in the delivery of functionality, not performance—hence, the argument for not putting the prototype into production as soon as it is completed. The prototype will lack performance that is required of production system.

The quick pace of the prototype release requires the right frame of mind. This should concern management as well as prototype developers and users. The prototype developers must be able to release immature versions, and potential users must be able to view a prototype for what it is. Nothing would be more disastrous to the process of delivering the final application system than management starting to have such misconceptions as: What is taking so long to develop the real system? They did three prototypes in two weeks' time!

8.8 TRAINING OF USERS AND SYSTEMS STAFF

The fifth step in prototyping planning, training, is vital. It should include users as well as technical staff. Training programs should be tailored to the fourth-generation tools and prototyping life cycle model selected for the specific application.

It is essential that the users and their managers thoroughly understand what prototyping is, how it differs from traditional methods, and what will be expected of them during the process. The most effective way to establish this understanding is through education prior to undertaking the project itself. Failure to provide this understanding can result in great confusion and dissatisfaction as the effort proceeds.

8.9 PROTOTYPING PITFALLS

The prototyping approach implies the need for the user to be actively involved in the development process. However, prototyping does not, in itself, offer any guarantee for user participation or for considering the interests of those affected by the development of a new system.

For example, like any other procedure, prototyping may be misused to manipulate users into cooperating in what can eventually amount to their job obsolescence or to the downgrading of their own work. By presenting prospective users with new technical gadgets, prototyping may conceal the fact that this type of user involvement can be a sophisticated way of turning the final system contrary to the users' interest.

Other problems are possible with prototyping, for example:

1. Lack of specific function during the tests may severely restrict the value of the test. For example, screen generators are excellent means for dealing with screen layout. They fail, however, to capture the psychological complexity of the dialogue communications.

2. The fundamental idea of prototyping can be misunderstood. For example, the danger sometimes exists that prototypes will take over the role played by the rigid, written specifications and become frozen. The essential role of the prototype is to improve on initial specifications. The fundamental idea of prototyping methodology is to iterate the design, not to freeze it.

3. An iteration in prototyping implies discarding one's own work. This requires from system designers a fundamental change of attitude toward one's work, and this change may not be easy to achieve (consider ego involvement).

4. Prototyping teams with high levels of prototyping enthusiasm sometimes tend to perform inadequate initial system analysis. Basic requirements gathering

cannot be shortcircuited. The appeal of an easily and rapidly developed prototype may encourage the prototyping team to move too quickly toward a working model without bothering even with a basic set of requirements.

5. User management sometime tends to embrace a premature prototype. A variety of factors can encourage this. Dissatisfaction with an old system and a need for an improved system are the two most common. These tendencies can be present even though the premature system uses computer resources poorly, inadequately interfaces with other systems, or delivers incomplete documentation.

8.10 PROTOTYPING SUCCESS STORIES

Enormous gains in productivity have been achieved through the use of the prototyping approach and fourth-generation tools. Some examples are as follows:

1. Prototyping combined with the Cullinet Software Inc. fourth-generation language ADS/Online tripled the productivity rates of fifteen communications applications at AT&T Communications in Cincinnati, Ohio. As a result of the productivity gains, prototyping is now a standard development method at AT&T Communications.

2. Developing computer-based system in a manufacturing environment can require expertise not normally possessed by engineers in this environment. Prototyping can solve this problem by putting computer-based design into the hands of engineers and users so they can give feedback on it. Lockheed-Georgia Co. used prototyping methodology in its Paperless Factory effort and in implementing the Assembly Control and Tracking System. The paperless concept was successfully demonstrated to potential users. Users and system designers interacted freely during the development process, thus making results satisfactory to all.

3. The experiences of the U.S. Army Information Systems Software Development Center at Fort Lee, Virginia, with evolutionary prototyping, as reported by Mary L. Cesena and Wendell O. Jones, were tremendous. Evolutionary prototyping produced four large systems in a record time with considerable savings, as shown in Figure 8.8. Estimated average savings in the development time, dollars, and man-months were 33 months, $1,460,000, and 467 man-months, respectively.

Some of the drawbacks of evolutionary prototyping forced the Army to refine the prototyping process and modify it into a methodology they call Contemporary Life Cycle Development. The prototyping approach plays a major role in it. (Details of Contemporary Life Cycle Development are described in the paper by M. L. Cesena and W. O. Jones [5].)

Based on historical data for projects of comparable size and system complexity, estimates of Contemporary Life Cycle Development savings are as summarized in

Development Time, Dollars, and Man-months
(Traditional vs. Accelerated)

System	Estimates Using Traditional Method			Results Using Accelerated Method		
	Development Time (months)	$$ (000)	Man-months	Development Time (months)	$$ (000)	Man-months
Repair Parts Supply	36	1785	612	6	297	102
Property Accountability	60	875	300	22	245	84
Retail Supply Operations	60	3500	1200	7	408	140
Personnel Management	28	1775	225	18	1135	144

Average Savings:
Development Time   32.75
Dollars ($000)   1460
Man-months   467

Figure 8.8 Savings in the Evolutionary Prototyping Project

Figure 8.9. The average reduction for the four major systems is reported as nearly 19 months in development time, $3,025,000 in cost, and 870 in man-months.

8.11 SUMMARY

The prototyping process starts with establishing prototyping objectives and plans. These are critical prerequisites for a successful prototyping project.

Relevant management issues for prototyping are:

1. Specifications management
2. Change management
3. Staffing of prototyping projects
4. Delivery Intervals

In the prototyping environment, change is not incidental—it is essential. It must be planned for and managed.

Prototyping puts special demands on the prototyping staff since it requires fast adaptation to change. The quick pace of the prototype release requires adaptations from management as well as from the prototype developers and users. Prototype

Development Time, Dollars, and Man-months
(Traditional vs. Accelerated)

System	Estimates Using Traditional Method			Estimates Using Accelerated Method		
	Development Time (months)	$$ (000)	Man-months	Development Time (months)	$$ (000)	Man-months
Facilities Engineering	36	4800	1460	18	2100	396
Food Service Management	36	5300	1944	10	100	320
Ammunition Management	36	3700	1224	30	1700	576
Retail Supply Management	45	6200	348	21	4000	206

Average Savings:
Development Time   18.5
Dollars ($000)   3025
Man-months   870

Figure 8.9   Estimates of Savings with Contemporary Life Cycle Development

developers must be able to release immature versions, and potential users must be able to view a prototype for what it is.

The essential role of the prototype is to improve on initial system specifications. The fundamental idea of the prototyping approach is to iterate the design, not to freeze it.

Exploratory, experimental, and evolutionary prototyping produce a tangible model of the system used as a feedback mechanism to help define the final system solution.

Planning the prototyping approach involves:

1. Assessing the application to see if gains will be made from the prototyping.

2. Developing and documenting a prototype life cycle model that makes sense for a particular application and environment.

3. Acquiring appropriate software tools and training the technical staff in their use.

4. Establishing the management and control procedures for the prototyping development process.

5. Training for both the users and the technical staff in the application prototype development procedures chosen.

Prototyping does not, in itself, offer any guarantee for user participation or for considering the interests of those affected by the development of a new system.

Prototyping failures are usually caused by one or more of the following problems:

1. Not selecting an appropriate business problem.
2. Not selecting the correct prototyping mode, which stems from misunderstanding the basic motivation for the particular prototyping development effort itself.
3. Not having the proper technical environment to support the prototyping process.
4. Lacking effective management methods and controls for prototyping.
5. Dealing with users who have no understanding of the prototyping process and who lack realistic expectations of prototyping outcomes.

Major guidelines for developing a prototype are to work in manageable modules and to build and to modify the prototype rapidly.

PROBLEMS AND EXERCISES

1. What are the objectives of prototyping?
2. Distinguish between the notion of a prototype and a production system. Would planning for each be different?
3. What skills are needed for a successful prototyping process, regardless of the prototyping mode? Who has to have those skills?
4. What is meant by a prototype that is a model containing some, but not all, of the essential features of the system?
5. List the disadvantages of using prototyping.
6. Can prototyping be considered a license to change one's mind? Discuss.
7. What are the criteria for deciding whether a system should be prototyped and how the prototyping process should be managed?
8. What may happen if the part of the system is prototyped, but no user feedback about it is incorporated into successive iterations?
9. Prototyping is immensely appealing as the first workable solution to the definition problem. Do you agree with this statement? Why or why not?
10. Could you dispense with SDLC and prototype every project?
11. Are any elements of the prototyping process difficult to manage?
12. To ensure a prompt delivery of the prototype, what elements of the prototyping process must be controlled?

13. In a paragraph, comment on the importance of fast turnaround time for delivery of models to be evaluated by the users.

14. If users expect to use prototypes "as is," what problems may arise?

15. List all the planning steps required for introducing prototyping in the development of computer information systems. How can people plan for a method they have not used before?

16. Briefly describe the major prototyping life cycle models.

17. What are the software development tools needed in a successful prototyping project?

18. Comment on the following notion: "Prototyping drastically reduces exposure to failure." Does this notion have any relation to the management of the prototyping projects? Discuss.

19. Why is training essential if you are trying to introduce the prototyping approach in an organization?

20. Who should be trained in the prototyping approach and why?

21. Describe the tasks with which the manager of the prototyping projects should be most concerned. Would this depend on the type of prototyping mode?

22. Prototyping is by nature volatile and cannot be predefined in terms of time and cost. Do you agree with this? Why or why not?

23. You are the project manager for the development of a new online order entry system. Your upper management has decided that prototyping will be appropriate to use. Describe how you will go about selecting your prototyping team.

24. How often should the new version of the prototype be released during the prototyping project? Would this depend on the type of prototype? On the number of people involved in the prototyping process?

25. Perhaps the best way to avoid building new application systems is to install application packages. Discuss this point of view.

26. Do you suppose that throwaway prototyping requires a change in attitude toward one's work? Whom (if any) does this change affect? Specify your position.

27. Comment on the following notion: "Designers who use prototyping to develop applications have difficulty controlling and managing the design process." Which of the many prototyping pitfalls may be involved here?

28. Comment on some obstacles standing in the way of prototyping.

29. Prototyping can be considered as much an art as a science. Would you agree with this statement? Why or why not?

30. Within the spirit of the prototyping method, most of the steps of the process can be measured and evaluated. Would you agree?

31. Should there be any standards in prototyping? If so, standards of what? Discuss.

32. Can organizational culture have an effect on the success of the use of the prototyping methodology?

33. What is the key focal point around which the prototyping process must be carried out? Try to give some specific examples.

PROJECTS

1. Refer to the article "Accelerated Information Systems Development in the Army" from the *SIM Spectrum*, Vol. 4, No. 3, 1987, and analyze the main steps of the Contemporary Life Cycle Development process. How does it differ from the prototyping approaches described so far? Why was this approach used? Why was it successful? Can it be used for any type of information system? Prepare a brief addressing each point.

2. Interview an information system manager of a business organization with which you are familiar. Ask about the current information systems under development. Is the traditional development life cycle approach used? Analyze why or why not. Include a brief on the nature of the planned application(s). Could prototyping be used? Is it used? If not, why not? What managerial issues are involved in his or her choice of the developmental approach? Report on your findings.

REFERENCES AND SUGGESTED READINGS

1. Babcock, C. "Prototyping, ADS/Online join to triple productivity." *Computerworld*, Vol. 20, No. 14, April 7, 1986, pp. 29-30.

2. Belardo, S., and Karwan, K. R. "The development of a disaster management support system through prototyping." *Information and Management*, Vol. 10, No. 2, February 1986, pp. 93-102.

3. Boar, B. H. *Application Prototyping: A Requirements Definition Strategy For the 80s*. New York: John Wiley & Sons, 1984.

4. Budde, R., et. al. *Approaches to Prototyping*. Berlin: Springer-Verlag, 1984.

5. Cesena, M. L., and Jones, W. O. "Accelerated information system development in the army." *SIM Spectrum*, Vol. 4, No. 3, September 1987, pp. 1-8.

6. Guimaraes, T. "Prototyping: Orchestrating for success." *Datamation*, Vol. 33, No. 23, December 1987, pp. 101-106.

7. Helander, G. A. "Improving system usability for business professionals." *IBM Systems Journal*, Vol. 20, No. 3, September 1981, pp. 294-305.

8. Hopmans, R. G. "Prototyping an expert system." *Computing Canada*, Vol. 13, No. 17, August 20, 1987, pp. 20-21.

9. Janson, M. A., and Smith, L. D. "Prototyping for systems development: A critical appraisal." *MIS Quarterly*, Vol. 9, No. 4, December 1985, pp. 305-315.

10. King, W. R. "Alternative designs in information systems development." *MIS Quarterly*, Vol. 6, No. 4, December 1982, pp. 31-42.

11. Lackman, M. "Controlling the project development cycle: Part 3—Tools for successful project management." *Journal of Systems Management*, Vol. 38, No. 2, 1987, pp. 16-27.

12. Lynch, B. "Job matching by computer." *Best's Review (Prop/Casualty)*, Vol. 87, No. 12, April 1987, pp. 84, 86.

13. Mason, R. E. A., and Carey, T. T. "Prototyping interactive information systems." *Communications of the ACM*, Vol. 26, No. 5, May 1983, pp. 347-354.

14. Medsker, L. R. "An interactive DSS for energy policy analysis." *Communications of the ACM*, November 1984.

15. Staw, B. M., and Ross, J. "Knowing when to pull the plug." *Harvard Business Review*, Vol. 65, No. 2, 1987, pp. 68-74.

16. Weisman, R. "Six steps to AI-based functional prototyping." *Datamation*, Vol. 33, No. 15, August 1, 1987, pp. 71-72.

17. Willis, T. H., Huston, C. R., and d'Ouville, E. L. "Project manager's responsibilities in a prototyping system analysis and design environment." *Project Management Journal*, Vol. 19, No. 1, February 1988, pp. 56-60.

PART III

INTRODUCTION TO A

FOURTH-GENERATION

LANGUAGE: NOMAD

Part III of this book describes how to use NOMAD on PC. In Chapters 9 through 19 we construct an application: A system for a ski rentals operation.

Chapter 9 gives an overview of the NOMAD environment.

Chapter 10 defines the application.

Chapter 11 describes NOMAD procedures.

Chapter 12 describes database definition process.

Chapter 13 considers interactive data entry and file maintenance.

Chapter 14 considers procedural data entry and file maintenance.

Chapter 15 discusses file maintenance using external files.

Chapter 16 describes file manipulation.

Chapter 17 considers standard reporting.

Chapter 18 considers customized reporting.

Chapter 19 discusses system integration.

In this part of the book we use several conventions. Those are:

NOMAD Command names are given in capital letters.

To differentiate between NOMAD's reserved words and the user's assigned words, we show the reserved words in uppercase letters and the assigned words in the lowercase letters. This convention is only for the reader, since NOMAD can accept both upper and lowercase forms.

Keystroke combinations are represented as, for example, CTR/ENTER. This means that keys CTR and ENTER are pressed together, both at the same time.

Defined terms are printed in italics.

CHAPTER 9

Overview of NOMAD Environment

Computers are simply a necessary and enjoyable part of life, like food and books.

Theodore Nelson

9.1 INTRODUCTION

The goals of this chapter are to introduce you to the NOMAD environment and to describe NOMAD in general terms. This general description includes a brief discussion of the cooperative processing capability. In addition, in this chapter, we

- Describe the window environment of NOMAD.
- List the system windows and describe their functions.
- Explain, in general, what a procedure is.
- Identify the basic commands used to move in and out of the NOMAD environment.
- Describe the control of the windows using the System menu.
- Explain what Forms are and list the basic commands used in their creation.
- Explain what an active data dictionary is and name the types of files maintained in a NOMAD data dictionary.
- List the steps required for the creation of an application with NOMAD.

9.2 THE USER PERSPECTIVE

With the advent of powerful personal computers and their proliferation in many organizations, a need has developed for users to communicate with the departmental minicomputer and with a corporate mainframe as well as with each other. In other words, users' applications now must run in and communicate across multiple operating environments. NOMAD supports this mode of operation, which is called cooperative processing.

Cooperative processing is the ability to distribute the processing of an application across multiple CPUs, which results in a multitiered environment of PCs, minis, and mainframes. For example, resource-intensive functions such as user interaction and data validation are processed on a PC. Data integrity and security are maintained in a *shared* environment of the mainframe.

In a cooperative processing application, the application, the processing, and possibly the data are split between the PC and what is often referred to as the *server*.

Cooperative processing technology is becoming important for data processing in many organizations. It can function in these environments: PC to mainframe, PC to database machine, PC to minicomputer, PC to PC.

4GLs such as NOMAD, which include communications facilities, make cooperative processing possible. This is a new technology and its full benefits have not yet been fully assessed. Some obvious benefits of cooperative processing are:

■ Reduced mainframe resource (CPU and memory) usage.

■ Fast response time in user dialogues due to the dedicated use of the PC's CPU.

■ The ability for PC applications to interact with files on databases external to its own.

Figure 9.1 schematically illustrates cooperative processing. Some of the terms that appear in the figure are defined as follows:

■ *User interface* represents the dialogue with the user through menus and forms.

■ *Local access* refers to the maintenance and manipulation of data locally on the PC. Cooperative processing allows the user to have data locally on the PC, as well as to access shared data on the server.

■ *Communications* refers to a 4GL's communications facility. Once the user's access is complete and an action such as add, update, or delete a record is requested from the server, a message is sent to the server through the 4GL's communications facility. Then the PC application can carry out other functions, or it can wait for the server's response.

■ *Language* refers to the 4GL used for all aspects of cooperative processing as well as the application itself.

■ *Data access* refers to the use of shared data sources on the server. Data sources can be data in other databases, for example, in the DB2 or SQL/DS or data on a database machine. (Which database external to its own is accessible depends on the given 4GL.)

The remaining part of this book concentrates on NOMAD, a 4GL with cooperative processing capabilities. NOMAD represents a family of products available for microcomputers, minicomputers, and mainframes. Once you master NOMAD on

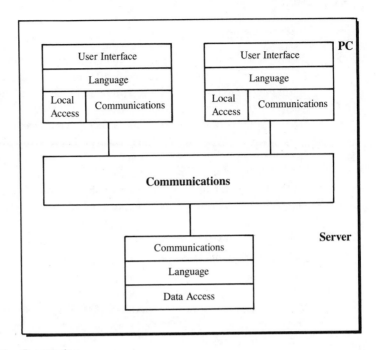

Figure 9.1   Cooperative Processing

a PC, it is easier to learn the form of NOMAD that is intended for the use on the mainframe. NOMAD on a PC complements mainframe NOMAD; it uses the same nonprocedural approaches and procedural syntax as the mainframe version.

9.3 THE NOMAD ENVIRONMENT

When you enter NOMAD on a PC you are in what is called the *Window environment*. Once there, NOMAD commands or procedures (we define procedures shortly) can be executed and the objectives of your specific computer application achieved.

You can work with NOMAD in two modes:

■ Interactive
■ Procedural

You are always in the window environment interactively or procedurally. In interactive mode, a set of system windows is available to you, including a Command window to enter commands. In procedural mode, you enter commands in the Command window.

Interactive Mode

In interactive mode (also called conversational mode), NOMAD commands are executed, one at a time, immediately after they are entered by the user. Think of the Window environment as if it represented a surface of your desk. The windows correspond to different parts of the working space, on which a variety of notes you need in your work are placed. This surface of your desk is very large, and you can keep many things on it, in layers. But you know where things are, and you can browse through your stacks of notes.

Windows are used for entering NOMAD commands and for viewing various types of output. You can customize windows to satisfy the special needs of your application. Windows can be manipulated and browsed through with:

1. A system menu of operations
2. Interactive function keys
3. Commands that operate on windows

Windows can overlap other windows. (The Windows and Forms section of this chapter describes NOMAD windows in detail and describes how to operate in the window environment.)

Procedural Mode

Very often your application may require that many commands be issued in the same sequence. In such a case, it is more efficient to issue them as a group. This group of commands is usually saved in a special file. In NOMAD the file of commands is called a *procedure*, and it can contain either simple one-line command statements or complex programs with hundreds of lines and with control logic. To activate the file, simply type its name and the NOMAD commands contained in that file are executed automatically.

9.4 MOVING IN AND OUT OF THE NOMAD ENVIRONMENT

Starting NOMAD

We assume that NOMAD is installed on your microcomputer and that it is residing in a directory named NOMAD. (To review how to install NOMAD on your microcomputer, refer to Appendix A.)

To start NOMAD you must give the name of the directory where your software is residing and then issue the invoking command: NOMAD. Thus, in the DOS environment, your steps will be as follows:

```
C> cd\NOMAD
C> NOMAD
```

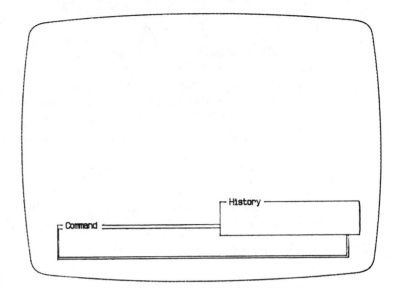

Figure 9.2 NOMAD Screen

The first command is the DOS command for changing the directory from the current directory to the NOMAD directory. The second command invokes NOMAD.

After the first screen (with the copyright information, software version number, and so on) is displayed, and after you have hit the ENTER key, you are placed in NOMAD's window environment.

The screen you then see is illustrated in Figure 9.2. This screen shows the Command and History windows. You enter all your commands in the Command window. When a command is accepted, it appears in the History window. More about the windows later.

NOMAD Commands

We start with the set of commands used for moving in and out of NOMAD. Other NOMAD commands are introduced throughout the rest of the book, when needed.

QUIT

The QUIT command shuts down the interactive NOMAD environment and returns control to the operating system. Access to NOMAD databases is then concluded. Type:

    QUIT

in the Command window, and you are returned to the system level.

SYSTEM

The SYSTEM command allows the execution of the operating system commands from within the NOMAD environment.

When you issue the SYSTEM command without any additional parameters, NOMAD switches you to the operating system environment. For example, if your operating system is DOS, you will be put in the DOS environment, ready to execute multiple DOS commands. If you then type:

```
EXIT
```

you will come back to where you started.

You can also execute a specific system command directly when you issue the SYSTEM command with additional parameters. For example, typing:

```
SYSTEM DIR C:\BOOK/W
```

automatically takes you to DOS and lists all the files on your hard disk, in your BOOK directory, in wide format.

The general format of the SYSTEM command is:

```
SYSTEM operating-system-command-name command-parameter
```

where operating-system-command-name is any valid command name in the accessed operating system and command-parameter is this specific command parameter. (Both operating-system-command-name and command-parameter are optional.)

EDIT

The EDIT command invokes the operating system editor from within the NOMAD environment. For example, if you type:

```
EDIT
```

the operating system editor is invoked. Because the name of a file to be edited was not specified this is done from the editor environment.

On the other hand, if you enter:

```
EDIT procski1
```

the file named procski1 becomes ready for editing right away.

Since you invoked your editor from the NOMAD environment, when you are finished editing you are automatically back to NOMAD. To start up consecutive editing session with the same file you only need to type:

```
EDIT
```

(since NOMAD automatically stores the name of the edited file).

Which editor is invoked depends on the value of the system variable specifying it. System variables are variables that allow you to define your system. The system variable used to store the name of the default editor is &EDITOR. [NOMAD uses the ampersand (&) to indicate a variable name.] In NOMAD, **EDLIN** (the DOS editor) is the default. Rather than use this default editor you can indicate different editor for your specific NOMAD session by entering:

```
&EDITOR = 'your editor name'
```

where **'your editor name'** is the name of the editor you want to use during the session.

If you want another editor to become the default editor for all your work with NOMAD, enter:

```
CHANGE SYSTEM EDITOR = 'your editor name'
```

where 'your editor name' is the name of the editor you want to become the default.

9.5 NOMAD WINDOWS AND FORMS

NOMAD Windows

NOMAD on the PC operates exclusively in the window environment. These windows are used to enter commands and data and to display information. Windows can be arranged in any way that seems best for your application. You have complete control over their size, location, format, and color.

When you work in the window environment, only one window is active at any specific moment. But you can freely switch from window to window. The currently active window is distinguished by a double border and it has the cursor in it. (See Figure 9.2.)

Windows can overlap other windows. The data in the covered windows is not lost; it is only hidden behind the window that is currently active.

The NOMAD window environment features a group of special windows called *system windows*. Some of them appear automatically when you first enter the window environment; some can be activated when you need them or they appear as the result of specific conditions such as errors and warnings. The NOMAD system windows are as follows:

- System Menu
- Command
- History
- Output
- Error
- List

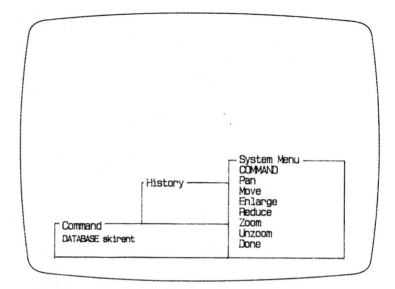

Figure 9.3 System Menu Window

When NOMAD is initiated, both the Command and History windows appear on your screen. The Command window is active. (Note in Figure 9.2. where the cursor is positioned.)

System Menu Window

The System menu is used to manipulate other windows. When the System menu is invoked, other activities are suspended. For example, NOMAD commands cannot be run while the System menu is displayed.

You invoke the System menu with the PF1 key (F1 key on the IBM PC keyboard). When you display the System Menu window, you are in system mode. The same key is used to return you to the other NOMAD windows and to leave the system mode. It acts like a toggle switch. Figure 9.3 illustrates the System menu window.

The choices available on the System menu and their meanings are as follows:

- *Window Name*—The entry that appears at the top of the System menu is the name of the window that will be manipulated with the operations listed in the System menu.

- *Pan*—Allows you to view "hidden" data by moving the window over the data currently outside of the area exposed by the window. The cursor disappears from the window and the directional arrow keys are used to move (pan) the window over the data.

- *Move*—Allows you to move the window to the new location on the screen by means of the directional arrow keys.

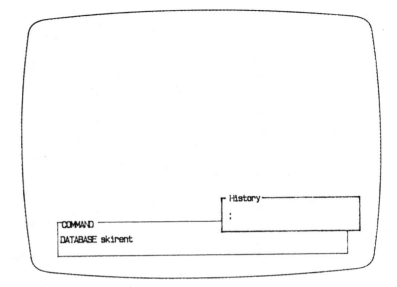

Figure 9.4 Command Window

- *Enlarge*—Expands the window to the size you indicate by using the directional arrow keys.
- *Reduce*—Reduces the window to the size you indicate.
- *Zoom*—Expands the window to the full size of your screen.
- *Unzoom*—Returns the window to the size and location it occupied prior to a ZOOM operation.
- *Done*—Terminates the System menu and returns control to the window from which the System menu was initially invoked.

Command Window

The primary way to communicate with NOMAD when you are in the window environment is through the Command window. In it you enter NOMAD commands, system commands, and names of files containing procedures.

You can enter several commands at once by stringing them together and using a semicolon (;) as a separator. A command can be continued over more than one line.

To execute the command in the Command window, press the ENTER key. Figure 9.4 illustrates an active Command window containing the command: DATABASE skirent.

History Window

The History window contains just that, a history or catalog (archive) of your successful NOMAD session. During a session with NOMAD each (syntactically

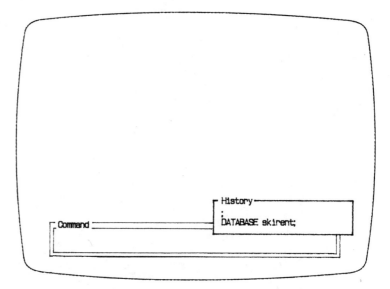

Figure 9.5 History Window

correct) command entered in the Command window is automatically recorded in the History window. (The History window archives all error-free commands. On the screen you see only a portion of the archive. Refer to the section on the NOMAD Window environment to recall how to access the full content of this and other windows.)

In addition, all recorded commands are automatically captured to a HIS-TORY.NOM file. (NOMAD automatically creates this filename including the extension .NOM.) The HISTORY.NOM file is updated each time a new command is appended to it. This file is kept only for the duration of the specific NOMAD session. When you exit NOMAD, the HISTORY.NOM file is automatically erased.

To build a permanent procedure from the commands saved in the HIS-TORY.NOM file, use the EDIT command to create a new file into which you can copy captured commands. (Do not edit the HISTORY.NOM file directly! NOMAD remembers the size of the HISTORY.NOM file, and it appends commands to the end of this file as they are archived in the History window. Editing and altering the size of the HISTORY.NOM file directly can produce unpredictable results.)

You can use the History window during your NOMAD session to review and recall previously executed commands. The commands from the History window can be recalled to the Command window by pressing the PF3 key (the processing function key F3 of the IBM PC keyboard). Figure 9.5 illustrates the History window for the command executed in Figure 9.4.

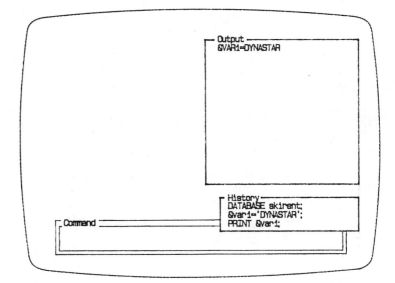

Figure 9.6   Output Window

Output Window

The Output window appears when NOMAD generates outputs in response to any output command (except the LIST command; more about this command later).

If the desired output is too large to be viewed in the Output window in its entirety, you can use the directional arrow keys or the [PAGE UP] and [PAGE DOWN] keys to pan the window over the data. Many different NOMAD commands can show a record of the output at any one time. We discuss them in later chapters.

A log of all output for the current NOMAD session is maintained automatically. The output is captured in a file called OUTPUT.LOG. This log file is saved permanently. It will remain in the directory until it is erased or replaced by a new OUTPUT.LOG file created in a subsequent NOMAD session. Figure 9.6 illustrates the Output window.

Error Window

The Error window appears only when an error is detected in the commands entered via the Command window. An error message is displayed in the Error window, and the cursor is placed under incorrect part of the command, in the Command window, with the incorrect part highlighted. This means the command is ready for correction.

The Error window is removed from the screen the moment the error is corrected or the incorrect command is cleared from the Command window.

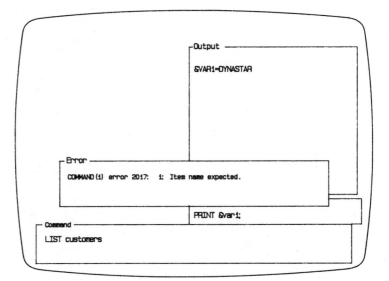

Figure 9.7 Error Window

As in the case of the Output window, NOMAD creates a permanent file called ERROR.LOG for storing all the error messages. This file also remains in the file directory until erased or replaced by a new file created by a subsequent NOMAD session. Figure 9.7 illustrates the Error window.

List Window

The List window appears when the LIST command is executed. The LIST command is a very powerful command used to generate formatted reports from the database. (Chapters 17 and 18 discuss the LIST command in detail and show how to use it to generate complex reports.)

The LIST.LOG file automatically captures all the output displayed in the List window. This file is permanently saved (as was the case for the OUTPUT.LOG and ERROR.LOG files), and it remains in the file directory until it is erased or replaced by a new LIST.LOG file created in a subsequent session.

The List window can be enlarged if necessary. You can use the directional arrow keys or the [PgUp] and [PgDn] keys to scroll through the information in the window as well. Figure 9.8 illustrates the output from a LIST command placed in the List window.

Controlling Windows in NOMAD

Operation on and control of windows can be performed by using one of the following methods:

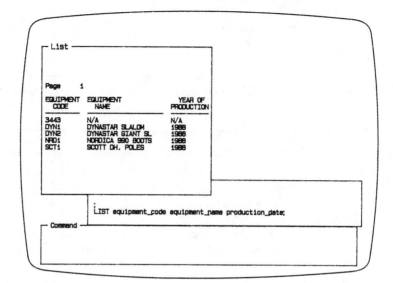

Figure 9.8   List Window

1. System menu
2. Function keys
3. Window commands

We consider the operation and control method involving the System menu in the next section. The function keys method is left to the reader (see the *NOMAD Reference Manual*). The window commands method is described in Chapter 14 of this book.

Manipulating the NOMAD Windows Using the System Menu

You first need to select the window you want to control. This is done by invoking the System menu. Press the PF1 function key to take you to the System menu. Next, position the cursor on the Window Name menu option (at the top of the System menu) and press the ENTER key repeatedly until the name of the desired window appears.

(There is another way of selecting the window you want to control. Before you invoke the System menu, move the cursor to the window you want to control and *then* press the PF1 function key. The System Menu automatically displays the name of the window in the Window Name menu option.)

Now you can activate any option of the System menu simply by moving (using directional cursor keys) to the desired option and pressing the ENTER key. If you select the Zoom, Unzoom, or Done option, the appropriate operation will be performed immediately, and the system will be ready for your next request. When you invoke Pan, Enlarge, Reduce, or Move, you need to use the directional keys to perform required function: left, right, up, down, HOME, END, [PgUp] and [PgDn].

For example, if you want to move the History window from its present position to another position on the screen and the cursor is currently in the Command window, you would take the following steps:

1. Press the PF2 key (the function key that moves the cursor from window to window) until the cursor enters the window you want, in this case the History window. Because the History window now contains the cursor, it has become the active window.

2. Activate the System menu by pressing the PF1 key.

Note: You can reverse the order of steps 1 and 2. That is, you can first activate the System menu, and then position the cursor on the Window Name option and press the ENTER key until the name "History Window" appears in this field.

3. Use the directional arrow keys to position the cursor on the Move option and press the ENTER key.

4. Use the directional arrow keys to move the window left, right, up, or down to the desired position.

5. Press the ENTER key. The History window is positioned where you want it. The System menu is now ready for your next selection.

6. Press the PF1 key. The System Menu disappears. (You are out of system mode.)

The task of moving the History window is finished. The History window will remain in this position to the end of the current NOMAD session unless you decide to change it again.

To make this new position permanent (that is, the default) for subsequent NOMAD sessions, you must execute the command:

    WINDOW SAVE SYSTEM

This command permanently saves the current position, size, and color of the window in the data dictionary or until you decide to change the attributes of the window again.

Keys Used for Editing in the Command Window

Some of the keyboard keys have special uses in the Command window. They are used for editing your sequence of commands. A few must be pressed simultaneously. For example, the notation CTRL/ENTER means that you need to press both keys at the same time. These editing keys or key combinations are as follows:

- **HOME**—Moves the cursor to the beginning of a current sequence of commands.

- **END**—Moves the cursor to the end of the current sequence of commands.

- **CTRL/ENTER**—Moves the cursor to the next line, without executing the current line.

- **PF3**—Retrieves the previous command from the History window. Press once for each command to be retrieved.

- **INS**—Allows any characters to be inserted (not overtyped) when you are typing in the Command window.

- **DEL**—Deletes the character at the cursor.

- **ALT/D**—Deletes the current line at the cursor.

- **CTRL/END**—Deletes everything from the current position of the cursor to the end of the line.

- **CTRL/HOME**—Deletes everything from the current position of the cursor to the end of the Command window.

NOMAD Forms

NOMAD creates System Menu, Command, History, List, Output, and Error windows for you automatically. However, you (the user) can create windows. These user-defined windows are called *Forms*. Forms allow you to create *your own* window environment. They usually represent the first step in the development of the customized interactive computer applications using NOMAD.

A Form can be larger than the physical screen of your terminal. The maximum size of a Form in NOMAD is 255 characters wide and 255 lines long. If you decide to not specify the size of the Form, NOMAD automatically sizes your Form to the smallest size that can contain all the fields and labels you specified for the Form.

Four basic commands are used to create Forms:

1. FORM—Starts the Form definition.
2. LABEL—Allows one to define annotation on a Form, such as headers, prompts, and instructions.
3. FIELD—Defines the input area of the Form.
4. FEND—Ends the Form definition and adds a given Form to the application's data dictionary.

The FORM, LABEL, and FIELD commands have many attributes that you can use to enhance the appearance of the Form or to satisfy a specific processing condition of the application. These attributes and examples of their usage are discussed extensively in Chapter 14. For now we concentrate on defining Forms.

A Form is defined in two ways:

1. You can use your system editor to create a file containing all the commands needed to build a Form. This file is called a *procedure*. You execute this procedure from the NOMAD Command window.

2. You can use NOMAD interactively. The necessary commands are entered and executed one at a time, allowing you to experiment with and prototype your Forms. For example, you can experiment with the visual aesthetics and the desired clarity for the intended use of the Form under construction. As each command is executed, it is checked for errors immediately, forcing you to correct errors one at a time.

Using NOMAD interactively can help to speed up the final Form development process. For example: assume you want to modify the Form you created in a current NOMAD session. From the History window, you will recall to the Command window all the commands you used to create this particular Form. Then you can edit the commands and introduce needed changes.

When you are satisfied with the appearance of the Form on the screen, store its definition in the application's data dictionary (discussed in the next section) by executing the FEND (FormEND) command. The Form is automatically stored, the screen is cleared, and you are ready for the next task.

9.6 NOMAD DATA DICTIONARY

The NOMAD data dictionary is the central depository of information about the databases and the applications you develop. The data dictionary records and maintains this information automatically. That is, every change you make to the databases or the application is recorded and put into effect in every place that is affected by the change. This type of dictionary is called an *active* data dictionary.

The NOMAD active data dictionary consists of three types of files:

1. System files (read-only files)

2. Application files

3. Database files

System files contain such information about the system as:

■ System variables [variables that define the system's default values (for example, a variable that holds the name of the system editor—see the example at the beginning of this chapter)]

■ Error messages

■ Default window descriptions (such as location, size, and color)

System files are identified by the .sdb extension in their name. For example, information on system variables is stored in a file called nomad.sdb. System files are read-only files, that is, you cannot change their content.

Application files store information on your specific application. They store information on:

- Application variables
- Forms definitions
- Applications procedures
- User-generated error messages
- Changes to the system defaults (such as windows size, color, and editor).

Application files are identified by their .udb ("u" stands for user) extension. For example, the nomad.udb file contains information about the system configuration that the application is using (information on the color and position of system windows, the editor to be used, and so on.)

Database files contain information about the application's database, that is, information on items, display formats, internal formats, and all other attributes of the application's database. These files, assigned the extension .ndb, are automatically created for each database. For example, if in your application you have a database with the name SKIRENT, NOMAD automatically creates the skirent.ndb file to hold all the information on this database.

Having an active, automatically maintained data dictionary offers the following benefits:

1. You do not have to perform any maintenance for your application's data dictionary. Since the data dictionary is active, all the maintenance is automatic.

2. You have easy access to information about your application, for example, standards, file and database definitions, cross-references, and documentation in the database schema.

3. Procedures and Forms are translated automatically. Translated versions are stored in the data dictionary the first time you execute them. From then on, the translated versions are used when you run procedures or Forms. That is why the execution is faster after the first run time.

We discuss how to query NOMAD's active data dictionary and how to use commands that directly affect the information stored in it in the later chapters.

Removing Database Information

Although NOMAD maintains the information in the data dictionary automatically, sometimes you may need to remove some items from it. For example, you may want to clean up and remove some database information that is no longer needed.

To remove an item from your database and at the same time from your data dictionary, follow these steps:

1. Edit your database schema (the description of the structure of your database) by making any required changes.
2. Issue the SCHEMA REORG command. (REORG stands for reorganize.)

With these two steps, the structure of the appropriate database is automatically changed, and the data dictionary is automatically updated.

Removing a Database

To remove a database from the data dictionary, issue the following command:

```
SCHEMA mydatabase DELETE;
```

where mydatabase is the name of database you want to remove. This command erases the data and the corresponding database structure information from the data dictionary.

Removing Non-Database Information

To remove non-database information from the data dictionary use the PURGE command. With this command you can remove procedures, Forms, or any defined items. Enter the following command:

```
PURGE myentity;
```

where myentity is the name of a procedure, a Form, or a defined item. The specified item is then removed from the data dictionary.

If, in your data dictionary, you have two or more entities with the same name (and this is quite possible), specify the type of entity you are removing. For example, the following command:

```
PURGE PROC myentity;
```

removes from the data dictionary only the procedure named myentity. All other entities with the same name remain.

9.7 STEPS NEEDED TO CREATE A COMPUTER APPLICATION WITH NOMAD

When using NOMAD to create an application, you should follow these steps:

1. *Database definition.* Define the data schema that contains a description of the data files, exact nature of the data items, physical data storage formats, output

formats, data integrity and control procedures, security and restrictions on data usage, and data accessing methods.

2. *Physical database creation and maintenance*. Create physical records in your database (this is called populating your database) by any of the following three methods:

  a. Enter data using NOMAD's interactive mode.

  b. Create custom Forms and procedures to be used for data entry.

  c. Enter data from the external transaction files.

3. *Database access and reporting*. Retrieve the data from the application's database and generate reports on these data. To do so, you can either use NOMAD's interactive mode or you can build custom procedures.

4. *System integration*. Construct a procedure that integrates the functions developed in all the previous steps so that it all works together.

The remaining chapters of this part of the book are devoted to each step of this process:

■ Chapter 10 defines our application.

■ Chapter 11 briefly looks at the NOMAD procedures and some of the commands associated with them.

■ Chapter 12 describes the database definition process.

■ Chapters 13 through 15 cover data entry and file maintenance.

■ Chapter 16 looks at data manipulation.

■ Chapters 17 and 18 describe the reporting process.

■ Chapter 19 describes system integration.

9.8 SUMMARY

NOMAD operates in the window environment, through which you enter and view information. The window with a cursor in it is the active window. The active window also has a double border around it. Only one window may be active at a time. You can scroll through the data within an active window. Windows may overlap each other. You can change the location, size, and color of the windows to suit your needs.

The system windows are:

■ *System Menu window*—lets you control other windows (size, position, and so on) and is activated with the PF1 key.

■ *Command window*—represents the primary way you communicate with NOMAD: You enter commands there.

■ *History window*—stores accepted and executed commands. This window acts as a log for all correct commands entered.

■ *Error window*—appears when an error is detected, is automatically removed when the incorrect command is corrected or cleared.

■ *Output window*—appears when you issue a command requesting an output. Output to this command is displayed. If the result is too large, you may enlarge this window or pan the data.

■ *List window*—appears when a LIST command is executed. In this window, report results are displayed.

The audit trail for your session with NOMAD is maintained in the session logs. Each log duplicates the information maintained in the specific window during your session. These log files (HISTORY.NOM, OUTPUT.LOG, LIST.LOG, and ERROR.LOG) capture all the information displayed in their respective windows.

You can create your own customized windows, called Forms. A Form is simply a user-defined format for entering and displaying information. Forms are built by using a combination of commands such as FORM, FIELD, LABEL, and FEND. They may be defined by using the Command window or procedures.

A procedure can be either a simple set of command statements or complex program with control logic. Procedures are used for a variety of processing tasks. You can execute the commands in a procedure by typing the procedure's name in the Command window. (Chapter 11 discusses procedures and procedural control commands in detail.)

The data dictionary is a central repository of information about your NOMAD environment and your application. It is an active dictionary—whenever you make changes that affect it, the data dictionary is automatically updated. It consists of three sets of files:

1. *System files*, which contain system information such as default values, and error messages.

2. *Application files*, which contain application information such as a detailed description of your database, relationships between entities, and application procedures.

3. *Database files*, which contain application database information such as display formats, internal formats, and all other attributes of the application's database.

When using NOMAD to create an application you should follow these steps:

1. Database definition

2. Physical database creation and maintenance

3. Database access and reporting

4. System integration

EXERCISES

1. Briefly describe the NOMAD environment.

2. List NOMAD system windows.

3. Assume that your screen displays many overlapping windows. How would you know which window is active?

4. What is the primary way to communicate with NOMAD?

5. Would the LIST command generate output in the Output window?

6. You cannot see all the data that resulted from the response to an output-generating command. What do you do?

7. What are the System menu choices? List them and briefly describe the function of each.

8. How is an audit trail of your NOMAD session maintained?

9. What do LIST.LOG, OUTPUT.LOG and ERROR.LOG files have in common?

10. Where do commands from the History window go?

11. How does the HISTORY.NOM file differ from the other log files?

12. How would you, using the Command window, permanently change to another editor?

13. What is an active data dictionary?

14. What information is stored in the NOMAD data dictionary?

15. List data dictionary files and briefly describe what they contain.

16. What is a Form? Why is it useful?

17. Do you think you can have multiple Forms on the screen at once? Can they overlap? Can user Forms be mixed with system windows (List window, for example)?

18. How can Forms be defined?

19. Which keys function in all the NOMAD windows?

20. You are in the Command window and you have entered several commands. What happens when you press the HOME key?

21. What happens when you select Pan from the System menu?

22. You are in the History window. You need to expand and center the window on the screen. Which of the System menu options allows you to do that?

23. Why and when do you need a Form that is larger than the physical screen of your terminal? Describe a hypothetical situation when a Form of this type can be useful.

24. Comment on the statement: "The data dictionary is a database about the database. An active data dictionary has an effect on database operations."

REFERENCES

NOMAD Reference Manual, *MUST Software International*, Division of U3S International, Ltd., Wilton, Connecticut, April 1988.

CHAPTER 10

Case Description

If one does not begin with a right attitude, there is little hope for a right ending.

Kung Fu meditation

10.1 INTRODUCTION

This chapter introduces our case study. The intent of this case study is to present a computer application that is sufficiently sophisticated (but not too complicated) that all the major 4GL commands can be gradually illustrated. We assume that the system analysis stage was already accomplished, and we use our 4GL for what it is intended—a programming tool.

This assumption leads to the next one, that is, that the design solution arrived at is what is needed. We do not discuss the efficacy of this particular solution (this is a subject for a text on system analysis and design). The design solution serves as a vehicle to introduce the use of a specific 4GL. Our focus is on the programming productivity tool: NOMAD on a PC. The tool is used in the coding stage of the system development process.

10.2 SKI SHOP RENTAL OPERATIONS

Bob's Ski Shop is a well-established, retail ski equipment store. Similar to most of the other ski shops, this store rents skis, boots, and poles to customers who like to try out new equipment before they decide to buy. The rental operation of this store is independent from its retail operations.

The management of the store decided to computerize the information flow in the rental portion of the operation for several reasons.

- Some customers complained of slow service.
- Rental shop managers said they needed quicker access to rental information (in order to perform their current marketing functions better and perhaps to better anticipate future opportunities) and improved inventory control.
- Other ski stores in this market had computerized their rental operations, and the management started to feel the pressure to "keep up with the Joneses."

The main goals of this rental shop are to equip each customer with proper equipment, to ensure customer safety, and at the same time to keep track of rented equipment.

Since a large portion of the customers are repeat customers, the quality of the rental services should improve markedly, if, for example, information on boot size and preferred equipment types is easily available. This would reduce service time and eliminate the need to collect these and other data each time the repeat customer comes in.

Most of the customers who rent equipment are beginning skiers. The store management feels that by giving these customers quality service and equipment, they eventually convert a renting customer to a buying one.

What's more, the information on who the present customers are and how often they rent their equipment can help management plan future advertising and promotional campaigns.

Therefore, the decision was made that the rental shop needed a computer-based system to manage the renting operation effectively, to keep track of inventories, and to improve customer services by substantially cutting the service time.

10.3 DATA PROCESSING NEEDS

The value of any computerized system can be measured only in terms of the output produced, but it is not the quantity or the variety of outputs that is most important. Our computerized rental system should not invent new and complex methods for performing routine tasks. Basically the system should give management better information on the rental inventory and customers. Its main function is to reduce service time.

During the design stage, the decision was made that the system must be totally interactive. It should guide its user through each function with menus, and query the user for any information it needs. No prior knowledge of computers or data processing should be required of the personnel operating the system. Also, no supplementary documentation should be needed once the intended users (that is, the rental shop technicians) obtain a minimal amount of experience in system operation.

10.4 MAIN MENU COMPONENTS

The main menu that appears on the screen when the Ski Rental System is first requested is shown in Figure 10.1. The user positions the cursor on the desired selection or enters the first letter of that selection and presses the ENTER key to invoke the specific module of the system.

Brief definitions of modules are as follows:

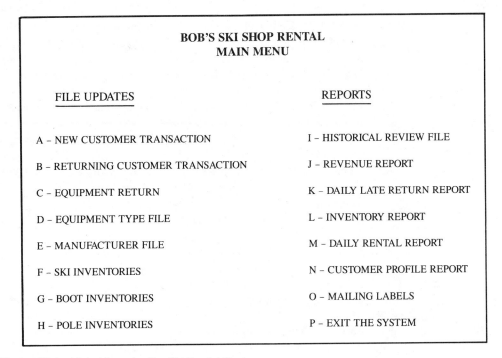

BOB'S SKI SHOP RENTAL
MAIN MENU

FILE UPDATES   REPORTS

A – NEW CUSTOMER TRANSACTION   I – HISTORICAL REVIEW FILE

B – RETURNING CUSTOMER TRANSACTION   J – REVENUE REPORT

C – EQUIPMENT RETURN   K – DAILY LATE RETURN REPORT

D – EQUIPMENT TYPE FILE   L – INVENTORY REPORT

E – MANUFACTURER FILE   M – DAILY RENTAL REPORT

F – SKI INVENTORIES   N – CUSTOMER PROFILE REPORT

G – BOOT INVENTORIES   O – MAILING LABELS

H – POLE INVENTORIES   P – EXIT THE SYSTEM

Figure 10.1   Main Menu for the Ski Rental System

A.   **NEW CUSTOMER TRANSACTION**—Captures detailed customer information and creates the renting transaction record for the first-time customer.

B.   **RETURNING CUSTOMER TRANSACTION**—Creates the renting transaction record for the returning customer. (Most of the detailed information is available from the customer's file which was created in the first module.)

C.   **EQUIPMENT RETURN**—Updates inventories and the renting transaction record (from the B module) when the customer returns equipment.

D.   **EQUIPMENT TYPE FILE**—Maintains a file on the type of equipment held in the ski store inventories.

E.   **MANUFACTURER FILE**—Maintains information on the manufacturers of the ski equipment kept in the store's inventories.

F.   **SKI INVENTORIES**—Maintains the Ski Inventory file.

G.   **BOOT INVENTORIES**—Maintains the Boot Inventory file.

H.   **POLE INVENTORIES**—Maintains the Poles Inventory file.

I.   **HISTORICAL REVENUE FILE**—Updates the Historical Revenue file which holds the weekly rental earnings from the previous year.

J. **REVENUE REPORT**—Creates the revenue report for any reporting period selected and gives comparisons and percent differences in the revenues earned from period to period.

K. **DAILY LATE RETURN REPORT**—Lists customers who have not returned rental equipment by the due date.

L. **INVENTORY REPORT**—Lists all the equipment available for renting at any time.

M. **DAILY RENTAL REPORT**—Lists all skis, boots, and poles rented during the day.

N. **CUSTOMER PROFILE REPORT**—Reports on who rental customers are and why, when, and where they are skiing. (The report can be useful in future advertising campaigns.)

O. **MAILING LABELS**—Creates mailing labels to be used in advertising campaigns.

P. **EXIT THE SYSTEM**—Allows the user of the rental system to terminate the processing and to exit the Ski Rental System.

The data flow diagram for the system is given in Figure 10.2. The Equipment Type and Manufacturer files are essentially table-lookups (described when we discuss these files) for the inventory files and are not included in the data flow diagram in Figure 10.2. The Historical Revenue file is not included either.

10.5 DESIGN SPECIFICATIONS

We now concentrate on the design specifications by which we define outputs, inputs, and procedures for processing the data. We look at:

■ Output (report) specifications
■ File designs
■ Input screens
■ Process specifications

Report Specifications

We start with specifications for the reports. For each report listed in Figure 10.1 the following subsections give a short description of the overall characteristics of the given report and specify the report variables.

Revenue Report

The Revenue Report has the following general characteristics:

■ Presents daily revenues for specified weeks in the present year and compares them with the revenues for the same calendar weeks of the previous year.

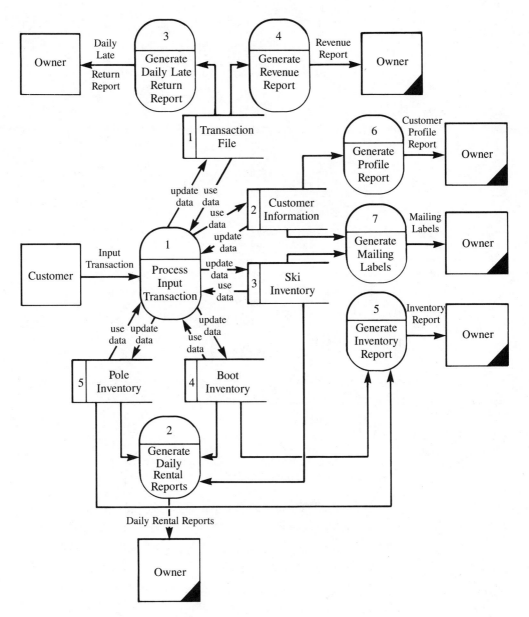

Figure 10.2   Data Flow Diagram for the Ski Rental System

- Provides quick comparison of revenues for management controls.
- Can be called up on the screen or printed out.
- Is arranged in order of date in the specified period or on a weekly basis for summaries and comparisons.

```
                          BOB'S SKI SHOP (1)
   Page: 1     (2)       DATE - 12/29/89   (3)
                         RENTING REVENUE REPORT (4)
                       FOR PERIOD 12/14/89 TO 12/27/89   (5)

          (6)                       (7)
          DATE                    REVENUES
   DECEMBER   14                    125.00
             15                    325.00
             16                    215.00
             17                    562.50
             18                    322.15
             19                    456.00
             20                    620.00

        WEEKLY SUBTOTAL -- 2,622.65    (8)
   LAST YEAR WEEKLY TOTAL -- 3,250.00     (9)
                   CHANGE -- -19.3%    (10)

   DECEMBER   21                    325.00
             22                    450.00
             23                    630.00
             24                    460.00
             25                    350.00
             26                    700.00
             27                    900.00
        WEEKLY SUBTOTAL -- 3,805.00
   LAST YEAR WEEKLY TOTAL -- 3,200.00
                   CHANGE --  18.9%

        TOTAL FOR PERIOD -- $6,427.65    (11)
          LAST YEAR TOTAL -- $6,450.00    (12)
                   CHANGE -- .03%        (13)
```

Figure 10.3 Revenue Report for an Arbitrary Period

Figure 10.3 shows the format of the Revenue Report.
The report contains the following items:

1. Major heading (the same for all reports from the system)
2. Report page number
3. Report request date (current date)
4. Report title
5. Requested reporting period (obtained by prompting the user)
6. Consecutive reporting dates
7. Daily revenues (from the daily rental Transaction file)
8. Weekly total (calculated)
9. Last year's weekly total (from the Historical Revenue file)
10. Revenue change (as percent) between current year's weekly total and last year's weekly total (calculated)
11. Total for the reporting period (calculated)

```
          BOB'S SKI SHOP  (1)
Page: 1   (2)           DATE - 12/29/89  (3)
                   DAILY LATE RETURN REPORT  (4)


    (5)          (6)        (7)    (8)    (9)      (10)
CUSTOMER NAME   TELEPHONE   SKI   BOOT   POLE   DAYS LATE
A.G. ADAMS     (208) 366-1230   X     X      X        2
M. BRENDT      (208) 461-5620   X     X      X        3
```

Figure 10.4   Daily Late Return Report

12. Total for last year's reporting period (calculated)

13. Total revenue change (as percent) for the reporting period between current year and last year (calculated)

Daily Late Return Report

The Daily Late Return Report has the following general characteristics:

■ Provides information on the customers who did not return rented equipment on time.

■ Can be called up on the screen or printed out.

■ Is arranged alphabetically by customer name.

Figure 10.4 shows the format of the Daily Late Return Report.
    The report contains the following items:

1-4. Same as items 1-4 in the Revenue Report

5. Customer name (from the Customer's file)

6. Telephone number (from the Customer's file)

7-9. Information on type of equipment rented (from the Transaction file)

10. Days late (calculated using due date in the Transaction file and the current date)

Inventory Report

The Inventory Report has the following general characteristics:

■ Provides information on ski inventories available for renting.

■ Can be called up on the screen or printed out.

■ Inventories corresponding to the specific manufacturers only can also be displayed.

■ Is arranged alphabetically by manufacturer's name and within that, by ski length.

```
                              BOB'S SKI SHOP       (1)
        PAGE: 1     (2)       DATE 02/02/89        (3)
                              SKI  INVENTORY  REPORT  (4)

            (5)                   (6)                 (7)
     MANUFACTURER               LENGTH           SERIAL NUMBER
     DYNASTAR                     165               001756
            TOTAL NUMBER OF DYNASTARS AT 165 -- 1               (8)

                                 170               001759
                                                   001760
                                                   001761
         TOTAL NUMBER OF DYNASTARS AT 170 -- 3
                       TOTAL NUMBER OF DYNASTARS -- 4       (9)

     DYNAMIC                     170               00234
                                                   00235
                                                   00236
                                                   00237
         TOTAL NUMBER OF DYNAMICS AT 170 -- 4
                                 200               00315
                                                   00316
                                                   00317
                                                   00318
         TOTAL NUMBER OF DYNAMICS AT 200 -- 4
                       TOTAL NUMBER OF DYNAMICS -- 8
                       TOTAL NUMBER OF SKIS -- 12      (10)
```

Figure 10.5 Inventory Report

Figure 10.5 shows the format of the Inventory Report. The report contains the following items:

1-4. Same as 1-4 items in the Revenue report

5. Manufacturer's name (from Ski Inventory file)

6. Ski length (from Ski Inventory file)

7. Serial number (from Ski Inventory file)

8. Total number of skis, at a given ski length, from a specific manufacturer (calculated)

9. Total number of skis for a specific manufacturer (calculated)

10. Total number of skis in the inventory (calculated)

Daily Rental Report

Daily Rental Report has the following general characteristics:

■ Provides information on daily transactions in the rental shop.

■ Can be called up on the screen or printed out.

■ Is arranged in descending order of due date.

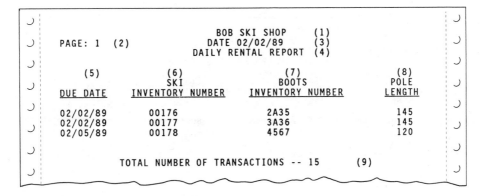

Figure 10.6 Daily Rental Report

Figure 10.6 shows the format of the Daily Rental Report.
The report contains:

1-4. Same as items 1-4 in the Revenue Report

5. Due date (from the Transaction file)

6. Rental ski inventory number (from the Transaction file)

7. Rented boots inventory number (from the Transaction file)

8. Rented pole length (from the Transaction file)

9. Total number of transactions (calculated)

Customer Profile Report

Customer Profile Report has the following general characteristics:

■ Provides information for targeting future advertising campaigns.

■ Can be called up on the screen or printed out.

■ Can report on all customers or select by age category, customer's home town, or skiing ability.

■ Is arranged alphabetically by customer name.

Figure 10.7 shows the format of the Customer Profile Report.
The report contains the following items:

1-4. Same as items 1-4 in the Revenue Report

5. Customer name (from the Customer's file)

6. Customer age (from the Customer's file)

7. Customer sex (from the Customer's file)

```
                              BOB'S SKI SHOP      (1)
       Page: 1 (2)             DATE  02/02/89     (3)
                            CUSTOMERS PROFILE REPORT (4)

        (5)              (6)       (7)       (8)        (9)
     CUSTOMER          CUSTOMER  CUSTOMER  CUSTOMER    CUSTOMER
       NAME              AGE       SEX       TOWN    SKIING ABILITY

     W.G.ANDERSON        35        M        BOISE      SKILLED

                        (10)                (11)        (12)
                        REASON
                        TO RENT              SKI         BOOTS

     TYPE OF RENTED
     EQUIPMENT    1. TRY NEW
                     EQUIPMENT        DYNASTAR SL    NORDICA X-747

                  2.                  DYNASTAR X-27  NORDICA X-747

                  3.                  DYNASTAR G-5   KESSEL 59

               TOTAL NUMBER OF SKIS TRIED:    3        (13)
               TOTAL NUMBER OF BOOTS TRIED:   2        (14)


     B.A.BROWN           27        F      NEW YORK    BEGINNER

                        REASON
                        TO RENT              SKI         BOOTS

     TYPE OF RENTED
     EQUIPMENT    1. NO EQUIPMENT   DYNAFLEX      NORDICA 727

               TOTAL NUMBER OF SKIS TRIED:    1
               TOTAL NUMBER OF BOOTS TRIED:   1
```

Figure 10.7 Customer's Profile Format

8. Customer home town (from the Customer's file)
9. Customer skiing ability (from the Customer's file)
10. Ski type (from the Transaction file and Ski Inventory file)
11. Boot type (from the Transaction file and Boots Inventory file)
12. Total number of ski styles rented (calculated)
13. Total number of boot styles rented (calculated)

Mailing Labels

The Mailing List Labels Report produces regular mailing labels. It uses the customer file. Specific customers can be selected on the basis of zip code, customer's age, or customer's skiing skills. This report is available in the printed form only.

Field Description	Field Type	Length
Customer identification type	AN	2
Customer identification number	AN	20
Customer last name	AN	20
Customer first name	AN	10
Customer middle initial	AN	1
Customer street address	AN	30
Customer city	AN	20
Customer state	AN	15
Customer zip	AN	9
Customer phone	AN	12
Local accommodations	AN	25
Customer height feet	N	1
Customer height inches	N	2
Customer weight	N	3
Customer age	N	3
Customer sex	AN	1
Customer skiing ability	AN	2
Binding L. toe	AN	3
Binding R. toe	AN	3
Binding L. heel	AN	3
Binding R. heel	AN	3

N – numeric
AN – Alphanumeric

Figure 10.8 Customer File Layout

File Designs

The data for the Ski Rental System can be organized in eight files. (Note that this is not a unique solution. We chose this approach to gradually introduce certain NOMAD commands.) A detailed data dictionary is given in the following eight sections.

Customer File

The layout for the Customer file is given in Figure 10.8.

A customer record must be created before any transaction record reflecting renting activity can be recorded. Thus the Transaction file's update program must detect any attempt to create any transaction record for customers not recorded in the Customer file. New customers records are created on the Customers File Update screen.

Transaction File

The layout for the Transaction file is given in Figure 10.9.

Field Description	Field Type	Length
Customer identification type	AN	2
Customer identification numbers	AN	20
Date out	AN	6
Date due	AN	6
Ski number	AN	8
Boot number	AN	4
Pole number	AN	4
Date return	AN	6
Technician ID	AN	2

Figure 10.9 Transaction File Layout

Field Description	Field Type	Length
Year	AN	4
Week's code	N	2
Ski rental weekly revenue	N	7
Boots rental weekly revenue	N	7
Poles rental weekly revenue	N	7

Figure 10.10 Historical Revenue File Layout

The transaction file is linked to the Customer file by a flag that is a concatenation of customer identification type and customer identification number. The updates of the Transaction file are done through the Transaction File screen.

Historical Revenue File

The layout for the historical revenue file is given in Figure 10.10.

The Transaction file and the Historical Revenue file are linked by a flag that is a concatenation of the year field and a code for a specific week. This is done to facilitate the Revenue Report. The Historical Revenue file should be updated once a year by running an update program with the Transaction file records.

Ski Inventory File

The layout for the Ski Inventory file is given in Figure 10.11.

The Ski Inventory file is linked to the Transaction file by a ski rental flag that is a concatenation of the customer identification type and customer identification number, which are fields in the Transaction file.

Boot Inventory File

The layout for the Boot Inventory file is given in Figure 10.12.

Field Description	Field Type	Length
Ski serial number	AN	8
Ski manufacturer	AN	4
Ski type	AN	4
Ski length	N	3
Ski rental charge	N	4
Ski rental flag	AN	22

Figure 10.11   Ski Inventory File Layout

Field Description	Field Type	Length
Boot serial number	AN	4
Boot manufacturer	AN	4
Boot type	AN	4
Boot size	N	3
Boot rental charge	N	4
Boot rental flag	AN	22

Figure 10.12   Boot Inventory File Layout

Field Description	Field Type	Length
Pole serial number	AN	4
Pole manufacturer	AN	4
Pole type	AN	4
Pole length	AN	3
Pole rental charge	N	4
Pole rental flag	AN	22

Figure 10.13   Pole Inventory File Layout

The Boot Inventory file is linked to the Transaction file by a flag in the same way that the Ski Inventory file was linked.

Pole Inventory File

The layout for the Pole Inventory file is given in Figure 10.13.

The Pole Inventory file is linked to the Transaction file by a flag in the same way that the Ski Inventory file was linked.

Field Description	Field Type	Length
Equipment code	AN	4
Equipment name	AN	20
Production date (year)	AN	4

Figure 10.14 Equipment Type File Layout

Field Description	Field Type	Length
Manufacturer code	AN	4
Manufacturer name	AN	25
Street	AN	20
City	AN	20
State	AN	15
Zip code	AN	9
Representative name	AN	30
Representative telephone	AN	12

Figure 10.15 Manufacturer File Layout

Equipment Type File

The layout for the Equipment Type file is given in Figure 10.14.

This file is used as a table-lookup for the inventory files. This substantially reduces redundant data entry. The information in this file is linked to the various inventory files by the equipment type code.

Manufacturer File

The layout for the Manufacturer file is given in Figure 10.15.

This file is also used as table-lookup for the various inventory files. The information in this file is linked to the inventory files by the manufacturer code.

Input Screens

For the input screens, we chose the very popular dialogue strategy of menu selection. Menu selection allows casual users to control processing without having to spend time learning a possibly complicated system structure and the processing order. Since specific menu items are self-explanatory with this technique, users can operate the system without extensive training.

This section describes only the sequence and variety of the screens the user views at the terminal. For this purpose we use the Ski Rental System dialogue chart shown in Figure 10.16. The details pertaining to specific screens are left for the reader to consider in the Exercises section.

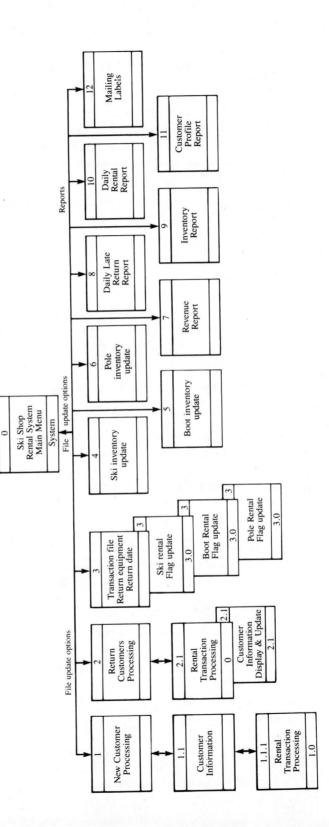

Figure 10.16 Dialogue Chart for the Ski Rental System

Note that to design a good dialogue requires a familiarity with the current technology of display terminals and the features they offer. These can be used to improve general dialogue design. In addition, one should check the capabilities of the specific 4GL used to code the application. For example, some 4GLs automatically handle escape procedures from screen to screen; HELP commands and HELP screens; error-messages, and a screen "repair" and printing of the screen content.

Process Specifications

This section concentrates on a few important facts concerning the modules used to update the Ski Rental Shop System files. Although other factors such as security measures, file backup and recovery, simultaneous processing controls, maintenance controls, physical security, and physical reliability are often discussed under the process specification topic, we will introduce them as needed in the other chapters.

We subdivide process specification into four basic areas:

1. Customer information processing
2. Equipment return processing
3. Equipment inventory processing
4. Historical revenue file processing

Customer Information Processing

Recall that customer information processing consists of two types of rental transactions: first-time customers and returning customers.

For the first-time customer, we start by creating the record in the file. Then we proceed to create a transaction record for the rental and simultaneously update the rental flags in the Ski Inventory file, Boot Inventory file, and Pole Inventory file. Each of these flags indicates that the specific equipment is rented out.

For returning customers, we first select the appropriate customer record from the Customer file and check the validity of all this information. We correct or update any invalid data. Then we proceed to create the rental transaction record and update the rental flags in the Inventory files.

Equipment Return Processing

This module updates the following files:

■ Rental Transaction file
■ Ski Inventory file
■ Boot Inventory file
■ Pole Inventory file

In the Transaction file we enter date of the return of the equipment and recalculate the rental charges, since the original due date for the equipment is not necessarily the same as the equipment return date.

In the various inventory files we update the rental flag by making it a blank field. The blank field in the rental flag means that the ski equipment is in the shop ready to be rented.

Equipment Inventories

The equipment inventory module updates records in the following files:

- Ski Inventory file
- Boot Inventory file
- Pole Inventory file
- Equipment type file
- Manufacturer file

Records are deleted when specific equipment is removed from the rental pool, and records are added when new equipment is acquired for rentals.

Historical Revenue File Processing

At the end of the ski season, this module summarizes the weekly revenue records in the Rental Transaction file. The weekly rental transactions are used to update the Historical Revenue file.

10.6 SUMMARY

This chapter described the Ski Rental System that we will use in the next chapters to illustrate 4GL statements and options. The chapter briefly discussed the Ski Shop rental operations, its data processing needs, and the design of the Ski Rental system. To keep the descriptions short, some of the design details were omitted, but those will be introduced throughout the text as needed.

The information in this chapter should allow you to understand, in general terms, how the system works and what its major components are.

EXERCISES

1. Design all the menu screens for the Ski Rental System.
2. Design data entry screens for all the files in the system.
3. Did the designer of the rental system include all the necessary procedures? Discuss the nature of this question. In your discussion, define "all the necessary procedures."
4. The Ski Rental System can be expanded or changed in many ways. Try to redesign this system by incorporating your own ideas. For example, you could combine the inventory files (ski, boots, and poles) into one file. Keep your new

design to use in practicing the NOMAD commands that are introduced in the later chapters.

5. "During the design stage, the decision was made that the system must be totally interactive. It should guide its user through each function with menus, and query the user for any information it needs. No prior knowledge of computers or data processing should be required of the personnel operating the system. Also, no supplementary documentation should be needed once the intended users (that is the rental shop technicians) obtain a minimal amount of experience in system operation." What analysis steps could have led to these design decisions? Why?

6. What else would you consider? What would your design specifications depend on?

7. In your opinion, is it all right to have this system totally interactive?

8. Would you add any other functions to the main menu of this system?

PROJECTS

1. State Parks Reservation/Registration System

Introduction

The Parks and Recreation Department in a western state is responsible for the management of state parks. The state system has ten parks holding several thousand campsites. These campsites can be reserved only by mail, and each campsite reservation must be confirmed. Reservations must be made several months in advance. This lag time is required because the reservation system is at present only manual.

Individual parks cannot make campsite reservations for sites located in other parks in the system. Last minute reservations are not possible either.

The management of Parks and Recreation realizes that customer services need to be improved. Also, a better reservation system would increase the campsites' occupancy rate. Management decided to acquire a computerized reservation and registration system. This system is to be accessible from all the state parks. In addition, the Tourist Information Centers located outside the parks' sites will now be able to take reservations.

Your Assignment

Assume that you are hired as an information system consultant to the Parks and Recreation Department. Your assignment is to help develop the computerized reservation system.

You have already held several meetings with the management of the Parks and Recreation Department, with administrators of each of the state parks, and with the key representatives of the Tourist Information Office. From this diversified group, you elicited, in a short period of time, initial requirements specifications for the proposed system. You accomplished this using NOMAD and the prototyping technique.

First, you established the reporting requirements of the system. Next, you decided what inputs and processing would be needed to generate the required reports. You also agreed on how screen displays for the reservation system are to look.

Reporting Requirements

After extensively analyzing the park system reservation and registration requirements, you consolidated the various information requirements into several outputs. Your analysis led you to various decisions concerning outputs as described in the following sections.

Campsite Availability Report

This report is to be generated in any locale where a reservation is taken. The reservation clerk can request this report by specifying the park site and the days for which the customer would like to place the reservation. This report is to be displayed on the video terminal screen and is to include the following information:

- Park description—The name and location of the park.
  - Park name—A 20-character field (maximum) giving the name of the park.
  - Park location—A 35 character (maximum) field giving the location of the park.
  - Park code—A 2-character code that represents the specific park in the system. (For example, BI represents Bold Island park.)
  - Dates of the desired reservation—The starting and ending dates (in MM/DD/YY format) for the reservation.
  - Site number—A 3-digit number that is unique for a given campsite in a specific park, but not unique for the whole state park system.
  - Site location description—A 40-character (maximum) description of the location of a specific site within the park, for example, near the beach, behind the showers and the games building, or 100 feet from the drinking water.
  - Site footage—A 4-digit numeric field specifying the size of the campsite.
  - Site type—A 2-character code describing the campsite amenities. These codes are:
    - AU = Amenities unavailable; camping space only
    - BA = Basic amenities (picnic table, fire pit, and/or grill)
    - FA = Full amenities (picnic table, fire pit, grill, and water faucet)
    - TU = Trailer site: amenities unavailable.
    - TA = Trailer site with amenities (electric hookup, water, picnic table, and fire pit)
  - Site rate—Rental price of the campsite

When this report is displayed on the screen, the reservation clerk must be able to use the reservation dates, park code, and site number as the input data for the reservation data entry screen without having to type in these input values again.

Confirmation Bill

After the reservation transaction is entered, the reservation clerk must be able to print a confirmation bill containing the following information:

- Name—First name, middle initial, and the last name of the person for whom the reservation is made.
- Address—The mailing address of the person for whom the site reservation is made (street, city, state, and zip code).
- Date of placing the reservation.
- Park Name—Name of the park where the site is reserved, as specified and described for the Campsite Availability Report.
- Site number—The unique number by which each campsite is identified, as described in the Campsite Availability Report.
- Site description—Complete description, including the site code, the site's location and type, as specified in the Campsite Availability Report.
- Dates of reservation period.
- Number of days for which the site is to be reserved (not to exceed 14 days).
- Total amount due for using the campsite.
- Deposit—Amount due to hold reservation (equal 20% of the total amount due).

Daily Reservation Pending

This report lists all the pending reservations by specific park or for all the parks in the park system. This information is to be available as a hard copy and on the screen. The report is to contain:

- Date—Report date (in MM/DD/YY format).
- Name—The name of the person for whom the reservation is made.
- Address—The address of the person who made the reservation (street address, city, state, and zip code).
- Site number—The unique identification number of the specific campsite.
- Park name—The name of the park where the site is reserved.
- Total number of reservations pending—A cumulative total by park.

Daily Site Use

This report is to allow park management to establish the daily occupancy of the park by site number. This report is to contain:

- Date—Report date.
- Site number—The unique number by which each campsite is identified.
- Name—The name of the campsite occupant (first name, middle initial, and last name).
- Car license number—A 10-character field holding the campsite occupants' car license number.
- State—The state where the campsite occupant has his or her car registered.

Monthly Use Summary Report

This report is to give information on monthly earnings from campsite rentals for a specific park or for all the parks in the system. The report is to be generated at the end of each month and only in printed form. The report is to include:

- Site number—The unique number by which each campsite is identified.
- Days used—The number of days in a month that the specific campsite was occupied.
- Revenue—The monthly earnings for the specific campsite.
- Total revenue—The total monthly revenue for a specific park.

Objectives for Your Work on this Project: First Stage

The main objective is to develop the prototype of the reservation system using NOMAD on a PC. In the first stage of the project, your tasks are to:

- Design all output reports and data entry screens (you have to determine the formats of these reports).
- Create the data dictionary for all the data elements in the park reservation and registration system.
- Identify all required files.
- Develop the main menu to be used for this online reservation system.

You will use the outcome of the first stage of this project throughout the rest of the book.

This application can be expanded and made more sophisticated in many ways. You are encouraged to think about designing such expansions.

2. System to Handle Properties, Water Rights, and Leases

Introduction

This case concerns the online storage and retrieval system required for the computerized legal information system on properties, water rights, and railroad leases of concern to one of the largest corporations in the state of Idaho.

One very important characteristic of the relationships among the various records (that is, the properties, water rights, and leases) in the database of this application is that they are "many-to-many" relationships. For example, some properties have multiple water rights or multiple railroad leases, and multiple properties may relate to railroad leases or water rights. When you design the database for this system, remember these many-to-many relationships.

Since these records represent legal data, each record is to include any required legal commentary.

Assume that you are the system analyst whose job is to develop this computer information system. You already had several meetings with the management of the legal department. You also met lawyers responsible for the issues concerning water rights, railroad leases, and real properties of this corporation. Using prototyping and NOMAD on a PC, you were able to establish the system requirements.

Reporting Requirements

After extensively analyzing the needs of the legal department for handling the information on properties, water rights, and railroad leases, you consolidated various information requirements into several outputs, as described in the following sections.

Properties Report

This report must be able to cover all properties or just selected properties, based on the following criteria:

1. All the properties belonging to a specified owner or owners.
2. All the properties in a specified state and county.

This report is to include the following information:

- State—The name of the state where the property is located.
- County—The name of the county where the property is located.
- Parcel owner—The name of the corporate division that owns the parcel, expressed in a 25-character alphanumeric field.
- Parcel user—The name of the corporate division using the parcel.
- Parcel number—An 8-character code that is unique within each county and is assigned by the county to keep track of property taxes. (The corporation owns properties in many states and counties.)
- Brief legal description—A description of the township, range, and section of the parcel.
- Parcel acreage—The acreage of the parcel expressed in a format nnnnn.nn, where n is positive integer.
- Comments lines—Optional lines of comments concerning the parcel. Up to 25 lines can be included for a parcel, and each line can contain 80 characters.

The report is to have summary lines that display the total acreage of parcels by county and by state. In addition, the cumulative total of acreage held by the corporation is to be displayed.

Water Rights Report

This report is sorted by parcels. Remember that parcels can have multiple water rights or multiple parcels can have one water right associated with them. This report is to contain:

- State—The name of the state where the water right is granted.
- County—The name of the county where the water right is granted.
- Water right number— A unique 12-character number identifying a specific water right in a given state.
- Usage type code—A 2-digit code describing the usage of the water. Possible usages are:
    DM = Domestic IN =   Industrial
    IR   = Irrigation ML =   Multiple use
- User—The 25-character (maximum) name of the user of the water (either a corporate division or an outside party).
- Parcel number—The parcel number that identifies the parcel where the water right is located, as specified in the Properties Report.
- Brief legal description—Short legal description of the parcel as described in the Properties Report.
- Comments lines—Optional comments concerning water rights. Up to 25 lines can be included, and each line can contain 80 characters.

Railroad Leases Report

This report lists all the railroad leases pertaining to corporate properties. This report is to include the following information:

- Lease legal number—A unique 8-character number describing a lease.
- Parcel number—The number of the parcel where the lease is located, as described in previous reports.
- Lease location—An additional 20-character (maximum) description of the location of the lease on the parcel.
- Type of lease—A 30-character (maximum) description of the lease that specifies the purpose of the lease, for example, the lease for the railroad loading ramp or the lease for the railroad tracks.
- Lease termination date—The date of the termination or renewal of the railroad lease, in MM/DD/YY format.

Case Objectives

Design all output reports and data entry screens. Create a data dictionary for all data elements in the firm's properties handling system.

Identify necessary files and develop menus to create this online system.

For some data, exact input or output format and validation rules are not specified. You are free to define those according to your judgment.

3. Local Business

Perhaps your instructor can arrange for you to conduct a class project for a local business. If this is possible, as a first stage of your work, prepare the design specifications in a manner similar to one presented in this chapter. These design specifications can be used to construct an application and to practice using NOMAD on a PC. We will refer to this project in some of the exercises given in the following chapters.

SUGGESTED READINGS

1. Dans, W. S. *Systems Analysis and Design: A Structured Approach*. Reading, Mass.: Addison-Wesley, 1983.

2. Licker, P. S. *Fundamentals of Systems Analysis with Application Design*. Boston: boyd & fraser, 1987.

3. Whitten, J. L., Bentley, L. D., and Ho, T. I. M. *System Analysis and Design Methods*. St. Louis, Mo.: Times Mirror/Mosby, 1986.

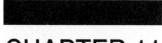

CHAPTER 11

Procedures

We can now reduce everything we do to a language to be acted upon by machines.

From an IBM exhibit

11.1 INTRODUCTION

The main objective of this chapter is to introduce you to the idea of procedures and the commands used in procedures. When you have completed this chapter, you will be able to:

■ Explain what a NOMAD procedure is.

■ List the methods of creating a procedure.

■ Describe, in general, procedure processing: translation and execution.

■ Explain, in general, the process of building procedures.

■ Classify and describe the statements used in a procedure: directive statements, command statements, and procedural control statements.

The process of building specific procedures is addressed in later chapters.

11.2 PROCEDURAL LANGUAGE

Procedural control commands, which perform various processing tasks such as controlling the flow of execution or handling processing error conditions, represent an integral part of NOMAD. A NOMAD procedure can be either a set of simple commands or a complex program containing not only command statements, but also sophisticated control logic.

A NOMAD procedure can be created in either of two ways:

1. With your system editor.

2. Online, in the interactive environment, with the NOMAD Command window.

In either case, the procedure is saved as a file and its filename is given a .NOM extension.

Procedures can be invoked from:

■ The NOMAD environment—Type the name of the file containing the procedure in the NOMAD Command window.

■ The PC operating system environment—Enter the command invoking NOMAD and follow it with the name of the file where the procedure is stored.

■ Another procedure—Use the CALL command, followed by the name of the file where the procedure is stored.

When the execution of the invoked procedure is completed, control is returned to the environment from which the procedure was invoked.

If your application requires that the same set of commands always be executed upon entering the NOMAD environment, one specially named procedure can be useful. This repeating set of commands should be stored in the PROFILE.NOM file. The PROFILE.NOM procedure is always automatically executed immediately after you invoke NOMAD.

NOMAD procedure processing is essentially a two-stage process:

1. *Translation*—After the syntax of the procedure's statements is verified, the procedure is translated into a form suitable for execution and is placed in the data dictionary.

2. *Execution*—Each translated command statement and procedural control command is executed in the order in which it occurs or in the order determined by such control statement as GOTO or CALL.

The formatting conventions for procedures are as follows:

■ Procedure statements can be entered in a free format without regard to column positioning. Statements can span multiple lines.

■ All statements must end with a semicolon, but the semicolon on the last statement in the whole procedure is optional.

■ Nonexecuting comments, which can continue from line to line, can be inserted anywhere in the procedure. They must either be delimited with an exclamation point (!) or start with a slash-asterisk (/*) and end with a asterisk-slash (*/).

For example,

```
!This is comment number one.!
```

or

```
/*This is comment number two.*/
```

Statements in a procedure can be classified as:

1. Directive statements
2. Command statements
3. Procedural control statements

Directive Statements

The directive statement's purpose is to direct the procedure translator to perform an *action* (execute specific command) during translation. The directive command statement will be executed immediately during translation time and before execution of the procedure, regardless of where it appears in the procedure.

For example, the directive:

```
DATABASE mybase;
```

specifies the name of the database to be loaded for use by the procedure. This directive allows NOMAD to check the validity of the database items referenced further on in the procedure.

The directive statements available in NOMAD are:

```
DATABASE        FEND
DBADD           LABEL
DBCLEAR         INCLUDE
DEFINE          SCHEMA
ERRFIELD        TRANS
FIELD           UNTRANS
FORM            WINDOW SAVE
FROM            WINDOW SET
```

Later sections of this chapter define these directive statements, give examples of their use, and discuss their application.

Command Statements

All NOMAD commands and many operating system commands can be used in procedures.

SYSTEM (or SYS) must precede the operating system command to be included in the NOMAD procedure. For example, the statement

```
SYSTEM dirprn;
```

prints your disk directory when executed in a procedure.

Two optional parameters can be placed in a command statement: a label and the OTHERWISE clause.

You can start a command with a *label*. A label can be up to 14 characters in length. The first character must be a hyphen (-) and the second must be any letter. The remaining characters can be letters, digits, or an underscore. Each label in the specific procedure must be unique within the procedure.

The label identifies a command statement's location in the procedure. Using the label, NOMAD can transfer execution flow to the labeled command. This can be done with the GOTO command or referenced with an ON condition. For example,

```
!1! -START_READ  READ myfile;
!2! . . .
!3! . . .
!4! . . .
!5! GOTO -START_READ;
```

In this example, line 1 (note that each line of this example is identified with a comment containing the line number) holds a label -START_READ and the NOMAD command READ myfile. This labeled command obtains a record from an external file named myfile and reads it into an input buffer area. Then it proceeds with the other commands. When line 5 is reached, the GOTO command switches control back to the command statement located on line 1.

You can also put the *OTHERWISE clause* after the command in the command statement. This parameter consists of the keyword OTHERWISE (or OTW) and a statement indicating what action is to be taken if the command preceding the OTHERWISE parameter cannot be performed.

Consider the following example:

```
!1! READ myfile OTW GOTO -DONE;
!2! . . .
!3! . . .
!4! -DONE FILE CLOSE myfile;
```

In the command statement on line 1 you are attempting to read records from an external file called MYFILE into the input buffer. If this cannot be done (OTW), control is switched to the labeled command statement (-DONE) residing on line 4.

The OTHERWISE clause may not appear after the following commands:

DO ... END	DATABASE
TRANS	CONTINUE
UNTRANS	DBADD
SCHEMA	DBCLEAR
DEFINE	INCLUDE
QUIT	EXIT
DECLARE	ON

Commands that control the translation and execution process are called procedure control statements. The rest of this chapter gives general comments on the commands used in procedures.

11.3 COMMANDS USED IN PROCEDURES

Commands used in procedures fall into one of these four categories:

1. Commands that control the process of procedure translation.
2. Commands that control the execution sequence in a procedure.
3. Error and condition testing commands.
4. All other NOMAD and operating system commands used in procedures.

For now we will concentrate on the commands that fall into the first three categories. All the other commands will be gradually introduced throughout the remainder of this book.

Commands That Control the Process of Procedure Translation

We start with the commands used to control the process of procedure translation.

INCLUDE Command

The INCLUDE command is used to modify a given procedure (including procedure) by copying and inserting all the statements from another (included) procedure.

The INCLUDE command can appear anywhere in a procedure except within the TRANS mode. (We will comment on the TRANS mode shortly.)

NOMAD makes no distinction between statements in the included procedure and those in including ones. Obviously, included statements must be compatible with the statements in the original including procedure. NOMAD translates and executes this combined set of statements as a single procedure.

Consider this example:

```
INCLUDE myproc;
```

Here, all commands from the myproc file will be inserted automatically.

The INCLUDE command can contain device and path information. For example,

```
INCLUDE c:\direct1\myproc;
```

PRESCAN Command

The PRESCAN command is used to compile a procedure and to save it in a NOMAD P code file (a file with the extension .NPC) for future use.

The compiled procedure is stored with the same name as that of the NOMAD procedure. (You can erase the original procedure to save storage space and still be able to produce the desired result from the original procedure by invoking its compiled version.)

For example, assume that you have a procedure file named proc1.nom, and it has the following statement in it:

```
print "BOB'S SKI HOUSE";
```

You can compile this procedure by using the PRESCAN command, that is,

```
PRESCAN proc1;
```

This command compiles the procedure and saves the result under the name proc1.

If you were to erase the original procedure (that is, you erase the file proc1.nom), its compiled version is still maintained in the file with the .NPC extension. Now if you run proc1, from NOMAD, you will see

```
BOB'S SKI HOUSE
```

displayed in the Output window. This is the result desired from the original procedure. You can run compiled procedures in this manner.

TRANS and UNTRANS Directives

The TRANS and UNTRANS directives control the translation of the procedure. Recall that the directive statements direct the procedure translator to perform an action during the process of translation. Normally, all the action is performed during translation, and no further action is taken during execution.

The TRANS directive causes the translation of statements that follow it to be postponed. When this directive is encountered, the process of translation is stopped.

The UNTRANS directive reverses this action. Statements that follow UNTRANS are translated normally.

All statements between the TRANS and UNTRANS directives are in the TRANS mode. They are called TRANS-mode statements. TRANS-mode processing is mostly used to:

1. Delay the translation and execution of the directive statements.

2. Perform symbolic substitution.

Since directive commands are normally executed at translation time, placing them in TRANS mode delays their execution until the procedure execution phase.

Consider this example:

```
TRANS;
IF &USERID = 'GREGORY'
     THEN DBADD SALEDATA;
UNTRANS;
```

The IF ... THEN command is placed in the TRANS mode and its translation is stopped. During execution, this statement is scanned for syntax errors and then executed. After this command is executed, the mode is changed with the UNTRANS directive, which causes the statements that follow UNTRANS to be translated normally.

Symbolic substitution allows you to modify procedure statements before they are executed. It is particulary useful in performing the following operations:

■ Passing symbolic parameters to a procedure.

■ Defining parameters to a NOMAD command.

■ Creating NOMAD commands while in a procedure.

Symbolic substitution is done with the ? function, which can be used only in the TRANS-mode statements. This substitution is done just prior to the statement's execution. The ? function can substitute for statements, keywords, items, names, and user variables.

User variables provide a method for saving values for use in calculations or logical expressions for the duration of the current NOMAD session. [The names of the user variables must start with the character & followed by up to 15 characters, the first of which must be a letter. Other valid characters are any letter, numeric digit, or an underscore (_). We will discuss general classes of variables, in depth, in Chapter 12.]

For example, assume that your user's variable (here called &var1) has a value equal to the string COMPANY. Assume that your procedure has statements in it that currently point to a specific record in the database that contains an item (field) called COMPANY. The *value* of that item for that specific record is BOISE STATE UNIVERSITY. The rest of the procedure is as follows:

```
TRANS;
PRINT 'I WORK FOR A ?(&VAR1)';
PRINT 'THE ?(&VAR1) NAME IS:' ?(&VAR1);
```

When this procedure is run, the results will look like this:

```
I WORK FOR A COMPANY
THE COMPANY NAME IS: COMPANY=BOISE STATE UNIVERSITY
```

In the first command, ?(&VAR1) is replaced by the literal string COMPANY. The translated statement is:

```
PRINT 'I WORK FOR A COMPANY';
```

and this PRINT statement prints exactly that.

In the second command, both occurrences of ?(&VAR1) are replaced, so the translated command statement is:

```
PRINT 'THE COMPANY NAME IS:' COMPANY;
```

The second substitution, which is not in quotes, tells NOMAD to print out the contents of the item COMPANY.

There is one restriction for symbolic substitution. The ? function cannot be used with labels for GOTO statements. The statement in the following example is illegal and will produce an error.

```
TRANS;
 . . .
 . . .
 . . .
GOTO ?(&VAR2);
```

CALL Command

This command causes another (CALLed) procedure to be translated together with the current procedure. For example, assume that we have a procedure that has many statements

```
 . . .
procedure statements
 . . .
 . . .
CALL test_1
 . . .
 . . .
```

The CALL command used in this procedure calls another procedure, test_1, and both are translated. CALL is also used to control the execution sequence.

Commands that Control the Execution Sequence in a Procedure

The procedural statements, with the exception of the directive statements, are executed in sequential order as they appear. However, this sequence of statement execution can be controlled.

CALL Command

This command has two different functions. Its outcome depends on when it is used. During translation, the `CALL` command causes the `CALLed` procedure to be translated (as in the preceding example). During the execution phase, the `CALL` command transfers control to the `CALLed` procedure.

You can issue the `CALL` command either from the NOMAD Command window or from within another procedure. After the `CALLed` procedure is completed, control returns to the environment from which the command was issued. In the following example,

```
CALL myproc1;
```

control passes to the procedure in a file named myproc1.

RETURN Command

This command stops the execution of a procedure and returns you to the calling procedure or environment. You can specify the number of procedure levels or the name of the procedure to which you would like to return. The procedure name must be an antecedent of the current procedure, or else a fatal error condition is raised.

In the following example,

```
RETURN TO myproc1;
```

control passes to the procedure with the name myproc1. In the following example,

```
RETURN 3;
```

control passes to the procedure or environment two levels in front of current calling procedure. If 3 is greater than the number of levels of calling procedures, the `RETURN 3;` is equivalent to the `EXIT` command. In the following example,

```
RETURN;
```

NOMAD defaults to level 1, and control passes to the current calling procedure or environment.

EXIT Command

This command stops the execution of the procedure and returns control to the NOMAD Command window environment or to the operating system environment, depending on the environment from which the procedure was invoked.

`EXIT` stops the execution of all processing. Note that in contrast to `RETURN`, `EXITing` from a called procedure does not return control to the calling procedure, but it does stop processing.

For example, assume that you executed your procedure from the Command window and now you issue the command

```
EXIT;
```

This stops execution of the procedural environment and returns control to the Command window, the environment from which the procedure was executed.

CONTINUE Command

This command is used to pass control to the next statement in line. Most often it is used in conjunction with the OTHERWISE clause, for example,

```
PRINT &I OTW CONTINUE;
```

The procedure including this statement will continue to run even if the PRINT command would raise an error condition. Without OTW CONTINUE, an error condition would have caused the procedure to terminate.

DO and END Commands

A DO command allows a series (a group) of statements to be used. For example, a DO group can be used to execute more than one statement when the end-of-file condition is reached. A group starts with the DO command and ends with the END command.

The DO group can contain:

■ Any executable statement.

■ Another DO group.

■ GOTO commands that transfer control to labels within or outside of the DO group. However, control cannot be transferred into the DO group from the outside. In the example:

```
ON ENDFILE;
    DO;
        PRINT 'WE ARE AT THE END OF FILE';
        PRINT 'NUMBER OF RECORDS READ' &Reads;
        EXIT;
    END;
```

three statements are executed after the end-of-file condition is reached.

FOR Command

This command is used to execute a statement or a group of statements for a specified number of iterations. When finished, the processing controls are passed to the statement immediately following the FOR command. There are two types of FOR commands:

- Computational FOR—Iteration is controlled by an &variable (user variable) value.
- Instance FOR—Iteration is controlled by positioning on instances (records) in a database.

In the *Computational FOR* command, iteration can be controlled in one of two ways:

1. By assigning successive numeric values to the &variable.
2. By performing one iteration for each value of the &variable.

To use the first method, you specify a starting number, an ending number, and an increment. The increment can be positive or negative, and it is an optional parameter. If it is not specified, NOMAD assumes a value of 1 for the increment.

Consider this example:

```
FOR &A = 10 TO 0 BY -2 PRINT &A;
```

The output from this command will be:

```
&A = 10
&A =  8
&A =  6
&A =  4
&A =  2
&A =  0
```

To use the second method for controlling iteration, you list the &variable values and do not use the BY clause. The values for the &variable can be alphanumeric or numeric. For example,

```
FOR &B = 'GREG','ALAN';
  DO;
      PRINT &B 'LIKES SKIING.'
        FOLD 'HE IS A GOOD SKIER.'
        FOLD 2;
  END;
PRINT 'THEY ARE BOTH GOOD SKIERS.';
```

Here we used a DO group in which we used a FOLD parameter. FOLD prints the next entry *n* lines down from the current line. For example, FOLD 2 means, "Insert 2 lines after the current line." The output from our example will look like this:

```
GREG LIKES SKIING.
HE IS A GOOD SKIER.

ALAN LIKES SKIING.
HE IS A GOOD SKIER.

THEY ARE BOTH GOOD SKIERS.
```

In the *Instance FOR command*, successive iterations are performed for each record (instance), starting with the first record of a database file (master) you have designated.

After execution, control passes (within the procedure) to the command directly following the FOR command, and the database is positioned as it was before the FOR was executed. Consider the example,

```
FOR EACH myfile PRINT &A;
```

where `myfile` is the name of a file (master) to be passed consecutively from the first to the last instance. The value of the &A variable will be printed as many times as there are records in the master myfile.

The Instance FOR command can be used with the SELECT command to process a specified subset of a designated master. Under this condition, the FOR command acts only on selected records. (We consider the use of the SELECT command later, in our extended example of an application.)

GOTO Command

This command interrupts the sequential flow of the NOMAD execution by unconditionally directing it to a labeled statement elsewhere in the procedure. The execution continues from there.

For example,

```
GOTO  -TAX;
```

interrupts normal execution and directs it to the point in the procedure that is labeled -TAX. Obviously, we assume that the -TAX label exists in the procedure; otherwise, NOMAD raises an error condition.

Because labels are local to procedures, NOMAD branches to a label only within the same procedure.

IF...THEN...ELSE Commands

This command allows for conditional control and execution of the flow in a procedure. For example,

```
OF &A >= 5 THEN GOTO -EXIT;
PRINT 'VALUE IS SMALLER THEN 5';
```

When the value of the &A variable is greater than or equal to 5, control switches to the statement with the label -EXIT. If &A is less than 5, the next statement (PRINT) is processed and the message VALUE IS SMALLER THAN 5 is printed. Consider this example:

```
IF &A >= 5 THEN GOTO -EXIT OTW -ERROR;
PRINT 'VALUE IS SMALLER THEN 5';
```

The output will be the same as in the previous example. The OTW clause is executed only when a portion of the IF command results in an *error* condition. It has no connection with the success or failure of the logical expression test &A = 5 and should not be confused with the function of the ELSE command, which is illustrated in the next example:

```
IF &A = 5 THEN GOTO -EXIT OTW -ERROR;
ELSE GOTO -START;
```

When the value of the &A variable is greater than or equal to 5 control switches to the statement with the label -EXIT. If &A is less than 5, control switches to the statement with the label -START.

The ELSE command is a separate statement. Therefore, the IF portion of the IF command must be followed by a semicolon. Multiple IF commands can be grouped (or nested) within one another. Each can have an associated ELSE command.

Error and Condition Testing Commands

In addition to the OTW clause, the ON command is used to handle specific conditions.

ON Command

This command specifies the action NOMAD should take when specific condition occurs. Specific conditions can include error handling.

NOMAD interrupts the procedure processing and executes the command or group of commands specified in the ON condition statement. After the ON condition statement is performed, processing continues.

ON commands are executed sequentially, so they can be redefined at different stages of the execution. Branching out of the ON statement or issuing a RETURN command ends the ON condition.

Normally, all error messages are suppressed when an error condition is handled by an ON command. If you want to display an error message, you have to use an optional parameter MSG. For example,

```
ON ERROR MSG GOTO -EXIT;
```

Here, the error message will be displayed along with the number of the statement that caused the error condition to occur. After the error message is printed, the GOTO command is executed, and control switches to the statement with the label -EXIT.

After the execution of the ON command, control passes to the statement following the one that caused the error condition to be raised, if no GOTO has been specified.

If there is more than one ON command that covers a specific condition, NOMAD executes the last appropriate ON command it finds.

You can control the point of return by including a GOTO, RETRY, RETURN, or EXIT command within the ON statement.

In general, NOMAD executes the actions specified in an ON command only if there is no OTW clause for that statement. The general format of the ON command is:

```
ON condition-name parameters MSG command or DO group
```

where

> *Condition-name* is a required parameter, and it identifies a condition that, if encountered, causes the execution of the commands that follow.
>
> *Parameters* are an optional entry that limit the condition to specific situations. Parameters can be items, &variables, statement labels, or data filenames.
>
> *MSG* is an optional parameter that causes error messages to be displayed along with the number of the statement that caused the error condition to occur. Normally all error messages are suppressed when an error condition is handled by an ON command. (We used this parameter in one of the preceding examples.)
>
> *Command* or *DO group* is (the action command or DO group of commands) to be performed whenever the required condition (specified by condition-name) is raised. If the ON command is issued without commands to be invoked, the default system action is performed.

The following condition names can be used with the ON command:

1. ON CONVERT occurs any time an assignment results in a data conversion error.

2. ON ENDFILE occurs when the end-of-file condition is detected during an execution of the READ command.

3. ON ERROR occurs when any general error condition arises and if the statement causing the error does not include an OTHERWISE clause.

4. ON FATAL occurs under either of the following conditions:
   a. NOMAD encounters a severe error while executing a procedure.
   b. Any abnormal condition occurs and there is no applicable OTHERWISE clause or ON command.

5. ON FUNCTIONKEY/FKEY n, m, . . . occurs when you press any of the function keys specified by the n, m, . . . list . If the FUNCTIONKEY command has no

numeric parameters, the FUNCTIONKEY condition is raised when you press any function key.

6. ON LIMIT occurs when a user tries to assign a value to an item, &item, or &variable that does not meet the limit specification established for it.

7. ON MASK occurs when a user tries to assign a value to an item, &item, or &variable that does not meet the MASK specification established in the application. MASK specifies the valid format to which alphanumeric item values must conform.

8. ON MEMBER occurs when a change to an item or an assignment to an &item or &variable fails a MEMBER test. The MEMBER parameter is used to restrict values for an item.

9. ON NOKEY occurs when NOMAD cannot find an instance in a master corresponding to the specified value. The &NOKEY variable contains the name of the item that did not match.

10. ON UNIQUE occurs when the database schema defines a master with the UNIQUE option and the user tries to store a duplicate record (nonunique data) in it. The variable &UNIQUE contains the name of the master file.

We will use these ON conditions and optional parameters associated with them in many examples in the later chapters.

11.4 SUMMARY

Procedures are an integral part of NOMAD. They provide control of the flow of execution; they can handle error conditions, and they perform a variety of processing tasks. Procedures can be either simple one-line command statements or complex programs.

To create a procedure, you enter the commands in the Command window or use your system editor to place the commands into a file. This file has the .NOM extension in its filename. Procedures can be invoked from the NOMAD Command window, your operating system, or from other procedures.

Procedure processing involves two phases: translation and execution. The translation process involves a check for syntax errors and translation into a form suitable for execution. Once a procedure has been translated (compiled), it is placed in the file with an .NPC extension and is executed. When the execution of the procedure is complete, control is returned to the environment from which the procedure was invoked.

The statements in the procedure can be classified into three categories:

1. Directive statements

2. Command statements

3. Procedural control statements

Directive statements direct the procedure translator to perform an action during the process of translation.

Command statements are commands used in the procedure. All NOMAD commands and many of the commands from your operating system can be used in the procedure. When operating system commands are included they must be preceded with the word SYSTEM.

Procedure control statements are commands that specifically control the translation and execution process of a procedure.

Commands that relate to the use of procedures fall into these general categories:

1. Those that control the process of procedure translation.
2. Those that control the execution sequence of the statements in the procedure.
3. Those that are error and condition testing statements.

Thus, procedural control commands that control the flow of execution and other processing tasks for the procedures comprise the procedural language of NOMAD.

EXERCISES

1. What is a procedure?
2. How do you set up a procedure in NOMAD?
3. If NOMAD procedures can be executed by typing the name of the procedure in the Command window and the name of a procedure can conceivably be the same as the name of a NOMAD command (or its abbreviation), what problems can you foresee from such naming?
4. Describe general formatting conventions for procedures.
5. How would you delimit the beginning and the end of the comment that is to contain the text: THIS IS AN EXAMPLE OF A COMMENT IN A NOMAD PROCEDURE?
6. What is involved in the translation phase? In the execution phase?
7. Classify the statements in the procedure and give an example of each.
8. Where can procedures be called from?
9. When the execution of the procedure is complete, where is the control returned?
10. List the commands that control the sequence of statement execution between procedures and environments.
11. What do the OTHERWISE clause and the ON command have in common?
12. Which command groups statements within a procedure?
13. List the commands that control procedure translation.
14. What is the function of the TRANS command? The UNTRANS command?
15. How would you invoke your operating system editor from within the NOMAD environment?

16. What is symbolic substitution?

17. A procedure has obtained the name of an item in a database and a value. Explain this part of the procedure:

```
TRANS
CHANGE ?(&ITEM)=&VAL;
```

18. What will be produced from the following procedure?

```
FOR &A= 'GREGORY','ALAN'
     DO;
     PRINT FOLD 'DEAR '&A ':'
     FOLD 'I WISH TO THANK YOU FOR THE GIFT.'
     FOLD 'THANKS, MOM'
     FOLD 2;
END;
```

CHAPTER 12

Database Definition

Intellectual control is the key to orderly development.

H. D. Mills

12.1 INTRODUCTION

The main objective of this chapter is to teach you how to define the database for our application.

When you have completed this chapter you should be able to:

- List the data types supported by NOMAD.
- Describe and classify the available display and storage formats.
- Describe, in general, the use and classification of the variables in NOMAD.
- Explain how to create a schema file.
- Identify the basic statements needed to construct the schema for our application, the Ski Rental System.
- Briefly describe the required as well as the optional parameters used in the MASTER and ITEM statements.
- Analyze an example of the database schema.
- Identify NOMAD commands used in creating, invoking, and reporting the database structure.

12.2 DATA STORAGE, DISPLAY FORMATS, AND VARIABLES

We start with a description of how NOMAD stores data. Next we show how to specify the display formats and how to declare and use variables.

Data Types

NOMAD supports several data types.

1. *Alphanumeric*—Contains letters, special characters (for example, *, &, #, +), and the numbers 0 through 9. Numbers stored as alphanumeric data cannot be used in algebraic calculations.
2. *Numeric*—Contains numeric data that are subject to algebraic calculations.
3. *Date*—Contains and manipulates calendar dates.
4. *Time*—Handles time intervals.
5. *DateTime*—Contains and manipulates calendar date and time of day.
6. *Logical*—Contains logical values such as true and false.

In addition, NOMAD supports `NOTAVAILABLE` values. `NOTAVAILABLE` means that a variable or an item does not contain any data value (and it is not a zero or a blank). When the `NOTAVAILABLE` value is printed, it appears as the string N/A. You can change this default representation to any other representation you require by changing the `&NOTAVAILABLE` system variable. For example:

```
&NOTAVAILABLE = 'NO DATA';
```

changes the printing of the variables with no (not available) values in them to the string NO DATA.

The `NOTAVAILABLE` value is also stored in another system variable called &NAV. This variable is used in assignment statements and in logical comparison testing (see the discussion later in this chapter).

Any mathematical or character string operation on variables with `NOTAVAILABLE` values results in a `NOTAVAILABLE` value. In logical comparison testing, only the comparison of `NOTAVAILABLE` with another `NOTAVAILABLE` results in a TRUE logical sentence.

Display Formats and Storage

NOMAD supports several data display formats necessary for the transformation and representation of the most common types of business data. Any display format can be specified by using the AS parameter in the following statements:

```
ITEM          FIELD
DECLARE       PRINT
DEFINE        LIST
DISPLAY       CREATE
```

For example, the statement:

```
PRINT (25/4 +12) AS $999.99;
```

prints:

$ 18.25

The available display formats are as follows:

1. *Alphanumeric format* is defined by using the letter A, followed by a number that specifies the length of the field, followed by the optional justification parameter. The justification options L, C, and R display data left, center, or right justified within the length of the specified field. For example,

    ITEM myitem as A24C;

defines the item named myitem as an alphanumeric field 24 characters long. The values of this item are to be displayed centered in the 24 characters.

   Internally, alphanumeric data is stored in ASCII format. Its internal length equals the length of the display format (default). You can override this default, specifying a larger internal format, by using the INTERNAL parameter. For example,

    ITEM myitem AS A24C INTERNAL A30;

causes the internal format to be 30 characters long.

   The maximum available length is 255 characters, and the default justification is left justified.

2. *Numeric format* displays data in two formats: numeric and scientific notation. In the numeric display format, you can display numbers up to 31 digits long. For larger numbers, you can use scientific notation, which can handle numbers up to 99 digits long.

   The length of the display field is determined by allocating one position for each formatting character. If the number to be displayed (counting any negative sign) is larger than the length of the field to be displayed, NOMAD prints asterisks in this field.

   The justification parameter is C, R, or L (center, right justified or left justified). The default justification for numeric values is right justified.

   The numeric display format is specified with special characters. The complete list of these characters is given in Appendix B.

   When no display format is specified, NOMAD displays in the default format. The default format is based on the internal storage format. Internal formats and their corresponding default display formats are given in the following list. *Note:* I specifies an integer, R a real number, and P any real number (of 15 or less digits) with decimals. For example, I4 stands for an integer taking up 4 bytes, R8 stands for a real number taking up 8 bytes and P15.2 for real number (of 15 or less digits) with two decimals. A specifies alphanumeric data not used in calculations.

All NOMAD's default internal formats, their size in bytes, usage, and displays, are listed in Appendix B.

Internal Format	Default Display Format
I2	999,999
I4	9,999,999,999
P15.2	9,999,999,999,999.99
R4	999,999,999.99
R8	999,999,999.99
An	An
IDATE	MM/DD/YY
IDATETIME	MM/DD/YY HH:MN:SS
ILOGICAL	t or f

3. *Date format* allows you to display and manipulate dates. Internally, dates are stored as the number of days since December 31, 1599. You cannot change this internal format, but you can change the date's display format. The following is a listing of some display formats for the date of March 12, 1944.

Display Format	Sample Output
DATE [default]	03/12/44
DATE 'MONTH DD:YYYY'	MARCH 12:1944
DATE 'YY.DDD'	44.072
DATE 'WEEKDAY the DDth of MONTH'	SUNDAY the 12th of MARCH
DATE 'The DDth of Month, YYYY'	The 12th of March, 1944
DATE 'The Moy of YYYY'	The Third month of 1944

The default format for the date value is MM/DD/YY.

As you can see, in a date display format you may describe how the month (for example, Moy = Month of the year), day, and year of the date value are to appear. A complete listing of the formatting keywords, characters, and phrases that can be a part of the date display format can be found in Appendix B.

4. *Time format* specifies that an item will be displayed as an interval of elapsed time. Time values are stored as R8 and are expressed in numbers of milliseconds in the time interval. This is an internal format which you cannot override. The following examples show how the time values of 125 days, 6 hours, and 25 minutes can be formatted and displayed. [*Note:* B specifies blanks, and parenthetical literal, for example, (Minutes), displays as specified. All keywords can be found in Appendix B.]

Display Format	Sample Output
TIME [default]	00125
	06:25:00:000
TIME 'For BHI (Hours)'	For 3006 Hours
[Rounded to the nearest hour]	
TIME 'BDDI HH:MN'	125 06:25
TIME 'MNI8 (Minutes)'	00180385 Minutes
TIME 'BMNI8 (Minutes)' 1	80385 Minutes

5. *DateTime format* is an extension of the Date data type. DateTime values are stored as R8. The value is the elapsed number of milliseconds since December 31, 1599, and this is the internal format of this data type.

A DateTime format can be assembled from any combination of the Date keywords and from any combination of the DateTime keywords listed in Appendix B. If a DateTime format is not specified, the default display format is:

```
MM/DD/YY HH:MN:SS
```

The following examples show some of the display formats for the date 03/12/44 and the time of the day 9:53:11.

Display Format	Sample Output
DATETIME [default]	03/12/44 09:53:11
DATETIME 'HH:MN:SS'	09:53:11
DATETIME 'MONTH'	MARCH
DATETIME 'HH:MN of the DDth of Mon YYYY'	09:53 of the 12th of Mar 1944
DATETIME 'DD/MM/YY at HH12.MN.SS M.'	12/03/44 at 09.53.11 AM

6. *Logical format* is used when Boolean data is needed. The value entered must be the result of the Boolean expression and can include any of the following:

```
true/false
t/f
yes/no
y/n
1/0
```

These values can be in either uppercase or lowercase. No matter which of the preceding choices you enter into the logical data type, the value displayed is t (t=true) or f (f= false).

12.3 VARIABLES

A variable is used for saving values that will be used in calculations, in logical expressions, or to characterize the environment of your NOMAD session. They are referenced by names that start with the ampersand (&) sign. The values of variables are saved only for the duration of the current NOMAD session. Variables work like the memory in your calculator.

NOMAD has several classes of variables:

1. *System Variables* have to do with the system; that is, they specify system parameters for a specific NOMAD session. They are used to monitor exception conditions, to maintain processing statistics. Two examples of the system variables are:

&EDITOR

Contains the name of the editor that can be invoked from NOMAD. The user can change the value of this system variable for the duration of the NOMAD session. (Recall from Chapter 9 the example of the command for changing your editor.)

&DATE

Contains the current date set by the system. The user cannot change it.

2. *User variables* contain temporary data values that you set. The name of the user variable must start with an ampersand (&), followed by up to 15 characters, the first of which must be a letter. Other valid characters are any letter, numeric digit, or an underscore (_).

   User variables with specific names can be declared only once. They can be assigned explicit display formats or internal formats. An example of a user variable name is &SALES1.

3. *&Items* relate to the database. They are the variables that NOMAD creates for each existing database item. These variables carry the same names as database items, preceded by an ampersand (&). The &item always has the same internal and display formats as the database item with the same name. (We discuss &items in more detail when we consider our application's database.)

NOMAD also has a set of predefined values, called system items, that are stored in the data dictionary. They are used to specify NOMAD default settings and can be referenced by predefined names.

DECLARE Command

All user &variables must be declared before they are used. This is done with the DECLARE command. The DECLARE command assigns a specific name and either a display format or an internal format to the user's variable.

Consider the following examples. In the statement

```
DECLARE &Ski_Rent_Rate AS 99.99;
```

we declare the &variable &Ski_Rent_Rate and specify its display format as 99.99. In the statement

```
DECLARE &Ski_Quantity INTERNAL I2;
```

the &Ski_Quantity &variable is declared to hold integer values. Its default display format is 999,999. In the statement

```
DECLARE &Ski_Type AS A4 INTERNAL A10;
```

both display format and internal format are defined for the alphanumeric &variable &Ski_Type. The display format is to be 4 characters long; the internal format is to be 10 characters long.

After the user &variable is declared, it has a value of NOTAVAILABLE (recall the data types we discussed at the beginning of this chapter). So, it has to be *assigned* a value.

The DECLARE command has other optional parameters:

1. *MASK* (mask format)—Specifies the valid format to which alphanumeric values must conform. If you assign a value to the &variable that does not conform to the mask format, NOMAD raises an error condition.

   The mask format is specified using the following characters:

   A   Restricts the designated position to alphabetic characters (A-Z).
   9   Restricts the designated position to numeric characters (0-9).
   X   Restricts the designated position to alphabetic or numeric characters.
   *   Allows the designated position to contain any character.

   For example, in the statement

   ```
   CREATE &Ski_Type_Name AS A10 MASK 'AAAAA-AAAA';
   ```

   the values that can be assigned to the &Ski_Type_Name can be 10 characters long. Each set of values must be formed from 5 letters followed by a hyphen (-), and then by 4 letters.

2. *LIMITS*—Specifies the valid values for the &variable. You can specify values as valid either within a range or individually.

   If you include the keyword NOTNAV in the LIMITS specification, the value of NOTAVAILABLE cannot be assigned to the &variable. For example in the statement

   ```
   DECLARE &Ski_Type AS A5
   LIMITS(NOTNAV,DYN-S,DYN-D,VOK-S);
   ```

   The &Ski_Type &variable is to be displayed as 5 characters long. Valid values are DYN-S, DYN-D, and VOK-S. NOTAVAILABLE cannot be assigned to the &Ski_Type. In the statement

   ```
   DECLARE &Ski_Rent_Rate AS 99.99
   LIMITS (8.50:14.50,20.00);
   ```

   the valid value for the &Ski_Rent_Rate &variable is any number in the range from 8.50 through 14.50, or a value of 20.00. Note that the specification of the range uses the colon (:), whereas single values are separated by a comma.

3. *ALIAS* (alias name)—Specifies an alternate name by which you can refer to the &variable. The name can be up to 15 characters long, beginning with a letter. It must be unique within a file. For example in the statement

   ```
   DECLARE &Ski_Type AS A5 ALIAS stype;
   ```

   the &Ski_Type &variable can be referred to by its alias which is stype.

4. *DOCUMENT* (character string)—Contains a 1- to 255-character description of the &variable. This parameter is useful when you need to document the sources and uses of the declared &variables. For example,

```
DECLARE &Ski_Type AS A5 ALIAS stype
DOCUMENT "Variable will contain the ski type descriptions";
```

Assigning Values to &Variables

Several methods are available for assigning values to the &variables. Although, for now, we will describe only two, we will introduce some of the others later.

An *assignment statement(=)* sets the &variable equal to the value of an expression on the right of the equality sign.

Once set, the value of the &variable remains the same until you change it with another assignment statement or delete it with the PURGE command.

In the following example of an assignment statement

```
&Ski_Value = &Ski_Price * &Ski_Quantity;
```

the value of the &Ski_Value variable is derived. It is a product of the value in the &Ski_Price variable and the value in the &Ski_Quantity variable.

An *ampset command* sets the &item equal to the value of the item on the currently positioned record in the database. It takes values directly from the database itself. Thus, this single command makes multiple assignments to &items from their corresponding items. For example, in the statement

```
AMPSET Skiinventory;
```

all &items will be set to the values corresponding to the items in a currently positioned record in the file Skiinventory.

There is a difference between the AMPSET command and the individual assignments. The individual assignments cause the values to be checked against any MASK, MEMBER, or LIMIT constraint parameter placed on the items. Since AMPSET takes the values directly from the database itself, it does not perform such a check.

CLEAR Command

&variables keep their value until they are explicitly assigned a new one. It is sometimes necessary to set them to the NOTAVALIABLE value, or in a case of the system variables, to their default values. Consider the following examples. The command

```
CLEAR all;
```

specifies that all user &variables are reset to the NOTAVAILABLE value. The command

```
CLEAR system;
```

resets all the system variables to their default values. The command

```
CLEAR skiinventory;
```

specifies that all &items associated with the file skiinventory are to be set to NOTAVAILABLE. In the command

```
CLEAR &Ski_Type &Ski_Type_Name &pwidth &plength;
```

the first two &variables (&Ski_Type and &Ski_Type_Name) are user-declared variables. The CLEAR command resets them to the NOTAVAILABLE value. &pwidth and &plength are system &variables. They are reset to 132 and 66 respectively, and are the default values for the page width and the page length.

12.4 DEFINING THE DATABASE IN NOMAD: CREATING A SCHEMA

The first step in creating your NOMAD application is to define the database. (The NOMAD database has a relational structure. The relationships between records of different master files are established not when the data is stored, but rather when the data is requested. Records are thus associated by matching specific fields in the records. When data is retrieved from a relational database, records from different files are matched and joined. The only restriction to the matching is that the item values matched must have the same data format.) The database is defined by creating a file called *schema*. The schema is a description of the data to be stored in the database and the format that is to be used for data storage and retrieval. You create this file using your system editor.

The required extension for this file is .SCH which is an abbreviation of the word "schema." NOMAD recognizes that the file with the .SCH extension contains the database definition statements. For example,

```
SKIRENT.SCH
```

is a valid filename. This file will contain special NOMAD statements describing the characteristics of your database.

Schema statements perform the following functions:

- Name the files in your database.
- Name fields (items) in each of your files.
- Describe the attributes, characteristics, and constraints on all items.
- Specify relationships among items.
- Provide data integrity checks.

■ Establish security of access to your database.

■ Allow you to predefine certain calculations.

To build a complete database schema for our application (the Ski Rental System, which was described in Chapter 10) you need to understand certain NOMAD statements.

In a stepwise manner, we start with basic statements using the default options and gradually increase the sophistication of the application until we have introduced all the other options.

The general rules used for building the statements in a schema are as follows:

1. Statements can be entered one statement to a line, one statement extending over multiple lines, or multiple statements on a single line.

2. The end of a statement is denoted by a semicolon (;).

3. Comments can be entered any place in the schema enclosed in exclamation points (!) or you can use the format of /* comment */. For example,

```
!This is an inventory system!
```

or

```
/*This is an inventory system*/.
```

4. The files in the database are called *master files.* Their names must be unique within the entire schema.

5. The names of items (fields, stored) and defines (calculated, derived fields, not stored) must be unique within the individual master files.

12.5 SCHEMA STATEMENTS: OPTIONS AND COMMANDS

Recall from Chapter 10 that our Ski Rental System requires the following eight files to store all the necessary information:

FILE NAME	CONTENTS
EQUIPMENT TYPE	Description of the equipment in the inventory
MANUFACTURERS	Data on the equipment manufacturers
CUSTOMER	Information on the Ski shop customers
SKIINVENTORY	Information on rental skis
BOOTINVENTORY	Information on rental boots
POLEINVENTORY	Information on rental poles
TRANSACTIONS	Information on the ski rental transactions
HISTORY	History of earnings from rentals in previous ski season

Each of these files will be used in turn to help introduce you to NOMAD's many statements and options.

Basic Statements with Required Parameters

To define a file in a schema, you will need at minimum these two statements:

- MASTER
- ITEM

The *MASTER statement* is used to specify a single file. It specifies the way that the instances of the data are to be stored and retrieved. Its required parameters are:

1. *Master-name*—The master name can be up to 15 characters long, beginning with a letter, followed by any alphanumeric character. The whole Master name must be unique within the data dictionary. The first 7 characters of each master name must be unique within a specific schema because the file created for each master uses these first 7 characters and an .NDB extension as its filename. There is no limit to the number of masters that can be defined in a database.

2. *KEYED*—Specifies an item or multiple items as a key. The master file is sorted in order of items specified as the key. When a key consists of multiple items, it is sorted first by the first key and then, within it, by the second key, and so on. The master is then said to be *multikeyed*. The default sorting order is ascending order. If you would like to keep your master in descending order, use the letter "D" after a specific keyed item.

   The keys are designated by listing the names of items enclosed in parentheses. Unique keys are the default. That is, no multiple records are allowed with the same value of a key. To allow duplicate records, place the NOTUNIQUE parameter after the list of keys.

   The following MASTER statement includes all the parameters just described:

   ```
   MASTER history KEYED(year,D,weekc) NOTUNIQUE;
   ```

   Here, the history file is multikeyed. Its key is composed of two items: the year and weekc. The records in the file are first sorted in descending order by year and then in ascending (default) order by weekc. Multiple records are allowed with the same value of a key.

The *ITEM statement* is used to describe the items (fields) in each master file. Such statements follow the MASTER statement. The total number of items and defines (defined calculated fields) in one master may not exceed 500. Its required parameters are:

1. *Item-name*—The item name is used to communicate with your database. It specifies the name of the item and must be unique within its master. Its maximum length is 15 characters, with the first character alphabetic and the remaining characters can be letters, numbers, and the underscore.

2. *AS display-format*—This parameter allows you to describe the format in which the values for the specific items are to be printed when the PRINT or the LIST command is used. NOMAD uses the display format to establish the requirements for the item's internal storage (the default). You can control an item's format by overriding the default internal storage format with the INTERNAL parameter.

Defining Our File

To differentiate between NOMAD's *reserved* words and the user's *assigned* words, we will show the reserved words in a uppercase letters and the assigned words in the lowercase letters. This convention is only for you, the reader, since NOMAD can accept both upper- and lowercase forms.

Before we define our first file, the EQUIPMENT_TYPE file, we need to consider what data are we going to store there. This file is to contain the information on the type of the rental equipment in the Ski Shop inventory, that is, the equipment type and the year of its production.

Since this information will be used in conjunction with the information in the SKI, BOOTS, and POLES inventory files, we need a field for linking records from those inventory files with the records in the EQUIPMENT_TYPE file. A good candidate for this linking field is the equipment code field. This field is also a good candidate for a key field in the EQUIPMENT_TYPE file.

Why should we not include the equipment name, the date of production, the data on the equipment manufacturer in the inventory of skis, boots, and poles files? We want to reduce the amount of data the user has to enter into these files. Note that these inventory files can contain multiple records on the equipment with the same equipment name and the same production date. It is much less work to type in the 4-digit equipment code than to type in the 20-character equipment name and the 4-digit year of production. The user should do it only once. The EQUIPMENT_TYPE file is a good place for it. When you avoid repeated entry of the same data, you also save the disk space.

Now we are ready to define our file. The schema statements for the EQUIP-MENT_TYPE file are:

```
/*This is the definition of the Equipment Type file*/
/*It contains information on the name of equipment*/
/*and the date of its manufacture*/
MASTER equipment_type  KEYED(equipment_code);
   ITEM equipment_code   AS A4;
   ITEM equipment_name   as A20;
   ITEM production_date   date'YYYY';
```

The first three lines are simply the comment statements. We have used them for documentation purposes to note what kind of information this file contains.

The fourth line is the MASTER statement. It assigns the name to a file (EQUIP-MENT-TYPE) and designates the item equipment_code as a key. NOMAD automatically makes the equipment_code a unique key, and the file will be sorted in the ascending order (by default).

The last three lines are ITEM statements specifying that the file will contain the following three fields:

1. equipment_code: A 4-characters alphanumeric field.
2. equipment_name: A 20-character alphanumeric field.
3. production_date: A date field that prints only the year as 4-digit number.

As you can see, very little is required to define this file.

Optional Parameters for the MASTER Statement

The MASTER statement has three optional parameters:

1. **ALIAS alias-name**—Allows you to specify an alternative name by which your master file can be referenced. The naming convention is the same as that for the regular filename, and the alias must be unique within the schema.

2. **DOCUMENT 'character string'**—Allows you to insert text that will appear whenever you issue the LIST command (more about this command shortly) for that master. The text can be up to 255 characters long and can be used to annotate MASTER statements for online documentation purposes.

3. **AMPDITEMS**—Causes, in a specified master file, automatic declaration of the variables (&ditems) associated with the defined items. (We will return to AMPDITEMS later and give an example of the use of this parameter when we describe the defines.)

Now, let us incorporate the first two optional parameters in our MASTER statement:

```
MASTER equipment-type KEYED(equipment_code) ALIAS equiptyp
DOCUMENT 'This file contains the description of the equipment
available for renting.';
```

We introduced the alias name for our file (equiptyp) and included a documentation sentence describing, in general, what our file contains.

Optional Parameters for the ITEM Statement

Many optional parameters are available for the ITEM statement. For clarity, we describe them in functionally related groups. Optional parameters are designed to perform the following functions:

1. Define a heading for the report column and a label for the data entry screen (HEADING, DESCRIPTION).
2. Implicitly define the output of the value of the item from another file (DISPLAY, MEMBER).
3. Define data integrity checks (MASK, LIMITS, and MEMBER).
4. Miscellaneous functions (ERRMSG, DOCUMENT, and ALIAS).
5. Control internal storage formats (INTERNAL).

HEADING

This parameter specifies the heading lines that are to appear at the top of a column on a report. To extend a heading to multiple lines, words in the heading are separated (for each line) by a colon (:). For example,

```
ITEM production_date  AS DATE 'YYYY'
    HEADING 'YEAR OF:PRODUCTION';
```

specifies the item, its display format, and the column heading for reports in which the values for the production_date item are displayed. This column heading is to be in two lines. The first line displays the text YEAR OF; the second displays PRODUCTION.

DESCRIPTION

This parameter specifies the description to appear at the left of the item when the item appears in a window specified by the WINDOW commands or by the FIELD statement. For example,

```
ITEM manufact_code  AS A4
    HEADING 'MANUFACTURERS:CODE'
    DESCRIPTION 'MANUFACTURERS CODE';
```

When the value of the item manufact_code appears on the screen, at the left of this value, a text MANUFACTURERS CODE will appear.

Descriptions can extend to multiple lines. To extend a DESCRIPTION to many lines, separate the words for each line with a colon (:).

If you do not specify a DESCRIPTION, NOMAD uses the item's HEADING. For example,

```
ITEM custident   AS A20  ALIAS cident
    HEADING 'CUSTOMER:IDENTIFICATION';
```

In this case, the value of the item custident (which can be referred to with an alias cident), when displayed in the window, is preceded by the text (in two lines):

```
CUSTOMER
IDENTIFICATION
```

If you do not specify a heading, NOMAD uses the item's name for a description. Any underscores that may be present are suppressed. For example,

```
ITEM zip_code
```

will have the description zip code.

DISPLAY

This parameter causes automatic look-up on another master just before it displays the value of the item. The form of this parameter is:

```
DISPLAY item-name2 FROM master-name.
```

For example,

```
ITEM pole_type AS DISPLAY 'equipment_name
     FROM equipment_type'
     HEADING 'POLE TYPE';
```

NOMAD locates the instance of the equipment_type master whose primary key equals the value of the item equipment_name (the item's value is matched with the primary key of the master). Then this value is displayed as the value of the item pole_type. (In our example, the report heading for the column of values of the pole_type item is to be POLE TYPE.) If there is no key match, the value displayed is the current setting of the &NOTAVAILABLE variable, which usually is set as N/A.

MEMBER

This parameter restricts values for an item to those specified as the primary key in a look-up master. For example,

```
ITEM pole_flag   AS MEMBER 'customer';
ITEM ski_flag    AS MEMBER 'customer';
```

When you assign a value for an item (pole_flag or ski_flag), automatic look-up is performed in the customer master for a matching key value.

Note that the MEMBER parameter also belongs to the third group of optional parameters: those used for the data integrity checks.

MASK

This parameter specifies the valid format to which alphanumeric item values must conform. The valid format is specified as follows:

A   Restricts the designated position to the letters (A-Z).
X   Restricts the designated position to the alphanumeric characters (letters or numbers).
9   Restricts the designated position to numbers (0-9).
*   Allows the designated position to contain any character.

You can specify characters other than A, X, 9, or * in a MASK format, but then the item value for that position must be precisely this specified character. For example,

```
ITEM rep_telephon  AS A12  MASK '999-999-9999'
     HEADING  'REPRESENTATIVE:TELEPHONE NO.'
     DESCRIPTION 'TELEPHONE NO';
```

The MASK format must match the length of the item, filled with asterisks (*), if necessary.

LIMITS

This parameter specifies the valid values for an item. The item subject to LIMITS can be alphanumeric, numeric, or a date.

You can specify the values as valid either within a range or individually. You set ranges for items by specifying the lower and upper limits (lower limit first), with a colon separating the two. In one LIMITS parameter you can use any number and combination of value specifications. You simply separate each specification from the next with a comma. For example,

```
ITEM skiing_ability  AS A2 LIMITS('EX','RE','IN','BG')
     ALIAS SKIA  HEADING 'SKIING:ABILITY';
```

specifies that the item skiing_ability can have as valid values only those specified in the LIMITS parameter. By the way, EX corresponds to the skiing ability of an expert skier (a racer); RE is an advanced skier (recreational expert); IN is an intermediate; and BG is a beginner.

ERRMSG

This parameter indicates an error message that is displayed when you make an error trying to update an item on a Form. For example,

```
ITEM skiing_ability  AS A2 LIMITS('EX','RE','IN','BG')
     ALIAS skia  HEADING 'SKIING:ABILITY'
     ERRMSG 'ERROR - VALID ENTRIES ARE EX, RE, IN and BG';
```

displays an error message:

```
ERROR - VALID ENTRIES ARE EX, RE, IN and BG
```

if an entry for the item SKIING_ABILITY is not one of those specified in the LIMITS parameter.

DOCUMENT

This parameter documents sources and uses of the item values. Its use and form are the same as those for the DOCUMENT parameter we defined for the MASTER statement.

ALIAS

This parameter specifies an alternate name by which you can refer to the item. Typically, ALIAS is the shorthand name for the item. It must be unique within the master.

Like the item-name, can be up to 15 characters long, beginning with a letter, and thereafter containing any combination of letters, digits, and underscore (_). For example,

```
ITEM ski_rentch AS $99.99 ALIAS skichar
     HEADING 'SKI RENTAL:CHARGE';
```

The item ski_rentch can be referred to by its alias, which is specified as skichar.

INTERNAL

This parameter specifies the internal format in which data values are stored. By default, the internal format is based on the display format. Specifying the INTERNAL parameter overrides this default. For example,

```
ITEM ski_sz AS 999 INTERNAL I2;
```

will be stored in I2 format. (Some of the internal formats are listed at the beginning of this chapter. For a detailed definition of the internal formats, refer to Appendix B.)

12.6 DEFINE STATEMENT

The DEFINE statement is similar to the ITEM statement, but there are some differences. The DEFINE statement allows you to establish items for which no data are stored in the database. Values for the defined items are derived. They are based on the computations, table look-ups, or specific tests performed each time the defined item is referenced.

The defined item can have any name. This name must be unique within its master.

Required Parameters for the DEFINE Statement

The following are required parameters.

Item-name

This parameter specifies the name of the item to be defined. Item-names must be unique within a master, and the number and the type of characters allowed are the same as for its use in the ITEM statement.

AS display format

This parameter specifies the default format in which the defined item is to be printed or listed. Its use is the same as in the ITEM statement.

EXPR = expression

This parameter specifies the expression required to yield a value for the defined item. For example,

```
DEFINE fee_paid  as $999.99
EXPR=ski_rent_paid + boot_rent_paid + pole_rent_paid;
```

The fee_paid item for which no data is stored in the database is thus defined; its display format is specified. The expression establishes how a value for this item is to be derived.

EXTRACT

This parameter specifies the data from another file to be looked up and used in the current file.

It is used to specify the value of the defined item. The value of the defined item can be specified by one of the two parameters: EXPR or EXTRACT. These parameters are mutually exclusive.

Consider this example:

```
DEFINE sman_name  AS EXTRACT 'manufact_name
         FROM manufacturers USING ski_manufact';
```

The value of the defined sman_name item is specified as the value of the manufact_name item from the file manufacturers.

NOMAD searches the manufacturers file for the record in which the value of the key field in this file matches the value of the ski_manufact item from the current file.

The value of manufact_name from this record becomes the value of the defined sman_name item.

Optional Parameters for the DEFINE Statement

All the optional parameters of the DEFINE statement are used in the same manner and have the same form as their corresponding parameters in the ITEM statement. These parameters are:

```
ALIAS
HEADING
DESCRIPTION
DOCUMENT
INTERNAL
```

Any display format that applies to an item can be used with a defined item as well. Any searching or reporting activity that can be performed on an item can also be performed on a defined item.

12.7 END STATEMENT

This statement denotes the end of a group of schema statements. It concludes the description of a master. Although it is an optional statement, it is advisable to use it for completeness. Its format is:

```
END;
```

12.8 SCHEMA FOR THE SKI SHOP RENTALS SYSTEM

We are ready to construct the schema for our application. The masters we need are:

EQUIPMENT_TYPE

The Equipment Type file contains the description of the equipment in the inventory. A portion of the schema for this file was created in this chapter. We only need to add some of the optional parameters to the item's definition to allow us to handle headers globally (heading option) and to document the items (description option).

MANUFACTURERS

The Manufacturers file contains data on the equipment manufacturers. As is the case with the Equipment Type file, the purpose of this file is to help reduce the amount of information the user has to enter into the equipment inventory files. The 4-digit manufacturer code provides a link to the inventory files.

CUSTOMER

The Customer file contains the information on the Ski Shop customers. Records in this file are organized by two key fields: IDENT_TYPE and CUSTIDENT.

SKIINVENTORY

The Ski Inventory file contains the information on rental skis. To the items introduced in the design specifications (Chapter 10) we add two defined items. The first defined item handles the name of manufacturers for a specific record in the rental inventory; the second handles the equipment type name. These defined items simplify the reporting process and reduce the amount of data to be entered into database. Defined items in NOMAD are used the same way as regular items, but they are not stored elements. They are recalculated each time you reposition the pointer on another record in the database.

The item SKI_FLAG is used to indicate if a specific pair of skis is rented or is in the inventory. The SKI_FLAG field is derived from the key fields of the Transactions file (customer id and the id type).

BOOTINVENTORY

The Boot Inventory file contains the information on rental boots. Its design construct is the same as that for the Ski Inventory file. The rental flag has the same values as the one in the Ski Inventory file, but here it is called the BOOT_FLAG.

POLEINVENTORY

The Pole Inventory file contains the information on rental poles. Its design construct is the same as that for the Ski Inventory and Boot Inventory files.

TRANSACTIONS

The Transactions file contains the information on the ski rental transactions. In addition to the items described in the design specification for this file (Chapter 10), several defined items are specified to handle daily rental charges, prepaid rental fees, and final rental fees for each type of rental equipment.

HISTORY

The Historical Revenue file contains the history of rental earnings from previous ski seasons. The records represent weekly earnings from the rental operation, for different categories of rental equipment.

Now we are ready for the database schema for our Ski Rental System application.

Each master file starts with the MASTER statement followed by the appropriate ITEM statements. Display formats are specified.

The MASK, HEADING, and DESCRIPTION parameters are used when they are needed in the ITEM statements. Aliases are used when this alternate reference will be referred to in the future.

Certain items have limits, so the LIMITS parameter is used for them. The ERMSG parameter is used to display specified customized error messages.

In the SKIINVENTORY, BOOTINVENTORY, POLEINVENTORY, and TRANSACTIONS master, defines (derived items) are stated and expressions for their calculations are specified.

Carefully analyze each statement in the following database schema file to see how it is constructed and what it states. This analysis will facilitate your learning by example.

```
SKIRENT.SCH

MASTER equipment_type     KEYED(equipment_code);
  ITEM equipment_code    AS A4  HEADING 'EQUIPMENT:CODE'
       DESCRIPTION 'EQUIPMENT CODE';
  ITEM equipment_name    AS A20 HEADING 'EQUIPMENT:NAME'
       DESCRIPTION 'EQUIPMENT NAME';
  ITEM production_date  AS DATE 'YYYY' HEADING 'YEAR
       OF:PRODUCTION' DESCRIPTION 'YEAR OF PRODUCTION';


MASTER manufacturers      KEYED(manufact_code);
  ITEM manufact_code     AS A4 HEADING 'MANUFACTURERS:CODE'
       DESCRIPTION 'MANUFACTURERS CODE';
  ITEM manufact_name     AS A25 HEADING 'MANUFACTURERS:NAME'
       DESCRIPTION 'MANUFACTURERS NAME';
  ITEM street            AS A20;
  ITEM city              AS A20;
  ITEM state             AS A15;
  ITEM zip_code          AS A9;
  ITEM rep_name          AS A30 HEADING 'REPRESENTATIVE:NAME'
       DESCRIPTION 'REPRESENTATIVE NAME';
  ITEM rep_telephon      AS A12 MASK '999-999-9999' HEADING
     'REPRESENTATIVE:TELEPHONE NO.'  DESCRIPTION 'TELEPHONE NO';


MASTER customer      KEYED(ident_type,custident);
  ITEM ident_type  AS A2 LIMITS('MC','DL','MX','VI','ST','OT')
       HEADING 'IDENTIFICATION:TYPE'
       ERRMSG 'ERROR - VALID IDENTIFICATIONS ARE MC,DL,MX,VI,ST,OT';
  ITEM custident    AS A20  ALIAS cident
       HEADING 'CUSTOMER:IDENTIFICATION';
  ITEM last_name   AS A20  ALIAS lname  HEADING 'LAST:NAME';
  ITEM first_name  AS A10  ALIAS fname  HEADING 'FIRST:NAME';
  ITEM middle_initial AS A1 ALIAS mname HEADING 'MIDDLE:INITIAL';
  ITEM street_address  AS A30 ALIAS stadd
       HEADING 'STREET:ADDRESS';
  ITEM city             AS A20;
  ITEM state            AS A15;
  ITEM zip_code         AS A9 ALIAS zip;
  ITEM phone            AS A12 MASK '999-999-9999'
       HEADING 'PHONE NUMBER';
  ITEM local_accom      AS A25   HEADING 'LOCAL:ACCOMMODATION';
  ITEM cust_height_f    AS 9        ALIAS custhgtf
       HEADING 'HEIGHT:FEET';
```

```
ITEM cust_height_i    AS 99        ALIAS custhgti
     HEADING 'HEIGHT:INCHES';
ITEM weight           AS 999;
ITEM age              AS 999;
ITEM sex              AS A1    LIMITS('F','M')
     ERRMSG 'ERROR - VALID ENTRY F OR M';
ITEM skiing_ability   AS A2 LIMITS('EX','RE','IN','BG')
     ALIAS skia     HEADING 'SKIING:ABILITY'
     ERRMSG 'ERROR - VALID ENTRIES ARE EX, RE, IN, and BG';
ITEM binding_l_toe    AS A3    ALIAS bindlt
     HEADING 'BINDING:L. TOE';
ITEM binding_r_toe    AS A3    ALIAS bindrt
     HEADING 'BINDING:R. TOE';
ITEM binding_l_heel   AS A3    ALIAS bindlh
     HEADING 'BINDING:L. HEEL';
ITEM binding_r_heel   AS A3    ALIAS bindrh
     HEADING 'BINDING:R. HEEL';


MASTER skiinventory        KEYED(skinum);
ITEM skinum        AS A8    HEADING 'SKI SERIAL:NUMBER';
ITEM ski_manufact AS MEMBER 'manufacturers'
     HEADING 'SKI MANUFACTURER';
ITEM ski_type      AS MEMBER 'equipment_type'
     HEADING 'SKI TYPE';
ITEM ski_length    AS 999        ALIAS skilen
     HEADING 'SKI LENGTH';
ITEM ski_rentch    AS $99.99    ALIAS skichar
     HEADING 'SKI RENTAL:CHARGE';
ITEM ski_flag      AS A22;
DEFINE sman_name    AS EXTRACT 'manufact_name FROM manufacturers
        USING ski_manufact'  HEADING  'SKI MANUFACTURER:NAME';
DEFINE st_name     AS EXTRACT 'equipment_name FROM equipment_type
        USING ski_type  HEADING  'SKI TYPE:NAME';


MASTER bootinventory        KEYED(bootnum);
ITEM bootnum       AS A4
     HEADING 'BOOT SERIAL:NUMBER';
ITEM boot_manufact AS MEMBER 'manufacturers'
     HEADING 'BOOT MANUFACTURER';
ITEM boot_type     AS MEMBER 'equipment_type'
     HEADING 'BOOT TYPE';
ITEM boot_size     AS 999      ALIAS bootsize
     HEADING 'BOOT SIZE';
```

```
    ITEM boot_rentch    AS $99.99  ALIAS bootchar
        HEADING 'BOOT RENTAL:CHARGE';
    ITEM boot_flag      AS A22;
    DEFINE bman_name    AS EXTRACT 'manufact_name FROM manufacturers
          USING boot_manufact'  HEADING 'BOOT MANUFACTURER:NAME';
    DEFINE bt_name    AS EXTRACT 'equipment_name FROM equipment_type
          USING boot_type' HEADING   'BOOT TYPE:NAME';


MASTER poleinventory        KEYED(polenum);
    ITEM polenum       AS A4  HEADING  'POLE SERIAL:NUMBER';
    ITEM pole_manufact AS MEMBER 'manufacturers'
        HEADING 'POLE MANUFACTURING';
    ITEM pole_type      AS MEMBER 'equipment_type'
        HEADING 'POLE TYPE';
    ITEM pole_length   AS 999      ALIAS poleleng
        HEADING 'POLE LENGTH';
    ITEM pole_rentch    AS $99.99  ALIAS polechar
        HEADING 'POLE RENTAL:CHARGE';
    ITEM pole_flag      AS A22;
    DEFINE pman_name    AS EXTRACT 'manufact_name FROM manufacturers
           USING pole_manufact'  HEADING 'POLE MANUFACTURER:NAME';
    DEFINE pt_name    AS EXTRACT 'equipment_name FROM equipment_type
           USING pole_type'  HEADING   'POLETYPE:NAME';


MASTER transactions              KEYED(ident_type,custident);
    ITEM ident_type  AS A2 LIMITS('MC','DL','MX','VI','ST','OT')
        HEADING 'IDENTIFICATION:TYPE'
        ERRMSG 'ERROR - VALID IDENTIFICATIONS ARE MC,DL,MX,VI,ST,OT';
    ITEM custident   AS A20  ALIAS cident
        HEADING 'CUSTOMER:IDENTIFICATION';
    ITEM date_out    AS DATE 'mmddyy' ALIAS dateo
        HEADING 'DATE OUT';
    ITEM date_due    AS DATE 'mmddyy' ALIAS dated
        HEADING 'DATE DUE';
    ITEM ski_num     AS MEMBER 'skiinventory'
        HEADING 'SKI INVENTORY:NUMBER';
    ITEM boot_num    AS MEMBER 'bootinventory'
        HEADING 'BOOT INVENTORY:NUMBER';
    ITEM pole_num    AS MEMBER 'poleinventory'
        HEADING 'POLE INVENTORY:NUMBER';
    ITEM date_ret    AS DATE 'mmddyy' ALIAS dater
        HEADING 'RETURN DATE';
    ITEM technician   AS A2  HEADING 'TECHNICIAN:ID';
```

```
DEFINE amount_ski   AS EXTRACT 'ski_rentch FROM skiinventory
        USING ski_num'  HEADING 'SKI RENTING:FEE PER DAY';
DEFINE amount_boot  AS EXTRACT 'boot_rentch FROM bootinventory
        USING boot_num'  HEADING 'BOOT RENTING:FEE PER DAY';
DEFINE amount_pole  AS EXTRACT 'pole_rentch FROM poleinventory
        USING pole_num' HEADING 'POLE RENTING:FEE PER DAY';
DEFINE ski_pre_paid AS $999.99
        EXPR=(date_due - date_out) * amount_ski
        HEADING  'SKI RENT:PRE-PAID';
DEFINE ski_rent_paid AS $999.99
        EXPR=(date_ret - date_out) * amount_ski
        HEADING  'SKI RENT:PAID';
DEFINE boot_pre_paid AS $999.99
        EXPR=(date_due - date_out) * amount_boot
        HEADING  'BOOT RENT:PRE-PAID';
DEFINE boot_rent_paid AS $999.99
        EXPR=(date_ret - date_out) * amount_boot
        HEADING  'BOOT RENT:PAID';
DEFINE pole_pre_paid AS $999.99
        EXPR=(date_due - date_out) * amount_pole
        HEADING  'POLE RENT:PRE-PAID';
DEFINE pole_rent_paid AS $999.99
        EXPR=(date_ret - date_out) * amount_pole
        HEADING  'POLE RENT:PAID';
DEFINE fee_pre_paid  AS $999.99
        EXPR=ski_pre_paid + boot_pre_paid + pole_pre_paid
        HEADING  'TOTAL RENTAL:FEE PRE-PAID';
DEFINE fee_paid  AS $999.99
        EXPR=ski_rent_paid + boot_rent_paid + pole_rent_paid
        HEADING  'TOTAL RENTAL:FEE PAID';


MASTER history             KEYED(year,weekc);
  item year       AS DATE 'YYYY'       HEADING 'YEAR';
  item weekc      AS 99                HEADING 'WEEK'S CODE';
  item ski_revenue AS $99,999.99 ALIAS skirev
      HEADING 'REVENUE:FROM SKI RENTAL';
  item boot_revenue AS $99,999.99 ALIAS bootrev
      HEADING 'REVENUE:FROM BOOTS RENTAL';
  item poles_revenue AS $99,999.99 ALIAS polesrev
      HEADING 'REVENUE:FROM BOOTS RENTAL';

END;
```

Having created the schema, you need to save it. Issue a SAVE command in your system editor and return to the NOMAD environment to create the database.

12.9 NOMAD COMMANDS FOR CREATING, INVOKING, AND REPORTING THE DATABASE STRUCTURE

The NOMAD schema contains the information about your application database. Such information is called *metadata*. Metadata is the information about your data descriptions. It can be thought of as the collection of all the attributes about a particular entity. For example, a particular entity may have, as its identifying characteristics, a name, the fact that it is an item in a particular master, a display format, an internal format, a heading, a description, and so on. All of this identifying information is the metadata for this entity.

Because of the presence of an active data dictionary, many attributes only need to be specified once to be recognized in other parts of NOMAD. For example, we placed integrity constraints including LIMITS and MEMBER in the schema. Since NOMAD knows that these integrity constraints exist, it ensures that they are validated each time the new record is created.

SCHEMA Command

The SCHEMA command translates your schema file and places the description of your database into the NOMAD dictionary.

The SCHEMA command is issued from the NOMAD Command window. Its required parameter is the database name, for example,

```
SCHEMA skirent;
```

We assume that the description of the database is already entered into the skirent.sch file. (The name of the database is skirent.) The SCHEMA command causes the description contained in skirent.sch to be put into the data dictionary file.

The SCHEMA command has several optional parameters.

```
NEW
REORG
CHECK
DELETE
```

They are used to indicate the specific action to be performed in the SCHEMA command.

NEW

The NEW parameter indicates a new database. You must use this parameter the first time you translate a database description (before entering the data). All metadata described in the schema statements is thus stored in the data dictionary.

When the NEW parameter is present in the SCHEMA command, NOMAD ensures that your database does not already exist. If any inconsistency is encountered during the processing of the schema description, an error message will appear.

REORG

The REORG parameter modifies the entries in the data dictionary and reorganizes the data in the database to correspond to the modified schema. It is used when you have made changes to the schema that require changing the storage of existing data. It compares a modified schema against the existing entries in the data dictionary.

When you use this parameter you can:

- Add new items to existing masters.
- Delete items from existing masters.
- Reorder items or masters.
- Delete existing masters.
- Change display formats, which become internal formats by default.
- Change internal formats.

However, you *cannot*:

- Change master names.
- Change item names.
- Add or delete keys.
- Change the sequence of keys.

If you change the name of an item and issue the SCHEMA command with the REORG parameter, the item is deleted under its former name and the schema will include a new item with a new name. A new item is generated with all its values set to NOTAVAILABLE. The old item values are deleted.

After you issue the SCHEMA command with the REORG parameter, NOMAD displays the changes you have requested and asks for a confirmation. If you answer yes, NOMAD makes the appropriate changes to the data dictionary and to the data. If you answer no, NOMAD leaves the old relations and data intact, and you can proceed with further editing of the schema.

CHECK

The CHECK parameter facilitates changes to the database definition that affect only metadata and do not affect the data from the database itself. The data dictionary is modified to reflect the schema changes.

When you use this parameter, you can:

- Add new masters.
- Reorder masters.
- Change item names.
- Change display formats, as long as the item's internal format is unchanged.
- Add, change, or delete parameters such as HEADING, AS, DESCRIPTION, DOCUMENT, MASK, LIMITS, and MEMBER. In general, you can add, delete, or change ITEM statement parameter options that do not affect the physical storage of the data.
- Add, change, or delete defines.

However, you *cannot*:

- Add, delete, or change the order of items and stored defines in an existing master.
- Change existing master names.
- Change the physical storage of the data.

If you change the name of an item and then issue the SCHEMA command with the CHECK parameter, NOMAD simply renames the item in the database. Only the name of the item is changed, unlike SCHEMA REORG, which would delete the old item and add the new one.

DELETE

The DELETE parameter erases all associated database files and the definitions of data structure in the data dictionary. The schema file is not deleted. In essence, this option causes the database to cease to exist because all metadata relating to the database that were subject to the DELETE option are removed from the data dictionary.

For example, assume that you have created the database called company and the schema for this database is contained in the company.sch file. When you issue the command:

    SCHEMA company DELETE

you are asked to confirm the deletion. After you confirm the deletion, all database files associated with the company database are deleted. The schema file company.sch is not erased, however.

DATABASE Command

This command specifies the database to be activated. It is required before any database activities can begin. For example, assume that the `skirent` database has been built. To activate the `skirent` database simply issue the following command:

```
DATABASE skirent;
```

The `DATABASE` command is usually the first command you will issue after you have entered the NOMAD environment.

Multiple `DATABASE` commands can be issued during a NOMAD session. In this way you can change from one database to another. For example, assume that your currently active database is the `company` database. You want to change to the `skirent` database. To do that, issue the following command:

```
DATABASE skirent;
```

Since this command specifies a database that is different from the currently active one

- The newly specified database `skirent` is now accessible.
- The `company` database is deactivated.
- Any open files are closed.
- All defined items associated with the deactivated database are no longer accessible.

If the `DATABASE` command were to specify a database that is already active, the command would simply be ignored, and the active database would remain accessible.

DBADD Command

This command specifies that an additional database is to be made active. As with the `DATABASE` command, the `DBADD` command is required before any database activity can be performed.

For example, assume that the currently active database is `skirent`. Now, if you issue the following command:

```
DBADD company;
```

the `company` database is also made active.

DBCLEAR Command

You can issue this command to deactivate all currently active databases. All defined items associated with the deactivated databases will no longer be accessible, and all open files will be closed.

You will be unable to access deactivated files unless you reissue the DATABASE or the DBADD command.

SLIST Command

This command displays a listing of the description of the database. When you specify the SLIST command without any parameters, the description of all currently active databases is displayed.

For example, assume that both the company and the skirent databases are currently active. If you issue the command:

```
SLIST;
```

a listing of the description of the company and the skirent database will be displayed.

To specify a particular listing, use one of the following parameters with the SLIST command.

- **Master-name**—Specifies the name of the master for which information is requested.
- **Item-name**—Specifies the name of the item for which information is requested.
- **ALLV**—Specifies a request for a listing of all system and user-defined variables. (Items are not listed.)
- **AMPV**—Specifies a request for a listing of all user variables. (Items are not listed.)
- **&variable**—Specifies the system variable (&variable), user-defined variable (&variable), or item (&item) for which information is requested.

For example, assume that you have made some changes to the **skirent** schema description. After all the changes were made, you used the SLIST command again to view specific changes you made to the data structure. To see a change you made to the manufact_name item, you could issue the following command:

```
SLIST manufact_name;
```

and the listing for the manufact_name item would be displayed.

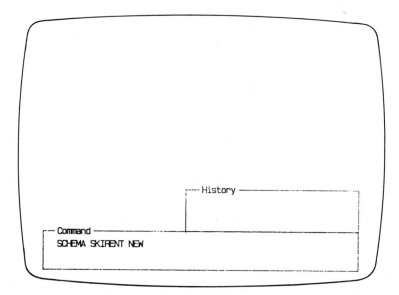

Figure 12.1 Translating a New Schema

12.10 SAMPLE SESSION WITH NOMAD

In this session you will encounter most of the features discussed thus far.

The Situation

You have constructed the schema for the ski rent database. The description of this database has been entered into the skirent.sch file. You used your system editor to do that, and you are back in the NOMAD environment. The Command and History windows are now displayed.

Translating a New Schema

Once you have entered the description of a new database, you can use the SCHEMA command to make the description known to the data dictionary. The screen and the command you enter are shown in Figure 12.1.

The NEW parameter tells NOMAD to

1. Check that another database with the name ski rent does not exist.
2. Check that the syntax for the MASTER and ITEM statements is correct.
3. Translate the file.
4. Store the file in the data dictionary.

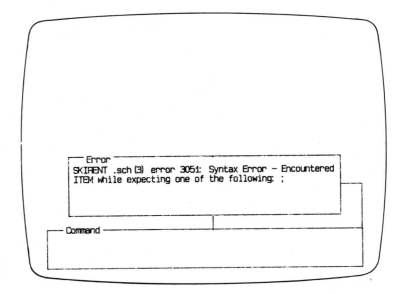

```
┌─ Error ──────────────────────────────────────────────┐
│ SKIRENT .sch (3) error 3051: Syntax Error - Encountered│
│ ITEM while expecting one of the following: ;           │
│                                                        │
│                                                        │
└──────────────────────────────────────────────────────┘
┌─ Command ────────────────────────────────────────────
│
│
```

Figure 12.2 First Error Window

Correcting Errors in Your Schema

Before your schema is placed in the data dictionary, NOMAD checks it for errors. You attempted to compile your schema, but a bright red Error window appeared on the screen (see Figure 12.2). The error window will be removed when you make the required correction.

From the error message, you can gather that the error is in line 3 of your schema description, as indicated by the (3) before the error's id. number. The nature of the error is also specified. To correct this error you will:

1. Invoke the EDIT command to return to the editor and correct the error.
2. Return to the NOMAD environment.
3. Reissue the SCHEMA skirent NEW command. Figure 12.3 shows the screen for step 1.

Having corrected the error you again invoke the SCHEMA command (step 3). The command and its parameters will be the same as in Figure 12.1.

However, suppose the Error window appeared again. This time the error is in line 20 (see Figure 12.4) and your database schema is not translated as yet.

To correct the error, you go back to your system editor (Figure 12.3) and complete steps 1 through 3 of error correction. Once all errors are corrected you are ready to translate the schema. Since the translation has not been successfully completed as yet, it is still considered a "new" translation.

Invoking the SCHEMA command (Figure 12.1) causes the description contained in skirent.sch to be put into the data dictionary.

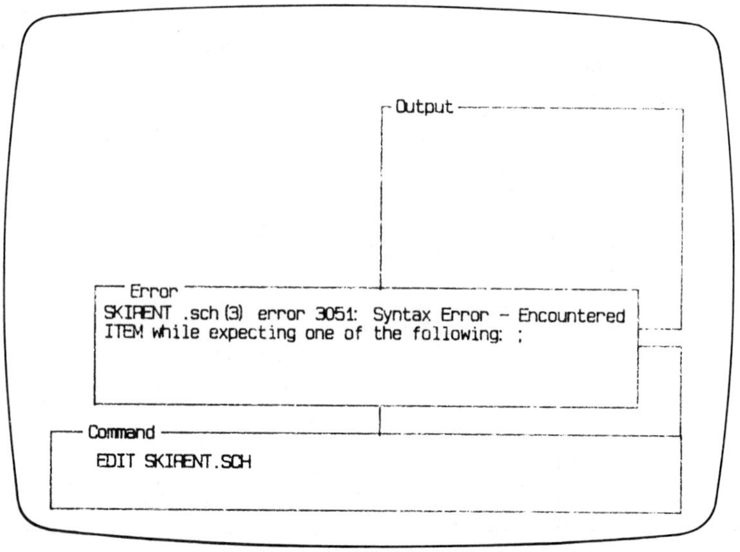

Figure 12.3 Correcting Errors in the Schema

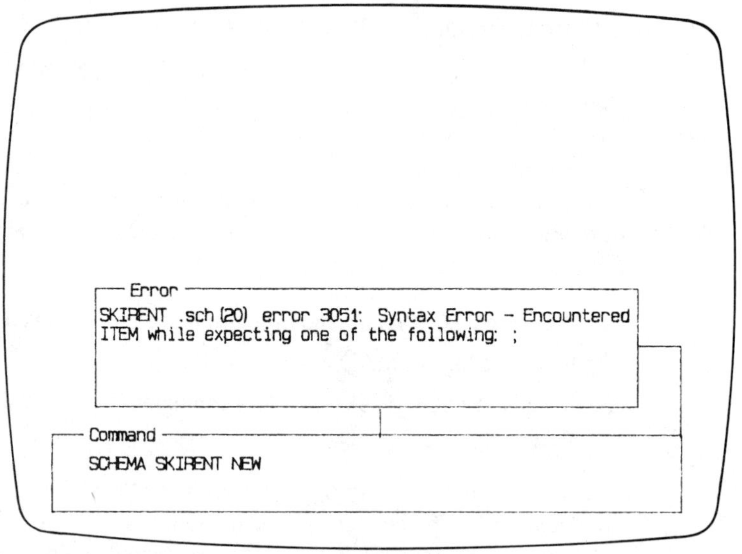

Figure 12.4 Second Error Window

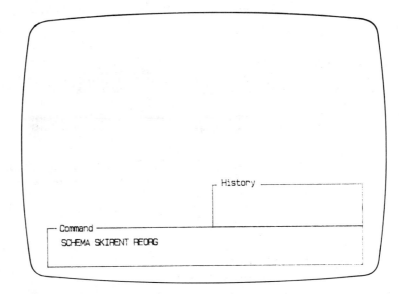

Figure 12.5   Reorganizing the Schema

Reorganizing the Schema Description

You have decided to change the database. If your change requires reorganization of the physical records, you will need to use the REORG parameter. Figure 12.5 shows your screen.

The Output window appears with all the masters listed and an indication that they are ready for reorganization. The Output window is partially overlapped by another window (Figure 12.6). This second window identifies the action you requested and you are asked to confirm it.

You will know that NOMAD has accepted your command when it appears in the History window (Figure 12.7). With all the reorganization done and the schema compiled, you are ready to activate the database.

Activating the Database

Before any database activities can be commenced, you need to activate your database. You do it with the DATABASE command. Figures 12.8 show the screen.

Activating Another Database

You decided to make another (skirent1) database active. Figure 12.9 shows the command you will use.
An Error window appears indicating that this database is not found (Figure 12.10). It is not found because it does not exist.

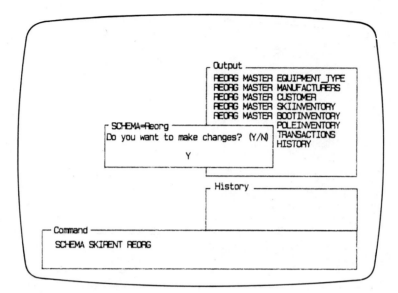

Figure 12.6 Confirmation Window

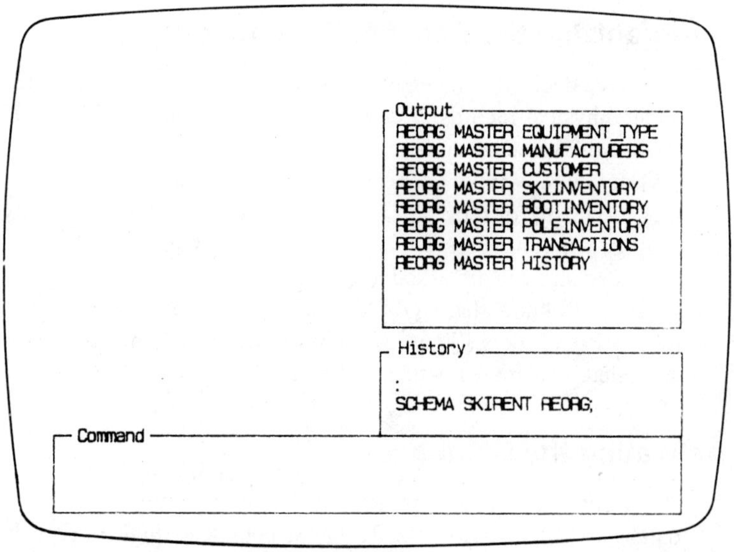

Figure 12.7 Accepted Command in the History Window

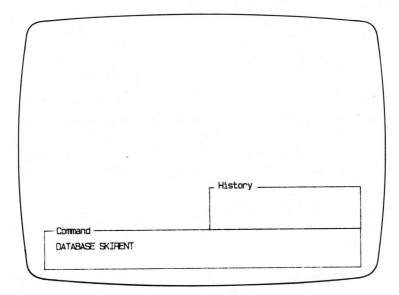

Figure 12.8 Activating the Database

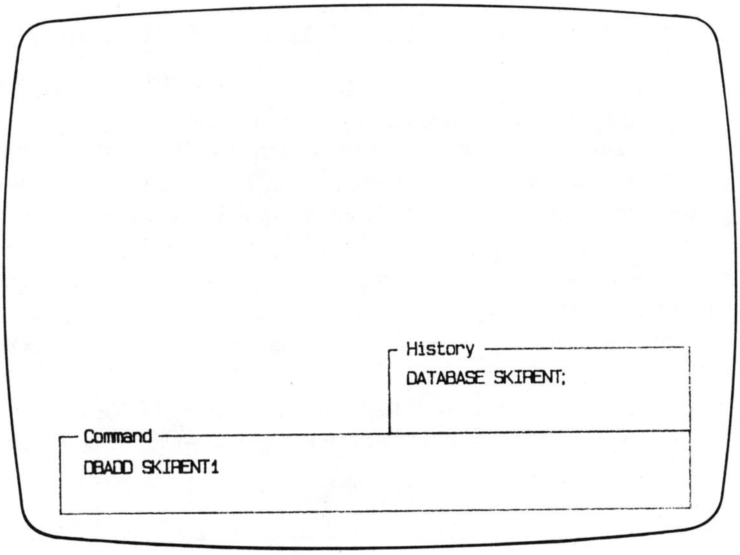

Figure 12.9 Activating Another Database

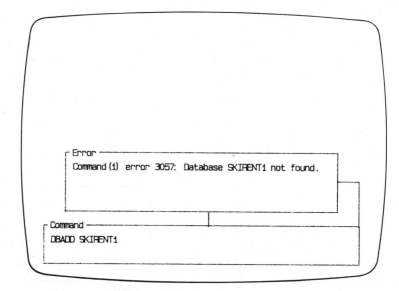

Figure 12.10   Error Window Indicating that the Database was Not Found

Listing of the Description of All Currently Active Databases

You want to see a listing of the description of all the active databases. You issue the SLIST command. Figure 12.11 shows your screen.

Your only active database at the moment is the skirent database. In the Output window you see the listing (partial) for this database. You could enlarge or pan through the Output window to see more of the description.

You are especially interested in the structure of the POLEINVENTORY master. Again you issue the SLIST command with an appropriate parameter. (See the Command window in Figure 12.11.) Your screen with the output will look like that shown in Figure 12.12. You have now successfully created the skirent database. This concludes our session.

As you can see, all communication through windows is simple and straightforward. Essentially, what you need to know is when to use which command and with what parameters.

12.11 SUMMARY

To construct a database, you need to know what data types your software supports and what display and storage formats are available.

NOMAD supports these data types:

1. Alphanumeric
2. Numeric

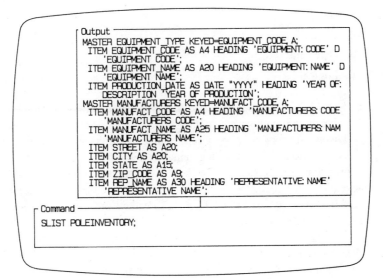

Figure 12.11   Listing of the Description of the Database

```
┌ Output ─────────────────────────────────────────────────────────────┐
│ MASTER POLEINVENTORY KEYED=POLENUM, A;                               │
│   ITEM POLENUM AS A4 HEADING 'POLE SERIAL: NUMBER';                  │
│   ITEM POLE_MANUFACT AS DISPLAY"MANUFACT_NAME from MANUFACTURERS" HEADING │
│       'POLE MANUFACTURING' INTERNAL A4;                              │
│   ITEM POLE_TYPE AS DISPLAY"EQUIPMENT_NAME from EQUIPMENT_TYPE" HEADING │
│       'POLE TYPE' INTERNAL A4;                                       │
│   ITEM POLE_LENGTH AS 999 HEADING 'POLE LENGTH' INTERNAL 14 ALIAS    │
│       POLELENG                                                       │
│   ITEM POLE_RENCH AS $99.99 HEADING 'POLE RENTAL: CHARGE' INTERNAL R8 ALIAS │
│       POLECHAR                                                       │
│   ITEM POLE_FLAG AS MEMBER"CUSTOMER";                                │
│                                                                     │
│                                                                     │
┌ Command ────────────────────────────────────────────────────────────┐
│                                                                     │
│                                                                     │
└─────────────────────────────────────────────────────────────────────┘
```

Figure 12.12   Listing the Description of the Master

3. Date

4. Time

5. DateTime

6. Logical

NOMAD also supports NOTAVAILABLE values. NOTAVAILABLE means that a variable or an item does not contain any data value (and it is not a zero or a blank).

Display formats are display representations of the supported data types.

A variable is used for saving values that will be used in calculations, in logical expressions, or to characterize the environment of your session. NOMAD has several classes of variables. This chapter discussed the *user variables*.

All user variables are declared before they are used. This is done with the DECLARE command, which assigns a specific name and the display format to it.

Several methods are available for assigning values. This chapter used the *Assignment statement*.

The application's database structure is defined by creating a file called a *schema*. The schema holds a description of the data to be stored in the database and the formats that are to be used for data storage and retrieval.

The schema statements perform the following functions:

1. Name the files in your database.

2. Name fields (items) in each of your files.

3. Describe the attributes, characteristics, and constraints on all items.

4. Specify relationships among items.

5. Provide data integrity checks.

6. Establish security of access to your database.

7. Allow you to predefine certain calculations.

To define a file in a schema, you need at least two statements: MASTER and ITEM.

When you carefully analyze the database schema constructed for our application, you will understand how to use the commands and statements introduced in this chapter.

Once the schema description is created and saved, you can issue the SCHEMA command. The SCHEMA command translates your schema file and places description of your database into the NOMAD data dictionary.

Before any database activities can begin you will need to use the DATABASE command.

To display a listing of the description of the database, you will use the SLIST command.

One of the most efficient ways to reinforce what you have learned about the creation of the database schema and the use of the commands needed for invoking and reporting the database structure is to follow the sample NOMAD session presented in this chapter. Going through the exercises is also very helpful.

EXERCISES

1. List all the data types NOMAD supports.

2. What are NOTAVAILABLE data?

3. What are display formats? Briefly describe those supported by NOMAD.

4. You want to display the date of April 9, 1988 as "The Fourth Month, and Ninth day." Specify the display format you will use to obtain this result.

5. For the date in Problem 4, you want to display "SATURDAY the 9th of APRIL." Specify the display format for this result.

6. What is a scaling factor? How it is used?

7. You want the value 12345.67 to be printed as
    a. 123.46
    b. $ 1,234,567.00
    What display format would you specify in each case?

8. What display format would you specify to print the value of 0 as a blank?

9. What are variables for? List those you encountered in this chapter.

10. How would you assign values to &variables?

11. What is a DEFINE?

12. What do the following two lines represent in the database schema?
    a. DEFINE pole_rent_paid AS $999.99
    b. EXPR=(date_ret - date_out) * amount_pole;

13. Why would you DECLARE different display and internal data formats?

14. Write a command that specifies that your data is to be alphanumeric and its display format is to be 15 characters long.

15. You are responsible for writing an application program for end users who have a very limited knowledge of computers. Why would you use a MASK parameter in your DECLARE command?

16. Write a command that specifies that: &Ski_Type variable is to be displayed as 7 characters long. Valid values are DYN-S, DYN-D, and VOK-S, and NOTAVAILABLE cannot be assigned to the &Ski_Type variable.

17. Specify all the optional parameters of the DECLARE command and describe how and for what purposes they are used.

18. Specify a command that declares that the data corresponding to the coded ski numbers in your inventory are to be displayed as numeric, 4 digits long. A variable that will hold code is to be referred to by the alias snumber. This command is also to document the source and possible uses of the declared &variable.

19. How can you change an ASSIGNMENT statement?

20. Is there a difference between individual ASSIGN and AMPSET commands?

21. Write a command that sets all &items to the values corresponding to the items in a currently positioned record in the Transactions file.

22. Write a command that resets the user-defined variables &SKI_TYPE and SKI_NUMBER to the NOTAVAILABLE values. This same command is to contain a reset of the report page width and page length to their default values.

23. What is the database schema?

24. Specify what schema statements are used for.

25. You are responsible for setting up the database for the operations of the jewelry store. Write the schema statements for the Customer file. Decide what type of information you need to have in this master. Do the same for the Transaction file, which is to contain the information on the customer's transactions. Annotate statements defining your masters for online documentation purposes.

26. What is the difference between the ITEM statement and the DEFINE statement?

27. Analyze this statement:

```
DEFINE sman_name  AS EXTRACT 'manufact_name
FROM manufacturers  USING ski_manufact';
```

28. Specify the use of these parameters:

```
NEW
REORG
CHECK
DELETE
```

PROJECTS

1. Write all the statements needed for the database schema for the State Parks Reservation System you designed for Project 1 of Chapter 10. Be sure to use the options for automatic validation of data entry, definitions of headings needed in future reports from that database, and online documentation of all the items.

2. Once you have constructed the schema for the State Parks database, do the following:
   a. Translate the database schema for Project 1 and place it in the data dictionary.
   b. If any errors appear, correct them.
   c. You discovered that you need to add headers to some of the items in your schema. Create missing headers and use an appropriate option in the SCHEMA command to translate this corrected schema.
   d. Now you discovered that you need to change the sizes of some of the items in your schema and add some new ones. Change and add what is needed and use an appropriate option in the SCHEMA command to translate this corrected schema.
   e. Display the content of this newly translated schema.

3. Write all the statements needed for the database schema for the Properties, Water Rights, and Leases System you designed for Project 2 of Chapter 10. Be sure to use the options for automatic validation of data entry, and online documentation of all the items and headings.

4. Translate the database schema for the Properties, Water Rights, and Leases System (as defined in Chapter 10) and place it in the data dictionary. Perform all the actions identified in steps (b) through (e) of Project 1.

5. For a project your instructor arranged for you with a local business, perform all the actions identified in Projects 1 and 2.

CHAPTER 13

Interactive Data Entry and File Maintenance

Awake! for Morning in the Bowl of Night
Has flung the Stone that puts the Stars to Flight:
And Lo! The Hunter of the East has caught
The Sultan's Turret in a Noose of Light.

Omar Khayyam, Rubaiyat
(Fitzgerald's 1859 text)

13.1 INTRODUCTION

The objective of this chapter is to teach you how to enter data into your NOMAD database and how to maintain this database.

You can enter data into your application's database and perform data maintenance in three ways:

1. By updating your database interactively, from the Command window, if you are dealing with a small amount of data. (Discussed in the present chapter.)

2. By using custom Forms if you are building the system for someone not familiar with NOMAD. By constructing Forms for data entry and maintenance procedures, you are building a screen-oriented, user-friendly application. (Discussed in Chapter 14.)

3. By performing transaction processing maintenance if you are dealing with large amounts of data coming from other files. (Discussed in Chapter 15.)

Assume here that you are dealing with a small amount of data, and thus that the interactive method applies. The commands you now need are of two functional types:

1. Those involved in locating and displaying specific records in your database.

2. Those needed for database maintenance.

13.2 INTERACTIVE MAINTENANCE

Database maintenance commands can be grouped according to the function they perform. They can:

1. Change individual records (instances) or parts of the records.
2. Control database modifications.
3. Update large volumes of data from external transaction files.

This chapter considers the commands used in functions 1 and 2 and the commands needed to modify data dictionary entities. Our approach will be to define NOMAD commands (and their options) in the order dictated by their use.

Recall that our application's database consists of eight files. However, to simplify matters while you are first learning about data maintenance commands, we concentrate on only one file, the Equipment Type file, to illustrate all the data entry and maintenance functions. The remaining seven files are left for you to use to practice what you have learned. (Refer to the exercises at the end of this chapter.)

Data Entry

At the start you have to tell NOMAD which database you will be working with. Your database is skirent. So, in the Command window you should type:

```
DATABASE skirent;
```

After execution, this command is placed in the History window (see Figure 13.1). The skirent database is now active and available for processing. You are ready to enter some records.

INSERT Command

The INSERT command adds new records to the database according to the insert parameters of the MASTER statement in the database schema. (For the format of the MASTER statements for the skirent database schema, refer to Chapter 12.) You can specify the item values being inserted in two ways:

1. Specify the items names and their values as parameters
2. Specify only the master name

If the names of the items in the file into which you are entering the data are unique for whole database (this is the case for items names in the EQUIPMENT_TYPE file), you specify the items and their values as parameters. The item(s) name must be unique in the database; otherwise, NOMAD will not be able to resolve the ambiguity. The value of any unspecified item comes from its &item equivalent. If

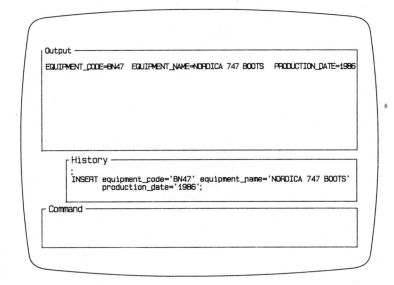

Figure 13.1   First Format of INSERT Command

the value for &item has not be assigned, the item is set to NOTAVAILABLE. (Figure 13.1 gives an example of this format.)

In the sample we inserted one record into the EQUIPMENT_TYPE file. The equipment_code, equipment_name, and production_date items occur only in this file. All values for these items are assigned in the INSERT statement. After the INSERT command is executed, NOMAD echoes the transaction in the Output window.

If you assign values to all &items before you issue the INSERT statement you can directly specify the name of a master where the records will be inserted. The items values are taken from the appropriate &items. Any item whose &item does not have a value is set to NOTAVAILABLE. (Figure 13.2 gives an example of this format.)

In our example those values are:

```
&equipment_code='BN97'
&equipment_name='NORDICA BOOTS'
&production_date='1987'
```

After values are assigned to &items then you issue the INSERT command (you only specify the name of the master where the record is to be inserted). After the INSERT command is executed, NOMAD echoes the transaction in the Output window.

We have used two forms of the INSERT command to show you how this command works. The EQUIPMENT_TYPE file now has two records in it.

```
┌─ Output ──────────────────────────────────────────────────────────┐
│                                                                    │
│  EQUIPMENT_CODE=BN97   EQUIPMENT_NAME=NORDICA 947 BOOTS   PRODUCTION_DATE=1967 │
│                                                                    │
│                                                                    │
│                                                                    │
│                                                                    │
│    ┌─ History ─────────────────────────────────────────────────┐  │
│    │  INSERT equipment_code='BN97' equipment_name='NORDICA 947 BOOTS' │
│    │         production_date='1967';                            │  │
│    │  INSERT equipment_type;                                    │  │
│  ┌─ Command ──────────────────────────────────────────────────┐   │
│  │                                                            │   │
│  │                                                            │   │
│  │                                                            │   │
│  └────────────────────────────────────────────────────────────┘  │
└────────────────────────────────────────────────────────────────────┘
```

Figure 13.2   Second Format of INSERT Command

Qualifying Database References

We now need to resolve the possible ambiguities arising from the naming convention used for items. Recall that NOMAD requires you to assign the names of items to be unique within one master. The same item, however, can occur in multiple masters. For example, in our application items, ident_type and custident occur in the customer and the transactions masters. The FROM command can help us control the selection of the master.

FROM Command

The FROM command specifies the master containing items that are subsequently referenced.

For example, items ident_type and custident occur in the customer as well as the transactions masters. If you want to specify that the items you plan to reference are to be from the customer master, you issue the following command:

```
FROM customer;
```

The FROM command now affects all commands issued from the keyboard and remains in effect until it is cleared by one of the following actions:

1. Issuing the FROM command without any parameters.

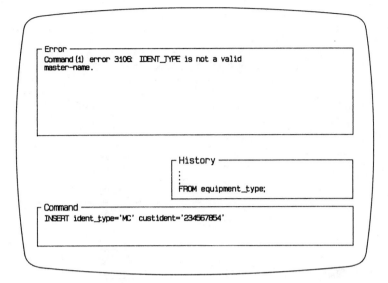

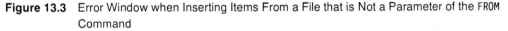

Figure 13.3 Error Window when Inserting Items From a File that is Not a Parameter of the FROM Command

2. Issuing the FROM command for a new master, for example,

FROM transactions;

3. Clearing the database.

Let us come back to our EQUIPMENT_TYPE file. Figure 13.3 shows the FROM command in the History window. Any subsequently issued command will refer to this particular file.

For example, if you were to attempt to INSERT items from a file that is not referred to in a FROM command (in this case, the EQUIPMENT_TYPE file), you will get an error message like the one shown in Figure 13.3. The error status is raised because the FROM command specifies the master that should be accessed for reference to all subsequent items. You cannot INSERT items from a file that is not referred to in the FROM command.

Figure 13.4 shows the appropriate use of the INSERT command after the FROM command (shown in the History window). With this command another record is added to the EQUIPMENT_TYPE file. To clear this particular FROM (to be able to refer to another file, for example), you issue the FROM command without any parameter (Figure 13.4).

If you now were to issue a command like the one shown in Figure 13.5, you would raise the error status again. Notice the nature of the error messages in the

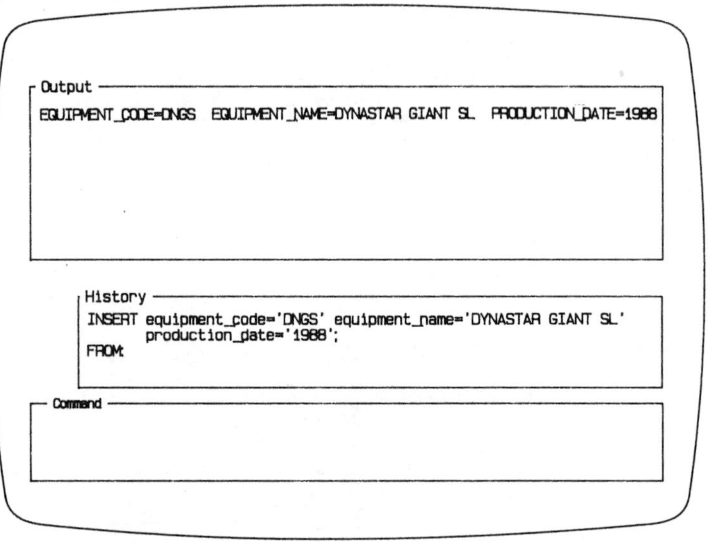

Figure 13.4 FROM Command without any Parameter

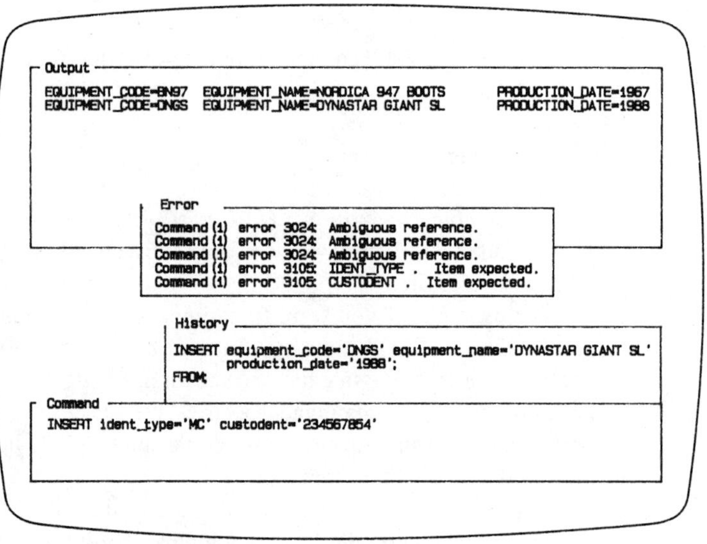

Figure 13.5 Error Status with Ambiguous Names of Files in INSERT Command

Error window. The INSERT command raises an error because there is no FROM command (specifying the master that should be accessed) to resolve any ambiguities in item references.

If you were to use the second form of the INSERT command, you would use FROM as a keyword to resolve any ambiguous reference (see Figure 13.6). Here, FROM

```
┌─ Output ─────────────────────────────────────────────────────────────┐
│ EQUIPMENT_CODE=BN97  EQUIPMENT_NAME=NORDICA 947 BOOTS    PRODUCTION_DATE=1967 │
│ EQUIPMENT_CODE=DNGS  EQUIPMENT_NAME=DYNASTAR GIANT SL    PRODUCTION_DATE=1988 │
│ IDENT_TYPE=MC  CUSTIDENT=234567854               LAST_NAME=N/A        │
│ FIRST_NAME=N/A          MIDDLE_INITIAL=N  STREET_ADDRESS=            │
│ N/A                     CITY=N/A                 STATE=N/A           │
│ ZIP_CODE=N/A       PHONE=N/A            LOCAL_ACCOM=N/A              │
│ CUST_HEIGHT_F=N  CUST_HEIGHT_I=N/  WEIGHT=N/A  AGE=N/A  SEX=N  SKIING_ABILITY= │
│ BINDING_L_TOE=N/A  BINDING_R_TOE=N/A  BINDING_L_HEEL=N/A  BINDING_R_HEEL=N/A │
└──────────────────────────────────────────────────────────────────────┘

  ┌─ History ────────────────────────────────────────────────────────┐
  │  production_date='1988';                                          │
  │  FROM;                                                            │
  └──────────────────────────────────────────────────────────────────┘
┌─ Command ────────────────────────────────────────────────────────────┐
│  INSERT FROM CUSTOMER ident_type='MC' custident='234567854';        │
└──────────────────────────────────────────────────────────────────────┘
```

Figure 13.6 Second Form of the INSERT Command with the FROM Keyword

specifies the master (customer) for which items are referenced. (Note that the FROM keyword applies only to the command in which it is included.) In the Output window in Figure 13.6 you can identify all items from the customer file for which an assignment was made. Those customer file items that were not assigned a value in the INSERT statement are assigned NOTAVAILABLE (N/A) values.

13.3 LOCATING AND DISPLAYING DATA FROM THE DATABASE

Assume that you have entered some more records into the EQUIPMENT_TYPE file, and now you want to list the contents of this file, displaying certain fields. You issue the command shown in Figure 13.7. Note that the column headings in the List window correspond to those specified (for these fields) in the database schema description.

Often you need to find specific data records in your database. To locate a particular record, you use one of the movement commands (commands that allow you to navigate through the database). When using the movement commands, you can see only one record (current record) at the time. Data contained in that record are automatically displayed. You remain at the current record until you issue another movement command or issue the LIST command.

If the movement commands you issue would have placed you before the first data record or beyond the last one, an END-OF-DATA message is displayed. Under these circumstances, an attempt to print the data results in the *NCI* (Not Current Instance) message.

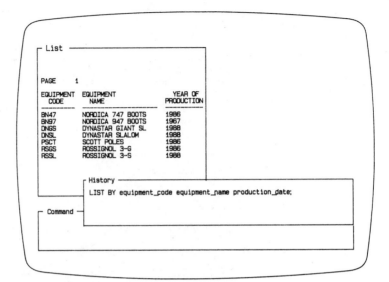

Figure 13.7   Content of the EQUIPMENT_TYPE File

Commands for Locating Specific Records in the Database

Commands that are used for locating specific records in the databases are of three types:

1. For absolute positioning (TOP, LAST, FIRST).
2. For relative positioning (NEXT, PREVIOUS).
3. For value-based positioning (LOCATE, TLOCATE, RKEY).

Absolute positioning means that you can position yourself at the beginning or at the end of the master.

Relative positioning commands position in relation to the current record. These commands are bit more involved in comparison to absolute commands. They also have some optional parameters.

Value-based positioning allows you to specify a search criteria for a particular record. You can search forward and backward in the master.

TOP Command

This command with no master reference positions you at the top of the database, that is, before the first record of the first master in the database. TOP with a master name positions you just before the first record instance in that master. Subsequent movement commands start with the first record of the specified master.

```
┌─ Output ──────────────────────────────────────────────────────────────────┐
│  EQUIPMENT_CODE=BN47   EQUIPMENT_NAME=NORDICA 747 BOOTS    PRODUCTION_DATE=1986
│  EQUIPMENT_CODE=BN97   EQUIPMENT_NAME=NORDICA 947 BOOTS    PRODUCTION_DATE=1967
│  EQUIPMENT_TYPE=DNGS   EQUIPMENT_NAME=DYNASTAR GIANT SL    PRODUCTION_DATE=1988
│  EQUIPMENT_TYPE=DNSL   EQUIPMENT_NAME=DYNASTAR SLALOM      PRODUCTION_DATE=1988
│  EQUIPMENT_TYPE=PSCT   EQUIPMENT_NAME=SCOTT POLES          PRODUCTION_DATE=1986
│
│
│       ┌─ History ─────────────────────────────────────────────────┐
│       │  TOP equipment_type;
│       │  NEXT equipment_type;
│       │  NEXT equipment_type;
│       │  NEXT equipment_type DO 3;
│  ┌─ Command ────────────────────────────────────────────────────────┐
│  │
│  │
│  │
```

Figure 13.8   TOP, NEXT and the NEXT Command with the DO Parameter

FIRST Command

You use this command to go to the first record of a specified master.

LAST Command

This command positions you at the last record of the specified master.

NEXT Command

When you use this command, you move forward from the current record and are positioned at the next record of the specified master.

The first two commands in the History window (TOP and NEXT) in Figure 13.8 show the use of both absolute and relative movement commands. With the first command, TOP, you move to the top of the EQUIPMENT_TYPE master; that is, you are now positioned before its first record. With the second command, NEXT, you are positioned at the next record, which is the first record of this master. This current record is automatically displayed in the Output window. Note that in this example the TOP (absolute) and the NEXT (relative) commands are equivalent to the single absolute command FIRST.

If you were to use the NEXT command again, you would move forward to the next record. (See the third command in the History window of Figure 13.8.)

The NEXT command has optional parameters: DO and BRIEF. The DO parameter causes the command to be repeated a specified number of times. The fourth command shown in the History window of Figure 13.8 illustrates the use the DO parameter.

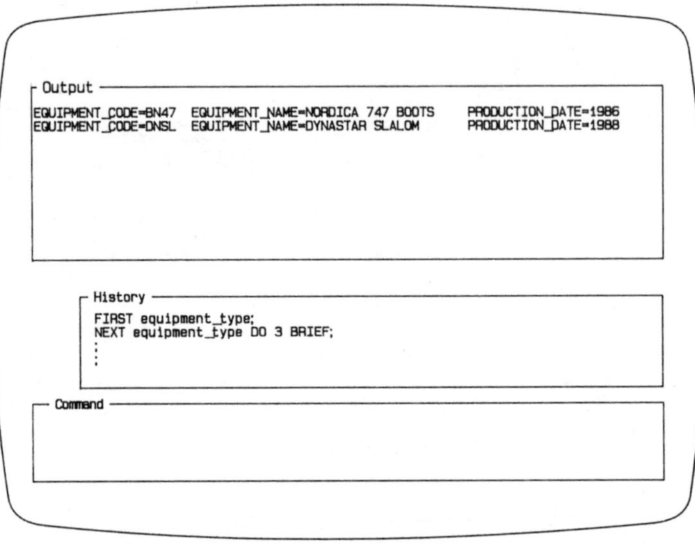

Figure 13.9 FIRST and NEXT Command with the BRIEF Parameter

Note that before this command is issued, the current record is the second record in the master. After we use the DO parameter (specifying that NEXT should be executed three times), the current record is the fifth one, as shown in the Output window. All accessed records are now displayed.

The BRIEF parameter can be used with the DO parameter to cancel the verification of all but the last accessed record.

An example of its usage is shown in Figure 13.9.

Here we use the FIRST command to position ourselves at the first record of the master. Next, the NEXT command is used with the BRIEF parameter to display only the last accessed record. This is why only the first and the fourth records are displayed in the Output window. The second and the third record verifications (output) are cancelled. After this set of commands is executed, the current record of this master is the fourth record.

PREVIOUS Command

You use this command to move backward from the current record and position yourself at the previous record of the specified master.

As with the NEXT command, you can use the DO and BRIEF parameters with PREVIOUS. DO n causes this command to be repeated n times. The BRIEF parameter used with the DO parameter cancels the verification of all but the nth accessed record. The second command in the History window in Figure 13.10 illustrates the use of the PREVIOUS command.

```
┌ Output ────────────────────────────────────────────────────────────┐
│ EQUIPMENT_CODE=DNSL   EQUIPMENT_NAME=DYNASTAR SLALOM    PRODUCTION_DATE=1988 │
│ EQUIPMENT_CODE=RSSL   EQUIPMENT_NAME=ROSSIGNOL 3-S      PRODUCTION_DATE=1988 │
│ EQUIPMENT_CODE=RSGS   EQUIPMENT_NAME=ROSSIGNOL 3-G      PRODUCTION_DATE=1986 │
│                                                                      │
│                                                                      │
│    ┌ History ──────────────────────────────────────────────┐        │
│    │ ⋮                                                       │        │
│    │ LAST equipment_type;                                    │        │
│    │ PREVIOUS equipment-type;                                │        │
│ ┌ Command ──────────────────────────────────────────────────┐       │
│ │                                                            │       │
│ │                                                            │       │
└─┴────────────────────────────────────────────────────────────┴───────┘
```

Figure 13.10 The LAST and PREVIOUS Commands

```
┌Output ──────────────────────────────────────────────────────────────┐
│ EQUIPMENT_CODE=RSSL   EQUIPMENT_NAME=ROSSIGNOL 3-S      PRODUCTION_DATE=1988 │
│ EQUIPMENT_CODE=DNSL   EQUIPMENT_NAME=DYNASTAR SLALOM    PRODUCTION_DATE=1988 │
│ EQUIPMENT_CODE=BN47   EQUIPMENT_NAME=NORDICA 747 BOOTS  PRODUCTION_DATE=1986 │
│         ┌ Error ───────────────────────────────────────────┐         │
│         │ Command (1) warning 6005: End of data (no next) on │         │
│         │ EQUIPMENT_TYPE                                     │         │
│         │ Command (1) error 4: Error occurred.              │         │
│         │                                                   │         │
│         ┌ History ─────────────────────────────────┐       │         │
│         │ FIRST equipment_type;                     │       │         │
│         │ ⋮                                         │       │         │
│         │ PREVIOUS equipment_type DO 3;             │       │         │
│ ┌ Command ──────────────────────────────────────────────────┐       │
│ │                                                            │       │
└─┴────────────────────────────────────────────────────────────┴───────┘
```

Figure 13.11 Error Condition Raised when the END OF DATA is Reached with the PREVIOUS Command

Now consider the example of the use of the PREVIOUS command given in Figure 13.11. In this example, the error condition is raised. The current record is the first record in the master (FIRST command). When the PREVIOUS command is issued (move backward), no records are found. Thus the END OF DATA is indicated.

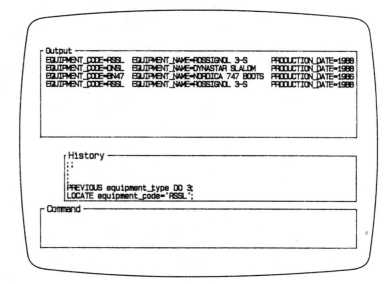

Figure 13.12 The LOCATE Command

LOCATE and TLOCATE Commands

These commands are used to search forward in the database for the record that satisfies the specified search conditions. LOCATE searches from the current position; TLOCATE starts searching from the first record (top) in the master.

The use of a logical expression specifies the search criteria required to locate a record. Assume that we issue the LOCATE command with the logical expression EQUIPMENT_CODE="RSSL". This causes NOMAD to search forward and to position at the first record that satisfies the search criterion. This record is now displayed in the output window.

When LOCATE (or TLOCATE) is issued without the logical expression, the command will use the search criteria from the most recent LOCATE (or TLOCATE) command. For example, if we continue with commands as in Figure 13.12 and now issue simply:

    LOCATE;

this command uses the EQUIPMENT_CODE="RSSL" expression for its search condition.

DO is also an optional parameter for the LOCATE command. Its function is the same as in the NEXT and the PREVIOUS commands.

Search starts from the first record in the database master; all records that satisfy the search condition are displayed in the Output window. If you were to use DO n in the TLOCATE command, it would be ignored because invoking it would call for the retrieval of the same record n times.

The use of the TLOCATE command is shown in Figure 13.13.

```
┌ Output ──────────────────────────────────────────────────────────┐
│ EQUIPMENT_CODE=DNGS  EQUIPMENT_NAME=DYNASTAR GIANT SL.  PRODUCTION_DATE=1988
│ EQUIPMENT_CODE=DNSL  EQUIPMENT_NAME=DYNASTAR SLALOM     PRODUCTION_DATE=1988
│ EQUIPMENT_CODE=RSSL  EQUIPMENT_NAME=ROSSIGNOL 3-S       PRODUCTION_DATE=1988
│ EQUIPMENT_CODE=DNGS  EQUIPMENT_NAME=DYNASTAR GIANT SL.  PRODUCTION_DATE=1988
│
│
│
│
│   ┌ History ──────────────────────────────────────────────────────┐
│   │ :
│   │ :
│   │ TLOCATE production_date='1988';
│   │
└───┴────────────────────────────────────────────────────────────────
  ┌ Command ────────────────────────────────────────────────────────┐
  │
  │                          ·
  │
  └──────────────────────────────────────────────────────────────────┘
```

Figure 13.13   TLOCATE Command

```
┌ Output ──────────────────────────────────────────────────────────┐
│ EQUIPMENT_CODE=RSSL  EQUIPMENT_NAME=ROSSIGNOL 3-S        PRODUCTION_DATE=1988
│ EQUIPMENT_CODE=DNGS  EQUIPMENT_NAME=DYNASTAR GIANT SL.   PRODUCTION_DATE=1988
│ EQUIPMENT_CODE=BN47  EQUIPMENT_NAME=NORDICA 747 BOOTS    PRODUCTION_DATE=1986
│ EQUIPMENT_CODE=DNSL  EQUIPMENT_NAME=DYNASTAR SLALOM      PRODUCTION_DATE=1988
│
│
│
│
│   ┌ History ──────────────────────────────────────────────────────┐
│   │ :
│   │ &equipment_code='DNSL';
│   │ RKEY equipment_code;
│   │ :
└───┴────────────────────────────────────────────────────────────────
  ┌ Command ────────────────────────────────────────────────────────┐
  │
  │
  │
  └──────────────────────────────────────────────────────────────────┘
```

Figure 13.14   The RKEY Command

RKEY Command

With this command you can search both forward and backward from the current record. You use the value of the key &item to position yourself at the appropriate record. Thus, before using this command, the value must be assigned to the &item. An example of the use of the RKEY command is shown in Figure 13.14.

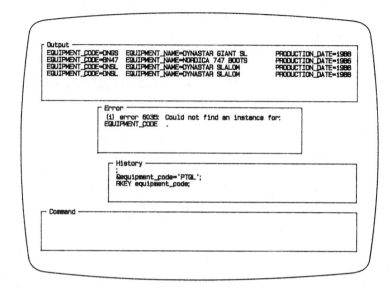

Figure 13.15 RKEY Command with Error Condition Raised

If the assigned value does not match the key item values in the master and the RKEY command is issued, the error condition is raised. (See Figure 13.15.)

If a position satisfying the key item value does not exist, NOMAD stops at the record previous to the record where the item value would have occurred if it had existed. For example, if you examine the contents of the EQUIPMENT_TYPE file shown in the List window of Figure 13.7, you will note that if the EQUIP-MENT_CODE="PQTL" value existed, it would be placed after the record with the EQUIPMENT_CODE="PSCT". The record with the EQUIPMENT_CODE= "PSCT" is the current record at which NOMAD stopped.

PRINT Command

This command is used to display current values of specified items. PRINT works only with the current record. If you were to request to PRINT an item that is not currently positioned, you would get the *NCI* (Not Current Instance) message. Figure 13.16 shows the use of the PRINT command.

The required parameter for the PRINT command is the name of the object to be displayed. It can be an item name, master name, &variable, or expression. It specifies the information to be printed. This command also has optional parameters:

■ **AS Parameter**—Specifies the display format of an item. If a format is not specifically stated, the display format defaults to the display format defined in the schema. Figure 13.17 shows how this parameter is used.

■ **Format Modifiers**—Specify the format of the printed output. These format modifiers include:

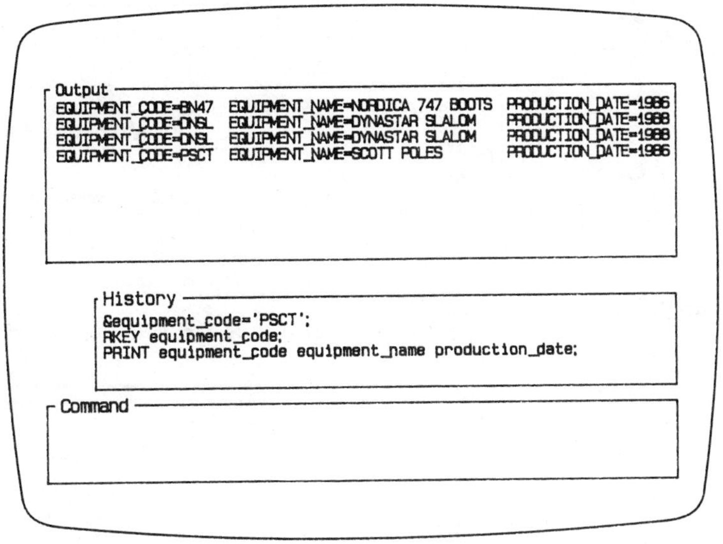

```
┌ Output ───────────────────────────────────────────────────────────
  EQUIPMENT_CODE=BN47   EQUIPMENT_NAME=NORDICA 747 BOOTS   PRODUCTION_DATE=1986
  EQUIPMENT_CODE=DNSL   EQUIPMENT_NAME=DYNASTAR SLALOM     PRODUCTION_DATE=1988
  EQUIPMENT_CODE=DNSL   EQUIPMENT_NAME=DYNASTAR SLALOM     PRODUCTION_DATE=1988
  EQUIPMENT_CODE=PSCT   EQUIPMENT_NAME=SCOTT POLES         PRODUCTION_DATE=1986




      ┌ History ────────────────────────────────────────────────
        &equipment_code='PSCT';
        RKEY equipment_code;
        PRINT equipment_code equipment_name production_date;

  ┌ Command ─────────────────────────────────────────────────────


```

Figure 13.16 PRINT Command

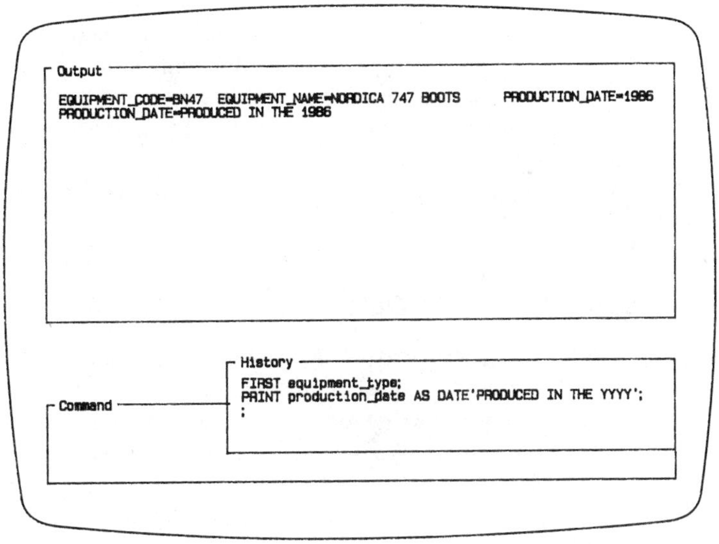

```
┌ Output ───────────────────────────────────────────────────────────

  EQUIPMENT_CODE=BN47  EQUIPMENT_NAME=NORDICA 747 BOOTS       PRODUCTION_DATE=1986
  PRODUCTION_DATE=PRODUCED IN THE 1986




      ┌ History ────────────────────────────────────────────────
        FIRST equipment_type;
  ┌ Command ──────   PRINT production_date AS DATE'PRODUCED IN THE YYYY';
                     :

```

Figure 13.17 PRINT Command with AS Formatting Option

■ COL, which specifies the exact column in which the next field prints.

■ SPACE n, which specifies the spacing between report columns on the report page. The default value is 2. To place columns directly next to each other, specify SPACE 0. To place them 10 spaces apart, you specify SPACE 10.

```
┌─ Output ─────────────────────────────────────────────────────────┐
│ EQUIPMENT_CODE=BN47        EQUIPMENT_NAME=NORDICA 747 BOOTS        │
│ PRODUCTION_DATE=1986                                               │
│                                                                   │
│                                                                   │
│   ┌─ History ─────────────────────────────────────────────────┐  │
│   :                                                              │
│   PRINT equipment_code COL 20 SPACE 10 equipment_name COL 40 FOLD │
│           production_date;                                        │
│ ┌─ Command ───────────────────────────────────────────────────┐  │
│ │                                                              │  │
│ │                                                              │  │
│ └──────────────────────────────────────────────────────────────┘ │
└───────────────────────────────────────────────────────────────────┘
```

Figure 13.18 PRINT Command with Format Modifiers

- FOLD, which prints the next entry of a report on the following line, starting in column 1. If you specify a number after FOLD, the next entry will be printed that many lines from the current line. For example, FOLD 3 specifies printing 3 lines down from the current line.

An example of the use of the PRINT command with format modifiers is shown in Figure 13.18.

Screening Your Data

So far we have discussed navigation through your master. The objective was to be able to position yourself at the specified record in the master. We also considered what commands to use to display the content of the master and how to use display format modifiers. We now turn to establishing screening criteria for your data in the master.

SELECT Command

This command can specify screening criteria for records or remove existing selection criteria. Some examples are:

1. The first command in Figure 13.19 establishes the selection criteria for the EQUIPMENT_TYPE master. Once this command is issued, the only instances from the EQUIPMENT_TYPE master that can be accessed are those with production_date='1988'. Any selection criteria in effect when you issued this command are removed.

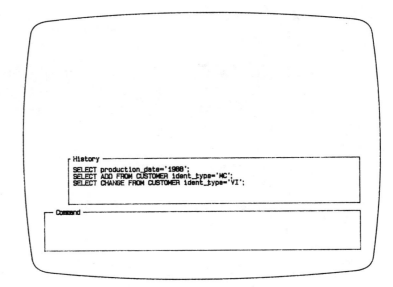

```
┌ History ─────────────────────────────────────────────────
  SELECT production_date='1988';
  SELECT ADD FROM CUSTOMER ident_type='MC';
  SELECT CHANGE FROM CUSTOMER ident_type='VI';



┌ Command ─────────────────────────────────────────────────

```

Figure 13.19   Examples of the SELECT Command

2. If the ADD parameter is used in the SELECT command, it will specify the selection criteria to be added to those currently in effect. The second command in Figure 13.19 shows the SELECT command with the ADD option together with the FROM parameter. This specification requests that all records with ident_type='MC' be selected, from the customer master, and that this selection be added to the current one. (Current selection criterion is as in the first statement of Figure 13.19.)

3. The selection criteria currently in effect can be changed with the CHANGE parameter. An example of the use of this parameter is shown in the third command of Figure 13.19. Here, the previous selection criterion (the second statement) is replaced with the new one, specified in the SELECT command with the CHANGE parameter. Note that in this command we have also used the FROM parameter to specify an item from the customer master.

The SELECT command can be used throughout the NOMAD session. SELECT causes only a subset of records to be made available for actions, such as:

```
LIST
NEXT
CHANGE
PRINT DO n
CREATE
```

To remove all SELECTs, use the following command:

```
SELECT CLEAR;
```

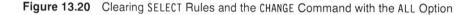

```
┌─ Output ──────────────────────────────────────────────────────────────────────┐
│  EQUIPMENT_CODE=BN47   EQUIPMENT_NAME=NORDICA 747 BOOTS   PRODUCTION_DATE=1989   │
│  EQUIPMENT_CODE=BN97   EQUIPMENT_NAME=NORDICA 947 BOOTS   PRODUCTION_DATE=1989   │
│  EQUIPMENT_CODE=DNGS   EQUIPMENT_NAME=DYNASTAR GIANT SL   PRODUCTION_DATE=1989   │
│  EQUIPMENT_CODE=DNSL   EQUIPMENT_NAME=DYNASTAR SLALOM     PRODUCTION_DATE=1989   │
│  EQUIPMENT_CODE=PSCT   EQUIPMENT_NAME=SCOTT POLES         PRODUCTION_DATE=1989   │
│  EQUIPMENT_CODE=RSGS   EQUIPMENT_NAME=ROSSIGNOL 3-G       PRODUCTION_DATE=1989   │
│  EQUIPMENT_CODE=RSSL   EQUIPMENT_NAME=ROSSIGNOL 3-S       PRODUCTION_DATE=1989   │
└────────────────────────────────────────────────────────────────────────────────┘

    ┌─ History ───────────────────────────────────────────────────────┐
    │  SELECT CLEAR equipment_type;                                    │
    │  :                                                               │
    │  CHANGE production_date='1989' ALL;                              │
    └─────────────────────────────────────────────────────────────────┘

  ┌─ Command ─────────────────────────────────────────────────────────┐
  │                                                                    │
  │                                                                    │
  └────────────────────────────────────────────────────────────────────┘
```

Figure 13.20   Clearing SELECT Rules and the CHANGE Command with the ALL Option

To clear SELECT rules for specific master only, specify the name of the master in the SELECT CLEAR command (for example, see the first command in Figure 13.20).

If you want to set the SELECT criterion for only one command, it is better to use the WHERE parameter in that command. because SELECT sets the SELECT criterion for the whole NOMAD session or until you clear it. For example, the request

```
LIST equipment_code equipment_name
     WHERE production_date= '1988';
```

creates the report with only those records for which the equipment production date (production_date) is 1988.

13.4 MODIFYING A DATABASE

The commands discussed in this section are CHANGE and REPLACE.

CHANGE command

The CHANGE command is used to modify the values of master records. For example, if you want to change the value of the production date item to 1989 for all the records in your EQUIPMENT_TYPE master, you can issue the commands as shown in Figure 13.20. The ALL parameter specifies that the scope of the change is to include all records. Since we have set up a specific SELECT criterion (Figure 13.19), we

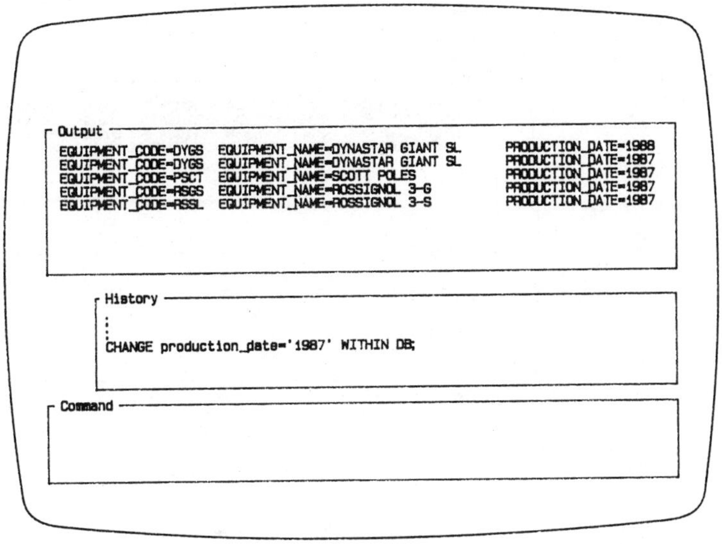

Figure 13.21 The CHANGE Command with the WITHIN DB Option

want to remove it now. To do that, we issue the SELECT command with the CLEAR parameter (see the first statement in Figure 13.20).

As you can see, through the use of this command we have modified all records in the master, starting with the first one.

The CHANGE command without any parameters changes the requested item values in a currently positioned record. After the CHANGE command is processed, the record pointer is on the just-modified record.

You can also request a change to take effect from the current record. Adding the WITHIN DB parameter to the CHANGE command will do this for you. Figure 13.21 illustrates its use.

As you can see, the WITHIN DB parameter affected all the records of the master, beginning with the current one. Again, the change is verified in the Output window.

We can also specify how many times the change is to be performed. We start with the currently positioned record. All the changed records are verified in the Output window. We do it with the DO parameter. An example of its use is shown in Figure 13.22.

In our case, the current record is the first record in the master. The required change is to be done three times (DO 3). That is why the production date value of the last three records equals the value that the CHANGE command has requested (1991).

We can also specify that the item to be changed is a KEY. This simply requires us to include the KEY parameter in the command. Its use is illustrated in Figure 13.23.

```
┌ Output ─────────────────────────────────────────────────────────────┐
│ EQUIPMENT_CODE=BN47   EQUIPMENT_NAME=NORDICA 747 BOOTS    PRODUCTION_DATE=1988 │
│ EQUIPMENT_CODE=BN47   EQUIPMENT_NAME=NORDICA 747 BOOTS    PRODUCTION_DATE=1991 │
│ EQUIPMENT_CODE=BN97   EQUIPMENT_NAME=NORDICA 947 BOOTS    PRODUCTION_DATE=1991 │
│ EQUIPMENT_CODE=DNGS   EQUIPMENT_NAME=DYNASTAR GIANT SL    PRODUCTION_DATE=1991 │
│                                                                      │
│                                                                      │
│   ┌ History ────────────────────────────────────────────────────┐   │
│   │ :                                                            │   │
│   │ CHANGE production_date='1991' DO 3;                          │   │
│   │                                                              │   │
│ ┌ Command ──────────────────────────────────────────────────────┐   │
│ │                                                                │   │
│ │                                                                │   │
└──────────────────────────────────────────────────────────────────────┘
```

Figure 13.22 The CHANGE Command with the DO Option

```
┌ Output ─────────────────────────────────────────────────────────────┐
│ EQUIPMENT_CODE=DNGS   EQUIPMENT_NAME=DYNASTAR GIANT SL    PRODUCTION_DATE=1988 │
│ EQUIPMENT_CODE=DYGS   EQUIPMENT_NAME=DYNASTAR GIANT SL    PRODUCTION_DATE=1988 │
│                                                                      │
│                                                                      │
│                                                                      │
│   ┌ History ────────────────────────────────────────────────────┐   │
│   │ :                                                            │   │
│   │ CHANGE KEY equipment_code='DYGS';                            │   │
│   │                                                              │   │
│ ┌ Command ──────────────────────────────────────────────────────┐   │
│ │                                                                │   │
│ │                                                                │   │
└──────────────────────────────────────────────────────────────────────┘
```

Figure 13.23 The Option for Changing KEY Field in a Record

After the CHANGE KEY command has been processed the record pointer is positioned at that changed record (current record). The change is verified in the Output window.

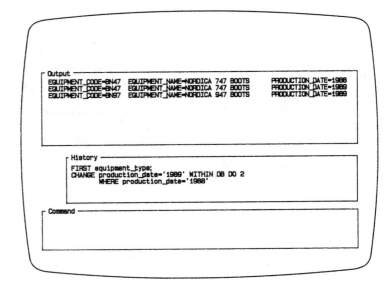

Figure 13.24 The CHANGE Command with all Options Discussed So Far

Figure 13.24 shows the use of the CHANGE command with all options we have discussed so far, in one statement.

Note that the exercises at the end of this chapter ask you to interpret the output in the Output window obtained when the CHANGE command is invoked with certain parameters.

REPLACE Command

Assume that you are positioned at a particular record in your database, and you want to replace it with a new one. To do this you can use the REPLACE command. You need to specify the master from which the current record is to be replaced. The first statement the History window of Figure 13.25 shows an example of its usage. Because you did not specify the values for the items of the new record, the equipment_name and production_date items are both set to NOTAVAIL-ABLE (N/A).

If you were to specify the value of the items to be placed in the new record, you would use the REPLACE command as in the second and third lines in the History window of Figure 13.25.

The REPLACE command replaces the current record of a master with a new record. Values of items are specified in the associated &items, and you are positioned on the last record displayed in the Output window.

Controlling Database Modifications

When commands are issued from the Command window, at the completion of each set of commands, by default, all updates are made permanent. To control whether these updates are permanent or temporary, use the SAVE and RESTORE commands.

```
┌ Output ─────────────────────────────────────────────────────────────────────┐
│ EQUIPMENT_CODE=DYSL  EQUIPMENT_NAME=DYNASTAR SLALOM      PRODUCTION_DATE=1988  │
│ EQUIPMENT_CODE=DYSL  EQUIPMENT_NAME=N/A                  PRODUCTION_DATE=N/A   │
│ EQUIPMENT_CODE=DYSL  EQUIPMENT_NAME=DYNASTAR SLALOM      PRODUCTION_DATE=1988  │
│                                                                               │
│                                                                               │
│                                                                               │
└───────────────────────────────────────────────────────────────────────────────┘

┌ History ────────────────────────────────────────────────────────────────────┐
│ REPLACE equipment_type;                                                        │
│ &equipment_name='DYNASTAR SLALOM'; &production_date='1988';                    │
│ REPLACE equipment_type;                                                        │
└───────────────────────────────────────────────────────────────────────────────┘

┌ Command ────────────────────────────────────────────────────────────────────┐
│                                                                               │
│                                                                               │
└───────────────────────────────────────────────────────────────────────────────┘
```

Figure 13.25   The REPLACE Command

SAVE Command

To control when your modifications are permanently saved, you can use the SAVE command with the optional parameter OFF. (This is shown in first statement of Figure 13.26.) The OFF option specifies that the updates from now on are going to be temporary. When you are ready to make your modifications permanent, you issue the SAVE command.

Assume that you want to delete all the records from the database, starting from the first record, regardless of the current position. For that purpose you use the DELETE command with the ALL parameter. (This is shown in second statement of Figure 13.26.) Now, if you wanted to check the status of your file with the LIST command (third statement), you would get the error message shown in Figure 13.26.

Although the changes you requested are not yet permanent, they are nevertheless made—hence the error message. If you wanted to quit now and you entered QUIT in the Command window, you would be prompted to specify whether you wanted to save or cancel the changes. (This is shown in Figure 13.27.)

If you want to save the changes, you specify SAVE. If you decide to cancel them, you specify RESTORE. Thus SAVEOFF allows you to control when the changes you specify are permanently saved.

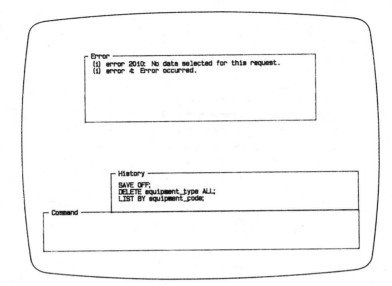

Figure 13.26 Status of Your File After the DELETE Command

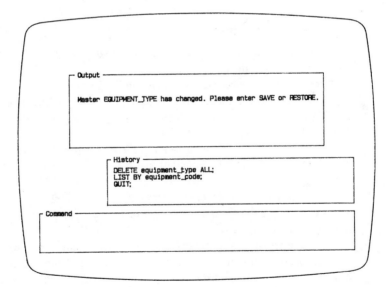

Figure 13.27 Quitting NOMAD with the SAVEOFF in Effect

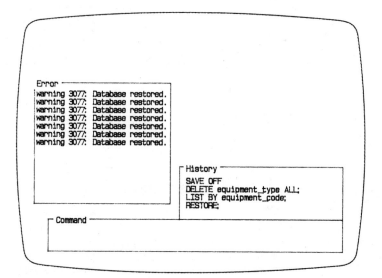

Figure 13.28 RESTORE Command

RESTORE Command

This command cancels all the modifications that were made. (An example of its use is shown in Figure 13.28.)

Here, a warning message is displayed in the Error window, indicating that the database is restored to its previous state. To check on the status of your file after the RESTORE, you could issue the LIST command. (An example is shown in Figure 13.29.)

As you can see, the file is restored to the previous state, and the RESTORE has cancelled the DELETE ALL command that was issued when the SAVE OFF was in effect.

If the NOMAD session were to terminate in the Command window mode as the result of an error, the system would automatically issue a RESTORE to cancel any temporary modifications.

During processing you cannot leave NOMAD if temporary database modifications are pending. If you attempt to do so, the message indicating that the database has been changed will be displayed (as in Figure 13.27), and you will be requested to issue either the SAVE or RESTORE.

Let us now specify that from now on all modifications are to be made permanent. The pointer is positioned at the first record of the EQUIPMENT_TYPE master, and you want to delete the first two records. You then verify this. The commands you will need to issue and the Output and List windows are shown in Figure 13.30.

The requested modifications are permanent because you specified SAVE ON to reverse the SAVE OFF specified previously. SAVE ON is the default in NOMAD'S interactive mode.

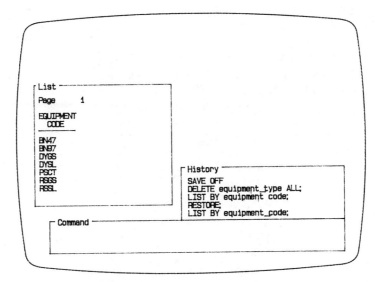

Figure 13.29 Status of Your File After the RESTORE Command

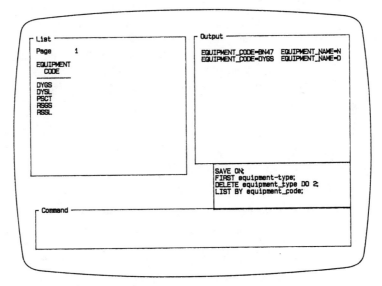

Figure 13.30 The DELETE Command When SAVE ON is in Effect

13.5 SUMMARY

To enter and maintain data in the database in an interactive mode you need commands that insert new records and locate old ones, so that the required changes can be brought about.

The INSERT command is used to add records to a database according to the insert criteria defined in the database schema.

Commands for locating specific records are:

- TOP, LAST, and FIRST for absolute positioning, that is, for locating at the beginning or at the end of the master.
- NEXT and PREVIOUS for relative positioning, that is, for locating in relation to the current record.
- LOCATE, TLOCATE, and RKEY for value-based positioning, that is, when locating search criterion (search value) is specified.

Once located, the data can be displayed with the use of the PRINT command. To modify the display, use the object modifiers COL, SPACE, and FOLD.

To restrict the database access by establishing the records selection criteria, use SELECT command. The SELECT command can be used throughout the NOMAD session. It causes only a subset of records to be made available for actions such as LIST, NEXT, CHANGE, PRINT, DO n, and CREATE.

The database records can be modified with the use of CHANGE and REPLACE commands. You control whether the modifications are permanent or temporary with the SAVE (using OFF and ON parameters) and RESTORE commands.

EXERCISES

1. What data types does NOMAD support?
2. What is a NOTAVAILABLE value? How it is handled?
3. What result will be provided by the command

   PRINT (5+&NAV)?

4. How is &NAV treated in logical comparisons tests?
5. What does NOMAD use to display a value that is not available? What is its default?
6. What will the result be of the command

   PRINT substr(&NAV,1,2) AS A3?

7. What do maintenance commands allow you to do?
8. What would you use the INSERT command for?

9. You have the following field values:

   ```
   &cno='0013'
   &cname='Gregory Good'
   &cphone='208-3851227'
   &caddr='1910 University Drive'
   &city='Boise'
   &cst='ID'
   &czip='83712'
   ```

   The master file is the Customer file. Recall that you can specify fields and their values as parameters. Show how the INSERT command can be used to enter this record. Make sure to use both formats of the INSERT command.

10. When would you use the FROM command?

11. Can FROM be used as a Keyword? When? Can it be used with any command?

12. The INVENTORY master has two items named SKICODE and SKINAME:

    ```
           master INVENTORY keyed(SKICODE);
     item SKICODE as a4   alias SCODE heading 'Ski:Code';
     item SKINAME as a20  alias SNAME heading 'Ski Name';
        .
        .
        .
    ```

    The SKIS master has two items with the same name:

    ```
           master SKIS keyed=SKICODE;
     item SKICODE as a4;
     item SKINAME as a30;
    ```

    Both of these masters are active at the same time.

    How would you use the FROM command to uniquely identify these items and to generate a report that contains the SKICODE and SKINAME from the INVENTORY master?

13. Consider the situation in Problem 12. Again, both masters are active at the same time. How would you use the FROM keyword to uniquely identify the SKICODE and the SKINAME items and to generate a report containing both items from the INVENTORY master?

14. Define and give an example of absolute, relative, and value-based positioning.

15. You want to position your pointer at the first record of the RENTALS database. What command would you use? Show how.

16. You want to position your pointer at the last record of the CUSTOMER database. What do you do?

17. Is the following command executed or ignored?

    ```
    TLOCATE SKI_TYPE= 'DYNAS'  DO 3;
    ```

18. Where are the following commands positioning you in the database?

    ```
    &skicode = 'D100'
    RKEY skicode
    ```

19. If you issue the command specified in Problem 18 from the Command window, where is your new position verified?

20. Which command do you use to change all the records in the master?

21. Why would you need to use the RESTORE command?

PROJECTS

Using data input commands from this chapter, enter all the necessary input data (you decide) into the database files you created for one of these projects:

- The State Parks and Recreation System
- The Properties, Water Rights, and Leases System
- The computer information system project that you and your instructor arranged for with your local business organization

CHAPTER 14

Procedural Data Entry and File Maintenance

Hierarchy is one of the central structural schemes that the architect of the complexity uses.

Herbert A. Simon

14.1 INTRODUCTION

The objective of this chapter is to teach you how to write NOMAD procedures for screen-oriented, user-friendly data entry and maintenance.

When you have completed this chapter, you should be able to:

■ Use interactive windows to write a procedure for user-defined Forms.

■ Understand the use of FORM, LABEL, FIELD, and FEND commands.

■ Construct a main menu for any application using the PICK and CHOICE commands.

■ Construct the update procedure using DECLARE, CLEAR, WINDOW READ with INSERT option, ASK, IF...THEN...ELSE, RETURN, and GOTO commands.

■ Construct the change procedure using WINDOW READ command with the CHANGE option.

■ Construct the procedure to delete records.

■ Query the database using partial key information.

■ Query the database and report on records satisfying a specified logical condition.

■ Create a menu for a procedure controlling integration process.

■ Understand the use of the FGET function.

■ Use the VERIFY command to affect the output of the PRINT command and request automatic verification of the current master records and defined items.

14.2 PROCEDURES FOR DATA ENTRY

If you are writing an application for a user who is not very familiar with NOMAD commands and you want this application to be user-friendly, you can construct interactive data entry and file maintenance procedures for this user. To do so, we will use all the data manipulation commands described so far as well as the commands required for building procedures.

The main elements of the data entry and maintenance procedures are the data entry windows (Forms) and the commands that are used to create and manipulate these windows.

User-Defined Windows (Forms)

The first step in building interactive data entry procedures is to define the application specific windows (Forms). Recall that there are two kinds of windows:

1. System-defined windows such as Command, Output, List, History, Error, and System windows.
2. User-defined windows such as Data Entry Forms to be used for entering application specific data and Menus used to control the selection of the flow of the application logic.

Our task now is to build user-defined windows for our application.

Let us start with a definition of a Form for updating the EQUIPMENT_TYPE master. Two approaches are possible:

1. You can use interactive system windows and type in individual commands, gradually building the application Form. Commands are entered and executed one at a time. You can use the WINDOW OPEN command (described later in this chapter) to view the form and get a better idea of its final appearance. You can experiment with its format for clarity and visual appeal. (We use this approach when explaining the Form building process.)
2. You can use your system editor, type in all commands needed for the Form, go back to the NOMAD environment, and run the created procedure as you would run any other procedure. The Form is thus created. To make any changes to it, you need to came back to the system editor and modify your procedure.

Let us start the Form building process with the first method: using interactive windows to build your Form and issuing the WINDOW OPEN command in the Command window to display the results on the screen.

Your application database is SKIRENT. First you need to activate it. Next you need to define the application specific window using the Form command.

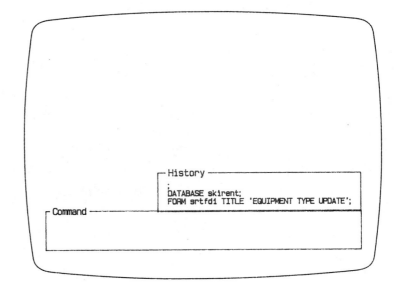

Figure 14.1 FORM Command

FORM Command

This command begins the definition of a Form. It can specify its basic attributes such as background, number of lines in the Form, visual attributes of the border, and so on. Its only required parameter is the name of the Form being defined. The name of the Form can be any valid DOS filename.

To specify that the title will appear in the upper left corner of the Form's window, use the optional parameter TITLE. An example of the FORM command is given in Figure 14.1.

Here the database SKIRENT is activated. The FORM statement is for a Form named SRTF01. Its title is EQUIPMENT TYPE UPDATE. You create this Form gradually with the appropriate commands.

LABEL Command

Now you can annotate the fields in this Form using the LABEL command. This command labels the data entry field corresponding to items in the database master. Its required parameter is a label value, which can be an item, &variable, any valid expression, or a character string. In our example, you specify a character string to be used as the label.

You can specify in which column of the Form the label is to be placed. For this you use the COLUMN parameter, which indicates the column number. You can also indicate on which line of the Form the label is to be placed by using *+n *-n, or n. LINE *+n indicates that the label is placed n lines past the current line. LINE *-n

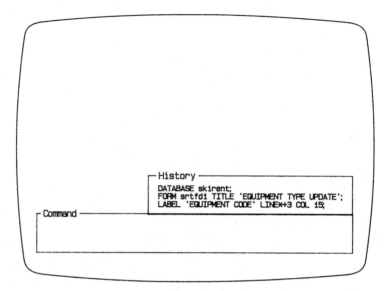

Figure 14.2 LABEL Command

indicates that the label is placed *n* lines before the current line, and LINE *n* indicates that the label is placed at the *n*th line, counting from the beginning of the Form.

An example of the LABEL command is given in Figure 14.2. Here, the label appears on the third line following the current line, starting in column 15.

FIELD Command

Now you are ready to define an area on the Form in which you will input or display your data. To define that area, you use the FIELD command. Its only required parameter is the field name, which names the area on the Form that corresponds to a specific item.

The FIELD command can have attributes defining the position of the field, for example. Figure 14.3 illustrates this command.

Here, the EQUIPMENT_CODE field starts in the fourth column past the current column position. The optional parameter UPPERCASE specifies that if the alphanumeric data for this field are entered in lowercase letters or in mixed lower- and uppercase, the data will be converted to uppercase.

Recall that EQUIPMENT_CODE is a key field in our master and is stored in uppercase. It does not matter how the user enters the data for this field, but to be processed or matched for any reason, the data in this field must be in uppercase. Therefore, we have used the UPPERCASE parameter to ensure conversion.

Figure 14.4 shows the statements needed to build a complete Form for the data entry (and display) for the EQUIPMENT_TYPE master. All field names correspond to appropriate items from the master. Their position is defined by line and column specification; each is given a label.

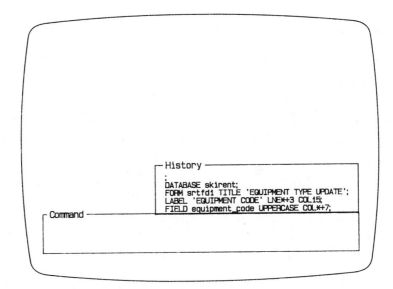

Figure 14.3 FIELD Command

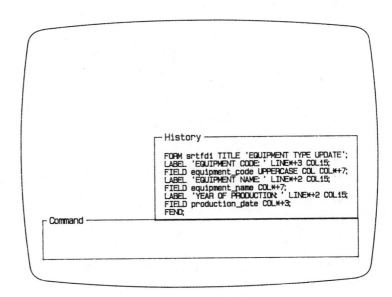

Figure 14.4 Completed Procedure for the EQUIPMENT_TYPE Master Form

FEND Command

As you can see in Figure 14.4, the FEND command indicates the end of the Form definition. This command has to be run together with the FORM command. Therefore, before you can do that, you should call back all the previously run statements

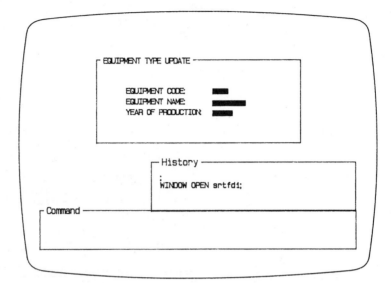

Figure 14.5   Created Form for `EQUIPMENT_TYPE` File

into the Command window and then run all the statements at the same time. Recall that you can bring commands from the History window to the Command window by pressing the Pf3 key. Press this key as many times as the number of statements you want to transfer.

Having constructed your Form, you can now see its format by using the `WINDOW OPEN` command. Figure 14.5 shows the format of the Form we have constructed. As you remember, the `HISTORY.NOM` file contains all the correct statements executed in the given session. Therefore, you can go to the editor and copy the set of commands for the Form from the `HISTORY.NOM` file to the user file for future use.

14.3 MENUS

Let us turn to building a menu. We start with the construction of the main menu for our application, the Ski Rental System. (The format of this menu was given earlier in Figure 10.1.)

To build a Form as a menu, you need two commands: `PICK` and `CHOICE`. You can build multiple menus in one Form by specifying several sets of `PICK` and `CHOICE` commands. One `PICK` command must be specified before each set of `CHOICE` commands.

PICK and CHOICE commands can be used in one of two ways:

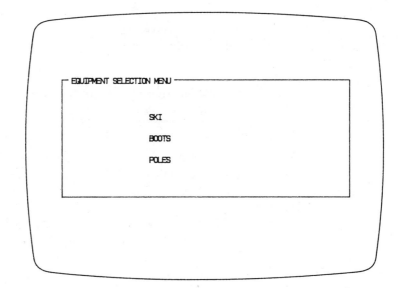

Figure 14.6 Equipment Selection Menu

1. As a permanent part of a Form definition. In this case, they are simply commands.

2. As a parameter to another command, the MENU command. In this case, they are attributes to the MENU command.

We start with the first method of using PICK and CHOICE and will return to the parameter method when we discuss the MENU command.

When the menu is initiated, the cursor is automatically placed on the first input field. You can move the cursor to the desired selection using the directional arrow keys or by typing the first letter of the text displayed on the screen that corresponds to the selection you want. To make your final choice and complete the menu process, press the [Enter] key.

Before you construct a menu, you need to designate (pick) how your menu operates. You need to do this because, when applications are run via menus, the nature of the application may demand different requirements for passing the values from the menu. In some cases, you may want to pass the exact value of the specified menu choice; in another, just the choice's index number from the menu of choices.

PICK Command

This command does not display anything on the Form. With it you just indicate the menu operation mode. To see how this command works, consider the simple menu example in Figure 14.6.

Depending on your applications needs, you can specify menu operations with the PICK command in one of two ways:

1. Use the PICK command with no option to pass the exact value of your menu choice to a specific procedure. The value from the selected menu option is stored in the specified variable or item. For example,

    PICK &var1;

    indicates that the value of the selected menu option will be stored in the variable &var1. The &var1 is declared (all &variables are declared before they are used). The choice value in a menu can be a character string or an expression.

    We can use Figure 14.6 to show how a menu operates if you have specified this form of the PICK command. If you position the cursor on the BOOTS choice the string BOOTS is returned and stored in &var1. This happens after you press [ENTER] to process the BOOTS menu choice.

2. Use the PICK command with the INDEX parameter to pass the index number of your menu choice to a specified procedure. The chronological (index) number of the choice in the menu is returned instead of the choice value itself. For example,

    PICK INDEX &number1;

    indicates that the index number of the selected option will be stored in the variable &number1.

    We again use Figure 14.6 to show how a menu operates if you specify this form of the PICK command. If you position the cursor on the BOOTS choice, since BOOTS is the second choice in this menu, the value 2 will be returned and stored in variable &number1. This happens after you press [ENTER] to process your menu choice.

When you have large menus (long lists of choices) and need to speed up menu choice execution, you can combine the two-step process of positioning on the menu choice and executing this choice in one step by using the AUTOPICK parameter in the PICK command. For example,

    PICK AUTOPICK INDEX &number1;

specifies that the menu choice will be executed when you enter the first character of this choice, and the returned value will be the index number of the selection. So, for the menu in Figure 14.6, if you type the letter "p", the POLES choice is automatically picked, and value 3 (since POLES is the third choice on the menu) is returned and stored in the variable &number1. Now you are ready to list the choices in your menu.

CHOICE Command

The CHOICE command is used to describe a choice in the menu. Multiple CHOICE commands are allowed for one PICK command.

The CHOICE command has only one required parameter: the choice value. The values can be literal, expressions, or &variables. For example, in the command

```
CHOICE 'RENT';
```

the choice value is the literal 'RENT'.

The CHOICE command has several optional parameters that can be used to more fully describe the menu choice or its position on the menu. Some examples of optional parameters are:

1. AS **display-format**—Specifies the format in which the menu choice is to be displayed on the Form. This option must be used when a format for choice value is unknown.

2. LINE **linenumber**—Specifies a line number of the Form where the menu choice is to be displayed. This specification can be done in two ways. You can give the absolute position of the line. For example,

```
LINE 10
```

puts the choice value on the line number 10. Another way is to give the position of the choice value in relation to the current position of the cursor. For example,

```
LINE *+6
```

positions the choice value six lines past the current line. If you were to specify LINE *-6, the choice value would be placed six lines before the current line.

3. COLUMN **column-number**—Specifies at which column of the Form the menu choice is to be displayed. The assignment of column numbers is done in the same way as it is for line numbers, in either relative or absolute fashion.

Sample Menu

Consider the Form defined in Figure 14.7. This Form defines the main menu for the Ski Shop System. Analyze especially the use of the PICK and the CHOICE commands.

Recall that our objective was to generate the main menu illustrated in Figure 10.1. The Form in Figure 14.7 accomplishes just that. The Form's name is MENU1. It spans one full screen (24 lines, 80 columns).

```
Form MENU1 LINESIZE 24 COLSIZE 80;
LABEL 'BOB SKI SHOP RENTAL SYSTEM' LINE 4 COL 28;
LABEL 'MAIN MENU' LINE *+2 COL 36;
LABEL 'FILE UPDATES' LINE *+3 COL 10;
LABEL 'REPORTS' COL 50;
LABEL '_____' LINE *+1 COL 10;
LABEL '_____' COL 50;
DECLARE &selection_n AS 99;
PICK INDEX &selection_n;
CHOICE 'A - NEW CUSTOMER TRANSACTION' LINE *+2 COL 2;
CHOICE 'B - RETURNING CUSTOMER TRANSACTION' LINE *+1 COL 2;
CHOICE 'C - EQUIPMENT RETURN' LINE *+1 COL 2;
CHOICE 'D - EQUIPMENT TYPE FILE' LINE *+1 COL 2;
CHOICE 'E - MANUFACTURER FILE' LINE *+1 COL 2;
CHOICE 'F - SKI INVENTORIES' LINE *+1 COL 2;
CHOICE 'G - BOOT INVENTORIES' LINE *+1 COL 2;
CHOICE 'H - POLE INVENTORIES' LINE *+1 COL 2;
CHOICE 'I - HISTORICAL REVENUE FILE' LINE *+1 COL 2;
CHOICE 'J - REVENUE REPORT' LINE *-8 COL 47;
CHOICE 'K - DAILY LATE RETURN REPORT' LINE *+1 COL 47;
CHOICE 'L - INVENTORY REPORT' LINE *+1 COL 47;
CHOICE 'M - DAILY RENTAL REPORT' LINE *+1 COL 47;
CHOICE 'N - CUSTOMER PROFILE REPORT' LINE *+1 COL 47;
CHOICE 'O - MAILING LABELS' LINE *+1 COL 47;
CHOICE 'P - EXIT THE SYSTEM' LINE *+5 COL 30;
FEND;
```

Figure 14.7 Form Definition for the Main Menu

At this point you should understand that:

■ The variable &selection_n is declared. It will hold numeric values.

■ The method of menu choice selection is specified as passing an index number of the selected menu choice (PICK INDEX &selection_n;).

■ All of the sixteen menu choices have literal values (A through P).

■ This menu has the header BOB SKI SHOP RENTAL SYSTEM placed in line 4, column 28, of the screen.

■ The MAIN MENU subheader is placed two lines below the header.

■ This menu has its list of choices placed in two columns. Note how LINE *-8 is used to position the next set of choices (K through O) in the second column. The two column titles are FILE UPDATES and REPORTS.

■ The choice P is positioned in a column by itself.

14.4 DATA ENTRY SCREENS FOR THE SKI RENTAL SYSTEM: SOURCE CODE AND FORMS

With your main menu constructed, you are ready to consider the data entry screens (Forms) for the seven masters in the Ski Rental System.

Recall that in the beginning of this chapter you learned how to construct a data entry and display Form for the EQUIPMENT_TYPE master. Data entry screens for all other masters are essentially the same; they use the same construct.

EQUIPMENT TYPE UPDATE

EQUIPMENT CODE:

EQUIPMENT NAME:

YEAR OF PRODUCTION:

Figure 14.8   EQUIPMENT_TYPE Data Entry Screen

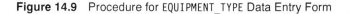

```
FORM srtf01 TITLE 'EQUIPMENT TYPE UPDATE';
LABEL 'EQUIPMENT CODE:'    LINE *+3  COL 15;
FIELD equipment_code UPPERCASE  COL *+7;
LABEL 'EQUIPMENT NAME:'    LINE *+2    COL 15;
FIELD equipment_name    COL *+7;
LABEL 'YEAR OF PRODUCTION:'    LINE *+2    COL 15;
FIELD production_date  COL *+3;
FEND;
```

Figure 14.9   Procedure for EQUIPMENT_TYPE Data Entry Form

At this point you are familiar with all the required commands. To facilitate your learning by example, we present completed source codes and brief explanations for the required Forms.

Form for the EQUIPMENT_TYPE Master

Figure 14.8 illustrates the data entry screen for the EQUIPMENT_TYPE file. The procedure (source code) for this form is given in Figure 14.9.

The name of this Form is srtf01. Its title is EQUIPMENT TYPE UPDATE. It has three data entry fields. If the data for equipment_code is entered in lowercase or mixed form, it is converted to uppercase for processing.

Form for the MANUFACTURERS Master

Figure 14.10 illustrates the data entry screen for the MANUFACTURERS file. The procedure (source code) for this Form is given in Figure 14.11.

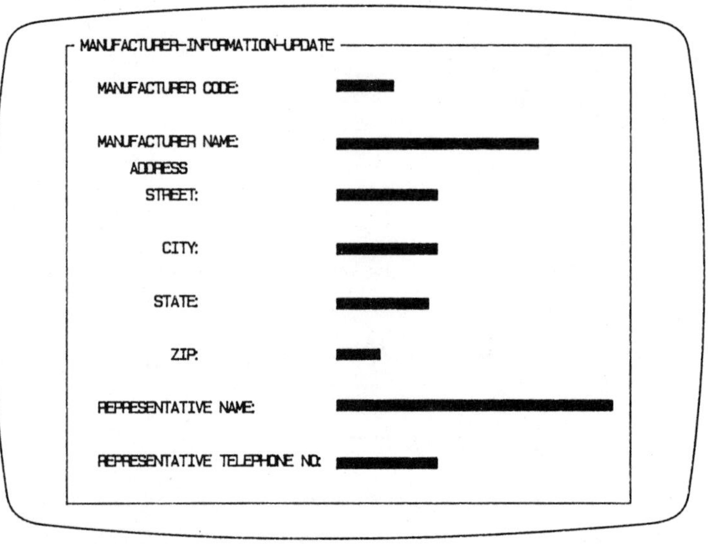

Figure 14.10   Data Entry Form for the MANUFACTURERS File

```
FORM srtf02  TITLE 'MANUFACTURER INFORMATION UPDATE';
LABEL 'MANUFACTURER CODE:'  LINE *+2 COL 10;
FIELD manufact_code    COL *+15;
LABEL 'MANUFACTURER NAME:'  LINE *+2 COL 10;
FIELD manufact_name    COL *+15;
LABEL 'ADDRESS' LINE *+1 COL 15;
FROM manufacturers;
LABEL 'STREET:'  LINE *+1 COL 12;
FIELD street    COL *+24;
LABEL 'CITY:' LINE *+2 COL 12;
FIELD city    COL *+26;
LABEL 'STATE:'  LINE *+2 COL 12;
FIELD state     COL *+25;
LABEL 'ZIP CODE:'  LINE *+2 COL 12;
FIELD zip_code    COL *+22;
FROM;
LABEL 'REPRESENTATIVE NAME:' LINE *+2 COL 2;
FIELD rep_name    COL *+13;
LABEL 'REPRESENTATIVE TELEPHONE NO:' LINE *+2 COL 2;
FIELD rep_telephon    COL *+5;
FEND;
```

Figure 14.11   Procedure for the Data Entry Form for the MANUFACTURERS File

The name of this Form is srtf02. Its title is MANUFACTURER INFORMATION UPDATE. Note the use of the FROM command to resolve possible ambiguity for the address data, since these fields also appear in the CUSTOMER master. The FROM command remains in effect until another FROM command is issued. Thus the FROM command without a parameter clears the command: FROM MANUFACTURERS.

Form for the CUSTOMER master

Figure 14.12 illustrates the data entry screen for the CUSTOMER file. The procedure (source code) for this Form is given in Figure 14.13.

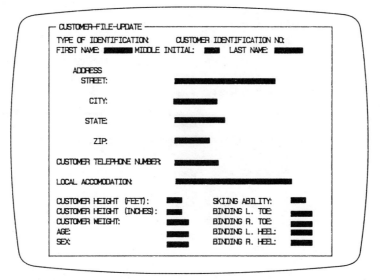

Figure 14.12 Data Entry Form for the CUSTOMER File

```
FORM srtf03  TITLE 'CUSTOMER FILE UPDATE';
LABEL 'TYPE OF IDENTIFICATION:' LINE *+1 COL 1; FROM customer;
FIELD ident_type    COL *+1;
LABEL 'CUSTOMER IDENTIFICATION NO:' COL *+2;
FIELD custident    COL *+1; LABEL 'FIRST NAME:' LINE *+2 COL 2;
FIELD first_name COL *+2; LABEL 'MIDDLE INITIAL:' COL *+2;
FIELD middle_initial COL *+1; LABEL 'LAST NAME:' COL *+2;
FIELD last_name COL *+1; LABEL 'ADDRESS' LINE *+2 COL 20;
LABEL 'STREET:'  LINE *+1 COL 12;
FIELD street_address   COL *+24;
LABEL 'CITY:' LINE *+2 COL 12;
FIELD city   COL *+26;
LABEL 'STATE:'  LINE *+2 COL 12;
FIELD state    COL *+25;
LABEL 'ZIP CODE:'  LINE *+2 COL 12;
FIELD zip_code    COL *+22;
LABEL 'CUSTOMER TELEPHONE NO:' LINE *+2 COL 12;
FIELD phone  COL *+9;
LABEL 'LOCAL ACCOMMODATION:'   LINE *+2 COL 12;
FIELD local_accom    COL *+12;
LABEL 'CUSTOMER HEIGHT (FEET):'  LINE *+2 COL 2;
FIELD cust_height_f  COL *+5;
LABEL 'CUSTOMER HEIGHT (INCHES):' LINE *+1 COL 2;
FIELD cust_height_i  COL *+3;
LABEL 'CUSTOMER WEIGHT:' LINE *+1  COL 2;
FIELD weight  COL *+11;
LABEL 'AGE:' LINE *+1 COL 2;
FIELD age COL *+23;
LABEL 'SEX:' LINE *+1 COL 2;
FIELD sex COL *+23;
LABEL 'SKIING ABILITY:'  LINE 19 COL 43;
FIELD skiing_ability COL *+3;
LABEL 'BINDING L. TOE:'  LINE *+1 COL 43;
FIELD binding_l_toe  COL *+3;
LABEL 'BINDING R. TOE:' LINE *+1 COL 43;
FIELD binding_r_toe  COL *+3;
LABEL 'BINDING L. HEEL:'  LINE *+1 COL 43;
FIELD binding_l_heel  COL *+2;
LABEL 'BINDING R. HEEL:'  LINE *+1 COL 43;
FIELD binding_r_heel  COL *+2;
FEND;
```

Figure 14.13 Procedure for the Data Entry Form for the CUSTOMER File

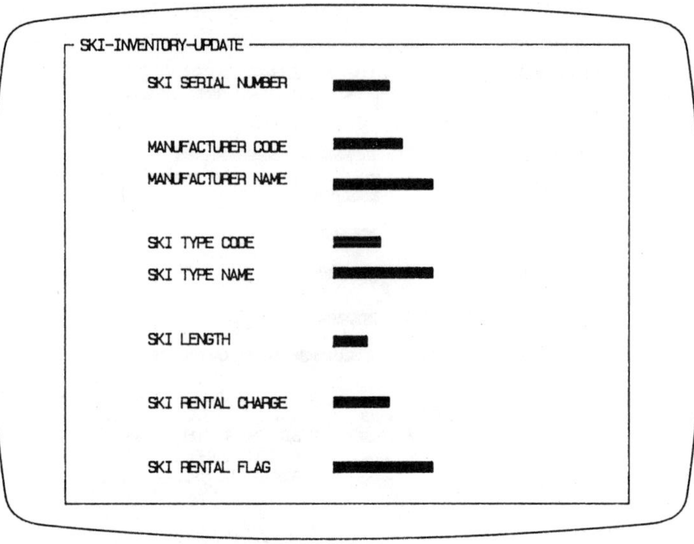

Figure 14.14 Data Entry Form for the SKIINVENTORY File

```
FORM srtf04 TITLE 'SKI INVENTORY UPDATE';
LABEL 'SKI SERIAL NUMBER' LINE *+5 COL 5;
FIELD skinum     COL *+3;
LABEL 'MANUFACTURER CODE' LINE *+2 COL 5;
FIELD ski_manufact    COL *+3;
LABEL 'MANUFACTURER NAME' LINE *+1 COL 5;
FIELD sman_name PROTECTED COL *+3;
LABEL 'SKI TYPE CODE' LINE *+2 COL 5;
FIELD ski_type    COL *+7;
LABEL 'SKI TYPE NAME' LINE *+1 COL 5;
FIELD st_name PROTECTED COL *+7;
LABEL 'SKI LENGTH' LINE *+2 COL 5;
FIELD ski_length    COL *+10;
LABEL 'SKI RENTAL CHARGE' LINE *+2 COL 5;
FIELD ski_rentch    COL *+3;
LABEL 'SKI RENTAL FLAG' LINE *+2 COL 5;
FIELD ski_flag PROTECTED    COL *+5;
FEND;
```

Figure 14.15 Procedure for the Data Entry Form for the SKIINVENTORY File

The name of this Form is srtf03. Its title is CUSTOMER FILE UPDATE. The construct used here is essentially the same as for the previous Form. There are more data entry fields here, and some of the lines of this procedure contain multiple commands separated by semicolons. Again the FROM command is used to resolve possible ambiguity. This FROM command remains in effect until the end of the procedure, so you do not need to issue another FROM command to nullify its effect.

Form for the SKIINVENTORY Master

Figure 14.14 illustrates the data entry screen for the SKIINVENTORY file. The procedure (source code) for this Form is given in Figure 14.15.

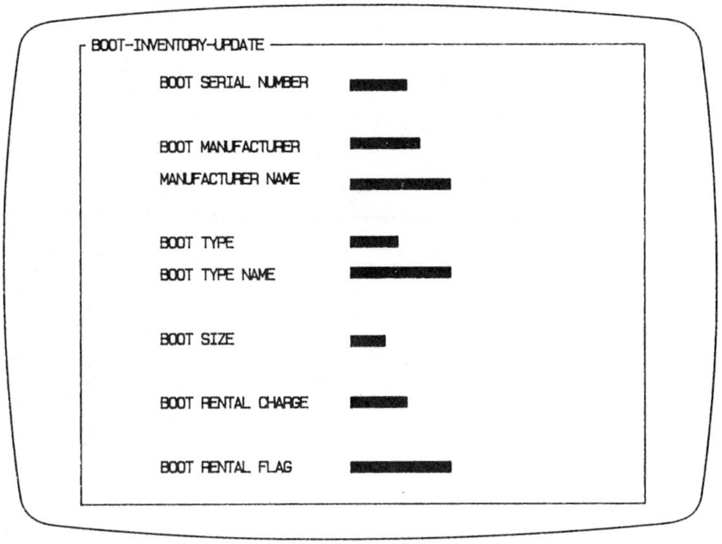

Figure 14.16   Data Entry Form for the BOOTINVENTORY File

```
FORM srtf05 TITLE 'BOOT INVENTORY UPDATE';
LABEL 'BOOT SERIAL NUMBER' LINE *+5 COL 5;
FIELD bootnum      COL *+3;
LABEL 'BOOT MANUFACTURER' LINE *+2 COL 5;
FIELD boot_manufact    COL *+4;
LABEL 'MANUFACTURER NAME' LINE *+1 COL 5;
FIELD bman_name PROTECTED COL *+4;
LABEL 'BOOT TYPE' LINE *+2 COL 5;
FIELD boot_type    COL *+12;
LABEL 'BOOT TYPE NAME' LINE *+1 COL 5;
FIELD bt_name   PROTECTED COL *+7;
LABEL 'BOOT SIZE' LINE *+2 COL 5;
FIELD boot_size    COL *+12;
LABEL 'BOOT RENTAL CHARGE' LINE *+2 COL 5;
FIELD boot_rench   COL *+3;
LABEL 'BOOT RENTAL FLAG' LINE *+2 COL 5;
FIELD boot_flag PROTECTED  COL *+5;
FEND;
```

Figure 14.17   Procedure for the Data Entry Form for the BOOTINVENTORY File

The name of this Form is srtf04. Its title is SKI INVENTORY UPDATE. There are eight data entry fields. Note that the fields such as sman_name, st_name, and ski_flag are protected from being changed by this Form since we used the FIELD option PROTECTED. This is done to prevent the user from entering information in these fields. This fields are only used for display.

Form for the BOOTINVENTORY Master

Figure 14.16 illustrates the data entry screen for the BOOTINVENTORY file. The procedure (source code) for this Form is given in Figure 14.17.

The name of this procedure is srtf05. Its title is BOOT INVENTORY UPDATE. Note that we also used the PROTECTED option to designate fields for display only.

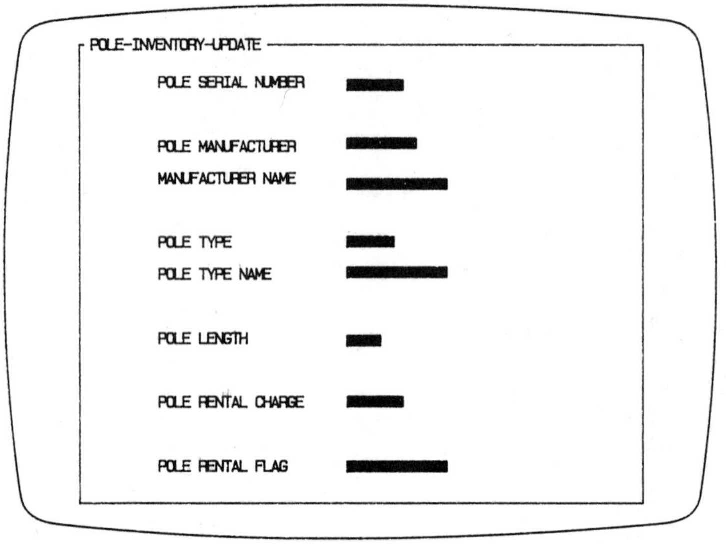

Figure 14.18 Data Entry Form for the POLEINVENTORY File

```
FORM srtf06 TITLE 'POLE INVENTORY UPDATE';
LABEL 'POLE SERIAL NUMBER' LINE *+5 COL 5;
FIELD polenum      COL *+3;
LABEL 'POLE MANUFACTURER' LINE *+2 COL 5;
FIELD pole_manufact    COL *+4;
LABEL 'MANUFACTURER NAME' LINE *+1 COL 5;
FIELD pman_name PROTECTED COL *+4;
LABEL 'POLE TYPE' LINE *+2 COL 5;
FIELD pole_type    COL *+12;
LABEL 'POLE TYPE NAME' LINE *+1 COL 5;
FIELD pt_name PROTECTED COL *+7;
LABEL 'POLE LENGTH' LINE *+2 COL 5;
FIELD pole_length    COL *+10;
LABEL 'POLE RENTAL CHARGE' LINE *+2 COL 5;
FIELD pole_rench    COL *+3;
LABEL 'POLE RENTAL FLAG' LINE *+2 COL 5;
FIELD pole_flag PROTECTED    COL *+5;
FEND;
```

Figure 14.19 Procedure for the Data Entry Form for the POLEINVENTORY File

Form for the POLEINVENTORY Master

Figure 14.18 illustrates the data entry screen for the POLEINVENTORY file. The procedure (source code) for this Form is given in Figure 14.19.

The name of this procedure is srtf06. Its title is POLE INVENTORY UPDATE.

Form for the TRANSACTIONS Master

Figure 14.20 illustrates the data entry screen for the TRANSACTIONS file. The procedure (source code) for this Form is given in Figure 14.21.

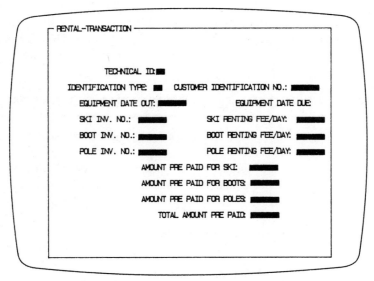

Figure 14.20 Data Entry Form for the TRANSACTIONS File

```
FORM srtf07 TITLE 'RENTAL TRANSACTION';
LABEL 'TECHNICIAN ID:' LINE *+1 COL 10;
FIELD technician COL *+3;
LABEL 'IDENTIFICATION TYPE:' LINE *+2 COL 2;
FROM transactions;
FIELD ident_type PROTECTED COL *+1;
LABEL 'CUSTOMER IDENTIFICATION NO.:' COL *+2;
FIELD custident PROTECTED COL *+1;
LABEL 'EQUIPMENT DATE OUT:' LINE *+3 COL 5;
FIELD date_out  COL *+2;
LABEL 'EQUIPMENT DATE DUE:' COL *+5;
FIELD date_due COL*+2;
LABEL 'SKI INV. NO.:' LINE *+2 COL 5;
FIELD ski_num COL *+3;
LABEL 'SKI RENTING FEE/DAY:' COL *+4;
FIELD amount_ski COL*+3;
LABEL 'BOOT INV. NO.:' LINE *+2 COL 5;
FIELD boot_num COL *+2;
LABEL 'BOOT RENTING FEE/DAY:' COL *+8;
FIELD amount_boot COL *+2;
LABEL 'POLE INV. NO.:' LINE *+2 COL 5;
FIELD pole_num COL *+2;
LABEL 'POLE RENTING FEE/DAY:' COL *+8;
FIELD amount_pole COL *+2;
LABEL 'AMOUNT PREPAID FOR SKIS:' LINE *+3 COL 15;
FIELD ski_pre_paid COL *+5;
LABEL 'AMOUNT PREPAID FOR BOOTS:' LINE *+2 COL 15;
FIELD boot_pre_paid COL *+3;
LABEL 'AMOUNT PREPAID FOR POLES:' LINE *+2 COL 15;
FIELD pole_pre_paid COL *+3;
LABEL 'TOTAL AMOUNT PREPAID:' LINE *+2 COL 20;
FIELD fee_pre_paid COL *+2;
FEND;
```

Figure 14.21 Procedure for the Data Entry Form for the TRANSACTIONS File

The name of this procedure is srtf07. Its title is RENTAL TRANSACTION. Note the use of the FROM command to specify the TRANSACTIONS master that contains the referenced fields, the names of which are not unique in the database.

14.5 UPDATING PROCEDURES FOR THE RENTAL SYSTEM

With your data entry Forms constructed, you are now ready to consider the Form control commands.

As you know, for real-world applications, the update procedure contains more than just one function. So we will create interactive procedures for the following functions:

1. Add a new record to the database.
2. Change the existing database record.
3. Delete a record from the database.
4. Query the database using partial key information.
5. Query and report on records satisfying a specified logical condition.
6. Control the flow for a procedure combining all of the preceding functions.

Initially we will code each of these functions as a separate update procedure to illustrate the building process and the necessary commands. Our final goal, though, is to combine all these procedures. For this we will build an integration procedure (see Function 6 in the preceding list). We start with the update procedures for the EQUIPMENT_TYPE file.

The ADD Procedure

To create a procedure for adding records to the EQUIPMENT_TYPE file, you need these commands:

```
DECLARE
CLEAR
WINDOW READ with INSERT option
ASK
IF...THEN...
RETURN
GOTO
```

The commands IF...THEN, RETURN, and GOTO were described in Chapter 11. The commands DECLARE and CLEAR were discussed in Chapter 12. Therefore, we need only discuss the WINDOW READ and the ASK commands.

WINDOW READ Command With INSERT Option

The WINDOW READ command loads a specified Form into memory and displays the Form on the screen so that the appropriate field values can be entered. After the data is entered, the specified file in your database is modified. The following example illustrates the Form of the WINDOW READ command.

```
WINDOW READ srtf01 INSERT LINE 4 COLUMN 5;
```

The parameters in this command are as follows:

1. FORM **name** is the only required parameter. SRTF01 is the name of the Form to be displayed.

   If the WINDOW READ command includes only a required parameter (WINDOW READ srtf01), it causes the srtf01 Form to be loaded into memory and displayed on the screen. After a user presses [ENTER], the WINDOW READ command is terminated, and the Form is removed from the screen and unloaded from memory. The data in the database is not modified.

2. INSERT inserts the entered data from the specified Form into the database as a new record. This is an optional parameter.

   When performing an insert, a newly created record in the database obtains its values from item fields displayed on the Form and from &items for the record items not displayed on the Form. NOMAD's handling of items and &items is very special. For each item in the database, an &item is declared (see Chapter 9).

   If you reference more than one file on the Form, NOMAD inserts the records into the database in the order you defined them on the Form. If the Form contains only &items or &variables, the INSERT option has no effect.

3. LINE **line number** indicates the line number on the screen where the Form is to begin. It is an optional parameter. If it is not specified, the vertical position of the Form is as it is specified in the Form's procedure code. In our example, the Form is to start on line 4.

4. COLUMN **column number** indicates the column number on the screen where the Form is to begin. This parameter is optional. It operates in the same way as the LINE parameter. In our example, the Form is to start at the column 5. When LINE and COLUMN options are used together, you can build such features as cascading forms (sequentially displaying multiple forms in the different part of a screen).

ASK Command

Use the ASK command in a procedure to request a response from the user before continuing the execution of the procedure.

The response Form is automatically created and opened and displayed on the screen for data entry. The ASK command automatically sizes its Form. Once the ASK

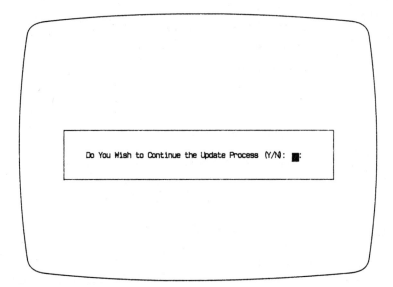

Figure 14.22 Response Form for the ASK Command

form is on the screen, you must enter a value (values), or press the [ENTER] key. If you switch to other windows using PF2 key, you will not be able to enter a command while the ASK is active.

The user's entry can update &variable values needed for subsequent action in the procedure. When entering information on the Form, use either the directional arrow keys or the Tab function to move from field to field. To process the data on the Form, press [ENTER]. After data is processed, the Form is automatically closed. It disappears from the screen.

Consider the following example:

```
ASK 'Do You Wish To Continue The Update Process(Y/N):'
&ans UPPERCASE;
```

The ask-values are the only required parameters of the ASK command.

In our example, the first ask-value is the text to be displayed on the response Form [Do You Wish to Continue the Update Process(Y/N):]. The second ask-value is &variable (&ans). Its current value (if any) will be displayed. A new value entered by the user will be accepted. The entry for the &ans will be transformed to uppercase letters for processing, as specified.

The corresponding response Form is shown in Figure 14.22. As you can see from this example, you can specify multiple ask-values with a single ASK command.

Several optional parameters allow you to control the appearance of the response Form. First we list the parameters that have to be placed directly after ASK and before the ask-values. They are:

```
        DECLARE &ans AS A1;
  -adds5
        CLEAR &equipment_code;
        WINDOW READ srtf01 INSERT LINE 4 COLUMN 5;
        ASK 'Do You Wish to Continue the Update Process(Y/N): '
            &ans UPPERCASE;
            IF &ans='N' THEN RETURN;
        GOTO -adds5;
```

Figure 14.23   Procedure that Adds New Records to EQUIPMENT_TYPE File

1. TITLE **title string** establishes the title for the Form. When TITLE is specified, it must be the first parameter after ASK. The title string will be displayed in the upper left corner of the Form window. If the TITLE parameter is not specified, the response Form has no default title.

2. LINESIZE n specifies the number of lines for the Form.

3. COLSIZE n specifies the number of columns for the Form. If the LINESIZE and COLSIZE are not specified, the response Form is automatically sized.

A second group of optional parameters deals with the ask-values. They are:

1. FOLD n places the ask-value *n* lines down from the current line, starting in column 1. The default for *n* is 1.

2. SPACE n places the ask-value *n* spaces to the right of the current column on the current line. The default for *n* is 1.

3. COLUMN **column number** sets the column position for an ask-value. Column 1 is the farthest left column on the Form.

4. AS **display format** displays the format of the ask-value. For values where the display format is unknown, such as an expression, you must specify its Format. AS can also be used to override an existing display format.

5. IN **column-count BY line-count** allows you to display a portion of the ask-value.

Procedure

The procedure to add new records in the EQUIPMENT_TYPE file is given in Figure 14.23.

The DECLARE command defines the alphanumeric &variable (&ans) as holding one character. –adds5 is a label.

The CLEAR command establishes the initial value for the &equipment_ code as not available; this fact will be displayed as a blank.

The WINDOW READ command with the INSERT option performs the tasks of displaying the srtf01 Form on the screen and allowing the new records to be inserted into the file. (The format of the srtf01 Form is shown in Figure 14.8.)

```
        DECLARE &ans AS A1;
-changes5
        CLEAR &equipment_code;
        ASK 'Enter Equipment Code to Locate a Record for Change: '
            &equipment_code UPPERCASE;
        RKEY equipment_code;
        WINDOW READ srtf01 CHANGE LINE 4 COLUMN 5;
        ASK 'Do You Wish to Continue the Update Process(Y/N): '
            &ans UPPERCASE;
        IF &ans='N' THEN RETURN;
        GOTO -changes5;
```

Figure 14.24 CHANGE Procedure for Data in the EQUIPMENT_TYPE File

The command specifies that the Form is to appear in the upper left corner of the screen, starting on line 4, column 5.

The ASK command displays the specified text. For the update process to continue, the user must respond and press the [ENTER] key. If the user only presses the [ENTER] key, &ans will equal &NAV (the system &variable holding symbol for a NOTAVAILABLE value). The user's response is converted to uppercase for processing.

The IF...THEN, RETURN, and GOTO commands control the flow of the execution of the procedure and allow the user to exit from the update loop.

The CHANGE Procedure

To change records in the database, make sure that you are positioned at the record you wish to change. If the database is not positioned, the update procedure will not execute and will give you an error message.

The actual change is accomplished with the WINDOW READ command using the CHANGE option. The option causes the display of the specified window with its fields of data from the current record of the database. (This is why you had to position yourself on the record you plan to change; you had to make it a current record.) All the unprotected fields now can be changed. After you press the [Enter] key, the WINDOW READ command updates the current record in the database with the corrected data.

Procedure

The procedure to change data in the EQUIPMENT_TYPE file is given in Figure 14.24.

The first two statements define the necessary &variable and initialize the &equipment_code variable, which is equivalent to the item equipment_code, the key field in the EQUIPMENT_TYPE file.

The ASK command queries the user for the value of the key field in the record the user wants to change.

The RKEY statement positions the database at the specific record the user has requested for change.

The WINDOW READ command displays the specified Form and allows you to enter changes to the record and to update the database with new values.

The remaining statements control the flow of logic in the procedure and allow the user to exit from the procedure.

The DELETE Procedure

In the DELETE procedure we use the DELETE command. In addition we will need some commands to control the user-defined windows. These commands can be used to control the system windows, too. They are:

1. WINDOW OPEN
2. WINDOW CLOSE

Before we construct the DELETE procedure, let us consider how these commands work.

Also, to delete a record, the construct is changed. There is no option in the WINDOW READ command for deletion; you must write procedural code. The reason for this requirement is that extra verification of the deletion is frequently desired, but cannot be accommodated easily in a command such as WINDOW READ.

WINDOW OPEN Command

The WINDOW OPEN command loads a Form (or system window) if it is not loaded already and displays it on the screen. To keep the window displayed continuously on the screen, issue a WINDOW OPEN command before specifying a WINDOW READ. Consider the following example:

```
WINDOW OPEN srtf01 LINE 1 COLUMN 5;
```

The srtf01 Form is loaded and displayed with the left upper corner of the Form starting at line 1 and column 5 of the screen.

In the WINDOW OPEN command, the only required parameter is the name of the Form to be displayed. The LINE and the COLUMN parameters are optional.

If you specify a LINE and a COLUMN that are too large for the Form to fit on the screen, NOMAD adjusts these parameters automatically so that the entire Form can be displayed on the screen.

WINDOW CLOSE Command

The WINDOW CLOSE command closes a Form (or a system window) and removes it from the screen. For example,

```
WINDOW CLOSE srtf01;
```

The srtf01 Form is closed and removed from the screen.

If the Form was forced into the memory with the WINDOW OPEN command, it is automatically unloaded.

```
        DECLARE &ans AS A1;
        WINDOW OPEN srtf01 LINE 1 COLUMN 5;
-deletes5
        CLEAR &equipment_code;
        ASK 'Enter Equipment Code to Delete a record: '
            &equipment_code UPPERCASE;
        RKEY equipment_code;
        DELETE equipment_code;
        ASK 'Do You Wish to Continue the Update Process(Y/N): '
            &ans UPPERCASE;
        IF &ans='N' THEN DO;
          WINDOW CLOSE srtf01;
          RETURN;
        END;
        GOTO -deletes5;
```

Figure 14.25   Procedure to DELETE Records in the EQUIPMENT_TYPE File

Procedure

The procedure to delete records in the EQUIPMENT_TYPE file is given in Figure 14.25.

The second statement of this procedure loads and opens the srtf01 Form. During the deletion process, the records are displayed.

Statements 4 through 6 perform the deletion of the records. The ASK statement queries the user for the key value of the record to be deleted. The RKEY statement positions the database at the record that will be deleted. The DELETE statement actually deletes the specified record.

If the delete process is successful, the fields in the srtf01 Form will change. The Form displays the values of the fields in the record that follows the deleted record.

The remaining ASK, IF...THEN, RETURN, and GOTO commands control the procedure's logic and allow the user to exit from the procedure loop. Before you exit the procedure, remove the srtf01 Form from the screen with the WINDOW CLOSE command.

The QUERY Procedure With a Partial Key

For this procedure we introduce several new window (Form) control commands:

1. WINDOW LOAD
2. WINDOW SIZE
3. WINDOW MOVE
4. WINDOW CLEAR

WINDOW LOAD Command

The WINDOW LOAD command loads a Form (window) into memory, but it does not display a Form on the screen.

When the Form is loaded, it is sized automatically to the smaller of either the full screen or the entire Form. So, when you request a display of the Form, it is displayed in its entirety. For example, if the Form is smaller than the screen, it is scaled and centered on the screen when it is displayed.

System windows can also be loaded. They are positioned as specified when you last used WINDOW SAVE SYSTEM, or if not specified, they are in the default positions for the system windows.

In the following example, the List window is loaded into memory:

```
WINDOW LOAD LIST;
```

WINDOW SIZE Command

The WINDOW SIZE command changes the size of a user Form or a system window. However, the command cannot make a user Form larger than specified in the Form definition.

This command can only be executed after the Form (window) is in memory. If a Form is open when this command is executed, the change will be seen immediately on the screen.

In the following example the List window is sized with 10 lines and 60 columns:

```
WINDOW SIZE LIST LINESIZE 10 COLSIZE 60;
```

LINESIZE and COLSIZE can be specified independently.

WINDOW MOVE Command

The WINDOW MOVE command changes the position of the user Form or system window. This command can be executed only when the Form (window) is in memory. If the Form (window) is open when the WINDOW MOVE command is executed, the change is seen immediately.

In the following example, the List window is moved to the position in which the upper left corner of the List window is located at line 2 and column 3:

```
WINDOW MOVE LIST LINE 2 COL 3;
```

If the LINE and COLUMN parameters are omitted, the WINDOW MOVE command moves the Form into the default position (line 1, column 1).

If the completed Form does not fit on the screen at the position specified by the WINDOW MOVE command, NOMAD moves the Form automatically so that its entire area is displayed on the screen, regardless of the user's specifications. (Specifications that do not allow the Form to be displayed in its entirety are ignored.)

WINDOW CLEAR Command

The WINDOW CLEAR command erases any data displayed in the window and places the cursor in the upper left corner of the screen. Its only required parameter is the name of the window. For example,

```
WINDOW CLEAR LIST;
```

clears all previous listings in the List window.

```
        DECLARE &ans AS A1;
        DECLARE &l_select AS A1;
        DEFINE equipment_code1 AS A1 EXPR=equipment_code;
        WINDOW LOAD LIST;
        WINDOW SIZE LIST LINESIZE 10 COLSIZE 60;
        WINDOW MOVE LIST LINE 2 COL 3;
        WINDOW OPEN LIST;
     -query1
        ASK 'Enter the First Letter of the Equipment Code: '
              &l_select;
        IF &l_select NOT=&NAV
           THEN SELECT equipment_code1=&l_select;
        LIST equipment_code equipment_name production_date;
        SELECT CLEAR;
        ASK 'Do You Wish to Continue the Query Procedure: ' &ans
              UPPERCASE;
        IF &ans='N' THEN DO;
          WINDOW CLOSE LIST;
          RETURN;
        END;
        WINDOW CLEAR LIST;
        GOTO -query1;
```

Figure 14.26 Retrieval Procedure with Partial Key

If the window has a file associated with it, both the window and the file are cleared when you issue the WINDOW CLEAR command. Obviously, if the window does not have a file associated with it, only the window is cleared when you issue this command.

Procedure

The procedure to retrieve the records from the EQUIPMENT_TYPE file using only the first letter (partial key) of the key item equipment_code is given in Figure 14.26.

In the second and third statements of the procedure, the DECLARE and DEFINE commands define the field that will contain the first letter of the item equipment_code.

The window control commands load, enlarge, and move the List window into the specified position.

The ASK command queries the user for the first letter of the equipment_code.

The next statement compares the letter supplied by the user with the first letter of the equipment_code in each record. The record is selected when the match occurs.

The LIST command reports selected records. As in all other procedures you have encountered so far, the remaining statements control the flow of the procedure and allow the user to exit from the query.

You might just notice that error handling has been left out to simplify the example. In certain situations, the SELECT and LIST commands can fail and the procedure will be aborted. All of the remaining procedure in this chapter will be without the error controls (user proofing) as this will be discussed in Chapter 19.

The Query Procedure With a Logical Condition

This procedure serves as another example of querying the database for specific information. Here we specify the production date. The reports on the equipment manufactured on this particular date are this query's output.

```
          DECLARE &ans AS A1;
          DECLARE &date_select AS DATE'yyyy';
          WINDOW LOAD LIST;
          WINDOW SIZE LIST LINESIZE 10 COLSIZE 60;
          WINDOW MOVE LIST LINE 2 COL 3;
          WINDOW OPEN LIST;
       -query2
          ASK 'Enter Production Date for Your Selection: '
              &date_select;
          IF &date_select NOT=&NAV
            THEN SELECT production_date=&date_select;
          LIST equipment_code equipment_name production_date;
          SELECT CLEAR;
          ASK 'Do You Wish to Continue the Query Procedure: '
              &ans UPPERCASE;
          IF &ans='N' THEN DO;
            WINDOW CLOSE LIST;
            RETURN;
          END;
          WINDOW CLEAR LIST;
          GOTO -query2;
```

Figure 14.27 Query Procedure with a Logical Condition

When you analyze this procedure, note that it contains all the NOMAD commands you have encountered so far. The procedure is given in Figure 14.27.

The Integration Procedure

The five procedures introduced so far in this chapter constitute separate entities. Each of them is capable of carrying out a separate task. To integrate these separate pieces, a procedure to control the integration process is required.

In the integration procedure we introduce a new command, MENU. The MENU command displays available choices in the window and accepts a choice from the user. Recall that the MENU command represents the second method of menu building. The first method, described earlier in this chapter, required the PICK and CHOICE commands.

MENU Command

The MENU command enables you to create a menu. Its required parameters are CHOICE and PICK, which operate very much as they do when they are used as commands. That is, PICK indicates the &variable name, and CHOICE indicates one of the number of choices that you must make if you have included PICK in your command. As before, the choice can be specified with a character string, a &variable, or an expression. For example,

```
     MENU
          PICK INDEX &s5_choice_n FOLD
          CHOICE "A - ADD RECORDS " SPACE 30 FOLD
          CHOICE "B - CHANGE RECORDS " SPACE 30 FOLD
          CHOICE "C - DELETE RECORDS " SPACE 30 FOLD;
```

The MENU command defines the window of choices, so you can pick the function you want. PICK INDEX indicates the choice number of the selected menu choice (1, 2, or 3 in this example). CHOICE indicates the choices that you make.

The optional parameters SPACE and FOLD operate as described previously.

The optional parameter FOLD is used to place a field or label (in our case, a label) *n* lines from the current line, starting in column 1. Recall that the default for FOLD is 1.

The optional parameter SPACE places a field or label (again, in our example, a label) *n* spaces to the right of the current column on the current line. The default for *n* is 1.

The MENU command of our example will produce a screen display with these choices for the user's selection:

```
A - ADD RECORDS
B - CHANGE RECORDS
C - DELETE RECORDS
```

You can add visual attributes to your menu screen with other optional parameters available for the MENU command. For example, you can establish a title for your menu by using the TITLE 'title string' parameter in the MENU command as follows:

```
MENU TITLE 'TYPE OF UPDATE'
```

This specifies the title of your menu as TYPE OF UPDATE.

Procedure

The integration procedure is shown in Figure 14.28.

The MENU command displays the available choices and accepts the answer from the user. When the user presses the [ENTER] key, control passes to the GOTO command. The expression is evaluated to determine which function to call based on the choice entered. The test is performed on a value of the index returned by the PICK command and stored in the &s5_choice_n variable declared as 9. The format of this menu is illustrated in Figure 14.29.

This concludes our discussion of the process of building the integration procedure needed for the maintenance of the EQUIPMENT_TYPE file. Similar procedures are required for the integrated updating of the MANUFACTURERS, SKIINVENTORY, BOOTINVENTORY, and POLEINVENTORY files. Essentially these integrating procedures will be very similar. They will differ only because of the Form each file uses.

The associated Forms and procedures were described earlier in this chapter. Writing the integrating procedures for the MANUFACTURERS, SKIINVENTORY, BOOTINVENTORY, and the POLEINVENTORY files is left for you as an exercise.

```
        DECLARE &s5_choice_n AS 9;
    -menus5
      MENU TITLE 'TYPE OF UPDATE'
        PICK INDEX &s5_choice_n FOLD
          CHOICE 'A - ADD RECORDS ' SPACE 30 FOLD
          CHOICE 'B - CHANGE RECORDS ' SPACE 30 FOLD
          CHOICE 'C - DELETE RECORDS ' SPACE 30 FOLD
          CHOICE 'D - LOCATE RECORDS WITH SPECIFIED:
                 FIRST CHARACTER IN KEY-FIELD' SPACE 30 FOLD
          CHOICE 'E - LOCATE RECORDS WITH SPECIFIED:
                 PRODUCTION DATE ' SPACE 30 FOLD 3
          CHOICE 'F - RETURN TO MAIN MENU ';
      GOTO (-add, -change, -delete, -query1, -query2)
              &s5_choice_n;
    -add
        CALL adds5;
        GOTO -menus5;
    -change
        CALL changes5;
        GOTO -menus5;
    -delete
        CALL deletes5;
        GOTO -menus5;
    -query1
        CALL query1s5;
        GOTO -menus5;
    -query2
        CALL query2s5;
        GOTO -menus5;
    -EXIT
        RETURN;
```

Figure 14.28   The Integration Procedure

```
 ┌─ TYPE OF UPDATE ──────────────────────────────────────┐

   A-ADD RECORDS
   B-CHANGE RECORDS
   C-DELETE RECORDS
   D-LOCATE RECORDS WITH SPECIFIED:   FIRST CHARACTER IN KEY-FIELD
   E-LOCATE RECORDS WITH SPECIFIED:   PRODUCTION DATE
   F-RETURN TO MAIN MENU

 └───────────────────────────────────────────────────────┘
```

Figure 14.29   Format of a Menu For Integrating Procedure

14.6 PROCEDURES FOR TRANSACTIONS

Now we will build the procedures for the first three choices of the main menu (see Figure 10.1). These procedures are:

1. Capture of the transaction with the first time customer (New Customer).
2. Capture of the transaction with the returning customer (Returning Customer).
3. Equipment return.

Procedures concerned with reports will be discussed in Chapter 18, and the procedures needed for the historical file update will be treated in Chapters 15 and 16.

New Customer Transaction Procedure

To construct this procedure, in addition to commands you already know, you will also need the WINDOW LOAD command and the FGET function. So far, we have been handling data that is gained through ASK or is entered into database. However, very often, you will have to be able to query and get information from individual fields on your Form. This is done with the FGET function.

WINDOW UNLOAD Command

The WINDOW UNLOAD command removes a Form from memory. The memory used by the Form is now made available for other use. (*Note:* The user Forms can be unloaded, but the system windows cannot.)

In the following example, the srtf07 Form is unloaded from memory:

```
WINDOW UNLOAD srtf07;
```

FGET Function

FGET returns the value of the specified field. The value displayed in the specified field of the Form is retrieved and put into a user-defined &variable or printed. Obviously, the specific Form has to be loaded into the window.

You can specify which data you want to get from a Form in three ways:

1. By specifying the name of the field on a Form. For example,

```
&skinum = FGET(srtf07,ski_num);
```

The value of the field ski_num from the srtf07 Form is retrieved and stored in the variable &skinum. Note that, in the argument of this function, the Form is specified first and then the field.

2. By specifying the Form's line number. For example,

```
PRINT FGET(srtf07,15);
```

The data from line number 15 of the srtf07 Form will be retrieved and printed.

3. By specifying the CURSOR parameter. For example,

```
PRINT FGET(srtf07,CURSOR);
```

The retrieval of data is from the line on the srtf07 Form where the cursor is currently positioned. The CURSOR option is the default option, so the word "CURSOR" can be omitted. For example,

```
PRINT FGET(srtf07);
```

is equivalent to the previous example.

Like with any function in NOMAD, FGET can be used within an expression, which can be assigned to an &variable, or used elsewhere.

Procedure

The new customer transaction procedure performs the following functions:

1. Creates the record in the CUSTOMER file.
2. Creates the rental transaction record.
3. Updates the rental flag in the SKIINVENTORY, BOOTINVENTORY, and POLEIN-VENTORY files to designate that specific equipment is rented.

Since the procedure is long, we have numbered each line by means of comments to make it easier to reference the statements. For clarity, specific functional groups in this procedure are separated by a blank line. This procedure is given in Figure 14.30.

The procedure starts with the declaration statements for all the variables needed (lines 1-3).

The statements in lines 4-15 represent the updating. This part of the procedure creates a new record in the CUSTOMER file.

If you enter the record correctly, the controls are passed to line 21; otherwise, you have a chance to make corrections. Control is passed to line 16.

The statements in lines 16-20 allow you to change the customer record just entered. After you confirm that the changes are as you wanted them, control switches to line 21.

The statements in lines 21-27 allow you to pass the identification key fields from the customer record into the rental transaction. The operator does not need to enter the same data twice.

On line 22 the FROM command is issued without any parameters. Therefore, it nullifies the command issued on line 5. The statements on lines 23-24 are FGET functions that retrieve specified values from the SRTF03 Form.

Lines 25-26 contain statements that assign values to the &ident_type and &custident variables from the TRANSACTIONS file.

```
! 1! DECLARE &ans AS A1;
! 2! DECLARE &ident1 AS A2;
! 3! DECLARE &ident2 AS A20;

! 4! -start
! 5!    FROM customer;
! 6!    CLEAR ALL;
! 7!    WINDOW LOAD srtf03;
! 8! -custcr
! 9!    WINDOW READ srtf03 INSERT ;
!10!    ASK 'Is Your Data Entered Correctly? (Y/N): '
!11!        &ans UPPERCASE;
!12!    IF &ans='N' THEN DO;
!13!      GOTO -custchan;
!14!    END;
!15!    GOTO -initial;

!16! -custchan
!17!    WINDOW READ srtf03 CHANGE ;
!18!    ASK ' Is Your Data Correct, Now ? (Y/N): '
!19!        &ans UPPERCASE;
!20!    IF &ans='N' THEN GOTO -custchan;

!21! -initial
!22!    FROM;
!23!    &ident1= FGET(srtf03,ident_type);
!24!    &ident2= FGET(srtf03,custident);
!25!    FROM transactions &ident_type = &ident1;
!26!    FROM transactions &custident = &ident2;
!27!    WINDOW UNLOAD srtf03;

!28! -transcr
!29!    WINDOW LOAD srtf07;
!30!    WINDOW READ srtf07 INSERT ;
!31!    PREVIOUS transactions OTW TOP transactions;
!32!    NEXT transactions;
!33!    WINDOW OPEN srtf07;
!34!    ASK 'Is Your Transaction Typed Correctly? (Y/N): '
!35!        &ans UPPERCASE;
!36!    IF &ans='N' THEN DO;
!37!       WINDOW CLOSE srtf07;
!38!       GOTO -transchan;
!39!    END;
!40!    GOTO -upinv;

!41! -transchan
!42!    WINDOW READ srtf07 CHANGE;
!43!    PREVIOUS transactions OTW TOP transactions;
!44!    NEXT tramsactions;
!45!    WINDOW OPEN srtf07;
!46!    ASK 'Is Your Transaction Correct, Now? (Y/N): '
!47!        &ans UPPERCASE;
!48!    IF &ans='N' THEN DO;
!49!       WINDOW CLOSE srtf07;
```

Figure 14.30   New Customers Transaction Procedure

The statement on line 27 unloads the srtf03 Form and thus releases space in the working buffer.

The statements in lines 28-40 update the TRANSACTIONS file with the new rental transaction. After the rental transaction is entered into the database (line 30), rental charges have to be calculated. To do that, you reposition the record pointer in the TRANSACTIONS file, since the rental charges are defined items in this file. Statements in lines 31-32 move the pointer and cause the calculation of these defined items.

If the data in a newly created rental transaction is correct, control is switched to line 52; otherwise, control is redirected to line 41.

```
!50!       GOTO -transchan,
!51!     END;

!52! -upinv
!53!     FROM skiinventory;
!54!     &ski_flag = &ident1 CAT &ident2;
!55!     &skinum = FGET(srtf07,ski_num);
!56!     RKEY skinum;
!57!     CHANGE ski_flag;
!58!     FROM bootinventory;
!59!     &bootnum = FGET(srtf07,boot_num);
!60!     &boot_flag = &ident1 CAT &ident2;
!61!     RKEY bootnum;
!62!     CHANGE boot_flag;
!63!     FROM poleinventory;
!64!     &polenum = FGET(srtf07,pole_num);
!65!     &pole_flag = &ident1 CAT &ident2;
!66!     RKEY polenum;
!67!     CHANGE pole_flag;
!68!     WINDOW CLOSE srtf07;
!69!     WINDOW UNLOAD srtf07;
!70!     FROM;
!71!     ASK 'Do  You Wish to Continue the Entry For a New
!72!          Customer (Y/N): ' &ans UPPERCASE;
!73!     IF &ans='N' THEN RETURN;
!74!     GOTO -start;
```

Figure 14.30 *continued*

The statements in lines 41-51 allow corrections to the rental transaction just entered. This part is very similar to the update part just described. (Recall that the update part resides in lines 28-40.) The only difference is in the statement on line 42. Here, the WINDOW READ command has a CHANGE parameter instead of a INSERT parameter.

The statements in lines 52-57 update the rental flag in the SKIINVENTORY file to denote that the specific pair of skis is rented.

The rental flag is built in line 54 by concatenating the key items from the rental transaction record. The statement in line 55 gets the rented ski serial number from the rental transaction. The statement in line 56 positions the SKIINVENTORY file pointer at the record with this serial number. The statement in line 57 changes the rental flag.

Using the same constructs, the statements in lines 58-62 update the rental flag in the BOOTINVENTORY file. The statements in lines 63-67 update the rental flag in the POLEINVENTORY file.

The statements in lines 68-70 close and unload the window and nullify the FROM POLEINVENTORY command.

The statements in lines 71-74 control the exit from the procedure. You have two choices here: to go back to the beginning of the procedure and enter another transaction, or to exit the procedure and to go back to the main menu.

Returning Customer Transaction Procedure

This procedure handles transactions concerning returning customers. These are customers who have rented ski equipment before; the records pertaining to these customers exist in the CUSTOMER file. The functions needed in this procedure are as follows:

1. For the returning customer, find the appropriate record in the CUSTOMER file.
2. Determine if this data is correct, and if necessary, change it.
3. Pass required data from the CUSTOMER record to the TRANSACTIONS record so that the operator does not need to type them in again.
4. Create the rental transaction record.
5. Update the rental flag in the inventory files to denote the fact that specific pieces of equipment are rented.
6. Return to the beginning of the procedure to process another customer or exit the procedure.

When you compare this procedure with the new customer transaction procedure, they differ in the construct of step 1 only. All the other functions are exactly the same. For example, the code in lines 25-83 of the returning customer procedure is the same as code in lines 16-74 of the procedure for handling rental transactions for new customers.

In the procedure for returning customers, we will use a command you have not encountered as yet. This is the VERIFY command.

VERIFY Command

The VERIFY command allows you to request automatic verification of the current master records and defined items. It can also be used to affect the output from the PRINT command.

NOMAD can confirm &variables and items values by displaying them in the Output window, when:

1. The record is repositioned, changed, deleted, or inserted.
2. The PRINT command is issued.

This confirmation depends on the current setting of the VERIFY command. The default settings are as follows:

1. ON for commands issued from the Command window. To suppress automatic verification of information from the commands entered within the Command window, specify:

   ```
   VERIFY CONV OFF;
   ```

   (CONV stands for conversational.) To return to the default status, specify:

   ```
   VERIFY CONV ON;
   ```

2. OFF for commands in a procedure. To request the automatic display of information from commands in a procedure, specify:

VERIFY PROC ON;

To return to the default setting, specify:

VERIFY PROC OFF;

The VERIFY command has the following optional parameters:

1. LONG/SHORT—Controls how much information is displayed for an item. If you specify:

VERIFY LONG;

the item or &variable name will be printed with its value. If you specify:

VERIFY SHORT;

only the value will be printed. The default verification is LONG.

2. DEFINES ON/OFF—Specifies whether or not defined items will be verified.

Procedure

The returning customer rental transaction procedure is given in Figure 14.31.

In lines 4-24 of the procedure, the appropriate record from the CUSTOMER file is located. This part of the procedure differs from constructs you have encountered before.

Lines 4-5 are DECLARE statements. They define variables holding the last and the first name of the returning customer, when the creation of the rental transaction starts.

Lines 6-7 load the Output window and adjust its size.

Lines 8-9 load the srtf03 window, which is used for entering the customer data. Recall that you have created this Form to update the CUSTOMER file.

Line 10 opens the Output window.

In lines 11-12, the system operator is asked to enter the last and the first name of the customer being served.

To resolve possible ambiguities arising from the last names in the CUSTOMER file, you use the FROM command. This command is used in line 13.

The statement in line 14 positions the record pointer at the top of the CUSTOMER file.

In line 15, the VERIFY command is used to verify and display information processed by the LOCATE statements. The LOCATE statement is in lines 16-18.

The statement in line 21 controls the flow of the procedure. If the record displayed in the Output window is the correct record (data on the customer being served), control is passed to the next function—line 25.

```
! 1! DECLARE &ans AS A1;
! 2! DECLARE &ident1 AS A2;
! 3! DECLARE &ident2 AS A20;
! 4! DECLARE &last_name1 AS A20;
! 5! DECLARE &first_name1 AS A10;
! 6! WINDOW LOAD OUTPUT;
! 7! WINDOW SIZE OUTPUT LINESIZE 5 COLSIZE 60;

! 8! -start
! 9!    WINDOW LOAD srtf03;
!10!    WINDOW OPEN OUTPUT LINE 2 COL 2;
!11!    ASK 'What is customer's last name?' &last_name1
          UPPERCASE;
!12!    ASK 'What is customer's first name?' &first_name1
          UPPERCASE;
!13!    FROM customer;
!14!    TOP customer;
!15!    VERIFY PROC ON;

!16! -search
!17!    LOCATE last_name = &last_name1
!18!         AND first_name = &first_name1;
!19!    ASK 'Is this correct record for customer? (Y/N)'
!20!         &ans UPPERCASE;
!21!    IF &ans='N' THEN GOTO -search;
!22!    VERIFY PROC OFF;
!23!    WINDOW CLEAR OUTPUT;
!24!    WINDOW CLOSE OUTPUT;

!25! -custchan
!26!    WINDOW READ srtf03 CHANGE ;
!27!    ASK ' Is Your Data Correct, Now ? (Y/N): '
!28!         &ans UPPERCASE;
!29!    IF &ans='N' THEN GOTO -custchan;

!30! -initial
!31!    FROM;
!32!    &ident1= FGET(srtf03,ident_type);
!33!    &ident2= FGET(srtf03,custident);
!34!    FROM transactions &ident_type = &ident1;
!35!    FROM transactions &custident = &ident2;
!36!    WINDOW UNLOAD srtf03;

!37! -transcr
!38!    WINDOW LOAD srtf07;
!39!    WINDOW READ srtf07 INSERT ;
!40!    PREVIOUS transactions OTW TOP transactions;
!41!    NEXT transactions;
!42!    WINDOW OPEN srtf07;
!43!    ASK 'Is Your Transaction Typed Correctly? (Y/N): '
!44!         &ans UPPERCASE;
!45!    IF &ans='N' THEN DO;
!46!        WINDOW CLOSE srtf07;
!47!        GOTO -transchan;
```

Figure 14.31   The Returning Customer Transaction Procedure

If the record is not correct, controls are passed back to line 16 to locate the customer record correctly.

The statement on line 22 turns off the verifying process.

And finally, lines 23-24 hold statements that clear and close the Output window.

Equipment Return Procedure

Our last procedure deals with the rental information when rented equipment is returned to the store. The functions needed in this procedure are as follows:

1. Locate the appropriate transaction record to enter the date of the equipment return and the rental charges.

```
!48!    END;
!49!    GOTO -upinv;

!50! -transchan
!51!    WINDOW READ srtf07 CHANGE;
!52!    PREVIOUS transactions OTW TOP transactions;
!53!    NEXT transactions;
!54!    WINDOW OPEN srtf07;
!55!    ASK 'Is Your Transaction Correct, Now? (Y/N): '
!56!         &ans UPPERCASE;
!57!    IF &ans='N' THEN DO;
!58!       WINDOW CLOSE srtf07;
!59!       GOTO -transchan;
!60!    END;

!61! -upinv
!62!    FROM skiinventory;
!63!    &ski_flag = &ident1 CAT &ident2;
!64!    &skinum = FGET(srtf07,ski_num);
!65!    RKEY skinum;
!66!    CHANGE ski_flag;
!67!    FROM bootinventory;
!68!    &bootnum = FGET(srtf07,boot_num);
!69!    &boot_flag = &ident1 CAT &ident2;
!70!    RKEY bootnum;
!71!    CHANGE boot_flag;
!72!    FROM poleinventory;
!73!    &polenum = FGET(srtf07,pole_num);
!74!    &pole_flag = &ident1 CAT &ident2;
!75!    RKEY polenum;
!76!    CHANGE pole_flag;
!77!    WINDOW CLOSE srtf07;
!78!    WINDOW UNLOAD srtf07;
!79!    FROM;
!80!    ASK 'Do You Wish to Continue the Entry For a New
!81!         Customer (Y/N): ' &ans UPPERCASE;
!82!    IF &ans='N' THEN RETURN;
!83!    GOTO -start;
```

Figure 14.31 *continued*

2. Update the located transaction with the equipment return date and calculate rental charges.

3. Update the rental flag in the SKIINVENTORY, BOOTINVENTORY, and POLEINVENTORY files to indicate that the equipment is returned.

Again, in this procedure, we use commands and functions you have encountered already.

Procedure

The equipment return procedure is given in Figure 14.32.

We describe this procedure only in general terms because you are already familiar with most of the statements used here. We have introduced them all in the procedures constructed so far.

The statements in lines 1-3 declare the user &variables that pass values to the procedure.

The statements in lines 4-5 load the Output window and change its size.

The statements in lines 6-22 form a part of the procedure for locating the appropriate transaction record when a customer returns rented equipment. The transaction record is located using one of the equipment codes: a ski, boot, or pole

```
! 1! DECLARE &ans AS A1;
! 2! DECLARE &tdate_out AS DATE'mmddyy';
! 3! DECLARE &tnumber AS A8;
! 4! WINDOW LOAD OUTPUT;
! 5! WINDOW SIZE OUTPUT LINESIZE 5 COLSIZE 60;

! 6! -start
! 7!    WINDOW LOAD srtf07;
! 8!    WINDOW OPEN OUTPUT LINE 2 COL 2;
! 9!    ASK 'What is Equipment Code?' &tnumber;
!10!    ASK 'What is the date when equipment was rented?'
!11!        &tdate_out;
!12!    TOP transactions;
!13!    VERIFY PROC ON;

!14! -search
!15!    LOCATE date_out=&tdate_out AND (ski_num=&tnumber OR
!16!           boot_num=&tnumber OR pole_num=&tnumber);
!17!    ASK 'Is this correct transaction record? (Y/N)'
!18!        &ans UPPERCASE;
!19!    IF &ans='N' THEN GOTO -search;
!20!    VERIFY PROC OFF;
!21!    WINDOW CLEAR OUTPUT;
!22!    WINDOW CLOSE OUTPUT;

!23! -transchan
!24!    WINDOW READ srtf07 CHANGE;
!25!    PREVIOUS transactions OTW TOP transactions;
!26!    NEXT transactions;
!27!    WINDOW OPEN srtf07;
!28!    ASK 'Is Your Transaction Completed Now? (Y/N): '
!29!        &ans UPPERCASE;
!30!    IF &ans='N' THEN DO;
!31!       WINDOW CLOSE srtf07;
!32!       GOTO -transchan;
!33!    END;

!34! -upinv
!35!    FROM skiinventory;
!36!    &ski_flag = &NAV
!37!    &skinum = FGET(srtf07,ski_num);
!38!    IF &skinum = &NAV THEN GOTO -next1;
!39!    RKEY skinum;
!40!    CHANGE ski_flag;
!41! -next1
!42!    FROM bootinventory;
!43!    &bootnum = FGET(srtf07,boot_num);
!44!    IF &bootnum = &NAV THEN GOTO -next2;
!45!    &boot_flag = &NAV;
!46!    RKEY bootnum;
!47!    CHANGE boot_flag;
!48! -next2
!49!    FROM poleinventory;
!50!    &polenum = FGET(srtf07,pole_num);
!51!    IF &polenum = &NAV THEN GOTO -end;
!52!    &pole_flag = &NAV;
!53!    RKEY polenum;
!54!    CHANGE pole_flag;
!55! -end
!56!    WINDOW CLOSE srtf07;
!57!    WINDOW UNLOAD srtf07;
!58!    FROM;
!59!    ASK 'Do You Wish to Enter Another Transaction?
!60!        (Y/N): ' &ans UPPERCASE;
!61!    IF &ans='N' THEN RETURN;
!62!    GOTO -start;
```

Figure 14.32   Equipment Return Procedure

inventory code plus the date when that equipment was rented. When the appropriate record is located, the control is passed to line 23.

The statements in lines 23-33 form the part of the procedure that enters the date of the equipment return and calculates rental charges. When your transaction is completed, controls are passed to line 34.

The statements in lines 34-54 form a procedure that updates the SKI, BOOT, and POLE inventory files to denote that the ski equipment is returned and available for renting. This is done by changing the field values in the rental flags, in the appropriate files, to the NOTAVAILABLE (N/A) value. This means that the rental flags do not contain any values. The equipment is ready for renting.

Finally, the statements in lines 55-62 close and unload the srtf07 (Form) window. Control is passed to the beginning of the procedure if you indicate that you want to enter another return transaction; otherwise, the control is passed to the calling procedure.

14.7 SUMMARY

Procedural screen-oriented file maintenance was discussed in this chapter.

The first step in building interactive data entry procedures is to define the application specific windows (Forms). Essential commands needed to build a Form are:

```
FORM
LABEL
FIELD
FEND
```

The data entry screens (Forms) for all the masters in the Rental System can be constructed using these commands.

Data entry Forms were constructed for these masters:

```
EQUIPMENT_TYPE
MANUFACTURERS
CUSTOMER
SKIINVENTORY
BOOTINVENTORY
POLEINVENTORY
TRANSACTIONS
```

Menus can also be built as Forms. To construct a Form as a menu, in addition to the Form building commands, you need the PICK and CHOICE commands. We constructed the main menu of our application as a Form.

The interactive data entry procedures require these functions:

1. Add a new record to the database.
2. Change the existing database record.
3. Delete a record from the database.
4. Query the database using partial key information.
5. Query and report on records satisfying a specified logical condition.

These functions were incorporated into five separate data entry procedures: ADD, CHANGE, DELETE, QUERY with a partial key and QUERY under specified condition procedures.

To build these procedures, you need all the flow of logic control commands defined in previous chapters as well as the Form building commands introduced in this chapter.

An ADD or CHANGE of record could be done procedurally (as with DELETE), but we have a WINDOW READ command to do this automatically. These commands are:

> WINDOW READ with INSERT option
> WINDOW READ with CHANGE option

To be able to construct a query for a user, you need the ASK command.

Forms are controlled through the window control commands. Some of those commands are:

> WINDOW LOAD
> WINDOW OPEN
> WINDOW CLOSE
> WINDOW UNLOAD
> WINDOW SIZE
> WINDOW MOVE
> WINDOW CLEAR

Separate data entry and maintenance procedures need to be integrated. The integration procedure can be constructed as a menu. We have constructed it using the MENU command.

The MENU command represents the second method of menu building. It requires the PICK and CHOICE commands. In the MENU command, PICK and CHOICE serve as the required parameters. Their function is the same as it was in the FORM command.

The integration of all interactive, screen-oriented data entry procedures completed our discussion.

EXERCISES

1. Which commands do you need to build a Form?

2. Analyze and describe the purpose of these statements:

```
DECLARE &data as A15;
&data = 'abcdefg';
LABEL 'data';
FIELD &data;
FEND;
```

3. Which command is needed to display the Form in Problem 1 on the screen?

4. What does this statement define?

```
FIELD equip_code COLUMN *+3 PROTECTED;
```

5. According to the following statement, where does the field e_ski start on the screen?

```
FIELD e_ski COLUMN 1 LINE *+2
            UPPERCASE
            ERRMSG 'invalid  equipment code';
```

6. What is the following statement defining?

```
FORM fr2 TITLE 'INVENTORY UPDATE' COLSIZE 70 LINESIZE 16;
```

7. Write a statement that annotates a line on a Form. The label is to appear on the line following the current line, starting at column 13.

8. Explain the work of each of the following commands and identify what this set of statements will produce.

```
DECLARE &1pick as A8;
FORM choice1 TITLE 'PAYMENT TYPE'
PICK &1pick;
CHOICE  'cash  ' line *+1 col 3;
CHOICE  'check ' line *+1 col 3;
FEND;
WINDOW READ choice1;
```

9. What values can &pick1 have here?

```
DECLARE &pick1 AS 99;
FORM pick1 TITLE 'REPORT';
CHOICE  'WEEKLY REPORT'  LINE *+1 COLUMN 6;
CHOICE  'MONTHLY REPORT' LINE *+1 COLUMN 6;
CHOICE  'ANNUAL REPORT'  LINE *+1 COLUMN 6;
FEND;
WINDOW READ pick1;
```

10. When and why would you use an ASK command?

11. Write all the statements necessary to generate this window:

```
VERIFICATION

INVALID SELECTION.
TYPE 1, OR 2, OR 3.
PRESS [ENTER] TO TRY AGAIN
```

12. How do you use the FGET function?

13. Assume that you loaded a Form named `form1` into a window. A field on this Form, say, the C1 field, has a value of 123. Write the statements needed to retrieve and to print the value of this field.

14. Briefly describe two ways of writing a menu.

15. Can you include several `PICK` and `CHOICE` options in one `MENU` command?

16. What is generated by this set of statements?

```
MENU PICK &ecolor FOLD;
CHOICE  'RED' FOLD;
CHOICE  'WHITE' FOLD;
CHOICE  'BLUE' FOLD;
PICK  &icolor FOLD
CHOICE  'WHITE' FOLD;
CHOICE  'GREEN' FOLD;
CHOICE  'BLUE' FOLD;
CHOICE  'ORANGE' FOLD;
```

17. List and briefly describe window control commands.

18. How can the `WINDOW CLOSE` command be used in a procedure?

19. Write a complete procedure to update the `CUSTOMER` master.

20. Write a procedure to update the `MANUFACTURERS` master.

21. Write updating procedures for the three inventory masters. Construct a menu for integrating these procedures. The masters are:

   ■ `SKIINVENTORY`

   ■ `BOOTINVENTORY`

   ■ `POLEINVENTORY`

PROJECTS

Develop all the updating procedures for the projects you designed in Chapter 10. Use menus and data entry screens (custom Forms). If you wish, you can omit all the error control procedures.

1. For the State Parks and Recreation System.

2. For the Properties, Water Rights, and Leases System.

3. For the computer information system project that you and your instructor arranged for with your local business organization.

CHAPTER 15

File Maintenance Using External Files

It was just what it ought to be and it looked what it was.

Jane Austen

15.1 INTRODUCTION

The main objective of this chapter is to show you how to construct procedures for maintaining a NOMAD database using external transaction files. Large-volume database maintenance is done in this fashion.

When you have completed this chapter you, should be able to:

- List the tasks required for database maintenance with an external transaction file.
- Identify the NOMAD commands (and their required parameters) used for this type of maintenance.
- Specify how to obtain statistics from the update process.
- Construct a maintenance procedure with a single transaction type.
- Construct a maintenance procedure with multiple transaction types.

15.2 UPDATING FROM EXTERNAL FILES

Often, to update the database, you need to use external transaction files. This happens when you need to update a large volume of records, to pass data from other applications into your NOMAD application, or to download the data from the corporate database into the PC application.

You are already familiar with some of the NOMAD commands required to create such an update procedure: CHANGE, DELETE, INSERT, REPLACE, and RKEY. These commands were discussed in Chapter 12. This chapter presents the CLOSE, FILE, LOAD, READ, and SET commands.

To update the NOMAD database from an external file requires the following tasks:

1. Open the external file. (Use the FILE command.)
2. Read a record into an input buffer area. (Use the READ command.)
3. Place the values from the read transaction record, now located in the input buffer, into appropriate &items and/or &variables. (Use the SET command.)
4. Locate the appropriate record in the database if you are going to change, delete, or replace the record. (Use the RKEY command.) Locating is not required if you are inserting records; this is automatically done based on key values.
5. Modify the database with the values of the &items. (Use CHANGE, DELETE, INSERT, or REPLACE.)
6. Repeat tasks 2 through 5 for each record in the transaction file. (Use the procedure control loop.)
7. Close the transaction file when the database maintenance is completed. (Use the CLOSE or FILE CLOSE commands.)

If the transaction file deals with only one type of transaction, for example, only delete or only insert, there is a simpler and more efficient alternative to the update tasks just described. This efficient method uses the LOAD command to perform tasks 2 through 6 automatically. We will discuss this command in some detail later.

When constructing a procedure that maintains the database using external transaction file, it is important to consider the format of the records in this file. There are two types of file formats: fixed and free. Both are handled by NOMAD. Which format is better depends on the application.

Fixed-format records have fixed-length fields placed in specific columns of the record. In free-format records, the fields are not restricted to specific columns and are separated with delimiters. In NOMAD, the delimiters can be defined by the user. The delimiter can be any character or a space.

We start our discussion of the database update procedures with the update from the fixed-format transaction file. This file contains a single type transaction. Next we consider a procedure for a maintenance of a database with the free-format transaction file. This file contains multiple type transactions, including deletion, replacement, insertion, and change of records transactions.

15.3 MAINTENANCE PROCEDURE WITH A SINGLE TRANSACTION TYPE

The maintenance procedure you will develop is for the Ski Rental System's HISTORY file. You need to start with the description of the format of the transaction file that updates the HISTORY file.

```
Item Name          Format       Length
---------          ------       ------

WEEK CODE          N2           2

SKI REVENUE        N8.2         8

BOOT REVENUE       N8.2         8

POLE REVENUE       N8.2         8
```

Figure 15.1   Record Format for the External Transaction File

```
0101000.5600567.7500154.50
0202345.0001238.5000372.50
0302910.3400589.0000500.00
0405625.5001240.0000254.50
0502340.7500500.0000150.50
0607843.7502310.0000345.00
0708256.0003000.0000235.00
0809210.1503200.0000500.00
0910150.4504523.0000782.00
1011346.5004570.0000700.00
1112349.0005000.0000679.00
1213458.0005200.0000760.00
1314520.0005670.0000780.00
1414000.0005600.0000700.00
1514000.0005689.7500689.00
1613880.0005300.7500630.00
1711200.7504300.1500300.00
1810000.6502365.0000200.00
1909823.0001289.0000200.00
2007893.0000865.0000150.00
2104329.0000700.0000100.00
2201230.0000500.0000080.00
2300735.0000325.0000060.00
2400320.0000150.0000025.00
```

Figure 15.2   Listing of the External Transaction File

Historical Transaction File

The HISTORY file is updated once a year, at the end of the ski season. To update the HISTORY file, the external transaction file is used. Records in this external file contain information on revenue from renting skis, boots, and poles, summarized on a weekly basis. The transaction file record format and its content are illustrated in Figure 15.1.

Every ski season represents 24 weeks of data. If the season is shortened, due to lack of snow, for example, you create appropriate records indicating revenue of zero. This way weekly revenues can be compared from year to year. A complete listing of the external transaction file for our example is given in Figure 15.2. (We show you in detail how to build this file in Chapter 16.)

Each record in this transaction file creates a record in the HISTORY file. Recall the structure of the HISTORY file (Chapter 10). To create a complete record in this file, you need to supply a value for the year which you can obtain by prompting the user of the maintenance procedure.

To build a complete maintenance procedure, we need two commands:

1. FILE **command**—Use this command to establish the identity and attributes of the external transaction file and to prepare for reading from or writing to this file.
2. LOAD **command**—Use this command to automatically perform tasks 2-6 of the database maintenance procedure.

FILE Command

This command is used to perform the following functions:

1. Determine the existence of an external file.
2. Create an external file.
3. Prepare a file for reading or writing.
4. Modify specified attributes of an external file.
5. Delete an external file.

The FILE command when used with the DEFINE, OPEN, CLEAR, or CLOSE parameters performs functions 2, 3, and 5. The FILE command with the DELETE parameter performs function 5. The FILE command with the STATUS parameter performs function 1.

FILE Command with DEFINE Parameter

This option establishes attributes for the file as described by the file-id name. These attributes remain in effect for the duration of the current session or until another FILE DEFINE changes them. They are deactivated by the FILE CLEAR command.

The only required parameter for this option is file-id. This file-id can be a character string up to 256 characters in length. You use this identification in subsequent references to the file. For example,

```
FILE DEFINE transaction_records;
```

Here, the identification name of the defined file is transaction_records.

NOMAD automatically assigns this name to a physical file by taking the first 8 characters of the identification name and supplying the extension .FIL. For our file-id example, the name of the physical file will be TRANSACT.FIL.

The DEFINE parameter allows the following options:

1. **File Name.** This allows you to specify the name of the physical file, including the device, directory, and extension. For example,

```
FILE DEFINE transaction_records
c:\nomad\data.dat;
```

specifies that the physical file for the transaction_record file is located on drive c, in the nomad directory under the filename data, and with the extension .dat.

2. **File Attributes.** File attributes are defined by the following keywords:

APPEND—Specifies that the file is to be opened for writing records. New records will be added to the end of the file. For example,

```
FILE DEFINE myfile APPEND;
```

specifies that the file myfile will be opened for appending records to the end of the file.

BINARY/TEXT—Specifies that files will contain either binary or textual data. The default attribute is TEXT. For example,

```
FILE DEFINE myfile APPEND BINARY;
```

specifies that the myfile file will be appended and will contain binary data.

CHANGE—Specifies that the file is open for both read and write. When a record is written to the file, the new record replaces the last record read. For example,

```
FILE DEFINE myfile CHANGE;
```

specifies that the myfile file is open for both read and write.

CREATE—Indicates that a file is to be opened only for writing. With this option a new file is created even if an old one with the same name exists. The old file is automatically deleted. For example,

```
FILE DEFINE myfile CREATE;
```

specifies that although the myfile file exists, a new file is created and is ready to be open for writing. The old myfile file is automatically deleted.

PAD—Specifies the value used to pad records short of their length, when writing to a record file. The defaults for the padding value are zero for binary files and space for the textual files. For example,

```
FILE DEFINE myfile CREATE RECORD
     LENGTH 125 PAD 9;
```

specifies that records shorter than the specified record length will be padded with the character 9.

READ—Specifies that a file is to be opened for reading only. For example,

```
FILE DEFINE myfile READ;
```

specifies that the myfile file is opened only for reading from; you cannot write to this file.

APPEND, CHANGE, CREATE, and READ are the access keywords. You cannot specify multiple attributes. That is, only one of these can be stated for each FILE DEFINE command.

If you do not specify an access keyword for the FILE DEFINE, the command you used to access this file automatically provides the default attribute. For example, the default provided by the READ and FILE OPEN commands is READ. The default provided by the WRITE and LIST commands is CREATE.

3. WINDOW. You use this parameter to specify the name of a previously created textual window to be associated with the file-id. For example,

```
FILE DEFINE myfile READ WINDOW 'screen1';
```

Specifies that the previously defined textual window screen1 is now associated with the myfile file. This file is to be open for read only.

4. **Communication Parameters.** NOMAD allows you to define several communication parameters, such as communication type, port, speed of communication link, parity, and so on. We do not specify these parameters in detail because they are beyond the scope of this book, but you should be aware of their presence in NOMAD.

FILE Command with OPEN Parameter

The OPEN parameter explicitly opens a file. All of the parameters described in the FILE DEFINE option are valid for the FILE OPEN option.

If a FILE DEFINE command has already specified a connection between the file-id and the physical file, FILE OPEN merely opens this file. On the other hand, if no FILE DEFINE was issued, FILE OPEN opens and establishes attributes for this file.

The attributes specified by the FILE OPEN command supersede the default attributes specified by the FILE DEFINE command. They remain in effect until the file is closed.

If you specify FILE OPEN for a file that is already open and if the attributes you defined are different than before, an attempt is made to modify the attributes of the open file. For example, in the command

```
FILE OPEN transaction_records;
```

the transaction_records file is explicitly open, so its attributes are automatically taken from the previously issued FILE DEFINE command.

FILE Command with CLEAR Parameter

If you issue the command

```
FILE CLEAR;
```

all previous FILE DEFINE commands are deactivated. All data provided by the FILE DEFINE are now deleted and all files are closed. What's more, the FILE CLEAR command resets the system windows. That is, the List, Output, Error, and History windows are reset.

FILE command with CLOSE Parameter

If you issue the command

```
FILE CLOSE transaction_records;
```

the `transaction_records` file is now closed. The same closing operation can be performed with the CLOSE command, as follows:

```
CLOSE transaction_records;
```

If none of these commands is issued, the file is automatically closed when you exit a procedure or when you quit NOMAD.

FILE Command with DELETE Parameter

If you issue the command

```
FILE DELETE c:\nomad\data.dat;
```

you are removing a specified physical file from the disk on drive c. Note that in this command you define your file by its name, not by the file-id.

FILE Command with STATUS Parameter

This option allows you to verify whether or not a specified file exists on the disk. The system &variable &RC is set to 1 if the file does not exist. The following example illustrates how to issue this command:

```
FILE STATUS c:\nomad\data.dat;
```

Note again that the file is referenced by its filename, not by its file-id.

LOAD Command

The LOAD command inserts, changes, or deletes records in the NOMAD database, according to the data in an external file. This command automatically performs several functions:

1. Reads a transaction record.
2. Sets values for &variables from the record read. If this setting fails due to the automatic data validation rules (set in the NOMAD database with the MEMBER or LIMIT parameters), the transaction record is rejected for this update.
3. Reads again if the IF condition specified in the LOAD command fails.
4. Keys into a specified NOMAD database.
5. Performs one of the ONMATCH operations such as reject, replace, delete, or change if the keying is successful and a matching record is found.

6. Performs one of the NOMATCH operations as insert a record or do not insert a record if the matching record is not found.

7. Reduces the DO count if the DO option is set.

8. Repeats steps 1-6 until the DO count is zero or the end of file in the external transaction file is reached, whichever occurs first.

You could write a NOMAD procedure that would perform all these functions, however, the LOAD command is simpler and more efficient.

The LOAD command does have some limitations. The LOAD command can process only one type of transaction because only one setting of &variables is applied to each transaction record, using a single ONMATCH or NOMATCH operation. (Later in this chapter we will show how to handle multiple transaction types with the READ and SET commands.)

The LOAD command operates in one of two modes. The nature of the operational mode depends on the specification of the DO option. The operational modes are as follows:

1. **DO option is not specified**. In this case, the LOAD command automatically issues a TOP command to position itself at the start of the NOMAD database. It automatically sets the associated system &variables to zero (we describe these system &variables later in this section). It closes the external transaction file if open, then opens it and carries out successive read operations and updates from the beginning of this external file. It closes the file when the end of file is reached.

   When the updating process is done, you can request a print of the updating statistics. For example, you can request the number of records read, the number of records inserted, and the number of records rejected. You do this by specifying the appropriate system &variables in the PRINT command. For example, assume that the LOAD command is executed and you issue the following PRINT command:

   ```
   PRINT (&reads)  (&inserts)  (&rejects);
   ```

   The output from this command could look like this:

   ```
   &READS=7 &INSERTS=6 &REJECTS=1
   ```

   which gives you a statistic of your LOAD procedure, indicating that 6 inserts and 1 reject took place during the execution of this update.

2. **DO option is specified**. The DO option assigns the number of transaction records that are to be processed by the LOAD command. With the DO option, an automatic TOP command is not issued and the current database position remains intact. The LOAD system &variables are not set to zero, and the external transaction file is not closed first because this is done in the LOAD operational mode without the DO option.

   For the LOAD command with the DO option, the external file is read from its current position. In this mode, database movement is forward from the current

```
FILE DEFINE historical_transactions=c:\nomad\transac1.dat:

LOAD history

    READ historical_transactions

    SET &year

        &weekc

        &ski_revenue

    &boot_revenue

    &poles_revenue;
```

Figure 15.3   Updating Procedure for History Master

position. The system-defined &variables are automatically incremented from the values they had when the LOAD command was issued. The external transaction file remains open if the end of file has not been reached after the LOAD command processes all the transaction records set in the DO option. Thus, the external file remains open.

To issue the LOAD command, three parameters are required:

1. **File Name**. The name of the file to be modified. The name is as specified in the schema of the NOMAD database.
2. READ **file-id.** Specifies that the external file (identified by the file-id) is to be read to the transaction buffer. You defined this external file previously with the FILE DEFINE command.
3. SET **set-parameters.** This parameter assigns the values from the records in the transaction buffer to &variables and &items in the record being modified. The only required parameter is the list of names of the &variables or &items being set.

Now let us illustrate the simplest example of the LOAD command. Assume that the internal formats of all items from the NOMAD file (which is to be updated) are the same as the formats of the elements in the records of the external file. The updating procedure, including the FILE DEFINE and LOAD commands, is shown in Figure 15.3.

The first command defines the external transaction file historical_transaction (this is its file-id) and its physical file (transac1.dat) as residing on the device c, in the NOMAD directory. The LOAD command will add data to the HISTORY master.

From the external file historical_transaction, the records are read into the transaction buffer. Finally, the SET parameter assigns values from the transaction buffer to the corresponding &items listed, and the HISTORY file is updated with these values.

This process is repeated until the end of file condition is reached in the transaction file.

Parameters for the SET Command

All of the following parameters are used in the SET command:

FREEFORM

This parameter specifies free format for the transaction file, with fields separated by a delimiter. The default delimiter is a blank or a comma. If you want to use another delimiter, you assign the value of the new delimiter to the system &variable &FREEFORM before you issue the LOAD command. The following examples illustrate the use of the FREEFORM parameter.

Example 1

File1 is the file-id for the external transaction file. The content of this file is:

```
1   DYNASTAR   25.5
2   DYNAMICS   30.6
3   NORDIC     12.5
    .
    .
    .
```

All the fields in this file are separated by the default delimiter (which is a blank). Multiple blanks are treated as one delimiter.

The ski_inventory is the NOMAD database to be updated. For this case, the LOAD command is:

```
LOAD ski_inventory
     READ file1
     SET FREEFORM
          &record_code
          &equipment_name
          &rental_charge;
```

The FREEFORM parameter tells the LOAD command that the transaction buffer is in the free format, with the default delimiter (a blank).

Example 2

You want to change the delimiter to a colon (:) because the transaction file content is as follows:

```
1:DYNASTAR:25.5
2:DYNAMICS:30.6
3:NORDIC:12.5
   .
   .
   .
```

For this case the LOAD command is:

```
&FREEFORM = ':' ;
LOAD ski_inventory
      READ file1
      SET FREEFORM
            &record_code
            &equipment_name
            &rental_charge;
```

Note the position of the assignment statement. The assignment is done before the LOAD command is executed. The value of the system &variable &FREEFORM defines the delimiter as a colon (:). The reminder of the update procedure is the same as in Example 1.

Assigning a value to the &FREEFORM changes the rules used by the SET parameter for scanning free-format fields in the transaction buffer. When the assignment is made, blanks are treated in the same manner as any other character. All leading, embedded, and trailing blanks are thus considered to be part of the input data.

A field is terminated only by the delimiter value in the &FREEFORM or by the end of the transaction buffer.

To reset the free-format delimiter back to the default commas or blanks, issue the following assignment statement:

```
&FREEFORM = &NAV;
```

When the default delimiters of commas or blanks are in effect, the following free-format rules apply:

1. Leading blanks are ignored.

2. An input field is terminated by one of the following delimiters:

   ■ One or more blanks

   ■ A comma

   ■ Blanks followed by a comma

   ■ Blanks followed by the end of the buffer

   ■ The end of the buffer

3. If the field is empty and a delimiter is encountered immediately, the &variable retains the value it had before the SET option was executed.

4. If the end of the buffer is reached and there are additional &variables to be assigned some values, these &variables remain unchanged.

5. The succeeding input field starts at the position after the previous delimiter.

6. To input commas or blanks as part of the data in a field, surround the field with single quotes (').

Positioning Modifiers

These modifiers allow you to adjust the current position in the buffer in three ways:

1. **CC +/- n**—This option moves the current position in buffer *n* positions forward (+) or backward (–) relative to the prior position. When CC is specified without an *n*, the current position is not moved.

   For example, assume that the transaction buffer contains the data for these three &items:

   ■ &PHONE, 11 digits long (area code plus phone number)

   ■ &AREA_CODE, 3 digits long

   ■ &ZIP_CODE, 5 digits long

   The record in the transaction buffer looks as follows:

   208345650083712

   where the first 3 digits represent the area code, the next 8 digits correspond to the local phone number, and the last 5 digits are the zip code. To set the value for the &area_code and the &zip_code use the SET parameter for the LOAD command as follows:

   SET &area_code CC +7 &zip_code;

   The &area_code is set first. After reading the value of the &area_code, the pointer is moved 7 positions forward (skipping the read of the local phone number). The current position is now at the first digit of the &zip_code and the &zip_code is set.

2. **SPACE +/- n**—This option is similar to the CC option, It moves the current position in the buffer *n* spaces forward (+) or backward (–). When SPACE is specified without an *n*, the default is 1. For example,

   SET &phone SPACE –12 &area_code;

   This command works in the same way that the SET &phone CC –11 &area_code; command does.

3. **COLUMN n**—This option allows you to move the pointer in the buffer to column *n*, regardless of prior position. For example,

   SET &area_code COLUMN 11 &zip_code;

```
FILE DEFINE historical_transactions=c:\nomad\transac1.dat;

LOAD history

READ historical_transactions

SET &weekc FORM N2

    &ski_revenue FORM N8.2

    &boot_revenue FORM N8.2

    &poles_revenue FORM N8.2;
```

Figure 15.4   Procedure Using a Form Input Format Option

First the &area_code is read; next the pointer is moved to the 11 column (position of the first digit of the &zip_code); and finally the &zip_code is set. This command is equivalent to the SET &area_code CC +8 &zip_code; command.

FORM Input Format

When you specify the input format, data can be read in from an external file and used to build or maintain a database. FORM identifies the input format for the &variable specified in the SET parameter. The use of the FORM input format option is illustrated in Figure 15.4.

The input format for &WEEKC is a 2-digit numeric field (N2). For all other &items the input format is the same, that is, a decimal field that is 8 digits long, with 2 digits after the decimal point (N8.2).

NOMAD internal formats are described in Appendix B. For external files, the following types of formats are provided:

1. An—Alphanumeric input format with n characters. For example,

   SET &text FORM A120;

2. I1—Binary input format. A 1-byte integer or binary field with values from 0 through 255. For example,

   SET &numeric FORM I1;

3. Nn—Integer number with n digits. The n number specified must be between 1 and 255 (inclusively). Leading and trailing blanks are ignored. For example,

   SET &numeric FORM N12;

4. Nn.m—A decimal number that is n digits long. For example,

   SET &ski_revenue FORMAT N8.2;

5. Free-format input format—The SET parameter provides free-format capabilities. An A or N without a length specification designates a free-format al-

phanumeric or numeric input format. The FREE FORM option will also do the same. For example,

```
SET &numeric FORM N &text FORM A;
```

6. NOMAD supports the LOGICAL, DATE, TIME, and DATETIME types of formats for the external files. (These types of formats were described in Chapter 12.)

BLANKNAV

This parameter sets &variable to NOTAVAILABLE if the field is entirely blank.

FIXTONAV

This parameter sets &variable to NOTAVAILABLE if a conversion error occurs when setting a specific &variable.

NAV9S

This parameter sets &variable to NOTAVAILABLE if the field is all 9's.

Optional Parameters for the LOAD Command

Now we describe and illustrate how some of the optional parameters function in the LOAD command. Several examples show how optional parameters can be combined.

ACCEPT ON

If you want to specify the file to which records *accepted* by the LOAD command are written during processing, use this option. For example,

```
ACCEPT ON file1
```

Accepted records are placed in this file. FILE1 is a file-id previously defined with the FILE DEFINE command.

REJECT ON

If you want to specify the name of a file to which records *rejected* by the LOAD command are written during processing, use this option. For example,

```
REJECT ON file2
```

FILE2 is a file-id. It is assumed that it was previously defined with the FILE DEFINE command.

A 24-character explanation of how each transaction was processed is appended to each record that is either accepted or rejected. This explanation is also written into the acceptance or the rejection file.

IF logical-expression

This option allows you to specify the selection criteria for the transaction records. If the expression is not TRUE for a specific record, the record is skipped in the LOAD command processing. Note that you can process multiple transaction types using selection criteria. The following example illustrates the use of the IF option.

First let us describe the format of the external transaction file. The file-id for this file is Transaction_file1. This file has two types of records. The type of the record is identified by a value (either "I" or "D") appearing in the first column of each record.

During your NOMAD file update procedure, you decide to insert all the records from the external file that are identified with the value "I". You do not want to process records of the other type. The records in this file might look like this:

```
I023.5234
I237.0546
D11234560
I100.9333
D34098894
```

Thus, you are dealing with 8 columns in each record: the &record_code starts at column 1, &number1 starts at column 2, and &number2 starts at column 7. &number1 and &number2 are two elements of FILE1 in the NOMAD database. FILE1 is to be updated with the external transaction file we have just described.

The procedure to process only selected records from the external transaction file is shown in Figure 15.5.

First, you declare the &record_code since it is not a NOMAD database item. Then you define all needed files and LOAD the file to be updated. The external file is read. Transactions rejected by the LOAD command are written to the REJECTS file.

The IF &records_code="I" in the LOAD command causes READ to skip over records that do not have an "I" in their first column. Note that the rejected transactions are not those eliminated by the IF condition.

DO n

This option limits the number of records processed to *n* records. Records read and skipped over because of the IF condition are not counted. In the example in Figure 15.6, only ten records will be processed by the LOAD command. Records skipped by the IF condition are not counted. This option also can be used to build test databases.

ONMATCH Parameter

This parameter is used to designate the action to be taken when the key (or keys) in the external file match the key (or keys) in the NOMAD database file being updated. You can select one of four different actions:

```
DECLARE &record_code AS A1;
        FILE DEFINE transaction_file1=tran1.dat;
        FILE DEFINE rejects=reject1.dat;
        LOAD file1
        READ transaction_file1
        SET &record_code
            &number1 FORM N5.1
            &number2 FORM N3
        REJECT ON rejects
        IF &record_code="I";
        CLOSE rejects;
```

Figure 15.5   Procedure to Process Selected Records From External Transaction File

```
LOAD File1
        READ transaction_file1
        SET &record_code
            &number1 FORM N5.1
            &number2 FORM N3
        REJECT ON rejects
        IF &record_code="I"
        DO 10;
```

Figure 15.6   Procedure with DO N Option

1. REJECT—Rejects the transaction record. This is the default if ONMATCH is not used.

2. REPLACE—Replaces the matching database file record.

3. DELETE—Removes the record from the NOMAD database file.

4. CHANGE—This parameter can be used in two ways:
   a. CHANGE without options can be used to modify the item values in the NOMAD database file being updated to the values in the corresponding &items of the external file. &items must have been set or have had values assigned to them. Key items cannot be changed using the LOAD command. An example of this command is:

   ONMATCH CHANGE

   When the matching record in the NOMAD database is found, it is changed according to the external transaction record.

b. CHANGE followed by the item names changes only those items. The items are changed to the values of the corresponding &items in the external transaction file.

For example,

```
ONMATCH CHANGE item1 item2
```

Only item1 and item2 values of the records in the file being updated are changed; all other items remain unchanged.

You can specify an "=expression" to change item values. For example,

```
ONMATCH CHANGE item1 = 1234.59
```

Only the value of item1 is changed. It specifically is changed to the value of 1234.59.

Note: If you specify ONMATCH CHANGE, it should be the last parameter in the LOAD command.

You can also specify the NOTIFNAV parameter with ONMATCH. This parameter prevents the item values from being changed to NOTAVAILABLE. For example,

```
ONMATCH REPLACE NOTIFNAV
```

specifies that if the match is found, items values will be replaced with the values in the &items in the external file, but not changed if these &items hold a NOTAVAILABLE value.

NOMATCH Parameter

This option specifies one of the two actions (INSERT or NOINSERT) to be taken when the key in the external transaction file does not match a NOMAD database file key. For example,

```
NOMATCH INSERT
```

inserts a record into the file being updated when no match is found for the external transaction file. NOINSERT rejects the transaction.

System &Variables Used by the LOAD Command

The LOAD command increments the following system &variables to automatically provide you with the statistics of the actions performed during the processing of the LOAD command:

```
! 1! DECLARE &hyear AS DATE'yyyy';
! 2! FILE DEFINE historical_transactions=c:\nomad\transac1.dat;
! 3! FILE DEFINE out=reject.dat;
! 4! ASK "What is the Year for historical transactions? " &hyear;
! 5! &year = &hyear;
! 6! LOAD history
! 7!    NOMATCH INSERT
! 8!    READ historical_transactions
! 9!    SET &weekc FORM N2
!10!        &ski_revenue FORM N8.2
!11!        &boot_revenue FORM N8.2
!12!        &poles_revenue FORM N8.2
!13!    REJECT ON out;
!14! FILE CLOSE out OTW;
!15! PRINT "RECORDS READ: "(&READS)
!16' FOLD"RECORDS INSERTED: "(&INSERTS);
```

Figure 15.7 Loading Procedure for History Master

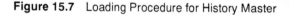

&variable	Statistic stored
&READS	Number of READ operations performed.
&ACCEPTS	Number of transaction records accepted.
&REJECTS	Number of transaction records rejected.
&CHANGES	Number of CHANGE operations performed.
&INSERTS	Number of INSERT operations performed.
&DELETES	Number of DELETE operations performed.
&REPLACES	Number of REPLACE operations performed.

We now examine the procedure that updates (using the external transaction file) the HISTORY file of the Ski Rental System. (The external transaction file was described at the beginning of this chapter.)

Procedure To Load Data Into the History File

Each line of the update procedure is numbered to help us refer to the specific constructs. The updating procedure is given in Figure 15.7.

In line 1 we declare the &variable &HYEAR as a 4-digit date field. It will hold the value for the transaction year. This variable will be needed when the user is prompted to enter the transaction year.

Lines 2-3 are the FILE DEFINE statements. The transaction file HISTORI-CAL_TRANSACTIONS is defined as well as the OUT file. The OUT file will hold records rejected by the LOAD command.

Lines 4-5 are used to prompt the user for the transaction year and assign this value to the &item &YEAR in the HISTORY file.

Lines 6-13 hold the LOAD command. In addition to the required parameters, we use the NOMATCH INSERT and the REJECT ON OUT optional parameters.

Note that with the SET parameter, we define the structure of the input transaction file by using the FORM option.

In line 14, the file holding rejected transactions (the OUT file) is closed.

In lines 15-16 the run statistics are printed. We specified to only print the number of records read and the number of records inserted.

15.4 MAINTENANCE PROCEDURE WITH MULTIPLE TRANSACTION TYPES

To illustrate this type of procedure, we will update the SKIINVENTORY file.

The external transaction file contains the following multipurpose transaction records:

- Transaction records that will be inserted into the SKIINVENTORY file.

- Transaction records that will be used to delete records from the SKIINVENTORY file.

- Transaction records that will be used to change some of the values in the existing inventory records.

Ski Inventory Transaction File

This file is supplied by a ski manufacturer once a year, when the new equipment is introduced. The existence of this file completely eliminates the need to update the ski inventory file using data entry screens.

The Ski Inventory Transaction file contains the following information: ski serial number, ski manufacturer code, ski type code, ski length, and suggested daily rental fee.

In addition, the first character in each record contains the information identifying transaction type. Valid transaction types are:

I—Insert a record into the database

D—Delete a record from the database

C—Change the values of certain fields in the existing records

The format of the transaction records is variable and the separator between fields is ";".

The external transaction file has three types of record formats:

1. The transaction record intended for insertion contains the following complete information on a specific rental unit:

Item Name	Format	Length
TRANSACTION TYPE CODE	A1	1
SKI SERIAL NUMBER (KEY)	A8	8
SKI MANUFACTURER CODE	A4	4
SKI TYPE CODE	A4	4
SKI LENGTH	999	3
SKI RENTAL CHARGE	99.99	5

2. The transaction records intended for deletion contain only two fields:

Item Name	Format	Length
TRANSACTION TYPE CODE	A1	1
SKI SERIAL NUMBER (KEY)	A8	8

3. The transaction records intended for change contain only three fields:

Item Name	Format	Length
TRANSACTION TYPE CODE	A1	1
SKI SERIAL NUMBER (KEY)	A8	8
SKI RENTAL CHARGE	99.99	5

To give you an idea how this file may look, we now present a short listing of the transaction file containing all three types of transactions. We also inserted two empty records, which we will use to illustrate some of NOMAD's control capabilities. In the following listing, the empty records are numbers 5 and 8.

Transaction File

Record Number	Record Content
1	D;QWW44444;
2	C;2222222S;40.2;
3	I;WWHG4444;DYNA;DYN2;205;31.60;
4	D;44444444;
5	
6	I;12121223;DYNA;DYN1;185;8.5;
7	C;23232323;25.5;
8	
9	I;W234VB67;DYNA;DYN2;210;35.0;

Before we can construct the update procedure for the ski inventory file, we need to introduce two new NOMAD commands. (All the other commands necessary to construct the procedure have already been covered in previous chapters.) These two new commands are:

1. READ **command**—Allows you to read the transaction record into the transaction buffer from where the values of &variables and &items can be set.

2. SET **command**—Allows you to assign the values of the &variables and of the &items from the transaction buffer that contains the last record read.

READ and SET were already described as required parameters in the LOAD command, but not as separate commands.

READ Command

The READ command transfers the data from the external file into a buffer, making this data available for processing. The READ command has only one required parameter: the file-id of the external transaction file to be read.

For example,

```
FILE DEFINE my_file = c:\nomad\transac1.dat;
READ my_file;
```

The external file with the file-id my_file (the physical file is transac1.dat and it is located in the NOMAD directory on the c disk) will be read into the buffer for further processing.

Before using the READ command, you should define this external file with the FILE DEFINE command to connect the file-id to the name of the physical file. If you do not issue a FILE DEFINE command, NOMAD will try to read the physical file with the default name (the first 8 characters of the file-id and an extension .FIL).

For example, assume that you issued just

```
READ transactions_file;
```

and have not defined the connection between file-id and the physical filename using the FILE DEFINE command before the READ command. So NOMAD automatically assumes that the name of the physical file is transact.fil and looks for it.

NOMAD has a system &variable named &LL which contains the length of the current record in the buffer. When you are reading from a file that has null lines (as is the case in our example), check the content of the &LL variable to see if it is 0. This will indicate that the line is null, and the assignment of &variables and &items should not be performed.

Each time a READ command is issued during the NOMAD session, the system &variable &READS is automatically incremented by 1.

To control the statistics of reads for the specific procedure, reset the &READS to 0 at the beginning of the procedure. This reset is accomplished with the &READS = 0; or with the CLEAR &READS; command.

To handle the end-of-file condition when you use the READ command, you have two choices: use the ON ENDFILE statement at the beginning of the procedure or use the OTHERWISE (OTW) clause in the READ command. (Both the ON ENDFILE statement and the OTW clause were described in Chapter 11.)

```
! 1! DECLARE &rec_code AS A1;
! 2! DECLARE &pskinum AS A8;
! 3! DECLARE &null AS 9999;
! 4! FILE DEFINE ski_transactions = c:\nomad\transki.dat;
! 5! ON ENDFILE(ski_transactions) GOTO -end;
! 6! ON CONVERT DO;
! 7!      PRINT &convert 'INVALID FORMAT. RECORD REJECTED'
! 8!           (&reads);
! 9!      &rejects = &rejects + 1;
!10!      GOTO -start;
!11!    END;
!12! ON UNIQUE DO;
!13!      PRINT 'DUPLICATE KEY. RECORD REJECTED '
!14!           (&reads);
!15!      &rejects=&rejects+1;
!16!      GOTO -start;
!17!    END;
!18! &inserts = 0;
!19! &reads = 0;
!20! &rejects = 0;
!21! &changes = 0;
!22! &deletes = 0;
!23! &null =0;
!24! &freeform = ";";
!25! -start
!26! READ ski_transactions;
!27! IF &ll=0 THEN DO;
!28!      &null= &null+1;
!29!      GOTO -start;
!30!    END;
!31! SET FREEFORM  &rec_code;
!32! IF &rec_code = "I" THEN GOTO -insert;
!33! IF &rec_code = "D" THEN GOTO -delete;
!34! IF &rec_code = "C" THEN GOTO -change;
!35! PRINT 'INVALID TRANSACTION CODE. RECORD REJECTED '
!36!          (&reads);
!37! &rejects=&rejects+1;
!38! GOTO -start;
```

Figure 15.8   Update Procedure for SKIINVENTORY File Using External File

SET Command

The SET command assigns values to &variables and &items from the buffer. The buffer is filled with data from the READ command.

The parameters of this SET command are the same as for the SET parameter of the LOAD command introduced earlier in this chapter. Here we review them briefly.

1. FREEFORM—Designates the free-format input, with fields separated by a delimiter.

2. Positioning modifiers—Designate the location of the data field to be set.

3. FORM input format—Is used to specify the format of the fields in the buffer.

4. BLANKNAV—Sets &name to NOTAVAILABLE if the value of the specific &variable or &item is blank.

5. FIXTONAV—Sets &name to NOTAVAILABLE if a conversion error occurs.

7. NAV9S—Sets &name to NOTAVAILABLE if the field is all 9's.

```
!39! -insert
!40!      SET FREEFORM  COLUMN 3  &skinum &ski_manufact &ski_type
!41!          &ski_length &ski_rentch;
!42!      INSERT skiinventory;
!43!      GOTO -start;
!44! -delete
!45!      SET FREEFORM COLUMN 3 &pskinum;
!46!      tlocate skinum = &pskinum OTW DO;
!47!          PRINT 'INVALID  TRANSACTION.  RECORD  NOT  FOUND.
!48!               '(&reads);
!49!          &rejects=&rejects+1;
!50!          GOTO -start;
!51!      END;
!52!      DELETE skiinventory;
!53!      &deletes=&deletes+1;
!54!      GOTO -start;
!55! -change
!56!      SET FREEFORM COLUMN 3 &pskinum &ski_rentch;
!57!      tlocate skinum = &pskinum OTW DO;
!58!          PRINT 'INVALID  TRANSACTION.  RECORD  NOT  FOUND.
!59!               '(&reads);
!60!          &rejects=&rejects+1;
!61!          GOTO -start;
!62!      END;
!63!      CHANGE ski_rentch;
!64!      &changes=&changes+1;
!65!      GOTO -start;
!66! -end
!67!      FILE CLOSE ski_transactions;
!68!      PRINT 'RECORDS READ : ' (&reads)
!69!          FOLD  'RECORDS INSERTED : '  (&inserts)
!70!          FOLD 'RECORDS DELETED : '  (&deletes)
!71!          FOLD 'RECORDS CHANGED : '  (&changes)
!72!          FOLD 'RECORDS REJECTED : '  (&rejects)
!73!          FOLD 'NULL RECORDS : ' (&null);
```

Figure 15.8 *continued*

In the following example of the SET command, we assume that the READ
statement was already issued:

```
SET FREEFORM COLUMN 7 &field1 &field2 &field3;
```

The SET command moves through the buffer, obtains values, and assigns them to
the &variables and to the &items. The fields of the input buffer are set to be in free
format and to be separated with default delimiters. Three &variables are set, and
the first one starts in column 7 of the input buffer.

Between READ commands you can issue any number of SET commands. Each
SET command starts at the beginning of the buffer, unless a positioning modifier
specifies otherwise. This is the case in the preceding example. Here, the input field
for the first &variable starts at the seventh column.

Procedure To Update the Ski Inventory File

We are ready to build the update procedure for the SKIINVENTORY file using the
external transaction file SKI_TRANSACTIONS. The record formats for the transaction file were described at the beginning of this section. We have numbered each
line of this procedure to clarify the description of its structure. The updating
procedure is given in Figure 15.8.

Lines 1-3 are declaration statements defining the three &variables. These variables are to hold values for the transaction type code, the ski serial number, and the number of null records in the external transaction file.

In line 4, the external transaction file is defined. Its file-id is SKI_TRANS-ACTIONS.

Line 5 holds a control statement specifying that at the end of the external transaction file, control passes to the line in the procedure that holds the label –END.

Lines 6-11 hold the error-handling routine for the format conversion. This particular routine is to be executed when NOMAD encounters an error when it attempts to convert the input record data to a specified data form as defined by the SET commands. This routine prints the warning message, counts the number of rejected records, and reads the next transaction record into the input buffer.

Lines 12-17 hold another error routine. This routine is activated every time the updating procedure tries to insert a record with a nonunique key. The routine includes the display of the warning message, a count of the number of rejected records, and the return of control to the statement with the label –START so that another transaction record can be read.

Lines 18-23 initialize to 0 all system &variables that hold processing statistics for this procedure.

Line 24 defines the semicolon (;) as the transaction records delimiter.

Line 25 holds the label –START and line 26 has the READ statement that transfers the records from the external transaction file to the input buffer.

Lines 27-30 contain a routine that determines whether the input buffer's length is zero. If the length is zero, the transaction record in the buffer is null. If the record is null, the number of null records is incremented by 1 and control is returned to the –START statement. Another transaction record can now be read.

Line 31 holds the SET command. It assigns the value to the &variable transaction type code.

In lines 32-34 are the IF conditions that check the value of the transaction type code and allow you to transfer the controls of the procedure to the appropriate processes (insert a record, delete a record, or change the rental fee in an existing record).

Lines 35-38 hold a routine that controls the flow of the updating procedure when the transaction type code is different from the allowed values I, D, or C.

Lines 39-43 form a routine that sets all the necessary &items from the SKIIN-VENTORY file and inserts a record into this file. Note how we used the position modifiers in the SET command. If we do not specify the position modifiers, each SET command will start at the beginning of the record in the buffer. In our case, the &items values start in column 3 of the input buffer. Lines 44-54 hold a routine that deletes the records in the NOMAD database. If invalid transactions are encountered, this routine displays the warning message. The controls return to the read of another record.

Lines 55-65 hold a routine that changes the rental fee values for specific records in the NOMAD database.

Finally, lines 66-73 hold the closing routine. The external transaction file is closed and the update statistics are displayed.

15.5 SUMMARY

For large volume database maintenance, transactions are read from an external data file. The most efficient way to do this is with a procedure.

Updating from an external file procedure involves these tasks:

1. Opening the file with the FILE command.

2. Reading a record with the READ command.

3. Placing the values from an external file record into &items and &variables using the SET command.

4. Positioning the database when CHANGE, DELETE, and REPLACE are required. For the INSERT command, positioning is not needed.

5. Modifying the database with the values of the &items by using the INSERT, REPLACE, CHANGE, or DELETE commands.

6. Repeating tasks 2 through 5 for each record in the file.

7. Closing the file with the CLOSE command when the database maintenance is completed.

Sometimes the LOAD command is an alternative to writing your own update procedure. The LOAD command can be used to replace tasks 2 through 5 of the update procedure if the transaction file deals only with one type of transaction. If the transaction file contains multiple transaction types (deletes, changes, or adds), we have to code all 7 steps separately.

There are two types of file formats to consider when maintaining the database with transactions from an external file: fixed and free. Which format is better depends on the application.

There are two types of update procedures you can construct: a maintenance procedure with a single transaction type and a maintenance procedure with multiple transaction types. Their nature depends on the transaction types of the external transaction file.

The following commands are used for updating with external transaction files.

Command	Description
FILE	Establishes the identity and attributes of an external file.
LOAD	Inserts, updates, and deletes instances in the NOMAD database, according to the data in an external file.

The LOAD command increments the following system &variables to automatically provide you with the statistics of the actions performed during the processing of the LOAD.

&Variable	Description
&READS	Stores the number of READ operations performed.
&ACCEPTS	Stores the number of transaction records accepted.
&REJECTS	Stores the number of transaction records rejected.
&CHANGES	Stores the number of CHANGE operations performed.
&INSERTS	Stores the number of INSERT operations performed.
&DELETES	Stores the number of DELETE operations performed.
&REPLACES	Stores the number of REPLACE operations performed.

The most efficient way of updating with external transaction files is to do it with a procedure. The following commands are used:

Command	Description
READ	Obtains a record from an external file and reads it into an input buffer area.
SET	Assigns values to &variables and &items from the buffer area.
INSERT	Inserts the values of &items into the database items. Positioning is not required.
DELETE	Deletes a database instance. Positioning is required before the DELETE action to locate the correct database instance.
CHANGE	Changes the values of the database items to the values in &items. Positioning is required.
REPLACE	Replaces the values of a database instance with the values in &items. Positioning is required.
RKEY	Positions NOMAD at the requested instance of the database.
CLOSE	Closes an external file.

EXERCISES

1. List all the functions of the FILE command.

2. What are required parameters for:
   a. FILE command
   b. LOAD command
   c. SET command

3. The record length of an external transaction file is 500 bytes. You want to create a file to store all rejected transactions and a file to store all accepted transactions.
   a. What is the record length for these files?
   b. Write all the statements needed to completely define these files.
   c. How would this statement differ if the record length of the transaction file were 488 bytes?

4. How do you open a specific file in NOMAD? For how long?

5. What are the functions of the LOAD command?

6. Using the LOAD command, write a routine inserting records to a file in the NOMAD database. Make your own assumptions about the format of the records in the external transaction file and the formats of the items in the NOMAD database file.

7. Rewrite the routine created for Problem 6 using the READ and SET commands.

8. List the steps performed by the LOAD command.

9. Write a procedure that loads an external file into an existing database. The data is to be loaded into the RENTALS master in the FENCING database. The transaction file contains information on fencing equipment rentals. Each record contains a rental customer number, followed by rental date, the equipment code number, the rental fee, the date the equipment was due back, and whether or not it was returned (Y or N). Assume that TRANIN is the filename of the input transaction file, and OUT is the filename of the file that will have rejected transactions in it.

10. After the LOAD procedure of the previous problem is executed, what command would you issue to display number of &READS, &INSERTS, and &REJECTS?

11. What function does the IF logical expression play in the LOAD command?

12. Assume that the RENTALS master can be updated with transactions in a file named TRANUPD. Each record in this file contains a code (one letter, A or B) in its first field to indicate whether to add a record (A) or reject it (B), a rental customer number, the rental date, the equipment code number, the rental fee, the date the equipment was due back, and whether or not it was returned (Y or N). Write a procedure using the LOAD command with the IF option that will cause READ to skip over records that do not have an 'A' in the first field of the record.

13. Can the LOAD command be used to load very large transaction files? Would it be useful to do a SAVE after a certain number of records are read? If yes, why? If not, why not? In addition, assume that rejected transactions are kept in a REJECT file.

14. List the tasks required for updating a database from an external file using the READ, SET, and INSERT methods.

15. List the system variables that the LOAD command increments automatically.

16. Why is this automatic incrementing of the system variables useful?

17. Is positioning in the database required when using CHANGE and REPLACE?

18. What is specified in this SET command?

```
SET &XX FORM A10 &YY FORM N;
```

19. Specify what is accomplished with the following set of statements:

    a. FIRST CUSTOMERS
    AMPSET CUSTOMERS
    &CPHONE = '208-3365322'
    &CZIP = '38512'
    REPLACE CUSTOMERS

    b. FIRST CUSTOMERS
    AMPSET CUSTOMERS
    REPLACE CUSTOMERS CPHONE ='208-3365322' CZIP = '38512'

20. Specify two ways in which item values can be assigned with the INSERT command. Give an example for each.

PROJECTS

1. Develop a procedure for updating information in the reservation master of the State Park Reservation System. The external transaction file contains information on the customer placing, changing, or cancelling the reservation. The necessary parameters for the files involved can be taken from Project 1 of Chapter 10. You choose the format for the transaction file.

2. Write the updating procedure for Project 1 if we assume that the records for placing, changing, or deleting the reservation are sorted into three separate transaction files.

CHAPTER 16

Data Manipulation

When we try to pick out anything by itself, we find it hitched to everything else in the universe.

John Muir

16.1 INTRODUCTION

In this chapter we introduce the NOMAD commands required to manipulate and transfer data in the database. We also discuss how to perform calculations on these data and list some functions available in NOMAD.

The manipulation and transformation of data through calculations is very important for reporting. Details of reporting are described in the next two chapters.

16.2 MANIPULATING AND TRANSFERRING DATA

NOMAD supports four commands for manipulating and transferring data in a database. Two of these commands, the CREATE and WRITE commands, are described in this chapter. The other two, the IMPORT and EXPORT commands, have been left out because they are used to communicate with software other than NOMAD on the PC. Since we are building our application entirely in NOMAD on the PC, we do not have any immediate need to import or export data. (If you find you need to use these commands, consult the NOMAD software manual.)

The commands described here are:

1. CREATE—Allows you to build a new database from an existing one in several ways. This new database can be

   ■ A copy of the old database.

   ■ A subset of the old database.

   ■ A summary of records from a file or multiple files in a database.

   ■ A combination of multiple databases.

   The new database then can be used for reporting. The CREATE command can be used in conjunction with LIST to produce complex custom reports. (We come back to this command in Chapter 18.)

2. WRITE—Transfers data from a database to an external transaction file, which then can be used to update database files, for example, our HISTORY file.

16.3 CREATE COMMAND

The CREATE command is used to generate a new database, which is a smaller subset, a copy, or a combination of existing databases.

The CREATE command functions like the LIST command, except that the output from the CREATE is not printed. CREATE is sometimes used with LIST to produce complex reports or a subset of data that could be used with more than one LIST.

Recall that the LIST command in NOMAD is used for reporting. This is a very powerful command, with many optional parameters, that is used to create complex, customized reports. (Chapters 17 and 18 are devoted entirely to the functioning of the LIST command.)

When you use the CREATE command, all active databases remain active, and the newly created database becomes active as well. The created database contains a single master file. The items in this master appear in the order specified by the CREATE command. With the CREATE command, names and aliases are automatically assigned to each item in the created database. For example, assume that the name of the newly created database (and a master) is REVENUE_SUMMARY. The record in this file is composed of the three items, which will appear in the CREATE command in the following order: Ski_revenue, Boot_revenue, and Pole_revenue. The names of the items and their aliases (automatically created) can be seen in Figure 16.1.

From this example you can gather that the format for the alias is

```
File-id(n)
```

where *n* is the sequential position of the item in the CREATE command, and File-id is the name of a newly created database. The alias ensures that each item has a unique identifier. Note that the item name can be the same as the name of the item from which the CREATE was performed. The sources of data for the created database can be items, defined items, or expressions from an active database.

Many parameters of the CREATE command are the same as those for the LIST command. Some are described in this chapter; the others are discussed in Chapters 17 and 18.

Required Parameters

We begin with three required clauses. At least one of these must be specified.

1. BY **clause**—Specifies the items used to sort the data. The items in the BY clause are used to define the order of records in the master created with the CREATE command.

```
      Item                    Alias
      ----                    -----

      SKI_REVENUE             REVENUE_SUMMARY(1)

      BOOT_REVENUE            REVENUE_SUMMARY(2)

      POLE_REVENUE            REVENUE_SUMMARY(3)
```

Figure 16.1 Item Names and Aliases Automatically Generated

2. **ACROSS clause**—Allows you to sort data and to create multiple items (fields in the database that are displayed as columns in a report).
3. **Object clause**—Specifies database item values. It identifies the information that is to appear as new database record items (for the CREATE command) or as columns in a report (for the LIST command).

BY Clause

Let us start with an example. The following CREATE command produces a new database:

```
CREATE BY date_out BY ski_num;
```

The master is created with two items: date_out and ski_num. Recall that both items are from the TRANSACTIONS file (look up the database definition for the Rental System database).

This newly created file is sorted in ascending (default) order by the date_out values and then by the ski_num values. Its file_id is TEMP, which is assigned automatically since we do not specify its id.

Moreover, we do not state how to dispose (that is, whether or not to save, and so on) this file. For the CREATE command in our example, the file is saved temporarily, until the end of the NOMAD session, or when the DATABASE or DBCLEAR commands are executed.

If you want to create a file with some items in an order different from the ascending (default) sort order, specify:

```
CREATE BY date_out BY ski_num DESC;
```

Note the use of the DESC parameter. This file is sorted first by the date_out values in ascending order and then by the ski_num values in descending order.

ACROSS Clause

You use ACROSS to sort data and display it in columns across the pages of a report. When using ACROSS, specify an item or defined item in a currently active database. Consider the following example:

```
CREATE BY date_out ACROSS technician SUM(fee_pre_paid);
```

If we are dealing with three technicians, the record of the created master contains:

- `DATE_OUT`—The order of the data.
- Sum of number one's of pre-paid fees—A total of pre-paid rental fees collected on a given date (`date_out`) by the first technician.
- Sum of number two's pre-paid fees—A total of pre-paid rental fees collected on a given date (`date_out`) by the second technician.
- Sum of number three's pre-paid fees—A total of pre-paid rental fees collected on a given date (`date_out`) by the third technician.

Note that the sort is by the `date_out` and then by the technician. In this file, the item is created for each technician. The value of each item is a total (sum) of pre-paid fees collected on that date by this technician.

Let us consider in more detail the format of the `ACROSS` clause in our example. After the keyword `ACROSS`, the name of the item from the old database appears. The data will be sorted by that item, and the item in the new file is created for each value of this item in the old database.

The next entry in the `ACROSS` clause is the specification of the values to be placed in the newly created item named `technician`. In general, this specification can be an item in the old database, a function, or an expression. In our example, it is a sum of values of the `fee_pre_paid` item.

Optional parameters of the `ACROSS` clause include:

1. `DESC`—Sorts the values of the items in the `ACROSS` clause in the descending order.
2. `ROWTOT`—Creates an additional item in the new record that contains the total of the items created across the record (if the values of these items are numeric). It is formed by contracting the two words "row" and "total".

Consider a second example:

```
CREATE BY date_out ACROSS technician
    DESC SUM(fee_pre_paid) ROWTOT;
```

This example differs from the previous one in two ways:

1. Created items (`technician`) are sorted in the descending order (note the use of the `DESC` parameter). So, the first item is the sum of the fees collected by the third technician, not by the first one, as was the case in the previous example.
2. An additional item is created by the use of the `ROWTOT` parameter. This item holds the total of the fees collected by all technicians.

Object Clause

The Object clause specifies the database values and information that are to appear as items in the created file. An object can be:

■ An item—A named or a defined item from the database.

■ A report function—An item whose value is derived from a calculation performed on a record in the database during the reporting process.

■ An expression—An operation performed on items. An expression can be a calculation, a constant, or a table lookup that results in a value.

The only required parameter for this clause is the object-item name. Several object-items can be defined at once. The object-item can be any of the following:

■ **Item**—An item or defined item name from the old database. For example,

```
CREATE BY date_out ski_num ski_pre_paid;
```

Recall that ski_num is an item in the TRANSACTIONS file. The newly created file will contain three items: date_out (key for the new file), ski_num (from the old file), and ski_pre_paid (a defined item in the same file).

■ **Expression**—An operation performed on items in the old database resulting in a new item. The expression can be a calculation, constant, or a table lookup that results in a value. When used in the CREATE command, the expression is enclosed in parentheses. For example,

```
CREATE BY date_out
(ski_pre_paid+boot_pre_paid)
      named fee_collected;
```

The new file contains two items: date_out and the fee_collected for rental of both skis and boots for a specific date (date_out).

■ **Function**—An item whose value is derived from a calculation performed on all records in a specific file (or files) from the old database. The function can be an AVERAGE, NUMBER, COUNT, STDDEV (standard deviation), MAX, MIN, SUM, or VARIANCE. For example,

```
CREATE BY date_out SUM(fee_pre_paid);
```

The created file will contain two items: the date_out and the total rental charges collected for a specific date (date_out).

■ **Master**—A filename from the old database. If master is used, all items from the old file will be included in the new file, in the same order as in the old database. For example,

```
CREATE transactions;
```

Here all the items from the TRANSACTIONS file (but not the defined items) are to be included in the new file. To include defined items, you must use optional parameters.

Optional parameters for the Object clause include:

1. DEFINES—Causes defined items from the old file to be included in the new record. Placed after the master (object-item is a filename). For example,

    ```
    CREATE transactions DEFINES;
    ```

   Both the items and the defined items of the TRANSACTIONS file will be the items in the created file.

2. EXCEPT—Allows you to exclude specified items or defined items from the new record. For example,

    ```
    CREATE transactions DEFINES EXCEPT ski_num
    ski_pre_paid;
    ```

   All items and defined items, except the ski_num item and ski_pre_paid defined items from the TRANSACTIONS file, are to be included in the new record.

Object Modifiers

These modifiers apply only to the object items (items, masters, expressions, and report functions) in Object and ACROSS clauses. They do not apply to the sorting items in the BY and ACROSS clauses.

Their function is to control the way NOMAD totals numeric items and formats them for reporting. You can use them to override the CREATE and LIST command defaults. With the use of the object modifiers, you can customize for display formats, printing of the object-items in subtotal lines, and so on. Some of the object-modifiers are SUBTOTAL, TOTAL, and CUM. Consider this example of the use of the object modifier:

```
CREATE BY date_out fee_pre_paid
    fee_pre_paid AS $99,999.99 CUM;
```

This command specifies that each new record is to contain three items: date_out, fee_pre_paid, and fee_pre_paid, where the last item will have a value equal to the cumulative total of all the pre-paid fees.

Chapter 17 gives a complete listing and detailed description of the object-modifiers.

Optional Parameters

Optional parameters of the Object clause include:

NAMED new name

This is used to give a new name to an item in the created database. For example,

```
CREATE BY date_out NAMED date
        SUM(fee_pre_paid) NAMED collected_fee;
```

Note how the items have new names: date and collected_fee.

Relational operators

These operators are used to interrelate data. The operations they perform are also called joining data operations. Relational operators create records that contain data associated with equivalent items from multiple related files. These operators are:

■ EXTRACT—This operator causes the inclusion of all the item values of the BY clause. Only the first value of the item in the MATCHING clause that is the same as the BY value together with its corresponding object data will be included. For example,

```
CREATE BY equipment_code
        equipment_name production_date
        EXTRACT MATCHING ski_type ski_rentch;
```

The new records will contain data from two files: EQUIPMENT_TYPE and SKIINVENTORY (recall our database schema). For each value of the equipment_code item in the EQUIPMENT_TYPE file, a new record is created in the new file containing the following items: equipment_code, equipment_name, production_date, and ski_rentch. Since the EXTRACTS option creates only the first matching record from the MATCHING clause, the value for the ski_rentch is from the first record in the SKIINVENTORY file that matches (has the same value) the ski_type item with the equipment_code item in the EQUIPMENT_TYPE file.

■ EXTRACT ALL—When you use this operator you are extracting all item values of the BY clause, as well as all item values of the MATCHING clause that match each BY value. For example,

```
CREATE BY equipment_code equipment_name
        EXTRACT ALL MATCHING ski_type ski_rentch;
```

The new records are created for all of the matches between the equipment_code and ski_type items (in contrast to the first match only when just the EXTRACT operator is used). New records will contain equipment_code and equipment_name items from the EQUIPMENT_TYPE file. The item ski_rentch comes from the SKIINVENTORY file.

■ REJECT—You use this operator if you want to create the new record for the values of the BY clause that does not match values of the MATCHING clause. You need these types of records for exception reporting. For example, consider:

```
CREATE BY equipment_code equipment_name
   REJECT MATCHING ski_type;
```

This statement creates a file of types of skis for which we do not have inventory. The values for `equipment_code` and `equipment_name` are from the EQUIP-MENT_TYPE master, and that for `ski_type` is from the SKIINVENTORY master.

- SUBSET—Use this operator when you want to create records that are common to both masters. Only the first record of the matching clause that is equivalent to each selected BY value is included. For example,

```
CREATE BY equipment_code equipment_name
   SUBSET MATCHING ski_type ski_rentch;
```

All skis with the `equipment_code` in the EQUIPMENT_TYPE master that have a corresponding `ski_type` in the SKIINVENTORY master are chosen. SUBSET creates only those records from the BY clause that have a match in the matching clause, and only for the first match.

- SUBSET ALL—This operator differs from SUBSET in that it picks up all of the matching values, not only the first match. For example,

```
CREATE BY equipment_code equipment_name
   SUBSET ALL MATCHING ski_type ski_rentch;
```

All the skis with an equipment code that matches the `ski_type` in the SKIINVENTORY master are chosen.

You can use multiple relational operators and matching clauses in the CREATE request. Each MATCHING clause is treated as an independent CREATE request. CREATE processes the relational operators individually, working from left to right within the command. When the evaluation of a relational operation is finished, the result is matched with the data obtained from the previous relational operation. Note that only the first relational operator uses the BY clause data. We come back to this notion when discussing the LIST command in Chapter 17.

Screening Options

You can reduce the data that NOMAD initially retrieved (when creating new records) with screening parameters. The screening parameters are:

1. LIMIT n—With this parameter you can screen for the number of new records to be created. For example,

```
CREATE BY equipment_code DESC
   equipment_name
   LIMIT 10;
```

The created records are sorted in descending order by `equipment_code`, and only ten records are available for output.

2. OUTPUT WHERE—This parameter uses a logical expression to specify the limiting criteria. You must use &variable in the OUTPUT WHERE clause. For example,

```
CREATE BY date_out technician
       SUM(fee_pre_paid)  SET &tot
       OUTPUT WHERE &tot>0;
```

Only those technicians who have collected rental fees appear in the created records.

We come back to this and other screening options in Chapter 17.

Other Optional Parameters

KEEP

If you want to permanently save the newly created database, you use the KEEP parameter as follows:

```
CREATE BY ski_num ski_rentch st_name KEEP;
```

Recall that the newly created file is automatically given the filename TEMP. When you use the KEEP parameter, you request that TEMP is to be saved permanently. Now, if you want to remove this database, use the following command:

```
SCHEMA temp DELETE;
```

If you do not specify KEEP in the CREATE command, you remove this newly created database when you issue the DATABASE, DBCLEAR, or the QUIT command. Without KEEP, the database is only kept temporarily for the duration of the session with NOMAD.

ZERONAV

If you want to change the NOTAVAILABLE value of the items in your database to a zero for numeric values and to a blank for the alphanumeric ones, use the ZERONAV parameter as follows:

```
CREATE BY ski_num ski_rentch ski_type ZERONAV;
```

For items that had NOTAVAILABLE values in the old database, the newly created records have:

■ Zero for the ski_rentch item since it is numeric.
■ Blank for the ski_type item since it is alphanumeric.

ON file-id

If you want to specifically assign the name to your newly created file (that is, not to refer to it by its default name TEMP), you use the ON file-id parameter as follows:

```
CREATE BY ski_num ski_rentch ski_type
    ON ski_charges KEEP;
```

This newly created file now has a name different from its default name TEMP. Its name is ski_charges, and it is permanently saved (KEEP) on the disk for any future references.

16.4 WRITE COMMAND

If you want to place the contents of one or more records into an external file, you can use the WRITE command.

Any external file defined with the FILE command is automatically open by the first WRITE referring to it. If, in the FILE command, you did not specify the LENGTH of the record, this length is also established by the first WRITE for this external file.

Required Parameters

The following two parameters are required:

1. An object—The information that you write to the external file. An object can be a name of a specific file from the NOMAD database, a name of an item, an expression, an alphanumeric string, or a &variable.
2. ON file-id—The referenced file that establishes a connection with the previously issued FILE command. It identifies the external file to which the data is to be written.

The use of the WRITE command is illustrated in this first example:

```
WRITE equipment_type ON transfer_file;
```

The object, equipment_type, identifies the file from our Rental System. All records from the equipment_type are to be written to an external file, which is identified with the file-id, transfer_file.

Consider this second example:

```
WRITE ski_num date_out date_in
ski_rent_paid*0.45 "1989" ON profit;
```

The first three objects, the ski_num, the date_out, and the date_in, are items from the TRANSACTIONS file of the Rental System. The next object, `ski_rent_paid*0.45`, is an expression. It calculates profit realized from the rental of a specific pair of skis. The last object is the alphanumeric string "1989". All are to be written to an external file with the file-id `profit`.

Optional Parameters

AS display format

This parameter allows you to describe how item values are to be written using any acceptable display format. (The data formats were described in Chapter 12.) For example,

```
WRITE ski_num AS A8 date_out AS DATE 'dd/mm/yy'
      date_in AS DATE'dd/mm/yy'
      ski_rent_paid*0.45 AS $99,999.99 '1989' AS A4
      ON profit;
```

Formats are described for all five objects.

Recall that if you do not explicitly specify an item's position in the new record, the default position is assigned. The default is the starting position in column 1. As objects are added, the current position is incremented by the object's length. In our example (where there is no explicit assignment of the positions; therefore, the default assignment applies) the object `ski_num` is written in columns 1-8, the object `date_out` in columns 9-16, the object `date_in` in columns 17-24, the object `profit` in columns 25-34, and the string object "1989" in columns 35-38. `profit` is the external file-id.

COLUMN n

You can explicitly specify the current column position using this parameter. This can be done regardless of the previous column position in the output record. If n is not specified, the default value is 1. For example,

```
WRITE ski_num AS A8 COLUMN 20 ski_rent_paid*0.45
      AS $99,999.99 ON profit;
```

The expression `ski_rent_paid*0.45` is to be written in columns 20-29.

SPACE n

You can place n blanks into the output record. If you do not specify the number of blanks, the default value is 1. For example,

```
WRITE ski_num AS A8 SPACE 5 ski_rent_paid*0.45
      AS $99,999.99 ON profit;
```

Here the object `ski_rent_paid` is written in columns 14-23.

TRANSMIT

Sometimes, after you write to a file, you need to transmit your records immediately. You can do this with the TRANSMIT parameter. Otherwise, if you fail to transmit you records immediately, the record data is placed in the output buffer and transmitted when the buffers become full or the READ or CLOSE command is issued. For example,

```
WRITE transactions ON transfer_file TRANSMIT;
```

writes the records to the external file transfer_file and transmits them immediately, one record at a time.

16.5 CALCULATIONS WITH NOMAD

We briefly considered calculations when we discussed expressions and functions. We now turn to the details of performing calculations with NOMAD.

In NOMAD an expression can be an algebraic equation, a logical comparison, or a built-in function. The order in which expressions are evaluated is the standard order used in computing. An outcome of an expression can be any data value allowed in NOMAD. The outcome can also be the TRUE or the FALSE value.

If you assign the result of the expression to an item or an &variable, their data types must be compatible. For example, do not assign an alphanumeric result of an expression to a numeric type &variable.

The rules that control the results of expressions are as follows:

1. If any element of the expression is a real number, the result is also a real number.

2. If all elements of the expression are integers, the result is an integer.

3. When a numeric expression results in more significant digits than can be stored or printed, the outcome is rounded to the nearest integer.

4. If one of the elements in an expression has a NOTAVAILABLE value, the result is usually NOTAVAILABLE. (We consider later in this chapter a few exceptions to this rule.)

NOMAD allows the use of dates in certain algebraic expressions. For example, assume you want to calculate and print a date 28 days past March 16, 1989. The following statements accomplishes this task:

```
DECLARE &date AS DATE'mm/dd/yy';
&date ='03/16/89';
PRINT (&date + 28) AS DATE'dd/mm/yyyy';
```

The expression in the PRINT statement calculates the required date. The output generated by this command is:

11/04/1989

If you want to specify the date when 28 weeks elapsed, the expression you use is:

PRINT (&date +28*7) AS DATE'dd/mm/yyyy';

The printed output is:

28/09/1989

In general, you can add or subtract days and weeks to or from a date value. The value of the resulting expression will be a date. However, you cannot add two dates. The result will raise an error.

You can subtract one date from the other, and the output is an integer representing the number of days between these two dates. For example, if you need to find out how many days passed between April 18, 1989, and June 14, 1989, these are the statements you need:

&date='04/18/89';
&newdate='06/14/89';
&days=&newdate - &date;

The variable &days will hold a value of 49.

Operators Used in Expressions

Operators are grouped into the following categories:

1. **Arithmetic Operators**—Perform ordinary arithmetic calculations, that is, addition, subtraction, multiplication, division, and exponentiation. They operate on two numeric values and return another numeric value as the result.

2. **Simple Logical Operators**—Compare two values and return a logical TRUE or FALSE value.

3. **Special Logical Operators**—Compare a value with several other values and return a logical TRUE or FALSE value.

4. **Logical Connectors**—Combine two logical expressions to create a new logical expression.

5. **Decoding Operators**—Replace coded values with values they obtain from a list of substitute (decoded) values.

6. **Concatenation Operators**—Combine alphanumeric strings to create new strings.

Operator	Function
+	Addition
−	Subtraction
*	Multiplication
/	Division
**	Exponentiation

Figure 16.2 Arithmetic Operators and Their Functions

Arithmetic Operators

NOMAD supports all standard arithmetic operators. Operators and their appropriate functions are given in Figure 16.2.

Arithmetic operators can be combined with functions, other operators, and parentheses to form complex mathematical expressions. For clarity in printed expressions, we use a space on either side of the arithmetic operators, but this space is not required. Here are some examples of mathematical expressions with valid arithmetic operators:

```
a * c − 5
var1 / (var2 ** 4)
a + c − (sqrt x + log x) ** (−2)
```

Simple Logical Operators

Simple logical operators compare two numeric or alphanumeric values and return the TRUE or FALSE condition, depending on the outcome of the evaluation. You can also combine simple logical operators with parentheses and arithmetic operators to form complex logical expressions.

Most logical operators have two names. One name is mnemonic, for example, LT (lesser than); the other is a mathematical symbol, for example, <. You can use either of them in NOMAD statements.

If NOTAVAILABLE data values are present in the logical expressions, the following rules apply:

1. If you compare a NOTAVAILABLE to another NOTAVAILABLE, the result is always TRUE.

2. If you compare a NOTAVAILABLE to any other value, the result is always FALSE.

Figure 16.3 shows simple logical operators and their mnemonic and symbolic representation in NOMAD.

To illustrate the use of simple logical operators, let us analyze some NOMAD commands. Consider this first example:

```
IF &ans  'N' THEN GOTO -start;
```

```
      Mathematical    Mnemonic
      Symbol          Name       Meaning
      ------------    --------   -------

      LT              <          Less than

      GT              >          Greater than

      EQ              =          Equal

      LE              <=         Less than or equal to

      GE              >=         Greater than or equal to

      NE              <>         Not equal to
```

Figure 16.3 Simple Logical Operators Supported by NOMAD

Here NOMAD compares the value of the &variable &ans with the string "N". If the value of &ans is not equal to N, NOMAD returns the logical TRUE value. Control is redirected to the statement labeled −start.

Consider a second NOMAD command:

```
SELECT production_date = &date_select;
```

Here the production_date is an item in the EQUIPMENT_TYPE file in our Ski Rental System. Only records in which the value of the production_date is equal to the value in the &variable &date_select are to be selected.

Consider a final example:

```
CREATE BY skinum ski_rentch WHERE ski_length LE 180;
```

Here new records are created from the records in the old database for which the value of the item ski_length is less than or equal to 180. These new records have two items: skinum and ski_rentch.

Special Logical Operators

There are several special logical operators in NOMAD. The operators AMONG, BETWEEN, and CONTAINS compare one value with many other values and return a logical value of TRUE or FALSE, depending on the results of the comparison.

The operator LIKE determines whether or not a character expression matches a specified pattern. It also returns a value of TRUE or FALSE.

■ AMONG—Determines if the specified expression is contained in a list of other expressions. You may use character strings, numeric values, database items, or any other valid expression with AMONG. To illustrate, assume that &var1 has a value of "DYNASTAR", &var2 has a value "ROSSIGNOL", and &var3 has a value "DYNAMICS". In the statement:

```
'K2' AMONG(&var1,&var2,&var3);
```

the expression "K2" is compared to the AMONG values. If the first expression is found in the list, the returned result is TRUE. If this expression is not found, the result is FALSE. For example, the result will be FALSE since "K2" is not in the list. You can integrate the AMONG operator into other NOMAD statements. For example,

```
&test = 'DYNASTAR';
IF &test AMONG(var1,var2,var3)
THEN GOTO -start;
```

The value of the &test is DYNASTAR. This value is in the list (we assume that DYNASTAR is the value of &var1, as in the previous example), thus control will be passed to the statement with the label –start.

- BETWEEN—Determines if one expression lies between two other expressions, inclusively. You may use character strings, numeric values, or any other valid data types with BETWEEN. For example,

```
PRINT IF 12 BETWEEN(11,21)
THEN 'CORRECT' ELSE "ERROR";
```

Since the number 12 is greater than or equal to 11 and less than or equal to 21, the word CORRECT will appear in the Output window after this statement is executed. With the BETWEEN operator you can compare strings, dates, or times. In the case of strings of different lengths, the BETWEEN operator automatically pads the shorter string with blanks before making the comparison. For example,

```
DECLARE &type AS A2;
&type = 'K2';
IF &type BETWEEN('DYNASTAR','ROSSIGNOL')
THEN GOTO -start;
```

The "K2   " string (padded with seven blanks after the character K2) is compared with "DYNASTAR " (DYNASTAR followed by one blank) and "ROSSIGNOL". Since K(2) is between D(ynastar) and R(ossingnol), control is passed to the statement with the label –start.

- CONTAINS—Determines if the first expression of the command contains a string of characters present in one of the other expressions listed. The comparison expressions are enclosed in parentheses and are separated by commas. If the characters in any of the comparison expressions match all or part of the first expression, CONTAINS returns a TRUE; otherwise, it returns a FALSE.

  For example, if &var1 has a value of "DYNAMIC-SLALOM", the command:

```
PRINT (IF &var1 CONTAINS
('SKI','SL','DH')
    THEN 'CORRECT'
    ELSE 'ERROR');
```

Character Expression First Argument	Pattern Second Argument	Result Returned
DYNASTAR	D%S%	TRUE
DYNASTAR	D_S%	FALSE
ROSSIGNOL	%SSI_N%	TRUE
DYNAMICS	DYNAMICS	TRUE
DYNAMICS	_YN_C%	FALSE

Figure 16.4   Like Operator Argument Samples and Their Results

determines whether or not the strings "SKI","SL", and "DH" are part of the string in &var1. Since "SL" is part of "DYNAMIC-SLALOM", when this command is executed, the word CORRECT will appear in the Output window.

■ LIKE—Determines whether characters in the expression match the specified pattern. The format of this operator is:

Character-expression LIKE pattern;

LIKE returns a TRUE logical condition if the pattern in the second argument (the pattern argument) is found in the first argument (character-expression). The pattern argument is defined using any combination of the following three elements:

1. Putting a specific character in the pattern. A true condition arises when the value and the location of the character specified in the second argument is exactly the same as those in the first argument.
2. Putting an underscore (_) in the pattern. This indicates that any single character in the first argument, located in the underscore position of the second argument, matches the underscore. The underscore is used as a wildcard character to match *a single* character.
3. Putting a percent sign (%) in the pattern. This matches zero or more arbitrary characters in the first argument with the % in the pattern. All other characters must match exactly or the result is FALSE. The % is used as a wildcard character to match *zero or more* characters.

The list in Figure 16.4 illustrates the possible construction patterns for the second argument, given the first argument. The result of the LIKE operation for each set of arguments is also shown.

The following example illustrates the use of the LIKE operator to test the pattern of an &test variable:

```
DECLARE &test AS A9;
&test = 'ROSSIGNOL';
PRINT IF &test LIKE '%SS%L' THEN 'OLD' ELSE 'NEW';
```

When this set of statements is executed, "OLD" appears in the Output window because the value of &test ("ROSSIGNOL") matches the pattern "%SS%L".

```
Connector             Returns a TRUE If:
---------             ------------------
AND                   Both values are TRUE.

OR                    Either value is TRUE.

XOR                   Only one value is TRUE.

NOT                   The value is not TRUE.

IMP(IMPLIES)          The first value cannot

                      disprove the second valu

EQV(EQUIVALENCE)      Both values are equal.
```

Figure 16.5   Logical Connectors Supported by NOMAD

Logical Connectors

Logical connectors test the validity of logical expressions that make the statement. They return a logical TRUE or FALSE value depending on the validity of the statement.

You can use logical connectors to combine two logical values and return a new logical value. Logical connectors supported by NOMAD are listed in Figure 16.5.

The following examples illustrate the use of the logical connectors:

```
&var1 LE &var2 OR &var1 = 6
A < > &var3 AND NOT B LT 10
Y = 5 XOR X = 30
```

Decoding Operators

Decoding operators translate old values to new values based on a specified list of old and new value pairs.

NOMAD supports two decoding operators: DECODE and RANGE. DECODE is similar to RANGE except that DECODE looks in the table for an old value that is *equal to* that of the old expression (first parameter of the operator), whereas RANGE looks in the table for an old value that is *greater than or equal to* that of the old expression.

DECODE searches the old-value side of the list and returns the new value when it finds a match. An example of format for these operators is as follows:

```
            expression DECODE
(old1=new1, old2=new2,..., oldN=newN, ELSE=newN+1);
```

When the old expression has numeric values 1 through *N*, you do not need to specify the old values. The result of the search depends on the ordinal position of the new value in the list. The format for this case is as follows:

```
            expression DECODE
(new1, new2,..., newN, ELSE=newN+1);
```

Parameters used with these operators form a list of old and new pairs. You can assign these pairs in any order. The data types of the old and new values do not have to be the same. The following rules govern the data type returned.

1. If the newN parameter is numeric, the result is numeric.
2. If the newN parameter is alphanumeric, the result is alphanumeric.
3. If the receiving object is specified as a date, the result is a date value.

DECODE (or RANGE) compares the expression value to each of the old values and:

■ If it finds a match, it returns the new value (newN).
■ If it does not find a match, it returns the value of newN+1 if ELSE is specified.
■ If ELSE is not specified, DECODE (or RANGE) returns a NOTAVAILABLE value.
■ If the expression being decoded is specified as a date, it is assumed that the oldN search arguments are dates.

To illustrate the use of the decoding operators, we present two examples. In the first example, assume that the value of &type is "SL".

```
    &ski_type = &type
DECODE('SL'='SLALOM', 'GS'='GIANT SLALOM',
'DH'='DOWN HILL', ELSE='OTHER');
```

The DECODE operation returns the value of "SLALOM" to the &ski_type.

For the second example, assume that &index is equal to 2. Since the old values are numbers, we use an alternate format of DECODE:

```
    &ski_type = &index
DECODE('SLALOM', 'GIANT SLALOM', 'DOWN HILL', ELSE='OTHER');
```

The returned value for the &ski_type in this case is "GIANT SLALOM".

If, in the last example, you use the RANGE operator, the following results are returned:

■ For &index values greater than or equal to 1 and less than 2, the value returned for the &ski_type is "SLALOM".
■ For &index values greater than or equal to 2 and less than 3, the value returned is "GIANT SLALOM".
■ For &index values greater than or equal to 3 and less than 4, the value returned is "DOWN HILL".
■ For &index values greater than or equal to 4, the value returned is "OTHER".

You can use the RANGE operator to set up a table of associations. For example, in the SKIRENT database, a field called REVCAT (representing Revenue Category)

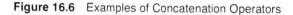

```
     NOMAD Statement              Result
     ----------------             ------

     "WED " CAT "RT12"            WED RT12

     "DIT5" CAT &NAV             DIT5

     &NAV CAT "DIT5"             DIT5

     "WED   " CATB "RT12"        WEDRT12

     &NAV CATB "DTRT"            DTRT

     "DERT    " CATB &NAV CAT "AS"  DERTAS
```

Figure 16.6 Examples of Concatenation Operators

can be added. Then a table of associations showing revenue categories can be constructed.

```
DEFINE revcat AS A12
EXPR=totrev RANGE(10000='POOR', 100000='SUCCESS',
ELSE='BLOCKBUSTER');
```

This sets up a table of associations where equipment that grossed up to $10,000 is considered Poor, equipment that grossed between $10,000 and $100,000 is considered a Success, and everything over $100,000 is considered a Blockbuster. A list request could therefore show, in part:

Equipment	TOTREV	REVCAT
Dynastar	120,000	BLOCKBUSTER
Rossignol	100,000	SUCCESS
Zap	9,000	POOR

Concatenation Operators

Concatenation operators bring together two or more character expressions to form a single character string. The following two operators are used:

1. CAT—Joins two character expressions and treats any blanks present as characters.

2. CATB—Joins two character expressions after having removed any trailing blanks from the first expression.

Both operators treat a NOTAVAILABLE value as a null string. Figure 16.6 lists examples of the use of the CAT and CATB operators.

16.6 FUNCTIONS IN NOMAD

For computations and for the string processing, NOMAD provides many built-in functions. To use a function, you specify the function name followed by a list of arguments in parentheses.

The function name and a short description of its use is presented in this section. The functions are grouped by class. This grouping is related to the data types used and to the usage in specific NOMAD commands. (The general formats for all functions supported by NOMAD and examples of their use are given in Appendix C.)

Functions Used With Character Data

The following functions are used with character data:

Function Name	Description
ALPHA	Determines whether a character expression contains letters or only blanks. The returned value is TRUE or FALSE. A FALSE value is returned when the expression contains numbers, punctuation marks, or special characters, for example, @, %, or *.
DDQUERY	Obtains the attributes of the database entity, for example, a file or an item from the data dictionary.
DISPLAY	Converts a numeric value to a character value.
INDEX	Locates the beginning of a substring within a longer character string, and returns the character number of the beginning of a substring.
LIKE	Determines whether or not a character expression matches a specified pattern.
LENGTH	Returns the length of a character expression, including trailing blanks.
LENGTHB	Returns the length of a character string, excluding trailing blanks.
MASK	Determines whether or not a character value conforms to a particular format pattern.
NUMBER	Determines whether or not a character expression contains only numeric digits.
SUBSTR	Returns a specified portion of a character string.
UPPER	Converts lowercase characters to uppercase equivalents.
VALUE	Converts a character value to a numeric value.

Functions Used with Numeric Data

The following functions are used with numeric data:

Function Name	Description
ABSVAL	Returns the absolute value of a number.
ATAN	Computes the arc tangent of the numeric expression. (Returned value is given in radians.)
COS	Calculates the cosine of a numeric expression.
DEGREE	Converts radians to degrees.
EXP	Exponentiates.
INT	Returns the integer portion of a number.
LOG	Calculates the natural log of the numeric expression.
LOGX	Calculates the natural log of the first numeric expression to the base of the second expression.
LOG10	Calculates the common log (base 10) of the numeric expression.
RADIAN	Converts degrees to radians.
SIGN	Determines whether an expression is positive or negative. For negative numbers, it returns –1; for positive numbers, it returns 1.
SIN	Computes the sine of the numeric expression.
SQRT	Computes the square root of the numeric expression.
TAN	Computes the tangent of the numeric expression.
ZNAV	Converts NOTAVAILABLE values to zero (for numerics) or blanks (for alphanumeric data).

Function Used with Date Data

The following function is used with date data:

Function Name	Description
ADDDATE	Adds or subtracts months or years to date values.

Functions Used With LIST and CREATE Commands

The following functions are used only with the LIST or CREATE commands. If you limit the scope (with SELECT or WHERE) of the LIST or CREATE command containing the function, the scope of the function will also be limited.

Function Name	Description
AVERAGE/AVG	Calculates the arithmetic mean of the values, excluding NOTAVAILABLE.
COUNT/CNT	Determines the number of values, excluding NOTAVAILABLE values.
FIRST	Returns the first occurrence of the data value.
LAST	Returns the last occurrence of a data value.
MAX	Finds the highest data value encountered for an item.
MIN	Finds the lowest data value encountered for an item.
NUMBER/NUM	Determines the total number of item values, including NOTAVAILABLE values.
STDDEV	Calculates the standard deviation of the item values.
SUM	Calculates the sum of the item values, excluding NOTAVAILABLE values.
VARIANCE	Calculates the arithmetic variance of the item values.

```
Page    1
DATE OUT  RETURN DATE   SKI RENT PAID   BOOT RENT PAID   POLE RENT PAID

031988    032188            $70.00          $30.00          $11.00
032088    032288            $70.00          $30.00          $11.40
032188    032688           $175.00          $75.00          $28.50
120387    120587            $17.00          $25.00          $11.40
110387    110687            $25.50          $37.50          $17.10
110487    110687            $17.00          $30.00          $11.40
111287    111587            $25.50          $45.00          $17.10
111387    111587            $70.00          $30.00          $11.40
011388    011588            $70.00          $30.00          $11.40
012088    012388           $105.00          $45.00          $17.10
012188    012688           $175.00          $75.00          $28.50
022188    022699           $175.00          $75.00          $28.50
```

Figure 16.7   Listing of Records From the TRANSACTIONS File with Values of Items Required for Processing

16.7 CREATION PROCEDURE FOR THE HISTORY TRANSACTIONS FILE

We are now ready to use commands discussed in this chapter in our Ski Rental System. We use these commands in a procedure that builds the transaction file for the HISTORY master. The tasks we need to accomplish are:

■ Process records from the TRANSACTIONS file (individual rental transaction).

■ Calculate the week's code (for each transaction record).

■ Create summary records on a weekly basis and write them to the external file (in the format required for the transaction file).

The items we need to process the TRANSACTIONS file are:

■ date_out—Date when equipment was rented.

■ date_ret—Date when equipment was returned.

■ ski_rent_paid—Charges for ski rental.

■ boot_rent_paid—Charges for boot rental.

■ pole_rent_paid—Charges for pole rental.

Figure 16.7 lists the values of these items for several records in the TRANSACTIONS file.

```
! 1! DECLARE &start_time AS DATE"mm/dd/yy";

! 2! DEFINE week_code AS 99
! 3!        EXPR = (INT((date_out - &start_time)/7)+1);

! 4! ASK "ENTER STARTING PERIOD FOR TRANSACTION YEAR MM/DD/YY :"
! 5!        &start_time;

! 6! CREATE BY week_code NAMED week_code1
! 7!        SUM(ski_rent_paid) NAMED sum_ski_paid AS 99,999.99
! 8!        SUM(boot_rent_paid) NAMED sum_boot_paid AS 99,999.99
! 9!        SUM(pole_rent_paid) NAMED sum_pole_paid AS 99,999.99
!10!        ON transact KEEP;

!11!    TRANS;

!12! FROM transact;

!13! FILE DEFINE ski1 = c:\nomad\transki1.dat CREATE;
!14! FILE OPEN ski1;

!15!    -start
!16!      NEXT transact OTW GOTO -end;
!17!    WRITE week_code1 AS 99
!18!        sum_ski_paid AS 99999.99
!19!        sum_boot_paid AS 99999.99
!20!        sum_pole_paid AS 99999.99
!21!        ON ski1 ;         .
!22!    GOTO -start;

!23!    -end
!24!        FILE CLOSE ski1;
!25! FROM;
!26! UNTRANS;
```

Figure 16.8 Procedure to Create an External Transaction File for the History Master

Figure 16.8 contains the procedure for creating a transaction file for the HISTORY master.

Line 1 declares the &variable &start_time. This variable is to hold the starting date of the ski rental season.

Lines 2-3 are the DEFINE statement that will calculate the week_code for each record from TRANSACTIONS master.

A specific start date is to be entered by the user in response to a query. Lines 4-5 (the ASK command) represent this query. A user enters the season's start date into the Form automatically created by the ASK command. Figure 16.9 illustrates this Form.

In lines 6-10, the CREATE command creates a new database (TRANSACT). Since the KEEP parameter is specified (after ON TRANSACT in line 10), this new database is to be kept permanently.

TRANSACT is to contain weekly summary records for the rental fees. The summaries are calculated using the SUM function. The list of records in this database is given in Figure 16.10.

In line 11, the TRANS command halts the compilation of statements succeeding it until the procedure is executed. To understand why we have to have this command, experiment by removing the command in line 11 and running the procedure to see what happens. If you attempt to compile the procedure without this particular statement, you will raise an error condition (see Problem 25).

The part of the procedure that processes the TRANSACT database and creates the external transaction file (with the required format) resides in lines 12-22. First we

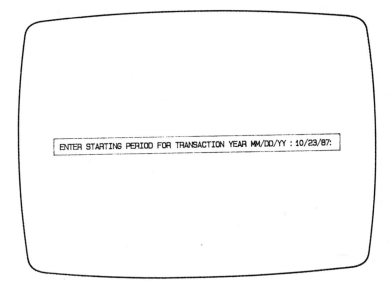

```
ENTER STARTING PERIOD FOR TRANSACTION YEAR MM/DD/YY : 10/23/87:
```

Figure 16.9   Form to Enter a Value for the &start_date

```
Page     1
                 SUM              SUM              SUM
WEEK CODE   SKI RENT PAID   BOOT RENT PAID   POLE RENT PAID
----------  -------------   --------------   --------------
        1          42.50            67.50            28.50
        2          95.50            75.00            28.50
        5          17.00            25.00            11.40
       11          70.00            30.00            11.40
       12         280.00           120.00            45.60
       16         175.00            75.00            28.50
       20         140.00            60.00            22.80
       21         175.00            75.00            28.50
```

Figure 16.10   Records in the TRANSACT Database Created by the CREATE Command

have to position ourselves at the top of the TRANSACT (line 12). Next we define and open the physical file that holds the external transaction file (lines 13-14). In lines 15-22 we process all records from the TRANSACT and write them to the external file. Note the use of the WRITE command.

```
 1    42.50    67.50    28.50
 2    95.50    75.00    28.50
 5    17.00    25.00    11.40
11    70.00    30.00    11.40
12   280.00   120.00    45.60
16   175.00    75.00    28.50
20   140.00    60.00    22.80
21   175.00    75.00    28.50
```

Figure 16.11   Listing of the Records in the External Transaction File

In line 24, the external file is closed.

In line 25, the FROM condition (from line 12) is cleared.

The listing of records in the external file is given in Figure 16.11. Note that the format is as described in Chapter 15.

Line 26 contains the UNTRANS command, which will cause all the NOMAD statements that are placed after it to be compiled before the execution of the procedure. In our procedure this statement is not absolutely necessary since this is a last statement, and there are no statements after it. We included it to make a point. If you use the TRANS command in the procedure, you want this command to be applicable only to certain statements. Since you want other statements in the procedure to be compiled, you have to reverse the process. You can do this with the UNTRANS command. For a detailed discussion of TRANS and UNTRANS usage, refer to Chapter 11.)

16.8 SUMMARY

The manipulation and transfer of data in a database is one of the most important operations in NOMAD. The CREATE, WRITE, EXPORT, and IMPORT commands allow to you to build a new database from one or more existing databases, transfer data to an external file, and receive or transfer information from or to another database product.

Expressions derive their results from a combination of data values and operations performed on these data values. Generally speaking, you can use expressions whenever a NOMAD &variable can be used. An expression can be an algebraic equation, a logical comparison, or a built-in NOMAD function. You can also include expressions within other expressions. Data values can be

■ Items
■ &variables
■ Constants

Operations can be defined with:

■ Operators (+,−,*,/, and so on)
■ Functions (AVG, ZNAV, ADDATE, and so on)

Functions are built-in facilities for performing computations for statistical analysis, financial analysis, and string processing. Functions are used with

■ Numeric data
■ Character data
■ Date data
■ LIST and CREATE commands

When NOMAD evaluates an expression, it proceeds from left to right and follows an order of precedence; that is, it first evaluates elements within parentheses, then it evaluates functions, then signed numbers, then decoding operators, then exponentiation, then multiplication and division, and so on.

Expressions return data values or, by default, TRUE or FALSE values.

If you assign the results of an expression to an item or &variable, the data type of the item or &variable must be compatible. For example, you cannot assign an alphanumeric result to a numeric data type.

You can use date values in expressions to:

■ Perform calculations with dates.
■ Add or subtract days or weeks to or from a date value.

Operators used in expressions specify actions or computations to be performed on data values. They perform the following functions:

■ Simple arithmetic calculations
■ Concatenation operations
■ Logical comparisons

Operators are organized into the following groups:

■ Arithmetic operators—Operate on two numeric values and return another numeric value.

■ Decoding operators (DECODE and RANGE)—Replace values with values they obtain from a list of substitute values.

■ Concatenation operators (CAT and CATB)—Combine alphanumeric strings to create new strings.

■ Simple logical operators—Compare two values and return a logical RUE or FALSE value. They can be represented in mnemonic form or in symbolic form, for example, LT or <.

■ Special logical operators (AMONG, BETWEEN, CONTAINS, and LIKE)—Compare a value with several other values and return a logical value.

Armed with this knowledge, you can build procedures that create external transaction files.

EXERCISES

1. When using the CREATE command, your newly created database is kept only temporarily. Why would you do that?

2. How is the name assigned to your newly created database?

3. What do you do to keep this newly created file permanently on the disk for any future references?

4. Under what circumstances (describe possible organizational scenario) would you keep a file created with the CREATE command permanently?

5. What will result from the following CREATE request?

```
CREATE BY equipment_code equipment_name
        SUBSET MATCHING ski_type ski_rentch
        REJECT MATCHING ski_type;
```

6. Explain what is accomplished with this CREATE request:

```
CREATE BY ski_rentch DESC
    equipment_name
        LIMIT 20;
```

7. What is OUTPUT WHERE screening used for in this command?

```
CREATE BY director
SUM(AWARDS) SET &hold_awards
OUTPUT WHERE &hold_awards=3;
```

8. Identify data transfers possible with NOMAD on the PC.

9. When would you use the WRITE command? What other commands have to be used in order for the WRITE command to function properly?

10. Comment on the following statement: "The WRITE command can update a file if you specify the CHANGE option with the FILE command for the file-id."

11. Could you use the WRITE command to transfer data from system to system? Describe how and give a structure of a command that uses NOMLINK.

12. Identify the output file and specify formatting and column placement for this command:

```
WRITE i_ski
      COLUMN 10 i_number AS 9999
      i_date AS DATE 'mm/dd/yy'
      ON outfile;
```

13. What is FOLD used for in a WRITE command?

14. Consider a possible scenario in your organization. You are working in a department that does a lot of what is called departmental computing. Could you conceive of circumstances when you would immediately need to transmit the records you just wrote to an external file? Describe the situation.

15. You require an immediate transmission of your newly written record. Which parameter of the WRITE command you use to accomplish this?

16. What is the output generated by this command?

```
DECLARE &date AS DATE'mm/dd/yy';
&date='06/09/89';
PRINT (&date + 28*7) AS DATE'dd/mm/yyyy';
```

17. Identify an error present in this statement:

```
DECLARE &date1 AS DATE'mm/dd/yy';
DECLARE &date2 AS DATE'mm/dd/yy';
&date1='03/16/89';
&date2='06/09/89';
PRINT (&date1 + &date2) AS DATE'dd/mm/yyyy';
```

18. Correct this short procedure so that the result generated from it is TRUE.

```
DECLARE &x AS A6;
&x='ABCD';
PRINT IF &x LIKE 'ABCD' THEN TRUE
                        ELSE FALSE;
```

19. List the special logical operators and specify their usage.

20. Assume that &a has a value of 'a', &b has a value of 'b', and &c has a value of 'c'. What will be printed in the Output window when this statement is executed?

```
PRINT IF 'd' AMONG(&a,&b,&c) THEN 'FOUND' ELSE 'NOT FOUND';
```

21. What will appear in the Output window when this statement is executed?

    ```
    PRINT IF 5 BETWEEN (1,10) THEN 'YES' ELSE 'NO';
    ```

22. Assume that A is a NOTAVAILABLE value and B contains a value. Specify and explain the reason for the value returned when these expressions are executed:
    a. NOT A LT B
    b. A NL B

23. Assume that &amt has a value of 15. What is the value of &amt1 after this statement is executed?

    ```
    &amt1=&amt RANGE(10='0-10', 20='11-20', 30='21-30',
                      ELSE='30+);
    ```

24. When would you use the DDQUERY function?

25. In the procedure shown in Figure 16.8, remove the statement

    ```
    !11!  TRANS;
    ```

    Run this procedure without this statement in it. What error condition is raised? Why? (*Hint*: When this procedure is compiled, are you referencing files that already exist?)

PROJECTS

1. The management of the State Park System requested from each of the park's managers information on the weekly revenues for the last year. The request is for the information in the file form. This information is to be used for the update of the park system head office's database. The file is to contain the following items:

   Park Designation Code
   Week Designation Code
   Campsite Type
   Weekly Revenue

   Your assignment is to write a procedure that creates this external file. The parameters needed for this file are to come from the design specification of the State Park Reservation System as developed Project 1 in Chapter 10. If some of the information does not exist there, you may define such information using your own judgement.

2. Write a procedure that creates the external file containing information from the Properties, Water Rights, and Leases System. The data items in the record of the external file are:

   1. State where the property is located
   2. County where the property is located
   3. Parcel Owner

4. Parcel Number
5. Parcel Acreage
6. Water Right Number
7. Usage Type Code

Remember that you can have multiple water rights on the same property. All other necessary information is specified in or can be derived from your work on Project 2 in Chapter 10.

CHAPTER 17

Standard Reporting

For business is not disposed to wait until the doer of business is at leisure; but the doer must follow up what he is doing, and make the business his first object.

Plato, *The Republic*

17.1 INTRODUCTION

This chapter discusses how to create standard reports from the data stored in a NOMAD database. By "standard" we mean that NOMAD automatically formats the reports according to default formats. Creating custom reports (where the user controls the format of the report as well as the format of the items displayed in the report) is discussed in Chapter 18.

All standard reports are created with the use of one command and its various parameters. This command is a very powerful LIST command. The use of its parameters allows us to automatically generate a variety of reports.

The CREATE command operates with the same parameters as the LIST command. Most of the parameters of the CREATE command were considered in Chapter 16. The remaining parameters of the LIST (and CREATE) command are the subject of this chapter.

Essentially, we concentrate on the standard reporting features of the LIST command. That is, we consider how to select the data for reporting, how to sort, how to perform calculations, and how to combine data from several master files. We show how to obtain printed reports and how to store created reports, on disk, for future use.

When you complete this chapter you should be able to:

■ Describe what is a standard report
■ Generate standard reports using the powerful LIST command
■ Store on disk or print out generated reports

Figure 17.1 Manufacturers of the Equipment Rented by Bob's Ski Shop

---

17.2 STANDARD REPORTS

We start with reports created with the basic LIST command. The LIST command uses headings, display formats, titles, justification, and other formatting information, as specified within the descriptions of the items in the database schema. The LIST command uses all the default formatting features, automatically producing a report with the default format of page numbers, column spacing, page breaks, and so on.

Let us start with a simple request: Who manufactures the equipment that the Bob's Ski Shop rents? To create the report that answers this question, the following command is issued:

```
LIST manufact_name;
```

The only parameter needed in the LIST command is the name of the item manufact_name. The report automatically appears in the List window. The report lines are in the same order as the database records. The format of this report is shown in Figure 17.1.

Note that the LIST command automatically produced the page number, column heading, spacing, and underlining. The header came from the item description in the MANUFACTURERS master, where it is defined as

```
'MANUFACTURERS:NAME'
```

The colon (:) causes the header on the report to be printed in two lines.

Next, we want a report listing the rental fee charged for the equipment rented as well as the rental date and the return date. All these are to be presented in an ascending order, sorted according to rental date.

Recall that all the necessary items (date_out, date_ret, and fee_paid) are in the TRANSACTIONS master. Thus, the LIST command that will create the required report is as follows:

```
LIST BY date_out date_ret fee_paid;
```

The report, which will appear in the List window, is shown in Figure 17.2.

```
Page        1


DATE OUT    RETURN DATE    FEE_PAID
--------    -----------    --------
012389      012689         $95.50
            012489         $70.20
012889      020589         $65.00
            020389         $185.60
020189      020289         $47.50
```

Figure 17.2   NOMAD Report Request with Sorting

```
Page        1


DATE OUT    RETURN DATE    FEE_PAID
--------    -----------    --------
012389      012489         $70.20
            012689         $95.50
012889      020389         $185.60
            020589         $65.00
020189      020289         $47.50
```

Figure 17.3   Report for a Request with Multiple Sort Keys

To sort, you specify the name of the item (after the reserved word "BY") by which sorting is required. Note that the value of the BY item is not printed if it is the same as that in the previous print line.

If you wanted to sort on multiple items, repeat the reserved word "BY" for each item to be sorted. For example, assume that the items in the previous report are to be sorted in the order of the rental date first, and then in the order of the return date. The statement that accomplishes this is:

```
LIST BY date_out BY date_ret fee_paid;
```

The report is shown in Figure 17.3. Note that the data in the report are sorted first by date_out and then by date_ret.

Next, let us see how we can solve the following problem in NOMAD. The owners of the Ski Shop want a report that lists daily rental revenues calculated for each technician in the shop. Three technicians work in the shop. Each column of the report is to correspond to the revenues collected by a specific technician. The report data are to be sorted by rental date. The statement

```
LIST BY date_out ACROSS technician SUM(fee_paid);
```

creates the requested report which is shown in Figure 17.4.

The report contains four columns. The keyword "BY" in the LIST command causes the rental dates to be printed down the report page in the first column. The keyword "ACROSS" causes the initials of the three technicians to print across the page, in the column headings. There are two other lines in the column headings.

```
Page      1


              AF          GW          WW

              SUM         SUM         SUM

DATE OUT   FEE PAID    FEE PAID    FEE PAID
--------   --------    --------    --------
011289     $592.50      $98.15     &254.00
           $783.23     $269.20     $540.50
011389     $155.00     $189.50       $0.00
011589     $348.00     $450.00     $189.00
011689     $891.00     $530.00     $499.00
```

Figure 17.4   Report on Daily Rental Revenues by Technician

The SUM line indicates that the values printed in the columns of the report are sums [NOMAD picks this up from the description of the function SUM(fee_paid).] The last line corresponds to the headers for the item fee_paid.

The values of SUM(fee_paid) are the totals of the rental fees, for a given day, collected by a given technician. They are printed in the appropriate column. Note that the columns are sorted in alphabetical order by the technician's initials.

All of the preceding reporting statements illustrate the use of the following required parameters of the LIST command:

■ Object clause

■ BY clause

■ ACROSS clause

Note that exactly the same parameters are used in the CREATE command (Chapter 16). Thus, most of the options for these parameters were discussed earlier. Remember that since they are required parameters, at least one of them must be included in the LIST statement.

In addition, any combination of these parameters can be used in one LIST statement. The combined use of the BY and ACROSS clauses was illustrated in the last example given.

Object Clause

Object modifiers of the object clause control the way NOMAD totals numeric items and the way it reports values. Modifiers are used to override the defaults of the LIST command for display formats, for calculation methods, and for the printing of items, expressions, and report functions in subtotal lines.

Object modifiers apply only to objects in the Object and ACROSS clauses. They do not apply to the sorting of items in the BY or the ACROSS clauses.

The modifiers are placed in the command immediately after the object being modified. Multiple modifiers can be used to modify a single object. The following object modifiers are discussed:

```
Page       1


                     PCT
 SKI  INVENTORY      SKI
        NUMBER     RENT PAID
 --------------    ---------
 00287436            14.84
 00987245             8.16
 11239880            22.40
 11540000            23.95
 22350000            17.44
 34110000            13.21
```

Figure 17.5 Report with PCT Modifier

```
PCT
SUBTOTAL
SUBTOTAL FULLST
SUBTOTAL ALL (ST ALL)
SUBTOTAL FOR BY item
TOTAL
TOTAL ALL
RECOMP
```

PCT

PCT computes and prints percentages. That is, it computes the proportion each value of the object contributes to the total value of the object. For example, the following LIST request uses PCT to calculate each rental ski's percentage of the total ski rental revenue:

```
LIST BY ski_num ski_rent_paid PCT;
```

The report created by this statement is shown in Figure 17.5. The PCT SKI RENT PAID column contains percentages of the total ski rental revenues for each pair of skis in the rental pool.

SUBTOTAL

SUBTOTAL causes a subtotal value to be calculated as each instance is processed and prints a subtotal for an object each time the value of an item in a preceding BY clause changes. NOTAVAILABLE values are treated as zeros.

To illustrate the use of the SUBTOTAL modifier, let us create a report that displays rental transactions, summarizing the subtotals of the skis and boots rental fees for each customer. (Pole rental fees are not to be shown.) Customer identification, rental date, and fee paid for rental of skis, boots, and poles are to be displayed. The following statement creates this report:

```
LIST BY custident date_out ski_rent_paid SUBTOTAL
                 boot_rent_paid SUBTOTAL
                 pole_rent_paid;
```

CUSTOMER IDENTIFICATION	DATE OUT	SKI RENT PAID	BOOT RENT PAID	POLE RENT PAID
234-3450-34990	011289	$65.50	$25.00	$8.50
	012089	$87.00	$30.20	$12,80
	031589	$150.00	$59.00	$21.00
		----------	----------	
*		$302.50	$114.20	
3456-222-34590	012589	$25.50	$10.00	$5.50
54780-3333-000	021589	$30.00	$15.00	$5.50
	021589	$75.00	$30.00	$15.60
		----------	----------	
*		$105.00	$45.00	

Page   1

Figure 17.6   Report Showing Calculated Subtotals

The report is shown in Figure 17.6.

An asterisk appears in the CUSTOMER IDENTIFICATION column to indicate that the subtotal is printed in this line. Note that the subtotal is not printed when only one valid numeric value is to be subtotaled. For example, the second customer rented only once, so no subtotal needs to be calculated and none is printed.

SUBTOTAL FULLST

Quite often the need arises to print subtotals for each BY value, regardless of the number of Object clause values. The SUBTOTAL FULLST modifier allows such subtotals to be printed whenever the value of the BY items changes. For example,

```
LIST BY custident date_out ski_rent_paid SUBTOTAL FULLST
                    Boot_rent_paid SUBTOTAL FULLST
                    pole_rent_paid;
```

In the report generated by this LIST command, a subtotal line prints even if there is only one line item. Without FULLST, such a subtotal would not be generated.

For each report column (that is, for each subtotal), dashes print automatically on the line immediately above the subtotal. The display format for the subtotal is the same as the display format for the object being subtotaled. After the subtotals are printed, one blank line is automatically inserted before the data for the next customer are printed. This improves the appearance and clarity of the report.

SUBTOTAL ALL

To print subtotals for all items in a LIST request you use SUBTOTAL ALL. SUBTOTAL ALL can be abbreviated in a statement as ST ALL. When you use this formatting option, you do not have to use the SUBTOTAL modifier for each of the object items. For example,

```
Page      1


   CUSTOMER      SKI INVENTORY               SKI
 IDENTIFICATION     NUMBER      DATE OUT   RENT PAID
 --------------   ------------  --------   ---------
 234-3450-34990   05634692      011289      $65.50
                                012089      $87.00
                                           ---------
                      *                     $152.00

                  93453436      031589      $150.00
                                           ---------
      *                                     $302.50

 3456-222-34590   30958300      012589       $25.50

 54780-3333-000   32991290      021589       $30.00
                                021589       $75.00
                                           ---------
                      *                     $105.00

                                           ---------
      *                                     $105.00
```

Figure 17.7   Report with Subtotals Calculated for Multiple BY Clauses

```
LIST BY custident date_out ski_rent_paid
        boot_rent_paid pole_rent_paid ST ALL;
```

Here, ST ALL generates subtotals for all three numeric items: ski_rent_paid, boot_rent_paid, and pole_rent_paid.

SUBTOTAL FOR

If you are dealing with multiple BY clauses, SUBTOTAL FOR allows you to specify the subtotaling of specific items.

Again let us consider an example. The ski shop owners would like to know if certain skis are rented more often than others and by whom. They would also want to know how much was collected in rental fees for each day. A report that lists rental transactions and subtotals them by the ski code and then by the customer will supply this information.

This report is to be sorted not only by the customer and by the ski code, but also by the date of the rental. To create such a report, we can use the following statement:

```
LIST BY custident BY ski_num BY date_out ski_rent_paid
        SUBTOTAL FOR (ski_num,custident);
```

The report is illustrated in Figure 17.7. The SUBTOTAL FOR (ski_num,custident) parameter in the LIST command caused a subtotal to print for the ski_num and the custident, rather than for all the BY clauses, which is the default.

```
Page       1




                    SUM
    SKI INVENTORY    SKI
       NUMBER     RENT PAID
    --------------  ---------
     19023433     $1,569.50
     19545390     $8,439.00
     24592030    $10,008.00
     30900000       $569.50
     49204500     $1,522.00
                 ===========
                 $22,108.00
```

Figure 17.8 Report with Calculated Grand Total

TOTAL

TOTAL calculates and prints a grand total for an object. The report that provides information on rental revenue for each pair of skis and the information on the total rental revenue requires the use of the TOTAL object modifier. The following statement illustrates the use of TOTAL:

```
LIST BY ski_num SUM(ski_rent_paid) AS $99,999.99 TOTAL;
```

The report is shown in Figure 17.8. For the line that is totaled, double dashes print automatically on the line immediately above the total value. The total value prints using the display format of the object being totaled. When the total value exceeds the size set by the display format, NOMAD prints a line of asterisks.

If the total cannot fit on the report column of the original item, use the AS modifier to change the display format. (This is what we did in our example.)

TOTAL ALL

The TOTAL modifier may be applied globally to all numeric objects in the LIST request. To do this, use the TOTAL ALL modifier. For example,

```
LIST BY ski_num SUM(ski_rent_paid)
    SUM(ski_pre_paid) TOTAL ALL;
```

Here, TOTAL ALL generates totals for both SUM(ski_rent_paid) and SUM(ski_pre_paid).

RECOMP

RECOMP recalculates subtotals and total values for objects that involve computations such as report functions and expressions.

```
Page       1

                   AVG
SKI INVENTORY      SKI
   NUMBER       RENT PAID
---------------  ---------
 19023433        $156.95
 19545390        $167.53
 24592030        $164.06
 30900000        $284.75
 49204500        $217.43
                ===========
                 $990.72
```

Figure 17.9 Report Displaying Calculated Total of Average Rental Revenues

```
Page       1

                   AVG
SKI INVENTORY      SKI
   NUMBER       RENT PAID
---------------  ---------
 19023433        $156.95
 19545390        $167.53
 24592030        $164.06
 30900000        $284.75
 49204500        $217.43
                ===========
                 $176.86
```

Figure 17.10 Report Generated with the RECOMP Modifier

Consider the following example. The ski shop owners would like to have a report that prints average rental earnings for each pair of skis and the global average for all skis in the rental pool. Executing the following LIST statement:

```
LIST BY ski_num AVG(ski_rent_paid) AS 99,999.99 TOTAL;
```

will create the report shown in Figure 17.9.

This report shows $990.72 (a total of average revenues), which is not the global average required in the report. To create the report that the ski shop owners require, we need to execute the following statement:

```
LIST BY ski_num AVG(ski_rent_paid) AS 99,999.99 RECOMP TOTAL;
```

The resulting report is shown in Figure 17.10. RECOMP recalculates the reported AVERAGE by dividing the grand total of rentals revenue by the total transactions count.

When used with the FIRST, LAST, MIN, or MAX report function, RECOMP retrieves the appropriate value from all the instances of the object. RECOMP does not affect the SUM, NUMBER, and COUNT report functions.

```
Page      1


SKI INVENTORY       SKI
   NUMBER       RENT PAID
--------------    ---------
03459940          $123.00
03459940          $245.50
03459940         $1120.00
                 ---------
  $              $1488.50


■■■■■■■■■■■■■■■■■■■■■■■■■■■■■■■■■

Page      2


SKI INVENTORY       SKI
   NUMBER       RENT PAID
--------------    ---------
13499940         $2123.00


■■■■■■■■■■■■■■■■■■■■■■■■■■■■■■■■■

Page      3


SKI INVENTORY       SKI
   NUMBER       RENT PAID
--------------    ---------
23900000          $643.00
23900000          $759.00
23900000         $5127.00
                 ---------
  $              $6529.00
```

Figure 17.11   Report with the BY Clause with Optional Parameters DUP and NEWPAGE

BY Clause

Three other optional parameters are:

1. DUP—Prints the current BY-item value on each line of the report.
2. NEWPAGE—Begins a new report page each time the value of the BY-item changes.
3. SKIP[n]—Skips *n* lines in the report each time the BY-item value changes. When you use the SKIP parameter without specifying *n*, it defaults to SKIP 1. If you specify SKIP 0, LIST suppresses the extra report line skipped after a subtotal value.

The following statement illustrates the use of the DUP and the NEWPAGE parameters:

```
LIST BY ski_num DUP NEWPAGE SKIP[0] ski_rent_paid SUBTOTAL;
```

The report created by this statement is shown in Figure 17.11. This report has three pages. The ski_num is printed on all lines of the report. Each time the value of ski_num changes, the report starts on a new page.

ACROSS Clause

The ACROSS clause sorts data in ascending order and displays them in columns across the pages of the report.

In Chapter 16, when describing the CREATE command through examples of its use, we considered the following required parameters:

1. ACROSS—A keyword that begins an ACROSS clause and causes sorting by the item specified directly after the ACROSS keyword.
2. Item—An item or defined item in a currently active database that the LIST command uses to sort the data in a report. It prints in the report's column headings.
3. Object—An item, report function, or expression that specifies the data to appear in the body of the report.

We also described some optional parameters:

1. DESC—Sorts the values of the item in the ACROSS clause in descending order across the report page.
2. ROWTOT—Computes the total of a numeric object in an ACROSS clause and prints it as an extra column at the end of the report. If ROWTOT ALL is specified, the totals for all objects in the ACROSS clause are calculated and printed.

Some additional parameters that we now consider are as follows:

1. Object modifiers—Specify how NOMAD should total numeric items in the ACROSS clause. The ACROSS clause object modifiers are the same as the object modifiers for the Object clause. Recall that the Object clause specifies the database values and information to appear in a report. (We discussed these at the beginning of this chapter.)
2. DUP—Causes the current ACROSS item value to be printed in each column heading of the report. For example,

```
LIST BY date_out ACROSS technician
     SUM(ski_rent_paid)
     SUM(boot_rent_paid) DUP;
```

The ACROSS item is technician. The value of this item, in our application, is a specific technician's initials (AF, GW, or WW). Because the DUP parameter is specified, the requested report will have an appropriate initial in each column heading.

3. NOPRINT—Suppresses the printing of the ACROSS item values in the column headings.
4. ENDAC—Terminates an ACROSS clause and re-establishes sorting within the preceding BY clause of a LIST request.

```
     SKI         SKI         SKI         SKI         SKI         SKI
   RENT PAID   RENT PAID   RENT PAID   RENT PAID   RENT PAID   RENT PAID
   ---------   ---------   ---------   ---------   ---------   ---------

================================================================

Page       1.2


     VI
     SUM
     SKI
   RENT PAID
   ---------
```

Figure 17.12   Column Headings Generated with the Multiple ACROSS Clauses

Multiple ACROSS clauses and multiple objects in the ACROSS clause can be specified. For example, assume that two technicians (their initials are AF and GW) are renting the ski equipment, and that six values (MC, DL, MX, VI, ST, and OT) identify the ski types (values of the ident_type item). We want to report the rental fee collected by each technician for each ski type. The statement

```
LIST BY date_out ACROSS technician ACROSS ident_type
              SUM(ski_rent_paid);
```

has two ACROSS clauses. The second ACROSS clause has two objects. The report produced by this statement will have twelve columns. The column headings generated for this report are shown in Figure 17.12.

When multiple objects are specified in an ACROSS clause, a column prints every time the ACROSS item value changes. Note that if you specify multiple ACROSS clauses in a LIST request, the data for each item is sorted within the item of the preceding ACROSS clause. Each column then has multiline headings that list the item values, in order, according to the priority of the sort. Note also that the page numbers become 1.1 and 1.2 as the report becomes too wide and is wrapped.

The following statement produces a report for which column headings are shown in Figure 17.13 (assume again that we have two technicians):

```
LIST BY date_out ACROSS technician SUM(ski_rent_paid)
        SUM(boot_rent_paid) SUM (pole_rent_paid) DUP;
```

Since the DUP parameter is used, the values of the technician are printed in all columns of the report.

If the DUP parameter in this statement is replaced with the NOPRINT parameter, the printing of the values for the item technician (in all of the columns of the report) will be suppressed.

When specifying ACROSS clauses, two restrictions must be considered:

1. You cannot precede an ACROSS clause with any object-item except a report function because LIST produces a disjointed report. (Disjointed reports are described in the next section of this chapter.)

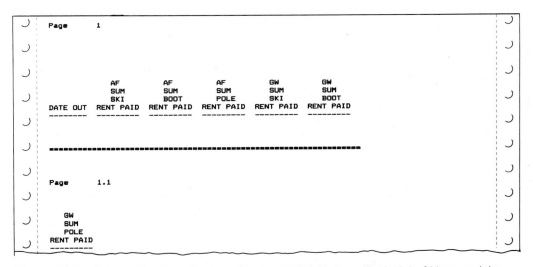

```
Page       1




              AF          AF          AF          GW          GW
              SUM         SUM         SUM         SUM         SUM
              SKI         BOOT        POLE        SKI         BOOT
DATE OUT   RENT PAID   RENT PAID   RENT PAID   RENT PAID   RENT PAID
--------   ---------   ---------   ---------   ---------   ---------



============================================================


Page       1.1


   GW
   SUM
   POLE
RENT PAID
---------
```

Figure 17.13 Column Headings Produced by the ACROSS Clause with Multiple Objects and the DUP Parameter

A report function can precede an ACROSS clause because the report function returns a single value and does not cause a disjointed report. For example,

```
LIST MAX(ski_rent_paid) ACROSS technician
     SUM(ski_rent_paid);
```

The MAX report function computes a single maximum value, which prints down the page of the report. Formatting of the report is automatically correct. The MAX single value is related to the other single values appearing within the report's columns, which run across the page of the report.

2. An ACROSS clause cannot precede a BY clause. Recall that the keyword "BY" causes the item values to be sorted and printed *down* the page. The keyword "ACROSS" causes the appropriate item values to be printed *across* the page. The values in BY have to relate to values in ACROSS, which generates appropriate intersections in the body of the report. Otherwise, the report will be disjointed and an error message will appear. For example,

```
LIST ACROSS ski_type
     SUM(ski_rent_paid) BY date_out;
```

is an invalid LIST command.

Now, let us say that we need to create the report shown in Figure 17.14. The command that generates this report is:

```
LIST ACROSS technician AVG(ski_rent_paid)
     ENDAC AVG(ski_rent_paid);
```

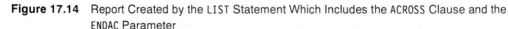

```
    Page     1


      AF           GW
      AVG          AVG          AVG
      SKI          SKI          SKI
  RENT PAID    RENT PAID    RENT PAID
  ---------    ---------    ---------
    $248.80      $198.50      $205.60
```

Figure 17.14   Report Created by the LIST Statement Which Includes the ACROSS Clause and the ENDAC Parameter

Note that to generate this report we use the ENDAC parameter. The ENDAC parameter terminates an ACROSS clause.

The last column of the report shows the average of all the rental transactions in the TRANSACTIONS master (average value for all the rental fees collected). The ENDAC parameter is necessary to terminate the ACROSS clause, so that the average of all of the appropriate data can be calculated.

Disjointed Reports

A report is *disjointed* when the data values printed on the same line of the report are not related. The idea is to combine data that relate generally, but not necessarily line by line.

Note that a disjoint report is easy to misinterpret if it is not titled correctly and labeled with the appropriate column headings.

Disjoint reports are created when you specify:

1. An object clause before the first BY clause in a LIST statement. For example,

   LIST SKI_RENT_PAID BY DATE_OUT;

   generates a report that lists, in its first column, the fees paid for the ski rental. This listing is in the order in which it is stored in the TRANSACTIONS master. The values for the date of the rental are listed in a sorted order, in the second column of the report, and may not relate to the values printed on the same detail line of the first column.

2. The LIST keyword in a LIST statement. For example,

   LIST BY DATE_OUT SUM(SKI_RENT_PAID) LIST
        BY SKI_NUM SUM(SKI_RENT_PAID);

   generates two adjacent reports. The first two columns show rental date and daily rental fees sorted by rental date. The next two columns show the ski inventory number and ski rental fees for a specific pair of skis, sorted by ski inventory number. On each of the detail lines of the report, the values in the first two columns are not related to the values of the last two columns.

Printing or Creating a File Copy of a Report

Reports produced by a LIST statement are displayed in the List window. This is done by default. To change this default and to direct a report to a printer or a file instead of the screen, you can specify the ON modifier (with the destination device) at the end of the LIST statement. Then the report prints at the specified destination device and does not appear in the List window.

To produce a report copy at the printer, specify ON PRN or ON PTR at the end of the LIST statement. For example,

```
LIST BY date_out SUM(ski_rent_paid) ON PTR;
```

creates a hard copy (printed) report that lists rental dates and daily ski rental fees.

To create a copy of the report on the external file, specify the filename after the ON modifier at the end of the LIST statement. In this case, each line of the report becomes a record in the generated file. Also, prior to using the file, issue a FILE command to connect the filename to the physical file on the disk. For example,

```
FILE DEFINE ski_fee_report = c:\ski\skirpt.fil;
LIST BY date_out SUM(ski_rent_paid) ON ski_fee_report;
```

Here, the FILE command establishes a file identification for the ski_fee_report file, which is the name used with the ON modifier in the LIST statement. The actual physical file generated on disk c in the directory ski is skirpt.fil.

If you do not issue a FILE command, NOMAD issues one for you. NOMAD uses the first eight characters of the filename specified after ON and automatically gives it the extension .FIL.

If desired, you can assign the destination device for all your reports by changing the value of the system &variable &LISTON. This change can be done within a procedure or from the Command window, before issuing the LIST request. If you specifically set the &LISTON, NOMAD directs all subsequent LIST statements outputs to the specified device until you reassign the &LISTON variable or return this system &variable to its screen default. For example,

```
&LISTON = 'PTR';
LIST BY date_out SUM(ski_rent_paid);
```

Here, the specified report is to be output to the printer. All subsequent reports created by any other LIST statements are also directed to the printer.

Screening Options

Quite often you need to limit the number of records to be printed in the reports. That is, you need to screen your data. There are two ways to do this.

First, you can limit access to the data before the report is produced. This is done with the help of the SELECT command (as discussed in Chapter 13). This can also be done with the WHERE screening option of the LIST command. The WHERE parameter screens the NOMAD database records to be retrieved and printed in a report. It applies to the entire LIST request.

Second, you can limit the printing of records but not the access. This is done with the screening options of the LIST statement. The screening options provide ways of reducing the data that are initially retrieved for a report. Only the data values that meet the criteria or limits specified by the screening options will appear in the report. These screening options are:

■ LIMIT n—Specifies the number of lines (*n*) to print in a report.

■ OUTPUT WHERE—Establishes the screening criteria that control the printing of lines in a report. It is specified with a logical expression.

WHERE

You can only use the WHERE option once in a LIST statement. Whenever NOMAD retrieves data from the database, it evaluates the WHERE logical expression. If the result of the logical expression is true, the data is included; otherwise, the data is excluded. WHERE follows the last item in the LIST request. Although WHERE can contain only one logical expression, logical connectors can be used to test for several conditions.

For example, the following LIST statement extracts and lists only rental fees that are greater than or equal to $100.00 and then subtotals them.

```
LIST BY ski_num ski_rent_paid SUBTOTAL
     WHERE ski_rent_paid GE 100;
```

LIMIT n

This option allows you to limit the number of detail lines to be printed in the report. This option can be very handy when you want to verify, for example, the format of the report or the format of the calculated and reported values. Under such circumstances you do not need to print test reports that include all the records retrieved for reporting.

With LIMIT n, the line count is performed after NOMAD gathers and sorts the report data. This line count does not include lines generated by such modifiers and options as HEADING, TITLE, SUBTOTAL, BYFOOT, and BYHEAD. Multilines created by modifiers such as FOLD, LINE, OVER, and SKIP are considered to be one line in the count. (We describe these modifiers in Chapter 18.)

The use of the LIMIT parameter is illustrated in the following statement:

```
LIST BY ski_num ski_rent_paid SUBTOTAL LIMIT 5;
```

```
  Page      1


  SKI INVENTORY      SKI
     NUMBER      RENT PAID
  -------------   ---------
   00349890        $123.50
                    $85.00
                   $150.00
                   --------
        $          $358.50

   10023000         $90.00
                   $180.00
                   --------
        $          $270.00

   24590000        $143.50
```

Figure 17.15   Report Created by the LIST Statement Which Includes the LIMIT Parameter

The report produced by this statement is shown in Figure 17.15. The LIMIT 5 parameter present in the LIST request that creates this report limits the number of detail lines printed on the report to the first five. Lines created by modifiers, that is, lines of dashes, subtotals, and skip lines, are not counted.

OUTPUT WHERE

If the OUTPUT WHERE parameter (specified with a logical expression) is present in the LIST request, NOMAD evaluates the OUTPUT WHERE expression before printing a detail line. If the logical expression is TRUE, the detail line is printed. If the expression is FALSE, the detail line is not printed. However, the data in this detail line is included in totals and subtotals. You can only use &variables in the logical expression specified with the OUTPUT WHERE parameter.

To illustrate the use of this parameter, consider the following example. The ski shop owners are interested in obtaining a report that lists rental fees for each pair of skis that were rented together with boots. At the same time they want a display of subtotal and total rental fees for all rental transactions. The following statement produces required report:

```
LIST BY ski_num ski_rent_paid SUBTOTAL TOTAL
     boot_num NOPRINT SET &boot_num
     OUTPUT WHERE &boot_num NE &NAV;
```

The NOPRINT and SET options of the LIST command are described in Chapter 18. The report is shown in Figure 17.16.

Only those pairs of skis that were rented together with boots appear in the report as detail lines. The subtotal and total rental fees are calculated regardless of whether the skis were rented with or without boots. This is why the subtotal and total detail lines are not sums of the values appearing in the printed detail lines. Note that we use the &boot_num as an &variable in the logical expression specified with the OUTPUT WHERE parameter.

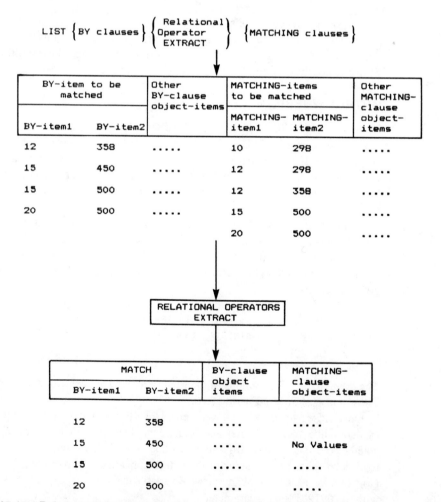

```
Page     1


SKI INVENTORY       SKI
    NUMBER       RENT PAID
--------------   ---------
00349890           $123.50
                   $150.00
                   ---------
  $                $358.50

10023000            $90.00
                   ---------
  $                $270.00

24590000           $145.50
                   =========
                   $774.00
```

Figure 17.16   Report Created by LIST Statement with OUTPUT WHERE Parameter

LIST {BY clauses} {Relational Operator / EXTRACT} {MATCHING clauses}

BY-item to be matched		Other BY-clause object-items	MATCHING-items to be matched		Other MATCHING-clause object-items
BY-item1	BY-item2		MATCHING-item1	MATCHING-item2	
12	358	.....	10	298	.....
15	450	.....	12	298	.....
15	500	.....	12	358	.....
20	500	.....	15	500	.....
			20	500	.....

RELATIONAL OPERATORS EXTRACT

MATCH		BY-clause object items	MATCHING-clause object-items
BY-item1	BY-item2		
12	358	.....	.....
15	450	.....	No Values
15	500	.....	.....
20	500	.....	.....

Figure 17.17   Relationship Between BY Clause and MATCHING Clause in the LIST Command

```
SKI INVENTORY MASTER            SKI RENTAL TRANSACTION MASTER
SKIINVENTORY                    TRANSACTIONS



SKI                             SKI                 SKI
SERIAL                SKI TYPE  SERIAL   DATE        FEE
NUMBER   SKI LENGTH   NAME      NUMBER   RENTED      PAID
SKINUM   SKI_LENGTH   ST_NAME   SKI_NUM  DATE_OUT    SKI_RENT_PAID
-------  ----------   --------  -------  --------    -------------
00134589     175      DYNAMICS SL  00134589  112389     $125.00
00256790     180      DYNAMICS SL  00134589  120189     $ 90.50
00445900     215      DYNAMICS DH  00134589  122789     $150.00
11335600     155      DYNASTAR SL  00256790  111589     $ 80.00
11555000     185      DYNASTAR SL  11555000  111089     $ 35.00
11659999     200      DYNASTAR SL  11555000  112089     $ 70.00
11778888     190      DYNASTAR GS  11555000  120189     $175.00
22298700     190      ROSSIGNOL SL 11778888  113089     $ 50.00
22349000     200      ROSSIGNOL GS 11778888  120389     $ 75.00
22789000     225      ROSSIGNOL DH 22298700  121589     $150.00
                                   22298700  122589     $ 30.00
                                   22600000  120189     $120.00
                                   22600000  123089     $ 80.00
                                   22789000  121589     $125.00
                                   22789000  122889     $125.00
                                   33000000  120589     $150.00
```

Figure 17.18   Content of the Selected Items in the Ski Inventory File and Rental Transactions File

Since we cannot use the item BOOT_NUM (the boot inventory number) in the logical expression, we use the SET parameter to assign the value to &BOOT_NUM. If the &BOOT_NUM value is not NOTAVAILABLE, the skis and boots are rented together. This is a condition for printing a detail line in the requested report.

Relational Operators

Relational operators are used to produce reports that contain data associated with equivalent items from two related masters. Each relational operator specifies different criteria for data to be included in the report.

Figure 17.17 shows the relationship imposed by a particular relational operator (EXTRACT) between items of one master (specified in a BY clause) and equivalent items of another master (specified in a MATCHING clause) of the LIST command.

The LIST command accepts multiple BY clauses and MATCHING clauses. The item of the first BY clause corresponds to the item of the first MATCHING clause; the item of the second BY clause corresponds to the item of the second MATCHING clause; and so on. Items being matched must have the same internal format.

Note that three of the four records have a match. The one that does not (15 450) will have no values brought from the second file.

NOMAD has several relational operators. To explain how they work, we show some examples of their use. We use the sets of data values that come from the ski inventory file and the rental transaction file of our Ski Rental System database. The fields needed in our examples and the content of the selected items in those files are given in Figure 17.18.

```
Page      1


SKI SERIAL                  SKI TYPE                      SKI RENT
NUMBER        SKI LENGTH    NAME              DATE OUT    PAID
-------       ----------    -----------       --------    --------
00134589             175    DYNAMICS SL       112389      $125.00
00256790             180    DYNAMICS SL       111589      $ 80.00
00445900             215    DYNAMICS DH
11335600             155    DYNASTAR SL
11555000             185    DYNASTAR SL       111089      $ 35.00
11659999             200    DYNASTAR SL
11778888             190    DYNASTAR GS       113089      $ 50.00
22298700             190    ROSSIGNOL SL      121589      $150.00
22349000             200    ROSSIGNOL GS
22789000             225    ROSSIGNOL DH      121589      $125.00
```

Figure 17.19   Output From the List Request Which Includes the EXTRACT Relational Operator

As you read the following sections, you may want to refer to the relationships imposed by particular relational operators (Figure 17.17) as well as to the data set shown in Figure 17.18.

EXTRACT

To illustrate the use of the EXTRACT operator in the LIST command, consider the following request from the the ski shop owners. They would like to obtain a report that lists all the skis in the inventory and prints the ski inventory number, ski type description, and ski length. This report is also to display the following information: whether or not the skis were ever rented, the date of the first rental transaction, and the amount of the rental fee collected in that transaction. As you can see, the request is for reporting on the items from both files, the ski inventory file and the rental transaction file. To create this report, we need to access all the records in the ski inventory file, but only the first matching record in the transaction file.

Let us now consider what can be accomplished with the EXTRACT relational operator. This operator retrieves all item values of the BY clause in the LIST command (with their associated object data). It extracts only the first item value of the MATCHING clause that is the same as the BY value (with its corresponding object data).

We can use the EXTRACT relational parameter to do exactly what is required in the report requested by the ski shop owners. The following LIST command will do the job:

```
LIST BY skinum ski_length st_name
     EXTRACT MATCHING ski_num date_out ski_rent_paid;
```

The report is shown in Figure 17.19.

The EXTRACT operator shows all the records from the BY clause and only the first matching record from the MATCHING clause. Blanks occur when EXTRACT cannot match item values between masters. For example, DYNASTAR SL serial number

```
Page      1

                                              SUM
     SKI SERIAL              SKI TYPE         SKI RENT
     NUMBER      SKI LENGTH  NAME             PAID
     ------      ----------  ----------------  --------
     00134589         175    DYNAMICS SL      $365.50
     00256790         180    DYNAMICS SL      $ 80.00
     00445900         215    DYNAMICS DH
     11335600         155    DYNASTAR SL
     11555000         185    DYNASTAR SL      $280.00
     11659999         200    DYNASTAR SL
     11778888         190    DYNASTAR GS      $125.00
     22298700         190    ROSSIGNOL SL     $180.00
     22349000         200    ROSSIGNOL GS
     22789000         225    ROSSIGNOL DH     $250.00
```

Figure 17.20 Output From the List Request with the EXTRACT ALL Relational Operator

11335600 has never been rented (there is no rental transaction record for this pair of skis). Also, the skis that are not in the inventory but are in the rental transactions file are not included in the report, for example, a pair of skis with serial number 22600000.

EXTRACT ALL

Assume that the ski shop owners would like to see a report that lists the following information for all skis in the inventory: ski serial number, ski length, ski type description, and appropriate total rental fees collected to date. This listing is to be by ski serial number.

To create such a report, we have to include all the matching records from the MATCHING clause (ski_num; ski serial number from TRANSACTIONS master) by using the EXTRACT ALL relational operator. This operator extracts all item values of the BY clause and all item values of the MATCHING clause that are equivalent to each BY value.

The following statement creates the required report:

```
LIST BY skinum ski_length st_name
     EXTRACT ALL MATCHING ski_num SUM(ski_rent_paid);
```

The report (shown in Figure 17.20) lists all the records from the SKIINVENTORY master and summarizes all the matching records from the TRANSACTIONS master.

Note, for example, the difference between total rental revenue in Figures 17.19 and 17.20 for the skis with the ski serial number 11555000. In Figure 17.19, the total is $35.00 because we used the EXTRACT operator, which only retrieved the first occurrence of the matching records. In Figure 17.20 the total is $280.00 because we used the EXTRACT ALL operator, which retrieved all the occurrences of the matching records.

The rental transaction records for the skis that do not exist in the inventory file are not included in the report.

```
   Page      1

                                                  SUM
        SKI SERIAL                 SKI TYPE        SKI RENT
        NUMBER      SKI LENGTH     NAME            PAID
        ------      ----------     ------------    --------
        00134389           175     DYNAMICS SL     $365.50
        00256790           180     DYNAMICS SL     $ 80.00
        00445900           215     DYNAMICS DH
        11335600           155     DYNASTAR SL
        11555000           185     DYNASTAR SL     $280.00
        11659999           200     DYNASTAR SL
        11778888           190     DYNASTAR GS     $125.00
        22298700           190     ROSSIGNOL SL    $180.00
        22349000           200     ROSSIGNOL GS
        22600000                                   $200.00
        22789000           225     ROSSIGNOL DH    $250.00
        33000000                                   $150.00
```

Figure 17.21   Output From the LIST Command with MERGE Relational Operator

MERGE

Now, assume that a report is requested that displays rental totals collected for each pair of skis listed in the rental transaction file. The rental transaction is to be reported even if the data on a given pair of skis does not exist in the inventory file. The ski type name and the ski length, if available, are also to be printed. The MERGE relational operator is useful for this type of report.

MERGE selects all the item values of both the BY and the MATCHING clauses, regardless of the match between item values of the two masters.

The following LIST statement produces the required report:

```
LIST BY skinum ski_length st_name
     MERGE MATCHING ski_num SUM(ski_rent_paid);
```

The output from this LIST request is shown in Figure 17.21

In this report, the use of the MERGE operator allows you to display all the records from the BY clause (SKIINVENTORY master) and all the records from the MATCHING clause (TRANSACTIONS master), regardless of a match. Blanks in the columns of the report can occur when:

- The pair of skis in the inventory was never rented.

- The pair of skis was rented but is not listed in the inventory. For example, a pair of damaged skis may have been removed from the inventory, but the skis were rented before the damage was incurred.

In the report in Figure 17.21, for example, the pair of DYNASTAR SL with serial number 11335600 was never rented, and the pair of skis with serial number 22600000 was rented twice (see Figure 17.18), even though it does not now exist in the inventory.

```
Page       1


SKI SERIAL              SKI TYPE
NUMBER       SKI LENGTH NAME
------       ---------- --------------------
00445900            215 DYNAMICS DH
11335600            155 DYNASTAR SL
11659999            200 DYNASTAR SL
22349000            200 ROSSIGNOL GS
```

Figure 17.22   Output From the LIST Command with REJECT Relational Operator

REJECT

Suppose that the ski shop owners want a report on all the skis in the inventory that have never been rented. This report can be generated by using the REJECT relational operator.

The REJECT operator extracts only the item values of the BY clause that have no match with item values of the MATCHING clause. The following LIST statement shows the use of the REJECT operator in a LIST request:

```
LIST BY skinum ski_length st_name
     REJECT MATCHING ski_num;
```

The produced report (shown in Figure 17.22) lists all the pairs of skis in the inventory that were never rented.

SUBSET

Consider the request to list only pairs of skis (from the ski inventory file) that were rented at least once. The rental date as well as the rental fee collected for the first rental occurrence should appear in the report. The LIST request that includes the SUBSET relational operator will do this job.

SUBSET extracts only those values of the BY clause that match item values of the MATCHING clause. Only the first item value of the MATCHING clause appears in the report.

The following statement shows the use of SUBSET operator in the LIST request:

```
LIST BY skinum ski_length st_name
     SUBSET MATCHING ski_num date_out ski_rent_paid;
```

The report generated by this request is shown in Figure 17.23. Note that all the pairs of skis that were never rented do not appear in this report (see Figure 17.22).

SUBSET ALL

Suppose now that the ski shop owners requested a report that lists only those pairs of skis from the ski inventory file that were rented at least once. The date of rental

```
Page      1


SKI SERIAL                    SKI TYPE                         SKI RENT
NUMBER        SKI LENGTH      NAME                DATE OUT     PAID
-------       ----------      --------------------  --------   --------
00134589             175      DYNAMICS SL         112389       $125.00
00256790             180      DYNAMICS SL         111589       $ 80.00
11555000             185      DYNASTAR SL         111089       $ 35.00
11778888             190      DYNASTAR GS         113089       $ 50.00
22298700             190      ROSSIGNOL SL        121589       $150.00
22789000             225      ROSSIGNOL DH        121589       $125.00
```

Figure 17.23 Output from the LIST Request with the SUBSET Relational Operator

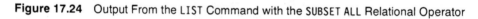

```
Page      1


SKI SERIAL                    SKI TYPE                         SKI RENT
NUMBER        SKI LENGTH      NAME                DATE OUT     PAID
-------       ----------      --------------------  --------   --------
00134589             175      DYNAMICS SL         112389       $125.00
                     175      DYNAMICS SL         120189       $ 90.50
                     175      DYNAMICS SL         122789       $150.00
00256790             180      DYNAMICS SL         111589       $ 80.00
11555000             185      DYNASTAR SL         111089       $ 35.00
                     185      DYNASTAR SL         112089       $ 70.00
                     185      DYNASTAR SL         120189       $175.00
11778888             190      DYNASTAR GS         113089       $ 50.00
                     190      DYNASTAR GS         120389       $ 75.00
22298700             190      ROSSIGNOL SL        121589       $150.00
                     190      ROSSIGNOL SL        122589       $ 30.00
22789000             225      ROSSIGNOL DH        121589       $125.00
                     225      ROSSIGNOL DH        122889       $125.00
```

Figure 17.24 Output From the LIST Command with the SUBSET ALL Relational Operator

and the rental fee for all the rental occurrences should appear in the report. The LIST command that includes the SUBSET ALL operator will create a report displaying this requested information.

The SUBSET ALL operator includes only those values of the BY clause that match item values of the MATCHING clause. All the matching item values of the MATCHING clause appear in the report. For example,

```
LIST BY skinum ski_length st_name
     SUBSET ALL MATCHING ski_num date_out ski_rent_paid;
```

The report produced by this LIST request is given in Figure 17.24. All the matching records appear in this report. For example, a pair of DYNAMICS SL skis with serial number 00134589 occurs three times in the rental transactions file. It is listed three times in the report.

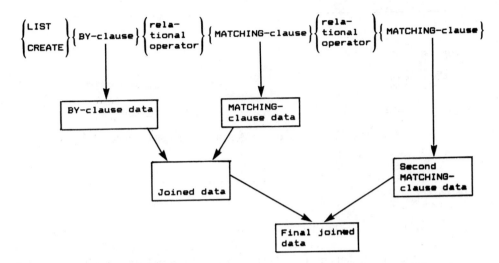

Figure 17.25 Processing Order in the LIST Command with Multiple Relational Operators

Multiple Relational Operators and MATCHING Clauses

You can use multiple relational operators and multiple MATCHING clauses in one LIST command. The relational operators are processed individually, working from left to right within the request.

When NOMAD finishes evaluating a relational operator, it matches the results with the data obtained from the previous relational operation. Only the first relational operator in the LIST command uses the BY clause data.

Figure 17.25 shows the processing sequence that occurs when a LIST command with multiple relational operators is executed.

To illustrate the use of the LIST command with multiple relational operators, let us create a report that lists the serial numbers for the pairs of skis that do not exist in the ski inventory file. The total rental fees for all the rental occurrences in the rental transactions file should appear in the report.

This report is created by using the LIST statement with multiple relational operators as follows:

```
LIST BY ski_num REJECT MATCHING skinum
EXTRACT ALL ski_num SUM(ski_rent_paid);
```

The report (shown in Figure 17.26) lists only total rental fees for the pairs of skis that are not in the inventory file.

```
Page      1

              SUM
SKI SERIAL  SKI RENT
NUMBER      PAID
------      --------
22600000    $200.00
33000000    $150.00
```

Figure 17.26   Output From the LIST Command with Multiple Relational Operators

17.3 SUMMARY

Creating standard reports with a 4GL such as NOMAD is simple and fast compared to creating the same standard reports with a 3GL.

Statements that create a standard report in NOMAD require only the use of the LIST command. The LIST command extracts the data from a database and generates a formatted report. Different types of standard reports can be generated with the many different parameters available for this command.

The basic LIST request consists of the word LIST followed by the items the user wants to include in a report.

LIST uses the headings, display formats, titles, justifications, and so on as specified within the descriptions of the items in the schema.

The LIST command automatically produces a report with page numbers, column spacing, page breaks, and all other formatting features.

There are many ways to specify the data selection, sort order, calculations, titles, headings for the report columns, and other reporting options. The LIST command offers this wide range of capabilities.

LIST generates a report directly on an output device such as a screen, printer, or disk. A report produced on a disk creates a file that is actually an electronic print image of the report.

This chapter considered the following topics:

- General LIST command syntax and usage
- Object modifiers
- Screening options
- Disjoint Reports
- Relational Operators
- Producing a printed or file copy of a report

EXERCISES

1. Assume that the values for the item in the following ACROSS clause are DW, TW, WW, HW, and GW. Specify column headings for the report generated with this LIST command:

   ```
   LIST BY date_out ACROSS technician SUM(ski_rent_paid)
                     SUM(boot_rent_paid) DUP;
   ```

2. What effect on the appearance of column headings of the LIST request in Problem 1 would the NOPRINT parameter have?

3. Is this a valid LIST command?

   ```
   LIST ACROSS technician SUM(ski_rent_paid) BY date_out;
   ```

4. What can follow the ENDAC parameter in the LIST request?

5. Specify column headings and the nature of the data to be printed in the body of the report when the following request is issued:

   ```
   LIST ACROSS film_desc AVG(box_office_rev) ENDAC
        AVG(box_office_rev);
   ```

   Note that the values for film_desc are Musical, Horror, and Comedy.

6. Briefly describe the restrictions that apply to the ACROSS clause as it is used in the LIST command.

7. Would this request generate an error message?

   ```
   LIST ski_type ACROSS technician SUM(ski_rent_paid)
        SUM(boot_rent_paid);
   ```

   Explain your answer.

8. Explain why the following request would generate a report that formats properly.

   ```
   LIST MAX(ski_rent_paid) ACROSS technician
        SUM(ski_rent_paid);
   ```

9. When would you generate a disjointed report?

10. Why are disjointed reports easy to misinterpret?

11. What type of a report is generated by this statement?

    ```
    LIST BY filename box_office_rev
         LIST BY director SUM(awards);
    ```

    Are the values in the first two columns related to the values in the last two?

12. What type of a report is generated by this request?

    ```
    LIST technician BY ski_code;
    ```

    Briefly describe the content of each of the columns of this report. Do values printed on the same detail line relate to each other?

13. What parameter do you need to use to redirect the generated report to the printer?

14. How do you write a report to an external file?

15. What is the &LISTON variable and how it can be used to redirect the output from the LIST request?

16. What is the effect of the &LISTON assignment on all subsequent LIST requests results?

17. Why would you use screening options in the LIST request? Give examples of reports from the database that would lend themselves to the use of screening options.

18. List all the screening options available in the LIST command, and briefly comment on the function of each.

19. Describe the report produced by this request:

    ```
    LIST BY ski_rent_fee DESC ski_type LIMIT 10;
    ```

20. Comment on why the OUTPUT WHERE parameter is useful in producing reports displaying totals and subtotals.

21. Why do you need to use an &variable in the logical expressions specified with the OUTPUT WHERE parameter?

22. Explain why NE &NAV is used in the following LIST request.

    ```
    LIST BY ski_num ski_rent_paid SUBTOTAL TOTAL
         boot_num NOPRINT SET &boot_num
         OUTPUT WHERE &boot_num NE &NAV;
    ```

23. Describe in detail the report generated by the statement:

    ```
    LIST BY ski_num ski_rent_paid SUBTOTAL TOTAL
         boot_num NOPRINT SET &boot_num
         OUTPUT WHERE &boot_num &NAV;
    ```

24. What is generated by this statement?

    ```
    LIST BY ski_num ski_rent_paid WHERE ski_rent_paid GE 500;
    ```

25. When would you use the EXTRACT relational operator?

26. Analyze the effect of the EXTRACT relational operator in this LIST request:

    ```
    LIST BY skinum ski_length st_name EXTRACT MATCHING
         date_out ski_rent_paid;
    ```

27. Comment on the difference between the effects of the EXTRACT and EXTRACT ALL relational operators in a LIST request.

28. Describe how the relational operator MERGE operates in the LIST command.

29. Create a LIST request that generates a report showing all of the skis that are in the INVENTORY master and counts the times the skis have been rented (from the TRANSACTIONS master). The columns of this report are to be:

```
SKI SERIAL        SKI TYPE        COUNT
NUMBER            NAME            RENT
```

30. For what types of reports would you use the SUBSET operator in the LIST request?

PROJECTS

1. For the State Parks Reservation system, create LIST requests that generate the following reports (designed for Project 1 in Chapter 10):

   ■ Campsite Availability Report

   ■ Daily Reservation Pending Report

   ■ Daily Site Use Report

   ■ Monthly Use Summary Report

   Use standard NOMAD reporting facilities.

2. For the Properties, Water Rights, and Leases System, create LIST requests that generate reports for Project 2 of Chapter 10. Use standard NOMAD reporting facilities.

3. Create all standard reports that you designed for the project your instructor arranged with a local business.

CHAPTER 18

Customized Reporting

Glendower: I can call spirits from the vasty deep.
Hotspur: Why so can I, or so can any man;
But will they come when you do call them?

Shakespeare, *Henry IV*

18.1 INTRODUCTION

This chapter considers how to control formats of report items. That is, we show how to control formats of titles, spacing, page breaks, footing, and so on.

We start with the formatting options for individual report items and continue with a discussion of global formatting that affects the entire report.

To practice the use of these commands, we complete the next stage of building the Ski Rental System and show how to construct all the necessary reports.

18.2 ITEM MODIFIERS AND FORMATTING OPTIONS

You can modify items that appear in BY, ACROSS, and Object clauses in the LIST command. Item modifiers are used for the following formatting functions:

Modifier	Function
AS	To change the display format of any item in the LIST command.
NOPRINT	To suppress the printing of the LIST items.
HEADING and HEADASIS	To modify column headings.
CENTER	To center data and column headings.
SET	To save results from one portion of the report for use elsewhere.

You can override report defaults so that the location of data on the report page is controlled. You can control the following:

■ Positioning items across a report page (COLUMN n and SPACE n formatting options).

```
Page      1


                      SUM
   SKI INVENTORY    SKI RENT
   NUMBER           PAID
   --------------   ----------

   00134900           $3,560.00
   00349999           $5,890.00
   12400000           $1,900.00
   16888888             $890.50
   23900000             $500.00
   45999000           $3,900.50
                      ==========
                     $16,641.00
```

Figure 18.1 Output From the LIST Command with the AS Modifier

■ Positioning items down a report page (FOLD n, LINE n, and OVER n formatting options).

■ Embedding character strings anywhere in the LIST command and controlling character string printing rules (DUP, SUBTOTAL, and TOTAL modifiers with character string).

Item Modifiers

Changing an Item Display Format

To change an item display format on a report, use the AS modifier followed by a new display format. The AS modifier also determines the internal data type of the expressions used in the LIST command, of the &variable types assigned with the SET parameter, and of the values maintained for totals.

Without an AS modifier, the components of an expression determine internal data formats. Internal data types affect rounding rules.

To illustrate the use of the AS modifier, consider the following LIST statement:

LIST BY ski_num SUM(ski_rent_paid) AS $99,999.99 TOTAL;

The report produced by this statement is shown in Figure 18.1.

If the AS modifier were not used in this LIST command, the format for SUM(ski_rent_paid) and the format for the grand total would be the same as those for ski_rent_paid as defined in the database schema, which is $999.99. This format is insufficient to hold values for SUM(ski_rent_paid) and the value for the grand total. That is why the AS modifier is needed.

Suppressing the Printing of LIST Items

In some cases, you may wish to use an item for sorting or some other use, but you do not wish to see it printed in the report. To suppress the printing of such items in a report, use the NOPRINT modifier.

```
   Page      1


      SUM
   SKI  RENT
   PAID
   ----------

   $3,560.00
   $5,890.00
   $1,900.00
     $890.50
     $500.00
   $3,900.50
   ==========
  $16,641.00
```

Figure 18.2   Output From the LIST Command with the NOPRINT Modifier

The following statement illustrates the use of the NOPRINT modifier:

```
LIST BY ski_num NOPRINT SUM(ski_rent_paid)
       AS $99,999.99 TOTAL;
```

The report created by this statement contains only one column. The report is shown in Figure 18.2. This report is printed in order by ski_num, but the NOPRINT modifier suppressed the printing of a column for this item.

Modifying Column Headings

NOMAD has two modifiers that can change a column heading. The HEADING modifier assigns a new column heading which overrides the default heading in the schema. This new heading is specified as a character string enclosed in quotes or as an alphanumeric item placed after the HEADING modifier.

To create multiline headings, use a colon to separate the lines. For example, the heading 'SKI:RENTAL:FEE' will be printed as a heading composed of three lines.

Recall that when the report function is used, NOMAD automatically includes the name of this function as a part of the column heading. See, for example, Figure 18.1, where the SUM report function is included in the heading of the second column. To suppress the printing of the report function in the heading, use the HEADASIS modifier. Note that the HEADING and HEADASIS modifiers cannot be specified for the same item.

The following LIST statement illustrates the use of heading modifiers:

```
LIST BY ski_num HEADING 'SERIAL CODE'
       SUM(ski_rent_paid) AS $99,999.99 HEADASIS
       TOTAL;
```

The report created by this LIST statement is shown in Figure 18.3. In this report, the first column has the heading 'SERIAL CODE', as specified in the HEADING modifier, and the HEADASIS modifier suppressed the printing of the report function (SUM) in the heading of the second column.

```
  Page     1


              SKI  RENT
  SERIAL CODE  PAID
  -----------  ----------

  00134900     $3,560.00
  00349999     $5,890.00
  12400000     $1,900.00
  16888888       $890.50
  23900000       $500.00
  45999000     $3,900.50
               ==========
              $16,641.00
```

Figure 18.3 Output From the LIST Command with the HEADING and HEADASIS Modifiers

Centering Data or Column Heading

Within report columns the alphanumeric fields are left-justified and numeric fields are right-justified. To override this default and center column headings or data within report columns, you can use the CENTER modifier.

The width of a report column equals the width of the data's display format or the width of the column heading, whichever is wider. The column heading width equals the width of the longest line in the heading. For example, the two-line heading 'SKI SERIAL:NUMBER' has a width of ten characters because, of the two-lines, SKI SERIAL is the longer line and it contains ten characters, including blank space. The other heading line, NUMBER will appear centered within this same width.

When the CENTER modifier is specified, NOMAD takes one of the following actions:

1. Centers the heading within the report column if the display format of the data is wider than the column heading.

2. Centers the data within the report column if the column heading is wider than the display format of the data.

The following LIST statement illustrates how the data or the heading is centered:

```
LIST BY ski_num CENTER SUM(ski_rent_paid) AS $99,999.99
     HEADING 'FEE:PAID' CENTER TOTAL;
```

The report resulting from this LIST statement is shown in Figure 18.4.

Because the heading of the first column is wider than the display format of the data, the width of the column is determined by the size of the heading and the data is centered within the column. Because the heading of the second column is narrower than the display format of the data, the width of the column is determined by the size of the data format and the column heading is centered over the data. The data starts in the left-most position.

```
Page    1


                      SUM
      SKI INVENTORY   FEE
        NUMBER        PAID
      --------------  ----------

        00134900     $3,560.00
        00349999     $5,890.00
        12400000     $1,900.00
        16888888      $890.50
        23900000      $500.00
        45999000     $3,900.50
                     ===========
                     $16,641.00
```

Figure 18.4   Output From the LIST Command with the CENTER Modifier

Saving LIST Command Items for Later Use in the Same Command

You may often need to save some of the information for use in a later part of the LIST command. For example, you may need to calculate and report rental fees for each pair of skis as a percentage of total rental fees. To be able to do this in a third-generation language, you must have your data read twice: first to calculate the total fee and second to calculate the percentages. In NOMAD, however, this is done in one LIST command with the SET modifier. The double reading of the file is completely transparent to the user. The SET modifier assigns values to &variables and stores the results for use in later calculations, as specified in the LIST command. The SET modifier can be used after an item in a BY clause or an Object clause.

If you use the SET modifier to assign a numeric value to an &variable, NOMAD automatically subtotals the values of the &variable within the preceding BY clause. If the value is alphanumeric, NOMAD assigns the last occurrence within the preceding BY clause to the &variable.

To understand the use of the SET modifier, consider the following LIST statement:

```
DECLARE &fee_total AS 99,999.99;
    DECLARE &fee_collected AS 99,999.99;

LIST SUM(ski_rent_paid) NOPRINT SET &fee_total
    BY ski_num
    ski_rent_paid NOPRINT SET &fee_collected
    (100 * &fee_collected/&fee_total) AS 999.99
    HEADING '% OF TOTAL:FEES COLLECTED';
```

The output from this LIST statement is shown in Figure 18.5.

In this example, the first SET modifier saves the total value of rental fees collected to date in the &variable &fee_total. This value will not be printed in the report because the NOPRINT modifier is specified. The second SET modifier saves

```
Page      1



SKI INVENTORY   % OF TOTAL
   NUMBER       FEES COLLECTED
-------------   --------------

    00134900         21.39
    00349999         35.39
    12400000         11.42
    16888888          5.36
    23900000          3.00
    45999000         23.44
```

Figure 18.5   Output From the LIST Command with the SET Modifier

the total of rental fees collected to date, for a given pair of skis, in the &variable &fee_collected. This value is not printed either.

The LIST command uses these two values to compute the expression (100 * &fee_collected/&fee_total) for each pair of skis that were rented to date. In the report a new column is generated containing the value of this expression.

Item Formatting Options

Positioning Items Across a Report Page

NOMAD offers several modifiers to position items across the page of the report. Two of the most often used modifiers are as follows:

1. COLUMN n (or COL n)—The number *n* specifies the page column in which you want the next item to print. If items overlap when COLUMN is used, the second item replaces the first. Overprinting does not occur.

2. SPACE n—This modifier specifies spacing (*n* spaces) between report columns. You can specify SPACE 0 to place columns next to each other with no space between them.

If you do not specify COLUMN n or SPACE n, the &RSPACE system variable value is used to establish the spacing between columns. (The default value for &RSPACE is 2 spaces.)

The following LIST statement illustrates the use of these two modifiers:

```
LIST BY ski_num SPACE 10 SUM(ski_rent_paid)
     COLUMN 50 MAX(ski_rent_paid);
```

The output from this statement is given in Figure 18.6.

The SPACE 10 modifier causes the values of the ski rental fees collected for a given pair of skis [SUM(ski_rent_paid)] to be printed 10 spaces to the right of the ski serial number value (ski_num). The COLUMN 50 modifier causes the maximum ski rental fee collected for one rental transaction for the specific pair of skis [MAX(ski_rent_paid)] to be printed starting in column 50.

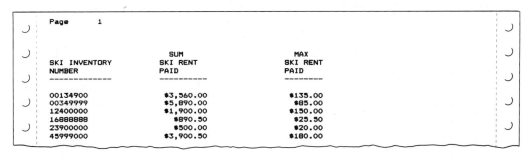

Figure 18.6   Output From the LIST Command with the COLUMN and SPACE Modifiers

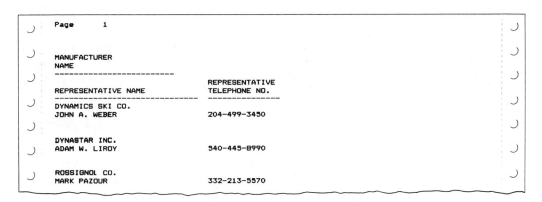

Figure 18.7   Output From the LIST Command with the FOLD Modifier

Positioning Items Down a Report Page

The positioning of print items down the page can be controlled in three ways:

1. The FOLD modifier—Places the next entry in column 1 on the following line. If you specify *n* with FOLD, the next entry prints *n* lines down from the current line. The column headings are also formatted according to the specified FOLDs. The use of the FOLD modifier is illustrated in the following LIST statement:

```
LIST BY manufact_name FOLD rep_name
     rep_telephon FOLD 3;
```

The FOLD following manufact_name tells NOMAD to print manufact_name and then skip to a new line before printing rep_name and rep_telephon. The FOLD 3 after rep_telephon causes NOMAD to skip two lines (three carriage returns) before printing the next occurrence of manufact_name. The column headings follow the same formatting rule. The generated report is shown in Figure 18.7.

```
Page      1



00123590  DYNAMICS SLALOM
     170  DYNAMICS SKI CO.
  $29.00

00349990  DYNAMICS DH.
     215  DYNAMICS SKI CO.
  $35.50

23899999  ROSSIGNOL SL.
     195  ROSSIGNOL INC.
  $28.00
```

Figure 18.8 Output From the LIST Command with the LINE Modifier

2. The LINE modifier—Places a character string or an item following LINE on the *n*th line in the first column and continues assigning consecutive column numbers to the next items in the LIST command. NOMAD ignores headings of items modified with the LINE modifier, unless specifically requested with the use of the HEADING modifier.

   The use of the LINE modifier to format a report is illustrated in the following example:

```
LIST LINE 1 BY skinum st_name
     LINE 2 ski_length sman_name
     LINE 3 ski_rentch FOLD 3;
```

   Here, LINE specifies the line number on which the items are to appear. No column heading is printed. The report resulting from this statement is shown in Figure 18.8.

3. The OVER modifier—Skips to the next report line and prints the next entry directly underneath the previous one. If you specify *n* with OVER, NOMAD skips *n* lines before printing the next entry. Column headings are also suppressed for the items modified by the OVER modifier. OVER differs from FOLD in that only one item (the one after the OVER modifier) prints one line below. All the other items print on the same line as the item before the OVER modifier (rather than one line down, as would be the case with the FOLD modifier).

   The use of the OVER modifier is illustrated in the following example:

```
LIST BY skinum ski_type OVER
     st_name ski_length ski_rentch;
```

   Here, ski_type prints over st_name. Also, LIST suppressed the column heading for the items that OVER modified, but not for the other items. The output is shown in Figure 18.9.

```
   Page     1



      SKI SERIAL                            SKI RENTAL
      NUMBER                   SKI LENGTH   CHARGE
      ----------               ----------   ----------
      00134990    SDYG               170    $28.00
                  DYNAMICS GS.
      00222390    SDYS               200    $30.00
                  DYNAMICS SLALOM
      11188000    SROS               195    $35.50
                  ROSSIGNOL SLALOM
```

Figure 18.9 Output From the LIST Command with the OVER Modifier

Embedding and Controlling the Printing of Character Strings

Character strings can be embedded anywhere in the LIST statement. They will appear in the report exactly as they appear in the LIST statement.

Character strings are treated as objects and can be modified by item and object modifiers such as HEADING and SUBTOTAL. The spacing set by the system variable &RSPACE is not used between a character string and the adjacent columns of data. To effect a space, embed spaces at the end of the character string.

Where character strings appear in a NOMAD report depends on where they were positioned in the LIST statement. NOMAD follows this convention:

1. Character strings specified *before* BY and Object clauses in a LIST statement will appear on every line of the report.

2. Character strings specified *after* BY and Object clauses in a LIST statement will appear each time the value of the item or object that immediately precedes the character string prints.

The following statement illustrates how to embed a character string in a report:

```
LIST '***' BY date_out ' Rental Fee Collected: '
           ski_rent_paid;
```

The character string '***' prints on every line of the report since it is specified before BY and Object clauses. The character string ' Rental Fee Collected: ' only prints when the value of the rental date (date_out) changes. There is no space between the character string and the adjacent columns unless *you* include it yourself, as it is in the example ' Rental Fee Collected: '. The report generated by this statement is given in Figure 18.10.

To control the printing of character strings and to override the NOMAD rule, you can place any of the following three modifiers after a character string:

```
Page      1


                             SKI RENTAL
        DATE OUT             CHARGE
        --------             ----------
    ###111589   Rental Fee Collected:  $150.50
    ###                                $89.00
    ###                                $125.00
    ###112089   Rental Fee Collected:  $245.00
    ###113089   Rental Fee Collected:  $155.00
    ###                                $230.00
    ###                                $35.00
```

Figure 18.10   Output From the LIST Command with Embedded Character String

```
Page      1



    SKI TYPE
    NAME
    ----------------------
    DYNAMICS DH         Length - 205 Rental Charge - $25.50
                        Length - 215 Rental Charge - $30.00
                        Length - 215 Rental Charge - $30.00
    DYNAMICS SLALOM     Length - 195 Rental Charge - $25.00
                        Length - 200 Rental Charge - $30.00
    DYNASTAR GS         Length - 200 Rental Charge - $35.00
                        Length - 205 Rental Charge - $35.00
    ROSSIGNOL SLALOM    Length - 200 Rental Charge - $35.00
```

Figure 18.11   Controlling the Printing of the Character String with the DUP Modifier

1. The DUP modifier—Forces the character string to be printed on every logical line of the report regardless of whether or not the preceding item or object prints. For example,

```
LIST BY st_name ' Length - ' DUP ski_length
    ' Rental Charge - ' ski_rentch;
```

The DUP modifier causes the character string ' Length - ' to print even when the value of the item ski type name (st_name) does not print. The report is shown in Figure 18.11.

2. The SUBTOTAL (ST) modifier—Prints when the value of an item in a preceding BY clause changes and when any subtotal lines print for that item. For example,

```
LIST BY ski_num ' ### ' SUBTOTAL
    ski_rent_paid SUBTOTAL;
```

The character string ' ### ' appears when the ski serial number (ski_num) changes and on a subtotal line. The output is shown in Figure 18.12.

3. The TOTAL (TOT) modifier—Causes the character string to print each time the value of a preceding LIST item changes and when the grand total line prints for that item.

```
 ⌣       Page      1                                                       ⌣

 ⌣                                                                         ⌣

         SKI SERIAL        SKI RENTAL
         NUMBER            CHARGE
 ⌣       ----------        ----------                                      ⌣
         00003440   ###        $86.00
                              $150.00
 ⌣                            $100.00                                      ⌣
                              --------
         $          ###       $336.00
 ⌣                                                                         ⌣
         01122200   ###       $180.00

 ⌣       02229900   ###       $240.00                                      ⌣
                              $160.00
                              --------
 ⌣       $          ###       $400.00                                      ⌣
```

Figure 18.12   Controlling the Printing of the Character String with the SUBTOTAL Modifier

---

18.3 REPORT FORMATTING OPTIONS

We have been concentrating on somewhat simple reports, that use many of NOMAD's defaults. However, the real world often presents nonstandard situations that may require you to change the default layout of the report. This is done with report formatting options.

Report formatting options allow global control of report parameters and creation of customized reports. These options affect the entire LIST request and can be specified individually or together at the end of the LIST statement. Here are some common formatting requirements:

■ Global control of the report attributes to override the general LIST formatting features (NOPAGENO, NOHEAD, CENTER ALL, HEADASIS ALL, LABELST, and LABELTOT report attributes).

■ Printing or performing calculations outside the detail lines of the report, that is, at the top or the bottom of each report page, or when control breaks occur, or in the end of the report (TITLE, FOOTING, BYHEAD, BYFOOT, and SUMMARY options).

■ Global control of printing items (NOPRINT ALL option).

■ Control of the printing operation (NOEJECT, FORMS, and STOP options).

Global Report Attributes

NOPAGENO

In some cases you may want to distribute individual pages of the report to different users and the page numbers actually can be misleading information. To suppresses the printing of page numbers, you can use the NOPAGENO report attribute. For example,

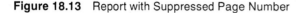

```
                   SUM
     SKI INVENTORY  SKI RENT
     NUMBER         PAID
     --------------  --------
       00239000      $689.00
       00590000      $954.00
       02389000      $800.00
       05909090      $980.50
```

Figure 18.13   Report with Suppressed Page Number

```
       00239000      $689.00
       00590000      $954.00
       02389000      $800.00
       05909090      $980.50
```

Figure 18.14   Report with Suppressed Page Number and Headings

```
LIST BY ski_num SUM(ski_rent_paid) NOPAGENO;
```

creates a report with no page numbers on it. (See Figure 18.13.)

NOHEAD

Similarly, if you want to suppress headings and page numbers at the top of each page, use the NOHEAD option. For example,

```
LIST BY ski_num SUM(ski_rent_paid) NOHEAD;
```

creates a report that contains no page numbers and no column headings. (See Figure 18.14.)

CENTER ALL and HEADASIS ALL

CENTER ALL and HEADASIS ALL are global modifiers that perform modifications on all report columns or functions. These modifiers work similarly to CENTER and HEADASIS, described at the beginning of this chapter.

The CENTER ALL modifier centers all columns. (As before, the column heading is centered over the data column if the data entry is wider than the heading. The data is centered if the column heading is wider than the data.)

The HEADASIS ALL modifier suppresses the report function name in the headings for all the columns generated by report functions.

The report generated by the following LIST statement illustrates the use of these two modifiers:

```
LIST BY ski_num SUM(ski_rent_paid)
       SUM(boot_rent_paid)
       CENTER ALL HEADASIS All;
```

```
Page      1


SKI INVENTORY  SKI RENT  BOOT RENT
   NUMBER        PAID       PAID
---------------  --------  ---------
   00239000     $689.00    $20.00
   00590000     $954.00    $90.50
   02389000     $800.00    $80.00
   05909090     $980.50    $35.00
```

Figure 18.15   Report Generated by the LIST Statement with the CENTER ALL and HEADASIS ALL Modifiers

```
Page      1

            TECHNICIAN  SKI RENT
DATE OUT    ID          PAID
--------    ----------  --------
112089      AF           $85.00
                         $60.00
                         $45.00
                        --------
$TOTAL AF               $190.00

            SW           $56.00
                        --------
$TOTAL 112089           $246.00

112589      AF           $74.00
                        ========
$Total Ski Fees         $320.00
```

Figure 18.16   Report Generated by the LIST Statement with the LABELST and LABELTOT Modifier

In this report, the data are centered in all three columns because the column headings are wider than the data. The report function (SUM) is removed from the heading of the second and third columns. The report is shown in Figure 18.15.

LABELST and LABELTOT

These modifiers are used to annotate the subtotal and total lines on the report.

The LABELST modifier creates a label using the value of the item for which the subtotal was calculated. This label prints on the subtotal line starting at column 1.

The LABELTOT modifier allows the user to annotate the total line with the user-defined character string. The printing of this character string starts at column 1 of the total line.

The use of both modifiers is illustrated in the following statement:

```
LIST BY date_out BY technician ski_rent_paid
     SUBTOTAL TOTAL LABELST
     LABELTOT 'Total Ski Fees';
```

Each subtotal line is automatically labeled by NOMAD with the character string '*TOTAL', followed by the value of the BY item (the value for which the total was calculated). The grand total line is labeled with the character string 'Total Ski Fees'. The generated report is shown in Figure 18.16.

Printing or Performing Calculations Outside the Detail Lines of the Report

TITLE

A title is the information you want to print at the top of each report page after the page number line. The information can consist of &variables values, expressions, and/or character strings. To print such information, you can use the TITLE clause. A blank line appears between the title and the heading lines unless you specify the NOSKIP parameter in the TITLE clause. The TITLE clause can consist of multiple lines, but only one TITLE clause can be specified for each LIST statement.

By default, the text of the title is centered over the report. To change the position of the text on the title line, use the LEFT, RIGHT, COLUMN, or SPACE modifiers. Multiple lines in the title can be positioned separately by using modifiers.

To illustrate the use of the TITLE option with some of the modifiers we described earlier, consider the following example:

```
LIST BY ski_num SUM(ski_rent_paid)
        TITLE 'SKI RENTAL FEES' FOLD 3
            LEFT 'MONTHLY REPORT' SPACE 5
            'PREPARED FOR: ALLEN FRANKEL';
```

This report has two lines in a title. The first line of the title ('SKI RENTAL FEES') is centered on the page of the report (default). The second line, created by FOLD 3, prints three lines down the page from the first title line and starts at the left margin of the report. There are two parts to the second line, separated by a space 5 characters long. The report is shown in Figure 18.17.

If we had multiple shops and wanted to have the name of the store or the store manager for whom this report is intended in the title (in the preceding example we only have one shop), we could use the following LIST statement:

```
LIST BY store_mgr SET &stm NOPRINT NEWPAGE
     BY ski_num SUM(ski_rent_paid)
     TITLE 'SKI RENTAL FEES' FOLD 3
         LEFT 'MONTHLY REPORT' SPACE 5
         'PREPARED FOR: ' &stm;
```

TITLE prints user information at the top of each page, whereas FOOTING prints it at the bottom of each page. LIST processes TITLE and FOOTING lines at the beginning of the next page rather than at the page on which they appear. Therefore, the values of the &variables assigned with SET reflect the values at the beginning of page $n+1$ in the TITLE and FOOTING on page n. If the BY clause modifier NEWPAGE advances to page $n+1$, TITLE and FOOTING use the &variable value last assigned on page n to print the value correctly on page n before advancing. On the last report page, TITLE and FOOTING show the last value of the assigned &variable.

```
Page 1
                        SKI RENTAL FEES

MONTHLY REPORT      PREPARED FOR: ALLEN FRANKEL

                        SUM
SKI INVENTORY   SKI RENT
NUMBER          PAID
--------------  --------
00239000        $689.00
00590000        $954.00
02389000        $800.00
05909090        $980.50
```

Figure 18.17   Report with the TITLE Option

```
Page        1

                        SUM
SKI INVENTORY   SKI RENT
NUMBER          PAID
--------------  --------
00239000        $689.00
00590000        $954.00
02389000        $800.00
05909090        $980.50

      Rental Fees
```

Figure 18.18   Report Created by the LIST Statement with the FOOTING Option

FOOTING

Typically FOOTING is used for footnotes or lines such as "CONFIDENTIAL." FOOTING prints the user text in the center of the line unless you specify COL, SPACE, LEFT, or RIGHT. It can consist of multiple lines, but only one FOOTING can be specified for each LIST statement.

The LIST statement skips one line between the body of the report and the first FOOTING line. To suppress this line, specify the NOSKIP option in the FOOTING clause.

The use of FOOTING to annotate a report is illustrated in the following statement:

```
LIST BY ski_num SUM(ski_rent_paid)
     FOOTING 'Rental Fees';
```

The character string 'Rental Fees' appears at the bottom of every page of the report. The report is shown in Figure 18.18.

BYHEAD

BYHEAD allows you to insert information or perform operations immediately before a value of the control break variable (a BY clause variable) changes to a new value.

Multiple BYHEAD modifiers can be specified for a BY item in one LIST statement. NEWPAGE and IF clauses can be used with BYHEAD modifiers. For example, if the IF expression in the BYHEAD modifier is true, NOMAD performs the associated operation. If you use multiple BYHEAD modifiers, the operations that are performed depend on the results of separate IF tests.

The SPACE, COLUMN, FOLD, and OVER formatting options can be used to format the report line created by BYHEAD.

When the &variable assigned with SET is used with BYHEAD, its value is equal to the first value of the &variable associated with a given value of a BY clause variable.

The use of the BYHEAD modifier is illustrated in the following statement:

```
DECLARE &ski_name AS A20;

LIST BY st_name NOPRINT SET &ski_name
    ski_length ski_rentch
    BYHEAD st_name FOLD 2
    '===================='
    FOLD &ski_name
    FOLD '====================';
```

In this report, all the skis of different length and the rental charges (per day) associated with them are listed under the appropriate ski names. The report is sorted by ski names (st_name). SET &ski_name stores the value of st_name for use in the BYHEAD. Whenever the value of the control break (st_name) changes, the formatting and printing specified in the BYHEAD is performed. One line is skipped because of FOLD 2. Then, a line of equal signs (=) is printed. On the next line, the value in &ski_name is printed, followed by another line of equal signs. The next line of the report starts immediately afterwards. The report is shown in Figure 18.19.

BYFOOT

BYFOOT specifies the information to be inserted or operations to be performed after the last line of data associated with a BY value (given value of the control variable). The BYFOOT modifier works similarly to the BYHEAD modifier. Thus all the rules and formatting options of the BYHEAD modifier apply to the BYFOOT modifier.

When used in BYFOOT, the value of the &variable (assigned by SET modifier) depends on the following:

```
Page       1


                SKI RENTAL
SKI LENGTH   CHARGE
----------   ----------


====================
DYNAMICS SLALOM
====================
        185      $25.50
        200      $30.00
        195      $28.00
        175      $22.00

====================
DYNASTAR GS
====================
        195      $30.00
        200      $35.00
        205      $35.00
        210      $38.00

====================
DYNASTAR SLALOM
====================
        195      $30.00
        200      $35.00
```

Figure 18.19   Report Illustrating the BYHEAD Modifier

1. If the &variable is alphanumeric or numeric with a NOSUBTOTAL modifier specified, the value of the &variable is the last value assigned by the SET for a given value of the BY clause variable.

2. If the &variable is numeric without a NOSUBTOTAL modifier specified, the value of the &variable is the current subtotal of all values assigned by the SET for a given value of the BY clause variable.

The following LIST statement illustrates the use of the BYFOOT modifier:

```
DECLARE &paid AS 99,999.99;

LIST BY ski_num  ski_rent_paid SET &paid
     BYFOOT ski_num
     (IF &paid GT 100 THEN '** GOOD RENTAL' ELSE ' ')
     FOLD 2;
```

This report lists rental skis by their number and the amount of the rental fee collected. &paid stores the total value of ski_rent_paid for the given ski type, to be used in the BYFOOT. Whenever the value of ski_num changes, the formatting specified in the BYFOOT is performed. If the total rental fee collected is greater than $100.00 (IF &paid GT 100), the character string '** GOOD RENTAL' prints; otherwise, a blank space prints and two lines are skipped. The report is shown in Figure 18.20.

```
   Page       1

   SKI INVENTORY  SKI RENT
   NUMBER         PAID
   --------------  --------
   12121212        $105.00
                    $17.00
                    $25.50
   ** good rental

   12121223        $25.50

   12345678         $70.00
                    $70.00
                   $175.00
                    $70.00
                    $70.00
                   $105.00
                   $175.00
       ** good rental
```

Figure 18.20   Report Illustrating the Use of the BYFOOT Formatting Option

SUMMARY

SUMMARY specifies the information to be printed or calculated in the end of the report. We can repeat the SUMMARY option within a LIST command.

The NEWPAGE modifier and IF clause can be used with the SUMMARY option. For example, we can specify NEWPAGE (to start printing a new page) with an IF clause that tests the conditions before the lines of the SUMMARY print. If the IF expression is true, NOMAD performs the associated SUMMARY operation.

The SPACE, COLUMN, FOLD, and OVER formatting options can be used to format report lines from the SUMMARY option. The SUMMARY option can contain &variables, expressions, and character strings.

The &variable value assigned with SET used in the SUMMARY option is the last &variable value (for the alphanumeric &variable or for the numeric &variable with NOTOTAL modifier specified). It is the grand total for numeric &variable with no NOTOTAL specified.

An example of the SUMMARY option is as follows:

```
DECLARE &ski_total AS $99,999.99;

LIST BY ski_num SUM(ski_rent_paid) SET &ski_total
     SUMMARY NEWPAGE FOLD 10 COLUMN 10
          'TOTAL RENTAL REVENUE IS  ' &ski_total;
```

The report generated by the preceding LIST command shows the ski rental revenue by rental skis in the rental inventory. Also, the grand total for rental revenue will be printed on a separate page with the annotation 'TOTAL RENTAL REVENUE IS ' located ten lines down the page and starting at the column 10.

```
NOT RETURNED!
12121212
WAS RENTED ON 12/03/87.

NOT RETURNED!
12121223
WAS RENTED ON 11/03/87.

NOT RETURNED!
12345678
WAS RENTED ON 03/19/88.
```

Figure 18.21 Customized Report Illustrating the Use of the `NOPRINT ALL` Option

Global Control of Printing Items

Global control refers to controls that apply to all items in a LIST request. To produce a special customized report, sometimes you need to suppress the standard printing of all LIST items (detail lines). Use NOPRINT ALL to suppress the printing of page numbers, column headings, and all the items. Use BYHEAD and BYFOOT to format the details of the report. For example,

```
DECLARE &hold_snum AS A8;
DECLARE &hold_date AS DATE'mm/dd/yy';

SELECT date_ret EQ &NAV;

LIST BY ski_num SET &hold_snum date_out SET &hold_date
     NOPRINT ALL
     BYHEAD ski_num
            FOLD 2 'NOT RETURNED!' FOLD &hold_snum
            FOLD 'WAS RENTED ON ' &hold_date '.';
```

Note that NOPRINT ALL suppressed the printing of the page number, the column headings, and all the items. Here the SET option is used to hold values of items to be used with the BYHEAD. The BYHEAD modifier, in turn, is used to format lines of this customized report. The need for and the use of the DECLARE command was explained in previous chapters. The SELECT statement reduces available records for the report to only those for which the return date field (`date_ret`) has no value. This means that the equipment has not yet been returned. The report is shown in Figure 18.21.

Controlling Printing Operation

You can control the printing of the reports on the printer with the use of three modifiers:

```
NOEJECT
FORMS
STOP
```

NOEJECT

When you print reports on the printer, NOMAD skips to the top of a new page. This is done before and after printing the output from the LIST request. At times you may want to have multiple short reports print on one page, so you would not want NOMAD to skip to a new page. To eliminate this skipping to a new page, you can use the NOEJECT modifier in your LIST request.

You can also prevent skipping to the top of a new page before you start to print a report. In this case you can use the NOEJECT BEGIN modifier. For example,

```
LIST BY ski_code ski_name NOEJECT BEGIN;
```

To prevent skipping to a new page at the end of the output from a LIST request, you can use the NOEJECT END modifier. For example,

```
LIST BY date_out BY ski_code NOEJECT END;
```

prevents skipping to a new page at the end of the report generated with this LIST request.

If you use the NOEJECT BOTH modifier, you prevent skipping to a new page before *and* after the printing of the LIST request. For example,

```
LIST BY ski_code ski_name NOEJECT BOTH;
```

FORMS

FORMS is used when you want to control when the report starts to print. It allows you to do a form alignment, or to start a fresh page. Recall that the system variable &PLENGTH, whose default value is 24, determines the number of lines on the page. For example;

```
LIST BY ski_code ski_name ski_num fee_rent
    FORMS OTW CONTINUE;
```

Note that we specified OTW CONTINUE in this request.

When using the FORMS print modifier, the following message appears:

```
ALIGN PAPER AND HIT RETURN OR TYPE:SETUP OR QUIT
```

To start printing the entire report, starting with page 1, you need to align the paper and to press the RETURN key. If you type SETUP, only the first page of the report prints. The TYPE SETUP OR QUIT prompt appears after this printing. If you type QUIT, the report does not print, but an error condition is raised and processing stops. To prevent that error condition from being raised, we used the OTW (OTHER-WISE) clause.

STOP

Sometimes there is a need to print a report on individual sheets of paper. Obviously, before printing you need to make sure that the proper length and page width are specified so that your report can be printed on one page. You can control printing and stop it at the end of each page with the STOP print modifier. For example,

```
&TLENGTH=55;
&RLENGTH=55;
&TWIDTH=80;
LIST BY ski_code ski_name ON PRN STOP;
```

This LIST request stops printing at the end of each page. When STOP is specified in this LIST request, the following prompt appears before printing:

```
ALIGN PAPER AND HIT RETURN
```

To start printing, press the RETURN key. After each page is printed, you can insert and align a new sheet of paper and resume printing.

18.4 REPORTS FOR THE SKI SHOP RENTAL SYSTEM

In this section we apply what we have learned. We construct five reports that are needed for the Ski Rental System. (These are the first five reports of the main menu in Figure 10.1; their content and format are in Figures 10.3 through 10.7.) The sixth report (mailing labels) is left for you as an exercise.

Revenue Report

The report shows the daily rental revenue for a prespecified period. The format of the report and its content were given in Figure 10.3. The data for this report are located in two masters: the TRANSACTIONS master and the HISTORY master. The procedure that creates this report is presented in Figure 18.22.

In lines 1-6, we declare all the &variables used in the procedure.

In lines 7-10, we define two items. The first item is the week_code, which transforms rental date (date_out) into weekly code to be compared with an appropriate weekly code (weekc) from the History file. The second item is week_revenue, which represents the historical weekly total revenue for skis, boots, and poles.

Lines 11-17 are used to gather report parameters (date for the beginning of the rental season, starting date for the reporting period, ending date for the reporting period, and the date of the report).

Statements in lines 18-19 are the statements that select transaction records. Only those records are selected for which the rental date (date_out) corresponds to the reporting period.

```
! 1! DECLARE &rep_date AS DATE'mm/dd/yy';
! 2! DECLARE &start_time_rep as DATE'mm/dd/yy';
! 3! DECLARE &end_time_rep as date'mm/dd/yy';
! 4! DECLARE &totrev as 999,999.99;
! 5! DECLARE &drevenue as 99,999.99;
! 6! DECLARE &start_time AS DATE'mm/dd/yy';

! 7! DEFINE week_code AS 99
! 8!        EXPR = (INT((date_out-&start_time)/7)+1);
! 9! DEFINE week_revenue AS 99,999.99
!10! EXPR=(ski_revenue+boot_revenue+poles_revenue);

!11! ASK 'ENTER STARTING PERIOD FOR TRANSACTION YEAR (MM/DD/YY):'
!12!        &start_time FOLD
!13!        'ENTER STARTING PERIOD FOR REPORT (MM/DD/YY) : '
!14!        &start_time_rep FOLD
!15!        'ENTER END PERIOD FOR REPORT (MM/DD/YY) : '
!16!        &end_time_rep FOLD
!17!        'ENTER REPORT DATE (MM/DD/YY) :' &rep_date;

!18! SELECT date_out GE &start_time_rep AND date_out LE
!19! &end_time_rep;

!20! CREATE BY week_code NAMED wcode AS 99
!21!        date_out NAMED date1 AS DATE'mm/dd/yy'
!22!        fee_payed NAMED revenue AS 99,999.99
!23!        SUBSET MATCHING weekc week_revenue
!24!        ON transrev;
!25! TRANS;
!26! LIST BY date1 AS DATE'MONTH DD' HEADING 'DATE'
!27!    BY wcode NOPRINT NEWPAGE SUM(revenue) HEADING 'REVENUES'
!28!    SET &drevenue MAX(week_revenue) NOPRINT SET &totrev

!29!    TITLE  FOLD 3 COL 13 'BOB'S SKI SHOP'
!30!           FOLD COL 12 'DATE - ' &rep_date
!31!           FOLD COL 9 'RENTAL REVENUE REPORT'
!32!           FOLD COL 4 'FOR PERIOD ' &start_time_rep
!33!           ' TO ' &end_time_rep FOLD 2

!34!    BYFOOT wcode FOLD 2
!35!           'WEEKLY SUBTOTAL              ---' SPACE 2 &drevenue
!36!           FOLD 'LAST YEAR WEEKLY SUBTOTAL --- ' &totrev FOLD
!37!           'CHANGE                 --- ' SPACE 3
!38!           (100$(&drevenue-&totrev)/&totrev) AS 99.99 ' %'
!           FOLD 3

!39!    SUMMARY FOLD 3
!40!           'TOTAL PER PERIOD             ---' SPACE 2 &drevenue
!41!           FOLD 'LAST YEAR TOTAL PER PERIOD --- ' &totrev
!42!           FOLD 'CHANGE                 --- ' SPACE 3
!43!           (100$(&drevenue-&totrev)/&totrev) AS 99.99 ' %';
```

Figure 18.22   Procedure to Create a Revenue Report for an Arbitrary Period

In lines 20-24, the CREATE command combines data from two masters (TRANS-ACTIONS and HISTORY) into a temporary master (TRANSREV). Note that the relational operator with a matching clause is used here.

Line 25 contains the TRANS command needed to stop the translation of the LIST command until LIST is executed. Without the TRANS command, the LIST request will raise the error condition because we are using items from the TRANSREV (temporary) master that does not exist until execution time.

Lines 26-43 correspond to the LIST request that generates the requested report. Note the use of the MAX function to reduce the redundancy of the historical revenue data. The historical weekly revenue value appears in seven daily records; we only need one.

```
! 1! DECLARE &rep_date AS DATE'mm/dd/yy';

! 2! DEFINE late AS 999
! 3!        EXPR = (&rep_date - date_due);
! 4! DEFINE ski_mark AS A1
! 5!        EXPR= (IF ski_num EQ &NAV THEN ' ' ELSE 'X');
! 6! DEFINE boot_mark AS A1
! 7!        EXPR= (IF boot_num EQ &NAV THEN ' ' ELSE 'X');
! 8! DEFINE pole_mark AS A1
! 9!        EXPR= (IF pole_num EQ &NAV THEN ' ' ELSE 'X');

!10! ASK 'ENTER REPORT DATE (MM/DD/YY) :' &rep_date;

!11! SELECT date_ret EQ &NAV AND date_due LE &rep_date;

!12! LIST  FROM customer BY custident NOPRINT
!13!         last_name HEADING 'CUSTOMER:LAST NAME'
!14!         first_name HEADING 'CUSTOMER:FIRST NAME'
!15!         phone HEADING 'TELEPHONE NO'
!16!         SUBSET ALL MATCHING FROM transactions custident
!17!         NOPRINT ski_mark HEADING 'SKI'
!18!         boot_mark HEADING 'BOOTS'
!19!         pole_mark  HEADING 'POLES'
!20!         late HEADING 'DAYS:LATE'

!21!     TITLE FOLD 3 'BOB'S SKI SHOP'
!22!           FOLD  'DATE -  ' &rep_date
!23!           FOLD  'DAILY LATE RETURN REPORT'
!24!           FOLD 3;
```

Figure 18.23   Procedure to Create a Daily Late Return Report

Daily Late Return Report

The format and content for this report were given in Figure 10.4. This report accesses the customer information master (CUSTOMER) and the rental transaction master (TRANSACTIONS). The procedure that creates this report is shown in Figure 18.23.

In line 1, we declare the &variable that will hold the value of the report date. This &variable will be used in line 10 to query the user for it (with the ASK command).

In lines 2-3, we define how to calculate the number of days the rental equipment is overdue.

In lines 4-9, we define the &variables that will hold symbols that indicate whether or not the equipment is rented.

Line 11 contains the command that selects only those transaction records for which rented equipment is overdue.

Lines 12-24 represent the LIST request that produces the desired report.

Inventory Report

This report is a simple ski inventory report. Its format and content were given in Figure 10.5. Information is extracted from only one file (SKIINVENTORY master). The procedure that generates this report is shown in Figure 18.24.

In lines 1-6, we declare all &variables used in this procedure.

In line 7, we ask for the report date.

In lines 8-24, the LIST request creates the ski inventory report. Note the use of multiple BYFOOT options.

```
! 1! DECLARE &rep_date AS DATE'mm/dd/yy';
! 2! DECLARE &total AS 999;
! 3! DECLARE &skiname AS A20;
! 4! DECLARE &subski AS 999;
! 5! DECLARE &slength AS 999;
! 6! DECLARE &sublength AS 999;

! 7! ASK 'ENTER REPORT DATE (MM/DD/YY) :' &rep_date;

! 8! LIST COUNT(st_name) NOPRINT SET &total
! 9!      BY st_name HEADING 'SKI TYPE' SET &skiname
!10!      COUNT (st_name) NOPRINT SET &subski
!11!      BY ski_length SET &slength COUNT(ski_length) NOPRINT
!12!      SET &sublength skinum

!13!      BYFOOT ski_length FOLD 1
!14!         'TOTAL NUMBER OF ' &skiname ' AT ' &slength '--- '
!15!         &sublength FOLD 1

!16!      BYFOOT st_name FOLD 1
!17!         'TOTAL NUMBER OF ' &skiname ' ---' &subski
!18!         FOLD 1

!19!      SUMMARY FOLD 1
!20!         'TOTAL NUMBER OF SKIS --- ' &total

!21!      TITLE FOLD 3 'BOB'S SKI SHOP'
!22!         FOLD 'DATE - ' &rep_date
!23!         FOLD 'SKI INVENTORY REPORT'
!24!         FOLD 3;
```

Figure 18.24 Procedure to Create an Inventory Report

Daily Rental Report

The daily rental report accesses only the rental transaction master (TRANSACTIONS). The format and content of this report were given in Figure 10.6. The procedure for this report is shown in Figure 18.25.

Lines 1-2 declare the &variables needed for the procedure.

Line 3 contains the ASK command to query the user for the report date.

In line 4, the SELECT command selects the rental transaction records for the rental date (date_out), which is equal to the date of the report.

In lines 5-12, the LIST request creates the required report.

Customer Profile Report

This report gives certain information on customers who rented the equipment in the period from the beginning of the rental season to the time of the report. The content and the format of this report were given in Figure 10.7. This report accesses the TRANSACTIONS master and the CUSTOMER master directly. It accesses indirectly (via the DEFINE command) the SKIINVENTORY, BOOTINVENTORY, and EQUIPMENT_TYPE masters. The procedure for this report is shown in Figure 18.26.

In lines 1-3, we declare some of the &variables needed in this procedure. Note that not all the &variables are declared in these lines. Some of the &variables will be declared by the SET option in the LIST request (except the &totski and &totboot for which we want to control the display format).

The DEFINE commands in lines 4-7 allow us to extract the names of the ski and boots types without directly accessing the SKIINVENTORY, BOOTINVENTORY, and EQUIPMENT_TYPE masters.

```
! 1! DECLARE &rep_date AS DATE'mm/dd/yy';
! 2! DECLARE &total AS 999;

! 3! ASK 'ENTER REPORT DATE (MM/DD/YY) :' &rep_date;

! 4! SELECT date_out EQ &rep_date;

! 5! LIST date_due COUNT(date_out) NOPRINT SET &total ski_num
! 6!      boot_num pole_num

! 7!    SUMMARY FOLD 3
! 8!            'TOTAL NUMBER OF RENTAL TRANSACTIONS --- ' &total


! 9!    TITLE FOLD 3 'BOB'S SKI SHOP'
!10!         FOLD 'DATE - ' &rep_date
!11!         FOLD 'DAILY RENTAL REPORT'
!12!         FOLD 3;
```

Figure 18.25 Procedure to Create a Daily Rental Report

```
! 1! DECLARE &rep_date AS DATE'mm/dd/yy';
! 2! DECLARE &totski AS 99;
! 3! DECLARE &totboot AS 99;

! 4! DEFINE ski_name AS EXTRACT'st_name FROM skiinventory
! 5!       USING ski_num';
! 6! DEFINE boot_name AS EXTRACT'bt_name FROM bootinventory
! 7!       USING boot_num';

! 8! ASK 'ENTER REPORT DATE (MM/DD/YY) :' &rep_date;

! 9! SELECT date_out LE &rep_date;

!10! LIST FROM transactions BY custident NOPRINT
!11!      'TYPE OF EQUIPMENT RENTED' SPACE 5
!12!      ski_name COUNT(ski_name) NOPRINT SET &totski
!13!      boot_name COUNT(boot_name) NOPRINT SET &totboot
!14!      SUBSET MATCHING FROM customer custident NOPRINT
!15!      first_name NOPRINT SET &fname last_name NOPRINT
!16!      SET &lname city NOPRINT SET &rcity age NOPRINT
!17!      SET &rage sex NOPRINT SET &rsex skiing_ability NOPRINT
!18!      SET &rski_ability NOHEAD

!19!    BYHEAD custident
!20!            'CUSTOMER NAME' SPACE 19 'AGE' SPACE 2 'SEX'
!21!            SPACE 2 'TOWN' SPACE 16 'SKIING ABILITY' FOLD
!22!            '------------------------------' SPACE 2 '---'
!23!            SPACE 2 '---' SPACE 2 '--------------------'
!24!            SPACE 2 '--------------' FOLD 2 &fname SPACE 0
!25!            &lname SPACE 2 &rage SPACE 4 &rsex SPACE 3 &rcity
!26!            &rski_ability FOLD 2 SPACE 29 'SKI' SPACE 19
!27!            'BOOTS' FOLD SPACE 29 '--------------------'
!28!            SPACE 2 '--------------------' FOLD

!29!    BYFOOT custident
!30!            FOLD 3 SPACE 10 'TOTAL NUMBER OF SKIS TRIED: '
!31!            &totski FOLD 2
!32!            SPACE 10 'TOTAL NUMBER OF BOOTS TRIED:' &totboot
!33!            FOLD 3

!34!    TITLE FOLD 3 'BOB'S SKI SHOP'
!35!            FOLD 'DATE - ' &rep_date
!36!            FOLD 'CUSTOMER PROFILE REPORT'
!37!            FOLD 3;
```

Figure 18.26 Procedure to Create a Customer's Profile Report

Line 8 asks for the report date. This date is also used in the SELECT command in line 9, where only those records are extracted for which the rental date (date_out) is less than or equal to the reporting date.

In lines 10-37, the LIST request generates the required report.

18.5 SUMMARY

The LIST command extracts data from a database and generates a formatted report. LIST uses the headings, display formats, titles, justification, and other information specified within the descriptions of the items in the schema.

There are also numerous defaults. The real power of a 4GL is that it can do a lot for the user without forcing the user to worry about the details. In other words,

    LIST ski_num;

generates a very basic report, but it will be formatted and will have a page number and column heading due to defaults. If you want to go beyond the basic report, numerous keywords can help you customize the report.

The LIST command offers a wide range of capabilities. There are many ways to specify the sort order, data selection, calculations, titles, spacing, page breaks, footings and other reporting options.

LIST has various options to control formats of titles, spacing, page breaks, footing, and so on.

Formatting options can be for individual report items or formatting can be global, affecting entire report.

Item modifiers (for items appearing in the BY, ACROSS, and Object clauses of the LIST request) perform the following functions:

■ Change the display format of LIST items (AS).

■ Suppress the printing of LIST items (NOPRINT).

■ Modify column headings (HEADASIS, HEADING).

■ Center data and column headings (CENTER).

■ Save results from one portion of LIST command for use elsewhere in the LIST command (SET).

Report formatting options allow you to produce customized reports and affect the entire LIST request. Thus they represent global formatting options. In this chapter we discussed:

NOPAGE	NOTITLE
NOHEAD	FOOTING
CENTER ALL	BYHEAD
HEADASIS ALL	BYFOOT
LABELST	SUMMARY
LABELTOT	NOPRINT

The printed output is controlled with:

    NOEJECT
    FORMS
    STOP

EXERCISES

1. What functions are performed by item modifiers?

2. Without an AS modifier, what determines the display formats?

3. Assume that the rev has a display format of $999,999,999 as specified in the database schema. Analyze the following LIST statement, and describe the report produced by it.

   ```
   LIST BY stname rev AS 999,999,999.99;
   ```

4. Briefly describe how either data or headings can be centered.

5. How do you change the column heading by using the HEADING modifier?

6. When using a report function, NOMAD automatically includes the name of the report function as part of the column heading. What do you need to do to cause the heading to be displayed as it is defined for the item, without the report function name?

7. Can HEADING and HEADASIS be specified for the same item?

8. Describe the report generated by the following LIST request:

   ```
   LIST BY box_office_revenue DESC NOPRINT filmname;
   ```

9. What would you use the SET modifier for?

10. Analyze the following LIST request and determine whether or not it calculates the percentage as requested. Specify especially how the SET parameter is used in this statement.

    ```
    LIST SUM(ski_rent_paid) NOPRINT SET &fee_total
         BY ski_num
         ski_rent_paid NOPRINT SET &fee_collected
         (100 * &fee_collected/&fee_total) AS 999.99
         HEADING '% OF TOTAL: FEES COLLECTED';
    ```

11. What are item formatting options?

12. Can item formatting options appear anywhere in a LIST request?

13. Identify what LINE specifies in the following LIST request:

    ```
    LIST LINE 1 BY ski_type ski_number
         LINE 2 i_tot_rented i_cost;
    ```

14. Explain why you would use the NOPRINT ALL formatting option, and give an example of a report that requires its use.

15. If a LIST request with NOEJECT BEGIN follows a LIST request with NOEJECT END, where does the output from the second LIST request begin on the printed page?

16. Are ON PRN and ON PTR synonymous?

17. Describe the output from the following:

```
&TLENGTH = 50;
&TWIDTH  = 60;
LIST BY ski_code ski_name ON PRN STOP;
```

18. Write the LIST request to create mailing labels for the customers who rented ski equipment in the past three months.

19. Write the LIST request to create the mailing labels for all the customers in the CUSTOMER master.

20. Add the following capabilities to the customer's profile report:
    a. Ability to generate the report for customers in any arbitrary age bracket. The user will be queried for the specific age bracket.
    b. Ability to generate the report by customers' home town.
    c. Ability to call out the report to a printer or a to a screen.

21. Create the report that lists the ten pairs of skis that earn the largest amount in rental fees. This report should list ski type, length, manufacturer's name, and total to-date rental fee collected. Sort the report by total rental fee in descending order.

22. Generate the report that lists the total monthly rental fees for each pair of skis in the inventory. List the ski type, length, and daily rental charge. The report is to be generated for the time period specified by the user.

23. Generate the report that lists total monthly rental equipment fees (for all skis, boots, and poles) and compares this total with the appropriate total monthly rental fees from the previous year (use the History file).

24. Generate the report that lists all the inventory information on skis, boots, and poles that were rented only once. Sort the report in order of equipment type code, but do not list this item on the report.

25. Create a report similar to that in Problem 23 for the equipment that was never rented. Allow the user to specify the reporting time interval.

26. Generate the report that lists customers who spend at least $150.00 on the rental of the equipment. Report their name, address, age, and the to-date total equipment rental. Sort by customer's name.

27. Create mailing labels for the customers in the report from Problem 26.

PROJECTS

1. For the State Parks Reservation System, improve the reports created in Project 1 in Chapter 17. Use the NOMAD reporting facilities introduced in this chapter. Create all the reports that you were unable to create with standard NOMAD options.

2. Try to improve the reports that you developed for the Properties, Water Rights, and Leases System. Use the NOMAD reporting facilities introduced in this chapter.

3. Create all the reports that you omitted in Project 3 in Chapter 17 due to your lack of familiarity with advanced NOMAD reporting facilities. Use all the reporting facilities introduced in Chapter 18.

CHAPTER 19

System Integration

*The meaning of a whole and a part will concurrently exist in our
mind only when we think about the relationship between them
instead of about the things themselves.*

Tiao Chang

*The word is a mirror, an imagining of Love's perfection.
No man has ever seen a part greater than the whole.*

Jelaluddin Rumi

*She is a friend of my mind. She gather me, man. The pieces I am,
she gather them and give them back to me in all the right order.*

Toni Morrison

19.1 INTRODUCTION

The objective of this chapter is to show you how to construct NOMAD procedures that control the integration of our Inventory Ski System application and how to enhance each constructed component with some of the production system features.

When you have completed this chapter, you should be able to:

- Create an integration control procedure that connects all the existing system components.
- Enhance each existing component with:
    - Error-handling routines.
    - Simple exits from existing loops.
    - User-assistance windows.
    - HELP facilities.
- Understand the need for and perform final system cleanup so that it becomes a working production system.

19.2 SET UP OF THE PRODUCTION SYSTEMS

Our Ski Rental System was designed to function in an interactive environment. So far we have constructed several separate procedures (components) that are capable of carrying out a specific task. We constructed:

■ A procedure to create our application's database.

■ A procedure to enter, change, and delete records in the database.

■ A procedure to create reports that management requires.

When constructing these components, we concentrated on the job of explaining major NOMAD commands and their available options, leaving the construction of an integrated, thus multifunctional, working (production) system for later.

Since the job of explaining the basic properties of NOMAD's commands is done, we now can concentrate on building the integrated production system. We need to perform several tasks:

1. Create an integration control procedure that connects all the existing components of the system.

2. Enhance each existing component with:

   ■ Error-handling routines.

   ■ Simple exits from loops using user-defined function keys (PF keys).

   ■ Windows that handle the user-assistance information that can be used in online documentation.

   ■ HELP facilities constructed with the DDQUERY function or the SLIST command.

3. Perform system cleanup and group the integrated system code according to functionality. To accomplish this,

   ■ Place all system DEFINES and DECLARES into a separate .NOM file. Execute this .NOM file at the beginning of the control procedure.

   ■ Place all user-defined Forms into a separate .NOM file.

To perform these tasks, we use all the NOMAD commands introduced throughout the text.

Integrating Procedure

The integrating procedure (control procedure) combines all the components of the system developed in the preceding chapters of this book. Thus, our system's separate components are combined into a working (production) whole.

The major components of the integrating procedure that need to be assembled are:

1. Activation of the system's database.
2. Initialization of all user-defined &variables, defined items, and Forms.
3. Error handling on the system level.
4. Closing all NOMAD windows.
5. Control of the interactive process and main menu logic.
6. System exit procedure.

Some of these components were developed previously; others need to be constructed now.

Activation of the system's database and initialization of the user-defined &variables, defined items, and Forms were discussed in previous chapters.

Error handling on the system level corresponds to the handling of the major system errors that can occur during system execution. For example, a lack of disk space (to write an output file to or to update the database) can result in a system-level error. Other error-handling routines will be included in our system as system enhancements.

Closing all NOMAD windows corresponds to the removal of all NOMAD interactive windows from the display.

The system user determines the passing of control in the integrating procedure by making selections from the main menu that is a part of the control procedure we are going to develop.

The system exit procedure closes all user-defined windows, removes them from the memory buffer, and reopens the NOMAD Command and History windows.

Enhancing Each Component of the System

To speed up development time, the first prototype of the application system is usually developed without such functions as error-handling routines, shortcuts in switching from one part of the system to the other with user-defined function keys, and user-assistance facilities such as online HELP and online documentation.

Error Handling

Error handling is an integral part of a well-written procedure. To keep our explanations of NOMAD commands and construction of procedures on a manageable level, we initially omitted error-handling routines. To make our system a production system, we need to consider them now.

The most commonly used technique to handle errors in NOMAD is the OTHER-WISE (OTW) clause described in Chapter 11. This clause is used to define the action to be taken when an error occurs in the execution of the specific NOMAD statement. The command or group of commands following the OTW clause takes over control if the command preceding the OTW cannot execute its task successfully.

Another means of handling errors is provided by ON... statements. ON is used, for example, when an attempt is made to read a record when the end of the file is reached (ON ENDFILE) or when a user attempts to assign an alphanumeric value to a numeric variable (ON CONVERT). (A complete list of available ON conditions is given in Chapter 11.) Some of the rules that govern the execution of the ON... statements are:

1. When a specific error occurs, NOMAD interrupts the procedure that is processing and executes the command or group of commands specified in the ON... statement.

2. ON... statements are executed sequentially, so they can be redefined at different parts of the integrated system. If there is more than one ON... statement that covers a specific condition, NOMAD executes the last appropriate ON... statement it finds.

3. Branching out of the ON... statement or issuing a RETURN command ends the actions specified in the ON... statement.

4. After the ON... statement is performed, processing continues and control passes to the statement following the one that caused the error condition to be raised, if no GOTO has been specified.

5. NOMAD executes the actions specified in an ON... statement only if there is no OTW clause for that statement.

Exit From Loops

The processing of any task on the computer is generally an iterative operation (loop). In any procedure that handles the specific task repeatedly, a code must be added to allow exiting from a loop. In all the procedures we have created so far, we used the ASK command, followed by the IF... THEN test, to terminate a specific procedure. That technique can prove to be cumbersome in a production system. Handling the flow of system operation via a set of menus can become cumbersome as well, especially for experienced users. Experienced users need some switching shortcuts from one part of the system to another.

The technique of defining and using processing function keys (PF keys) to exit a loop in the procedure or to switch from one part of the system to another serves this purpose. (The function keys definition is accomplished with the ON FUNCTIONKEY command, which was described in Chapter 11.)

User-Assistance Facilities

In addition to providing error-handling routines, user-assistance information plays an important part in an interactive environment. Two methods can generate user-assistance information:

1. **HELP facility with user-defined assistance windows**—FORM commands are used to define such windows. You can design these windows, both size and location, based on the needs of your application. These windows may be used to display messages, instructions, status conditions, and online documentation. The user-assistance information that appears in these windows is assigned to &variables. These &variables are defined as fields in the user-assistance Form. Every time the &variable value changes, it is immediately redisplayed in the window.

    You can also display online documentation that is stored in the schema file with the DOCUMENT attribute in the ITEM statement. Recall that the DOCUMENT attribute allows you to store up to 255 characters of information on the specific item. You can retrieve this information using the DDQUERY function, described in Chapter 16 and Appendix C.

    To invoke the HELP facility (to display the user-assistance window), you can use the predefined function key, for example, function key 10 (PF10). To set up the required code, you can use the ON FUNCTIONKEY condition.

2. **HELP facility using the SLIST command**—NOMAD's Output window and the SLIST command are used to create HELP facilities. A predefined function key can invoke these facilities as well. In this case, the SLIST command retrieves information about the items from the data dictionary. Results of an SLIST command are automatically displayed in NOMAD's Output window. Using this technique saves you from having to define another window (user-assistance window). However, you need to be sure that you open the Output window prior to requesting HELP for an item; otherwise, the result of the SLIST will not appear anywhere on the screen because the Output window has been closed.

General Cleanup

You perform a general cleanup by removing any redundant code and by grouping (modularizing) code according to its functionality. This modularization is recommended for ease of maintenance and for possible future trouble-shooting. In this final step of construction of the integrated production system, you need to do the following:

- Move all the DEFINEs and DECLAREs to the top section of the procedure or split them into separate .NOM files.
- Move all code that defines user windows to separate .NOM files or place this code after the DEFINEs and DECLAREs.

Separate DEFINES and DECLARES

Another reason that we separate DEFINES and DECLARES into the separate procedures is because of the data dictionary. Once these entities are translated, they are stored in an active data dictionary. This means that you only need to translate them once. If you try to redefine an item with a different data type, NOMAD stops the procedure scanning process and displays an error message. To prevent the error condition, you must first purge the item from the data dictionary (using the PURGE command) before redefining it. If the DEFINES and DECLARES are in a common procedure, their execution is easier to control.

Put All Forms in One Procedure

NOMAD requires that all user windows be reinitialized before they are used. If you keep them in a separate file, it will be easier to maintain and run them.

19.3 INTEGRATED SKI RENTAL SYSTEM

To facilitate learning by example, we conclude with the code that integrates the modules of the Ski Rental System created in Chapters 10 through 18 of this book. We specifically show what is needed to make this system a production system (that is, an integrated system, as described in this chapter).

By now you are aware of the fact that there are many possible solutions to any data processing problem and that the solutions are not unique. Thus, the Ski Rental System we created does not represent the one and only possible solution to the data processing problem specified in Chapter 10. You are encouraged to consider other possible solutions in the Exercises section at the end of this chapter.

The integration code that follows is included on the data disk (the Ski Rental System data disk) that comes with this book. The names of the files on this disk correspond to the filenames displayed at the tops of the figures of this chapter.

Control Procedure

The main control procedure, RENTAL.NOM, operates the entire application. Therefore, to start our online Ski Rental System, enter

    RENTAL

in the Command window. (We assume that you have already copied the data disk into the NOMAD directory on the hard disk.) This procedure is listed in Figure 19.1.

```
!   1! !Control procedure for the Ski Rental System!

!   2!     DECLARE &ferror_msg1 AS A72;
!   3!     DECLARE &ferror_msg2 AS A72;
!   4!     DECLARE &ferror_msg3 AS A72;
!   5!     DECLARE &system_msg AS A72;
!   6!     DECLARE &selection_n AS 99;
!   7!     DECLARE &system_msg1 AS A35;
!   8!     DECLARE &system_msg2 AS A35;
!   9!     DECLARE &system_msg3 AS A35;
!  10!     DECLARE &help1 AS A70;
!  11!     DECLARE &help2 AS A70;

!  12!     FORM srtmsg1 TITLE 'USER MESSAGE';
!  13!     FIELD &system_msg1 LINE #+1;
!  14!     FIELD &system_msg2 LINE #+1 COL 1;
!  15!     FIELD &system_msg3 LINE #+1 COL 1;
!  16!     FEND;

!  17!     FORM shelp TITLE 'HELP WINDOW';
!  18!     FIELD &help1 PROTECTED LINE #+1 COL 1;
!  19!     FIELD &help2 PROTECTED LINE #+1 COL 1;
!  20!     FEND;

!  21!     FORM srterror TITLE 'FATAL ERROR MESSAGE';
!  22!     FIELD &ferror_msg1 PROTECTED LINE #+2;
!  23!     FIELD &ferror_msg2 PROTECTED LINE #+2 COL 1;
!  24!     FIELD &ferror_msg3 PROTECTED LINE #+2 COL 1;
!  25!     FEND;

!  26!     FORM srtmsg TITLE 'USER MESSAGE';
!  27!     FIELD &system_msg PROTECTED;
!  28!     FEND;

!  29!     ON FKEY(1,9,10,11) DO;
!  30!       &system_msg='Sorry, that function key is not used here. Press ENTER to continue. ;
!  31!     WINDOW READ srtmsg LINE 20 COL 1 OTW;
!  32!       &system_msg='Please select the function that you want to work with.';
!  33!     RETRY;
!  34!     END;

!  35!       &system_msg='Wait, NOMAD is processing';
!  36!     WINDOW CLOSE LIST    OTW;
!  37!     WINDOW CLOSE OUTPUT   OTW;
!  38!     WINDOW CLOSE COMMAND OTW;
!  39!     WINDOW CLOSE HISTORY OTW;
!  40!     WINDOW OPEN srtmsg LINE 21 OTW;

!  41!     DATABASE skirent;
!  42!     CALL initial;
!  43!     CALL forms;

!  44! FORM menu1 LINESIZE 15 COLSIZE 74;
!  45! LABEL  BOB S SKI SHOP RENTAL SYSTEM' LINE 1 COL 28;
```

Figure 19.1   Control Procedure for Ski Rental System

Lines 2-11 are declaration statements defining all &variables needed to handle user messages, error messages, and help information. These &variables will be used throughout the system.

Lines 12-28 define four user windows (Forms) that will display customized user, error, and help information. These custom Forms definitions are placed in the control procedure to separate them from all the other Ski Rental System Forms.

```
!46!|LABEL 'MAIN MENU' LINE *+1 COL 36;
!47! LABEL 'FILE UPDATES' LINE *+1 COL 10;
!48! LABEL 'REPORTS' COL 50;
!49! LABEL '_____' LINE *+1 COL 10;
!50! LABEL '_____' COL 50;
!51! PICK INDEX &selection_n;
!52! CHOICE  'A - NEW CUSTOMER TRANSACTION' LINE *+2 COL 2;
!53! CHOICE  'B - RETURNING CUSTOMER TRANSACTION' LINE *+1 COL 2;
!54! CHOICE  'C - EQUIPMENT RETURN' LINE *+1 COL 2;
!55! CHOICE  'D - EQUIPMENT TYPE FILE' LINE *+1 COL 2;
!56! CHOICE  'E - MANUFACTURER FILE' LINE *+1 COL 2;
!57! CHOICE  'F - SKI INVENTORIES' LINE *+1 COL 2;
!58! CHOICE  'G - BOOT INVENTORIES' LINE *+1 COL 2;
!59! CHOICE  'H - POLE INVENTORIES' LINE *+1 COL 2;
!60! CHOICE  'I - HISTORICAL REVENUE FILE' LINE *+1 COL 2;
!61! CHOICE  'J - REVENUE REPORT' LINE *-8 COL 47;
!62! CHOICE  'K - DAILY LATE RETURN REPORT' LINE *+1 COL 47;
!63! CHOICE  'L - INVENTORY REPORT' LINE *+1 COL 47;
!64! CHOICE  'M - DAILY RENTAL REPORT' LINE *+1 COL 47;
!65! CHOICE  'N - CUSTOMER PROFILE REPORT' LINE *+1 COL 47;
!66! CHOICE  'O - MAILING LABELS' LINE *+1 COL 47;
!67! CHOICE  'P - EXIT THE SYSTEM' LINE *+4 COL 30;
!68! FEND;

!69!         ON FATAL MSG DO;
!70!           CALL sysexit;
!71!           &ferror_msg1='Warning, Fatal system error';
!72!           &ferror_msg2='Please, contact your system support people';
!73!           &ferror_msg3='Please, press ENTER key to return to NOMAD';
!74!           WINDOW READ srterror LINE 5;
!75!           WINDOW OPEN error;
!76!           GOTO -exit;
!77!         END;

!78! -main
!79!     &system_msg='Please select the function you want to work with.';
!80!     WINDOW READ menu1 LINE 1 OTW GOTO -exit;
!81!     &system_msg='Waiting';
!82!     GOTO (-s1, -s2, -s3, -s4, -s5, -s6, -s7, -s8, -s9,
!83!           -s10, -s11, -s12, -s13, -s14, -s15, -exit)
!84!           &selection_n;

!85! -s1
!86!     CALL proc1;
!87!     GOTO -main;
!88! -s2
!89!     CALL proc2;
!90!     GOTO -main;
!91! -s3
!92!     CALL proc3;
!93!     GOTO -main;
!94! -s4
!95!     CALL proc4;
!96!     GOTO -main;
!97! -s5
!98!     CALL proc5;
!99!     GOTO -main;
!100! -s6
!101!     CALL proc6;
!102!     GOTO -main;
!103! -s7
!104!     CALL proc7;
!105!     GOTO -main;
```

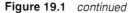

Figure 19.1 *continued*

Lines 29-34 contain code that deactivates the function keys to be used in the lower levels of the system (that is, not on the level of the control procedure). If, during the execution of the control procedure, the user presses the PF1, PF9, PF10, or PF11 key, a special user message appears. After the user presses the ENTER key, as requested in the displayed message, control automatically returns to the place in the control procedure where the specific function key was activated.

```
!106!    -s8
!107!        CALL proc8;
!108!        GOTO -main;
!109!    -s9
!110!        CALL proc9;
!111!        GOTO -main;
!112!    -s10
!113!        CALL rep1;
!114!        GOTO -main;
!115!    -s11
!116!        CALL rep2;
!117!        GOTO -main;
!118!    -s12
!119!        CALL rep3;
!120!        GOTO -main;
!121!    -s13
!122!        CALL rep4;
!123!        GOTO -main;
!124!    -s14
!125!        CALL rep5;
!126!        GOTO -main;
!127!    -s15
!128!        CALL rep6;
!129!        GOTO -main;
!130!    -exit
!131!        CALL sysexit OTW;
!132!        WINDOW CLOSE ERROR OTW;
!133!        WINDOW CLOSE srtmsg OTW;
!134!        WINDOW OPEN COMMAND OTW;
!135!        WINDOW OPEN HISTORY OTW;
!136!        RETURN;
```

Figure 19.1 *continued*

Lines 35-40 contain statements that close all the NOMAD system windows and open the srtmsg window to be used for user messages. All the statements in this block contain the OTW clause. This clause causes control to pass to the next statement if, for some reason, the specified statement cannot be executed. For example, at the moment you initialize the Ski Rental System, the Output window is closed. Thus, if statement 39 does not include the OTW clause, an error condition could be raised (you cannot close a window that is already closed). The presence of the OTW clause in the statement in line 39 causes control to pass to the next statement (in this case, 40, 41, and then 42).

Line 41 holds a statement that opens the Ski Rental System database.

Line 42 calls a procedure that contains all the DECLARE and DEFINE statements for the entire Ski Rental System.

Line 43 calls a procedure that initializes all Forms used in the system.

Lines 44-68 define the main menu used to control the flow of the entire system. (This is the menu from Figure 10.1.)

Lines 69-77 define the action to be taken if, for some reason, a fatal error occurs during processing. After the error message is displayed and the user presses the ENTER key, the Ski Rental System is terminated (exited) and control passes to the NOMAD Command window.

Lines 78-129 contain the main control procedure in which the main menu is initialized (line 86). Control then passes to option that the user selects. After this option is executed, control returns to the main menu.

```
! 1!     WINDOW CLOSE menu1 OTW;
! 2!     WINDOW CLOSE srtf01 OTW;
! 3!     WINDOW CLOSE srtf02 OTW;
! 4!     WINDOW CLOSE srtf03 OTW;
! 5!     WINDOW CLOSE srtf04 OTW;
! 6!     WINDOW CLOSE srtf05 OTW;
! 7!     WINDOW CLOSE srtf06 OTW;
! 8!     WINDOW CLOSE srtf07 OTW;
! 9!     WINDOW CLOSE srtf09 OTW;
!10!     WINDOW CLOSE LIST OTW;
!11!     WINDOW CLOSE OUTPUT OTW;
```

Figure 19.2 Exit Procedure

```
! 1! DECLARE &prtsg AS A6;
! 2! DECLARE &tdate_out AS DATE'mmddyy';
! 3! DECLARE &tnumber AS A8;
! 4! DECLARE &last_name1 AS A20;
! 5! DECLARE &first_name1 AS A10;
! 6! DECLARE &ans AS A1;
! 7! DECLARE &ident1 AS A2;
! 8! DECLARE &ident2 AS A20;
! 9! DECLARE &sys_key AS 99;
!10! DECLARE &l_select AS A1;
!11! DECLARE &date_select AS DATE'yyyy';
!12! DECLARE &s5_choice_n AS 9;
!13! DECLARE &start_time AS DATE'mm/dd/yy';
!14! DECLARE &hyear AS DATE'yyyy';
!15! DECLARE &rep_date AS DATE'mm/dd/yy';
!16! DECLARE &start_time_rep as DATE'mm/dd/yy';
!17! DECLARE &end_time_rep as date'mm/dd/yy';
!18! DECLARE &totrev as 999,999.99;
!19! DECLARE &drevenue as 99,999.99;
!20! DECLARE &total AS 999;
!21! DECLARE &skiname AS A20;
!22! DECLARE &subski AS 999;
!23! DECLARE &slength AS 999;
!24! DECLARE &sublength AS 999;
!25! DECLARE &totski AS 99;
!26! DECLARE &totboot AS 99;

!27! DEFINE ski_name AS EXTRACT'st_name FROM skiinventory USING ski_num';
!28! DEFINE boot_name AS EXTRACT'bt_name FROM bootinventory USING boot_num';
!29! DEFINE late AS 999 EXPR = (&rep_date-date_due);
!30! DEFINE ski_mark AS A1 EXPR= (IF ski_num EQ &NAV THEN ' ' ELSE 'X');
!31! DEFINE boot_mark AS A1 EXPR= (IF boot_num EQ &NAV THEN ' ' ELSE 'X');
!32! DEFINE pole_mark AS A1 EXPR= (IF pole_num EQ &NAV THEN ' ' ELSE 'X');
!33! DEFINE week_code AS 99 EXPR = (INT((date_out-&start_time)/7)+1);
!34! DEFINE week_revenue AS 99,999.99 EXPR=(ski_revenue+boot_revenue+poles_revenue);
!35! DEFINE manufact_code1 AS A1 EXPR=manufact_code;
!36! DEFINE equipment_code1 AS A1 EXPR=equipment_code;
```

Figure 19.3 Ski Rental System's DECLARES and DEFINES

Lines 130-136 contain the closing procedure that closes all user-defined windows and opens the NOMAD Command and History windows. The closing of user-defined windows (line 131) is accomplished with statements located in the SYSEXIT.NOM procedure. This procedure is listed in Figure 19.2.

DEFINES and DECLARES

All the DEFINEs and DECLAREs for the Ski Rental System are grouped in one procedure for ease of maintenance. The procedure is contained in the INITIAL.NOM file. The procedure is listed in Figure 19.3.

```
!  1! FORM srtf01 TITLE 'EQUIPMENT TYPE UPDATE';
!  2! LABEL 'EQUIPMENT CODE:'      LINE *+3  COL 15;
!  3! FIELD equipment_code UPPERCASE  COL *+7;
!  4! LABEL 'EQUIPMENT NAME:'      LINE *+2    COL 15;
!  5! FIELD equipment_name      COL*+7;
!  6! LABEL 'YEAR OF PRODUCTION:'    LINE *+2    COL 15;
!  7! FIELD production_date  COL *+3;
!  8! FEND;

!  9! FORM srtf02  TITLE 'MANUFACTURER INFORMATION UPDATE';
! 10! LABEL 'MANUFACTURER CODE:'  LINE *+2 COL 10;
! 11! FIELD manufact_code      COL *+15;
! 12! LABEL 'MANUFACTURER NAME:'  LINE *+2 COL 10;
! 13! FIELD manufact_name     COL *+15;
! 14! LABEL 'ADDRESS' LINE *+1 COL 15;
! 15! FROM manufacturers;
! 16! LABEL 'STREET:'   LINE *+1 COL 12;
! 17! FIELD street      COL *+24;
! 18! LABEL 'CITY:' LINE *+2 COL 12;
! 19! FIELD city     COL *+26;
! 20! LABEL 'STATE:'   LINE *+2 COL 12;
! 21! FIELD state      COL *+25;
! 22! LABEL 'ZIP CODE:'  LINE *+2 COL 12;
! 23! FIELD zip_code      COL *+22;
! 24! LABEL 'REPRESENTATIVE NAME:' LINE *+2 COL 2;
! 25! FIELD rep_name      COL *+13;
! 26! LABEL 'REPRESENTATIVE TELEPHONE NO:' LINE *+2 COL 2;
! 27! FIELD rep_telephone      COL *+5;
! 28! FEND;

! 29! FORM srtf03  TITLE 'CUSTOMER FILE UPDATE';
! 30! LABEL 'TYPE OF IDENTIFICATION:' LINE *+1 COL 1;
! 31! FROM CUSTOMER;
! 32! FIELD ident_type      COL *+1;
! 33! LABEL 'CUSTOMER IDENTIFICATION NO:'   COL *+2;
! 34! FIELD custident COL *+1; LABEL 'FIRST NAME:' LINE *+2 COL 2;
! 35! FIELD first_name COL *+2; LABEL 'MIDDLE  INITIAL:'  COL *+2;
! 36! FIELD middle_initial COL *+1; LABEL 'LAST NAME:'  COL *+2;
! 37! FIELD last_name COL *+1; LABEL 'ADDRESS' LINE *+2 COL 20;
! 38! LABEL 'STREET:'   LINE *+1 COL 12;
! 39! FIELD street_address      COL *+24;
! 40! LABEL 'CITY:' LINE *+2 COL 12;
! 41! FIELD city    COL *+26;
! 42! LABEL 'STATE:'   LINE *+2 COL 12;
! 43! FIELD state      COL *+25;
! 44! LABEL 'ZIP CODE:'   LINE *+2 COL 12;
! 45! FIELD zip_code      COL *+22;
! 46! LABEL 'CUSTOMER TELEPHONE NO:' LINE *+2 COL 12;
! 47! FIELD phone  COL *+9;
! 48! LABEL 'LOCAL ACCOMMODATION:'   LINE *+2 COL 12;
! 49! FIELD local_accom      COL *+12;
! 50! LABEL 'CUSTOMER HEIGHT (FEET):'  LINE *+2 COL 2;
! 51! FIELD cust_height_f  COL *+5;
! 52! LABEL 'CUSTOMER HEIGHT (INCHES):'  LINE *+1 COL 2;
! 53! FIELD cust_height_i  COL *+3;
! 54! LABEL 'CUSTOMER WEIGHT:' LINE *+1  COL 2;
! 55! FIELD weight  COL *+11;
! 56! LABEL 'AGE:' LINE *+1 COL 2;
! 57! FIELD age COL *+23;
! 58! LABEL 'SEX:' LINE *+1 COL 2;
! 59! FIELD sex COL *+23;
! 60! LABEL 'SKIING ABILITY:'  LINE 19 COL 43;
! 61! FIELD skiing_ability COL *+3;
```

Figure 19.4 *User-Defined Forms*

Procedure To Initialize All User-Defined FORMS

All the Forms that were defined in Chapter 14 are combined in one procedure listed in Figure 19.4. All the Forms are combined in one procedure for ease of maintenance and to simplify the initialization process (as specified in the control procedure). The user-defined Form procedure is contained in the FORMS.NOM file.

```
! 62! LABEL 'BINDING L. TOE:'  LINE *+1 COL 43;
! 63! FIELD binding_1_toe  COL *+3;
! 64! LABEL 'BINDING R. TOE:' LINE *+1 COL 43;
! 65! FIELD binding_r_toe  COL *+3;
! 66! LABEL 'BINDING L. HEEL:'  LINE *+1 COL 43;
! 67! FIELD binding_l_heel  COL *+2;
! 68! LABEL 'BINDING R. HEEL:'  LINE *+1 COL 43;
! 69! FIELD binding_r_heel  COL *+2;
! 70! FROM;
! 71! FEND;

! 72! FORM srtf04 TITLE 'SKI INVENTORY UPDATE';
! 73! LABEL 'SKI SERIAL NUMBER' LINE *+5 COL 5;
! 74! FIELD skinum    COL *+3;
! 75! LABEL 'MANUFACTURER CODE' LINE *+2 COL 5;
! 76! FIELD ski_manufact   COL *+3;
! 77! LABEL 'MANUFACTURER NAME' LINE *+1 COL 5;
! 78! FIELD sman_name PROTECTED COL *+3;
! 79! LABEL 'SKI TYPE CODE' LINE *+2 COL 5;
! 80! FIELD ski_type    COL *+7;
! 81! LABEL 'SKI TYPE NAME' LINE *+1 COL 5;
! 82! FIELD st_name PROTECTED COL *+7;
! 83! LABEL 'SKI LENGTH' LINE *+2 COL 5;
! 84! FIELD ski_length   COL *+10;
! 85! LABEL 'SKI RENTAL CHARGE' LINE *+2 COL 5;
! 86! FIELD ski_rentch   COL *+3;
! 87! LABEL 'SKI RENTAL FLAG' LINE *+2 COL 5;
! 88! FIELD ski_flag PROTECTED  COL *+5;
! 89! FEND;

! 90! FORM srtf05 TITLE 'BOOT INVENTORY UPDATE';
! 91! LABEL 'BOOT SERIAL NUMBER' LINE *+5 COL 5;
! 92! FIELD bootnum    COL *+3;
! 93! LABEL 'BOOT MANUFACTURER' LINE *+2 COL 5;
! 94! FIELD boot_manufact   COL *+4;
! 95! LABEL 'MANUFACTURER NAME' LINE *+1 COL 5;
! 96! FIELD bman_name PROTECTED COL *+4;
! 97! LABEL 'BOOT TYPE' LINE *+2 COL 5;
! 98! FIELD boot_type   COL *+12;
! 99! LABEL 'BOOT TYPE NAME' LINE *+1 COL 5;
!100! FIELD bt_name  PROTECTED COL *+7;
!101! LABEL 'BOOT SIZE' LINE *+2 COL 5;
!102! FIELD boot_size   COL *+12;
!103! LABEL 'BOOT RENTAL CHARGE' LINE *+2 COL 5;
!104! FIELD boot_rentch   COL *+3;
!105! LABEL 'BOOT RENTAL FLAG' LINE *+2 COL 5;
!106! FIELD boot_flag PROTECTED  COL *+5;
!107! FEND;

!108! FORM srtf06 TITLE 'POLE INVENTORY UPDATE';
!109! LABEL 'POLE SERIAL NUMBER' LINE *+5 COL 5;
!110! FIELD polenum    COL *+3;
!111! LABEL 'POLE MANUFACTURER' LINE *+2 COL 5;
!112! FIELD pole_manufact   COL *+4;
!113! LABEL 'MANUFACTURER NAME' LINE *+1 COL 5;
!114! FIELD pman_name PROTECTED COL *+4;
!115! LABEL 'POLE TYPE' LINE *+2 COL 5;
!116! FIELD pole_type   COL *+12;
!117! LABEL 'POLE TYPE NAME' LINE *+1 COL 5;
!118! FIELD pt_name PROTECTED COL *+7;
!119! LABEL 'POLE LENGTH' LINE *+2 COL 5;
!120! FIELD pole_length   COL *+10;
!121! LABEL 'POLE RENTAL CHARGE' LINE *+2 COL 5;
```

Figure 19.4 *continued*

```
!122! FIELD pole_rentch  COL #+3;
!123! LABEL 'POLE RENTAL FLAG' LINE #+2 COL 5;
!124! FIELD pole_flag PROTECTED  COL #+5;
!125! FEND;

!126! FORM srtf07 TITLE 'RENTAL TRANSACTION';
!127! LABEL 'TECHNICIAN ID:' LINE #+1 COL 10;
!128! FIELD technician COL #+3;
!129! LABEL 'IDENTIFICATION TYPE:' LINE #+2 COL 2;
!130! FROM transactions;
!131! FIELD ident_type PROTECTED COL #+1;
!132! LABEL 'CUSTOMER IDENTIFICATION NO.:' COL #+2;
!133! FIELD custident PROTECTED COL #+1;
!134! LABEL 'EQUIPMENT DATE OUT:' LINE #+3 COL 5;
!135! FIELD date_out  COL #+2;
!136! LABEL 'EQUIPMENT DATE DUE:' COL #+5;
!137! FIELD date_due COL#+2;
!138! LABEL 'SKI INV. NO.:' LINE #+2 COL 5;
!139! FIELD ski_num COL #+3;
!140! LABEL 'SKI RENTING FEE/DAY:' COL #+4;
!141! FIELD amount_ski COL #+3;
!142! LABEL 'BOOT INV. NO.:' LINE #+2 COL 5;
!143! FIELD boot_num COL #+2;
!144! LABEL 'BOOT RENTING FEE/DAY:' COL #+8;
!145! FIELD amount_boot COL #+2;
!146! LABEL 'POLE INV. NO.:' LINE #+2 COL 5;
!147! FIELD pole_num COL #+2;
!148! LABEL 'POLE RENTING FEE/DAY:' COL #+8;
!149! FIELD amount_pole COL #+2;
!150! LABEL 'AMOUNT PREPAID FOR SKIS:' LINE #+3 COL 15;
!151! FIELD ski_pre_paid COL #+5;
!152! LABEL 'AMOUNT PREPAID FOR BOOTS:' LINE #+2 COL 15;
!153! FIELD boot_pre_paid COL #+3;
!154! LABEL 'AMOUNT PREPAID FOR POLES:' LINE #+2 COL 15;
!155! FIELD pole_pre_paid COL #+3;
!156! LABEL 'TOTAL AMOUNT PREPAID:' LINE #+2 COL 20;
!157! FIELD fee_pre_paid COL #+2;
!158! FROM;
!159! FEND;

!160! FORM srtf09 TITLE 'RENTAL TRANSACTION';
!161! LABEL 'TECHNICIAN ID:' LINE 1 COL 10;
!162! FIELD technician COL #+3;
!163! LABEL 'IDENTIFICATION TYPE:' LINE #+2 COL 2;
!164! FROM transactions;
!165! FIELD ident_type PROTECTED COL #+1;
!166! LABEL 'CUSTOMER IDENTIFICATION NO.:' COL #+2;
!167! FIELD custident PROTECTED COL #+1;
!168! LABEL 'EQUIPMENT DATE OUT:' LINE #+2 COL 5;
!169! FIELD date_out  COL #+2;
!170! LABEL 'EQUIPMENT DATE DUE:' COL #+5;
!171! FIELD date_due COL#+2;
!172! LABEL 'SKI INV. NO.:' LINE #+2 COL 5;
!173! FIELD ski_num COL #+3;
!174! LABEL 'SKI RENTING FEE/DAY:' COL #+4;
!175! FIELD amount_ski COL#+3;
!176! LABEL 'BOOT INV. NO.:' LINE #+2 COL 5;
!177! FIELD boot_num COL #+2;
!178! LABEL 'BOOT RENTING FEE/DAY:' COL #+8;
!179! FIELD amount_boot COL #+2;
!180! LABEL 'POLE INV. NO.:' LINE #+2 COL 5;
!181! FIELD pole_num COL #+2;
```

Figure 19.4 *continued*

```
!182! LABEL 'POLE RENTING FEE/DAY:' COL *+8;
!183! FIELD amount_pole COL *+2;
!184! LABEL 'EQUIPMENT DATE RETURN' LINE *+2  COL 15;
!185! FIELD date_ret COL *+2;
!186! LABEL 'AMOUNT PREPAID FOR SKIS:' LINE *+2 COL 1;
!187! FIELD ski_pre_paid COL *+5;
!188! LABEL 'AMOUNT PAID FOR SKIS:' COL *+3;
!189! FIELD ski_rent_paid COL *+5;
!190! LABEL 'AMOUNT PREPAID FOR BOOTS:' LINE *+2 COL 1;
!191! FIELD boot_pre_paid COL *+3;
!192! LABEL 'AMOUNT PAID FOR BOOTS:' COL *+3;
!193! FIELD boot_rent_paid COL *+3;
!194! LABEL 'AMOUNT PREPAID FOR POLES:' LINE *+2 COL 1;
!195! FIELD pole_pre_paid COL *+3;
!196! LABEL 'AMOUNT PAID FOR POLES:' COL *+3;
!197! FIELD pole_rent_paid COL *+3;
!198! LABEL 'TOTAL AMOUNT PREPAID:' LINE *+2 COL 1;
!199! FIELD fee_pre_paid COL *+2;
!200! LABEL 'TOTAL AMOUNT PAID:' COL *+5;
!201! FIELD fee_paid COL *+2;
!202! FROM;
!203! FEND;
```

Figure 19.4   *continued*

Enhanced System Components

We now list enhanced procedures. For each procedure we discuss only the enhancements. The basic contents of each procedure were considered in previous chapters.

The enhanced procedures are discussed in the order in which they appear on the main menu. Three procedures that update the SKIINVENTORY, BOOTINVENTORY, and POLEINVENTORY files and the procedure that creates mailing labels for all the customers on file are left for you as exercises to practice using NOMAD.

New Customer Transaction Procedure

Recall that this procedure allows you to create a rental transaction for the new customer and to create a record in the CUSTOMER file. We enhanced this procedure by allowing the user to control exits from loops by means of the function keys. We also allow the user to exit from this procedure at any point; the originally entered information can be deleted or saved at any point up to the moment when the exit process was initiated.

This procedure is contained in the PROC1.NOM file on your data disk and is listed in Figure 19.5.

Lines 2-3 hold statements that move the Error window to the new location. This way the Error window will not cover the user-defined windows.

Control of exits from loops is done with the PF1 function key. Lines 4-7 hold the statements that define the operation of the PF1 key. To see how this function key operates, we can trace its use in specific places in the procedure. For example, consider the select statements held in lines 32-37.

```
! 1!     WINDOW CLOSE srtmsg OTW;
! 2!     WINDOW LOAD ERROR OTW;
! 3!     WINDOW MOVE ERROR LINE 17 OTW;

! 4!         ON FKEY(1) DO;
! 5!             &sys_key=&&FUNCTIONKEY;
! 6!             RETURN;
! 7!         END;

! 8! ON FKEY(9,10) DO;
! 9!   &system_msg='Sorry, that function key is not used here. Press ENTER to continue.';
! 10!  WINDOW READ srtmsg LINE 20 COL 1 OTW;
! 11!  RETRY;
! 12! END;

! 13!  ON FKEY(11) DO;
! 14! ASK 'Do you want to delete all created transactions? (Y/N)'
! 15!     &ANS UPPERCASE;
! 16!     IF &ANS = 'N' THEN DO;
! 17!     SAVE;
! 18!     CLEAR ALL;
! 19!     GOTO -return;
! 20!    END;
! 21!    RESTORE;
! 22!    GOTO -return;
! 23!   END;

! 24!    -start
! 25!       SAVE OFF;
! 26!       FROM customer;
! 27!       CLEAR ALL;
! 28!       WINDOW LOAD srtf03 OTW;

! 29!    -custcr
! 30!       WINDOW READ srtf03 INSERT;
! 31!       WINDOW OPEN srtf03;
! 32!       &system_msg1='If record correct';
! 33!       &system_msg2='press PF1';
! 34!       &system_msg3='else press ENTER';
! 35!       WINDOW READ srtmsg1 LINE 7 COL 1 OTW;
! 36!       WINDOW CLOSE srtf03 OTW;
! 37!       IF &sys_key=1 THEN GOTO -initial;

! 38!    -custchan
! 39!       WINDOW CLOSE srtmsg1 OTW;
! 40!       CLEAR &sys_key;
! 41!       WINDOW READ srtf03 CHANGE OTW;
! 42!       WINDOW OPEN srtf03 OTW;
! 43!       WINDOW READ srtmsg1 LINE 7 COL 1 OTW;
! 44!       WINDOW CLOSE srtf03 OTW;
! 45!       IF &sys_key=1 THEN GOTO -initial;
! 46!       GOTO -custchan;

! 47!   -initial
! 48!       CLEAR &sys_key;
! 49!       FROM;
! 50!       &ident1= FGET(srtf03,ident_type);
! 51!       &ident2= FGET(srtf03,custident);
! 52!       FROM transactions &ident_type = &ident1;
! 53!       FROM transactions &custident = &ident2;
! 54!       WINDOW UNLOAD srtf03;
```

Figure 19.5   New Customer Transaction Procedure

```
! 55!    -transcr
! 56!       WINDOW LOAD srtf07 OTW;
! 57!       WINDOW READ srtf07 INSERT ;
! 58!       PREVIOUS transactions OTW TOP transactions;
! 59!       NEXT transactions;
! 60!       WINDOW OPEN srtf07;
! 61!       WINDOW READ srtmsg1 LINE 1 COL 1 OTW;
! 62!       WINDOW CLOSE srtf07 OTW;
! 63!       IF &sys_key=1 THEN GOTO -upinv;

! 64!    -transchan
! 65!       CLEAR &sys_key;
! 66!       WINDOW READ srtf07 CHANGE;
! 67!       PREVIOUS transactions OTW TOP transactions;
! 68!       NEXT transactions;
! 69!       WINDOW OPEN srtf07;
! 70!       WINDOW READ srtmsg1 LINE 1 COL 1 OTW;
! 71!       WINDOW CLOSE srtf07;
! 72!       IF &sys_key=1 THEN GOTO -upinv;
! 73!       GOTO -transchan;

! 74!    -upinv
! 75!       FROM skiinventory;
! 76!       &ski_flag = &ident1 CAT &ident2;
! 77!       &skinum = FGET(srtf07,ski_num);
! 78!       RKEY skinum OTW GOTO -F1;
! 79!       CHANGE ski_flag;
! 80!       -F1
! 81!       FROM bootinventory;
! 82!       &boot_flag = &ident1 CAT &ident2;
! 83!       &bootnum = FGET(srtf07,boot_num);
! 84!       RKEY bootnum OTW GOTO -F2;
! 85!       CHANGE boot_flag;
! 86!       -F2
! 87!       FROM poleinventory;
! 88!       &pole_flag = &ident1 CAT &ident2;
! 89!       &polenum = FGET(srtf07,pole_num);
! 90!       RKEY polenum OTW GOTO -F3;
! 91!       CHANGE pole_flag;
! 92!       -F3
! 93!       WINDOW CLOSE srtf07 OTW;
! 94!       WINDOW UNLOAD srtf07 OTW;
! 95!       FROM;
! 96!       CLEAR &sys_key;
! 97!       &system_msg1='If you wish to enter next customer';
! 98!       &system_msg2='data, press PF1,';
! 99!       &system_msg3='else press ENTER';
!100!       WINDOW READ srtmsg1 OTW;
!101!       IF &sys_key=1 THEN DO;
!102!          SAVE;
!103!          GOTO -start;
!104!       END;
!105!       SAVE;
!106!    -return
!107!       CLEAR ALL;
!108!       WINDOW CLOSE srtf03 OTW;
!109!       WINDOW CLOSE srtf07 OTW;
!110!       WINDOW OPEN srtmsg LINE 20 COL 1 OTW;
!111!       RETURN;
```

Figure 19.5 *continued*

The statements in lines 32-34 initialize the &system_msg1, &system_msg2, and &system_msg3 variables with a message to the user specifying what to do next. The user is instructed to press the PF1 key if the information on the screen is correct or to press the ENTER key if the information is to be changed. (This user message is generated by the statement in line 35.)

If the user presses the PF1 key, the ON FKEY(1) condition is raised and the statements in lines 4-7 are executed. In this case, the &sys_key variable is initialized to the value of 1, and control returns to the statement that follows the one where PF1 was activated. This statement is in line 36. Line 36 contains the statement that closes the srtf03 window. Where the control is directed depends on the value of the &sys_key variable (line 37). Since, in our example, the value is 1, control passes to the statement with the label -initial (line 47).

If the user presses the ENTER key, the ON FKEY condition is not raised. In this case, processing continues with the statement in line 36; the &sys_key variable is not initialized with a value of 1; and processing continues with the statement in line 38.

We use this technique of exiting the loops for all procedures in the Ski Rental System.

We allow the user to exit the entire procedure by using PF11 key (Shift/PF1). The user has two options: all the information entered can be either erased or saved. The operation of the PF11 key is defined in lines 13-23.

Entered data can be saved upon exit from the procedure or when the user enters a new customer transaction. This is achieved with the following statements: SAVE, when exiting the procedure with the PF11 key (line 17); RESTORE (line 21); SAVE OFF (line 25); and SAVE, when ending the transaction (line 105).

The OTW clause is used in several places in the procedure to control error handling.

Returning Customer Transaction Procedure

Here you do not create a new record, but rather you search the CUSTOMER file for the information on the returning customer. You can update this information as well. Then you create the rental transaction record.

All the enhancements used in this procedure are the same as those for the previous procedure. Analyze the code to reinforce what you have learned. This procedure is contained in the PROC2.NOM file on your data disk and is listed in Figure 19.6.

```
! 1!        WINDOW LOAD OUTPUT OTW;
! 2!        WINDOW SIZE OUTPUT LINESIZE 8 COLSIZE 76;
! 3!        WINDOW LOAD ERROR OTW;
! 4!        WINDOW MOVE ERROR LINE 17 OTW;

! 5!     ON FKEY(1) DO;
! 6!        &sys_key=&&FUNCTIONKEY;
! 7!        RETURN;
! 8!       END;

! 9!     ON FKEY(9,10) DO;
! 10!    &system_msg='Sorry, that function key is not used here. Press ENTER to continue.';
! 11!       WINDOW READ srtmsg LINE 20 COL 1 OTW;
! 12!       RETRY;
! 13!    END;
! 14!

! 15!    ON FKEY(11) DO;
! 16!       ASK 'Do you want to delete all created transactions? (Y/N)
! 17!          &ANS UPPERCASE;
! 18!       IF &ANS = 'N' THEN DO;
! 19!          SAVE;
! 20!          CLEAR ALL;
! 21!          GOTO -return;
! 22!       END;
! 23!       RESTORE;
! 24!       GOTO -return;
! 25!    END;

! 26!      -start
! 27!         SAVE OFF;
! 28!         WINDOW LOAD srtf03 OTW;
! 29!         WINDOW CLEAR OUTPUT;
! 30!         WINDOW OPEN OUTPUT LINE 2 COL 2 OTW;
! 31!       ASK 'Customer's last name?' &last_name1 UPPERCASE;
! 32!       ASK 'Customer's first name?' &first_name1 UPPERCASE;
! 33!         FROM customer;
! 34!         TOP customer;
! 35!         VERIFY PROC ON;

! 36!      -search
! 37!         CLEAR &sys_key;
! 38!         LOCATE last_name = &last_name1
! 39!            AND first_name = &first_name1 OTW DO;
! 40!         &system_msg1='No more customers with the name:';
! 41!         &system_msg2=(&last_name1 CATB ' press PF1 to');
! 42!         &system_msg3='enter new name, press ENTER to exit';
! 43!         WINDOW READ srtmsg1 LINE 12 COL 1;
! 44!         IF &sys_key=1 THEN GOTO -start;
! 45!            SAVE;
! 46!            WINDOW CLEAR OUTPUT;
! 47!            WINDOW CLOSE OUTPUT OTW;
! 48!            RETURN rental;
! 48!         END;
```

Figure 19.6 Returning Customer Transaction Procedure

```
! 49!        &system_msg='If the record is correct press PF1, else press ENTER';
! 50!            WINDOW READ srtmsg LINE 19 OTW;
! 51!        IF &sys_key=1 THEN DO;
! 52!            VERIFY PROC OFF;
! 53!            WINDOW CLEAR OUTPUT OTW;
! 54!            WINDOW CLOSE OUTPUT OTW;
! 55!            GOTO -custchan;
! 56!        END;
! 57!            GOTO -search;
! 58!
! 59!        -custchan
! 60!            CLEAR &sys_key;
! 61!            WINDOW READ srtf03 CHANGE;
!      !        WINDOW OPEN srtf03 OTW;
! 62!            &system_msg='If the data is correct press PF1, else press ENTER and retype';
! 63!            WINDOW READ srtmsg LINE 1 OTW;
! 64!            WINDOW CLOSE srtf03 OTW;
! 65!        IF &sys_key=1 THEN GOTO -initial;
! 66!            GOTO -custchan;
! 67!
! 68!        -initial
! 69!            FROM;
!      !        &IDENT1= FGET(srtf03,ident_type);
! 70!            &IDENT2= FGET(srtf03,custident);
! 71!            FROM transactions &ident_type = &ident1;
! 72!            FROM transactions &custident = &ident2;
! 73!            WINDOW UNLOAD srtf03 OTW;
! 74!
! 75!        -transcr
! 76!            CLEAR &sys_key;
!      !        WINDOW LOAD srtf07 OTW;
! 77!            WINDOW READ srtf07 INSERT;
! 78!            PREVIOUS transactions OTW TOP transactions;
! 79!            NEXT transactions;
! 80!            WINDOW OPEN srtf07 OTW;
! 81!            &system_msg='If the data is correct press PF1, else press ENTER and retype';
! 82!            WINDOW READ srtmsg LINE 19 OTW;
! 83!        IF &sys_key=1 THEN GOTO -upinv;
! 84!            WINDOW CLOSE srtf07;
! 85!
! 86!        -transchan
! 87!            CLEAR &sys_key;
! 88!            WINDOW READ srtf07 CHANGE;
!      !        PREVIOUS transactions OTW TOP transactions;
! 89!            NEXT transactions;
! 90!            WINDOW OPEN srtf07 OTW;
! 91!            &system_msg='If the data is correct press PF1, else press ENTER and retype';
! 92!            WINDOW READ srtmsg LINE 19 OTW;
! 93!        IF &sys_key=1 THEN GOTO -upinv;
! 94!            WINDOW CLOSE srtf07 OTW;
! 95!            GOTO -transchan;
! 96!
! 97!        -upinv
! 98!            CLEAR &sys_key;
! 99!            FROM skiinventory;
!100!            &ski_flag = &ident1 CAT &ident2;
!      !        &skinum = FGET(srtf07,ski_num);
!101!            RKEY skinum OTW GOTO -F1;
!102!            CHANGE ski_flag;
```

Figure 19.6   *continued*

```
!103!      -F1
!104!         FROM bootinventory;
!105!         &boot_flag = &ident1 CAT &ident2;
!106!         &bootnum = FGET(srtf07,boot_num);
!107!         RKEY bootnum OTW GOTO -F2;
!108!         CHANGE boot_flag;
!109!      -F2
!110!         FROM poleinventory;
!111!         &pole_flag = &ident1 CAT &ident2;
!112!         &polenum = FGET(srtf07,pole_num);
!113!         RKEY polenum OTW GOTO -F3;
!114!         CHANGE pole_flag;
!115!      -F3
!116!         WINDOW CLOSE srtf07;
!117!         WINDOW UNLOAD srtf07;
!118!         FROM;

!119!         &system_msg='If you wish  to  continue   press PF1, else press ENTER';
!120!         WINDOW READ srtmsg LINE 19 OTW;
!121!      IF &sys_key=1 THEN DO;
!122!         SAVE;
!123!         GOTO -start;
!124!      END;

!125!   -return
!126!         WINDOW CLOSE srtf03 OTW;
!127!         WINDOW CLOSE srtf07 OTW;
!128!         WINDOW CLOSE OUTPUT OTW;
!129!         RETURN;
```

Figure 19.6 *continued*

Equipment Return Procedure

This procedure allows you to enter the return date (of the rental transaction), calculates fees to be collected, and updates all rental flags in the equipment inventory files.

Again, all the enhancements are similar to those described previously. This procedure is contained in the PROC3.NOM file on your data disk and is listed in Figure 19.7.

Equipment Type File Updating Procedure

This procedure is the combination of all the procedures developed in Chapter 14. This procedure allows you to add, change, and delete records as well as to create reports (printed or displayed on the screen) containing information from the EQUIPMENT_TYPE master.

In this procedure we introduce HELP facilities. We define the PF10 key as the HELP key and use the DDQUERY function to display the information on individual items from the DOCUMENT option in the schema of the Ski Rental System. (Lines 10-16 of the porcedure hold the defining statements.) The retrieved information is

```
!  1!          ON FKEY(1) DO;
!  2!            &sys_key=&&FUNCTIONKEY;
!  3!            RETURN;
!  4!          END;

!  5!          ON FKEY(9,10) DO;
!  6!    &system_msg='Sorry, that function key is not used here. Press ENTER to continue.';
!  7!            WINDOW READ srtmsg LINE 2 COL 1 OTW;
!  8!            RETRY;
!  9!          END;

! 10!          ON FKEY(11) DO;
! 11!          ASK 'Do you want to delete all created transactions? (Y/N)'
! 12!            &ANS UPPERCASE;
! 13!            IF &ANS = 'N' THEN DO;
! 14!              SAVE;
! 15!              CLEAR ALL;
! 16!              GOTO -return;
! 17!            END;
! 18!            RESTORE;
! 19!            GOTO -return;
! 20!          END;

! 21!          WINDOW CLOSE srtmsg OTW;
! 22!    -start
! 23!          WINDOW LOAD ERROR OTW;
! 24!          WINDOW MOVE ERROR LINE 17 OTW;
! 25!          SAVE OFF;

! 26!          CLEAR &sys_key;
! 27!          WINDOW LOAD srtf09 OTW;
! 28!          ASK 'Equipment Code?' &tnumber;
! 29!          ASK 'The date when equipment was rented?'
! 30!             &tdate_out;

! 31!    -search
! 32!            FROM transactions;
! 33!            TOP transactions;
! 34!    LOCATE DATE_OUT=&tdate_out AND (ski_num=&tnumber OR
! 35!      boot_num=&tnumber OR pole_num=&tnumber) OTW DO;
! 36!            &system_msg1='No transaction with this date and equipment code.';
! 37!            &system_msg2=' press PF1 to enter new data';
! 38!            &system_msg3=' press ENTER to exit';
! 39!            WINDOW READ srtmsg1 LINE 2 COL 1;
! 40!            IF &sys_key=1 THEN GOTO -START;
! 41!            GOTO -return;
! 42!          END;

! 43!    -transchan
! 44!            CLEAR &sys_key;
! 45!            WINDOW READ srtf09 CHANGE;
! 46!    PREVIOUS transactions OTW TOP transactions;
! 47!            NEXT transactions;
! 48!            WINDOW OPEN srtf09 OTW;
! 49!            &system_msg='If your transaction is completed press PF1, else press ENTER and
              retype';
! 50!            WINDOW READ srtmsg LINE 2 OTW;
! 51!            WINDOW CLOSE srtf09 OTW;
! 52!            IF &sys_key=1 THEN GOTO -upinv;
! 53!            GOTO -transchan;
```

Figure 19.7   Equipment Return Procedure

```
! 54!    -upinv
! 55!         FROM skiinventory;
! 56!         &ski_flag = &NAV;
! 57!         &skinum = FGET(srtf09,ski_num);
! 58!         IF &skinum = &NAV THEN GOTO -next1;
! 59!         RKEY skinum OTW GOTO -next1;
! 60!         CHANGE ski_flag;
! 61!    -next1
! 62!         FROM bootinventory;
! 63!         &bootnum = FGET(srtf09,boot_num);
! 64!         IF &bootnum = &NAV THEN GOTO -next2;
! 65!         &boot_flag = &NAV;
! 66!         RKEY bootnum OTW GOTO -next2;
! 67!         CHANGE boot_flag;
! 68!    -next2
! 69!         FROM poleinventory;
! 70!         &polenum = FGET(srtf09,pole_num);
! 71!         IF &polenum = &NAV THEN GOTO -end;
! 72!         &pole_flag = &NAV;
! 73!         RKEY polenum OTW GOTO -end;
! 74!         CHANGE pole_flag;
! 75!    -end
! 76!         WINDOW UNLOAD srtf09 OTW;
! 77!         FROM;
! 78!         CLEAR ALL;
! 79!         &system_msg='If you wish to continue press PF1, else press ENTER';
! 80!         WINDOW READ srtmsg LINE 2 OTW;
! 81!         SAVE;
! 82!         IF &sys_key=1 THEN GOTO -start;
! 83!    -return
! 84!         WINDOW OPEN srtmsg LINE 20 COL 1 OTW;
! 85!         WINDOW CLOSE srtf09 OTW;
! 86!         RETURN;
```

Figure 19.7 *continued*

for the item in &CURSORFIELD. (&CURSORFIELD contains the name of the item on which the cursor is positioned when the PF10 function key is activated.) All the other enhancements are the same as those in previous procedures.

This procedure is contained in the PROC4.NOM file on your data disk and is listed in Figure 19.8.

Manufacturer File Updating Procedure

This procedure allows you to add, change, and delete records in the MANUFAC-TURERS master and to report on certain information from this master. The procedure is very similar to the previous procedure. The procedures differ in the way in which the HELP facility is generated. In the MANUFACTURER file updating procedure, we use the SLIST command instead of the DDQUERY function. The HELP facility is defined in lines 11-26 and can be invoked by pressing the PF10 key during the data entry, change, or delete processes.

```
!  1!            ON FKEY(1) DO;
!  2!               &sys_key=&&FUNCTIONKEY;
!  3!               RETURN;
!  4!            END;

!  5!            ON FKEY(9) DO;
!  6!     &system_msg='Sorry, that function key is not used here. Press ENTER to continue. ;
!  7!               WINDOW READ srtmsg LINE 20 COL 1 OTW;
!  8!               RETRY;
!  9!            END;

! 10!            ON FKEY(10) DO;
! 11!               &help1=DDQUERY('DOCUMENT',&CURSORFIELD);
! 12!               IF &help1=&NAV THEN &help1='No  help available';
! 13!        &help2='Press  ENTER  to  return  to  the  data  entry  screen';
! 14!               WINDOW READ shelp LINE 18 OTW;
! 15!               RETRY;
! 16!            END;

! 17!            ON FKEY(11) DO;
! 18!            ASK  'Do   you   want   to   delete   all  created   transactions? (Y/N)'
! 19!               &ANS UPPERCASE;
! 20!               IF &ANS = 'N' THEN DO;
! 21!                  SAVE;
! 22!                  CLEAR ALL;
! 23!                  WINDOW OPEN srtmsg LINE 20 COL 1 OTW;
! 24!                  RETURN rental;
! 25!               END;
! 26!               RESTORE;
! 27!               WINDOW OPEN srtmsg LINE 20 COL 1 OTW;
! 28!               RETURN rental;
! 29!            END;

! 30!            WINDOW LOAD LIST OTW;
! 31!            WINDOW SIZE LIST LINESIZE 10 COLSIZE 60;
! 32!            WINDOW MOVE LIST LINE 2 COL 3;

! 33!     -menus5
! 34!               &system_msg='Please  select  the function you want to work with.';

! 35!            WINDOW OPEN srtmsg LINE 20 COL 1 OTW;

! 36!     MENU TITLE 'TYPE OF UPDATE'
! 37!     PICK INDEX &s5_choice_n FOLD
! 38!        CHOICE 'A - ADD RECORDS ' SPACE 30 FOLD
! 39!        CHOICE 'B - CHANGE RECORDS ' SPACE 30 FOLD
! 40!        CHOICE 'C - DELETE RECORDS ' SPACE 30 FOLD
! 41!        CHOICE  'D  -  LOCATE  RECORDS  WITH  SPECIFIED:FIRST CHARACTER IN KEY-FIELD'
! 42!                 SPACE 30 FOLD
! 43!        CHOICE 'E  - LOCATE RECORDS WITH SPECIFIED:PRODUCTION DATE
! 44!                 SPACE 30 FOLD 3
! 45!        CHOICE 'F - RETURN TO MAIN MENU ';
! 46!     GOTO (-add, -change, -delete,  -query1, -query2, -exit)
! 47!               &s5_choice_n;

! 48!     -add
! 49!        GOTO -adds5;

! 50!     -change
! 51!        GOTO -changes5;
```

Figure 19.8 Equipment Type File Updating Procedure

```
! 52!     -delete
! 53!        GOTO -deletes5;

! 54!     -query1
! 55!        GOTO -query1s5;

! 56!     -query2
! 57!        GOTO -query2s5;

! 58!     -exit
! 59!        RETURN;

! 60!     -adds5
! 61!       CLEAR &sys_key &equipment_code;
! 62!        SAVE OFF;
! 63!        WINDOW CLOSE srtmsg OTW;
! 64!        WINDOW READ srtf01 INSERT LINE 4 COLUMN 5;
! 65!        &system_msg='If you  want add another record press PF1, else press ENTER';
! 66!        WINDOW READ srtmsg LINE 20 OTW;
! 67!        SAVE;
! 68!        IF &sys_key=1 THEN GOTO -adds5;
! 69!        GOTO -menus5;

! 70!     -changes5
! 71!        CLEAR &sys_key &equipment_code;
! 72!        SAVE OFF;
! 73!        WINDOW CLOSE srtmsg OTW;
! 74!        ASK 'Enter equipment code to locate a record: '
! 75!        &equipment_code UPPERCASE;
! 76!        RKEY equipment_code OTW DO;
! 77!        &system_msg='Record not found, press  PF1 to enter new equipment code,
          else press ENTER';
! 78!        WINDOW READ srtmsg LINE 20 OTW;
! 79!        IF &sys_key=1 THEN GOTO -changes5;
! 80!        SAVE;
! 81!        GOTO -menus5;
! 82!      END;
! 83!        WINDOW READ srtf01 CHANGE LINE 4 COLUMN 5;
! 84!        &system_msg='Locate another  record? If yes, press PF1, else press ENTER';
! 85!        WINDOW READ srtmsg LINE 20 OTW;
! 86!        SAVE;
! 87!        IF &sys_key=1 THEN GOTO -changes5;
! 88!        GOTO -menus5;

! 89!     -deletes5
! 90!        CLEAR ALL;
! 91!        SAVE OFF;
! 92!        WINDOW CLOSE srtmsg OTW;
! 93!        ASK 'Enter equipment code to locate  the record: '
! 94!        &equipment_code UPPERCASE;
! 95!        RKEY equipment_code OTW DO;
! 96!        &system_msg='Record not  found, press PF1 to enter new equipment code else
          press ENTER';
! 97!        WINDOW READ srtmsg LINE 20 OTW;
! 98!        IF &sys_key=1 THEN GOTO -deletes5;
! 99!        SAVE;
!100!        GOTO -menus5;
!101!      END;
!102!        WINDOW OPEN srtf01 LINE 1 COLUMN 5 OTW;
!103!        &system_msg='Press ENTER  to  delete  this record, press Pf1 to exit';
!104!        WINDOW READ srtmsg LINE 20 OTW;
!105!        WINDOW CLOSE srtf01 OTW;
!106!        IF &sys_key=1 THEN GOTO -menus5;
```

Figure 19.8 *continued*

```
!107!          DELETE equipment_code;
!108!          &system_msg='If you want to delete another record press PF1, else press ENTER';
!109!          WINDOW READ srtmsg LINE 20 OTW;
!110!          SAVE;
!111!     IF &sys_key=1 THEN GOTO -deletes5;
!112!          GOTO -menus5;

!113!       -query1s5
!114!          CLEAR &sys_key;
!115!          WINDOW CLEAR LIST;
!116!          WINDOW CLOSE srtmsg OTW;
!117!          WINDOW OPEN LIST OTW;
!118!          ASK 'Enter first letter of the equipment code:'
!119!             &l_select;
!120!          IF &l_select NOT=&NAV
!121!          THEN SELECT equipment_code1=&l_select;
!122!     &system_msg='For printed  report press  PF1, to display on the screen press ENTER';
!123!          WINDOW READ srtmsg LINE 20 OTW;
!124!          IF &sys_key=1 THEN GOTO -print;
!125!          LIST equipment_code equipment_name production_date
!126!     OTW DO;
!127!          &system_msg='No record  selected  for  the report, press ENTER to continue';
!128!          WINDOW READ srtmsg LINE 20 OTW;
!129!     END;
!130!          GOTO -next;
!131!        -print
!132!          LIST equipment_code equipment_name production_date
!133!          ON PTR OTW DO;
!134!           &system_msg='No record selected  for  the report, press ENTER to continue';
!135!           WINDOW READ srtmsg LINE 20 OTW;
!136!          END;
!137!        -next
!138!          CLEAR &sys_key;
!139!          SELECT CLEAR;
!140!          &system_msg='If you want to continue the query press PF1, else press ENTER';
!141!          WINDOW READ srtmsg LINE 20 OTW;
!142!          IF &sys_key=1 THEN GOTO -query1s5;
!143!          WINDOW CLOSE LIST OTW;
!144!          WINDOW CLEAR LIST;
!145!          GOTO -menus5;

!146!       -query2s5
!147!          CLEAR &sys_key;
!148!          WINDOW CLOSE srtmsg OTW;
!149!          WINDOW OPEN LIST OTW;
!150!          ASK 'Enter production date: '
!151!             &date_select;
!152!          IF &date_select NOT=&NAV
!153!          THEN SELECT production_date=&date_select;
!154!          &system_msg='For  printed  report  press  PF1,  to  display on the screen
             press ENTER';
!155!          WINDOW READ srtmsg LINE 20 OTW;
!156!          IF &sys_key=1 THEN GOTO -print1;
!157!          LIST equipment_code equipment_name production_date
!158!     OTW DO;
!159!          &system_msg='No record  selected  for  the report, press ENTER to continue';
!160!          WINDOW READ srtmsg LINE 20 OTW;
!161!     END;
!162!          GOTO -next1;
!163!        -print1
!164!          LIST equipment_code equipment_name production_date
```

Figure 19.8 *continued*

```
!165!          ON PTR OTW DO;
!166!          &system_msg='No record  selected  for  the report, press ENTER to continue';
!167!          WINDOW READ srtmsg LINE 20 OTW;
!168!     END;
!169!        -next1
!170!          CLEAR &sys_key;
!171!          SELECT CLEAR;
!172!          &system_msg='If you want to continue the query press PF1, else press ENTER';
!173!          WINDOW READ srtmsg LINE 20 OTW;
!174!          IF &sys_key=1 THEN GOTO -query2s5;
!175!          WINDOW CLOSE LIST OTW;
!176!          WINDOW CLEAR LIST;
!177!          GOTO -menus5;
```

Figure 9.8 *continued*

```
!  1!        ON FKEY(1) DO;
!  2!            &sys_key=&&FUNCTIONKEY;
!  3!            RETURN;
!  4!        END;

!  5!        ON FKEY(9) DO;
!  6!        &system_msg='Sorry, that function key is not used here, press ENTER to continue';
!  7!            WINDOW READ srtmsg LINE 20 COL 1 OTW;
!  8!            RETRY;
!  9!        END;

! 10!        ON FKEY(10) DO;
! 11!            WINDOW LOAD OUTPUT OTW;
! 12!            WINDOW CLEAR OUTPUT;
! 13!            WINDOW SIZE OUTPUT LINESIZE 18 COLSIZE 72;
! 14!            WINDOW MOVE OUTPUT LINE 1 COL 1;
! 15!            WINDOW CLOSE srtf02 OTW;
! 16!            WINDOW OPEN OUTPUT OTW;
! 17!        TRANS;
! 18!            SLIST ?(&CURSORFIELD);
! 19!        UNTRANS;
! 20!        &system_msg='If you want to return to the data entry screen, press ENTER';
! 21!            WINDOW READ srtmsg LINE 20 OTW;
! 22!            WINDOW CLOSE OUTPUT OTW;
! 23!            WINDOW OPEN srtf02 OTW;
! 24!            RETRY;
! 25!        END;

! 26!        ON FKEY(11) DO;
! 27! ASK 'Do you want to delete all created transactions? (Y/N)'
! 28!            &ANS UPPERCASE;
! 29!        IF &ANS = 'N' THEN DO;
! 30!            SAVE;
! 31!            CLEAR ALL;
! 32!            WINDOW OPEN srtmsg LINE 20 COL 1 OTW;
! 33!            RETURN rental;
! 34!        END;
! 35!            RESTORE;
! 36!            WINDOW OPEN srtmsg LINE 20 COL 1 OTW;
! 37!            RETURN rental;
! 38!        END;

! 39!            WINDOW LOAD LIST OTW;
! 40!            WINDOW SIZE LIST LINESIZE 10 COLSIZE 78;
! 41!            WINDOW MOVE LIST LINE 2 COL 3;

! 42!        -MENUS4
! 43!            &system_msg='Please select the function you want to work with';
! 44!            WINDOW OPEN srtmsg LINE 20 COL 1 OTW;

! 45!        MENU TITLE 'TYPE OF UPDATE'
! 46!            PICK INDEX &s5_choice_n SPACE 30 FOLD
! 47!            CHOICE 'A - ADD RECORDS '    FOLD
! 48!            CHOICE 'B - CHANGE RECORDS '  FOLD
! 49!            CHOICE 'C - DELETE RECORDS '  FOLD
! 50!            CHOICE  'D  -  LOCATE RECORDS WITH SPECIFIED FIRST CHARACTER IN KEY-FIELD'
! 51!                FOLD
! 52!            CHOICE 'E - RETURN TO MAIN MENU ';
! 53!    GOTO (-add, -change, -delete, -query1, -exit)
! 54!            &s5_choice_n;
! 54!            &s5_choice_n;
```

Figure 19.9 MANUFACTURER File Updating Procedure

This procedure is contained in the PROC5.NOM file on your data disk and is listed in Figure 19.9. The development of the enhanced procedures for the SKIINVENTORY, BOOTINVENTORY, and POLEINVENTORY masters are left for you as an exercise. The files that can hold these enhanced procedures are the PROC6.NOM, PROC7.NOM, and PROC8.NOM files.

```
! 55!        -add
! 56!            GOTO -adds4;

! 57!        -change
! 58!            GOTO -changes4;

! 59!        -delete
! 60!            GOTO -deletes4;

! 61!        -query1
! 62!            GOTO -query14;

! 63!        -EXIT
! 64!            RETURN;

! 65!        -adds4
! 66!            CLEAR &sys_key &manufact_code;
! 67!            SAVE OFF;
! 68!            WINDOW CLOSE srtmsg OTW;
! 69!            WINDOW READ srtf02 INSERT LINE 4 COLUMN 5;
! 70!            &system_msg='If you want add another record, press  PF1 else press ENTER';
! 71!            WINDOW READ srtmsg LINE 20 OTW;
! 72!            SAVE;
! 73!            IF &sys_key=1 THEN GOTO -adds4;
! 74!            GOTO -menus4;

! 75!        -changes4
! 76!            CLEAR &sys_key &manufact_code;
! 77!            SAVE OFF;
! 78!            WINDOW CLOSE srtmsg OTW;
! 79!            ASK 'Enter  manufacturer code to locate a record:'

! 80!                  &manufact_code;
! 81!            RKEY manufact_code OTW DO;
! 82!            &system_msg='Record not found, press  PF1 to enter new manufacturer code,
                  else press ENTER';
! 83!            WINDOW READ srtmsg LINE 20 OTW;
! 84!            IF &sys_key=1 THEN GOTO -changes4;
! 85!            SAVE;
! 86!            GOTO -menus4;
! 87!            END;
! 88!        WINDOW READ srtf02 CHANGE LINE 4 COLUMN 5;
! 89'            &system_msg='If you want to change another record press PF1, else press ENTER';
! 90!            WINDOW READ srtmsg LINE 20 OTW;
! 91'            SAVE;
! 92!            IF &sys_key=1 THEN GOTO -changes4;
! 93!            GOTO -menus4;

! 94!        -deletes4
! 95'            CLEAR &sys_key &manufact_code;
! 96'            SAVE OFF;
! 97'            WINDOW CLOSE srtmsg OTW;
! 98'            ASK 'Enter manufacturer code to locate a record: '
! 99'                  &manufact_code;
!100'            RKEY manufact_code OTW DO;
!101'            &system_msg='Record not  found, press PF1 to enter new manufacturer code,
                  else press ENTER';
!102'            WINDOW READ srtmsg LINE 20 OTW;
!103'            IF &sys_key=1 THEN GOTO -deletes4;
!104'            SAVE;
!105'            GOTO -menus4;
!106'            END;
```

Figure 19.9   *continued*

```
!107!        WINDOW OPEN srtf02 LINE 1 COLUMN 5 OTW;
!108!        &system_msg='Press ENTER  to  delete  this record,' press Pf1 to exit';
!109!        WINDOW READ srtmsg LINE 20 OTW;
!110!        WINDOW CLOSE srtf02 OTW;
!111!        IF &sys_key=1 THEN GOTO -menus4;
!112!        CLEAR &sys_key;
!113!        DELETE manufact_code;
!114!        &system_msg='If you want delete another record press PF1, else press ENTER';
!115!        WINDOW READ srtmsg LINE 20 OTW;
!116!        SAVE;
!117!    IF &sys_key=1 THEN GOTO -deletes4;
!118!        GOTO -menus4;

!119!      -query14
!120!        WINDOW CLEAR LIST;
!121!        CLEAR &sys_key;
!122!        WINDOW CLOSE srtmsg OTW;
!123!        ASK 'Enter first letter of the  manufacturer code:

!124!        &l_select;
!125!        WINDOW OPEN LIST OTW;
!126!        IF &l_select NOT=&NAV
!127!        THEN SELECT manufact_code1=&l_select;
!128!        &system_msg='For  printed  report  press  PF1, for display on the screen
             press ENTER';
!129!        WINDOW READ srtmsg LINE 20 OTW;
!130!        IF &sys_key=1 THEN GOTO -print;
!131!        LIST    manufact_code    manufact_name    rep_name    rep_telephone
!132!             OTW DO;
!133!        &system_msg='No  record  selected  for the report, press ENTER to continue';
!134!        WINDOW READ srtmsg LINE 20 OTW;
!135!        END;
!136!        GOTO -next;
!137!      -print
!138!        LIST FROM manufacturers manufact_code
!139!             manufact_name rep_name rep_telephone
!140!        ON PTR OTW DO;
!141!        &system_msg='No record  selected  for  the report, press ENTER to continue';
!142!        WINDOW READ srtmsg LINE 20 OTW;
!143!        END;
!144!      -next
!145!        CLEAR &sys_key;
!146!        SELECT CLEAR;
!147!        &system_msg='If you want to continue the query press PF1, else press ENTER';
!148!        WINDOW READ srtmsg LINE 20 OTW;
!149!        IF &sys_key=1 THEN GOTO -query14;
!150!        WINDOW CLOSE LIST OTW;
!151!        GOTO -menus4;
```

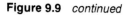

Figure 9.9 *continued*

History File Updating Procedure

This procedure is the combination of the procedures developed in Chapters 15 and 16. It allows you to generate the summary of the rental fees on a weekly basis for each type of equipment (skis, boots, and poles). This information is stored in the transaction file that is used to update the HISTORY master.

No new enhancements are introduced in this procedure. We performed general cleanup by removing the redundant code. The procedure is contained in the PROC9.NOM file on your data disk and is listed in Figure 19.10.

```
! 1!    !HISTORY file updating procedure!
! 2! FILE DEFINE out=reject.dat;

! 3!  ASK 'ENTER  STARTING PERIOD FOR TRANSACTION YEAR MM/DD/YY:'

! 4!      &start_time;

! 5! CREATE BY week_code NAMED week_code1
! 6!      SUM(ski_rent_paid) NAMED sum_ski_paid AS 99,999.99
! 7!      SUM(boot_rent_paid) NAMED sum_boot_paid AS 99,999.99
! 8!      SUM(pole_rent_paid) NAMED sum_pole_paid AS 99,999.99
! 9!      ON transact KEEP;

!10!   TRANS;
!11!     FROM transact;

!12!     FILE DEFINE ski1 = c:\nomad\transki1.dat CREATE;
!13!     FILE OPEN ski1 OTW;
!14! -start
!15!     NEXT transact OTW GOTO -end;
!16!     WRITE week_code1 AS 99
!17!         sum_ski_paid AS 99999.99
!18!         sum_boot_paid AS 99999.99
!19!         sum_pole_paid AS 99999.99
!20!         ON ski1;
!21!     GOTO -start;
!22! -end
!23!     FILE CLOSE ski1;
!24!     FROM;
!25!     ASK  'The year for these transactions? '
!26!         &hyear;
!27!     &year = &hyear;
!28!     FILE DEFINE ski2= c:\nomad\transki1.dat READ;
!29!     LOAD history
!30!     NOMATCH INSERT
!31!     READ ski2
!32!         SET &weekc FORM N2
!33!             &ski_revenue FORM N8.2
!34!             &boot_revenue FORM N8.2
!35!             &poles_revenue FORM N8.2
!36!         REJECT ON out;
!37!     FILE CLOSE out OTW;
!38!     WINDOW LOAD OUTPUT OTW;
!39!     WINDOW CLEAR OUTPUT;
!40!     WINDOW SIZE OUTPUT LINESIZE 5 COLSIZE 35;
!41!     WINDOW OPEN OUTPUT LINE 2 COL 15 OTW;
!42!     PRINT 'RECORDS READ: '(&READS)
!43!         FOLD'RECORDS INSERTED: '(&INSERTS);
!44! UNTRANS;

!45!     SELECT year = &hyear;
!46!     LIST weekc ski_revenue boot_revenue poles_revenue
!47!     ON PTR OTW;
!48!     WINDOW CLOSE srtmsg OTW;
!49!     &system_msg='Press ENTER to return';
!50!     WINDOW READ srtmsg LINE 15 OTW;
!51!     WINDOW CLOSE OUTPUT OTW;
!52!     WINDOW OPEN srtmsg LINE 20 COL 1 OTW;
!53!     SELECT CLEAR;
```

Figure 19.10 HISTORY File Updating Procedure

```
! 1!        ON FKEY(1) DO;
! 2!              &sys_key=&&FUNCTIONKEY;
! 3!              RETURN;
! 4!        END;
! 5! ASK 'ENTER STARTING PERIOD FOR TRANSACTION YEAR (MM/DD/YY):'
! 6!              &start_time FOLD
! 7!              'ENTER STARTING PERIOD FOR REPORT (MM/DD/YY):'
! 8!              &start_time_rep FOLD
! 9!              'ENTER END PERIOD FOR REPORT (MM/DD/YY):'
!10!              &end_time_rep FOLD
!11!              'ENTER REPORT DATE (MM/DD/YY):' &rep_date;
!12!              WINDOW LOAD LIST OTW;
!13!              WINDOW CLEAR LIST;
!14!              CLEAR &sys_key;
!15!        &system_msg='For printed report press PF1, for screen report press ENTER';
!16!              WINDOW READ srtmsg LINE 20 OTW;
!17!              IF &sys_key=1 THEN DO;
!18!                 &prtsg='ON PTR';
!19!                 &RLENGTH=56;
!20!                 &PLENGTH=66;
!21!                 CLEAR &sys_key;
!22!                 GOTO -print;
!23!              END;
!24!              &prtsg=' ';
!25!              CLEAR &sys_key;
!26!              WINDOW CLOSE srtmsg OTW;
!27!              WINDOW OPEN LIST OTW;
!28!              &RLENGTH=18;
!29!              &TLENGTH=20;
!30!        -print
!31!              SELECT date_out GE &start_time_rep AND date_out LE
!32!                    &end_time_rep;
!33!        CREATE BY week_code NAMED wcode AS 99
!34!              date_out NAMED date1 AS DATE'mm/dd/yy'
!35!              fee_paid NAMED revenue AS 99,999.99
!36!              SUBSET MATCHING weekc week_revenue
!37!              ON transrev;
!38!        TRANS;
!39!        LIST BY date1 AS DATE'MONTH DD' HEADING 'DATE'
!40!              BY wcode NOPRINT NEWPAGE SUM(revenue)
!41!              HEADING 'REVENUES' SET &drevenue MAX(week_revenue)
!42!              NOPRINT SET &totrev ?(&prtsg)
!43!              TITLE FOLD 3 COL 13 'BOB'S SKI SHOP'
!44!              FOLD COL 12 'DATE - ' &rep_date
!45!              FOLD COL 9 'RENTAL REVENUE REPORT'
!46!              FOLD COL 4 'FOR PERIOD ' &start_time_rep
!47!              ' TO ' &end_time_rep FOLD 2
!48!        BYFOOT wcode FOLD 2
!49!              'WEEKLY SUBTOTAL          ---' SPACE 2 &drevenue
!50!              FOLD 'LAST YEAR WEEKLY SUBTOTAL --- ' &totrev FOLD
!51!              'CHANGE                   --- ' SPACE 3
!52!              (100*(&drevenue-&totrev)/&totrev) AS 99.99 ' %'
!53!              FOLD 3
!54!        SUMMARY FOLD 3
!55!              'TOTAL PER PERIOD         ---' SPACE 2 &drevenue
!56!              FOLD 'LAST YEAR TOTAL PER PERIOD --- ' &totrev
!57!              FOLD 'CHANGE                  --- ' SPACE 3
```

Figure 19.11　Revenue Report Procedure

Revenue Report Procedure

The enhancements considered next all relate to the procedure developed in Chapter 18.

The revenue report procedure (contained in the REP1.NOM file on your data disk and listed in Figure 19.11) allows the revenue report to be displayed on the screen or to be printed. The printing option is selected by using the PF1 key and the ?(&prtsg) parameter assignment function.

```
!58!              (100#(&drevenue-&totrev)/&totrev) AS 99.99 ' %'
!59!              OTW DO;
!60!    &system_msg='No record  selected for  the report, press ENTER to continue';
!61!              WINDOW READ srtmsg LINE 20 OTW;
!62!           END;
!63!    UNTRANS;
!64!    &system_msg='Press ENTER to return to main menu';
!65!              WINDOW READ srtmsg LINE 20 OTW;
!66!              WINDOW CLOSE LIST OTW;
!67!              CLEAR ALL;
!68!              WINDOW OPEN srtmsg LINE 20 OTW;
```

Figure 19.11 *continued*

If the user presses the PF1 key, the value of the &prtsg variable becomes "ON PTR" (lines 15-18). When this value is substituted in the statement in line 42 (during the execution of the procedure), the report is routed to the printer. Note that because the substitution function is present, the code in lines 39-62 has to be in TRANS mode. (That is, this code is translated during the execution of the procedure.)

If the user presses the ENTER key, the value of the &prtsg variable becomes a blank (line 24). When the blank value is substituted in the statement in line 42, the report is routed to the screen.

To control the size of the report page, the following values are assigned to the system variables:

■ &RLENGTH=56—Assigns 56 lines to the report page (line 19).

■ &PLENGTH=66—Assigns 66 lines to the printed page. The &RLENGTH value has to be less than or equal to the value of &PLENGTH (line 20).

■ &TLENGTH=20—Assigns 20 lines to the screen. The &RLENGTH value has to be less than or equal to the value of &TLENGTH for the reports to be displayed only on the screen (lines 28-29).

Daily Late Return Report Procedure

The enhancements for this report are the same as those for the previous report. The Daily Late Return report displays information on customers who did not return rental equipment as promised. The display can be on the screen or printed.

This procedure is contained in the REP2.NOM file on your data disk and is listed in Figure 19.12.

```
 ! 1!        ON FKEY(1) DO;
 ! 2!               &sys_key=&&FUNCTIONKEY;
 ! 3!               RETURN;
 ! 4!        END;

 ! 5!               ASK 'ENTER REPORT DATE (MM/DD/YY) :' &rep_date;
 ! 6!               SELECT date_ret EQ &NAV AND date_due LE &rep_date;

 ! 7!               WINDOW LOAD LIST OTW;
 ! 8!               WINDOW CLEAR LIST;
 ! 9!               WINDOW SIZE LIST LINESIZE 18 COLSIZE 76;
 !10!               CLEAR &sys_key;
 !11!        &system_msg='For printed report press PF1, for display on the screen press ENTER';
 !12!               WINDOW READ srtmsg LINE 20 OTW;
 !13!           IF &sys_key=1 THEN DO;
 !14!               &prtsg='ON PTR';
 !15!               &RLENGTH=56;
 !16!               &PLENGTH=66;
 !17!               GOTO -print;
 !18!           END;
 !19!               &prtsg=' ';
 !20!               CLEAR &sys_key;
 !21!               WINDOW OPEN LIST OTW;
 !22!               &RLENGTH=18;
 !23!               &TLENGTH=20;

 !24!        -print
 !25!           TRANS;
 !26!           LIST FROM customer BY custident NOPRINT
 !27!               last_name HEADING 'CUSTOMER:LAST NAME'
 !28!               first_name HEADING 'CUSTOMER:FIRST NAME'
 !29!               phone HEADING 'TELEPHONE NO'
 !30!               SUBSET ALL MATCHING FROM transactions custident
 !31!               NOPRINT ski_mark HEADING 'SKI'
 !32!               boot_mark HEADING 'BOOTS'
 !33!               pole_mark  HEADING 'POLES'
 !34!               late HEADING 'DAYS:LATE'  ?(&prtsg)

 !35!           TITLE FOLD 3 'BOB'S SKI SHOP'
 !36!               FOLD  'DATE - ' &rep_date
 !37!               FOLD  'DAILY LATE RETURN REPORT'
 !38!               FOLD 3
 !39!           OTW DO;
 !40!        &system_msg='No record selected for the report, press ENTER to continue';
 !41!               WINDOW READ srtmsg LINE 20 OTW;
 !42!           END;
 !43!           FROM;
 !44!           UNTRANS;
 !45!               &system_msg='Press ENTER to return  to main menu';
 !46!               WINDOW READ srtmsg LINE 20 OTW;
 !47!               WINDOW CLOSE LIST OTW;
 !48!               CLEAR ALL;
 !49!               WINDOW OPEN srtmsg LINE 20 OTW;
```

Figure 19.12 Daily Late Return Report Procedure

Inventory Report Procedure

This procedure creates reports (to be printed or displayed on the screen) concerning the equipment in the rental pool. No new enhancements are introduced for this procedure.

The procedure is contained in the REP3.NOM file on your data disk and is listed in Figure 19.13.

```
! 1!        ON FKEY(1) DO;
! 2!            &sys_key=&&FUNCTIONKEY;
! 3!            RETURN;
! 4!        END;

! 5!            ASK 'ENTER REPORT DATE (MM/DD/YY):' &rep_date;
! 6!            WINDOW LOAD LIST OTW;
! 7!            WINDOW CLEAR LIST;
! 8!            WINDOW SIZE LIST LINESIZE 18 COLSIZE 76;
! 9!            CLEAR &sys_key;
!10!            &system_msg='For printed report press PF1, for display on the screen
                press ENTER';
!11!            WINDOW READ srtmsg LINE 20 OTW;
!12!        IF &sys_key=1 THEN DO;
!13!            &RLENGTH=56;
!14!            &PLENGTH=66;
!15!            CLEAR &sys_key;
!16!            &prtsg='ON PTR';
!17!            GOTO -print;
!18!        END;
!19!            &prtsg=' ';
!20!            CLEAR &sys_key;
!21!            WINDOW CLOSE srtmsg OTW;
!22!            WINDOW OPEN LIST OTW;
!23!            &RLENGTH=18;
!24!            &TLENGTH=20;
!25!        -print
!26!          TRANS;
!27!            LIST COUNT(st_name) NOPRINT SET &total
!28!                BY st_name HEADING 'SKI TYPE' SET  &skiname
!29!                COUNT (st_name) NOPRINT SET &subski
!30!                BY ski_length SET &slength COUNT(ski_length)
!31!                NOPRINT SET &sublength skinum ?(&prtsg)

!32!        BYFOOT ski_length FOLD 1
!33!                'TOTAL NUMBER OF ' &skiname ' AT '
!34!                &slength '--- ' &sublength FOLD 1

!35!        BYFOOT st_name FOLD 1
!36!                'TOTAL NUMBER  OF ' &skiname ' ---' &subski
!37!                FOLD 1

!38!            SUMMARY FOLD 1
!39!                'TOTAL NUMBER OF SKIS --- ' &total

!40!                TITLE FOLD 3 'BOB'S SKI SHOP'
!41!                FOLD  'DATE - ' &rep_date
!42!                FOLD  'SKI INVENTORY REPORT'
!43!                FOLD 3
!44!            OTW DO;
!45!            &system_msg='No record selected for the report, press ENTER to continue';
!46!            WINDOW READ srtmsg LINE 20 OTW;
!47!            END;
!48!        UNTRANS;
!49!            &system_msg='Press ENTER  to return to main menu';
!50!            WINDOW READ srtmsg LINE 20 OTW;
!51!            WINDOW CLOSE LIST OTW;
!52!            CLEAR ALL;
!53!            WINDOW OPEN srtmsg LINE 20 OTW;
```

Figure 19.13 Inventory Report Procedure

```
! 1!    ON FKEY(1) DO;
! 2!         &sys_key=&&FUNCTIONKEY;
! 3!         RETURN;
! 4!    END;

! 5!         ASK 'ENTER REPORT DATE (MM/DD/YY) :' &rep_date;
! 6!         SELECT date_out EQ &rep_date;
! 7!         WINDOW LOAD LIST OTW;
! 8!         WINDOW CLEAR LIST;
! 9!         WINDOW SIZE LIST LINESIZE 18 COLSIZE 76;
!10!         CLEAR &sys_key;
!11!         &system_msg='For printed report press PF1, for display on the screen  press ENTER';
!12!         WINDOW READ srtmsg LINE 20 OTW;
!13!      IF &sys_key=1 THEN DO;
!14!         &prtsg='ON PTR';
!15!         &RLENGTH=56;
!16!         &PLENGTH=66;
!17!         CLEAR &sys_key;
!18!         GOTO -print;
!19!      END;
!20!         &prtsg=' ';
!21!         CLEAR &sys_key;
!22!         WINDOW CLOSE srtmsg OTW;
!23!         WINDOW OPEN LIST OTW;
!24!         &RLENGTH=18;
!25!         &TLENGTH=20;
!26!    -print
!27!       TRANS;
!28!        LIST date_due COUNT(date_out) NOPRINT SET &total
!29!            ski_num boot_num pole_num ?(&prtsg)

!30!    SUMMARY FOLD 3
!31!         'TOTAL NUMBER OF RENTAL TRANSACTIONS --- ' &total

!32!    TITLE FOLD 3 'BOB'S SKI SHOP'
!33!         FOLD   'DATE -  ' &rep_date
!34!         FOLD   'DAILY RENTAL REPORT'
!35!         FOLD 3
!36!      OTW DO;
!37!         &system_msg='No record selected for the report, press ENTER to continue';
!38!         WINDOW READ srtmsg LINE 20 OTW;
!39!      END;
!40!      UNTRANS;
!41!         &system_msg='Press ENTER to return  to main menu';
!42!         WINDOW READ srtmsg LINE 20 OTW;
!43!         WINDOW CLOSE LIST OTW;
!44!         CLEAR ALL;
!45!         WINDOW OPEN srtmsg LINE 20 OTW;
```

Figure 19.14   Daily Rental Report Procedure

Daily Rental Report Procedure

This procedure has no new enhancements. It is contained in the REP4.NOM file on your data disk and is listed in Figure 19.14.

Customer Profile Report Procedure

This procedure corresponds to the last report discussed and developed in Chapter 18. The enhanced procedure allows the report to be displayed on the screen or printed. The report contains information on the rental customers and their ski equipment preferences.

This procedure is contained in the REP5.NOM file on your data disk and is listed in Figure 19.15. The report that creates the mailing labels is left to you as exercise (the REP6.NOM file).

```
! 1!        ON FKEY(1) DO;
! 2!            &sys_key=&&FUNCTIONKEY;
! 3!            RETURN;
! 4!        END;

! 5!            ASK 'ENTER REPORT DATE (MM/DD/YY):' &rep_date;
! 6!            SELECT date_out LE &rep_date;
! 7!            WINDOW LOAD LIST OTW;
! 8!            WINDOW CLEAR LIST;
! 9!            WINDOW SIZE LIST LINESIZE 18 COLSIZE 76;
!10!            CLEAR &sys_key;
!11!       &system_msg='For printed report press PF1, for display on the screen press ENTER';
!12!            WINDOW READ srtmsg LINE 20 OTW;
!13!          IF &sys_key=1 THEN DO;
!14!            &prtsg='ON PTR';
!15!            &RLENGTH=56;
!16!            &PLENGTH=66;
!17!            CLEAR &sys_key;
!18!            GOTO -print;
!19!          END;
!20!            &prtsg=' ';
!21!            CLEAR &sys_key;
!22!            WINDOW CLOSE srtmsg OTW;
!23!            WINDOW OPEN LIST OTW;
!24!            &RLENGTH=18;
!25!            &TLENGTH=20;
!26!         -print
!27!           TRANS;
!28!           LIST FROM transactions BY custident NOPRINT
!29!                'TYPE OF EQUIPMENT RENTED' SPACE 5
!30!                ski_name COUNT(ski_name)  NOPRINT SET &totski
!31!                boot_name COUNT(boot_name) NOPRINT SET
!32!                &totboot SUBSET MATCHING FROM customer
!33!                custident NOPRINT first_name NOPRINT SET
!34!                &fname last_name NOPRINT SET &lname city
!35!                NOPRINT SET  &rcity age NOPRINT SET &rage sex
!36!                NOPRINT SET &rsex skiing_ability NOPRINT
!37!                SET &rski_ability NOHEAD ?(&prtsg)

!38!                BYHEAD custident
!39!                 'CUSTOMER NAME' SPACE 19 'AGE' SPACE 2 'SEX'

!40!                 SPACE 2 'TOWN' SPACE 16 'SKIING ABILITY'
!41!                 FOLD '--- -----------------------------'
!42!                 SPACE 2 '---' SPACE 2 '---' SPACE 2
!43!                 '-----------------' SPACE 2
!44!                 '-----------------' FOLD 2 &fname SPACE 0
!45!                 &lname SPACE 2 &rage SPACE 4 &rsex SPACE 3
!46!                 &rcity &rski_ability FOLD 2 SPACE 29 'SKI'
!47!                 SPACE 19 'BOOTS' FOLD SPACE 29
!48!                 '--------------------' SPACE 2
!49!                 '--------------------' FOLD

!50!         BYFOOT custident
!51!                 FOLD 3 SPACE 10 'TOTAL NUMBER OF SKIS TRIED:'
!52!                 &totski FOLD 2 SPACE 10
!53!                 'TOTAL NUMBER OF BOOTS TRIED:' &totboot
!54!                 FOLD 3

!55!         TITLE  FOLD 3 'BOB'S SKI SHOP'
!56!                 FOLD  'DATE - ' &rep_date
!57!                 FOLD  'CUSTOMER PROFILE REPORT'
!58!                 FOLD 3
```

```
!59!            OTW DO;
!60!            &system_msg='No record  selected  for the report, press ENTER to continue';
!61!            WINDOW READ srtmsg LINE 20 OTW;
!62!            END;
!63!         UNTRANS;

!64!            &system_msg='Press ENTER to return  to main menu';
!65!            WINDOW READ srtmsg LINE 20 OTW;
!66!            WINDOW CLOSE LIST OTW;
!67!            CLEAR ALL;
!68!            WINDOW OPEN srtmsg LINE 20 OTW;
```

Figure 19.15 Customer Profile Report Procedure

19.4 SUMMARY

When we are satisfied that individual system modules (components) are working correctly and meet our established objectives, we enhance them and combine the modules into a working (production) system. The entire system is now viewed as a hierarchy of components. We do a final cleanup, put the components together, and make sure that they work properly when they are joined with others.

The components of our Ski Inventory System were enhanced with:

- Error-handling routines.
- Exits from loops in procedures with user-defined function keys (PF keys).
- Windows that handle the user-assistance information used in online documentation.
- HELP facilities constructed with the DDQUERY function or the SLIST command.

The final cleanup of our system is accomplished by:

- Placing all system DEFINEs and DECLAREs into a separate .NOM file.
- Placing all user-defined Forms into a separate .NOM file.

To join components with others and to make sure that they all work together, we created an integration control procedure that connects all the existing components of the system.

And now we have an integrated Ski Inventory System.

EXERCISES

1. What is a main control procedure? Why do you need it and what does it do?
2. Briefly describe a procedure that controls the interactive process.
3. Suggest enhancements other than those discussed in the text for the components you have constructed.
4. Comment on how the OTW clause works and why it can be used in error-handling routines.
5. For error handling, when would you use the ON... condition and when would you use the OTW clause? Be specific.
6. Discuss two methods for creating user-assistance facilities.
7. How are the FORM and DDQUERY commands useful in creating customized user-assistance screens?
8. How can the SLIST command be used to construct a system's HELP facility?
9. Comment on the notion of a general system cleanup.

10. Why is it necessary to do a general system cleanup when integrating the system? What could happen if this is not done?

11. What needs to be done in a final step of constructing the integrated production system? Be specific.

12. The procedure that updates the SKIINVENTORY file from the external file (as developed in the Chapter 15) is to be integrated with the Ski Rental System. The code for this procedure was given in Figure 15.8. For your integration procedure remember to change the main menu and to use the ON ENDFILE condition to detect the end of the transaction file.

13. Implement the online documentation that describes (in detail) each option available in the Ski Rental System. The documentation is to be invoked with the function keys. Generate two levels of documentation. On the first level, have brief description of each option. On the second level, have a detailed description of each available option that can be invoked. Invoke one option at a time, depending on the cursor's location on the menu.

14. Revise the new customer transaction procedure (PROC1.NOM) so that it contains the following options:
    a. Documentation (use the DDQUERY function).
    b. Customized handling of errors that result from the violation of the LIMIT conditions set in the database schema.
    c. Customized handling of errors that result from an attempt by the user to enter a record possessing a key that already exists in the database.
    d. Customized handling of errors that result from an attempt by the user to enter, for example, some alphanumeric data into the numeric field.

15. Create the procedure that saves the log of the transactions processed during the execution of the new customer transaction procedure. Integrate this procedure into the PROC1.NOM procedure.

16. Change the new customer transaction procedure in such a way that the total prepaid rental fee is displayed for all rental situations. This procedure currently displays the prepaid fee only if all three types of equipment are rented (that is, skis, boots, and poles). (*Hint*: Use the ZNAV function.)

17. Change the returning customer transaction procedure (PROC2.NOM) so that it incorporates the improvements requested in Problems 15 and 17.

18. Change the returning customer transaction procedure (PROC2.NOM) so that the display of the records from the CUSTOMER file (during the search for the specific customer) is in the user-defined window. At present the output appears in the Output window.

19. Integrate into the returned equipment procedure (PROC3.NOM) a routine that calculates and displays the fee to be paid when the equipment is returned (total fee due minus the prepaid fee). Make sure that all items are displayed for all rental situations (see Problem 16).

20. Change the returned equipment procedure (PROC3.NOM) in such a way that only the return date field can be entered by the user of this procedure. All other fields are now for display purposes only and cannot be changed. As it is now, the user can change all the fields in this procedure.

21. Design and integrate with the returned equipment procedure (PROC3.NOM) an error-handling routine that captures incorrect return date. For example, an incorrect date is a return date that falls before the equipment rental date or one that does not correspond to the specified rental season.

22. Design and integrate with the Ski Rental System an updating procedure for the SKIINVENTORY master.

23. Design and integrate with the Ski Rental System an updating procedure for the BOOTINVENTORY master.

24. Design and integrate with the Ski Rental System an updating procedure for the POLEINVENTORY master.

25. Design and integrate with the Ski Rental System a procedure that generates mailing labels for the customers that rented the ski equipment. Give the user of the procedure a choice of generating the mailing labels for the customers who:
    a. Rented the equipment in a prespecified period of time.
    b. Are in a specified age bracket.
    c. Rented a specific type of equipment, for example DYNASTAR skis.
    Note that the time, age bracket, and equipment type are specified by the user.

PROJECTS

Create the integrated production system for one of the projects you designed and developed in the previous chapters. That is, for:

1. The State Parks Reservation System.
2. The Properties, Water Rights, and Leases System.
3. The information system project that you and your instructor arranged with your local business organization.

Follow all the rules set and explained in this chapter.

APPENDIX A

NOMAD Installation Notes

We assume that you are familiar with basic operation of a personal computer.

A.1 HARDWARE AND SOFTWARE REQUIREMENTS

PC NOMAD is a 4GL/DBMS that runs on IBM XT, IBM AT, or IBM PS/2. It also runs on IBM compatibles: Compaq Deskpro 360/20, Epson Equity III, AT&T 6300, Tandy 1200 HD, and Compaq Portable 386.

The minimum hardware configuration required is:

> 640K OF MEMORY
> 2 MEG OF STORAGE
> MONOCHROME OR COLOR MONITOR

A printer is optional.

The software required is PC DOS Version 3.0, or later. Your students' version of NOMAD comes on seven (7) diskettes (5 1/4″).

A.2 INSTALLATION PROCEDURE: DEFAULT INSTALL

To install NOMAD on the hard disk of your personal computer, insert diskette 1 (1 of 7) into drive a. At the DOS prompt (we assume that DOS is installed on your hard disk) type in:

```
a:install
```

and press the [ENTER] key.

Install is the name of the .exe file that begins the installation program. (*Note*: The drive designation can be changed to specify drive from which you are installing NOMAD.)

The installation program starts automatically. It is window-driven: once you begin the installation program, a series of windows appear that enable you to select the parameters for your installation.

From the first window in the installation program choose

```
DEFAULT INSTALL
```

This option automatically installs the NOMAD base product and all its components as well as tutorials, NOMAD Assistant, and communications, all with their default settings. (Customized installation options are described in the NOMAD Reference Manual.)

After you select the Default Install option, the default directory for NOMAD is displayed:

```
\NOMAD
```

Accept this default and begin the installation process. (*Note*: You can change the default directory if you wish and then start the installation.) Each installation window will guide you through the process.

Keys

The bottom of each window in the Installation program lists the keys available for that window. These keys are:

[F1]   Activates the online HELP; explains a specific menu, field, or checklist selection. The first time you press the [F1] key, the information displayed describes the current menu selection. The second time you press the [F1] key from the same position, the information displayed describes the overall window.

[ENTER] Processes a window and goes to the next window.

[ESC]   Cancels the processed menu selection and goes back to the previous window.

After you have installed all of the NOMAD diskettes (7 of 7), the last window in the installation program appears. The last window contains information on how to access NOMAD from the DOS level. When you reach the last window, your installation is complete.

Note: Any adjustments to the config.sys file must be made before you can access NOMAD. If you have not already created a config.sys file, you can create one as in this example:

■ Access the directory you use when you start your computer (a: with DOS in drive a for dual floppy disk users; c:\ for hard disk users)

■ Type **copy con config.sys** and press the [ENTER] key.

■ Type **files=30** and press the [ENTER] key.

■ Press F6 and then press the [ENTER] key to end the copy procedure.

■ Press CTRL/ALT/DEL to reboot your system using the new config.sys file. The file will be accessed automatically.

(For more information on the config.sys file, see your DOS manual.)

A.3 STARTING NOMAD

To access NOMAD and to verify that the installation has been successful, follow these two steps:

STEP	ACTION	RESULTS
1	*type* cd\NOMAD and press [ENTER]	This puts you in the NOMAD directory. You can specify whatever the appropriate directory is for NOMAD.
2	*type* NOMAD and press [ENTER]	The system calls NOMAD and the copyright screen is displayed. Next, the screen is cleared, and two NOMAD windows, Command and History, are displayed. You are in the NOMAD environment, ready to do your work.

If, for any reason, the specified results do not occur, return to the \NOMAD directory and repeat steps 1 and 2. If the error persists, reinstall NOMAD and repeat steps 1 and 2.

A.4 ENDING THE NOMAD SESSION

The recommended method of ending the NOMAD session is to type **quit** in the Command window, and press the [ENTER] key. **You should avoid using any of the [CTRL]/[BREAK], [CTRL/C] or [CTRL/ALT/DEL] key combinations to exit NOMAD because these methods of exiting NOMAD may leave your database in an *unusable format.***

If for any reasons you used these key combinations, do the *schema check* before accessing your database to make it usable again.

APPENDIX B

Notes on the Display and Internal Formats in NOMAD

B.1 NUMERIC DISPLAY FORMAT

9   Specifies a digit in a display field. (Leading zeros are suppressed.)

For example, for the display format specified as 999999, number 345 will be displayed in the field of 6 digits with 3 blanks in front of it (default, right justified).

B   Specifies a blank fill.

For example, a display format B9999 will specify a display field 5 digits long. Number 00056 will be displayed as right-justified 56 with all leading zeros suppressed. Note that for this display format, the entire field will be blank-filled if the value is 0.

0   Specifies a zero fill.

For example, a display format of 09999 gives a display field 5 digits long. Leading zeros will not be suppressed. Number 56 displays as 00056. Number 0 will display as 00000.

,   Specifies that numbers are to be displayed with commas in designated positions.

For example, display format 99,999 will generate a display field 6 digits long. Number 12454 displays as 12,454.

.   Specifies printing of the decimal point.

For example, if a display format is 99.99, number 12.457 will be displayed as 12.46.

V   Specifies a virtual decimal point. The number will be printed without a decimal point.

For example, for the display format 999V99, number 123.47 will be printed as 12347.

*   Specifies printing of an asterisk for each leading zero.

For example, for the display format *999,999, number 5629 will be printed as **5,629.

$ Specifies printing of a dollar sign one space to the left of the number.
For example, for the display format **$999,999.99**, number 2345.25 will be printed as **$ 2,345.25**.

−   Specifies that a space be reserved for a leading minus sign.
For example, for the display format of **-*999,999**, the number −1254 will be printed as ****−1,254**.

+   Specifies that a plus or minus sign will always appear in front of the number.
For example, for the display format **+999**, the number 134 will be printed as **+134**.

MI   The **MI** follows last 9 in a display format; it specifies printing of the minus sign to the right of the negative number.
For example, for the display format of **999MI**, the number −150 will be printed as **150−**.

CR   The **CR** follows last 9 in a display format; it specifies printing of **CR** to the right of the negative number.
For example, for the display format **999CR**, the number −150 will be printed as **150CR**.

PR   The **PR** follows last 9 in a display format; it specifies that the negative numbers will be enclosed in parentheses.
For example, for the display format **999PR**, the number −150 will be printed as **(150)**.

%   The % follows last 9 in the format; it specifies printing of a percent sign directly to the right of the last digit.
For example, for the display format **999%**, the number 36 will be printed as **36%**.

(n)   n is an integer, a scaling factor; it follows the last 9 in the display format; it specifies how many places the decimal point is moved. Shift is to the right if n is a positive integer and to the left if n is a negative integer.
For example, for the display format **999,999(3)**, the number 123.56 will be printed as **123,560**. For the display format ***999.999(−3)**, it will be printed as *****.124**.

B.2 DATE DISPLAY FORMAT

The **DATE** display format provides keywords for specifying how the day, month, and year of the date value are to appear. These keywords can include certain characters and phrases.

Characters

Keyword		Example of Output
blank		
/	slash	/
-	dash	-
'	quote	'
,	comma	,
:	colon	:
.	period	.
(	left parenthesis	(
)	right parenthesis	)

Day Values

Keyword		Example of Output
DDD		001, 002, ..., 365 (Julian date)
DD		01, 02, ..., 31
BD		1, 2, ..., 31
DDTH		1ST, 2ND, ..., 31ST
DDth		1st, 2nd, ..., 31st
DOM	(day of month)	FIRST, SECOND, ..., THIRTY-FIRST
Dom		First, Second, ..., Thirty-first
dom		first, second, ..., thirty-first
DAYS		ONE, TWO, ..., THIRTY-ONE
Days		One, Two, ..., Thirty-one
days		one, two, ..., thirty-one
WEEKDAY		MONDAY, ..., SUNDAY
Weekday		Monday, ..., Sunday
weekday		monday, ..., sunday

Month Values

Keyword	Example of Output
MM	01, 02, ..., 12
BM	1, 2, ..., 12
MMTH	1ST, 2ND, ..., 12TH
MMth	1st, 2nd, ..., 12th
MONTH, Month, month	MARCH, March, march
MON, Mon, mon	MAR, Mar, mar
MOY (month of year)	FIRST, ..., TWELFTH
Moy	First, ..., Twelfth
moy	first, ..., twelfth
MONTHS	ONE, ..., TWELVE
Months	One, ..., Twelve
months	one, ..., twelve

Quarter Values

Keyword	Example of Output
Q	1, 2, 3, 4
QTH	1ST, 2ND, 3RD, 4TH
Qth	1st, 2nd, 3rd, 4th
QOY	FIRST, SECOND, THIRD, FOURTH
Qoy	First, Second, Third, Fourth
qoy	first, second, third, fourth
QUARTER	ONE, TWO, THREE, FOUR
Quarter	One, Two, Three, Four
quarter	one, two, three, four

Year Values

Keyword	Example of Output
YYYY	1989
YY	89
YYTH	44TH, 82ND, 31ST
YYth	44th, 82nd, 31st
YEARS	ONE, TWO, ..., NINETY-NINE
Years	One, Two, ..., Ninety-nine
years	one, two, ..., ninety-nine
YOC (year of century)	FIRST, SECOND, ..., NINETY-NINTH
Yoc	First, Second, ..., Ninety-ninth
yoc	first, second, ..., ninety-ninth

DATETIME Display Format

This format can only be used with DATETIME and TIME values. A DATETIME format can be assembled from any combination of the DATE keywords and from any combination of the DATETIME keywords. DATETIME keywords are listed below. The n in this list is the integer between 1 and 16 that specifies the number of digits displayed. The space for the minus sign is counted as one digit. If you assign insufficient space for the display of a specific field, NOMAD displays asterisks (***) in that field.

Keyword	Explanation	Displayed with Leading
WKIn	weeks	zeroes
BWKIn	weeks	blanks
DDDIn	days	zeroes
BDDIn	days	blanks
HHIn	hours	zeroes
BHIn	hours	blanks
MNIn	minutes	zeroes
BNIn	minutes	blanks
SSIn	seconds	zeroes
BSIn	seconds	blanks
MSIn	milliseconds	zeroes
BMSIn	milliseconds	blanks

Parenthetical Literal

To have keywords corresponding to the date or the time values appear literally in the display output, specify them within parentheses. Some of the keywords are given below.

Keyword	Example of Output
(hours), (HOURS)	hours, HOURS
(hrs), (HRS)	hrs, HRS
(hr), (HR)	hr, HR
(h), (H)	h, H
(minutes), (MINUTES)	minutes, MINUTES
(minute), (MINUTE)	minute, MINUTE
(min), (MIN)	min, MIN
(mins), (MINS)	mins, MINS
(m), (M)	m, M
(seconds), (SECONDS)	seconds, SECONDS
(second), (SECOND)	second, SECOND
(secs), (SECS)	secs, SECS
(sec), (SEC)	sec, SEC
(s), (S)	s, S
(milliseconds)	milliseconds
(MILLISECONDS)	MILLISECONDS

Hour Expressions

Keyword	Example of Output
HH	00, 01,..., 23
BH	0, 1,..., 23
HHTH	0TH, 1ST,..., 23RD
HHth	0th, 1st,..., 23rd
HH12	00, 01,..., 12
BH12	0, 1,..., 12
HH12TH	0TH, 1ST,..., 12TH
HHth	0th, 1st,..., 12th
HOURS/HRS	ZERO, ONE, TWO,..., TWENTY-FOUR
hours/hrs	zero, one, two,..., twenty-four
HOD (HOUR OF DAY)	FIRST, SECOND,..., TWENTY-FOURTH
hod	first, second,..., twenty-fourth

Minute Expressions

Keyword	Example of Output
MN	00, 01,..., 59
BN	0, 1, 2,..., 59
MNth	0th, 1st,..., 59th
MNTH	0TH, 1ST,..., 59TH
minutes/mins	zero, one,..., fifty-nine
MINUTES/MINS	ZERO, ONE,..., FIFTY-NINE
moh (minute of hour)	zeroth, first,..., fifty-ninth
MOH	ZEROTH, FIRST, ..., FIFTY-NINTH

Second Expressions

Keyword	Example of Output
SS	00, 01,..., 59
BS	0, 1,..., 59
SSTH	0TH, 1ST,..., 59TH
ssth	0th, 1th,..., 59th
SECONDS/SECS	ZERO, ONE, FIFTY-NINE
seconds/secs	zero, one,..., fifty-nine
som (second of minute)	zeroth, first,..., fifty-ninth
SOM	ZEROTH, FIRST,..., FIFTY-NINTH

Millisecond Expressions

Keyword	Example of Output
MS	001, 002,..., 999
BM	S1, 2,..., 999

Meridian Expressions

Keyword	Example of Output
M	AM, PM, NOON, MIDNIGHT
m	am, pm, noon, midnight
M.	A.M., P.M., NOON, MIDNIGHT.
m.	a.m., p.m., noon, midnight.

B.3 NAME DISPLAY FORMAT

Nomad can distinguish between a first name, last name, title, initial, prefix, and suffix. This is done with a NAME format that specifies that an item will be displayed as a name when it is printed. A maximum of 14 keywords/characters can be specified with the NAME format. The following keywords/characters can be used:

Character/Keyword	Meaning
	blank
.	period
,	comma
(	left parenthesis
)	right parenthesis
–	dash
F	first name
M	middle name
L	last name
P	prefix
S	suffix
N	nickname
FI	first initial
MI	middle initial
LI	last initial

To use the NAME display format options, the database value must be in the following format:

    LASTNAME, FIRSTNAME MIDDLENAME;PREFIX;SUFFIX;NICKNAME

Appropriate delimiters must be included as part of the database value. For example,

    Voigt, Dorothy Esther;MS.;MD;Cava

Parts of names can be omitted, but the semicolon must be included in any parts that follow it. For example,

    Voigt, Thea Agnes;;Ph.D;Busia

Here prefix MS is omitted.

The default display length for a full name display format is 30 characters. To override this default, specify a length value as the first entry in the NAME format. The NAME format is:

```
AS NAME 'n name format'
```

where n specifies the length for the display format. Examples of the NAME format keywords and resulting outputs are given below.

Name Format	Example of Output
AS NAME '50'	WOJTKOWSKI, THEA AGNES; MS.;PHD;BUSIA
AS NAME 'L,F MI.'	WOJTKOWSKI, THEA A.
AS NAME 'F MI.L-N'	THEA A. WOJTKOWSKI-BUSIA
AS NAME 'P FI.MI.L'	MS. T.A.WOJTKOWSKI
AS NAME 'L,F MI.,S'	WOJTKOWSKI, THEA A.,PHD
AS NAME '(FIMILI)'	(TAW)

B.4 INTERNAL FORMATS

The internal format describes how NOMAD stores data. Internal format is established by an ITEM statement, DECLARE command, or DEFINE statement, either explicitly with the INTERNAL parameter or implicitly with the AS parameter. When both (INTERNAL and AS) parameters are specified, NOMAD uses specified formats if they are compatible. If only the INTERNAL parameter is specified, NOMAD automatically assigns a compatible display format.

Internal formats provided by NOMAD are:

■ *Real (R)*—for storing real numbers.

■ *Integer (I)*—for storing integer values.

■ *Packed decimal (P)*—for storing values with a decimal.

■ *Alphanumeric (fixed length) (A)*—for storing values of variables with the alphanumeric (fixed length) display format.

■ *Alphanumeric (variable length) (A)*—for storing values of variables with the variable alphanumeric display format.

■ *Idate*—for storing values of variables with the date display format.

■ *Itime*—for storing values of variables with the TIME display format.

■ *Idatetime*—for storing values of variables with the DATETIME display formats.

■ *Ilogical*—for storing logical values.

Internal formats and compatible default display formats are listed below.

Internal Format	Default Display Format
R4	99,999,999.99
R8	99,999,999.99
I2	999,999
I4	99,999,999
P15.2	9,999,999,999,999.99
An	An
IDATE	MM/DD/YY
ITIME	BDDI6 HH:MN:SS
IDATETIME	MM/DD/YY HH:MN:SS
ILOGICAL	T OR F

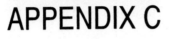

APPENDIX C

Functions in NOMAD

C.1 INTRODUCTION

NOMAD provides built-in functions (facilities) for performing statistical and financial computations. It also has functions for processing character (string) data, date data, and functions used with the LIST and CREATE commands. This Appendix describes the general formats of these functions and shows examples of their use in NOMAD.

Functions Used for Processing Numeric Data

The following functions (listed in an alphabetical order) are used in NOMAD with numeric data.

ABSVAL

Returns the absolute value of a number, or expression.

Format:

```
ABSVAL (numeric expression)
```

Examples:

1. &AMT=-20
   PRINT ABSVAL(&AMT);

   The result is 20.

2. PRINT ABSVAL(2-10);

   The result is 8.

ATAN

Computes the arc tangent of a numeric expression. Returns the angle in radians (over the range −pi/2 to +pi/2)

Format:

    ATAN (numeric expression)

Example:

    PRINT ATAN(10000);

The result is 1.5.

AVG

Computes the arithmetic mean.

Format:

    AVG (numeric expression)

Example:

    LIST AVG(SKI_RENT_PAID);

The result is the average rental revenue of all rentals in the TRANSACTIONS master.

COS

Calculates the cosine of a numeric expression (value in radians).

Format:

    COS (numeric expression)

Example:

    PRINT COS(500)

The result is −0.89.

CNT

Counts the number of elements (excluding NOTAVAILABLE values) in its expression.

Format:

    CNT(expression)

Example:

```
LIST CNT(EQUIPMENT_CODE);
```

The result is the count of EQUIPMENT_CODEs in the EQUIPMENT_TYPE master.

INT

Truncates a real number to an integer.

Format:

```
INT(numeric expression)
```

Example:

Assume that &tt has the value 15.25

```
PRINT INT(&tt) AS 999;
```

The result is 15 (integer portion of 15.25).

LOG

Calculates the log to base e (natural log) of a numeric expression.

Format:

```
LOG(numeric expression)
```

Example:

```
PRINT LOG(55);
```

The result is 4.01.

LOG10

Calculates the log to base 10 (common log) of a numeric expression.

Format:

```
LOG10(numeric expression)
```

Example:

```
PRINT LOG10(55) AS 99.9999
```

The result is 1.7404.

MAX

Finds the largest value of its argument.

Format:

```
MAX(expression)
```

Example:

```
LIST MAX(FEE_PAID);
```

The result is the largest available value of the FEE_PAID item from the TRANSAC-TIONS master.

MIN

Finds the smallest value of its argument.

Format:

```
MIN(expression)
```

Example:

```
LIST MIN(FEE_PAID);
```

The result is the smallest available value of the FEE_PAID item from the TRANSAC-TIONS master.

NUM

Counts the number of elements in its argument including NOTAVAILABLE values.

Format:

```
NUM(expression)
```

Example:

```
LIST NUM(SKI_CODE);
```

This request reports the number of SKI_CODEs in the EQUIPMENT master.

SIGN

Checks if an expression is positive or negative. If expression is positive it returns 1; if expression is negative it returns −1. For expression equal zero, it returns zero. For NOTAVAILABLE values, it returns a NOTAVAILABLE.

Format:

```
SIGN(numeric expression)
```

Example;

```
&X1=10; &Y2=-6; &Z1=0;
PRINT SIGN(&X1) SIGN(&Y2) SIGN(&Z1);
```

The results are:

```
1 -1 0
```

SQRT

Calculates the square root of a numeric expression.

Format:

```
SQRT(numeric expression)
```

Example:

```
PRINT SQRT(81);
```

The result is 9.

STDDEV

Computes the standard deviation (square root of the variance) of all the instances of the argument, excluding NOTAVAILABLE values.

Format:

```
STDDEV(numeric expression)
```

Example:

```
LIST BY MANUFACTURER SKI_TYPE STDDEV(TOTREV);
```

This request reports the standard deviation by manufacturer of the total revenue of SKI_TYPE, where the manufacturer has more than one type of equipment (skis) in the database.

SUM

Adds all the numeric instances of the argument, ignoring NOTAVAILABLE values.

Format:

```
SUM(numeric expression)
```

Example:

```
LIST SUM(FEE_RENTAL);
```

This request reports the sum of the FEE_RENTAL for the entire SKIRENT database.

VAR

Computes the arithmetic variance of all the numeric instances of the argument, excluding NOTAVAILABLE values.

Format:

```
VAR(numeric expression)
```

Example:

```
LIST BY SKI_NUM VAR(FEE_PAID)
```

This request reports, by ski number, the variance of the FEE_PAID fee, where the manufacturer has more than one ski type in the database.

ZNAV

Converts NOTAVAILABLE values to zeros if the NOTAVAILABLE value is numeric or to blanks if the NOTAVAILABLE value is a character.

Format:

```
ZNAV(expression)
```

Example:

(*Note:* If any argument in an arithmetic expression is a NOTAVAILABLE value, the result of the expression is a NOTAVAILABLE value.)
In the following example, the &FEE is a NOTAVAILABLE value.

```
DECLARE & AS 99,999; DECLARE &FEE AS 9999;
&REV=77000;
PRINT &REV &FEE
```

The result is:

```
&=77,000 &FEE=N/A
```

Calculation `PRINT &FEE+&REV;` produces N/A in the Output window. To get numerical results ZNAV needs to be used. That is:

```
PRINT ZNAV (&FEE)+ ZNAV(&REV);
```

The result is 77,000.

Functions Used for Processing Character Data

ALPHA

Determines whether a character expression contains only letters or blanks.

Format:

```
ALPHA(character expression)
```

Example:

Assume that &W has a value 'Dorothy'.

```
PRINT (IF ALPHA(&W) THEN 'ONLY LETTERS' ELSE 'CONTAINS NUMBERS';
```

The result of this statement is `'ONLY LETTERS'`.

DDQUERY

Determines the attributes of a database entity such as a master, item, define, or &variable from the data dictionary.

Format:

```
DDQUERY(attribute string, entity string)
```

An **entity string** is any character expression that is a valid entity, such as a master, defined item, &item, defined &item, and declared &variable. An **attribute string** is any character expression that is a valid attribute.

Valid attributes are:

ALIAS	Retrieves an existing alias of an entity.
DISPLAY	Retrieves the specified display format.
DOCUMENT	Retrieves a document string.
EXPRESSION	Retrieves the expression for the defined item.
HEADING	Retrieves the heading of an item.
INTERNAL	Retrieves the internal format of an item, &variable, or defined item.
ISKEY	Determines whether an item is or is not a key. The value returned depends on this determination, and is TRUE or FALSE.
ISUNIQUE	Determines if the master is keyed.
KEYLIST	Retrieves a list of keys in the master.
MASTER	Retrieves the masters name for an item.
TYPE	Retrieves the type of an entity. The type of an entity is item, master, or defined item.
NAME	Retrieves the name of the specified entity. You can use NAME to display the item name associated with an alias of an item.
NUMITEMS	Retrieves the number of items and defined items in a master.

Example:

```
PRINT DDQUERY
('DISPALY','MANUFACT_CODE')
```

The result is A4 displayed in the Output window.

INDEX

Used to locate the string position of a substring of characters within a longer string. If INDEX cannot locate the substring, it returns a zero.

Format:

```
INDEX(character expression1, character expression2)
```

Example:

Assume that item CNAME has a current value of 'Mary Nice'. To locate the character string 'Nice' within the item CNAME enter:

```
&WHERE=INDEX(CNAME,'Nice')
```

&WHERE has a value of 6.

If you searched for the string 'Nicer', INDEX would return a zero, since 'Nicer' is not contained in the string 'Mary Nice'.

LIKE

Determines whether all characters in the character expression match a specified pattern. The true condition is specified if the pattern matches.

The pattern can incorporate two wild card characters. The wild card character '_' is used to match a single character. The wild card character '%' is used to match zero or more characters. All other characters must be an exact match or the result is false.

Format:

character expression LIKE pattern

Example:

```
DECLARE &CUSTOMER AS A20;
&CUSTOMER='WARNER';
PRINT  IF &CUSTOMER LIKE 'WARN%' THEN 'TRUE'
ELSE 'FALSE';
```

The result is True.

LENGTH

Counts the number of positions allocated to a character expression. Counts leading, trailing, and embedded blanks.

Format:

```
LENGTH(character expression)
```

Example:

```
DECLARE &CUSTOMER AS 20;
&CUSTOMER='Chris Warner ';
PRINT LENGTH(&CUSTOMER);
```

The result that appears in the output window is 20.

LENGTHB

Counts the number of positions allocated to a character expression, excluding trailing blanks.

Format:

```
LENGTHB(character expression)
```

Example:

```
DECLARE &CUSTOMER AS 20;
&CUSTOMER='Chris Warner ';
PRINT LENGTHB(&CUSTOMER);
```

The result is 12.

MASK

Checks whether or not a character value conforms to a particular format pattern.

Format:

```
MASK(mask pattern,character expression)
```

Example:

```
&EQUIPMENT_CODE='123ABC123';
PRINT (IF MASK('**AB****',&EQUIPMENT_CODE)
THEN &EQUIPMENT_CODE
ELSE 'BAD DATA');
```

&EQUIPMENT_CODE does not fit the MASK pattern; the result is BAD DATA.

SUBSTR

Extracts substrings from character strings.

Format:

```
SUBSTR(character expression, starting position,[length])
```

Example:

Assume that &CITY= 'New Orleans'.

```
PRINT SUBSTR(&CITY,3,5)
```

The result is a substring 'w Orl' (starting in the 3rd position of the string 'New Orleans', 5-character long.

UPPER

Converts lowercase characters to uppercase.

Format:

```
UPPER(character expression)
```

Example:

Assume that &CITY='new york'

```
PRINT &CITY UPPER(&CITY);
```

The result is: new york NEW YORK.

Function Used for Processing DATE data

ADDATE

Adds (or subtracts) months or years to a date expression. Ordinary arithmetic is used to add days or weeks.

Format:

```
ADDATE(date expression, months,[years])
```

Example:

```
&DATE='January 19, 1989';
PRINT ADDATE(&DATE,2,1)
AS DATE 'Month dd, YYYY';
```

The ADDATE function adds 2 months and 1 year to &DATE. The result is March 19, 1990.

Report Functions Used with LIST and CREATE Commands

The following functions (report functions) are used with the LIST or CREATE commands to create reports. Use them to generate data values for BY items or ACROSS items. If you limit the scope of the LIST or CREATE command (with SELECT or WHERE), the scope of the function will also be limited.

AVG

Computes the arithmetic mean of all the instances of the argument within the preceding BY or ACROSS item, or within the scope of the command.

Format:

```
AVG(numeric expression)
```

Example:

```
LIST BY MANUFACTURER AVG(PRODUCTION_COST)
AS $999,999,999;
```

The result of this request from the database is the report (in the List window) listing manufacturers and their average production costs. Portion of this report can look like this:

```
                           AVG
MANUFACTURER       PRODUCTION COST
-----------------  ----------------
DYNASTAR              $16,055,300
N/A                   $17,555,333
ROSSIGNOL             $13,333,666
FOX                            $0
```

CNT

Counts all the instances of the argument within the preceding BY or ACROSS item, or within the scope of the command. NOTAVAILABLE value is not counted.

Format:

```
CNT(expression)
```

Example:

```
LIST CNT(CUSTOMER);
```

The result is the count of customers in the CUSTOMER master.

FIRST

Used as a parameter in the LIST or CREATE command to return the first available value within the preceding BY or ACROSS item.

Format:

```
FIRST(expression)
```

Example:

Assume that CUSTINDENT is an item in the CUSTOMER master.

```
LIST FIRST(CUSTIDENT)
```

This request displays (in the List window) first `CUSTINDENT` in the `CUSTOMER` master.

LAST

Used as a parameter in `LIST` or `CREATE` command to return the last available value.

Format:

`LAST(expression)`

Example:

Assume that `CUSTINDENT` is an item in the `CUSTOMER` master.

`LIST LAST(CUSTIDENT)`

This request displays (in the List window) last `CUSTIDENT` in the `CUSTOMER` master.

MAX

Used as a parameter with `LIST` command to return the largest available value.

Format:

`MAX(expression)`

Example:

Assume that `SKI_RENT_PAID` is a defined item in the `TRANSACTIONS` master.

`LIST MAX(SKI_RENT_PAID)`

The result of this request is the largest `SKI_RENT_PAID` from the `TRANSACTIONS` master.

MIN

Used as a parameter with `LIST` command to return the smallest available value.

Format:

`MIN(expression)`

Example:

Assume that `SKI_RENT_PAID` is a defined item in the `TRANSACTIONS` master.

`LIST MIN(SKI_RENT_PAID)`

The result of this request is the smallest SKI_RENT_PAID from the TRANSACTIONS master.

NUM

Counts all the instances (including NOTAVAILABLE values) of the argument within the preceding BY or ACROSS item and within the scope of the LIST or CREATE command.

Format:

```
NUM(expression)
```

Example:

Assume that CITY is an item in the CUSTOMER master.

```
LIST NUM(CITY);
```

The result of this request is the number of CITY instances, including NOTAVAILABLE values in the CUSTOMER master.

STDDEV

Computes the standard deviation of all the instances of the argument within the preceding BY or ACROSS item and within the scope of the request. Where there is only one instance of a BY or ACROSS item, STDDEV returns a value of zero.

Format:

```
STDDEV(numeric expression)
```

Example:

Assume that there is only one instance for the BY item in this example.

```
LIST BY DATE_OUT SKI_NUM STDDEV(FEE_PAID)
```

The result is zero since there is only one instance.

SUM

Adds all the instances of the argument within the preceding BY or ACROSS item and within the scope of the command.

Format:

```
SUM(numeric expression)
```

Example:

```
LIST SUM(FEE_PAID);
```

The result is the sum of FEE_PAID for the entire SKIRENT database.

VAR

Computes the arithmetic variance of all the instances of the argument within the preceding BY or ACROSS item and within the scope of the request. NOTAVAILABLE values are excluded.

Format:

```
VARIANCE(numeric expression)
```

Example:

```
LIST ACROSS SKI_NUM VAR(AMOUNT_SKI)
```

This request generates report which lists for each SKI_NUM the arithmetic variance of the AMOUNT_SKI rental charges.

APPENDIX D

Glossary of NOMAD Terminology

ACROSS clause A LIST statement clause that sorts the report data and displays it across the columns of a report page.

ALIAS An alternate item name that can be used to reference the item.

Alphanumeric data type Any valid ASCII character, including alphabetic letters (a through z), numbers (0 through 9), spaces, and special characters (*,&,%,@.$,#,).

Argument A value, item, defined item, or &variable passed to a NOMAD command, function, or procedure when the command, function, or procedure is performed.

Arithmetic expression An expression whose result is a numeric value.

Concatenation operators Operators that combine various strings of alphanumeric data values to obtain new strings. APPEND is a concatenation operator.

Constant A nonchanging value.

Cooperative processing The ability to distribute the processing of an application across multiple CPUs.

Current instance The instance where the master is positioned.

Database Interrelated data that can be retrieved and used in multiple applications on a computer.

Database management system A series of programs that can be used to establish, update, and query a database.

Data type A classification of the values for an &variable, item, or defined item. NOMAD data types are alphanumeric, numeric, date, time, datetime, and logical.

Date data type Data composed of calendar dates.

Defined item An item whose value is computed when the item is referenced. The value of a defined item is not stored.

Descending A series of values that begins with the largest value and proceeds to the smallest value.

Disjoint report A report in which data printed on the same line is not necessarily related.

Display format A specification of the form in which data values are to be displayed when NOMAD prints or writes them to the screen.

Entity Any one of the building blocks that can be used to construct a database.

Error window A window containing an error message that appears when a mistake is made entering or executing a NOMAD command.

Execute A command that performs an operation defined by command, or operations defined by statements in a procedure.

Expression A set of computations, logic tests, variables, or constants combined to generate a specific result. Arithmetic, logical, and string expressions are formed by combining items, operators, functions, constants, and &variables.

External file A non-NOMAD file. For example, a DOS file.

File A combination of records containing related information.

Fixed format A format wherein fields are of a fixed length and are restricted to specific column positions.

Form User-defined window.

Format The organization of data for storage and manipulation (internal use) or for display (external use).

Formatting option A list modifier that inserts lines of text into the body of a report, controls NOMAD formatting features, or affects the processing of all items specified in BY, ACROSS, or object clauses in a LIST statement.

Free format A format wherein fields are not restricted to specific columns.

Function A NOMAD built-in facility for performing computations, or actions, including string processing and date processing.

HEADING An item statement option in the schema that specifies a column heading for an item when it appears in a report.

History window Displays correct commands accepted by NOMAD from the Command window.

Instance A database record that includes defined items.

Integer An internal numeric format whose value has no fractional part.

Item A logical "piece of data."

Item modifier A LIST command option that alters the output format of an item specified in a BY, ACROSS, or object clause.

ITEM statement Specifies an item in the schema.

Internal format The format in which data is stored by the computer.

Key An item or items used to order the logical storage sequence of records in a master or segment of a database.

Keyword A reserved word having a specific meaning within a NOMAD command statement.

LABEL An annotation on a Form.

LIST modifier A LIST command option that either screens the data to appear in a report, or controls report format or layout.

List window A window that displays the output generated by the LIST command.

Literal An alphanumeric value usually enclosed in single quotation marks (').

Logical connectors Connectors that combine two logical expressions to obtain a new logical expression, allowing the formation of complex logical expressions from simple ones. AND, OR, and NOT are logical connectors.

Logical expression An expression that performs a logical comparison test using logical and comparison operators and returns TRUE or FALSE result.

Maintenance The act of updating information in a procedure or database, or the structure of the database.

Master A group of related items within a database.

Matching clause A LIST statement clause used as an argument for a relational operator.

Metadata Data that describes the database.

N/A The default character string signifying a NOTAVAILABLE value.

NOTAVAILABLE A value that represents a never-assigned (missing) value of an item or &variable. It is different from a value of zero or a blank. NOMAD stores and returns this value for an item or &variable when the value you want to retrieve is inappropriate, does not exist, or is not known to NOMAD.

Numeric data type Data that contains both integer and real numeric data.

Object A master, item, expression, or report function in a LIST request that specifies report values rather than sorting criteria.

Object clause A LIST statement clause that specifies the data to appear in a report. An object clause can consist of a master, defined items, report functions, expressions, or a combination of these parameters.

Optional parameters Command specifications that are not required.

Output window A window that displays the output generated by a command other than the LIST command.

Position NOMAD's location in a database.

Procedure A sequence of instructions that may consist of a command statement or a complex program consisting of a set of commands.

Prompt The computer's request for data from the user.

Prompt message An information line printed when a prompt is issued.

Real number An internal data format for storing decimal data values.

Record The basic component of any data file. A logical combination of data fields grouped together so they can be manipulated as a single unit.

Relational database A database structure of flat files (tables) in which relationships between data files can be specified when the database is accessed for data retrieval.

Report A formatted page of data from a NOMAD database that provides information for decisions.

Request A command issued to the computer.

Required parameters Command specifications that must be specified and entered.

Reserved word A NOMAD command or command parameter.

Schema A description of a database.

Scientific notation Numeric data in exponential notation.

Screening option A LIST modifier that temporarily limits the database values retrieved for inclusion in a report.

Significant digits Those digits to the left of the decimal point that are not leading zeros, continuing to the right of the decimal point to those that are not trailing blanks.

Simple logical operators Operators that compare two values (numeric or character) and return either a TRUE condition (if the result is true) or a FALSE condition (if the result is false). The notation for simple logical operators in NOMAD is:

LT or <	Less than	NL	Not less than
GT or >	Greater than	NG	Not greater than
EQ or =	Equal to	NE	Not equal to
LE or <=	Less than or equal to		
GE or >=	Greater than or equal to		

Special logical operators Operators that allow complicated logical expressions to be stated more simply than they would be with simple logical operators. Special logical operators compare a value with several other values and return a TRUE or

FALSE result. AMONG, BETWEEN, and CONTAINS are the special logical operators used in NOMAD.

String A combination of characters.

System item A system-defined item that specifies default settings for NOMAD.

System window A window that allows the user to control the size and placement of the other windows, and to scroll the data in the other windows.

System &variable An &variable initialized by NOMAD as the value stored in the corresponding system item.

Translation The process that changes a procedure into a form that NOMAD can understand.

User &variable An &variable containing a temporary data value set by the user.

Variable A data entity whose value can change.

&variable A data value temporarily stored during a current NOMAD session for use in calculations and logical expressions.

Window Area of the screen that allows you to view specified information. Various types of information can be viewed simultaneously on the screen. All communication between the user and NOMAD takes place through windows.

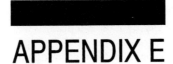

APPENDIX E

List of Acronyms

Acronyms introduced in the text and their meanings are listed in this Appendix.

ASCII	American standards code for information interchange
C	Computer language
COBOL	Common business oriented language
DASD	Direct access storage device
DBC	Database computer
DBMS	Database management system
DB2	Database 2 (IBM)
DD	Data dictionary
DDL	Data definition language
DEC	Digital Equipment Corporation
DL	Data language
DML	Data manipulation language
DOS	Disk operating system
DSS	Decision support system
EIS	Executive information system
ES	Expert system
FMS	Forms manangement system (DEC)
FORTRAN	Formula translator
GDDM	Graphical data display mananger (IBM)
IAG	Interactive application generator
IBM	International Business Machines Corporation
IDD	Integrated data dictionary
IDM	Intelligent database machine (Britton-Lee)
IDMS	Integrated database management system
IDMS/R	Integrated database management system/relational
IMS	Information management system (IBM)
ISAM	Indexed sequential access method
LAN	Local area network
MIPS	Millions of instructions per second
MIS	Management information system
MVS	Multiple virtual storage (IBM)
MVS/CICS	Multiple virtual storage/consumer information control system (IBM)
MVS/SP	Multiple virtual storage/system product (IBM)
MVS/TSO	Multiple virtual storage/time sharing option (IBM)
MVS/XA	Multiple virtual storage/extended architecture

PL/I	Programming language/one
QBE	Query-By-Example (IBM)
QMF	Query by Forms (IBM)
RDBMS	Relational database management system
RMS	Record manangement system (DEC)
SAM	Sequential access method
SDLC	System development life cycle
SQL	Structured query language
SQL/DS	Structured query language/data system
TSO	Time sharing option (IBM)
TPS	Transaction processing system
VAX	Virtual address extension (DEC)
VAX/CMS	VAX code management system (DEC)
VAX/VMS	VAX virtual memory system (DEC)
VM	Virtual machine (IBM)
VM/CMS	Virtual machine/conversational monitor system (IBM)
VM/SP	Virtual memory/system product (IBM)
VMS	Virtual memory system (DEC)
VSAM	Virtual sequential access method

APPENDIX F

Origins of NOMAD (and Other 4GLs)

In prior generations of languages, the user (programmer) of the language had to provide the functions, write the reports, carry out the database functions, and develop full-screen inquiries through procedural coding. With a 4GL, much of this functionality is built into the product.

Today's 4GLs can trace their beginnings to RAMIS (Rapid Management Information System), which began as a consulting project.

Many business organizations in the mid-1960s, having collected masses of data, encountered serious difficulties with obtaining reports on these data. Reporting programs had to be written in COBOL, professional programmers were needed for this task, and the end users who really needed the reports had no rapid access to their data. The available tools such as COBOL were essentially "user unfriendly," and could not be used by those outside the organization's data processing departments.

One organization, Allied Chemical, decided to do something about it. In 1963, Allied requested from Mathematica Inc., an operations research firm and data processing consultant to Allied, that they develop a product that could be used by the nonprogrammers to rapidly write reports. By 1967, RAMIS was ready, and the era of the 4GLs had begun.

RAMIS was so successful (because the end users could use it) that Mathematica upgraded its capabilities and in 1969 offered it as a separate product. Two companies, Nabisco and American Express, were the earliest users of the now commercially available RAMIS (in addition, Mathematica Inc. started to provide training and hot-line support of their product).

The RAMIS project became the basis for the development of two other 4GLs. NCSS (a time-sharing organization that was purchased later by D & B Computing Services, and then bought by MUST Software International) was formed by a group of Mathematica's senior technicians who had extensive time-sharing experience. NCSS acquired the right to market RAMIS in a time-sharing environment. With time, NCSS people started to feel that they had little control over adding new features and in deciding the future direction of the RAMIS product. Because of RAMIS' commercial success, they decided that a market niche existed for them as well. Thus, they decided to develop their own 4GL/DBMS. This is how NOMAD came to be. NOMAD became commercially available in 1975, two months before the second product (FOCUS) that was also spawned from the RAMIS project.

FOCUS was also developed by people who left Mathematica to form Information Builders Inc. Much of the development of FOCUS was done in conjunction with Tymshare, which had the exclusive rights to FOCUS in a time-sharing environment.

RAMIS, NOMAD, and FOCUS did very well in the time-sharing market. RAMIS (and its enhanced version, RAMIS II) flourished on NCSS's network and on other networks (for example, on GE's TELENET). Commercial sales of FOCUS, especially its standalone PC version, really took off in the 1980s; PC versions of the RAMIS and NOMAD products were released later. The early versions of RAMIS, NOMAD, and FOCUS are now significantly improved and new features are continually being added.

NOMAD has remained in the time-sharing environment for some time. In 1984, the MVS/TSO version of NOMAD became available. Eventually NOMAD became the first widely avilable 4GL/relational DBMS. NOMAD's support of a truly relational model is considered significantly better than that of its closest competitor, FOCUS.

Early 4GL development efforts, which started with RAMIS, benefitted other 4GL vendors, who entered the 4GL market much later. Today, hundreds of products can be classified as 4GLs. They all came about in response to the need to increase productivity (by professional programmers as well as by end users) beyond the capabilities of 3GLs. Not only is there probably a market niche for each one of these 4GLs, but they all can be considered stepping stones to a new generation of computer languages as well.

REFERENCE

Bernkopf J. "4GL by any other name would not be COBOL." *Information Center*, October 1985, pp. 21-28.

INDEX

NOTES